The Fifth Discipline Fieldbook

Strategies and Tools for Building
a Learning Organization

Also by Peter Senge

The Fifth Discipline: The Art and Practice of the Learning Organization

A CURRENCY BOOK

PUBLISHED BY DOUBLEDAY
a division of Bantam Doubleday Dell Publishing Group, Inc.
1540 Broadway, New York, New York 10036

CURRENCY and DOUBLEDAY are trademarks of Doubleday, a division of Bantam Doubleday Dell Publishing Group, Inc.

Book design by Chris Welch and Terry Karydes
Illustrations by Martie Holmer

Library of Congress Cataloging-in-Publication Data

The Fifth discipline fieldbook : strategies and tools for building a learning
    organization / Peter M. Senge, . . . [et al.].
        p.   cm.
    Includes bibliographical references and index.
    1. Organizational effectiveness—Handbooks, manuals, etc.   2. Work
groups—Handbooks, manuals, etc.   3. Senge, Peter M.   Fifth
discipline.   I. Senge, Peter M.   II. Title: 5th discipline
fieldbook.   III. Title: Learning organization.
    HD58.9.F54   1994
    658.4'02—dc20   93-50130
                                                          CIP

ISBN 0-385-47256-0

Contents

Personal Mastery

Mental Models

"Leadership and Mastery" workshops than any other team—it often seems like for much of our adult lives. She is a principal at Innovation Associates, where she codirects their quality-leadership practice. She has worked with a wide range of organizations, from manufacturing to hardware and software design to healthcare to local community groups. Her column "Managing People" ran for three years in the *Great Valley News* in the Philadelphia area. Based in Sherrills Ford, North Carolina, Charlotte brings a unique blend of Southern charm and style to the challenging work of organization change—and she possesses an engaging storyteller's wit, as a few thousand graduates of "Leadership and Mastery" workshops can attest.

■ Richard (Rick) Ross and I have worked together for ten years, engaging in regular dialogue about the nature of learning in organizations for most of that time. He is the most vocal champion among us for the practical manager's needs and concerns. He began his career as a neuroscientist, investigating where in the brain different types of learning occur. He went on to become a clinical psychologist, a practicing manager, and finally an organizational consultant. He has worked extensively with major corporations, focusing increasingly on the design and delivery of programs for intact teams, and on methods for implementing the learning disciplines. We sometimes think that all of this is merely preparation for his real calling—being a stand-up comic. Rick has served on the faculty of the University of Southern California and is currently the president of Ross Partners. He lives in San Diego, California.

■ Bryan Smith is president of Innovation Associates of Canada. He lives in Thornhill, Ontario. He and I have been good friends for almost fifteen years. A central focus of his work involves helping organizations become healthy, vibrant communities of common purpose, by applying the learning disciplines to strategic planning, team development, and organizational change. Bryan began his study of visionary leadership in his doctoral work seventeen years ago, and he is extraordinarily insightful into the dilemmas and strategies of effective leadership. He is without doubt one of the most thoughtful and experienced consultants in this field. In this project he took on the unofficial role of "team diplomat."

■ Art Kleiner has been a professional writer since 1985. He is a contributing editor of the *Whole Earth Review* and *Garbage Magazine,* a faculty member at New York University's Interactive Telecommunications Program, and a consulting editor at MIT's Center for Organi-

About the Authors

Peter Senge

Like my previous book, *The Fifth Discipline,* this "fieldbook" describes the experimentation, research, writing, and invention of hundreds of people. My colleagues in the organizations with which I am associated—the Center for Organizational Learning at MIT's Sloan School of Management, where I am director; the consulting and training firm Innovation Associates, where I continue to conduct "Leadership and Mastery" workshops; and the Learning Circle, a new organization founded to develop the worldwide community of learning organization practitioners—and I have come to know, and often participate in, many new stories of change. More than ever we are coming to believe that a "new type of management practitioner" is emerging today, a person who is willing to combine his or her own personal learning with broader collective action in an organization.

As we have met more and more people who fit this description, we realized the potential value of a book—or a series of books—sharing the learnings emerging in this growing community. Alone I would have been unable to realize this vision, in part because of the demands of my commitments in building the MIT Learning Center. Fortunately, a group of longtime collaborators shared the vision of the *Fieldbook.* Each had been involved in implementing or communicating about learning-organization principles and methods for ten years or longer. It was delightful to watch how we quickly became a coherent team, with each of us bringing his or her distinctive sensibility to the project.

The team of authors of the *Fieldbook* includes:

- Charlotte Roberts—a speaker, consultant, program designer, and writer whose work has focused on the executive team's role in a learning organization. Charlotte and I have probably co-led more

Endnotes

zational Learning. His book, *The Age of Heretics* (in progress for Currency Doubleday), is a history of the social movement of people trying to change large corporations for the better between 1970 and 1990. *The Fifth Discipline* never would have turned out as it did without Art's help. He is, in my experience, a unique combination of writer, editor, and coach—with a genuine commitment to helping people find their own voice. If he ever gets bored with writing, he'd be a great consultant. It is very nice that he can "come out from behind the curtain" for the *Fieldbook*, for which he serves as editorial director.

In addition, we have all drawn heavily upon contributions from many, many other people—colleagues from whom we have learned much, and contributors whose writing appears directly in this volume. A list of acknowledgments appears on page 567.

Getting Started

1 "I See You"

Among the tribes of northern Natal in South Africa, the most common greeting, equivalent to "hello" in English, is the expression: *Sawu bona*. It literally means, "I see you." If you are a member of the tribe, you might reply by saying *Sikhona,* "I am here." The order of the exchange is important: until you see me, I do not exist. It's as if, when you see me, you bring me into existence.

This meaning, implicit in the language, is part of the spirit of *ubuntu,* a frame of mind prevalent among native people in Africa below the Sahara. The word *ubuntu* stems from the folk saying *Umuntu ngumuntu nagabantu,* which, from Zulu, literally translates as: "A person is a person because of other people."* If you grow up with this perspective, your identity is based upon the fact that you are seen—that the people around you respect and acknowledge you as a person.

During the last few years in South Africa, many corporations have begun to employ managers who were raised in tribal regions. The *ubuntu* ethic often clashes subtly with the culture of those corporations. In an office, for instance, it's perfectly normal to pass someone in the hall, while preoccupied, and not greet him. This would be worse than a sign of disrespect under the *ubuntu* ethic; it would imply that you felt that person did not exist. Not long ago, an internal consultant who had been raised in a rural village became visibly upset after a meeting where nothing much had seemed to happen. When a project where he had

* Our understanding of the meaning of *sawu bona* and *ubuntu* derives from conversations with Louis van der Merwe and his colleagues James Nkosi and Andrew Mariti.

played a key part came up for discussion, his role was not mentioned or acknowledged. Asked later why it bothered him so much, he said, "You don't understand. When they spoke about the project, they did not say my name. They did not make me a person."

In putting this book together, we aspire to the mutual respect and openness that is embedded in the spirit of *ubuntu.* As a book of "notes from the field," this volume takes its shape and meaning from the aspiration and commitment of the people who will read these pages, the people who are working to build learning organizations. You could argue that we invoke each others' potential by our willingness to see the essence of each other. Therefore, we would like to offer a formal acknowledgment and welcome to this book:

We see you. We are glad you are here.

2 An Exchange of Lore and Learning

The Purpose of *The Fieldbook*

This book is for people who want to learn, especially while treading the fertile ground of organizational life. It is for people who want to make their organizations more effective, while realizing their personal visions. And it is for managers facing an array of problems which resist current ways of thinking, managers who want to know: "How do I fix things?" You can't just "fix things," at least not permanently. You can apply theories, methods, and tools, increasing your own skills in the process. You can find and instill new guiding ideas. And you can experiment with redesigning your organization's infrastructure. If you proceed in all these ways, you can gradually evolve a new type of organization. It will be able to deal with the problems and opportunities of today, and invest in its capacity to embrace tomorrow, because its members are continually focused on enhancing and expanding their collective awareness and capabilities. You can create, in other words, an organization which can learn.

The idea of a learning organization has become increasingly prominent over the last few years. This book's predecessor, *The Fifth Disci-*

pline°, helped give voice to that wave of interest by presenting the conceptual underpinnings of the work of building learning organizations. Since its publication in 1990, we have talked to thousands of people who have committed themselves to the idea of building a learning organization. Many of them are still not certain how to put the concepts into practice. "This is great," they say, "but what do we do Monday morning? What steps should we take to instill a sense of systemic awareness in a team of people? How can we integrate new types of skills and practices with other organizational improvement efforts, like total quality, sociotechnical systems, or selfmanaging teams? How do we navigate past the many barriers and roadblocks to collective learning? How do we discover exactly what type of learning organization we wish to create? How do we get started?"

No one person has *the* answers to these questions. But there are answers. They are emerging from the collective experience of people working to increase learning in a wide variety of settings. Thousands of us are evolving together into a worldwide community, with enormously powerful potential. In that sense, the readers of this book are pioneers. Some scout the edge of the learning organization frontier, while others settle the territory, testing new concepts in organization practice, perhaps building a new type of civilization in the process.

It would be nice to compile a definitive book of diagnosis and technique which could become the learning organization equivalent to *Architectural Graphic Standards* or the *Physicians' Desk Reference.* But architects, physicians, and other professions evolved their tools and methods over hundreds of years. Management, particularly the management of learning organizations, is much younger. It will take years of experimentation and testing for a full-fledged handbook to be published.

Instead it is time for a "fieldbook"—a collection of notes, reflections, and exercises "from the field." This volume, the first in what we hope will be an ongoing series, contains 172 pieces of writing by 67 authors, describing tools and methods, stories and reflections, guiding ideas, and exercises and resources which people are using effectively. Many of the pieces are intensely pragmatic, geared toward helping you solve particular problems. Many of them are deeply reflective, aimed at helping you productively change the ways you think and interact.

There are no "top ten" learning organization exemplars in this book—no excellent learning companies, no sterling *wunder-orgs* that do everything so well that the rest of us need only benchmark and copy them. Instead, we believe that the learning organization exists primarily

° *The Fifth Discipline: The Art & Practice of the Learning Organization* by Peter M. Senge (1990, New York: Currency Doubleday).

as a vision in our collective experience and imagination. Today, to an unprecedented degree in the history of the modern professionally managed organization, people are encouraged to look beyond their own organizational walls for ideas and support. Because no single organization has the resources to conduct *all* the necessary experiments on its own, managers seek avidly to learn about each others' attempts, results, and reflections. The people who develop and exchange this information are not merely *talking* about the learning organization; they use it as a springboard for experiments and initiatives. With each effort they make, they create a new facet of the overall image of what the learning organization can be.

The more detailed and clear that image becomes, the more easily and effectively we will be able to pursue it. Since the richness of this vision depends on conversations among people, the interrelationships of this "community of commitment" take on enormous strategic importance. We hope this *Fieldbook* will contribute to making the community stronger.

The five disciplines

THE CORE OF LEARNING ORGANIZATION WORK IS BASED UPON FIVE "learning disciplines"—lifelong programs of study and practice:

- Personal Mastery—learning to expand our personal capacity to create the results we most desire, and creating an organizational environment which encourages all its members to develop themselves toward the goals and purposes they choose.
- Mental Models—reflecting upon, continually clarifying, and improving our internal pictures of the world, and seeing how they shape our actions and decisions.
- Shared Vision—building a sense of commitment in a group, by developing shared images of the future we seek to create, and the principles and guiding practices by which we hope to get there.
- Team Learning—transforming conversational and collective thinking skills, so that groups of people can reliably develop intelligence and ability greater than the sum of individual members' talents.
- Systems Thinking—a way of thinking about, and a language for describing and understanding, the forces and interrelationships that shape the behavior of systems. This discipline helps us see how to

change systems more effectively, and to act more in tune with the larger processes of the natural and economic world.

To practice a discipline is to be a lifelong learner on a never-ending developmental path. A discipline is not simply a "subject of study." It is a body of technique, based on some underlying theory or understanding of the world, that must be studied and mastered to put into practice. As you develop proficiency, your perceptual capacity develops; you gradually surrender to new ways of looking at the world. For example, once you begin to master team learning or systems thinking, it is very difficult to play the old office game of optimizing your position at the expense of the whole.

Some people have an innate gift for a discipline, but an innate gift is not the key to mastery: many people have great artistic talent but never produce any art of consequence because they do not follow a lifelong process of honing and developing their talent. In organizations, we believe the people who contribute the most to an enterprise are the people who are committed to the practice of these disciplines for themselves—expanding their own capacity to hold and seek a vision, to reflect and inquire, to build collective capabilities, and to understand systems.

3 How to Read This Book

Start anywhere. Go anywhere

We HAVE DESIGNED THE BOOK TO REWARD BROWSING IN ANY DIRECTION. Cross-references, for example, point out meaningful links. Zoom in where you feel engaged. Here are some starting points:

- "Why Bother?"—The benefits of this work: pages 9 and 13.
- "Moving Forward"—Peter Senge's essay proposing a strategic framework for designing a learning organization effort: page 15.
- "Defining Your Learning Organization"—A solo exercise defining what kind of organization *you* want to create: page 50.
- "Designing a Learning Organization: First Steps"—A team exercise for getting started: page 53.
- "Opening Moves"—Entry paths for different organizations: page 77.

Make the book your own

MARK UP THE PAGES. WRITE ANSWERS TO THE EXERCISES IN THE MARgins. Draw. Scribble. Daydream. Note the results of what you have tried, and ideas of what you would like to try. Over time, as your field notes accumulate, they will become a record of effective practices—and a tool for reflecting on the design of the next initiative.

Do the practice

EXERCISES AND TECHNIQUES PRODUCE A DIFFERENT KIND OF LEARNING from simply reading about the work. If you feel "I already know that," ask yourself honestly: Does your knowledge about these skills and methods show up in your performance? If not, then we suggest trying the exercises and techniques that seem useful.

Margin icons

TO MAKE BROWSING THROUGH THE BOOK EASIER, WE USE MARGIN ICONS to indicate different types of material:

Solo Exercise

Solo Exercise: An exercise which you practice alone—to deepen understanding and capability, to bring forth an example from your own experience, to set personal direction, or to provoke an "aha!"

Team Exercise

Team Exercise: An exercise for a group of people working together, sometimes conducted by a facilitator or team leader.

Guiding Ideas

Guiding Ideas: A principle (or set of principles) which we find meaningful as a philosophical source of light and direction.

Infrastructure

Infrastructure: Innovations in organizational design which affect authority, structures, information flow, and the allocation of resources.

Theory and Methods: Techniques and the theoretical underpinnings which give those techniques their power.

Theory and Methods

Cameo: The voice of a guest contributor. We asked each "cameo" writer to discuss an issue that emerged in his own work, and what he discovered as he dealt with it.

Cameo

Lexicon: A guide to the roots of the words we use, and the way we use them now. Staking out the precise meaning of words is important in a field like management, where so much jargon is used so loosely.

Systems Story: Stories which incorporate systems archetypes or other applications of systems thinking.

Systems Story

Tool Kit: A practical device or technique.

Tool Kit

Resource: Recommendations of books, articles, and videotapes which we have found valuable.

Resources

4 Why Bother?

Why build a learning organization? Why commit ourselves to a lifelong attempt to understand and shift the ways we think and behave?

BECAUSE WE WANT SUPERIOR PERFORMANCE

Often it seems that the essence of management in the West is to extract ideas from the heads of people at the top of the organization and place them into the hands of people at the bottom. Konosuke Matsushita, the founder of the innovative company which bears his name, believed that this was the primary reason the West would never catch up with Japan economically.

Matsushita, who died in 1989, may have been right about Western management in the past; but in the last few years, at least, most organizations we know are trying to achieve what he described. Managers talk about it in different ways. Some say they want to build high-performance organizations or gain competitive advantage. Others talk about total quality management, fast cycle time systems, self-managing work teams, empowered organizations, improving their innovation and productivity, finding core competencies, or (as we do) building learning organizations. No matter what words they use, they are all really describing different facets of the same fundamental purpose: to marry the individual development of every person in the organization with superior economic performance.

TO IMPROVE QUALITY

One of the most powerful discoveries for us during the past several years has been seeing how closely our work on learning organizations dovetails with the "Total Quality" movement. Again and again we have found that organizations seriously committed to quality management are uniquely prepared to study the "learning disciplines."

FOR CUSTOMERS

Xerox Canada monitors some of the copiers it sells through a telecommunications link. If a machine isn't working right, technicians replace it for free—often before the users of the machine have noticed any problems. Xerox's marketing people estimate that the accumulated effect of customer gratitude and word of mouth is worth millions in advertising and promotion to the people they most want as customers.

To offer this service, Xerox had to be more than competent. They had to bring together people from throughout the company—marketing, research and development, technology, customer service, logistics, sales, purchasing, and accounting—in service of a common purpose.

Said former Xerox Canada CEO David McCamus during one of their shared vision sessions, "If we can genuinely satisfy customers, be part of their business, and be a real resource to people, then I can feel good about that at the end of my career."

FOR COMPETITIVE ADVANTAGE

In the long run, the only sustainable source of competitive advantage is your organization's ability to learn faster than its competition. No outside force can take the momentum of that advantage away from you. Arie de Geus, the former Coordinator of Group Planning at Royal Dutch/Shell, who articulated this idea in the late 1980s,° explains it this way: "Any insight or invention, whether it is a new way of marketing, a new product, or a new process, is really a learning process. At Shell, we saw we did not have to be too secretive—provided we were not standing still. If we continued to learn and generate new ideas, and incorporate them into our work, then by the time anyone had copied us we would be that much further along."

° ℙlanning as Learning," by Arie de Geus, *Harvard Business Review,* March/April 1988.

FOR AN ENERGIZED, COMMITTED WORK FORCE

Without learning about the business, as well as their own tasks, employees cannot make the contributions that they are capable of. This requires dramatic learning efforts, both for the employees who must learn to act in the interest of the whole enterprise, and for the senior managers who must learn how to extend mastery and self-determination throughout the organization.

TO MANAGE CHANGE

If there is one single thing a learning organization does well, it is helping people embrace change. People in learning organizations react more quickly when their environment changes because they know how to anticipate changes that are going to occur (which is different than trying to predict the future), and how to create the kinds of changes they want. Change and learning may not exactly be synonymous, but they are inextricably linked.

FOR THE TRUTH

"If I speak out," people realize when they begin building a learning organization, "now I won't be labeled as someone with a bad attitude. I can talk about the things that aren't going right, or come clean with my customers and suppliers, instead of having to just shut up and live with it."

In many cases, the most senior executives are the most eager of all to see the freedoms to speak the truth take hold. Now they can say, "I don't know the answer. And I have faith that we'll figure it out."

BECAUSE THE TIMES DEMAND IT

During the next thirty years, cutting-edge technological changes will spin out into everyday life. The importance of economies of scale may diminish. Factories might produce autos on Monday, refrigerators on Tuesday, and robots on Friday. New types of energy and communications grids will contribute to reshaping the political structure of local communities. People in learning organizations will be able to look forward to creating, instead of merely reacting to, the new world that emerges.

BECAUSE WE RECOGNIZE OUR INTERDEPENDENCE

Peter Senge

Throughout human history, the critical threats to survival came as dramatic external events: saber-toothed tigers, floods, earthquakes, attacks by rival tribes. Today, the most critical threats are slow, gradual processes to which we have contributed ourselves: environmental destruction, the global arms race (which continues unabated by the breakup of the Soviet Union), and the decay of educational, family, and community structures. These types of problems cannot be understood, given our conventional ways of thinking. There is no beast to slay, no villain to vanquish, no one to blame—just a need to think differently and to understand the underlying patterns of dependency. Individual change is vital, but not sufficient. If we are going to address these conditions in any significant way, it will have to be at the level of *collective* thinking and understanding—at the level of organizations, communities, and society.

BECAUSE WE WANT IT

Ultimately, the most compelling reason for building a learning organization is because we want to work in one. Or because there is nothing we would rather be doing with our lives right now than building a learning organization.

5 Why Bother? (A CEO's Perspective)

William O'Brien

William O'Brien, formerly the Chief Executive Officer of the Hanover Insurance Company, is now a member of the board of governors of the Center for Organizational Learning at MIT. (Also see page 306.)

Most people I talk to in business today agree that extraordinary changes are taking place in the business universe. These changes go beyond an imbalance between supply and demand, or the advance of new technology. They represent an adjustment to far-reaching forces, including an evolution of the global work force that is unprecedented in history.

In the period which we might call the modern industrial technology age—the time from 1920 to 1990, when Ford, General Motors, Du Pont, and many other large corporations were growing up—there were several driving forces behind the success of every winning company. The most important was efficiency of manufacturing; the ability to mass-produce, specialize work, and cut every cost down to the smallest tenth of a percent. Second, the winning companies learned to be effective mass marketers. A third attribute was rapid adoption of technology, and a fourth was financial acumen—the ability to analyze activity in detail, determine how to get the best rates of return, and keep capital moving. The fifth driving force was a set of elementary people skills, which companies developed through sincere efforts to move from Douglas McGregor's "Theory X" to "Theory Y." All these forces gave momentum to the wave of modern industrial technology.

Now, I believe, a new wave is forming: the beginning of a twenty-first-century era which is yet unnamed. It is difficult to see the potential of that era if you're a CEO of a major corporation (or of any organization), because right now, we are at the bottom of the trough. No one knows what their industry is going to look like at the top of the next wave, in the next century. If you're in insurance, my own business, you don't know how the legal and regulatory situation will change; if you're in manufacturing, every aspect of global competitiveness, trade, and technology is uncertain. For any group of people charged with corporate governance, it would be like playing Russian Roulette to base your business on any picture of what is going to happen during the next curve. If you think you can figure it out, then I suggest you are in dire need of humility.

Instead, the only prudent thing one can do in this position is to ask oneself, "What are the preconditions to cope with this change?" Personally, I bet that four abilities will be necessary. I don't say there are only four; nor am I sure they're the right four. But they are the four I bet on.

The first is learning how to disperse power on an orderly, nonchaotic basis. Right now the word "empowerment" is a very powerful buzzword. It's also very dangerous. Just granting power, without some method of replacing the discipline and order that come out of a command-and-control bureaucracy, produces chaos. We have to learn how to disperse power so self-discipline can largely replace imposed discipline. That immerses us in the area of culture: replacing the bureaucracy with aspirations, values, and visions.

The second attribute of winning companies will be systemic understanding. In the insurance industry, we have extensive information, large computers, and smart actuaries spreading risk; but when we put them all together, nobody's satisfied with the way the automobile insurance system is working. We're good at the type of problem which lends itself to a scientific solution and reductionistic thinking. We are absolutely illiterate in subjects that require us to understand systems and interrelationships.

The third attribute that twenty-first-century companies will need is conversation. This is the single greatest learning tool in your organization—more important than computers or sophisticated research. As a society, we know the art of small talk; we can talk about how the Red Sox are doing or where we went on vacation. But when we face contentious issues—when there are feelings about rights, or when two worthwhile principles come in conflict with one another—we have so many defense mechanisms that impede communications that we are absolutely terrible. To navigate this enormous change we're going through, a corporation must become good at conversation that isn't polite.

Finally, under our old system of governance, one could lead by mandate. If you had the ability to climb the ladder, gain power, and then control that power, you could enforce these changes in attributes. But the forthcoming kind of company is going to require voluntary followership. Most of our leaders don't think in terms of getting voluntary followers; they think in terms of control.

INGREDIENTS FOR SUCCESS

1920–1990

- Efficient manufacturing
- Effective mass marketing
- Rapid adoption of technology
- Financial acumen
- "Theory Y"

1990–the Future

- Distributing power while increasing self-discipline
- Systemic thinking skills as well developed as reductionist skills
- Improved conversation
- Voluntary followership

The abilities on the left of the chart will continue to be important. The bureaucratic way of life, after all, has done a great job in raising our material standard of living and relieving us from the oppression of hard, physical labor. But I don't think the new attributes will be a fad. Their essence, when you cut through all the propaganda, is marrying together individual growth and economic performance. You can never separate them. If you try to walk down one road without the other, you will not build a great organization. For me, personally, one of the turning points was the day I had to say to myself: What do I want to do with the rest of my life? Do I want to spend it coping with politics and other organizational diseases—or do I want to spend it working on building a great organization?

6 Moving Forward

Thinking Strategically About Building Learning Organizations

Peter Senge

How do you know what to do first, second, or third in this Fieldbook? No simple recipe can tell you, because everyone's needs are different. Hence this essay, the longest in the book, which presents a strategic framework—a conceptual map to guide your own decisions about how to proceed. You'll note that our icons throughout the book, listed on pages 8–9, are tagged directly to the "architectural elements" (the points of the triangle) described here.

"The most dangerous stage is respect"

When we try to bring about change in our societies, we are treated first with indifference, then with ridicule, then with abuse and then with oppression. And finally, the greatest challenge is thrown at us: We are treated with respect. This is the most dangerous stage.

—*A. T. Ariyaratne*°

° Speech made at International Community Leadership Summit, Winrock, Arkansas, March 1983. This quote paraphrases and expands upon a well-known statement made by Mahatma Gandhi in his book *Satyagraha in South Africa* (1928, 1979, Canton, Me.: Greenleaf Books).

A. T. Ariyaratne is one of the world's most successful community organizers. His organization, the Sarvodaya Shramadana, has mobilized millions of people in Sri Lanka in successful grass roots initiatives, with lasting benefits for Sri Lanka's economic and community development.

Ariyaratne reminds us that it is easier to begin initiatives than to bring enduring changes to fruition. At the early stages, excitement comes easily. Later, after you begin to make progress, opposition develops—which can actually mobilize your efforts. People see themselves fighting "a noble battle" against the entrenched forces preserving the status quo. A few small initial victories establish confidence that more progress is just around the corner. Eventually, the initiative is treated with respect: the "enemy outside" begins to espouse all the same goals, objectives, and ideals as those instigating the change. At this point, it is easy for people to think that the work is over. In fact, it may be just starting.

Today, there is a groundswell of interest in learning organizations. But in times of "respect," it becomes more important than ever to think and act strategically. Otherwise, all the talk about "learning organizations" will amount to little more than another management fad.

Thinking strategically starts with reflection on the deepest nature of an undertaking and on the central challenges it poses. It develops with understanding of focus and timing. Focus means knowing where to place one's attention. What is truly essential? What is secondary? What cannot be ignored without risking the success of the enterprise? Timing means having a sense of an unfolding dynamic. Although every organizational setting is unique, all organizations develop learning capabilities according to the same generic patterns. Some changes are intrinsically long term; they cannot be achieved quickly. Others can be started relatively quickly, but only assume lasting importance in concert with slower-occurring changes. Some changes can be achieved directly; others occur as by-products of effort focused elsewhere. Understanding such issues is the essence of strategic thinking.

Strategic thinking also addresses core dilemmas. Inevitably, one of the factors that makes significant change difficult is conflict among competing goals and norms: we want to distribute power and authority and yet we also want to improve control and coordination. We want organizations to be more responsive to changes in their environment and yet more stable and coherent in their sense of identity, purpose, and vision. We want high productivity and high creativity. Good strategic thinking brings such dilemmas to the surface, and uses them to catalyze imagination and innovation.

For the past fifteen years or longer, many of us have been struggling to understand what "learning organizations" are all about and how to make progress in moving organizations along this path. Out of these efforts, I believe, some insights are emerging to enhance our ability to think and act strategically. The purpose of this section is to share those ideas and to invite all of us, the growing community involved in doing this work, to help in testing and improving upon them.

The essence of "the learning organization"

At some time or another, most of us have been a member of a "great team." It might have been in sports, or the performing arts, or perhaps in our work. Regardless of the setting, we probably remember the trust, the relationships, the acceptance, the synergy—and the results that we achieved. But we often forget that great teams rarely start off as

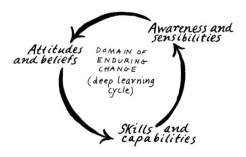

great. Usually, they start as a group of individuals. It takes time to develop the knowledge of working as a whole, just as it takes time to develop knowledge of walking or riding a bicycle. In other words, great teams are learning organizations—groups of people who, over time, enhance their capacity to create what they truly desire to create.

Looking more closely at the development of such a team, you see that people are changed, often profoundly. There is a deep learning cycle. Team members develop new skills and capabilities which alter what they can do and understand. As new capabilities develop, so too do new awarenesses and sensibilities. Over time, as people start to see and experience the world differently, new beliefs and assumptions begin to form, which enables further development of skills and capabilities.

This deep learning cycle constitutes the essence of a learning organization—the development not just of new capacities, but of fundamental shifts of mind, individually and collectively. The five basic learning disciplines are the means by which this deep learning cycle is activated. Sustained commitment to the disciplines keeps the cycle going. When this cycle begins to operate, the resulting changes are significant and enduring.

NEW SKILLS AND CAPABILITIES

We know that a genuine learning cycle is operating when we can do things we couldn't do before. Evidence of new skills and capabilities deepens our confidence that, in fact, real learning is occurring.

The skills and capabilities that characterize learning organizations fall into three natural groupings:

- **Aspiration:** the capacity of individuals, teams, and eventually larger organizations to orient themselves toward what they truly care about, and to change because they want to, not just because they need to. (All of the learning disciplines, but particularly the practice of personal mastery and building shared vision, develop these capabilities.)
- **Reflection and Conversation:** the capacity to reflect on deep assumptions and patterns of behavior, both individually and collectively. Developing capabilities for real conversation is not easy. Most of what passes for conversation in contemporary society is more like a Ping-Pong game than true talking and thinking together. Each individual tosses his or her view at the other. Each then responds. Often, we are preparing our response before we have even heard the

other person's view. In effect, we are "taking our shot" before we have even received the other's ball. "Learningful" conversations require individuals capable of reflecting on their own thinking. (These skills emerge especially strongly in the disciplines of mental models and team learning.)

〉〉 See the material on dialogue, page 357, and on reflection and inquiry skills, page 237.

■ **Conceptualization:** the capacity to see larger systems and forces at play and to construct public, testable ways of expressing these views. What seemed so simple from my individual point of view looks much less so when I see it from others' points of view. But constructing coherent descriptions of the whole requires conceptualization skills not found in traditional organizations. (Systems thinking is vital for these skills, especially in concert with the reflectiveness and openness fostered by working with mental models.)

〉〉 See "Brownie's Lamb," page 94.

Like any new skills, the skills and capabilities required in building learning organizations shape what we can understand and accomplish. But they are unusual because they affect us deeply. They are not skills of specialization, like learning "financial accounting for executives." They inevitably lead to new awarenesses because they bring about deep shifts in how we think and interact with one another.°

° A more in-depth discussion of these skills and capabilities appears in *The Fifth Discipline*, chapters 9 and 11 (aspiration), 10 and 12 (reflection and conversation), and 5 and 6 (conceptualization).

NEW AWARENESSES AND SENSIBILITIES

Over time, as our new skills and capabilities develop, the world we "see" literally shifts. For example, as we become better in systems thinking, we literally start to "see" underlying structures driving behavior. Where we might have leaped immediately to blame someone in the past, we now have an instinctive awareness of the forces compelling them to act as they do. Similarly, with increased awareness of our mental models, we become increasingly aware of the ways in which we continually construct our views of the world. Rather than "seeing" a customer as "tough to deal with," we are more able to hear the exact words she or he said, and recognize how their words trigger our own mental models. Rather than "seeing" a "mature market," we see assumptions and practices that have gone unquestioned for years—and perhaps begin to imagine alternatives.

Awareness and sensibilities

When a group begins to advance in the practice of dialogue, as William Isaacs points out, "a new type of listening emerges." People begin to "listen to the whole," hearing not only what individuals say, but deeper patterns of meaning that flow through the group. For example, it is quite common in advanced dialogues for people to report that someone else gave voice to the thoughts they were about to say. This eventually quiets our anxieties about "getting our points out." More importantly, it gradually builds a subtle awareness of collective thought that profoundly transforms our experience of what is possible in genuine conversation.

As we practice the disciplines of personal mastery and shared vision, we become increasingly aware of the presence or absence of spirit in an enterprise. We become more and more conscious of when we (and others) are operating based on our vision, versus when we are simply reacting to events. When a decision must be made by a team, people see the alternative in light of their vision and sense of purpose; and they often see new alternatives which would not have been visible if their deeper purpose were obscure.

Attitudes and beliefs

* See *Organizational Culture and Leadership* by Edgar H. Schein (1992, San Francisco: Jossey-Bass), p. 21 and following. See *Fieldbook,* p. 267.

NEW ATTITUDES AND BELIEFS

Gradually, new awarenesses are assimilated into basic shifts in attitudes and beliefs. This does not happen quickly. But, when it does, it represents change at the deepest level in an organization's culture—"the assumptions we don't see," as Edgar Schein puts it.*

Schein, who is the chairman of the Board of Governors of the MIT Center for Organizational Learning, distinguishes deep beliefs and assumptions from an organization's or a society's espoused values. For example, growing up in the United States, we are aware of our society's beliefs in the individual's innate rights and dignity. If, however, an American lives for some time in an Asian culture she becomes aware of a very different set of deep beliefs about loyalty to the group. She might discover that behind our espoused belief in the individual often lies a fear of losing our identity in a group—a fear that most Asian cultures do not engender.

Deep beliefs are often inconsistent with espoused values in organizations. The organization might espouse an ideal of "empowering" people, but an attitude that "they won't let us do it" prevails. Thus, even though espoused values change, the culture of the organization tends to remain the same. It is a testament to our naïveté about culture that we think that we can change it by simply declaring new values. Such declarations usually produce only cynicism.

But deep beliefs and assumptions can change as experience changes, and when this happens culture changes. The carrier of culture is, as author Daniel Quinn says, the story we tell ourselves over and over again. As we gradually see and experience the world anew, we start to tell a new story.°

The set of deep beliefs and assumptions—the story—that develops over time in a learning organization is so different from the traditional hierarchical, authoritarian organizational worldview that it seems to describe a completely different world. Indeed, in a way it does. For example, in this world we surrender the belief that a person must be "in control" to be effective. We become willing to reveal our uncertainties, to be ignorant, to show incompetence—knowing that these are essential preconditions to learning because they set free our innate capacity for curiosity, wonder, and experimentalism. We start to give up our faith in the analytic perspective as the answer to all of life's problems. Eventually, a deep confidence develops within us. We begin to see that we have far greater latitude to shape our future than is commonly believed. This is no naive arrogance. It develops in concert with awareness of the inherent uncertainties in life, and the knowledge that no plan, however well thought out, is ever adequate. This confidence is based simply on firsthand experience of the power of people living with integrity, openness, commitment, and collective intelligence—when contrasted to traditional organizational cultures based on fragmentation, compromise, defensiveness, and fear.

° *Ishmael* by Daniel Quinn (1992, New York: Bantam/Turner). See *Fieldbook*, p. 304.

The architecture of learning organizations

SINCE *THE FIFTH DISCIPLINE* WAS PUBLISHED, PERHAPS THE MOST OFTEN asked question has been, "How do we get started in practicing the learning disciplines?" People ask, "Do we simply need to get together and talk about the book? Or is it a matter of developing the right training programs?"

While the disciplines are vital, they do not in themselves provide much guidance on how to begin the journey of building a learning organization. The deep learning cycle is difficult to initiate. Skills involving fundamental new ways of thinking and interacting take years to master.

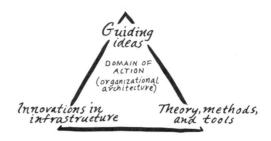

New sensibilities and perceptions of our world are a by-product of long-term growth and change. Deep beliefs and assumptions are not like light switches that can be turned on and off.

Imagine that we are standing in a beautiful open field, with the vision of building a new type of school—a school where children could continually develop their innate capabilities for learning. As architects, we would work with three critical elements. First, there would be materials needed in the construction. Second would be the tools with which we would design and eventually build the physical structure. Last would be our overarching ideas about how the school building should look, and how it could support the learning we desired to occur. Ultimately, many people will be involved in bringing the vision of the new school to fruition. But without the work of skilled and committed architects, they can never begin. The architecture is the "shell" within which the real work of the school will eventually take place.

In the same way, the real work of building learning organizations is the work of the deep learning cycle, and it is the province of all who engage in ongoing practice of the learning disciplines. But it takes place within a "shell," an architecture—of guiding ideas, innovations in infrastructure, and theory, methods, and tools.

GUIDING IDEAS

"Good ideas drive out bad ideas," says former Hanover Insurance CEO Bill O'Brien. "The problem with most companies is that they have no good ideas. Instead, they are driven by ideas like: 'The name of the game is climbing the corporate ladder,' or 'Do whatever it takes to win personally.' Like a bad ecology, these ideas pollute the organizational climate and become self-reinforcing."

Fortunately, guiding ideas can be developed and articulated deliberately. Indeed, this has long been a central function of genuine leader-

° Forgotten founders: Benjamin Franklin, the Iroquois, and the Rationale for the American Revolution by Bruce E. Johansen (1982, Ipswich, Mass.: Gambit Press).

history to the three-day retreats where management teams repair to author corporate mission or vision statements.°

To illustrate more serious efforts, consider the following statement by Bill O'Brien: "Our traditional organizations are designed to provide for the first three levels of Abraham Maslow's hierarchy of human needs — food, shelter, and belonging. Since these are now widely available to members of industrial society, these organizations do not provide anything particularly unique to command the loyalty and commitment of people. The ferment in management today will continue until organizations begin to address the higher order needs: self respect and self actualization."

In this statement, O'Brien articulates a larger context within which to consider the specifics of an organization's mission, vision, and values. He suggests that changes in the world offer a new opportunity for organizations to reach for higher aspirations. Regardless of whether you agree with his views, it is clear that they arise from considerable thought. They carry a sense of passionate conviction not captured in most mission statements. The fact that O'Brien and his colleagues at Hanover Insurance worked continually for twenty years to develop "a guiding philosophy" for the organization speaks eloquently for patience and perseverance.

The second distinguishing feature of powerful guiding ideas follows from the first—*seeing the process as ongoing*. Guiding ideas are not static. Their meaning, and sometimes their expression, evolve as people reflect and talk about them, and as they are applied to guide decisions and action. This, of course, is the central tenet of the discipline of building shared vision—that shared visions live in our ongoing conversations about what we seek together to create.

THREE KEY GUIDING IDEAS FOR LEARNING ORGANIZATIONS

° I am indebted to Fred Kofman for helping me to understand these three ideas and their potential significance (see "Communities of Commitment: The Heart of the Learning Organization" by Fred Kofman and Peter M. Senge, *Organizational Dynamics*, Fall 1993).

Are there guiding ideas relevant for all efforts to build learning organizations? A five-day introductory program developed for the member companies of the MIT Center for Organizational Learning offers one perspective. The program is organized around three interrelated ideas which constitute the philosophical core of the systems perspective. All three of these ideas question bedrock tacit assumptions of the Western cultural tradition.° Time will tell the merit of these as guiding ideas for a workable philosophy of management, but they seem to be pointing in the right direction.

ship. "We hold these truths to be self-evident . . ." With these simple words, the cornerstone ideas upon which the United States system of governance is based were articulated. Few acts of leadership have had greater impact.

Guiding ideas (or "governing ideas," as O'Brien calls them) for learning organizations start with vision, values, and purpose: what the organization stands for and what its members seek to create. Every organization, whether it deliberately creates them or not, is governed according to some explicit principles. They are not necessarily benign. Perhaps the most pernicious guiding idea to penetrate to the heart of Western business management over the past thirty to fifty years is that the *purpose* of the enterprise is to maximize return of the shareholders' investment. If people really come to believe this, then whatever ideas are articulated will, *by definition of the organization's purpose,* be subordinate to making money. Can there be little wonder that people in such organizations are uncommitted, that they view their jobs as mundane and uninspiring, and that they lack any deep sense of loyalty to the organization?

By contrast, management writer Ikujiro Nonaka describes the Japanese view that "A company is not a machine but a living organism, and, much like an individual, it can have a collective sense of identity and fundamental purpose. This is the organizational equivalent of self knowledge—a shared understanding of what the company stands for, where it's going, what kind of world it wants to live in, and, most importantly, how it intends to make that world a reality."°

But many attempts to articulate guiding ideas in organizations result in bland "motherhood and apple pie" mission or vision statements. What, then, distinguishes powerful guiding ideas? The first distinguishing feature is *philosophical depth*. Before the Founding Fathers could agree on the ideas articulated in the Declaration of Independence they literally invested years in study and conversation. They studied the evolution of democratic thinking in the West, the history of democratic governance systems among Native Americans, and hermeneutic philosophy, as transmitted through the Masonic order. Benjamin Franklin served as a colonial envoy to the Iroquois nation; during a three-decade period he wrote and published a number of works on Iroquois government practices. Only after five or ten years of patient and challenging conversation could they declare that "We hold these truths to be self-evident," jointly authoring a statement of precepts to which they were literally willing to commit "their lives, their fortunes, and their sacred honor." Contrast this

° "The Knowledge-Creating Company" by Ikujiro Nonaka, *Harvard Business Review,* November–December 1991, p. 313.

■ **The primacy of the whole** suggests that relationships are, in a genuine sense, more fundamental than things, and that wholes are primordial to parts. We do not have to create interrelatedness. The world is already interrelated.

In the West, we tend to think the opposite. We tend to assume that parts are primary, existing somehow independent of the wholes within which they are constituted. In fact, how we define "parts" is highly subjective, a matter of perspective and purpose. There is no intrinsic set of categories, no innate way to define elements that is built into the nature of the "real thing" we are looking at. Consider a simple mechanical system, like an airplane. Is it made up of a fuselage, wings, tail, and cockpit? Of metal parts and plastic parts? Or of a right half and a left half? There are an infinite number of ways to partition the plane. The categories we invoke depend upon whether we are a designer, a parts supplier, or a passenger. But what makes an airplane an airplane cannot be found in the parts. A submarine also has a fuselage and a tail; a large crane in a steel mill has a cockpit; and a blimp has all three. The identity of the airplane exists only in the function and design of the whole. The parts of the plane are neither absolute nor "out there." Rather, they arise as we as observers interact with the phenomenon we are observing.

The primacy of the whole is even more compelling when we consider living systems. Dividing a cow in half does not make two small cows. A person might be said to be comprised of a head, a torso, and limbs; or of bones, muscles, skin, and blood; or of the brain, lungs, heart, liver, and stomach; or of a digestive system, circulatory system, respiratory system, and nervous system; or of many, many cells. No matter what distinctions we choose, we cannot grasp what it is to be human by looking at the parts.

In the realm of management and leadership, many people are conditioned to see our "organizations" as things rather than as patterns of interaction. We look for solutions that will "fix problems," as if they are external and can be fixed without "fixing" that which is within us that led to their creation. Consequently, we are inevitably drawn into an endless spiral of superficial quick fixes, worsening difficulties in the long run, and an ever-deepening sense of powerlessness. In organizations, articulating the primacy of the whole as a guiding idea may be the first step in helping people break this vicious cycle.

*The Interpretation of Cultures by Clifford Geertz (1973, New York: Basic Books).

▪ **The community nature of the self** challenges us to see the interrelatedness that exists in us. Just as we tend to see parts as primordial to wholes, we tend to see the individual as primordial to the community in which the individual is embedded. "There is no such thing as human nature independent of culture," says anthropologist Clifford Geertz.*

When somebody asks us to talk about ourselves, we talk about family, work, things we care about, and what we do for fun. But in all of this talk, where is our "self"? The answer is nowhere, because the self is not a thing. The self is, as my colleague Fred Kofman says, "a point of view that unifies the flow of experience into a coherent narrative—a narrative striving to connect with other narratives." Moreover, the narrative is deeply informed by our culture. The stories we construct to make sense of our experience, to give meaning to our actions and thoughts, are stories that we have learned to construct.

When we forget the community nature of the self, we identify our self with our ego. We then assign a primordial value to the ego (part) and see the community (whole) as secondary. We see the community as nothing but a network of contractual commitments to symbolic and economic exchanges. Encounters with others become transactions that can add or subtract to the possessions of the ego.

The resulting loss is incalculable—isolation, loneliness, and loss of our "sense of place." We lose a sense of self which other cultures know very well. For example, in many indigenous cultures the essence of being a person is being in relationship to other people (like the culture of *ubuntu* described on page 3 of this book). In such cultures, our unquestionable "reality" of separation is not so "real." A culture where people greet one another with "I see you," and where speaking a person's name brings him or her into existence as a person, may seem "crazy" to us. But it is perfectly consistent with a systems view of life, which suggests that the self is never "given" and is always in a process of transformation.

As a guiding idea for learning organizations, the community nature of the self opens the door to powerful and beneficial changes in our underlying values. When we do not take other people as objects for our use, but see them as fellow human beings with whom we can learn and change, we open new possibilities for being ourselves more fully.

▪ **The generative power of language** illuminates the subtle interdependency operating whenever we interact with "reality" and implies a radical shift in how we see some of these changes coming about.

Werner Heisenberg shocked the world of classical physics in 1927 by claiming that when we measure the world we change it. With his uncertainty principle, Heisenberg gave "hard science" credibility to what philosophers had gradually come to understand over the preceding hundred years: that human beings cannot ever know what is "really real." We participate more deeply than we imagine in shaping the world that we perceive.

Philosophers have given the name "naive realism" to the worldview which holds rigid positions like the primacy of the parts and the isolated nature of the self. This worldview takes reality as a given entity outside our perception, and sees language as the tool through which we describe this external reality "out there." But as Heisenberg suggests, we have no actual way of ever knowing what is "out there." Whenever we articulate what we see, our language interacts with our direct experience. The "reality" we bring forth arises from this interaction.

The alternative to "naive realism" is recognizing the generative role of the traditions of observation and meaning shared by a community—and that these traditions are all that we ever have. When we are confronted by multiple interpretations of the "real world," the alternative to seeking to determine which is "right" is to admit multiple interpretations and seek those that are most useful for a particular purpose, knowing that there is no ultimately "correct" interpretation. The alternative to seeing language as describing an independent reality is to recognize the power of language that allows us to freshly interpret our experience—and might enable us to bring forth new realities.

When we forget the generative power of language, we quickly confuse our maps for the territory. We develop a level of certainty that robs us of the capacity for wonder, that stifles our ability to see new interpretations and new possibilities for action. Such are the roots of belief systems that become rigid, entrenched, and ultimately self-protective. When we forget the contingent nature of our understanding, who we are becomes our beliefs and views. This is why we defend against an attack on our beliefs as if it were against an attack on ourselves. In a very real sense, it is.

Theory, methods, and tools

THEORY, METHODS, AND TOOLS

Ideas such as these, which represent significant shifts in our predominant ways of thinking, can be daunting. The point of raising them is not to have people grasp them intellectually, nor to have people adopt them posthaste—but to find a way to pursue them meaningfully. It may be enough if they challenge all of us to think more deeply. If they stand the test of time, they will have to find their way into the way we conduct our work. How might this happen?

Buckminster Fuller used to say that if you want to teach people a new way of thinking, don't bother trying to teach them. Instead, give them a tool, the use of which will lead to new ways of thinking.

There are many tools and methods vital to developing learning organizations. Much of this book elaborates on methods and tools introduced originally in *The Fifth Discipline,* or presents new, complementary tools. All of these methods and tools help us enhance the capabilities that characterize learning organizations: aspiration, reflection and conversation, conceptualization.

Examples of methods and tools that help individuals, teams, and eventually larger organizations orient themselves toward what they truly care about (aspirations) include reflective practices for drawing out personal vision *(see "Drawing Forth Personal Vision," page 201),* and interactive practices for developing shared vision *(see "Building Shared Vision: How to Begin," page 312).* Examples of the methods and tools of reflective conversation include "Left-Hand Column Cases" *(see "The Left-Hand Column," page 247),* and dialogue exercises such as "Projector and Screen," and the use of blindfolds *(page 384).* Methods and tools for conceptualizing and understanding complex, interdependent issues include "system archetypes," *(see page 121),* and "management flight simulators" based on generic management structures such as new product development and service quality *(see page 530).*

Thinking in terms of theory, methods, and tools sheds new light on the meaning of the "disciplines for building learning organizations." These disciplines represent bodies of "actionable knowledge" comprised of underlying theories, and practical tools and methods derived from these theories.

The synergy between theories, methods, and tools lies at the heart of any field of human endeavor that truly builds knowledge. In music, the theory of sonata form has given rise to methods for developing sonata structures, as well as many instructional techniques for helping students understand and practice writing sonatas. In medicine, the theory of car-

THEORY, METHOD, TOOL

By the term "theory," I mean a fundamental set of propositions about how the world works, which has been subjected to repeated tests and in which we have gained some confidence. The English word "theory" comes from the Greek root word *theo-rós,* meaning spectator. This derives from the same root as the word "theater." Human beings invent theories for the same basic reasons they invent theater—to bring out into a public space a play of ideas that might help us better understand our world.

It is a shame that we have lost this sense of the deeper meaning of theory today. For most of us, theory has to do with "science." It suggests something cold, analytic, and impersonal. Nothing could be further from the truth. The process whereby scientists generate new theories is full of passion, imagination, and the excitement of seeing something new in the world. "Science," as Buckminster Fuller often said, "is about putting the data of our experience in order."

New theories penetrate into the world of practical affairs when they are translated into methods and tools. "Method" comes from the Greek *méthodos*—a means to pursue particular objectives. It gradually evolved into its current meaning: a set of systematic procedures and techniques for dealing with particular types of issues or problems.

"Tool" comes from a prehistoric Germanic word for "to make, to prepare, or to do." It still carries that meaning: tools are what you make, prepare, or do with.—PS

diac functioning—how a healthy heart functions and the irregularities that indicate a heart attack—has led to a long-standing methodology for cardiac monitoring to track heart attacks in progress and to avert those that are starting. The method advanced significantly when electronic cardiac monitors were developed—a tool which enabled much more precise and extensive monitoring.

Conversely, through developing practical tools and methods, theories are brought to practical tests, which in turn leads to the improvement of the theories. This continuous cycle—of creating theories, developing and applying practical methods and tools based on the theories, leading to new insights that improve the theories—is the primary engine of growth in science and technology.

The same basic connections between theory, method, and tools underlie each of the learning disciplines. Each embodies practical tools, which are grounded in underlying theory and methodology. In systems thinking, the tool of system archetypes is based on a general methodology, developed at MIT over the past 40 years, called "system dynamics," for understanding how the feedback structure of complex systems generates observed patterns of behavior. The methodology, in turn, is based on the theory of complex feedback systems that has been developing in engineering for the past 150 years. One part of that theory describes how complex systems involve reinforcing and balancing feedback processes (*see page 113*).

In the discipline of working with mental models, the "left-hand column case" (*page 247*) has proven to be a very useful tool to help managers begin to appreciate how underlying assumptions can sabotage conversations, especially when they go unrecognized and unarticulated. The tool derives from a general body of method which uses the actual "data" of conversations to unearth the reasoning which leads us to act in defensive or self-defeating ways. The power of the methodology, in turn, derives from underlying theories about the nature of mental models (such as "the ladder of inference," *page 242*), and about the sources of defensiveness when we perceive threat or potential embarrassment. These theories have their origins in developments in linguistics and in cognitive and social psychology over the past sixty years.

Why is it important for tools to be based on underlying theories? After all, isn't the most important aspect of a tool its usefulness?

Yes and no. It is hard to argue with a tool that seems helpful. Not long ago, an experienced management consultant presented his methods at an MIT seminar. When asked at the end of his presentation about the theoretical bases of his methods, he said that there were none. They were just tools that he had developed over his years of experience and they seemed to work. I left the seminar feeling uneasy. I believe there were several reasons for my concern.

First, such "theory-less" tools are not likely to significantly add to our store of generalizable knowledge. Without underlying theory, you get tools which might work in one situation, but you don't know why. They might fail in other situations, but you don't know why either. Ultimately the tool's usefulness may depend on unreproducible aspects of a particular person's skill. A really good consultant can make the tool work. But all the rest of the people in your company haven't got the foggiest idea how to apply it effectively.

Second, with no underlying theory, we may not always appreciate the limitations of a tool, or even its counterproductiveness if used inappropriately. In our rush to solve practical problems, we may grab at ready-made solutions that neither address the fundamental causes of a problem, nor stretch our thinking in important new directions.

Herein lies the strongest reason to look for tools based on important new theories: only such tools have the *power to change how we think*. Most tools introduced into management to solve problems, however innovative they may be, are based on conventional ways of thinking. After all, without an underlying theory, how could they be otherwise? Such tools may be useful, but they will not be transformative. They often leave deeper sources of problems unchanged. To paraphrase Albert Einstein, our present problems cannot be solved at the level of thinking at which they were created.

For example, many useful "systems analysis" tools are available for diagramming, analyzing, and redesigning organizational work flow processes. Some of these tools have been applied and refined over many years. But virtually all of them are based on a static way of seeing the world. They recognize that "everything in the system is connected," but they characterize that connectedness in terms of "detail complexity." They help to create a snapshot showing how a system works at a moment in time. This helps to rearrange the elements of that system into a more ideal picture.

But conventional static systems analysis tools offer no understanding of how the problems we have today have developed over time, especially if the causes are nonobvious. Nor will they help in understanding the likely consequences of our future efforts at change, especially where we might take actions that make things better today but worse tomorrow. Because they are a product of our present ways of thinking, static systems tools will tend to merely reinforce the notion that "somebody else" created our problems. They offer no penetrating insights into how our own actions may have caused our present problems—or how our own perspective led us to the obvious "fixes" that eventually made our problems worse. For this you need a dynamic, not a static, perspective.

Relying on our present ways of thinking, it is very difficult to develop tools that change that way of thinking. For this we must find or generate new theory. Although relatively rare, there are strong examples of the impact of managerial tools and methods supported by bringing in a new body of theory to a field where it had not yet been applied. For example, the total quality tools like control charts derive their usefulness from the theory of stationary statistical processes, a well-established field within mathematics.

Innovations in infrastructure

INNOVATIONS IN INFRASTRUCTURE

Infrastructure is the means through which an organization makes available resources to support people in their work. Just as an architect and contractor of a house must develop mechanisms to get the right building materials and bring them to the site, builders of learning organizations must develop and improve infrastructural mechanisms so that people have the resources they need: time, management support, money, information, ready contact with colleagues, and more.

Organizations seeking to enhance learning have experimented with diverse innovations in infrastructure. For example, in Japan quality management led to organizing front line workers in "quality circles" and setting up various management councils to support quality improvement. The innovations in infrastructure that will support emerging learning organizations encompass a broad range of changes in "social architecture"—including changes in organizational structures (such as self-managing work teams), new designs for work processes, new reward systems, information networks, and much more.

In his classic book *Out of the Crisis*, the eminent quality pioneer W. Edwards Deming suggested his own example of an innovation in infrastructure: "Efforts and methods for improvement of quality and productivity in most companies and in most government agencies are fragmented, with no overall competent guidance, no integrated system for continual improvement." He proposed a general "organization for quality" including a "leader for statistical methodology" reporting directly to top management and local counterparts throughout the organization, "with authority from top management to be a participant in any activity that in his judgment is worthy of his pursuit." The purpose of this leader would not be to dictate the quality techniques, but to make sure that people throughout the organization learned and understood them—such an important task, in Deming's view, that it took precedence over conventional line management.[*]

I first discovered the importance of infrastructure for learning through my experiences with the "group planning" office at Royal Dutch/Shell. Over the past twenty years, there has been a steady evolution of "planning as learning" throughout Shell's worldwide group of 150 operating companies. This evolution has encompassed a broad array of

[*] *Out of the Crisis*, by W. Edwards Deming (1982, 1986, Cambridge, Mass.: MIT Center for Advanced Engineering Study), pp. 466–67.

tools and methods, such as scenario analysis and systems modeling. But, more importantly, it has also led to a new understanding of the role of planning as an infrastructure to enhance learning throughout the organization. Planning is no longer primarily a staff function for coming up with the proper "answer" which managers must then implement, but a process "whereby management teams," says former planning head Arie de Geus, "change their shared mental models of their company, their markets, and their competitors."

During the past twenty-five years, Shell has steadily risen from one of the weakest to probably the strongest of the largest world oil companies. Throughout this period, the planning as learning approach has had first-order impacts on how the company recognized and responded to the turbulent, unpredictable world oil market. For example, Shell responded in a qualitatively different manner from other oil companies to the first round of OPEC oil-price shocks in the early 1970s. It rapidly decentralized operations while other oil companies were centralizing, and it worked hard to make refineries and trading operations more flexible, so that they could more quickly respond to changing availabilities. In the mid-1980s, Group Planning developed a "fictitious" case study involving a sudden *drop* in the world oil price, and managers throughout the world wrestled with how they would manage under such a change. Mental models that had adjusted to a world of twenty-eight dollars a barrel oil were challenged, and new assumptions had to be explored. As a result, Shell accelerated development of several key technologies to reduce cost in off-shore drilling, technologies which subsequently proved critical when oil prices fell to ten dollars a barrel in 1986 and stayed low in ensuing years.°

° "Planning as Learning" by Arie de Geus, *Harvard Business Review*, March–April 1988.

§§ To learn more about how this works in practice, see Kees van der Heijden's cameo, "Shell's
§§ Internal Consultancy," page 279.

Because learning is integral to planning, and because planning is inescapable to management, you cannot escape learning at Shell. It is not a marginal activity to be engaged in when one has spare time. In the Shell operating companies that participate, learning is no longer a concern of a handful of "experts" isolated from the mainstream of the business.

This contrasts sharply with many companies which attempt to drive learning through the training and education departments. While ongoing training and education are important, they are less integral to most business operations than planning is. Even though line managers may believe that an initiative pushed by training or human resources is worthwhile, in a world where people are already overcommitted and budgets are rarely abundant, what is not integral to the business often does not get done.

⟩⟩ See "A New Form of Corporate Planning" by Bryan Smith, page 80.

Other examples of learning integrated with the main work of the organization are beginning to emerge. When the Saturn division of General Motors developed its manufacturing facilities in Springhill, Tennessee, one of its first significant innovations was a "learning laboratory" adjacent to the manufacturing line. Called the Workplace Development Center, it was a complete mockup of an assembly line, where engineers and assembly line team members could try out new processes together, with videotape cameras, so people could study their own movements and relationship with the line. Said Saturn President Richard ("Skip") LeFauve: "Teams from the plant solve problems in simulated working conditions. We're passing on to employees design tools for assembly, manufacturing and synchronous operations. Traditionally, these tools were the property of management and were applied through an industrial engineering department. But at Saturn, they are common property."[*]

At AT&T, Chairman Bob Allen has established a variety of "forums" at different levels within the organization to encourage reflection and conversation about issues shaping the business's long-term health and vitality. This includes a "Chairman's Strategy Forum," which draws together the top 150 managers worldwide several times a year to examine key issues driving the business. In explaining the reason for the forums, Allen says, "We have plenty of infrastructure for decision making within AT&T. What we lack is infrastructure for learning."

These infrastructure innovations are not limited to the largest companies. At a home furnishings manufacturing firm, American Woodmark, the training department has been reshaped so that line managers are the principal trainers, and the content of the training is partly determined by conversations about the future of the organization.

⟩⟩ See "Training as Learning" by American Woodmark CEO Bill Brandt, on page 463.

The most important innovations in infrastructure for learning organizations will enable people to develop capabilities like systems thinking and collaborative inquiry *within the context of their jobs*. It matters little if we are masterful at inquiry in training sessions, but can only pontificate in real management meetings; or if we are accomplished in systems

[*] "Human Integrated Manufacturing (CE Roundtable)," *Chief Executive,* July–August 1992, p. 44; and "Saturn's Grand Experiment" by Beverly Geber, *Training,* June 1992, vol. 29, no. 6, p. 27.

thinking exercises but cannot apply them to real work settings. Until people can make their "work space" a learning space, learning will always be a "nice idea"—peripheral, not central.

PRACTICE FIELDS

Following this reasoning, we have focused much of our research at MIT on one potentially significant innovation in infrastructure—the managerial practice field. The underlying idea grows from comparing organizational settings where teams learn reliably with other settings where little team learning occurs. In sports and in the performing arts, two settings where teams consistently enhance their capabilities, players move regularly between a practice field and the real game, between rehearsal and performance. It is impossible to imagine a basketball team learning without practice, or a chamber music ensemble learning without rehearsal. Yet, that is exactly what we expect to occur in our organizations. We expect people to learn when the costs of failure are high, when personal threat is great, when there is no opportunity to "replay" an important decision, and when there is no way to simplify complexity and shorten time delays so as to better understand the consequences of actions. Is it any wonder that learning in organizations is rare?

At MIT, we are experimenting with two types of managerial practice fields. Our "learning laboratory projects" are focused on particular issue areas, like new product development and cycle time in complex supply chains. For example, several companies are collaborating at MIT in designing and testing a New Product Development Learning Laboratory.

Managers at one of these companies, Ford, describe their experience on page 554.

Other practice field projects, the "dialogue projects," focus on the quality of conversation and capability for collective thinking. In some cases these projects take place with intact teams, such as management teams; in other cases, the "teams" are diverse groups of people who need one another to take effective action in a broad area of concern, such as the health care system of a community. The dialogue projects create a different sort of practice field, which is not defined by a set of particular management issues but by a common commitment to generate deeper levels of conversation which can penetrate into whatever issues, both personal and substantive, need to be addressed.

In both types of practice field projects, the overarching principle is to establish a new cycle of learning that connects practice and performance. And, in both types of projects, initial evidence suggests that the practice field concept may, indeed, be a breakthrough in learning infrastructure. At Ford, the learning laboratory is making a significant impact on internal coordination, quality, productivity, and timing in a major new car project.

At GS Technologies, an ongoing dialogue project has led to a profound shift in union-management partnership and consequently the birth of a new organization.

⟨⟨ The GS story appears on page 364. For more about dialogue, see page 357 and following.

The next steps in both projects are to diffuse the practice fields more widely, to further test their merits, and to see if they may indeed constitute significant new infrastructures for *organizational* learning.

The integrity of the architecture

LEADERS INTENT ON DEVELOPING LEARNING ORGANIZATIONS MUST FOCUS on all three of the architectural design elements. Without all three, the triangle collapses.

Without *guiding ideas,* there is no passion, no overarching sense of direction or purpose. People ask, "Why are we doing this?" or "What's this change in infrastructure all about?" Top management gets fired up about "total quality management," "reengineering" or some other hot idea. Time and resources are poured into achieving intended changes. But, after a year, with little tangible to show for the effort, something else hot comes along and the effort is abandoned. Ultimately, the organization remains at the whim of circumstance and external conditions. This happens again and again unless people discover that leadership involves articulating transcendent guiding ideas to which they will stay committed.

Without *theory, methods, and tools,* people cannot develop the new skills and capabilities required for deeper learning. Efforts at change lack depth and are ultimately seen as superficial. For example, the CEO and managers through the organization may espouse a guiding idea about "openness," and the importance of surfacing mental models. But if people do not practice regularly with tools like left-hand column cases, conversations polarize when issues get hot. People withhold their genuine views to avoid uncontrollable conflict, trust erodes, and "openness" is seen as a facade of "nice ideas" inconsistent with what actually happens in the organization.

Without *innovations in infrastructure,* inspiring ideas and powerful tools lack credibility because people have neither the opportunity nor resources to pursue their visions or apply the tools. Changes cannot take root and become part of the fabric of organizational life. Learning is left to chance. It is not managed with the same commitment that other critical organizational activities are given. Efforts to promote systems thinking, reflection, or other learning capabilities have little, enduring organization-wide impact. Infrastructure that is incongruent with guiding ideas can also lead to cynicism. Managers may espouse that "Human beings are intrinsically motivated to learning," but if people feel that they must pursue learning only "on their own time" then they lose faith not just in the organization, but in the idea of learning.

The early days of the quality movement in U.S. manufacturing provide an example of the need for all three elements. In the early 1980s, there was a rush to implement "quality circles," an innovation in infrastructure. However, the quality circle fad faded quickly. Gradually, we discovered that people working in quality circles needed to learn how to employ new tools and methods so they could begin rigorous analysis, testing, and improvement of their processes. But even then, quality circles (and the quality movement which replaced them) fell short of creating transformative change. They needed the third corner of the architectural triangle: appropriate guiding ideas to energize and direct organization-wide improvement.

In the case of quality management, three sets of guiding ideas are critical. The first, according to W. Edwards Deming, concerns "constancy of purpose" for the enterprise as a whole. The second has to do with understanding the nature of variation. Lastly, there is a set of guiding ideas that concern human motivation. All human beings, said Dr. Deming, are born with "intrinsic motivation": an inner drive to learn, to take pride in their work, to experiment, and to improve.° Without this lasting guiding idea, managers think they must motivate people to study and improve, and that they must keep watch over people to make sure that learning is occurring.

° *The New Economics* by W. Edwards Deming (1993, Cambridge, MA: MIT Center for Advanced Study), p. 111ff.

In my judgment, few American firms have grasped all three of these guiding ideas. Consequently, rarely has quality management become the "thought revolution in management" envisioned by Japanese quality innovator Kaoru Ishikawa.

Interestingly, when these three sets of guiding ideas are all present, basic innovations in infrastructure typically occur far more easily and sustainably. Levels of supervisory management are removed and don't return. Quality inspectors are eliminated permanently. Authority to study and improve work processes is pushed down to front-line workers, who embrace it as their own. Guided by an overall philosophy, and empowered by effective tools and methods and by the authority to take action, the quality improvement process then begins to lead to significant change.

Moreover, pursuing all of the elements of the architecture simultaneously generates synergies that do not occur when attention is paid to only one of the elements alone.

Innovations in
infrastructure

Theory, methods,
and tools

AVOIDING THE STRUCTURAL "QUICK FIX"

In the early stages of the quality movement in Japan in the 1950s, quality control experts applied statistical tools to more reliably check the quality of products produced. This sparked Japan's quality ascent. But more significant breakthroughs came in the early 1960s, when a few companies, led by Toyota and Komatsu, began to break with tradition by getting rid of quality control checkers, teaching the tools and methods directly to front line workers, and giving them authority to analyze their own processes. This linking of new tools with a new level of authority ignited an engine for continuous improvement.

Today, in the arena of "reengineering," a similar synergy is needed between infrastructure innovation and theory, tools and methods. Organizations are attempting to reorganize more around "horizontal" processes that cut across traditional vertical functions. But such "horizontal process" organizations are much more interdependent than traditional functional organizations. This places a particular burden on people to learn together and practice systemic thinking.

For example, a common form of reengineering is to "co-locate" all the engineers of a large product development effort into one site, to alleviate traditional organizational "stovepipes" separating engineering subspecialties. But in itself, this "co-location" often fails to get at the real barriers to cross-functional problem solving—which are in people's heads, not within the organizational structure. Solutions to cross-functional barriers tend to emerge only when the newly "co-located" engineers can develop openness and systems thinking skills, and discover how their individual ways of working might unintentionally sabotage the development of the product as a whole.

See Daniel Kim's story of the "tragedy of the power supply," on page 142.

Without a well-articulated theory and set of tools, most reengineering efforts are driven instead by vague concerns to eliminate redundancy or reduce costs. Even if such early efforts are successful, they do not build an organization's capability to continually reengineer itself. Often, the organizations become dependent on expert reengineering consultants.

Already, critiques have begun to surface about the arbitrariness and unreliability of reengineering when it is not guided by clear theory. British management historian John Thackray has written, "Re-engineering is not exactly a tool box—more of a direction, a cause, a faith in the possibilities of top-down revolutions." And when McKinsey partner John Hagel recently offered a list of common causes of reengineering failures, every item on the list was a symptom of the absence of appropriate theory: "failure to understand the processes that are being demolished before the re-engineering is implemented; attacking too many processes—there are usually only about five or six that are truly significant; exclusion of some parts of the corporation from any impact or consequences—ie, sacred cows; and excessive speed—most successful re-engineering programmes take three to four years."°

° "Fads, Fixes & Fictions," by John Thackray, *Management Today,* June 1993, pp. 40–42.

PREPARING THE SOIL AND DEVELOPING THE SEEDS

Many of the methods and tools of learning organizations will be impossible to implement widely without changes in traditional guiding ideas in management. In turn, new guiding ideas will prove impossible to instill widely without a corresponding commitment to appropriate methods and tools.

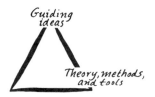

In the late 1960s, a major system dynamics study of a highly successful capital-goods manufacturer revealed that the firm had been losing market share because of its production policies. Whenever incoming orders declined, production schedules were cut back so aggressively that delivery times increased. The product was actually less available during recessions than during boom times. Disgruntled customers would turn to competitors, who would then retain their business once industry orders began to expand again.

Inspired by the insights of the study, the company's top management instituted a new production policy during the 1970 recession—to maintain production rates. Market share expanded and executives estimated a net profit gain of several million dollars. Unfortunately, four years later, when the major 1974 recession hit, the firm reverted to its traditional production policies, delivery times increased, and the decline in market share resumed.

The successful production policies failed to "stick" because three generations of CEO's had invested their reputations in developing aggressive inventory control policies. Inventory control had, in effect, become one of the company's preeminent guiding ideas. If you were a production manager, there was no more surefire way to ruin your career than to be responsible for overbuilding inventory. This fear could have been changed only through concerted effort by top management to articulate new guiding ideas that could gradually supplant it. But to champion such a change would require acknowledging that the old ideas were no longer appropriate—something top management was unwilling to do.

Despite its unhappy ending, the above case was more successful than many systems studies which never result in any changes in policies and practices, even temporary ones. The reason, again and again, is that the systemic insights are inconsistent with traditional guiding ideas. The precious seeds of new insight fall on barren soil.

For example, implementing systemic insights may require that diverse organizational interests cooperate in pursuing policies that might be suboptimal for individual functional areas. But such behavior can seemingly contradict traditions of functional excellence. Unless commitment to the mission and vision of the larger organization is greater than commitment to individual functional goals, functional goals will predominate.

Today, many executives are articulating a new philosophy revolving around "empowering people." But few organizations are working hard to introduce tools and methods to actually help people to make more intelligent decisions, especially decisions that improve systemwide performance. The result will likely be organizations which decentralize authority for a while, find that many poor and uncoordinated decisions result, and then abandon the "empowerment" fad and recentralize. The "empowered" soil will lie fallow, with no seeds to grow. This, of course, is precisely what many of the newly "empowered" workers, cynical from past management fads, fear.

Guiding ideas

Innovations in infrastructure

MAKING MEANING OF NEW STRUCTURES
In both political and corporate arenas, senior managers are often eager to make changes in infrastructure, believing that the more dramatic and quick the changes they make, the more long-lasting and positive the

effects may be. Yet, there is abundant evidence that changes in infrastructure, like reorganizations and changes in reward systems, often have far less impact than expected. One reason is that they conflict with established guiding ideas.

Despite the eagerness and political payoff that often come from changes in infrastructure, when we first work to articulate guiding ideas, and then design the infrastructure reform in harmony with those ideas, the results seem to be far more sustainable. Links to guiding ideas allow an infrastructure reform effort to move from a reactive to a creative orientation—to shift from a point of view which says (for example), "We've got to get rid of the structural barriers which are holding us back," to a point of view which says, "In the organization we really want to build, what structures (policies, reward systems, and resource-allocation mechanisms) would support our vision?"

For example, in 1990 the operations managers of Hill's Pet Nutrition, Inc. distributed a list of "guiding principles," including this statement about teamwork: "People will work as a team and cooperate when they share common goals, receive proper information, have the skills to recognize, utilize and balance others' strengths and weaknesses, value teamwork, are rewarded for doing so, [and] are recognized as a team for doing a good job." Having articulated that principle, they then instituted several infrastructural reforms which resonated with it. At a new "greenfield site," they began training all their employees *before* the equipment arrived in the plant. They insisted that the building's architect consider team learning in the design of the building. Union-management relationships, reward and appraisals, and all the other conventional mechanisms of "infrastructure" changed to match the growing understanding of guiding ideas by people throughout the organization. Most impressively, having a set of guiding principles allowed Hill's to develop infrastructural links between their four very different manufacturing facilities, allowing the management of all four sites to act together as members of a common team.

〳〵 Hill's vice president Joe Douglas and five other managers tell their story on page 429.

Putting it all together

THE POWER OF THE ABOVE IDEAS COMES WHEN WE PUT THE PIECES TOgether. An image emerges of the full scope of the work of building learn-

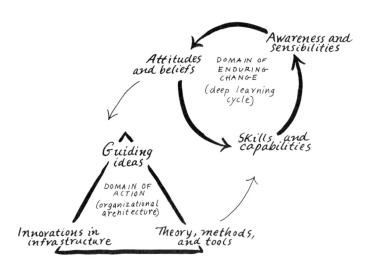

ing organizations; an image that is both more complete and more richly textured than can be seen from "the five disciplines" alone.

The triangle of organizational architecture represents the most tangible form of efforts. (Indeed, that is precisely why the triangle symbol is used: all physical structures start with the triangle. In three-dimensional construction, the most elementary physical structure is the triangle's cousin, the tetrahedron.) By contrast, the circle represents the more subtle underlying discipline-based learning cycle. (As a form, the circle is inherently abstract and intangible—with no edges or vertices, with no beginning and no end, an ancient symbol of ongoing movement.) The key focus for activity is in the triangle. The central causality of change is in the circle. Both continuously affect and influence one another. Together they represent the tangible and subtle changes involved in building learning organizations.

We tend to assume that which is most tangible is most substantial, and that which is intangible is insubstantial. In fact, the opposite is true. A set of guiding ideas articulated by one generation of management can be changed by another. An infrastructure developed and implemented today can be redesigned tomorrow. A current set of tools and methods can be supplanted by a new set of tools and methods. The very reasons why we focus on the triangle—because here is where we can make changes—also means that those changes can be short-lived.

By contrast, the deep learning cycle, which seems so evanescent and uncertain at first glance, endures. Once we begin to assimilate systems thinking as a way of seeing the world we become, in the words of one manager, "looped for life." Once we learn to distinguish our assumptions from the "data" upon which those assumptions are based, we are forever more aware of our own thinking. Once we begin to operate with a genuine sense of vision, we have a permanent understanding of the difference between reacting and creating. Once a group has participated in true dialogue, its members do not forget. Changes produced by the deep learning cycle are often irreversible.

I have seen countless cases where people continue to pursue their dreams even though there is no organizational reward, once they have developed enough confidence and competence to make progress. They simply do it because "it is the right thing to do." It sometimes becomes impossible for senior management to uproot a shared commitment to systems thinking and openness, once it has become established. Learning teams within organizations simply outlive unsympathetic bosses.

This does not mean that, having begun to practice the learning disciplines, we will retain high levels of mastery automatically. As in any discipline, our level of expertise ultimately depends on how far along our own developmental path we travel, and on our commitment to continual practice. But we do not forget the basic principles we have learned. The first deep effect of the learning cycle is orientational—we become oriented to a way of being that remains with us, as a sort of inner compass. We may not always operate in the manner of that discipline, but we tend to know when we are, and when we are not.

BALANCING ATTENTION BETWEEN TRIANGLE AND THE CIRCLE

When optical telescopes were the only form of astronomy, observers were trained to focus away from faint objects they were trying to detect, because the cones of the eye are actually more perceptive of objects on the periphery of our vision. Similarly, while changes in the circle are what really matters, attention is often best placed on the triangle of guiding ideas, infrastructure, and theory, methods and tools. These represent the operational changes where concentrated time and energy can produce results.

Yet, while we are focused on the triangle we are mindful of the circle. Buckminster Fuller used to talk about the "Principle of Precession" characteristic of many significant change processes. When you spin a top, the primary mode of movement is rotation around its axis. But, after a while, a secondary mode of movement develops. The top begins to *precess*, as the axis itself slowly, gradually begins to move around its original position. This precession is quite mysterious to the casual observer because it has no visible relation to the obvious rotation of the top. Unless we understand the dynamics of the top as a system, we might not even notice the precession, and we certainly wouldn't tend to connect this subtle movement to the spinning. So it is with the deep process of learning. For a long time it may appear that there is nothing going on except the surface activity of the triangle. People talk about new ideas. They practice the application of tools and methods. They design and implement changes in infrastructure. Yet, deeper changes are in the offing. When those deeper changes start to become evident, many people will not even notice them and those who do will often not connect them with the obvious activity.

Yet, the two are connected in subtle ways. The deeper changes are evoked only by sustaining the surface movement. If the rotation stops, so too will the precession. If we stop working to articulate guiding ideas, to improve infrastructure, and to apply the tools and methods embodied in the learning disciplines, the deeper learning cycle will not progress.

Similarly, the deeper changes will gradually affect the work on architecture. Potential guiding ideas like "openness" and "localness" will have little conviction until enough people experience the collective intelligence of the whole that is possible when capabilities for dialogue, mental models, shared vision, and systems thinking develop. This is one reason we generally advise against writing down mission or philosophy statements too hastily. A premature articulation can "freeze" people around principles which have not yet been experienced, precluding deeper understanding and conviction.

RESULTS

Ultimately, learning—whether it is learning to walk, ski, or compose symphonies—is judged by results. The rationale for any strategy for building a learning organization revolves around the premise that such organizations will produce dramatically improved results, compared to more traditional organizations. Whether the results include profit, time to market, customer loyalty, or other agreed-upon measures of effectiveness, learning must ultimately be assessed in terms of "how well the game is played." None of us would think a product development team was learning if it did not improve its products, or a sales team if it did not establish more loyal customers.

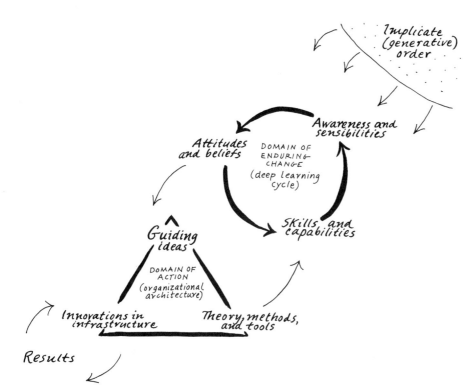

The problem is knowing how and when to measure important results. There are two interrelated issues in assessing results of learning processes: patience and quantification.

We need patience precisely because deeper learning often does not produce tangible evidence for considerable time. "You don't pull up the radishes to see how they're growing," says Bill O'Brien. Yet, in effect, impatient managers often do just that to assess whether or not learning processes are progressing. As a Ford manager pointed out in one of our recent core courses at MIT, "If calculus were invented today, our organizations would not be able to learn it. We'd send everyone off to the three-day intensive program. We'd then tell everyone to try to apply what they'd learned. After three to six months we'd assess whether it was working. We'd undoubtedly then conclude that this 'calculus stuff' wasn't all it was made out to be and go off and look for something else to improve results."

O'Brien states a simple guiding principle: "Time periods for measurement must be congruent with the gestation period of the learning." Measurements that are made prematurely will lead to erroneous conclusions. This principle, while easy to state, can be very difficult for impatient managers and organizations to practice.

The second problem with assessing results is quantification. Again, there is a simple guiding principle: "Measure quantitatively that which should be quantified; measure qualitatively that which should not be quantified." In almost all organizational learning settings there will be some important quantifiable results: sales, time to market, product quality, total cost (especially including many costs which are often hidden, like life cycle costs), and profit. But many of the most important results of organizational learning are not quantifiable: intelligence, openness, innovativeness, high moral quality, courage, confidence, genuine caring—for the customer, for one another, and for our shared aspirations. Despite the nonquantifiable nature of such results, they are not unknowable. There are many ways that people can come to agreement in making assessments of progress in producing such results. But there are also many dangers.

In particular, organizational "cultures that are saturated exclusively in scientific principles," says O'Brien," have an insatiable appetite for quantitative measurement—even when they misrepresent truth and reality." For example, management often uses quantitative "proxies" for qualitative results, such as the proxies used with operating staffs. "Managers," suggests O'Brien, often "become obsessed with the proxies and not with what the proxies are intended to represent. This often causes destructive games playing in companies," even to the point of causing people to do things to make the proxy look good counter to the desired result. "There are times," O'Brien concludes, "when the organization would have been better off without a measurement than with a faulty one." But this can be a difficult lesson for control-oriented cultures.

⌇⌇ See the "measurement trap" cameo by Edward Baker, page 454.

THE IMPLICATE ORDER

Lastly, there is also a level still more subtle than the deep learning cycle. This most subtle level is, however, also the most difficult to talk about. In fact, we may only infer its presence, since there is no tangible evidence of its existence. But ultimately it may prove vital to a full understanding of the deep shifts in awareness and capabilities of learning organizations.

The physicist David Bohm (one of the main contributors to the theory of dialogue) points out that the Western word "measure" and the Sanskrit "maya" appear to derive from the same origins. Yet, in the West, the concept of measure has come to mean "comparison to some fixed external unit," while maya means "illusion."

"In the prevailing philosophy in the Orient," says Bohm, "the immeasurable is regarded as the primary reality. In this view," he adds, "the entire structure and order of forms . . . that present themselves to ordinary perception and reason are regarded as a sort of veil, covering the true reality, which cannot be perceived by the senses and of which nothing can be said or thought."°

Bohm proposed a "new notion of order" to describe this deeper reality, the "implicate order," where "everything is enfolded into everything." In Bohm's view, the implicate order is continually "unfolding" into what we experience as the manifest world, "the explicate order." More importantly, human beings participate in this "unfoldment," as Bohm called it.

The most subtle aspect of "thinking strategically" lies in "knowing what needs to happen." This is extraordinarily difficult to describe, but I know that I and many others often feel that all we are ever doing is "listening" purposefully to what is needed. George Bernard Shaw said, "This is the true joy in life, [to be] used for a purpose recognized by yourself as a mighty one. . . . [to be] a force of nature . . ." Could Shaw's "being a force of nature" relate to Bohm's "participation" in the "unfolding" of the implicate order?" Is this what happens when we develop our sensibilities in the deep learning cycle?°

Such questions may hold a particular power as we stand here at the outset of the journey of learning about learning organizations. Bohm's quest in life was toward understanding the roots of fragmentation in our ways of thinking and being. "It should be said that wholeness is what is real, and that fragmentation is the response of this whole to man's action." Insofar as the quest for learning organizations might reestablish "the primacy of the whole" in human affairs, perhaps the quests are more intertwined than we can at present know.

° Bohm believed that this Eastern view may have been closer to the ancient Greek view, as still evident in an alternative history of the word "measure"—as in the phrase "the measure of the person." He noted that Latin precursors of the modern words "medicine," "moderation," and "meditate" are all based on the same Latin root meaning "to measure." See *Wholeness and the Implicate Order* by David Bohm (1980, London: Ark Paperbacks), p. 20 and pp. 176–81.

° Epistle Dedicatory to *Man and Superman* by George Bernard Shaw (1903, Cambridge, Mass.: The University Press), p. 32.

7 Core Concepts About Learning in Organizations

Rick Ross, Bryan Smith, Charlotte Roberts, Art Kleiner

AT ITS ESSENCE, EVERY ORGANIZATION IS A PRODUCT OF HOW ITS MEMBERS THINK AND INTERACT.

Thus, the primary leverage for any organizational learning effort lies not in policies, budgets, or organizational charts, but in ourselves. Even creating desired results is not a sign of learning. If you strike it rich by winning the lottery, you have achieved something extraordinary, but you have not expanded your capacity to win future lotteries.

This emphasis on thinking and interacting makes many people in mainstream organizations feel disoriented. It means shifting their point of orientation from outward to inward.°

To look inward, the first step is becoming aware of, and studying, the tacit "truths" that we take for granted, and the aspirations and expectations that govern what we choose from life. The disciplines of personal mastery, mental models, and systems thinking all help us to productively examine and change the way we think.

Changing the way we interact means redesigning not just the formal structures of the organization, but the hard-to-see patterns of interaction between people and processes. The disciplines of shared vision, systems thinking, and team learning are specifically aimed at changing interactions.

In the end, the premise that organizations are the product of our thinking and interacting is powerful and liberating. It suggests that individuals and teams *can* affect even the most daunting organizational barriers. These barriers didn't appear on the landscape like natural formations, like mountains and rivers. They were created by peoples' wishes, expectations, beliefs, and habits. They remained in place because they were reinforced and never challenged: eventually, they became invisible, because they were so taken for granted.

Once we start to become conscious of how we think and interact, and begin developing capacities to think and interact differently, we will already have begun to change our organizations for the better. Those changes will ripple out around us, and reinforce a growing sense of capability and confidence.

° Credit for first articulating the idea probably belongs to Karl Weick, in *The Social Psychology of Organizing* (1969, Reading, Mass.: Addison-Wesley).

Learning in organizations means the continuous testing of experience, and the transformation of that experience into knowledge—accessible to the whole organization, and relevant to its core purpose.

What do you do with a definition like this? Managers have used it to judge their own learning processes. It forms a sort of checklist:

- *Do you continuously test your experiences?* Are you willing to examine and challenge your sacred cows—not just during crises, but in good times? What kinds of structures have you designed for this testing? When people raise potentially negative information, do you "shoot the messenger"?

- *Are you producing knowledge?* Knowledge, in this case, means the capacity for effective action. Does your organization show capabilities it didn't have before? Do you feel as if what you know is qualitatively different—"value-added"—from the data you took in?

- *Is the knowledge shared?* Is it accessible to all of the organization's members? Or are people walking around saying, "You know, I could have sworn we put out a report on this subject two years ago"?

⟩⟩ See "The Destiny Factor," page 341.

- *Is the learning relevant?* Don't use the label "irrelevance" to screen out new ideas *per se*, but ask yourself: Is this learning aimed at the organization's core purpose? Can people make use of it? This is a great criterion, incidentally, for evaluating training programs.

LEARNING

These Chinese characters represent the word "learning." The first character means *to study.* It is composed of two parts: a symbol that means "to accumulate knowledge," above a symbol for a child in a doorway.

The second character means *to practice constantly,* and it shows a bird developing the ability to leave the nest. The upper symbol represents flying; the lower symbol, youth. For the oriental mind, learning is ongoing. "Study" and "practice constantly," together, suggest that learning should mean: "mastery of the way of self-improvement."—PS

The roots of the English word for learning suggest that it once held a similar meaning. It originated with the Indo-European *leis,* a noun meaning "track" or "furrow." To "learn" came to mean gaining experience by following a track—presumably for a lifetime.—AK

PRODUCTIVE WORKPLACES by Marvin Weisbord

(1987, San Francisco: Jossey-Bass)

The concept of a learning organization benefits from a hundred-year-long heritage of ideas about changing organizations for the better. This book opens up that history. The author, Marvin Weisbord, once ran a printing company founded by his father, then became an organizational development consultant. The first part of the book is a set of in-depth profiles of Frederick Taylor, Kurt Lewin (whose "action research" is an important foundation for all five disciplines), Douglas McGregor ("Theory X and Theory Y"), and the "open systems"/sociotechnical designers Fred Emery and Eric Trist. The second part describes how Weisbord himself used their techniques and practices. —AK

Defining Your Learning Organization

Charlotte Roberts, Rick Ross, Art Kleiner

PURPOSE

How do you know a learning organization when you run across it? And how do you measure your progress? You will get only limited usefulness from someone else's definition of what you are trying to achieve. This exercise helps you create your own definition. °

° **D**an Simpson (Director, Corporate Planning, Clorox), Libbi Lepow and Jeff Dooley contributed to this exercise.

STEP 1: "IF I HAD A LEARNING ORGANIZATION . . ."

Imagine that you are working in the learning organization you would like to build (or "quality," "ideal," or "great" organization).

On paper or computer, answer these questions:

a. What policies, events, or aspects of behavior in this new organization help it thrive and succeed?

b. How do people behave inside the organization? How do they interact with the outside world?

c. What are some of the differences between this ideal organization and the organization for which you work now?

Write brief answers in the present tense, as if you are in that organization now. ("People eagerly come to work," not "People will come to work more eagerly.") Be specific. Express the examples, images, possibilities, and details that cross your mind.

STEP 2: ENHANCING THE DEFINITION

You might like to know how other people have envisioned the learning organization. Take any definitions from this list that fit your image and add them (perhaps changing them in the process).

In a learning organization . . .

a. People feel they're doing something that matters—to them personally and to the larger world.

b. Every individual in the organization is somehow stretching, growing, or enhancing his capacity to create.

c. People are more intelligent together than they are apart. If you want something really creative done, you ask a team to do it—instead of sending one person off to do it on his or her own.

d. The organization continually becomes more aware of its underlying knowledge base—particularly the store of tacit, unarticulated knowledge in the hearts and minds of employees.

e. Visions of the direction of the enterprise emerge from all levels. The responsibility of top management is to manage the process whereby new emerging visions become shared visions.

f. Employees are invited to learn what is going on at every level of the organization, so they can understand how their actions influence others.

g. People feel free to inquire about each others' (and their own) assumptions and biases. There are few (if any) sacred cows or undiscussable subjects.

h. People treat each other as colleagues. There's a mutual respect and trust in the way they talk to each other, and work together, no matter what their positions may be.

i. People feel free to try experiments, take risks, and openly assess the results. No one is killed for making a mistake.

All together, between our list and your own, you may end up with a large list of characteristics. Make sure you have at least five. Number each of them so you can refer to them easily in the next step.

STEP 3: "WHAT WOULD IT BRING ME . . . ?" (FIFTEEN MINUTES OR MORE)

One by one, consider each of your choices from Step 2: If my organization had these new features, what sorts of things would happen as a result? What would it bring the organization? What would it bring you personally?

As you answer this question, some elements will command your attention. Make note of these and spend most of your time with them.

STEP 4: PICKING AND REFINING THE TOP FIVE

Based on what happened in Step 3, choose the *five* characteristics which are the most compelling to you and your organization. Don't worry about which characteristics seem plausible, or easy to achieve. (That comes later.) Try to include at least one or two elements that prompt you to think, "It feels right, but we could never do that here."

Why five? The number is large enough to allow for a diverse image, but small enough that you can keep all the characteristics in mind.

Take another look at your wording of each element. Rewrite as necessary to make sure your phrasing fits the image as you see it.

STEP 5: "WHAT STANDS IN OUR WAY . . ."

Now what would you have to do to achieve each of these components of your vision? What barriers and obstacles would have to be overcome?

For example, if you wrote: "People treat each other as colleagues," you may feel that, in your organization, the promotion system would have to be redesigned. What skills and new conceptions would you need to have to accomplish this?

You may feel daunted by the difficulty of overcoming these barriers and obstacles. Nonetheless, write out a preliminary set of ideas. What stands in your way? Articulate each point here.

STEP 6: "I'LL KNOW WE'RE MAKING PROGRESS IF . . ."

Now consider each of the five primary goals, and each of the obstacles you have described. Name one or more "indicators" for each set. An indicator is a sign or symptom which, *if* it took place, would signal you that some progress had been made.

This exercise, performed by members of a team, can lead into a skillful discussion (page 385), into the "Designing a Learning Organization" exercise (page 53), or into the first stages of a co-creating vision effort (see page 322). The exercises "What Do We Want to Create?" (page 337) contains questions that may help with this exercise.

Designing a Learning Organization: First Steps

Rick Ross, Charlotte Roberts, Bryan Smith

The exercise "Defining Your Learning Organization" (page 50) may be helpful as a preliminary to this.

STEP 1: ESTABLISHING THE GROUPS

Assemble a group with two types of participants: (1) people who seem to believe most wholeheartedly in improving the organization, and (2) people who, because of their position, will inevitably be involved first in any organizational learning effort.°

Typically, any individual will have met about half the other participants, and know most of the rest by name. This exercise is particularly effective when it brings a vertical slice of the organization—senior executives, line managers, staff people, and hourly employees—together into one discussion about optimizing the larger system. "It allowed us to dance to the same music," said a participant in one session, "at least for one round." Selected semioutsiders might be included: a union leader, retailer, dealer, supplier, or customer.

Divide the group into two sections, equal in size. Section A will operate as the keepers of the vision—the people who present an image of what the learning organization could be. Section B will maintain a grasp of current reality—the organization, with all its strengths and difficulties, as it exists today. Neither awareness, alone, is sufficient. Learning depends upon the dynamic cross-currents between them.

You will probably find that the B teams, making their lists of "policies sent from hell," have an easier time than the A's. On the other hand, the mood in the A sections may be sunnier and less sardonic. Both sections are essential; don't let either side slack off.

Divide Section A and Section B into working teams, each with a handful of people (five to six people, ideally representing several different parts of the organization).

STEP 2: DIVERGENT THINKING

For forty-five minutes or more, each team should deliberate on the following set of questions, not necessarily in the order given here. Write the answers on a flip chart:

° This long-standing exercise appears in different form in *The Learning Company* by Mike Pedler, John Burgoyne, and Tom Boydell, (1987, San Francisco, Jossey-Bass), p. 62. See *Fieldbook*, p. 59.

PURPOSE
One way of approaching the question "How do we get started?" is literally to ask your team to design its own process, based on its own priorities.

OVERVIEW
One half of the assemblage (Section A) develops a shared vision of their ideal learning organization. The other half (Section B) develops a picture of the obstacles and barriers to learning in their current reality.

PARTICIPANTS

10 to 200 people. They need not all work together, but their work should be interrelated enough so that their concerns are relevant to each other.

FACILITATOR

Could be someone within the organization, or an outside meeting facilitator.

TIME

From four hours to two days; the larger the group, or the less accustomed to working together closely, the more time is needed.

SUPPLIES

Flip charts and felt pens.

ENVIRONMENT

A large, undisturbed meeting place where at least two separate groups can gather at the same time, with wall space on which to hang flip-chart papers.

Section A:

1. What would we have, that we don't have now, if we had a learning organization?
2. What action steps might we take to achieve those visions? What policies and practices would be worthwhile?

Section B:

1. What are the present barriers and obstacles to becoming a learning organization?
2. What would we want to change or eliminate? What policies should be eliminated? What practices abandoned?
3. What elements of the organization already support learning?

Inevitably, you will move from descriptions of the situation to action steps: "What should we do about it? Who might champion this action?" As you discuss these, you will probably unearth previously unmentioned vision elements (Section A) or barriers (Section B). Continue adding those to your list.

STEP 3: CLARITY

Still in the same teams, begin consolidating the ideas from Step 2 into ten or twelve coherent points. Number each point.

Points might, for example, resemble this format:

What we would have as a learning organization (Section A):

1. A better system for disseminating financial and customer-survey information throughout the company.
2. Allowing a personal mastery program for every interested permanent employee.

Barriers to a learning organization (Section B):

1. The time delays in communications between the marketing and production functions.
2. Bringing in a new "guru" without showing how their message fits with the message of the *last* guru.

STEP 4: CONVERGENT THINKING

Still in working teams, winnow your list down to three items. Some can be eliminated immediately. Others will be defended—"Here is why I think this action step is particularly important." Give everyone an opportunity to explain his or her reasoning, and to challenge the reasoning of others.

〳〵 To get more out of this, use the protocols of skillful discussion; see page 385.

INSTANT PRIORITIES*

If you have difficulty winnowing the list, this ten-minute worksheet can help give you a quick snapshot of which statements the group really desires, which it feels tepid about, and which it would not accept.

The form printed here will handle up to ten alternatives; you can easily create larger charts with spreadsheet programs.

a. Agree on ten or fewer alternatives, and write them on the "alternatives" form so that each one is numbered.

b. Give every member of the team a photocopy of the form with the statements written on it.

c. As individuals, work your way through the chart. In every gray square, circle the number of the alternative you prefer. For instance, the top box gives you a choice between alternatives No. 1 and No. 2.

d. When finished choosing, enter the number of times you "voted" for each alternative in tally Column A.

e. Then, in Column B, identify your priorities by ranking the statements—1 for the statement for which you voted most (the highest number in Column A); 10 for the statement for which you voted least (the lowest number in Column A). If there are tie votes in Column A; pick one or the other as the higher-ranked item in Column B.

f. When all team members are finished, add their tallies (from Column A) together to get a group total. Column C is provided here to contain that group tally.

g. Once again, identify priorities by ranking the statements, but this time as a group. Put the group rankings (1 for the group's favorite, 10 for its least favorite) in Column D.

Column D gives you the group's decision. But Column C tells you how wide the gaps were between the top-ranked and bottom-ranked statements—a vital bit of information. It may show you, for instance, that the top three statements are the only ones really worth considering over the long run.

* The "Instant Priorities" technique was adapted, in part, from a survey method developed by Richard Bolles.

Priorities

Circle your preferred alternative for each combination of the statements listed below.

1	2								
1	3	2	3						
1	4	2	4	3	4				
1	5	2	5	3	5	4	5		
1	6	2	6	3	6	4	6	5	6
1	7	2	7	3	7	4	7	5	7	6	7
1	8	2	8	3	8	4	8	5	8	6	8	7	8
1	9	2	9	3	9	4	9	5	9	6	9	7	9	8	9
1	10	2	10	3	10	4	10	5	10	6	10	7	10	8	10	9	10

Alternatives	A Your totals	B Your priorities	C Group totals	D Group priorities
1 _____	____	____	____	____
2 _____	____	____	____	____
3 _____	____	____	____	____
4 _____	____	____	____	____
5 _____	____	____	____	____
6 _____	____	____	____	____
7 _____	____	____	____	____
8 _____	____	____	____	____
9 _____	____	____	____	____
10 _____	____	____	____	____

STEP 5: PRESENTATIONS AND PRIORITIES

Each A team presents its top three suggestions for what to create. Each B team presents the three most significant barriers or obstacles.

In large groups, you will need an intermediate step in which teams present to their own sections separately. In those sessions, the full A and B sections each develop a list of the top three priorities and then present them to each other.

Or, if the total group numbers twenty-five people or less, simply have the A and B teams present to the common plenary.

Follow every presentation with another skillful discussion. Your object is to end each session aligned around three key projects for getting started building a learning organization—goals to pursue, or obstacles to overcome.

You need not reach consensus, where everyone agrees. Make sure every person in the group feels that he has been heard and understood.

STEP 6: IMPLEMENTATION

Assign champions and create task forces for each of the chosen projects, ideally set up as experiments. In each of these experiments, the task force will attempt an action, note the results, learn, and report back to the larger group in thirty or sixty days.

From here, as you might move to more substantial work in developing a shared vision (see page 322) or working with mental models (see page 235).

How a hospital used "First Steps" to move from "teaching" to learning *Charlotte Roberts*

A GROUP OF TEN EXECUTIVE TEAMS FROM A REGIONAL HOSPITAL CONSOR-tium recently used a variation of the "Designing a Learning Organization" exercise. They all came from private community hospitals, located in middle-income neighborhoods. As is typical of these meetings, everyone knew the other attendees from their own hospital but had rarely, if ever, talked to them in depth. "When we talk," said one administrator, "it's always about a crisis: a financial problem, or a crisis on a unit. We never get to talk about the future." Thus, for this two-day session, we deliberately kept people together in intact teams from their own hospital.

Changing times had thrown all the hospitals into deep conflict. Their immediate neighborhoods were becoming far more diverse, with growing Spanish- and Chinese-speaking communities. Suburban residents were interested in "wellness"; they enthusiastically sought advice on nutrition, exercise, alternatives to surgery, and high-quality child care. AIDS had reinforced the demand for long-term and home care support. There was also a growing elderly community with increasing needs for medical services. City governments were raising environmental concerns about incineration and the disposal of medical waste. And top administrators had begun nervously wondering how to prepare for new political battles over health care costs and insurance. If hospitals could not learn to manage these issues well, they would face serious trouble.

At several hospitals, the administrative staff had flirted with Total Quality programs—only to meet derision from the other groups. Doctors argued that they already provided quality care; the hourly workers' unions said, in effect, "We aren't paid enough to take that responsibility." And since the other groups were balking, said the nursing leaders, why should they participate?

OUR INITIAL INQUIRY: HOW IS TEACHING DIFFERENT FROM LEARNING?

We began our meeting by sidestepping the interdepartmental rivalries. Instead, we asked everyone to name what the opposite of a learning hospital might be. The answer emerged through discussion: *all* hospitals, even if they don't train physicians and nurses, are "teaching hospitals." They see themselves as keepers and teachers of valuable secrets about health to their "clients." But information passes only one way; the hospital has no formal way to increase its own understanding of the people nearby and their needs. Would it serve hospitals to learn instead of teach? The participants weren't sure.

Working teams brainstormed examples of "teaching hospitals" (Section B) and "learning hospitals" (Section A). A teaching hospital "waits until people break down," as one nurse said, "and then tells them why they broke," protecting its professionals' expert status. A learning hospital might offer the same information, but it would continually test and refine it: What would reach people more effectively? There might be dial-in television programs, including on-air patient interviews about their health experiences. Professionals would be encouraged to admit when they don't have an answer.

One team suggested that a learning hospital would define health as a combination of five factors: mental, physical, emotional, social, and spiritual health. "And financial," added a senior physician who managed a burn center. He had seen burn victims, in addition to their other traumas, left financially devastated. A learning hospital might teach its patients not just how to buy health insurance, but how to establish solvency as a component of good health.

The Section A teams began to propose "market-in" solutions, in which the hospital brought the community and other customers (payers, physicians, etc.) into its planning process. One of the first policy changes implemented after the workshop was to encourage terminally ill patients to bring possessions from home, including small pieces of furniture, to make the hospital room more like their own. "When we really push total quality to the farthest limits in health care it is like art," said a physician. "We find ourselves honoring the spirit embodied in our forms of care—and then we find ourselves asking: 'Are there other forms we need to bring in?' Life is bigger than all of us."

THE LEARNING COMPANY by Mike Pedler, John Burgoyne, and Tom Boydell; (1991, London: McGraw-Hill Book Company);

TOWARDS THE LEARNING ORGANIZATION: A GUIDE by Jinny Belden, Marcia Hyatt, and Deb Ackley (1993; St. Paul, Minn.: Belden, Hyatt, and Ackley).

These are two excellent books of tools, techniques, and exercises which complement those in this *Fieldbook. The Learning Company*, written by three British consultants, contains dozens of short "glimpses" of learning organization theory and practice. *Towards the Learning Organization* is self-published, and it weaves together many of the traditional approaches to improving organizational effectiveness (Total Quality, participative management, empowerment) with powerful quotations, helpful exercises, and some new ways of developing multiple perspectives. — RR

8 The Wheel of Learning
Mastering the Rhythm of a Learning Organization

Rick Ross, Bryan Smith, Charlotte Roberts

If you ever have the chance to observe predators in the wild, you may notice that they operate in cycles. Most of the time, they display barely any movement. They project a sense of calm focus, as if they're waiting for a particular moment. Then it comes! Their muscles are charged with intensity as they sneak up on their prey and strike. When it's over, they return to their original calm. The cycle is back to its beginning.

People learn in similarly cyclical fashion. They pass between action and reflection, between activity and repose. To make effective change take place, managers need to find a way to tap this rhythm—to create not only time to think, but time for different types of thought and collective discussion. Our preferred tool for this is the "wheel of learning."[○]

How do you use the wheel? In any project or initiative, either individually or on a team, each stage demands deliberate attention before you move to the next:

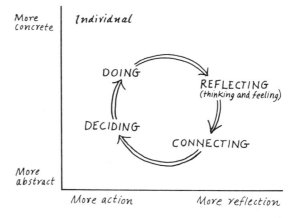

Reflecting: Becoming an observer of your own thinking and acting. This phase might start with a postmortem about a previous action: How well did it go? What were we thinking and feeling during the process? What underlying beliefs (what "theories in use") seemed to affect the way we handled it? Do we see our goals differently now? Many organizational cultures influence people to skip this stage, partly because of assumptions about the way people spend their time. If someone is reflecting, it's considered perfectly acceptable to interrupt them, because "they're not doing anything."

§§ For reflective techniques, see the "Left-Hand Column," page 246, and "Writing to Your
§§ Loyalties," page 268.

Connecting: Creating ideas and possibilities for action, and rearranging them into new forms. In this stage, you look for links between your potential actions and other patterns of behavior in the system around you. Scientists think of this stage as the time for generating hypotheses about the way the world works. What did our last action suggest might be a fruitful path to follow? What new understandings do we have about the world? Where should we be looking next?

[○] Our primary source on the learning cycle is *Experiential Learning: Experience as the Source of Learning and Development* by David Kolb (1984, Englewood Cliffs, N.J.: Prentice-Hall). Kolb synthesized and expanded upon theoretical work by American educational philosopher John Dewey, organization psychology pioneer Kurt Lewin, and learning philosopher Jean Piaget. Veterans of the quality movement will also recognize the "Shewhart cycle" (the "Plan-Do-Study-Act cycle") popularized by E. Edwards Deming. (Walter Shewhart was apparently aware of Dewey's concepts of reflective thinking.) British management writer Charles Handy coined the term "learning wheel" in his book *The Age of Unreason* (1989, 1990; Boston, Harvard Business School Press). Stephanie Spear of Innovation Associates developed a variation of the cycle that applies particularly well to teams. Joyce Ross helped articulate our description.

§§ Systems thinking has particular relevance at this stage. See page 103.

Deciding: Settling on a method for action. From alternatives and options generated in the connecting stage, you choose and refine your approach. "Deciding" incorporates an element of choice: "Here is the alternative we choose to take, and here are the reasons why."

Doing: Performing a task, with as much of an experimental frame of mind as possible. What you do may be hurried, but it will be supported by the three reflective stages which came before. When you finish the deed, you move immediately back to the reflecting stage, perhaps with a formal postmortem. How well did it work out?

Following the wheel of learning can ease a group of people out of a constant pattern of low-level frenzy, by setting aside time for reflection and creativity. Practiced regularly, it becomes a way of life, in the same way that the scientific method is a way of life for people in laboratories. Work done in rhythm with the learning wheel is reassuringly cyclical. No matter how frantic things get, you know your action will be mindful, because time for reflection is built in. Yet when it's time to act, you can move instantly.

When you are rushing to complete an action, but you feel mysteriously blocked, the cycle suggests alternatives to pushing harder. Chances are, you need to spend more time in one of the other phases. People who use the wheel recognize that they learn faster when they move slowly—when they are more thoughtful and take the time not just to react momentarily, but to try to understand more deeply what is going on at the moment. If you spend only a few minutes reflecting, you might spend days implementing—not so much to correct for mistakes, but to redesign in mid-action. Someone will ask, "Why wasn't I brought on board?" Someone else will demand a change that should have been anticipated. When you struggle to catch up, there's an inherent mismatch, because these reflective changes require deliberate, thoughtful attention, at the moment when your body is (as it were) springing through the air toward prey.

The team learning wheel

EACH POINT ON THE INDIVIDUAL WHEEL HAS A TEAM EQUIVALENT: THE "reflection" stage is "public" because it takes place over a common table. People talk about their mental models and beliefs, and challenge each other gently but relentlessly.

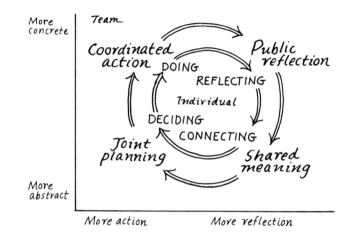

See "Skillful Discussion," page 385.

As common ground is established, the team can come to a mutual understanding. This ushers in the stage of shared meaning: "What is it that *we* know?" Stephanie Spear calls this stage "shared insight," and it is very good for refining shared vision and values.

Then comes joint planning—or, in less formal situations, joint design of an action step. "We're going to do a prototype now. And here's what it will look like." This stage may also include planning structural change, a key component step in systems thinking.

For more about this step, see "Enriching the Archetype," page 161.

Finally, there is coordinated action, which need not be joint action—it can be carried out independently by various members of the team, who may work in different functions and locations. All the time spent reflecting, building shared meaning, and jointly planning turns the action into a polished initiative.

Many people think they can skip the public reflection and shared meaning stages, but those are two most crucial stages. If you spend enough time reflecting together to build shared meaning, you will often end up with coordinated action without the need for planning.

Besides helping to coordinate team activities across vast distances, the team learning wheel continually reminds a team of its own weaknesses, in a way that compels the team to compensate for them naturally. As most people do with the individual wheel, most teams tend to "short-circuit" past one or more of the steps. In some organizations, teams continually leap off into new decisions and actions, without reflecting on the tests they've already conducted or considering (in the "shared meaning" stage) a full range of alternatives. It's as if they were performing experiment after experiment, but never stopping to check the results.

In other organizations, managers say, "I've got to figure this out completely before I make a move." They remain in "connecting" and "deciding," and miss the learning that comes from experimentation (acting), and considering the results. Other people feel comfortable brainstorming and conducting experiments, but never focus their attention on "deciding" on one alternative. Their efforts are scattered and diffuse.

Charles Handy points out that the key role of leaders is to keep the "wheel" moving. This is not an easy task; it requires energy and mental finesse, the ability to hold fast to a sense of purpose, and the willingness to understand mental models of people with learning styles other than your own.

Individual styles on the learning wheel *Rick Ross*

DAVID KOLB SUGGESTS THAT MOST PEOPLE "TAKE" NATURALLY TO ONE or two phases of the cycle:

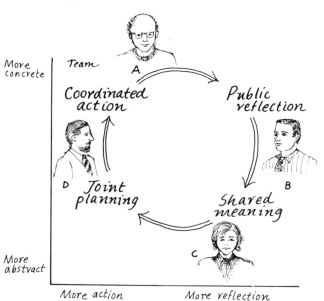

Kolb, in fact, based his taxonomy of learning styles on his version of this cycle. He labeled people who get personally involved in a lot of activities, like the gentleman at point B, as "divergent thinkers." They excel at problem analysis. I call them "brainstormers," because they're wonderful at seeing things from different perspectives. In the first part of problem solving, when you're trying to analyze a situation, these people are worth their weight in gold. Every time everybody else tries to close off discussion and move to a solution, they say, "Well, there's another way to look at this."

⟨⟨ For tools for uncovering learning styles in teams, see page 421.

But at some point you have to put duct tape over their mouths and allow people at point C to direct the discussion. They're the connection-makers. They draw hypotheses and suggest reasons why something happened. They're the most natural systems thinkers on the team. You don't have to shut them up; you have to draw them out.

You gradually move on to the solution-finders (Kolb called them "convergent thinkers") at point D. Like the connection-makers, they have a facility for abstraction, but they are also drawn to experiment. They intuitively feel that things should move to a point. They are great at solutions analysis. The action begins under their aegis.

The last group, up at point A, is Kolb's "accommodaters." He did not mean that they give in easily when challenged in the group—just the opposite. But they manage the process of accommodating the group's theory to reality; implementing the solution, and judging the hypotheses of the experiment against the facts. They are the most willing to dump the theory if the theory doesn't fit, which makes them essential.

The most powerful teams, as Kolb notes, have representatives from all four styles. And these teams drive their members crazy. Because while A is trying to bring things to a point, B's got seventeen different ideas about how to look at it. D wants to do something—"anything, for God's sake!"—and C has just noticed a new set of connections. The challenge is learning to value that diversity, and to help the team pace itself through the wheel: the team leader knows when to turn to the divergers at point B and give them their head, and when to shut them up and call on the connection-makers. Later, when everyone agrees on the basic solution, someone needs to turn to Jean the engineer, the accommodator at point A, and say: "O.K. What are our first steps? Who's going to talk to whom?"

THE AGE OF UNREASON by Charles Handy (1989, 1990, Boston: Harvard Business School Press).

Within the next fifteen years most organizations (says Charles Handy) will be thoroughly unrecognizable—downright "unreasonable"—by current standards. He offers a convincing portrayal of the turmoil which is changing business structures, and what new styles of organizations could (and should) emerge from it. For example, he describes the "shamrock" organization—equally attentive to developing core managers, part-timers, and temporary freelancers—and the federal organization, which follows the principle of "subsidiarity": power should always flow from the lowest possible level. Handy also gives a very compelling guide to using the wheel of learning. We recommend the book for people redesigning infrastructure, working in teams, or planning a learning organization effort.—RR, AK

9 Leadership Fields

Charlotte Roberts, Rick Ross, Bryan Smith

You can always sense the presence or absence of leadership when you begin working in a new organization. In some cases, you get a sense that something is off-kilter, though everyone is saying the "right" things. You also know that *they* know something's off-kilter. Other times you become aware that a field of competence and learning exists—enhancing and reinforcing people's efforts. A "field," in this case, is an unseen pattern of structure that is nonetheless real enough to influence behavior. We know about these fields—as we know about gravitational, electromagnetic, and quantum fields—not because we experience them directly, but because we see their effects.°

Developing a field that encourages learning is the primary task of leadership, and perhaps the only way that a leader can genuinely influence or inspire others. To build a field, you don't look first to bringing other people on board; you attend to the appropriate details within your sphere, and people eventually come on board themselves.

For more about the architectural components of these details, see "Moving Forward," particularly the section on the "Architectural Triangle," page 21.

° Our use of field theory steps off from the chapter on fields in *Leadership and the New Science* by Margaret Wheatley (1993, San Francisco: Berrett-Koehler), pp. 47–49. See *Fieldbook*, p. 96.

We see the value of creating a field in seminars we lead. On Day One, we have learned to be intensely focused on the details of presentation. The room is like a temple; there are no open boxes with papers visible, or people typing noisily on lap-tops in the back of the room. Even the arrangement of chairs is carefully considered—is it too stiff? Too scattered? Each of these details may seem insignificant at the time, but everything in the room adds to or detracts from the spirit we create.

If on Day One we've been successful as leaders, then by Day Two, the field no longer needs us. Other participants add details of their own, in the paired conversations and the relationships they build with each other, and produce results we could never have imagined, let alone produced. Every teacher of a successful class knows this feeling. It's as if there are flames lighting up within people all around the room, feeding into a large common flame. With that field intact, our need to control the scene disappears. We can devote attention to challenging the group further.

Many leaders, intuitively aware of the potency of the fields they generate, are known for their attentiveness to detail. For instance, many take a personal hand in designing the physical layout of their buildings. But not every leader recognizes that his or her role requires just as much attention, or more, to design the emotional ambience of the leadership field and to develop the capacity to sense its boundaries. The stronger the field gets, the more chance that it will extend to customers, shareholders, and the network of competitors, suppliers, and global allies.

The role of senior managers

EVERYONE FROM A CLERK ON A SHIPPING DOCK TO THE CHAIRMAN OF THE board contributes to an organization's culture. But senior managers have a particular responsibility. They are so influential already that whatever they do has a substantial impact on the organization's field. Every aspect of their performance, every conversation they hold, and every action they take demonstrates what values they believe are important to the organization. That is why a learning organization cannot exist without its senior managers' commitment and leadership.

The days are gone when senior managers predominantly felt that learning was the function of the Human Resources department; they know the strong relationship between their job and the task of promoting learning. But in many cases, they're still not certain how to proceed.

Some assume that it's enough to set an example: producing extraordinary results and visibly improving their own capabilities will inspire others. But in practice, this does not seem to be enough. It is necessary to demonstrate belief in the enterprise and the people who are members of it.

The learning disciplines are a vehicle for growing this kind of leadership. Rather than beginning a dozen simultaneous initiatives, we recommend focusing on three or four, always with an idea of what values you are trying to convey. You should always start with initiatives you care about deeply—which is why personal mastery is such a valuable discipline for senior leaders. You must be visibly willing to take a stand for the guiding ideas you consider important, while remaining open to involvement and points of view from others—which is why the communications skills of shared vision are so crucial. Truly understanding others' points of view will also demand practice in reflection and inquiry (mental models) skills. Translating this understanding into innovations in infrastructure will reinforce the field you create—which is why you need the design skills of systems thinking. Finally, the discipline of team learning will often be the arena in which your leadership is felt.

CHARISMA VERSUS THE FIELD OF INFLUENCE

This work of building a field has nothing to do with charisma; in fact, if you rely on your personal charisma and power to generate influence, you have no way to convert that power to the organization. When you die or leave the organization, the field of influence will shut down. For contrast, I recall a partner in a chartered accounting firm who had been introduced to me as one of the most exceptional leaders of the Toronto buisness community. When I first met him, I said to myself, "This man is as mousy as they come." He spoke almost in a whisper. He could have been cast for a movie role as a nervous, unprepossessing accountant.

An hour later, I almost wanted to quit my studies and become a chartered accountant myself. I've rarely been as excited about a subject in my life. He talked about accountants as coaches and mentors: "We are like priests to an organization," he said. "We will be anywhere where anyone wants advice on the business. We will give them the best insight; we will show them how they can get where they're going." This man attracted the most talented young accountants in North America. People loved working for him. They devoted their lives to his vision of accounting as a helping profession. His charisma came not from his personality but from what he saw, what he stood for, and his ability to express it in a field that influenced thousands of others. — BS

STEWARDSHIP **by Peter Block** (1993, San Francisco: Berrett-Koehler).

Peter Block makes the case eloquently that leadership in a learning organization is very different from the prevailing model of charismatic, strong leadership from the top. Stewardship, according to Block, is ". . . the willingness to be accountable for the well-being of the larger organization by operating in service, rather than in control, of those around us. It is accountability without control or compliance." He suggests a range of policy changes, including innovative redesigns of rules and rewards. The book's image of an organization led by stewardship is itself a vivid vision. — CR

CONTROL YOUR DESTINY OR SOMEONE ELSE WILL
by Noel Tichy and Stratford Sherman (1993, New York: Currency Doubleday).

Though General Electric CEO Jack Welch may never have heard of a "learning organization," per se, elements of his leadership reflect many of the practices in this book, within the context of a fiercely hierarchical company. Welch's Corporate Executive Council, for instance, comprised of all twelve GE company presidents and some key corporate staff members, is a prototype example of team learning and, specifically, skillful discussion. The members of Welch's team bring every conceivable type of business issue to the table, and consider them all in free-flowing conversation, without feeling they have to reach a decision.

Perhaps most impressively, as the authors in this business biography show, Welch learns. He moved from a top-down vision (the famous dictum that all GE businesses had to be #1 or #2 in their markets) to a much more learning-filled operation (his "Work-Out" system). — RR

10 Reinventing Relationships
Leverage for Dissolving Barriers to Collaboration

Charlotte Roberts

No matter how fervent our desires for team learning and collective intelligence, they are often undermined by the boundaries between people. In 1992, I was invited by the CEO of a large private hospital to spend a day with his executive team. Over the phone, he said that his team had fundamental problems with learning and communicating. But when the team gathered, his attitude was completely different. "Charlotte, we already *are* a learning organization," he said. "All we need is some fine-tuning of our action plans." The only factor that had changed was the presence of people with whom he had an ongoing boss/subordinate relationship. Thus, during the meeting, I kept alert for other signals of relationship problems among the team members.

At the CEO's request, we talked through a definition of learning. At a break, two executives told me it reminded them of debating how many angels dance on the head of a pin. Their deference before the boss, but cynicism out of his earshot, was another clue. Back in the meeting, one team member boldly declared that he did not think they were either a learning organization or a quality organization. The CEO quickly reminded him of the high marks given the hospital by a benchmarking committee he had appointed. Two other executives joined in to support the CEO's opinion. The bold speaker retreated like a frightened puppy. Apparently people were not free to disagree. After a few more such incidents, I asked whether people in the rest of the hospital were "unwilling to tell the truth about what really goes on? Or do they just tell you what they think you want to hear?" Nobody said anything; they either shuffled papers or looked away. Another clue, I thought; their discomfort was palpable.

Finally, after the first day was closed, a vice president (who had pummeled his peers with positivism at the meeting) pulled me aside. "No," he said softly, "we're not a learning organization." He could not even hire his own people, he said. The CEO approved all hires. Two final clues: what he said, and his choice of when to talk with me.

I am told this team still has trouble learning and communicating. Its problems are driven by the team members' own assumptions about human nature, and about how managers should conduct themselves together. To move forward, teams like these need to reinvent their models of appropriate human relationships. This may require deep reflections into fundamental beliefs about self, work, and power. It may also require changing the most carefully guarded structures of the organization, those which have to do with promotion and compensation. This is long, difficult work, particularly for an organization whose leaders resist facing their assumptions. But practically, the work can begin by addressing two leverage points: promoting intimacy and sharing authority.

INTIMACY

The word "intimacy" stems from the Latin *intimatus*, to make something known to someone else. (Another derivation is the verb "intimate," which originally meant "to notify.") In its original meaning, in other words, intimacy did not mean emotional closeness, but the willingness to pass on honest information. — **CR**

Intimacy

NOT LONG AGO, I SAW THE POWER OF INTIMACY AT A HIGH-TECH MANU-facturing company. Previously, any question about customer needs had to go through sales. But now, a group began meeting regularly over a project—the design, construction, and installation of one of their key customer's factories. The customer had a unique and complex request: to develop a group of interacting robots that would "read" each others' work as the product rapidly moved down the assembly line. Because the team members had spent time getting to know each other personally, they knew when to defer to each others' questions and opinions. They did not make promises the team could not keep. Their separate conversations with the customer didn't contradict; when misunderstandings or disagreements popped up, they could investigate without feeling paralyzed. They were a single unit committed to serving their customer, not a collection of egos and expertise vying for recognition and control of the situation.

Intimacy in organizations starts with a commitment to get to know people behind the mask of their job title, role, or function. Members of an intimate team know each others' preferences and predilections. They speak openly about what they believe, feel, think, and aspire to be. They are skilled at balancing inquiry and advocacy; this skill appears to be far easier to learn and practice when there is a threshold level of intimacy. If you are a leader of an intimate team, you may find yourself earning loyalty that accrues to more than just your position of authority. You may also notice a decline in turnover rates. Employees who feel valued are more likely to stay with the organization.

To produce intimacy, start conversing accordingly. This doesn't mean probing into secrets, stepping over the bounds of propriety, or invading privacy. Intimacy should never put anyone under pressure to unveil the details of his or her personal life or desires. More significant (and often more difficult) are your true opinions about an idea, your uncertainties, and your private opinions about your own (or others') failures and sacred cows. If someone expresses distaste or interest in something, ask for the source of this opinion. If someone asks you, answer honestly. Shared vision exercises also lead to a sense of intimacy: when we deeply care about the realization of a common purpose, we recognize the need for each others' contributions.

While intimacy offers a rich sense of involvement, it also implies vulnerability. As a learner exploring your mental models and personal vision and values, you will be mentally, emotionally, and socially "exposed." You will not be as free to sneak things by, to withhold information, to pretend you know something that you don't, or to propose and implement self-serving policies that undermine team goals. In intimate situations, you must be trustworthy, because you know that you are bound to your team in the long run by your shared purpose. The lack of trust pervasive in most organizations is not a *cause* of lack of intimacy, but a symptom of it.

Many senior managers are particularly skeptical of the value of intimacy—and doubtful of their capacity to handle it. "How can I be intimate with everyone on my team," they ask, "when I don't have time to talk to everyone now?" It may require more time and attention at the beginning, but it soon leads to great time savings. People who understand each other intimately waste less effort. They don't have to undo mistakes provoked by inaccurate second-guessing or write "cover-your-butt" memos to guard against each others' attacks. The quality of decisions increases, due to truth telling and commitment to common purpose. If there are fewer people to do a greater amount of work, then the project's survival often depends on achieving at least a minimum level of intimacy.

Some managers fear that if they act vulnerably they may unleash (or provoke) sexual overtones. Others are afraid of racism, or uncomfortable clashes of opinion. But intimacy is not sexuality in the workplace, nor does it mean giving free rein to every emotional impulse. Most people who have experience with intimacy know that expressing feeling is a skill, like any other. It improves with practice. A wide range of feelings can be expressed at work—from the genuine caring which we reserve for close friends to mutual respect for colleagues who contribute to the product or service. For whatever reasons, the generation of employees under age fifty appears to be more comfortable with this kind of expression. In many cases, they demand it. An organization hoping to attract the best of them has no choice but to permit the display of human feeling in the workplace, with consideration, but also with full acknowledgment of the whole person at work, not just his role.

Shared authority

AUTHORITY

Like the word "author," this word can be traced back to the Greek *authentikós,* which meant "do-er," master, or creator. The English meaning of "authority" (possession of the right and power to command) stems from the fact that the creator of a work of art or craft has the power to make decisions about it. — CR

Authority has been traditionally practiced as the boss's ability to command or make decisions. Because managers can tell people what to do, they are considered obligated to "author" all the critical decisions—much like benevolent dictators.

But in the new work relationship, authority is shared. This means being mutually responsible for the same effects, with or without explicit shared decision making. As the lexicon suggests, without shared authority there can be no shared creativity or authorship. If you and I work together, we see ourselves as co-creators. We may continue making individual decisions, but we do so with full knowledge of our shared purpose, and of what each other thinks and feels.

When I described this model of authority at one company, a manager asked me, "But who makes the *tough* decisions?" Implicit in his question was a widely held mental model of tough decisions: because they involve allocating painful effects (often including layoffs, pay cuts, and demotions), a team is incapable of understanding them, let alone making them. I hold a different mental model: that because these decisions are so critical, and affect so many people, they *demand* involvement from the people who will be affected or held accountable. How do you keep decision makers honest? By making sure that everyone is aware of the long-term implications, that no one's individual interest can dominate the proceedings, and the information shared by everyone is as complete and accurate as possible.

I know a bank that learned the benefits of sharing authority when a teller at a remote branch, alone on a Friday night, ran out of change thirty-five minutes before closing. With a long line of people cashing paychecks before her, she started rounding up her disbursements to the nearest dollar. When she ran out of ones, she rounded up to the nearest five. She even rounded up a few to the nearest $10 before she closed her window. When her supervisor counted the money, she had given out an extra $320. But the bank estimates that it gained 100 new customers that evening through referrals. The teller felt no fear of reprisals at any point; in fact, the bank singled her out as a heroine.

As a group moves into sharing authority, there is an added value to intimacy: it creates the climate to support tough decisions in tough times.

Promoting a new model of relationships

What, then, could an executive team do to promote new forms of relationships?

- Share relevant information, knowing this may involve educating people to comprehend the information. Because many people believe their authority comes from hiding information, *senior management must open up first.* The information that the top managers choose to share must be obviously important, ideally vital to team efforts—and perhaps heretofore undiscussable or privileged.

  }} For a good model of information sharing see "The Great Game of Business," page 542.

- Share credit. Collaboration, shared authority, and intimacy can't exist when one person—especially the "boss"—takes credit for the work.

- Reward and recognize honesty and openness. Senior managers must become role models for this in staff meetings and other interactions.
- Promote and reward partnering, particularly across functions, and at all levels of the organization.

⨝⨝ See "Finding a Partner," this page.

- Hold dialogues or skillful discussions focused on people's perceptions of their relationships. This should preferably be done *after* a group has had some exposure to team learning and articulating mental models. Not long ago, for instance, it helped one executive team going through a takeover to talk about their private fears of how the new organization could "push" them out.

    Each person finished the sentence, "I will leave this organization in a minute if . . ."

    ". . . if I am asked to wait for the new corporate people to tell me what to do," said one.

    ". . . if I don't have enough authority to make a difference," said another.

    ". . . if the president of our division leaves, who has shared my values in the past and has been my mentor."

    Declaring these boundaries and their potential loss was a critical element of joining into the new system. Having the freedom and safety to talk about their fears was a sign of the new relationships they had been forging with each other, and it gave them the mutual courage to approach the new organization honestly.

11 Finding a Partner

Bryan Smith, Charlotte Roberts

If you are trying to create a learning organization, you will often become painfully aware of how far away you are from your goals. This can be emotionally wrenching, especially during the inevitable stages where you meet up against resistance, hostility, and delays in the system. The ideal strategy is to move gently, continually toward your vision for the organization, learning to live with the feelings of stress and emotional tension. But it's not easy, and all the conventional strategies for dealing with that tension make matters worse. Executives faced with disappointment force themselves to "push harder"; they lower their vision ("We don't really need to make this reform complete"), or they deny that they have any emotional tension at all, for fear of burdening the organization ("Current reality is not so bad."). Any of these strategies will undermine your purpose. If only as a safety valve to preserve your change effort, you need to find a way to cultivate awareness of your own emotional tension, without giving in to it. You need to make sure you are taking care of yourself.

Some people claim that they can go off and meditate by themselves and clear the emotional tension they feel. But for most people in organizations, a better strategy is to find a partner whom they can trust. Leaders, regardless of "rank," need a partner to talk to and confide in while going through the often intense phases of change.

Why is the presence of this partner so important? Because if you are the leader, the rest of the people on your team or in your organization expect to see you project openness and honesty—including the confidence to say what you believe in, and to admit when you are uncertain. It is much easier to pull this off if you are in steady contact with someone who can help you uncover what you are thinking and feeling, including your misgivings.

As Larry Wilson, the founder of Wilson Learning puts it, your prospective partner should be a "nourishing person" for you: someone whose face lights up when you walk into the room and who has few, if any, plans for your improvement. Partners may have a vision of your potential, but they thoroughly accept you as you are now. As you sort through the close relationships in your life, you may discover that only one or two people meet these criteria—and your significant other or spouse may not be one of them!

This is a different dynamic from finding a sympathetic person on whom you can "dump" your bad feeling when you get away from work. In systems terms, when you "dump," you're shifting the burden of your feelings onto the dumpee. If you generate strong emotional tension at work, and take it home and spill it onto a friend or spouse, there's a cathartic release and the tension goes out of your system. Then you are ready to go back and build up more negative tension, while your friend or spouse copes with the fact that you have used him or her, once again, as a repository vessel for your negative feelings.

On the other hand, when you find a worthy partner associated with work, you are designing a more fundamental solution, in which the tension is named, witnessed, and used as energy to influence the system at work. Your goal is to forge an alliance, or create some form of mutual commitment, in which there is absolute trust and freedom of expression. Make a point of allowing your prospective partner to make an informed choice about taking on the role. Describe the changes you see ahead and make your expectations clear; ask if he or she is willing to serve as a sounding board, colleague, and personal consultant.

Given the current reality of the organization where you work, you may find it difficult to imagine having this kind of partnership. You may need to build it outside the organization in the beginning. Or you may stay on your own. But keep in mind that, over time, you are trying to build the capacity, in yourself and in the organization, to achieve this kind of partnership.

In a good "partner" conversation you can blow off steam without the burden of having to follow through. You may end up expressing your emotional tension in words, gestures, tears, or angry shouting—that's part of the process. Your partner may surprise you sometimes by saying something like: "I can see it's worse than you're letting on. You're deeply hurt." There is a moment of great release and awareness when you recognize that someone else has articulated what you've felt below the surface. A "partner" conversation will also remind you that while your feelings are absolutely legitimate, they may also change soon; your commitment, to paraphrase Gandhi, is to the truth as you see it each moment, not to consistency.

Always let your partner know how you would like her or him to listen that day. Partners may listen only as a sounding board, with no verbal response but lots of emotional response. They may listen and offer responses that show you how others will perceive your comments later. They may advise on strategies and tactics, or offer more wide-ranging insights. Whatever form they take, these conversations are a sort of transformer, temporarily adding capacity to your emotional circuits. That allows you to take your emotional tension, which is as directionless and jarring as static electricity, and transform it into usable energy. That is why your partner will not help you much by telling you how the other people in your team feel about the situation, or how "it does you no good to be angry." People need a partner precisely *because* they need help seeing their feelings. Similarly, it doesn't help to have someone say: "If you're feeling so angry, what are you going to do about it?" There is a profound difference between the actions that you might take when driven by the desire to reduce your emotional tension, and the strategic actions that will emerge after the tension has been transformed into positive creative energy.

Eventually, your partner will probably be the first to recognize the critical point when the organization is more than halfway planted in its new reality. Both of you can construct questions or metrics to test the assumption that your organization has indeed "turned the corner." Once you have evidence, you can do for your organization what your partner did for you—point to the light at the end of the tunnel.

12 Opening Moves

How to Find an Appropriate Path Through the Five Disciplines

Charlotte Roberts, Bryan Smith, Rick Ross

Pursue all five sometime during the first year

SOME MANAGERS SAY, "JUST TELL ME ABOUT SYSTEMS THINKING AND mental models. Don't give me personal mastery and shared vision." They crave an intellectual challenge, but don't want to tackle the "entangled" issues of intimacy and personal growth.

But every discipline makes the others' practice more effective. We compare the five disciplines to a hand. Sure, you can learn about just two fingers if you like—but have you ever tried to turn a doorknob with just two fingers?

It's difficult to practice all five disciplines—or more than two—at once. We recommend serial progression. Work on systems thinking leads naturally to work with mental models. From there, you may step easily to team learning. That may lead you to a shared vision effort, which in turn reminds you of the need for work on personal vision. Thinking about current reality, you return to systems thinking, and start the cycle over, or move to a different cycle.

Master basic prerequisites early on

A FEW PREREQUISITES MAKE UNIVERSAL SENSE:

- Before you throw people into a room to practice skillful discussion, dialogue, and other team learning skills, they should learn basic inquiry (see page 253) and reflection (see page 246) skills.
- People who have articulated a personal vision (see page 201) find it more natural to move on to shared vision work.
- Basic work on archetypes (see page 121) should precede any attempt to do systems modeling.

Keep a retrospective map

THERE IS NO SPECIFIC ROAD MAP: EACH TEAM CREATES ITS OWN STORY line. Sometime during the process, however, it's useful to look back and reconstruct a map, as a group. Why did you start where you started? What governed your choice of where to move? How would you redesign your next move forward? The collective memory of where you have been can reveal a great deal about where you should go.

ENTRY POINT #1: PERSONAL TO SHARED VISION

Start with individual vision (see "Personal Mastery," page 193), then move into "Co-creating" shared vision (see page 322). That shared vision then becomes a framework for designing the organization's next steps (using "Strategic Priorities," see page 344). Organizations which are not in crisis, and which maintain a reasonable level of internal communication, often do well starting here. The top managers must feel comfortable, right from the start, spending hours to draw forth employees and managers to collaboratively envision the future of the enterprise.

ENTRY POINT #2: SYSTEMS STUDY

Highly rational cultures, such as engineering or financial firms, appreciate this approach. Begin by modeling the structures of the firm and its relationship to the outside, looking for structures that are affected by the organization's unseen mental models. You might use computer modeling techniques (see page 173) which other companies find daunting. Eventually, this track leads to shared vision. "The system seems to be setting goals *for* us," you may decide. "We should set our own." We suggest "Backing into a Vision" (see page 340). From there, you move to personal mastery: How else can people set goals effectively? You make this move not as a "soft" altruistic gesture, but in the context of "hard" objectives grounded in your organization's strategic interest.

ENTRY POINT #3: A SELF-CONTAINED TEAM

Typically, when people are interested in starting here, there's some dirty laundry involved. "We can't move forward," people feel, "until we clean up our relationships." This prompts some organizations to begin working with dialogue (see page 357) or skillful discussion (see page 385). Team learning efforts invariably lead to discussion of roles: how people's behavior, attitudes, and positions can better fit together (see David Kantor's cameo, page 407). Eventually, the team recognizes that it is not isolated; it needs to filter its new understanding out to the rest of the organization. This typically requires work with systems thinking and shared vision, perhaps coupled with process mapping (see page 184).

ENTRY POINT #4: CURRENT REALITY (SELF-ASSESSMENT)

Begin with an analysis of the organization's current capacity and ability. Rely on systems thinking and other self-assessment tools to come to grips with the current systems (internal), the environment (external), and the character of the organization. Especially rely on points of view from people outside the organization (customers, suppliers, competitors). A useful technique is described in Kees van der Heijden's cameo (see page 279). Then move to other disciplines.

ENTRY POINT #5: STARTING AT THE TOP

If the organization is struck by a moral or financial crisis, the executive team may decide to begin a learning effort. This requires two simultaneous initiatives: team learning to reflect upon and learn from the executive team's own practice, and shared vision to understand the collective aspirations of the rest of the organization. The top team assumes most of the burden of change during the early stages; it must be willing to allow time for its own work with mental models and archetypes. See Charlie Kiefer's cameo "Executive Team Leadership," (page 435).

ENTRY POINT #6: CHRONIC PROBLEMS

Exercises like "the Five Why's" (see page 108) begin with chronic problems. As a team, can you identify fundamental causes? To understand the causes, you must involve people at every level of the system that creates the problem. From system dynamics, you can move into mental models and team learning work with representatives of the full process.

ENTRY POINT #7: INFRASTRUCTURE REVIEW

Some organizations begin with an overall analysis of the policies of the current system. Which aspects support learning? Which might inhibit or block learning? It's particularly promising to begin with the budgeting process: Why was it designed in this form? What was its purpose? Two useful techniques for this are "Double-loop Accounting" (see page 286) and the "Destiny Factor and History Chart" (see page 341).

ENTRY POINT #8: THROUGH A TOTAL QUALITY EFFORT

Momentum toward becoming learning organizations often starts with quality management (see page 445).

ENTRY POINT #9: YOUR OWN ENTRY POINT

Any point in this book can lead you into the five disciplines. If all else fails, we refer you to the first two exercises in the book, "Defining Your Learning Organization," (see page 50) and "Designing a Learning Organization: First Steps" (see page 53).

A new form of corporate planning

Bryan Smith

"I WOULD LIKE TO BEGIN WORKING WITH THE LEARNING DISCIPLINES," senior managers sometimes say, "but we don't have five days for people to learn dialogue or systems thinking. We don't even have an afternoon for a meeting." It often turns out that much of their time is tied up with the annual strategic planning and budgeting process—preparing for and carrying out endless efforts to measure the corporation's results, set objectives, inform the board and shareholders, create budgets, and bring the system under control. This planning and budgeting process, if you're willing to take the time and organize it differently, is one of the great unexamined sources of leverage for building a learning organization.

⟨⟨ "Double-loop Accounting" is particularly complementary to this design (see page 286).

Consider why traditional planning and budgeting, although well intentioned, fail in most organizations. The accounting system, where budget forecasts are created, is assumed to be "value-free." In fact, it has powerful, unintended influences on the direction and focus of the organization. For example, budgets often incorporate a pervasive bias toward whatever worked before. If functions like customer service, where the greatest leverage for improvement may lie, were underbudgeted in the past, they remain underbudgeted in the future.

There is often no opportunity to talk about creative ideas, corporate purpose, vision, or commitment. Instead, every number in each proposal becomes an implicit statement about the values of the organization. The only way people can express their values—and return with a substantial budget for their project—is by advocating their position, as forcefully as possible.

This intensely frustrating experience frequently leads to arbitrary decisions. The results satisfy no one, and represent no one's view of reality. But the action steps and budget restrictions which emerge from the meeting are driven deeply into the organization. There is no possible response except compliance. Any employee who is smart will not try to argue with the numbers, because you can't argue with assumptions which have not been made explicit. But from the moment they hear the objectives, they begin assembling plausible excuses for why they will not achieve them. Finally, since everyone has deliberately kept their personal thoughts, feelings, and aspirations from surfacing, people feel a remarkable lack of enthusiasm and goodwill about the plan. "Why isn't the commitment there?" wonder the accountants and the CEO. The answer is, because the process has systematically extracted any commitment from the very beginning.

STEP 1: PERSONAL VISION

All of this can be avoided with one relatively small change in the sequence of the planning cycle. Typically, individual departments spend six weeks or more preparing spreadsheets for a week-long executive planning team meeting—a duel over allocations. Instead, have the executive planning team meet first, to talk about the intangibles. Given the frustrations people feel with past sessions, I find most people are *very* open to suggestions for going at planning a different way.

Begin with three days off-site, with all the senior managers who will participate in the planning process present. Start by giving them an opportunity to talk about their personal vision for their life as a whole. What do they want to see, for themselves, in the future? With that as a starting point, how can their vision for the organization reflect and amplify their individual vision? It's important, as this conversation begins, to legitimize the notion that senior managers and executives are important stakeholders for the company. This is their chance to ask each other: What do you *really* think we should do with this organization to maximize its potential? Eliminate, from the beginning, the air of detachment and supposed "objectivity" that typically surrounds the planning process.

STEP 2: SHARED VISION

During that same off-site meeting, extend the conversation to create a shared vision for the organization (or for the division or unit whose plan is being prepared). Don't compress this conversation too much; the process of listening to each other is as important as the end product.

See the material on building shared vision on page 312.

STEP 3: A MAP OF CURRENT REALITY

Inevitably, the presence of that shared vision generates a much higher degree of openness, candor, and curiosity: What impediments keep us from getting where we want to go? Now a wide range of techniques for building a map of current reality can come into play: systems thinking, articulating mental models, and possibly scenario planning. By this point, the difference from former budget discussions is dramatically evident. Instead of keeping their intentions close to their chests, people begin to talk openly about the aspects of current reality they see.

STEP 4: HOW DO WE CLOSE THE GAP?

Having developed a common image of current reality, the team moves on to consider its strategic priorities. What are the primary areas of leverage? What action needs to be taken? And in the context of high-leverage actions, what decisions need to be made about funding? Now, and only now, the spreadsheet can emerge, to take the vision for the company and translate it into specific allocations: "How will we collectively allocate resources across the organization to achieve our vision?"

See "Strategic Priorities," page 344.

STEP 5: CHOICE AND IMPLEMENTATION

Steps 1 through 4 can all be accomplished in a carefully planned three-day session. At the end of that session, each participant has the opportunity to commit himself to the strategic plan—to choose it. Participants will go back to their parts of the organization to build the appropriate segments of the plan. They have a sense of their role in a synchronized organization-wide program. In regular meetings throughout the rest of the two- to three-month planning cycle, the senior team members can continue to compare notes, coordinate experiments they may have decided to run together, and chart the direction of the plan.

A planning method like this, of course, does not exist in a vacuum. It requires the use of all five learning disciplines, and it will not, in itself, produce the changes that the organization requires. But it will start the organization on a fundamentally different track, and trigger a powerful learning process. Because values and direction are brought into the open up front, you need to spend less time wrangling over numbers later. There is a higher level of commitment, and a greater sense of shared responsibility for meeting the total budget, not just each individual's allocation. Finally, if the learning disciplines are of value, the new planning process gives senior officers a chance to see that value for themselves, with no risk to their own group and no need for a frontal "change-agent-style" assault on the organization's policies and norms.

Systems
Thinking

13 Strategies for Systems Thinking

Jim Boswell, a friend of ours who grew up on a farm, points out that farm children learn naturally about the cycles of cause and effect that make up systems. They see the links among the milk the cow gives, the grass the cow eats, and the droppings which fertilize the fields. When a thunderstorm is on the horizon, even a small child knows to turn off the floodgate on a spring-water well, for fear that runoff carried downstream by the rains will foul it. They know that if they forget to turn off the gate, they'll have to boil their water, or carry it by bucket from far away. They easily accept a counterintuitive fact of life: the greatest floods represent the time when you must be *most* careful about conserving water.

Similar paradoxes crop up regularly in organizational life. The time of your greatest growth is the best moment to plan for harder times. The policies which gain the most for your position may ultimately drain your resources most quickly. The harder you strive for what you want, the more you may undermine your own chances of achieving it. Systems principles like these are meaningful not so much in themselves, but because they represent a more effective way of thinking and acting. Incorporating them into your behavior requires what David McCamus, former chairman and CEO of Xerox Canada, calls "peripheral vision": the ability to pay attention to the world as if through a wide-angle, not a telephoto lens, so you can see how your actions interrelate with other areas of activity.

A universal language

ALTHOUGH SYSTEMS THINKING IS SEEN BY MANY AS A POWERFUL PROB-lem-solving tool, we believe it is more powerful as a language, augmenting and changing the ordinary ways we think and talk about complex issues. The subject-verb-object constructions of most Western languages (where A causes B) make it difficult to talk about circumstances in which A causes B while B causes A, and both continually interrelate with C and D. The tools of systems thinking—causal loop diagrams, archetypes, and computer models—allow us to talk about interrelationships more easily, because they are based on the theoretical concept of feedback processes. The structure of channels by which elements of a system "feed" influence and information to each other over time may produce growth. That structure may produce decline. Or it may move naturally toward a state of balance and equilibrium.°

You know that you can "speak" the systems language skillfully, as our colleague Michael Goodman puts it, "when it becomes second nature; when you find yourself thinking in it; when you don't have to translate a causal circle or an archetype into English to figure it out."

Daniel Kim, publisher of *The Systems Thinker*, notes that in some multinational organizations, people who are not native speakers of the same language use archetype diagrams, with the elements labeled in each participant's language, to communicate effectively about sophisticated issues. The individuals may not be able to understand each other's words; but they understand how each other sees common patterns.

At Federal Express, work with systems thinking in a pilot learning laboratory has led to unprecedented improvements in relations between the company and a number of large customer accounts. These customers began to notice that their Fed Ex reps were more open, more willing to collaborate, and more capable of helping to solve strategic issues. "There was no dramatic policy change," says Pat Walls, a Federal Express managing director who is coordinator of the learning laboratory project there. "When you trace back the stories, you find out that all this change came from hundreds of little things that individuals were doing differently. It's like the old expression, 'You are what you eat.' If you start thinking differently, you see things differently. And all your actions start to change."

° To learn more about the history of the feedback concept, see *Feedback Thought in Social Science and Systems Theory* by George P. Richardson (1991, Philadelphia: University of Pennsylvania Press).

If the human body is "what we eat," then our organizations become the stories we tell ourselves. When we institutionalize the practice of systems thinking, ideally by using complementary combinations of the tools described in this part of the book, we end up telling ourselves a different set of stories. If those stories are credible and resonant, the organization's collective understanding changes, and its operations follow.

Supports for systems thinking

DURING THE LAST FEW YEARS, A NEW UNDERSTANDING OF THE PROCESS of organizational change has emerged. It is not top-down *or* bottom-up, but participative at all levels—aligned through common understanding of a system. This is possible because archetypes and other system-oriented tools have put system dynamics language into the hands of teams and on the walls of meeting rooms, where they can energize organizational learning at all levels. People are also exploring systems thinking in learning laboratories which fit their own cases and needs.

For another type of support, see "Systems Thinking and Process Mapping: A Natural Combination," page 184. For more about Learning Labs, see page 529.

SYSTEMS THINKING

At its broadest level, systems thinking encompasses a large and fairly amorphous body of methods, tools, and principles, all oriented to looking at the interrelatedness of forces, and seeing them as part of a common process. The field includes cybernetics and chaos theory; gestalt therapy; the work of Gregory Bateson, Russell Ackoff, Eric Trist, Ludwig von Bertallanfy, and the Santa Fe Institute; and the dozen or so practical techniques for "process mapping" flows of activity at work. All of these diverse approaches have one guiding idea in common: that behavior of all systems follows certain common principles, the nature of which are being discovered and articulated.

But one form of systems thinking has become particularly valuable as a language for describing how to achieve fruitful change in organizations. This form, called "system dynamics," has been developed by Professor Jay Forrester and his colleagues at Massachusetts Institute of Technology over the past forty years. The tools and methods which we describe in this part of the book—"links and loops," archetypes, and stock-and-flow modeling—all have their roots in the system dynamics understanding of how complex feedback processes can generate problematic patterns of behavior within organizations and large-scale human systems.—PS, AK

SYSTEM

A system is a perceived whole whose elements "hang together" because they continually affect each other over time and operate toward a common purpose. The word descends from the Greek verb *sunistánai,* which originally meant "to cause to stand together." As this origin suggests, the structure of a system includes the quality of perception with which you, the observer, cause it to stand together.

Examples of systems include biological organisms (including human bodies), the atmosphere, diseases, ecological niches, factories, chemical reactions, political entities, communities, industries, families, teams—and all organizations. You and your work are probably elements of dozens of different systems.—AK

SYSTEMIC STRUCTURE

Some people think the "structure" of an organization is the organization chart. Others think "structure" means the design of organizational work flow and processes. But in systems thinking, the "structure" is the pattern of interrelationships among key components of the system. That might include the hierarchy and process flows, but it also includes attitudes and perceptions, the quality of products, the ways in which decisions are made, and hundreds of other factors.

Systemic structures are often invisible—until someone points them out. For example, at a large bank we know, whenever the "efficiency ratio" goes down two points, departments are told to cut expenses and lay people off. But when bank employees are asked what the efficiency ratio means, they typically say, "It's just a number we use. It doesn't affect anything." If you ask yourself questions such as: "What happens if it changes?" you begin to see that every element is part of one or more systemic structures.

The word "structure" comes from the Latin *struere,* "to build." But structures in systems are not necessarily built consciously. They are built out of the choices people make consciously or unconsciously, over time.—RR, CR, AK

THE SYSTEMS THINKER, edited by Colleen Lannon-Kim, published by Pegasus Communications, Cambridge, Massachusetts

We recommend this newsletter wholeheartedly, both as a source for information about archetypes (including many archetypes which we did not have room to cover) and about all other systems-oriented methods. The editors are skilled, wide-ranging, and knowledgeable; their bailiwick includes all the learning disciplines, not just systems thinking.—**AK**

14 What You Can Expect . . . As You Practice Systems Thinking*

Charlotte Roberts, Jennifer Kemeny

* $\overset{\circ}{A}$ lso see "The Laws of the Fifth Discipline," in *The Fifth Discipline*, page 57.

There are no right answers

BECAUSE SYSTEM DYNAMICS ILLUSTRATES THE INTERDEPENDENCIES within the current system, there is never a single right answer to any question. Instead, the discipline reveals a variety of potential actions you may take: some high-leverage and some low-leverage. Each of these actions will produce some desired results and (almost certainly) some unintended consequences somewhere else in the system. The art of systems thinking includes learning to recognize the ramifications and trade-offs of the action you choose.

You won't be able to "divide your elephant in half"

YOU CAN'T REDESIGN YOUR SYSTEM (THE "ELEPHANT") BY DIVIDING IT into parts; everyone must look at the whole together. Thus, you can't practice systems thinking as an individual—not because the discipline itself is difficult, but because good results in a complex system depend on bringing in as many perspectives as possible. As you put together a team, make sure all necessary functions are represented, and gain clearance from top management to propose cross-functional solutions, regardless of sensitivities and politics. No area of the organization can be off-limits or protected. Also, try to include a variety of learning styles on the team.

} } For tools for studying your team's learning styles, see page 421.

By its nature, systems thinking points out interdependencies and the need for collaboration. Thus, as the team continues its work, it may become necessary to bring in new members—particularly people who were once seen as enemies, but are now obviously players on the same side in the same game.

Cause and effect will not be closely related in time and space

DON'T LOOK FOR LEVERAGE NEAR THE SYMPTOMS OF YOUR PROBLEM. GO upstream and back in time to ferret out the root cause. Often, the most effective action is the subtlest. Sometimes it's best to do nothing, letting the system make its own correction or guide the action. Other times, the highest leverage is found in a completely unexpected source.

The founder of the Cray supercomputer company, Seymour Cray, had originally assumed that his market was severely limited to a few supercomputer applications. By the early 1980s, to his surprise, customers with new kinds of needs began to appear. A systems thinking exercise showed that there would be unexpected leverage not in their proposed marketing strategy (advertising to technical audiences), but in promoting education for aeronautical engineering and movie animation, endeavors that would require supercomputers.

You'll have your cake and eat it too— but not all at once

IN PROPOSING SYSTEMS SOLUTIONS, MAKE SURE YOU TAKE INTO ACCOUNT the necessary time delays. For example, if you propose a staff expansion, how long will it take to train new people? How much will that training drain the time of your existing staff?

Years ago, we worked with an office supply manufacturer which developed a strategy of forming strategic alliances with independent dealers. On paper, it looked wonderful; but when we studied the delays in the system, we saw it could take two years for these individual dealerships to develop into high-flight entrepreneurial sales organizations. Because they had not prepared people for the need to ride out the expansion for two years without sales, the proponents of strategic alliances had to step away from their strategy.

Time delays and other subtle aspects of the system only become apparent with time and experimentation. Commit to continually examining how the system is working.

The easiest way out will lead back in

BEWARE THE EASIEST, FASTEST SOLUTION. MOST PEOPLE PREFER TO INtervene in a system at the level of rules, physical structure, work processes, material and information flows, reward systems, and control mechanisms—where the elements are more visible and it requires less skill to work with them. But as you move toward the more intangible elements, such as people's deep-seated attitudes and beliefs, your leverage for effective change increases. You come closer to looking at the underlying reasons why the rules, physical structure, and work processes take their current form.

Behavior will grow worse before it grows better

MORE OFTEN THAN NOT, AS A SYSTEMS EFFORT MAKES UNDERLYING structures clearer, members of the group may have moments of despair. Jay Forrester has called systems dynamics the "new dismal science," because it points out the vulnerabilities, limited understandings, and fallibilities of the past, and the assurance that today's thinking will be the source of tomorrow's problems. But actually, things are finally getting better. People see formerly "undiscussable" problems rising to the surface. They realize how their old, beloved ways of thinking have produced their current problems. Their new awareness reinforces their sense of hope about leading an effective change.

Organizational politics do not easily handle this new awareness. In a high-tech company, not long ago, a systems model disclosed two of the policies set by the founders as the root cause of their greatest problem — delivery delays. The middle managers who developed the model refused to present it publicly. They said, "We didn't sign up for confrontation. We don't want to step on people's toes." They asked if, instead, they could "tweak" the model to come up with a simple answer, such as "Speed up production line three." Delivery delays remained in place.

Select team members who are willing to take a stand and who know in advance that their advice will be unpopular. The team must have permission from top management to pursue its understanding, and clout to have its redesigns taken seriously. It must also have the ability to conduct experiments and take action; you cannot gain a systems understanding unless you can take part in changing it. Otherwise, you will continually see the system sabotage your well-intentioned efforts.

15 Brownie's Lamb: Learning to See the World Systemically

Donella Meadows

A system can comprise something as intangible as the deeply set attitudes of a ewe. This account of a systems intervention, by writer/farmer/systems modeler/biophysicist/Dartmouth College professor Donella (Dana) Meadows, was written in spring 1992. At first, Dana and her partners, Sylvia and Don, fought the system; gradually, they learned to work with it. Ultimately, patience with a delay made the difference.

Brownie, our yearling ewe, was the last to lamb this year. Yearlings are not quite full grown and are totally inexperienced, so you have to watch them very closely. Brownie managed to produce her lamb without any help, but then she didn't know what to do with it. In fact, she didn't recognize it as hers.

There's a miraculous moment right after birth when the ewe licks off her lamb, which dries it and stimulates its circulation, and which also produces some kind of powerful chemical lock. The ewe starts chuckling gently to the lamb—a low sound she never makes at any other time. The lamb bleats back in answer. At that moment they fall totally in love with each other. They can identify each other by smell and sound ever after, even in a barnyard that is jumping with identical-looking ewes and lambs. After that magic bonding, the ewe will drive away every other lamb, and she will rest content only when she knows that her own precious child is close to her.

Somehow that chemistry failed with Brownie. Sylvia found the lamb still partly wrapped in its amniotic sac, and Brownie cruising madly around the barnyard looking for something she knew she had lost, though she didn't know quite what it was. I've seen this happen before, especially with yearlings, and the outcome is what we call a "bummer"— an abandoned lamb. We have to adopt it and bottle-feed the poor thing every three or four hours, day and night. Bummer lambs are endearing, because they identify with people, not sheep. "Everywhere that Mary went, the lamb was sure to go," was surely written about a bummer; they follow you around with great insistence. But bummers are a lot of trouble in the short term, and in the long term, no matter how conscientiously you coddle them, they never grow well. Ewes just make better lamb mothers than people do.

Sylvia and Don knew it was essential to get the colostrum, the first antibody-rich milk, into that lamb. So they wrestled Brownie into a stall. Because it's a bother to milk a sheep by hand (they have such little udders you have to do it with three fingers and it takes forever), they rigged up a temporary stanchion, so Brownie was held tight standing up. Her lamb could nurse all it wanted without her butting it away. The lamb was strong and aggressive and took full advantage of the opportunity. By the time I got home twenty-four hours later, the skinny little newborn's tummy had filled right out, and the lamb was dancing around. Brownie was very unhappy, but the lamb was off to a good start.

We tried letting Brownie loose at that point, hoping she'd settle down with her baby. But she took one look at the lamb and knocked it off its feet. It's heartbreaking to watch a ewe "bum" a lamb. The sweet little thing runs enthusiastically up to its mother, and its mother slams it against the barn wall. It tries again and gets slammed again. Well, we couldn't let that go on. I was ready to give up, when Don came up with a brilliant idea. "Let her out of the stall and back with the other sheep," he said.

"That won't make any difference," I said, but there wasn't much else to do, so I grabbed the lamb and we let Brownie loose.

She ran straight back to the spot where the lamb had been born and began searching for it. We put the lamb back down, right there. She butted it away and kept searching, but the clever little lamb managed to sneak in behind her back legs and get some sucks in anyway. The lamb was bonded to the mother, and it was getting food, so we backed off and watched anxiously.

For a day that fool Brownie searched the barnyard bawling constantly for her lost lamb, with her lost lamb tagging right behind her. It was so frustrating to watch—like the search for happiness, when it's right there waiting for you to wise up. Somehow, sometime, the magical chemical signal clicked on, forty-eight hours after birth. I didn't know it was possible. By the next morning Brownie had stopped moaning and was chuckling to her lamb, who was getting bigger and stronger by the hour.°

° If you like this essay, adapted from Dana Meadow's correspondence, you would appreciate her book *The Global Citizen* (1991, Covelo, Calif.: Island Press).

BELONGING TO THE UNIVERSE by Fritjof Capra and David Steindl-Rast, with Thomas Madison (1991, San Francisco: Harper);

LEADERSHIP AND THE NEW SCIENCE by Margaret Wheatley (1993, San Francisco: Berrett-Koehler).

For years, I struggled with a question I thought important: In organizations, which is a more important influence on behavior—the system or the individual? The principles of quantum physics answered that question for me with an authoritative: "It depends." For me, two books have been particularly helpful.

Belonging to the Universe is a dialectic between science and theology written by Fritz Capra (author of *The Tao of Physics*) and two Benedictine monks, Brother David Steindl-Rast and Thomas Madison. They explain the changes involved in the shift from linear thinking to systems thinking—for example, the shift from seeing things as structures to seeing them as processes. A tree is not an object, but an expression of processes, such as photosynthesis, which connect the sun and the earth. The same is true of our bodies, our jobs, our organizations, and ourselves.

Margaret Wheatley's book, *Leadership and the New Science*, shows how twentieth-century scientific discoveries may apply to business and other organizations. She considers, for example, self-organizing systems (where order emerges from chaos) as a prototype for managing in turbulent environments. Wheatley's personal approach to this material makes her a good example of a learner. At one point, for instance, she sits down next to a stream and asks herself, "I wonder what the stream has to teach me?"—RR

16 Starting with Storytelling

The Acme story*
The four levels of a systems view

Jennifer Kemeny, Michael Goodman, Rick Karash

Goodman, Kemeny, and Karash, whose writing appears throughout this section, comprise the Systems Thinking consultation team at Innovation Associates. What started as a few discrete writing tasks for them developed into a collaborative effort with us to do something no one has ever attempted before: creating a comprehensive guide to nontechnical systems thinking practice. All three studied at MIT's Sloan School, where many of the methods described here were developed. All three drew on extensive experience developing models and applying systems approaches to business and organizations. All three, as various segments in this book attest, are innovators in the field. Michael Goodman, director of this team, helped coordinate this part of the book.

A good systems thinker, particularly in an organizational setting, is someone who can see four levels operating simultaneously: events, patterns of behavior, systems, and mental models.

The Acme Company sells high-quality industrial equipment, known both for its innovative design and its durability. Acme's principal customers tend to be purchasing departments within Fortune 1000 corporations. Many have been repeat customers for thirty years or more.

* This story (and material throughout the "Systems Thinking" section of this book) has its roots (in very different form) in material from *Systems Thinking: A Language for Learning and Acting: The Innovation Associates Systems Thinking Course Workbook* (1992, Framingham, Mass.: Innovation Associates).

Sales were steady all through the 1980s.

A

Late deliveries noticeably increased, beginning in 1989 and accelerating thereafter.

B

Time per sale (the time each sales person had to spend to make a sale) increased 16% in 1990.

C

Billing errors noticeably increased, beginning in 1991 and accelerating thereafter.

D

Sales took a dramatic downturn in 1991.

E

Time per sale continued to increase; it went up 21% in 1992.

F

Customer service staff complained of overwork and stress in 1992.

G

FIRST LEVEL: EVENTS AT ACME

In late 1992 Acme's senior management team met to consider some individual *events* which had recently troubled the company. After the presentation ended, the executives sat silently for five minutes. Then everyone began to speak at once.

"We're way off our sales targets," said the senior vice president of marketing. "We'd better remind the salespeople that they're still accountable for those targets if they want to get bonuses."

"We need new promotions and lower prices," said the senior vice president of sales. "Otherwise, we'll have a hard time replacing our lost customers with new ones. I'd like to see us start delivering outside our service area, too."

"I understand the need to sell at low cost," said the senior vice president of manufacturing, "but we're getting really behind. With all our new special orders, we can't do long production runs any more. That's slowing us down. We're also getting some technical problems with the equipment. We'll do our best, but I warn you, we may have to think about adding resources."

"No way," said the general manager. "Our finances are too tight right now. You'll have to make do with what you've got."

"Can't we be proactive about this?" asked the CEO. "We can accept some investment if it will pay off and solve these problems."

It's at this point, in many organizations, that problem-solving stops and people jump to solutions. Acme's senior managers did exactly that. They instituted a new system to speed up deliveries. To cut billing errors and improve customer service, they ordered improved training programs and rewrites of the operations manuals. To boost sales, they instituted new pricing promotions, allowed more nonstandard deliveries, established better sales incentives, and held motivational meetings, "to put fire under the sales force."

Unfortunately, profitability and sales dropped even more precipitously during the following three quarters.

SECOND LEVEL: PATTERNS OF BEHAVIOR

Six months later, the senior management team met again. As before, they began to brainstorm about possible solutions, and single out targets for blame. Then the CEO said, "This didn't get us anywhere last time. We need a different way to think about things."

"I've been curious about the trends," said the general manager. "We have a lot of seemingly unrelated factors here." They assigned a task force to research the *patterns of behavior* of the system over time. Instead of listing isolated events, the task force would select key variables and track them back three or four years.

Two weeks later, the general manager stood before them. "The trends are worse than we thought," he said. "When we put all the figures and reports together, look at how our service problems have increased in the last few years." And he projected this slide:

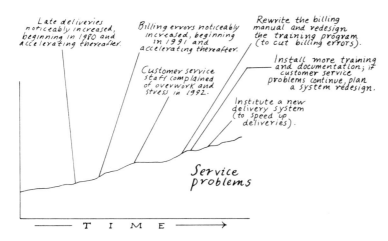

"Sales per year," he continued, "have dropped even more since 1991. And show no sign of turning around.

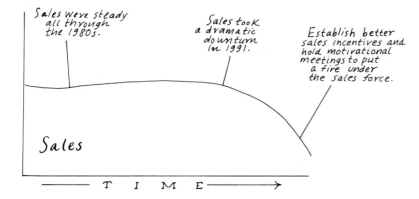

"Finally," he said, "here is one of our indicators of the effort our sales force puts into getting new accounts. It takes us more than twice as much time, counting all leads, to close a sale now than it did in the 1980s."

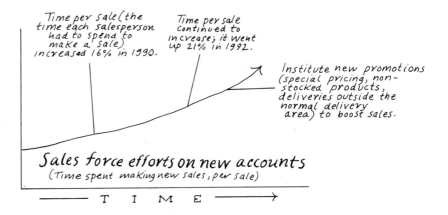

The trends, the managers quickly realized, did not suggest why some lines were falling while others were rising. Nor did it suggest any steps for action. The trends reinforced the feeling of urgency—but toward what?

THIRD LEVEL: SYSTEMIC STRUCTURE

Then the general manager said, "Is it possible that these trends influence each other in ways we haven't looked at before?"

"For instance?" asked the CEO.

"Well," said the sales manager, "every time sales go down, we redouble our effort to get new customers. Maybe there's a causal relationship there."

Over the next hour, they talked through some key interrelationships between these factors, considering and discarding hypotheses, until they ended up with a diagram of a simple system: the Acme sales system. It looked like this:

"Well," said the manufacturing vice president, tracing a path around the circle from the lower right, "I see why the sales force efforts cause service problems. We offer so many promises and special deals. If the customer wants it pink, we paint it. If they want it ten miles outside our normal delivery zone, we send the truck. This stresses the manufacturing and delivery functions"—pointing to the lower left—"and apparently it created havoc in customer service. But what's the link between our service problems and sales?"

"It's not a one-on-one correspondence," said the general manager. "Service problems can rise for a long time without any visible effect. But eventually customers hit a threshold point, where they're too irritated to stay with us. You can see that threshold here—" pointing to the top. "Despite our heroic efforts, they stopped buying from us."

"As a result," said the sales vice president, "we focus even more on gaining more new customers. Which means service problems continue to go up, and sales eventually drop again, and we try even harder to get new accounts."

"The harder we try to sell our products," said the marketing vice president gloomily, "the more sales we lose. It's a vicious spiral."

"Why do we keep doing this?" asked the CEO. He turned to the sales vice president. "How come, whenever sales drop, you push harder to get new customers?"

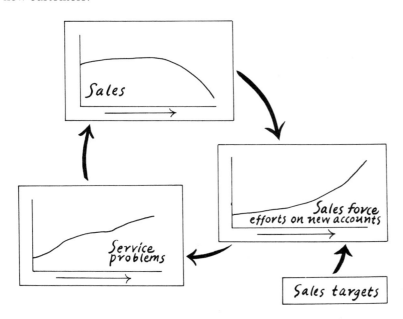

"Well, we have to!" said the sales VP, walking to the board. "We have to make our sales targets!"

There was no need to say more. Acme annually set sales targets as part of their planning process. As each year unfolded, management would monitor these. If sales fell below the targets, pressure would arrive, in the form of incentives and bonuses, to get sales "back on track."

FOURTH LEVEL: MENTAL MODELS

"We will have to change the system," said the CEO. Within two weeks, a new sales policy was announced at Acme. Special deals for new customers were forbidden. New incentives rewarded salespeople who won back old customers.

Sales figures dropped even more. With the end of the year approaching, sales and marketing managers throughout Acme began to complain about the new policy. How could they bring in the revenue the company needed, when they had no incentives to offer new customers? It soon became clear that quick policy reforms, in themselves, would not achieve the desired results.

Finally, the senior management group met once more. "Where is it written," asked the CEO, "that when sales go down we will make up the difference with new accounts?"

"In fact," said the vice president of marketing, "it's written in our beliefs." They would probably have to seek leverage, they all realized, in the mental models of their employees—the prevailing motivations and assumptions held (and generally unvoiced) by people, which had allowed this system to remain in place so long, despite the harm it was doing to the company:

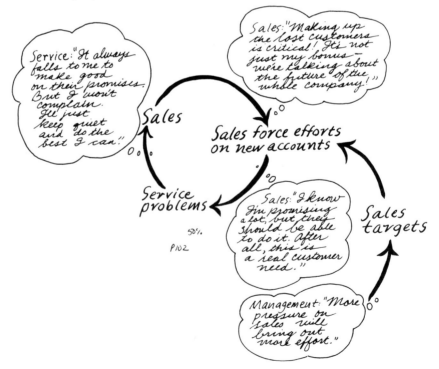

Underlying almost every link of the cycle is a key assumption, shown here by a thought balloon. Salespeople still tacitly assumed that their job was primarily to "do whatever it takes to get a new customer," which kept up the pressure on Customer Service. If they saw their job as retaining old customers they would probably start to become more aware of the service problems that were driving customers away. Changing this mental model might involve reshaping the compensation and incentive system, but it would also require shifting deeply held attitudes about the sales force's relationship with the rest of the company. The service staff generally assumed that salespeople were out of touch with the company's needs. Neither group felt any responsibility to understand the other group's activities or priorities.

It took Acme's senior management several months to find ways to deal effectively with their problem. They restructured sales targets: one of the few places where senior management had immediate leverage. They moved some of their marketing people to a customer service task force, and invested even more in customer surveys and increasing delivery reliability. They established a quality-oriented initiative in manufacturing, with an emphasis on increasing flexibility. Finally, they continued to track trends and patterns of behavior—with an eye to the systems underneath. This helped them keep close watch on which of their interventions were most worthwhile.

Exploring your own story *Michael Goodman, Rick Karash*

STEP 1: THE PROBLEM IS . . .

It generally takes no more than a few minutes to settle on a description of your problem, right now, as you see it. Start your sentence with the phrase: "The problem is . . ."

The problem is: We don't seem to be able to increase sales; all our special promotions just produce temporary "blips" of improvement.

The problem is: District marketing offices should be able to handle all their own technical support needs, but more and more, they've been requiring help from the corporate tech support group.

■ The issue should be important to you and your organization. Don't make this an academic exercise, but an inquiry into something you genuinely care about, and want to understand.

PURPOSE

To lay the groundwork for a systems understanding of your own situation.

OVERVIEW

Discerning a coherent story out of the interrelationships of seemingly random events.

PARTICIPANTS
An intact team with a problem.

TIME
Several hours.

SUPPLIES
Flip charts, markers, self-sticking notes.

■ Choose a chronic problem. Focus on a situation which has been around for a while, and which troubles you repeatedly, rather than on a one-time event.

■ Choose a problem of limited scope. If you cannot reduce the statement of the problem to one or two sentences, narrow your focus. You will find it easy to broaden the subject later, but with unlimited scope, you risk getting overwhelmed with the abstract realization that "everything is connected to everything."

■ Choose a problem whose history is known, and which you can describe. People have different notions about past patterns. Getting consensus on some key aspects of the history can be insightful. A description of a history can be as simple as a sentence:

> *The problem is: Profits were steady for two years, but have been declining for the last six months.*

> *The problem is: Productivity rose rapidly until about a year ago, when it leveled off.*

■ Make sure your description of the problem is as accurate as possible. Resist any temptation to sanitize it for political reasons, or bias it toward a particular solution. Systems thinking is a process of discovery and diagnosis—an inquiry into the governing processes underlying problems we face. Like any good detective, stick to the facts and evidence. Having "noncombatants" (neutral third parties) present, as participants, leaders, or coaches, can help you stay inquiring, especially if the issue is hot.

⟩⟩ See "Writing to Your Loyalties," page 268.

■ In stating your problem, don't jump to conclusions by including a suggestion of the solution in your statement of the problem. For instance, do not say:

> *The problem is: We just need to cut costs.*
> *The problem is: We need a new computer system.*

At this stage in the exercise, no one yet knows why the situation occurred, much less what the solution will be. For many, the discipline of not jumping to a solution is the most difficult part of this process. All you know is that the solution is not likely to be intuitively obvious, or else you would have already implemented it.

■ If possible, choose a problem which has been tackled before, with little or no success. This ensures that a systemic dynamic is at play.

■ Be nonjudgmental. Avoid blaming anyone or any particular policy. Don't assume you know the motives of any other participant, particularly if he or she is not present in the discussion. You might be tempted to say, "The technical department is being unreasonable. We can hardly bear the pressure they've put us under. We need to shake them back into line." The real problem, however, is the untenable pressure. The technical department may simply be passing it on; they may feel it as painfully as you do.

STEP 2: TELLING THE STORY

The next step is to bring the story or stories underlying your problem to the surface. This process is also known as model building; it can be a powerful learning process, especially for teams.

During this phase, you develop a theory or hypothesis that makes sense, is logically consistent, and could—if accurate—explain why the system is generating the problems you see. Then, in the spirit of the scientific method, you test the story you have created. As in all model building, when the theory can't explain observations, then it needs refinement or revision. We are all natural model builders but rarely get a forum and the tools to exchange and examine our theories. The loops and archetypes give us those tools.

The worst approach to take is classical problem solving—precisely defining a "problem statement" to quickly come up with the right "solution." Instead, the team should purposely maintain a great many divergent ideas for as long as possible, even if they seem to contradict at first. For many of us, this is the most difficult aspect of this stage.

The story you tell with loops and archetypes is not linear; it does not have a beginning, a middle, and an end. Instead, you view a series of events from many vantage points and identify key themes and recurring patterns. As you continue to consider the structure, your understanding of the underlying structure will deepen.

At the heart of the art of systems story telling is one question:

How did we (through our internal thinking, our processes, our practices, and our procedures) contribute to or create the circumstances (good and bad) we face now?

This question tends to yield significant answers only after sustained deliberation. We offer two ways of beginning that deliberation. You can use either of them, or both.

OPTION A: MAKE A LIST

Identify the "characters" of the story: key factors that seem likely to capture the problem or are critical to telling the story.

Some might be widespread and political in scope . . .

One key factor is, the national health care costs are out of control.

. . . while others pertain only to this particular organization . . .

One key factor is, we spend far too much time in redundant paperwork.

The point of this exercise is not to settle on any of these statements as "right" or "wrong." In fact, you should try to refrain from criticizing any of them at all. Instead, your purposes are:

- To begin talking about the problem; to plant stakes in the ground and identify people's assumptions and hypotheses about root causes.
- To establish a sense of boundaries: what are the dimensions of this problem? How far does it stretch? What will you have to consider?
- To illuminate the team's varied perspectives. You may discover that each member of the team focuses on a different set of factors, based on his or her own tacit assumptions or experience.
- To lay groundwork for selecting some key factors as variables.

To bring forward a wider range of key factors, consider questions like these:

1. *How would this issue look from an upper management viewpoint? What factors would be visible from that level?*
2. *How would this issue look from a front-line "shop floor," "office worker," or "service technician" perspective? What factors would be visible from that level?*
3. *How would other stakeholders, including customers, see the key factors?*
4. *Can you identify factors which your group created, or to which your group contributed?*

OPTION B: DRAW A PICTURE

Everyone in the room should be given pieces of paper—or, preferably, self-stick notes such as Post-it notes. Use 5 × 8-inch pages or larger. Clear your thoughts. Then, as individuals, draw the most important graph about your problem, and accompany it with a few words (spoken or written) describing its significance.

Use the "pattern-of-behavior" line-chart form, with "time" (the period of months, quarters, or years you care about) as the X-axis, and the key factor (variable) as the Y-axis. Don't worry about getting exact numbers; instead, just put down your impression of the general trend:

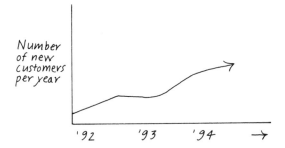

As accompaniment, you might say, "Our division is one of the growth divisions of the company. For three years we've been steadily bringing in new customers. *That's* our most important graph."

Until this stage, most people have only seen this situation in terms of the current moment. They have only felt its pressures. Drawing the most important graph moves you to a state of mind more sensitive to changes over time. It helps you see that the problem isn't brand-new.

Someone else in the room, meanwhile, has probably been working on a separate issue. "Each time we get a new customer," he or she might say, "we have to create special forms for that customer. For complex customers, we often have to check with the technical department. It must be a burden for them to answer our phone calls, and while our demand for their help has increased, their capacity has remained the same. These two graphs are equally important:"

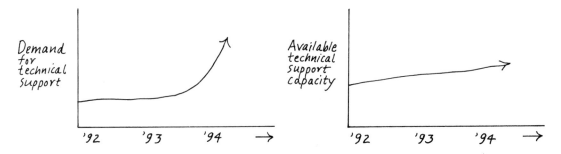

Suddenly, in the relationship between those graphs, a story is developing. You may have good reason to suspect, for instance, that the widening gap between the second graph and the third may be generating quality problems which eventually cause the number of customers to go down.

But if this story is typical, it's still incomplete. Other people chime in to flesh the story out, possibly with more graphs. You might try to ascertain how other key players see the situation. If, as in this case, there are no technical staff people in the room, then you might ask yourselves: "How *would* they see this if they were here? What would be *their* most important graph?"

You still won't be sure how to analyze the graphs or where the leverage might be; but you will begin to notice common themes. Does the trend go back a few years or a few months? Where do the trends seem to be headed? What will happen if they continue into the future? There may be a breaking point—a point after which the burden of the demand for technical support will be too difficult to bear.

Finally, as you consider the overall situation, how do the graphs relate to each other? What's the basic story, in words, that combines these graphs? If you drew them on self-stick notes, that will help you here— you can post them on a wall, and move them around to group the patterns of behavior which you think are related.

Soon, these groupings will become the basis for a larger systemic picture. You may also choose to refine your descriptions: changing "available technical support capacity" to "level of quality of technical support." But for now, their purpose is not to produce a diagram which everyone can agree upon, but to provoke a mutual sense of the story in the minds of people in the room. Notice how different your final understanding is from the "problem statement" you made in Stage 1. It may be appropriate at the end of this stage to reconsider the original problem statement.

You can move from here to "The Language of Systems Thinking," page 113, or "Applying an Archetype," page 121.

The Five Whys Rick Ross

THE FIVE WHYS' PERSPECTIVE

It's mid-afternoon, an hour before the shift changes at a manufacturing plant, and I'm the foreman. I'm walking through the plant, giving a tour to a friend who happens to be a systems thinker. Suddenly, I see a pool of oil on the floor. So I grab the nearest member of the assembly line crew: "Hey! There's oil on the floor! For Pete's sake, somebody could slip in that! Clean it up!"

When I'm finished, my systems thinking friend breaks in with a quiet question: "Why is there oil on the floor?"

"Yeah," I repeat to the crew member. "How'd the oil get on the floor?"

The crew member replies, "Well, the gabungie's leaking." All of us automatically look up. Sure enough, there's a visible leak up there in the gabungie."°

"Oh, okay," I sigh. "Well, clean up the oil and get the gabungie fixed right away."

My friend pulls me aside and murmurs, "But why is the gabungie broken?"

I say, "Yeah, well, the ga—" and turn to the crew member. "Why *is* the gabungie broken?"

"The gaskets are defective," is the reply.

"Oh well, then, look," I say. "Here. Clean the oil up, fix the gabungie, and, uh, do something about the gaskets!"

My friend adds: "And why are the gaskets defective?"

"Yeah," I say. "Just out of curiosity, how come we got defective gaskets in the gabungie?"

The shop floor crew member says, "Well, we were told that purchasing got a great deal on those gaskets."

I can see my friend start to open his mouth, but this time I get there first. "Why did purchasing get such a great deal?"

"How should I know?" says the crew member, wandering off to find a mop and bucket.

My friend and I go back to my office and make some phone calls. It turns out that we have a two-year-old policy in the company that encourages purchasing at the lowest price. Hence the defective gaskets—of which there is a five-year supply—along with the leaking gabungie and the pool of oil. In addition, this policy is probably causing other problems throughout the organization, not closely related in time or space to the root "cause."

STEP 1: THE FIRST WHY
Pick the symptom where you wish to start; the thread which you hope you can pull on to unravel the knot. Ask the first why of the group: "Why

° The gabungie is a big machine, mounted into the ceiling, which carries the whosis into the frammistat so it can be fribbulated.

PURPOSE
An alternative method for telling your story, by hunting backward for the root cause of pernicious, recurring problems. °

° This exercise is partly based on an established Japanese quality technique and its description by quality consultant Peter Scholtes.

OVERVIEW
Asking "Why," five times, in a team setting, with discussion.

PARTICIPANTS
Any number. Best done in an intact team, working on a real problem. Can also be done in pairs.

TIME
One hour or more.

SUPPLIES
Have plenty of flip chart paper, markers, and self-sticking notes handy, and deputize someone to write everything down.

is such-and-such taking place?" You will probably end up with three or four answers. Put them all on the wall, with plenty of room around them.

STEPS 2, 3, 4, 5: THE SUCCESSIVE WHYS

Repeat the process for every statement on the wall, asking "Why" about each one. Post each answer near its "parent." Follow up all the answers that seem likely. You will probably find them converging; a dozen separate symptoms may be traceable back to two or three systemic sources.

As you trace the Whys back to their root causes, you will find yourself tangling with issues that not only affect the gabungie (whatever that may be), but the entire organization. The policy to get the lowest price on supplies might have been caused by a battle in the finance office. It might result from a purchasing strategy, or from underinvestment in maintenance. The problem is not that the original policy was "wrong-headed," but that its long-term and far-flung effects remained unseen.

AVOIDING THE "FIXATION ON EVENTS"

To be effective, your answers to the Five Whys should steer away from blaming individuals. For example, in answer to the question: "Why is there oil on the floor?" someone may say: "Because the maintenance crew didn't clean it up."

"Why didn't they clean it up?"

"Because their supervisor didn't tell them to."

"Why didn't he do that?"

"Because the crew didn't tell him about it."

"Why didn't they tell him?"

"Because he didn't ask."

Blaming individual people leaves you with no option except to punish them; there's no chance for substantive change. One of the benefits of the Five Whys exercise is that it trains people to recognize the difference between an event-oriented explanation, and a systemic explanation. The systemic explanations are the ones which, as you trace them back, lead to the reasons *why* they didn't clean it up, or he didn't tell them to, or they didn't ask. (Maybe, for example, poor training of maintenance people contributed to the oil puddle problem; but even the best-trained, hardest-working custodians in the world could not stop the gasket from leaking.)

To avoid being distracted by event- and blame-related "answers," try this technique: as each answer is recorded, say: "Okay. Is that the only reason?"

}} Many Five Whys problems, including the gabungie problem, turn out to be cases of "Fixes
}} That Backfire." For more on this archetype, see page 125.

A real case of five whys: Sears Roebuck

WHEN A PROBLEM IS DENIED OR UNPROBED TOO LONG, FIVE WHYS IN-quiring may occur in embarrassing public forums. Sears Roebuck, for example, suffered in 1992 when a series of well-publicized Whys traced back an auto repair snafu to a high-level corporate policy decision.

STEP 1: THE FIRST WHY
Between 1990 and 1992, consumer complaints to the California State Department of Consumer Affairs (DCA) about Sears's auto repair service rose 50 percent. "Why?" asked staffers at DCA. To find out, they set up a sting operation, bringing in cars for repair. Sears salesmen, they found, overcharged an average of $223 per visit.

STEP 2: THE SECOND WHY
In June 1992, the DCA went public with its figures. Why, asked California newspaper reporters, did a company with Sears's reputation let such a breach of integrity take place? Interviewing mechanics, some reporters uncovered the fact that Sears had begun a fierce program of quotas and incentives several years before. Hourly wages had been partly replaced with commissions calculated according to the size of the bill and the mechanic's speed. Sears service "advisers" were given sales quotas ($147 per hour in one case), commissions for every part or service they recommended, and prizes or trips when they brought in more income than their counterparts in other Sears stores.

STEP 3: THE THIRD WHY
But why such an unrestrained program? Why so little apparent aware-ness of the danger of offending customers? To the reporters who repeat-

edly questioned them, Sears executives gradually admitted that they had established the quota and incentive policies at the corporate level, as part of a fervent national effort to slash expenses and improve profitability. Incentives had seemed like a faultless way to motivate workers and cut costs.

STEP 4: THE FOURTH WHY

The reason for the cost-cutting, according to several industry analysts whom the newspapers interviewed, had to do with the brutal financial pressure of recent years. The failure of other competitors like Carter Hawley Hale and Federated Department Stores showed how precarious department-store retailing had become—but worst of all, Sears's market share was slipping. In 1990, both Kmart and Wal-Mart passed Sears in store sales. Sears's department stores were considered far less successful than their other subsidiaries: Allstate Insurance, the Discover card—and Sears auto repair, which (as one analyst said) had been "leading the firm's strategic turnaround."

STEP 5: THE FIFTH WHY

And why was Sears's main business having difficulties? A full answer would probably depend on soul-searching and research within Sears itself—along the lines of the research done when you ask the Five Whys. Before the episode was over, the publicity (along with two class-action lawsuits) cost the retailer 15 percent of its auto repair business nationally, and 20 percent in California. In the end, Sears acknowledged its mistakes, corrected its policies, and agreed to an $8 million settlement, the largest of its type in the history of California.°

° Our information came from articles in the *San Francisco Chronicle:* September 3, June 23, June 13, June 12, and June 11, 1992; from articles written by Denise Gellene in the *Los Angeles Times:* September 3, September 2, July 22, July 10, June 23, June 19 (written with George White), June 17, June 16, June 13, June 12, June 11, 1992; from "Shape Up, Sears, and Do the Right Thing" by Gerald C. Meyers, *Los Angeles Times,* June 19, 1992; and from *Everybody's Business* by Milton Moskowitz, et al. (1990, New York: Currency Doubleday), pp. 196–98.

17 The Language of Systems Thinking: "Links" and "Loops"

Michael Goodman, Jennifer Kemeny, Charlotte Roberts

In systems thinking, every picture tells a story. From any element in a situation (or "variable"), you can trace arrows ("links") that represent influence on another element. These, in turn, reveal cycles that repeat themselves, time after time, making situations better or worse.

This image, for instance, from the Acme Company (page 97), shows the level of service influencing sales. Every time service grows poorer (when billing and delivery problems increase), sales will also decrease. Conversely, if the level of service improves, we can expect (eventually, at least) more sales.

But links never exist in isolation. They always comprise a circle of causality, a feedback "loop," in which every element is both "cause" and "effect"—influenced by some, and influencing others, so that every one of its effects, sooner or later, comes back to roost.

Here, for example, is a loop showing the entire Acme story:

HOW TO TELL THE STORY FROM A LOOP

1. Start anywhere. Pick the element, for instance, of most immediate concern. *Our sales are dropping . . .* Resist the temptation to explain why this is happening—yet.
2. Any element may go up or down at various points in time. What has the element been doing at this moment? Try out language which describes the movement: *As Acme's sales level goes up . . . goes down . . . improves . . . deteriorates . . . increases . . . decreases . . . rises . . . falls . . . soars . . . drops . . . waxes . . . wanes . . .*

3. Describe the impact this movement produces on the next element. *As Acme's sales level goes down, the number of efforts to sell new accounts goes up.*

4. Continue the story back to your starting place. Use phrases that show causal interrelationship: "This in turn, causes . . ." or ". . . which influences . . ." or ". . . then adversely affects . . ." *As Acme's sales level goes down, the number of efforts to sell new accounts goes up. This means the level of service drops, which in turn influences sales to continue falling . . .*

5. Try not to tell the story in cut-and-dried, mechanistic fashion. *When service problems rise, sales fall. As sales fall, sales force efforts rise.* Instead, make it come alive. Add illustrations and short anecdotes so others know exactly what you mean. . . . *This means the level of service drops. We just can't keep to the delivery schedules we promised. Loyal customers, in turn, become upset. Some stop doing business with us . . .*

Note that linear languages, like English, permit us to talk about the loop only one step at a time, as if we were following a train in a toy railroad around a track. In reality, however, all of these events occur at once. Seeing their simultaneity (*. . . sales continue to fall, while we spur even more efforts to sell new accounts . . .*) helps you recognize system behavior and develop a sense of timing.

Reinforcing loops: when small changes become big changes

THERE ARE BASICALLY TWO BUILDING BLOCKS OF ALL SYSTEMS REPRESENtations: reinforcing and balancing loops.

Reinforcing loops generate exponential growth and collapse, in which the growth or collapse continues at an ever-increasing rate. To grasp the often-surprising ramifications of exponential growth, consider an interest-bearing bank account. Your money grows much faster than it would if you merely put $100 each year into a piggy bank. At first, the difference seems small; interest would generate only a few extra dollars per year. But if you left the interest in the bank, the money would grow at an ever-faster rate. After fifty years (at 7 percent interest), you'd have more than $40,000, more than eight times as much as the piggy bank would generate by growing at the same rate, year after year.°

° From *Beyond the Limits*, by Donella H. Meadows, Dennis Meadows, and Jørgen Randers (1992, Post Hills, VT: Chelsea Green Publishing Company), pp. 16–18. See *Fieldbook*, p. 135.

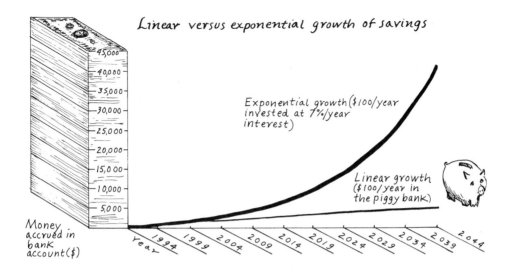

Linear versus exponential growth of savings

Exponential growth ($100/year invested at 7%/year interest)

Linear growth ($100/year in the piggy bank)

Money accrued in bank account ($)

Year — 1994 1999 2004 2009 2014 2019 2024 2029 2034 2039 2044

45,000 40,000 35,000 30,000 25,000 20,000 15,000 10,000 5,000

If you were unprepared for it, you'd reach a moment of surprise after perhaps fifteen years, when you saw how the growth of your money was building on itself—a truly virtuous spiral.

But you'd be caught in a vicious spiral if, instead of investing money, you went into debt for a long time. At first it would seem as if you were paying only small sums in interest. But over time, the balance you owed would grow with increasing speed.

In all reinforcing processes, as in the bank account, a small change builds on itself. High birth rates lead to higher birth rates; industrial growth begets more industrial growth. Don't underestimate the explosive power of these processes; in their presence, linear thinking can always get us into trouble. For example, organizations often assume that they will face steady, incremental growth in demand. They are startled to discover that when their new facilities come on line (be they factories, distribution systems, utility grids, jails, highways, or city services) the demand has already overshot the relief effort.

When someone remarks that, "The sky's the limit," or "We're on a roll," or "This is our ticket to heaven," you can bet there's a reinforcing loop nearby, headed in the "virtuous" direction they prefer.

When people say, "We're going to hell in a handbasket," or "We're taking a bobsled ride down the chute," or "We're spiraling to oblivion," you know they're caught in the other kind of reinforcing loop—the vicious cycle.

DRAWING THE REINFORCING LOOP

There can be any number of elements in a reinforcing loop—all in a circle, all propelling each others' growth. For example, this loop describes a "pile-up" of overwork on an overburdened team:

The team's agenda is full. The fuller the agenda, the less time people take to sit down and fully explore issues in depth. Therefore, the team's level of focus is scattered. The more scattered it is, the lower the level of shared understanding among team members. The lower the level of shared understanding, the more superficial the treatment of problems becomes. Thus, decisions that get made don't stick. Therefore, problems arise, adding to the team's agenda. Over time, as the team moves around the cycle, more and more problems pile up . . .

Note the "snowball" at the center of the loop. Reinforcing loop situations generally "snowball" into highly amplified growth or decline. If you prefer, use the letter *R* to mark a reinforcing loop.

A reinforcing loop, by definition, is incomplete. You never have a vicious or virtuous cycle by itself. Somewhere, sometime, it will run up against at least one balancing mechanism that limits it. The limit may not appear in our lifetime, but you can assume it will appear. Most of the time, there are multiple limits.*

*For more examples of reinforcing processes, see *The Fifth Discipline,* p. 80.

REINFORCING LOOP TEMPLATE (FOR PLOTTING YOUR OWN SITUATION):

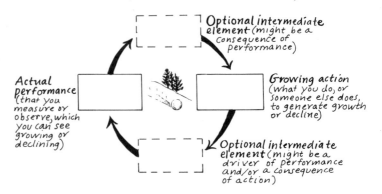

Balancing loops: pushing stability, resistance, and limits

BALANCING PROCESSES GENERATE THE FORCES OF RESISTANCE, WHICH eventually limit growth. But they are also the mechanisms, found in nature and all systems, that fix problems, maintain stability, and achieve equilibrium. They ensure that every system never strays far from its "natural" operating range—a human body's homeostatic state, an ecosystem's balance of predator and prey, or a company's "natural" expenses, which, whenever you cut them, seem to balloon up somewhere else.

Balancing loops are often found in situations which seem to be self-correcting and self-regulating, whether the participants like it or not. If people talk about "being on a roller coaster," or "being flung up and down like a yo-yo," then they are caught in one type of balancing structure. If caught in another type, they may say, "We're running into walls," or "We can't break through the barrier," or "No matter what we try, we can't change the system." Despite the frustration they often engender, balancing loops aren't innately bad: they ensure, for example, that there is usually some way to stop a runaway vicious spiral. Our survival depends on the many balancing processes which regulate the earth, the climate, and our bodies.

Balancing processes are always bound to a target—a constraint or goal which is often implicitly set by the forces of the system. Whenever current reality doesn't match the balancing loop's target, the resulting gap (between the target and the system's actual performance) generates a kind of pressure which the system cannot ignore. The greater the gap, the greater the pressure. It's as if the system itself has a single-minded awareness of "how things ought to be," and will do everything in its power to return to that state. Until you recognize the gap, and identify the goal or constraint which drives it, you won't understand the behavior of the balancing loop.

The North Millerfield Community Hospital (a pseudonym) in Connecticut opened a very attractive outpatient clinic in the late 1980s. The administrators knew that it was meeting a real need, and they assumed it would always be filled with patients, almost up to its capacity. That would make it a constant revenue generator. However, a few months after it opened, the number of patient visits (and thus revenues) leveled off, below the hospital's forecasts. The hospital started a community marketing campaign, and patient visits rose for a time, but soon dropped off again.

Finally, the administrators took a close look at their patient volume statistics. They spent time in the waiting room and surveyed staff at the front desk and patients. It turned out that when traffic was low, people were served quickly. Word got around, doctors and paramedics referred people, and North Millerfield's clinic became crowded. But people have an innate distaste for sitting in busy waiting rooms. Since they had a choice, they went elsewhere. The general lesson for all businesses is: if you don't adjust your service satisfaction to the level expected by your customers, the system will do it for you!

Sometimes, the target is clearly articulated and shared. Everyone in a sales force knows their sales targets. Other times, it is obscure, ill-defined, implicit, or assumed. The level of quality which customers would accept has driven the changes in the auto industry for the past twenty years, but no one has been able to agree on, or measure, that level of quality. A vision may drive the behavior of a team but never be articulated. Sometimes the target moves or changes, because it too is subject to influences from the system. In fact, discovering or creating new targets is often the key to overcoming the resistance that confronts you.

DRAWING THE BALANCING LOOP

Here is how you might represent North Millerfield's patient demand system in a balancing loop. Note that the comments in parentheses (Waiting time is "rising," while patient satisfaction is "going down") represent a snapshot of only one moment of the system. At other times,

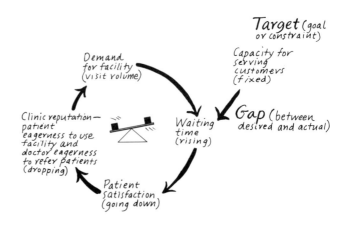

during the clinic's more unpopular periods, waiting time will fall, while patient satisfaction goes up.

We use a "balance beam" at the center of the loop, because it shows one common type of balancing loop behavior: "teeter-tottering" around a desired level, first overshooting a bit, then compensating in the other direction, and finally coming to rest at the target. If you prefer, label your balancing loops with the letter *B.*°

Delays: when things happen . . . eventually

DELAYS OCCUR OFTEN IN BOTH REINFORCING AND BALANCING LOOPS. These are points where the link (the chain of influence) takes a particularly long time to play out. Throughout this book, we represent delays with a pair of parallel lines, with an hourglass icon nearby as a reminder that time is passing (see drawing in margin).

Delay can have enormous influence in a system, frequently accentuating the impact of other forces. This happens because delays are subtle: usually taken for granted, often ignored altogether, always under-estimated. In reinforcing loops, delays can shake our confidence, because growth doesn't come as quickly as expected. In balancing loops, delays can dramatically change the behavior of the system. When unacknowledged delays occur, people tend to react impatiently, usually redoubling their efforts to get what they want. This results in unnecessarily violent oscillations. One of the purposes of drawing systems diagrams is to flag the delays which you might otherwise miss. In addition, delays are often a source of waste; removing delays is a key method for speeding up cycle time.

To see a simple demonstration of the impact of delays on system behavior, see "Moving into Computer Modeling," page 173.

When drawing systems archetypes, you may choose to mark more than one delay. But it is most helpful to identify the most significant delays—particularly the longest delays, relative to the other links.

For example, in the North Millerfield Hospital story, there are at least two significant delays:

■ The delay before customer satisfaction goes down. ("The first time I visited the clinic, I assumed the long waits were just a fluke. The second time I visited, I wanted to go somewhere else, but my spouse insisted.")

° For more examples of balancing processes, see *The Fifth Discipline*, p. 84.

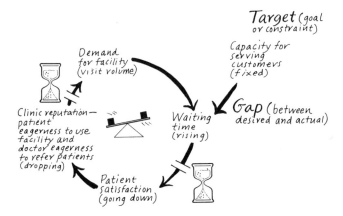

- The delay before the impact is felt of the clinic's lost reputation. ("That was the end for us. We haven't been back in months. I drove by last week and noticed that they've started advertising for patients.")

The underlying dynamic, of course, applies not just to hospital emergency rooms, but to restaurants, fast-food windows, stores, supermarkets, banks, gas stations, government agencies, and anyone who drives away customers by missing a key component of good service.

BALANCING LOOP TEMPLATE

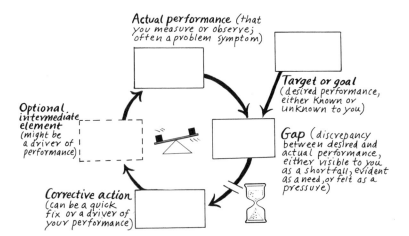

ARCHETYPES

The word comes from the Greek *archetypos,* meaning "first of its kind." A stepchild of the field of systems thinking, systems archetypes were developed at Innovation Associates in the mid-1980s. At that time, the study of systems dynamics depended upon complex causal loop mapping and computer modeling, using mathematical equations to define the relationships between variables. Charles Kiefer, I.A.'s president, suggested trying to convey the concepts more simply. Jennifer Kemeny (with Michael Goodman and Peter Senge, based in part upon notes developed by John Sterman) developed eight diagrams that would help catalogue the most commonly seen behaviors. Some archetypes, including "Limits to Growth" and "Shifting the Burden," were translations of "generic structures"—mechanisms which Jay Forrester and other systems thinking pioneers had described in the 1960s and 1970s.—**AK**

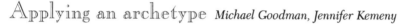

Applying an archetype *Michael Goodman, Jennifer Kemeny*

THIS STAGE PROMPTS US TO FILL IN GAPS IN OUR THINKING, AND TO TELL fuller, more complete stories. By showing feedback (reinforcing and balancing) relationships, the templates visually portray the interconnected nature of our world.

Archetypes are accessible tools with which managers can quickly construct credible and consistent hypotheses about the governing forces of their systems. Archetypes are also a natural vehicle for clarifying and testing mental models about those systems. They are powerful tools for coping with the astonishing number of details that frequently overwhelm beginning systems thinkers. As you work with archetypes, and they become second nature, they will become part of your diagnostic repertoire. You will be able to talk about systemic issues at a surprisingly sophisticated level, without the need for computers or other elaborate modeling tools. If you move on to more complex systems dynamics work (such as computer modeling), we believe that beginning with archetypes is the most effective way to develop your capacity.

STEP 1: CHOOSING AN ARCHETYPE

You start by making guesses. You may have to trust your intuition at first. Some people worry that they will apply the "wrong" archetype, misdi-

PURPOSE
To take the verbal and graphical descriptions of your story—the theories you are constructing— and capture the key elements into one or more of the "classic stories" of the systems archetypes.

OVERVIEW
Examining your situation in terms of typical combinations of feedback (reinforcing and balancing) relationships.

PARTICIPANTS
An intact team, perhaps alternating between solo- and teamwork.

TIME
Several hours.

SUPPLIES
The material left from "Exploring Your Own Story" (page 103).

agnose the problem, and make things worse. In practice, this doesn't happen, because by definition, people initially pick archetypes that hold interest for them. The fact that you are interested in one particular systems story is a clue that it probably applies, at least enough to start there.

Read through examples of each archetype in action. Keep alert for the stories which seem to ring analogously to your own story, no matter how different the circumstances may be. Generalizing your story—omitting some details to simplify it and look at it from a more distant perspective—can help you place it.°

One good clue to a pertinent archetype is finding a pattern of performance that seems to sum up the behavior of your entire system. Check that performance against this chart:

° For more material on archetypes, see *Systems Archetypes: Diagnosing Systemic Issues and Designing High-Leverage Interventions* by Daniel H. Kim (1993, Cambridge, Mass.: Pegasus Communications), and *The Fifth Discipline*, pp. 93–113 and 378–390.

BEHAVIOR AND ARCHETYPES COMPARISON CHART

For these patterns of behavior . . . These archetypes may apply:

An important variable accelerates up (or down), with exponential growth or collapse . . . . *Reinforcing loop*

There is movement toward a target (without delay), or else oscillation, hovering around a single target (with delay) . . . . *Balancing loop*

A problem symptom alternately improves (the problem variable goes down) and deteriorates (the problem goes up, worse than before) . . . . *"Fixes That Backfire"*

There is growth (sometimes dramatic growth), leveling off or falling into decline . . . . *"Limits to Growth"*

Three patterns exist side by side. The reliance on the short-term fix grows stronger, while efforts to fundamentally correct the real problem grow weaker, and the problem symptom alternately improves and deteriorates . . . .*"Shifting the Burden"*

Total activity grows, but the gains from individual activities are dropping . . . . *"Tragedy of the Commons"*

Each side's performance either declines or stays level and low, while enmity or competitiveness increases over time . . *"Accidental Adversaries"*

A good strategy is not to settle on one "answer" right away, but to look at your situation through the lens of several different archetypes. Two or three may fit together, each highlighting a different aspect.

The "Archetype Family Tree" (see page 149) can help you see how the archetypes fit together.

ADDING YOUR ELEMENTS TO THE STORY

First, try to match the elements of your story to the archetype. Start with the core or governing loop, the loop which seems to drive the behavior of the system. This loop often closely matches the pattern of behavior over time, and often depicts what people in the system are paying the most attention to.

CORE LOOPS OF KEY ARCHETYPES

the quick-fix balancing loop in "Fixes That Backfire,"

the reinforcing growth loop in "Limits to Growth,"

the quick-fix loop in "Shifting the Burden,"

and the individual actor loops in "Tragedy of the Commons."

See the archetype descriptions beginning on page 125.

Now pick a key variable and start building the loop by asking what affects that variable. ("Our investment in training is affected by our revenues.") You can, if you wish, fill in the names of your elements by drawing directly on a copy of an archetype template. If your story implies more variables than the template has, go ahead and draw in extra boxes. Any loop may have any number of elements.

Work backward around the structure. ("Our revenue depends upon service quality.") About each element, ask: What's causing changes in this element? What influences it to vary?

Or, if you get stuck, try working forward: What is the effect when this variable changes? What other elements must change?

If you still feel stuck, go back to the story. Are there key elements which you have left out? Where do they link to the archetype?

Draw arrows to show the direction of movement in the loops. Put a snowball or a letter *R* at the center of each reinforcing (growing) loop, and a balance beam or letter *B* at the center of each balancing loop. Remember that reinforcing loops always grow or decline. Balancing loops always move toward a target or goal level.

Give your variables names which represent levels of activity which may go up or down sometime in the future, even if that movement seems implausible to you now. Write in: "Level of sales" rather than "We're selling less this year" or "Our sales have dropped in half." As a reminder of your problem, you may want to put the current behavior in parentheses: "Level of sales (falling)."

It's particularly valuable to include any elements which are at least partly under your influence: if you can change the relationship of your company with suppliers, seeing that element as part of a vicious cycle may lead to insights about how you can influence the whole system.

Don't force your story into a template if it doesn't fit. Switch to another archetype. Or start with just a simple balancing or reinforcing loop that tells one important part of the story. Then add more elements, one link at a time, working forward or backward around a structure you create from scratch.

⸮⸮ For more about creating structures from scratch, see "Beyond Training Wheels," page 177.

When you have applied an archetype, turn back to the archetype description and check the patterns of behavior you would expect to see. Does it match the patterns you have seen in your own history? In a "Fixes That Backfire" structure, for example, do you see a continuing series of fixes to a stubborn problem that improves only momentarily?

Archetype 1: "Fixes That Backfire"

Daniel Kim, Michael Goodman, Charlotte Roberts, Jennifer Kemeny

Daniel Kim contributed extensively to the Fieldbook, particularly on archetypes and learning labs. He generously allowed us to adapt and incorporate much of his writing that originally appeared in The Systems Thinker *(reviewed on msp 88), a newsletter which he founded and publishes. Dan is a researcher at the Center for Organizational Learning at MIT; his 1993 thesis was an innovative inquiry into the underlying relationships between Systems Thinking and other management tools, such as Total Quality, process mapping, and strategy design.*

How many times have you heard the saying, "The squeaky wheel gets the oil?" Whoever or whatever makes the most "noise" will often grab our attention. Now imagine someone who knows nothing at all about mechanics—and who, told hastily to grab oil, mistakenly picks up a can of water and splashes it on the wheel. With great relief, he'll hear the squeaking stop. But after a brief time, it will return more loudly as the air and water join forces to rust the joint. Once again, before doing anything else, he rushes to "fix" the problem—reaching for the can of water again, because it worked the last time. That person might stay busy all day, splashing water on all the squeaky wheels in the area. And eventually some wheels do stop squeaking permanently—because instead of being fixed, they are encased in rust.

Suppose the "squeaky wheel" is a customer screaming for a product that is two weeks late. How do we know whether we are applying oil or water when we respond? In our frenzy to stop the irritation, are we throwing oil on the flames and applying water to the rust?

The central theme of this archetype is that almost any decision carries long-term *and* short-term consequences, and the two are often diametrically opposed. As shown in the template, the problem symptom cries out (squeaks) for resolution. A solution is quickly implemented (the fix) which alleviates the symptom (in the balancing loop). *But the unintended consequences of the fix (the vicious cycle of the reinforcing loop) actually worsen the performance or condition which we are attempting to correct.*

"FIXES THAT BACKFIRE" TEMPLATE

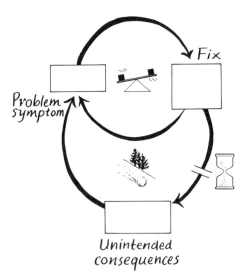

Often, people are aware of the negative consequences of applying this quick fix. But they do it anyway, because the pain of not doing something right away is more urgent, and feels more powerful . . . than the delayed negative effects. Sure enough, the relief is temporary, and the symptom returns, often worse than before. This happens because the unintended consequences (in the reinforcing loop) snowball slowly over a long period of time, often unnoticed at first but continuing to accumulate (like rust) as the wrong solution is repeatedly applied.

"Fixes That Backfire" is one of the easiest archetypes to see. Look at the performance involved with your worst current problem. If there are small triumphs and long troughs, there may be a "Fixes That Backfire" structure involved. You will notice a pattern of behavior something like this:

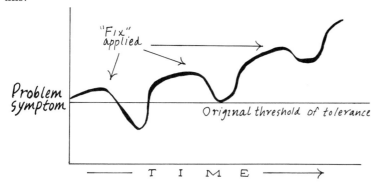

One indicator is your feeling that you need to try the same solution just a little more, and then a little more, and then one more time . . . until you catch yourself resisting the idea of trying anything else.

You can also recognize a "Fixes That Backfire" dynamic by the feeling of powerlessness people have when confronted with the consequences of their actions. People often see the dangers of what they're doing, but they feel they have no choice. People who sink over their heads in debt are a good example: they know they should stop borrowing more money, but how can they stop? Their immediate cash flow problems still remain, and override all other concerns.

TYPICAL "FIXES THAT BACKFIRE" SITUATIONS

"Downsizing to improve profits:" a company reduces staff (the fix) to reduce costs and raise profitability (the problem symptom). The most leverage seems to come from encouraging older workers, who generally have higher wages, to take early retirement. To everyone's delight, profitability immediately improves. However, the staffing cuts also eliminate some of the older, more experienced staff. Morale problems from layoffs drain enthusiasm. Production costs increase through error and overwork. These factors contribute to lowered productivity (the unintended consequence) and drain away all the added profitability from the "layoff fix," and then some. Management decides, with a heavy heart, that it has no choice but to make more staffing cuts . . .

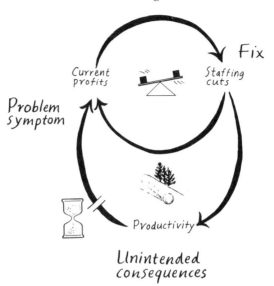

This is a sadly typical story. In one 1991 study of 850 companies which had cut staff drastically, only 41 percent had achieved the savings they hoped for.°

"Expediting customer orders": A large semiconductor manufacturer experiences production problems and runs behind schedule on some shipments. The company knows its customers (computer makers) will have to shut down production lines until the chips are delivered. The Moon Computer Company calls demanding that its chips be delivered immediately, so the semiconductor manufacturer assigns an expediter to track down Moon's order and push it through the line (the fix). Of course, it's not simply a matter of finding the right chip and escorting it to the loading docks; expediting Moon's order means wading through the entire factory, and repeatedly disrupting the production line, at great extra cost and effort. Unfortunately, no sooner has Moon's order left the warehouse when the LaSt Computer Company calls, demanding *its* shipments. Another department, meanwhile, is expediting for Conneq Computers. As a result, the production line is continually disrupted— leading to more missed delivery dates, and more customer calls.

° **A**mputating Assets: Companies That Slash Jobs Often End Up with More Problems Than Profits," *U.S. News & World Report,* May 4, 1992.

STRATEGIES FOR A "FIXES THAT BACKFIRE" SITUATION

- Increase awareness of the unintended consequences: open up people's mental models by acknowledging openly that the "fix" is merely alleviating a symptom. Make a commitment to address the real problem now.
- Cut back on the frequency with which you apply the "fix" and the number of "fixes" you apply at one time. (As with prescription drugs, the number of unintended side effects multiplies dramatically when "solutions" to problems are combined.) Select the interventions that produce the least harmful or most manageable consequences.
- Can you manage or minimize the undesirable consequences? Are there alternative "fixes" in which the undesirable or unintended consequences are not as devastating? Do you actually need to fix the problem? Or will the system take care of itself in the long run?
- Reframe and address the root problem: give up the fix that works only on the symptom. Every fix that backfires is driven by an implicit target in the balancing loop. So make it explicit. What's the problem you are *really* trying to fix? If the problem is current profits, for example, are short-term financial results the best goal? Or is the game really about creating long-term financial health for the company?

This may help you see the leverage that comes from changing your aspirations:

Work on "Fixes That Backfire" often leads people to a shared vision exercise: Is your vision present in the fixes that you are doggedly pursuing? Or are you trying to solve a problem which has little to do with where you actually want to go?

Archetype 2: "Limits to Growth" *Daniel Kim,*

Michael Goodman, Jennifer Kemeny, Charlotte Roberts, Art Kleiner

"It was the best of times, it was the worst of times, it was the age of foolishness," wrote Charles Dickens in *A Tale of Two Cities.* Life often seems full of such paradoxes. When we are busy earning lots of money, we have little time to enjoy it. When we do have time available, it seems we don't have much money to spend. A rapidly growing company finds itself so busy planning for more growth, it doesn't invest its profits in the development it might need if growth slowed down. When growth does slow down, and it becomes more obvious how some fundamental improvements could spur that growth again, the company no longer has the necessary money or people available. If only you could anticipate the "worst of times" while you're still in the "best of times." Recognizing this paradox can help individuals and companies avoid the trap of "Limits to Growth."

The truth is, we never grow without limits. In every aspect of life, patterns of growth and limits come together in various combinations. Sometimes growth dominates; sometimes limits dominate; and often the degree of influence shifts back and forth between them.

In the template, the growth process is usually shown as a virtuous reinforcing loop on the left. The limiting process is usually shown as a balancing loop on the right, which reacts to imbalances imposed on it by the growth loop. The balancing loop is also driven to move toward its target—a limit or constraint on the whole system, difficult to see because it is so far removed from the growth process.

"LIMITS TO GROWTH" TEMPLATE

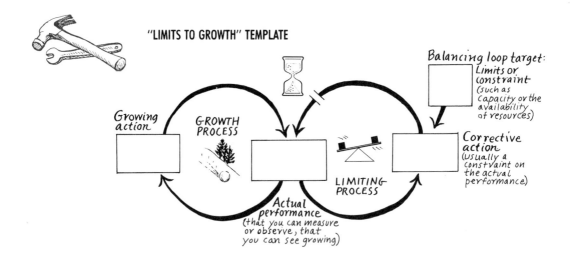

The "Limits to Growth" archetype helps us see how the balance between these elements shifts over time. It particularly helps us come to terms with the ways in which, by pushing hard to overcome the constraints on our lives, we make the effects of those constraints even worse than they otherwise would be.

If you feel as though you've suddenly run into a brick wall, or bumped your head on a glass ceiling, then a "Limits to Growth" situation is at play in your life. Typically, there has been a boom—an acceleration of growth and performance, usually the result of your hard work. But the growth mysteriously levels off. Your natural reaction is to increase the same efforts that worked so well before. But now, the harder you push, the harder the system seems to push back. It has reached some source of resistance which prevents further improvements. Even though everyone works harder and harder, the earlier boom does not return.

At this point, instead of your expected growth, you will notice one of two patterns of behavior:

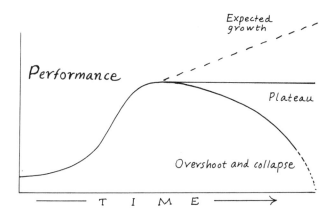

Sometimes the boom merely reaches a plateau, after which your performance remains in equilibrium, even though there continues to be a high level of effort. Other times, your performance zooms past its natural constraints and completely crashes. System dynamics modelers call this phenomenon "overshoot and collapse."

TYPICAL "LIMITS TO GROWTH" SITUATIONS

"Picking the low-hanging fruit": At the beginning of a quality improvement campaign, the first efforts (such as training in the statistical process control tools) lead to significant gains in the quality of products, services, and processes. This lends cachet, support, and impetus to the quality efforts. But as the easy changes (known as "low-hanging fruit" among quality veterans) are completed, the level of improvement plateaus, much to everyone's disappointment. The next wave of improvements are more complex and tougher to manage; they involve coordinating several different parts of the organization. The lack of organization-wide support, and the attitudes of senior management, now become limits. Unless the company makes more widespread changes at higher levels, its quality gains will be limited.

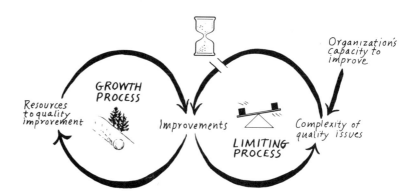

"The software artists": Computer hardware continues getting "faster, cheaper, and better," at an astonishing rate, virtually without limits. However, the production of software for these increasingly complex machines lags behind, often years behind. Without sufficiently sophisticated software, there are limits to the usefulness and popularity of computers. Faced with this limit, hardware producers push to make even faster, better, and cheaper machines.[*]

"Reformers creating distance": School administrators and teachers in a community develop an innovative "restructuring" education reform effort. However, as the number of restructured schools goes up, the increased community awareness generates a backlash from parents and other community members who don't want innovation and reform. This is aggravated by the fact that the community perceives it had little to say in the reforms. The educators begin to fight harder to get their point across . . .

[*] This case is based on a study by David H. Mason and James Herman, Northeast Consulting Resources, Inc., Boston, Massachusetts.

STRATEGIES FOR A "LIMITS TO GROWTH" SITUATION

- Beware of doing more of what worked in the past. Resist the temptation to invest more heavily in the reinforcing process, rather than trying to understand the balancing process. For every reinforcing process, there are probably ten or more balancing processes waiting to happen, but they are nearly all invisible. We don't notice what keeps things stable; we notice only when things dramatically grow or decline.

- If your growth has stalled, look at both the reinforcing and balancing loops to try to find interrelationships between your success strategies and potential limits. The limits might be within the organization (exhausting your financial, human, or technological resources); they might be within yourselves (if you are held back by mental models, traditions, or norms); or they might be external (a saturated market or a commodity market which attracts new competitors). For every limit, there are effective strategies, but we usually don't see them. Our natural tendency is to look for what worked in the past and to keep redoubling our efforts, instead of paying attention to the constraints.

- The choice between plateauing or peaking and crashing often depends on the length of the balancing loop delay and our response to it. A long delay in the balancing loop means the growth cycle can push the system well beyond its capacity before it is heeded.

- The real leverage in a "Limits to Growth" scenario lies in its early phases, while you still have time and resources to maneuver. Anticipate upcoming limiting forces, which are small now, but which will increase as time goes on. You cannot eliminate the limits. You can, however, work with them more effectively, and incorporate them into your next wave of expansion. Ask yourself: What measures can you take so that, as you continue to grow, your capacity to handle your limits also grows?

- Look for other potential engines of growth—other virtuous circles which could bolster and sustain the growth as it falters. Can you strengthen the resources which are driving your own growth?

Should growth be a guiding idea for your organization? *Michael Goodman*

MANY LEADERS OF ORGANIZATIONS, MOVEMENTS, OR INDUSTRIES SEEM troubled by the notion that their growth has limits. "If we don't grow," they seem to feel, "we die." But there is evidence to suggest that this model of the world isn't true. After all, nothing can grow forever, and it may be counterproductive to try. Where, then, does the "grow or die" model come from?

I often ask people what type of growth they have in mind. More sales? More profits? More people? Usually, what they *really* want to grow is their own horizon—their opportunities to learn, their chance to develop skills, their quality of life, and their impact on the world. They assume that to accomplish these things, they need to keep their budget growing, boost their staff, and acquire more resources. That means their organization must grow, the faster the better.

In our culture, this is a predominant, and successful, governing idea. People who live according to the idea spend their lives playing the "growth game": every time they run up against constraints, they work hard to overcome them, and then they move on to the next hurdle. The highest rewards in our society go to the masters of this game.

But the game itself has a built-in limit, which has to do with the nature of constraints, particularly in business. In the early stages of most managers' careers, the constraints are relatively easy to overcome: a limited production capacity, a weak market share for a brand, or a budget that reins in their decisions. "Conquering" these limits helps convince these managers that growth is the means to success, and that they can play the game well.

Then the game changes. The constraints become more complex. Now, to grow further, the manager must learn how to work cross-functionally, to raise quality, to create more innovative products, or to reengineer the work processes. Gradually, the constraints become more intangible; the limits are now the managers' own mental models, beliefs, and culture. Now the well-honed skills of pushing against tangible hurdles no longer work as well—solving separate problems can't, for example, guarantee that people will work together as colleagues across functions. The more aware the manager becomes of interrelationships, the more incongruous becomes the idea that "bigger is better"—without an awareness of purpose, or the balance of the natural order. As managers recognize examples of this, they begin to see through the game of growth; unfortunately, by now, they've exhausted themselves playing it.

Is there another way to set up the game? In a world where people recognize limits, what might desirable growth—sustainable organizational growth, lasting not just for years but for lifetimes—turn out to be? Success in this game might mean increasing the skills of our people, our own capacity to learn, the quality of what we produce, or the quality of our workplace. The business would be rewarded for growing better instead of bigger.

In her syndicated newspaper column, Donella Meadows quotes from one company which follows this strategy. The highly regarded Patagonia sports clothing company deliberately dropped 30 percent of its clothing line in 1990, partly out of concern for ecological impact ("We need to use fewer materials. Period.") and partly for fear of the effects of runaway growth. "During the eighties," wrote founder/president Yvon Chouinard in the Patagonia catalogue, "most of us managed to exceed our limits. Patagonia . . . was no exception. By the end of 1989 we . . .

had nearly outgrown our natural niche, the specialty outdoor market, and we were on our way to becoming much larger than we wanted to be . . . Last fall you had a choice of five ski pants, now you may choose between two . . . The fewer styles we make, the more we can focus on quality. We think the future of clothing will be less is more, a few good clothes that will last a long time. We have never wanted to be the largest outdoor clothing company in the world, we have only wanted to be the best."

Would investors support such a strategy? Would customers? Would employees? Because so many people believe that slow growth means no advancement, no new opportunities, and stagnation, there are not enough cases by which to judge. But we do have evidence that emphasis on growing bigger, with no thought to growing better, is a sure way to squander our energies and resources in the all-consuming dynamic of "Limits to Growth."

BEYOND THE LIMITS by Donella H. Meadows, Dennis Meadows, and Jørgen Randers (1992, Post Hills, Vt.: Chelsea Green Publishing Company).

Sometime during the next fifty years, worldwide economic and population growth will hit limits inherent in our environmental capacity. As in all "Limits to Growth" situations, how we manage the approach to those limits will determine the severity with which those limits "push back." The worse approach is to push hard toward as much of the same kind of growth as possible. This book explains why, based on (and updating) the original "Limits to Growth" system dynamics model which first posed these issues in the early 1970s. —**AK**

Archetype 3: "Shifting the Burden"

Daniel Kim, Michael Goodman, Jennifer Kemeny, Charlotte Roberts

MOST OF US WOULD PROBABLY SYMPATHIZE WITH HELEN KELLER'S PARENTS, whose overprotection of their handicapped daughter seemed not only compassionate but necessary. How could a blind and deaf child ever be expected to take care of herself? Thus, Helen learned that no matter what problem she faced, her parents would rush to her aid, eroding her ability, and desire, to cope with the world. Each incident reinforced her parents' belief that the child was helpless. Fortunately, her teacher, Anne Sullivan, refused to let the child's handicaps prevent her from becoming self-reliant. Helen Keller went on to graduate from Radcliffe College and become an author as well as a spokesperson and role model for many of the nation's handicapped.

Helen Keller's two choices—between being protected from harm and distress, and learning to live on her own—illustrate a pervasive dynamic which we call "Shifting the Burden." The well-intentioned actions of Keller's parents *shifted the burden* of responsibility for her welfare to themselves.

A "Shifting the Burden" story, like a "Fixes That Backfire" situation, usually begins with a problem symptom that prompts someone to intervene and "solve" it. The solution (or solutions) are obvious and immediate; they relieve the problem symptom quickly. But they divert attention away from the real or fundamental source of the problem, which becomes weaker as less attention is paid to it. This reinforces the perception that there is no other way out except the symptomatic solution. If Helen Keller had grown to an adult age with every need still taken

"SHIFTING THE BURDEN" TEMPLATE

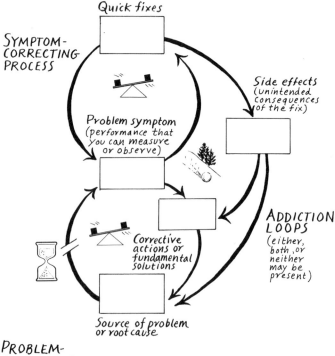

care of by her parents, it would have been far more difficult for a prospective Anne Sullivan to teach her to be self-reliant.

The basic "Shifting the Burden" template has two balancing loops. Each represents a different type of "fix" for the problem symptom. The upper loop is a symptomatic quick fix; the bottom loop represents measures which take longer (note the delay) and are often more difficult, but ultimately address the real problem.

In many "Shifting the Burden" structures, there are additional reinforcing loops which degrade the system into a pattern we call "addiction." Like the "unintended consequences" loop in "Fixes That Backfire," these addiction loops represent unintended consequences that compound the problem. The addiction becomes worse than the original problem, because of the devastation it wreaks on the fundamental ability to address the problem symptom. Organizational addiction can take the form of automatic, knee-jerk dependence on certain policies, procedures, departments, individuals, or ways of thinking.

There are three simultaneous patterns of behavior in a "Shifting the Burden" situation. The quick fix continues upward, especially with the onset of addiction. The symptom oscillates; sometimes up, sometimes down, but always gradually rising (as in "Fixes That Backfire"). Since the symptom is sometimes above, and sometimes below, the threshold of irritation, the problem seems to come and go. The third variable, the corrective action or fundamental solutions—the capacity of the system to fix itself—declines. At moments of reflection and self-awareness, you suddenly notice that your capabilities are atrophying.

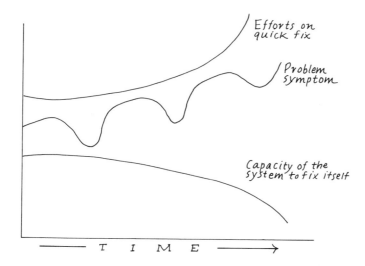

Efforts on quick fix

Problem symptom

Capacity of the system to fix itself

T I M E

All of these together add up to a powerful tendency toward addictive denial. When you hear someone say, "I can get out of this any time I want," you are probably listening to someone caught in a addictive "Shifting the Burden" pattern.

TYPICAL "SHIFTING THE BURDEN" SITUATIONS

"Crisis heroism": When a crisis (such as delays in a product launch) hits, the "crisis" manager is given enormous flexibility to "do whatever it takes" to get the product out. Ordinary roadblocks and formalities are swept aside. All this comprises the upper, symptom-correcting loop: the product is launched on time, and the crisis manager is touted as the hero of the day.

Meanwhile, several people have suggested the more fundamental solution of the bottom loop: redesigning the entire project management system, and rethinking the ordinary roadblocks and formalities. But this strategy would take longer, and less attention is given to it, so it has less effect on the problem symptom.

Most cases of "crisis heroism" include an addictive side effect: People see that if they want to be recognized for accomplishment, they'll have to be "heroes," too. Gradually, the company becomes addicted to "heroically" creating crises at the expense of making fundamental long-term changes.

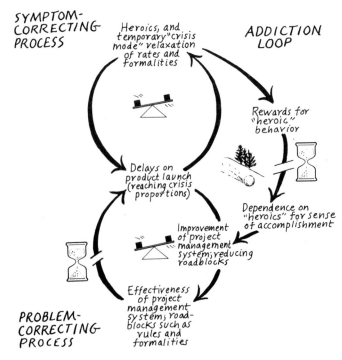

SYMPTOM-CORRECTING PROCESS — Heroics, and temporary "crisis mode" relaxation of rates and formalities — ADDICTION LOOP — Rewards for "heroic" behavior — Delays on product launch (reaching crisis proportions) — Dependence on "heroics" for sense of accomplishment — Improvement of project management system; reducing roadblocks — Effectiveness of project management system; roadblocks such as rules and formalities — PROBLEM-CORRECTING PROCESS

" 'Shifting the Burden' to the intervenor": This is a very common variation of "Shifting the Burden," found in many circumstances. An outside entity is called in to help solve a difficult problem: a quality consultant to an organization, a technical trainer to a rural village, a welfare program to a poor family, or a price subsidy to farmers of a particular crop. The "intervenor's" role is meant to be temporary, but gradually the people with the problem become dependent on the intervention, and never learn to solve the problems themselves. This is not simply a matter of passing the buck. If the outsider could genuinely solve the problem, that would be acceptable. But the insiders, in the long run, are the only people who can make the fundamental changes necessary to solve the problem.

The intervenor need not be a literal outsider. A quality consultant, for example, might be an internal expert who may indeed produce some clear gains in quality. But because the "fires were quickly put out," there is no incentive for the nonexperts to struggle with the quality problems, to experiment, and to learn how to prevent future quality problems from arising in the first place. The next time quality issues arise, everyone in the organization knows they will once again depend on expert help.

STRATEGIES FOR A "SHIFTING THE BURDEN" SITUATION

- In trying to understand a "Shifting the Burden" situation, start the same way as you would with "Fixes That Backfire": What is the problem symptom which you tried to fix? What is the fix you tried? What were the unexpected results, and how did they affect the original source or root cause of the problem?

  Then comes the leap: What alternative solutions might you have tried, if the quick-fix avenue were not available to you? Would any of those alternatives have been more fundamentally satisfying? And how do you know that these corrective actions would truly address the source of the problem?

- Use the archetype as a tool for inquiry, not as a tool for advocacy. There is a temptation to assume that your preferred solution, whether you tried it or not, is the "right" solution—and to simply write that solution into the slot. In many cases, top management sees one solution as fundamental, while front-line workers see another, and marketing sees a third. Each "fundamental solution" would suggest a different sense of appropriate leverage. That's why, especially in teams, it's important to suspend your preconceptions about which "solution" fits the slot, and instead try to explore, as an interfunctional group, the deeper sources of the problem. This type of sustained dialogue often unearths mental models and cultural assumptions as the real root causes of the problem.

> ⟨⟨ This is a good use of Skillful Discussion (page 385) or Dialogue (page 357).

- Strengthen the long-term solution. If you are not achieving your fundamental goals, then you may require a more clearly articulated goal. A good first step is simply seeking to investigate why it takes so long, or seems so difficult, to approach the deeper sources of the problem.
- If possible, support only the long-term solution; overlook the symptoms and "go cold turkey" on your addiction. If you must address the problem symptoms right away, do so with restraint. Keep aware of your main purpose: to gain time to work on the fundamental solution.
- Articulate your long-term vision or goals around this problem. People sometimes ask, "Is the moral of 'Shifting the Burden' that I have to do everything myself? Can't I hire a tax adviser, instead of figuring out the forms on my own?" Certainly you can delegate work to others—but make the choice about what you are delegating. Hiring an accountant to handle the papers would be "Shifting the Burden" *if* (a) you want to be skilled at tax finance yourself, and (b) you didn't set up a structure from which you could learn.
- As you strengthen long-term capability, do what you can to reduce dependency on the short-term fix. That may mean supplementing the fundamental solution with other support for the organization: support that seems to have little to do with the problem symptom, but helps the organization deepen its capacity generally. Watch out for underlying "addictive" mental models such as, "Oh, we can quit doing that any time we want," which make it hard to give up the symptom-relieving activities.

Archetype 4: "Tragedy of the Commons"

Daniel Kim, Michael Goodman, Jennifer Kemeny, Charlotte Roberts

HAVE YOU EVER BEEN CAUGHT IN A RUSH HOUR TRAFFIC JAM IN A LARGE metropolitan city such as Los Angeles? Everyone who wishes to get to work quickly uses the freeway, because it is the most direct route. At first there is room for everyone, but after some critical threshold of traffic is reached, each additional driver brings about a decrease in the average speed. Eventually, there are so many drivers that traffic crawls at a snail's pace. As individuals, each person feels he or she is a victim of the traffic. But in effect, they all conspired as a group to create the traffic which blocks them. The value of the "public" good, as it is overused, lessens for everyone.

The "Tragedy of the Commons" always opens with people benefiting individually by sharing a common resource—a brand-new freeway, for example. But at some point, the amount of activity grows too large for the "commons" to support. In many cases, the commons seems immeasurably large and bountiful at first, but it is either nonrenewable or takes a great deal of time and effort to replenish. The commons might be natural resources, open space, human effort, financial capital, production capacity, or market size—anything which groups of individuals depend upon in common.

When you have a "Tragedy of the Commons" issue, the system is sending you a signal that you cannot solve the problem or your own, in isolation from your fellow competitors, users, or consumers. Typically this signal comes in the form of increased difficulty in getting your share of the common resource. Sometimes you can recognize it by your feeling of powerlessness. It's a little tougher to extract minerals from the ground; a little more difficult to fund projects or hire truly qualified people. You're compelled to step up your own efforts—to be a bit smarter and more aggressive than your peers. You see others around you acting the same way, which of course accelerates consumption of "the common."

When this archetype is active, two indicators of performance change simultaneously. The total activity, using up the "common" resource, rises robustly. But the gain you feel for your effort—the individual gain per action—hits a peak and begins to fall. Eventually, if the dynamic continues too long, the total activity will also hit a peak and crash.

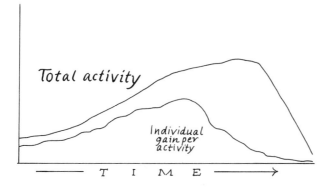

What makes the "Tragedy" tragic is the "crash" dynamic—the destruction or degeneration of the commons' ability to regenerate itself. Putting increasing numbers of cattle on rangeland eventually undermines the ability of the soil to grow grass. Draining the financial resources of an enterprise, past a certain point, threatens the life of the enterprise. When the commons is not actually damaged, there is still tragedy in the low level of performance that everyone must accept, no matter how hard they try to boost it. Often, because of the delays in the system, the poor performance is not observable until it is too late.

The "Tragedy of the Commons" template consists of two or more linked "Limits to Growth" archetypes, all sharing a common constraint or finite limit (the implicit target of all the balancing loops). The "gain per individual activity," or the average productivity of the entire system, goes down much faster than it would if only one "growth loop" were operating. This affects the performance that each player measures or observes, and prompts the players to step up their growing action. There may also be an added "tragic" reinforcing cycle at play (the long, thick arrow leading to "limits or constraints"), as the total activity of the system gradually depletes the available resources.

TYPICAL "TRAGEDY OF THE COMMONS" SITUATIONS

"The tragedy of the power supply": In Ford's 1994 Lincoln Continental project (see page 554), the number of electricity-draining components designed for the car overloaded the battery power available. None of the component designers would back down and reduce their power consumption, because it was in their interest to design electrical components with high functionality. Recognizing the limits, each design team, within its own group, added even more functionality, to justify being allotted as much battery power as possible from the common good.

As Nick Zeniuk, business planning manager for the project, tells the story, the team members finally realized that "each person would still look out for his or her own interest unless a) somebody discovered new technology, which wasn't going to happen in the next few months, or b) somebody from the outside came in and dictated. What did we do? I came from the outside and dictated." "Dictating from the outside" worked here only because of the effort Ford's team made to discover the "Tragedy of the Commons" dynamic. Everyone had seen themselves that the system encouraged them to pursue their own individual rewards, not the optimization of the whole.

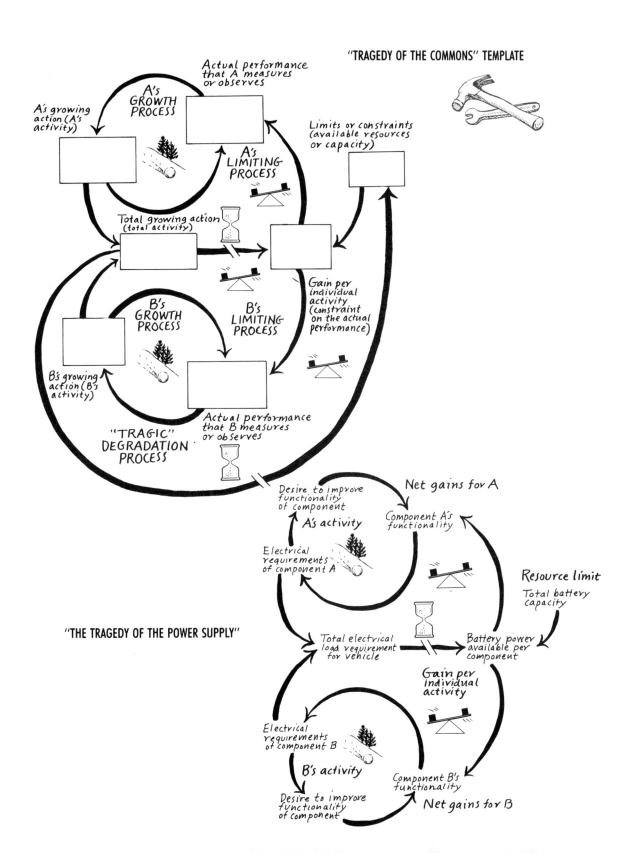

"TRAGEDY OF THE COMMONS" TEMPLATE

Actual performance that A measures or observes

A's growing action (A's activity)

A's GROWTH PROCESS

A's LIMITING PROCESS

Limits or constraints (available resources or capacity)

Total growing action (total activity)

B's GROWTH PROCESS

B's LIMITING PROCESS

Gain per individual activity (constraint on the actual performance)

B's growing action (B's activity)

"TRAGIC" DEGRADATION PROCESS

Actual performance that B measures or observes

Desire to improve functionality of component

Net gains for A

A's activity

Component A's functionality

Electrical requirements of component A

Resource limit
Total battery capacity

"THE TRAGEDY OF THE POWER SUPPLY"

Total electrical load requirement for vehicle

Battery power available per component

Gain per individual activity

Electrical requirements of component B

B's activity

Component B's functionality

Desire to improve functionality of component

Net gains for B

"The centralized sales force": In a company with a centralized sales force, the Division A people know that if they insist on "high priority" from the central sales support they will get a speedy response, so they label more and more of their requests as high priority. Divisions B, C, D, and E all have the same idea. The central sales staff grows increasingly burdened by all the field requests, and the net gains for each division are greatly diminished. The same story can be told about centralized engineering, training, maintenance, and many other functions.

STRATEGIES FOR A "TRAGEDY OF THE COMMONS" SITUATION

■ Beware of the temptation to assume that every seeming "Tragedy of the Commons" requires an intervention from a higher authority. Use this archetype to distinguish between true "tragedies of the commons" and situations where you "shift the burden" of a painful decision to the next level up. It's a true "tragedy" if the incentives at the individual level must work at cross-purposes when you look at the collective outcome.

■ There are three potential forms of leverage. In some cases (such as many corporate situations), the collective costs of their efforts can be brought to the attention of individual actors. The more clearly they see the structure, the more likely they are to stop. In other cases (such as many ecological situations), the common resource must be closed off until it has time to replenish itself. Finally, it is sometimes possible to replenish the common resource directly, or (especially in technological cases) to remove the constraints which set the limit on the common resource.

■ In any of these situations, there must be an overriding legislation for the common good, mandating some common goal or focal point. It can't be managed individually, because each individual faces overwhelming pressure to keep using up the resource. One car driver can't unilaterally fix gridlock by staying off the freeway; that will merely help the next driver get to work a tiny bit faster.

One argument for undertaking the pains of government reform is that only effective, responsive governments can deal with the increasing number of "Tragedy of the Commons" situations emerging in the world today. But it would be a mistake to depend upon government, or upon any authority, for leverage. Ultimately, we are inventing one source of leverage for "Tragedy of the Commons" problems now, through our efforts to create learning organizations.*

*The concept behind this archetype was described by Garrett Hardin in "The Tragedy of the Commons," *Science,* December 13, 1968.

Archetype 5: Accidental Adversaries

Jennifer Kemeny

THIS ARCHETYPE EXPLAINS HOW GROUPS OF PEOPLE WHO OUGHT TO BE in partnership with each other, and who *want* to be in partnership with each other (or at least state they do), end up bitterly opposed. It applies to teams working across functions, joint ventures between organizations, union-management battles, suppliers and manufacturers, family disputes, and even civil wars. I developed this archetype, in fact, because of the need to understand a puzzling dynamic which my colleagues and I saw again and again in our consulting work. It had become a wry joke with us: whenever there were two groups with much to gain from working together, we could expect to see them locked in fierce combat and resentment. Was there a structural reason for this?

TYPICAL "ACCIDENTAL ADVERSARIES" SITUATIONS

One classic case, where this structure was first recognized and articulated, concerned the largest consumer products and retailing companies in the world. Procter & Gamble and Wal-Mart both had the same goal—improving the effectiveness and profitability of their production/distribution system—but they each felt the other was acting (perhaps deliberately) in self-serving ways that damaged the industry. These perceptions were not unique to P&G and Wal-Mart; they were rampant in the industry.

As two of the most capable corporations in the world, Procter & Gamble and Wal-Mart had long been aware of the advantages of cooperating closely with (respectively) their distributors and their suppliers. (This cooperation, which gently reinforced itself, forms the outer reinforcing loop in the diagram.)

In the mid-1980s, however, both companies realized that their relationships had deteriorated, partly as a result of a fifteen-year-long pattern of behavior. Manufacturers (like Procter) had learned through the 1970s and 1980s to heavily discount their goods and use lots of price promotions in marketing, to boost market share and value, and thereby improve profits. (This is shown in P&G's balancing loop, the small circle at upper left.)

But price promotions created extra costs and difficulties for distributors (like Wal-Mart), which coped by "stocking up," also known as "forward buying"—buying large quantities of the product during the dis-

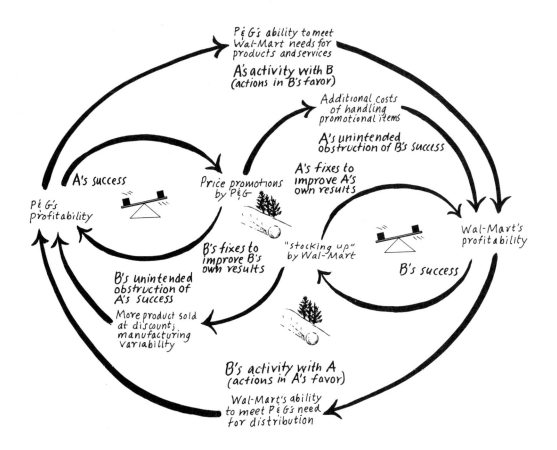

count period, selling it at regular price when the promotion ended, and using that extra income to improve their margins. (This strategy is shown in Wal-Mart's balancing loop at lower right.) This, of course, deeply undermined the manufacturer's profitability, because the retailer discounted many times the manufacturer's intended amount of product. Worse still, it created great swings in manufacturing volume, adding to costs, because distributors (being already stocked up) wouldn't order more product for months. To improve their results, the manufacturers pushed even more heavily on promotions, blaming the distributors for their troubles; and the distributors, blaming the manufacturers, stocked up even more.

Eventually, consumer products companies found themselves putting effort into promotions at the expense of new product development, while distributors concentrated on buying and storing promoted prod-

ucts instead of basic operations. Much of the short-term profits from promotions were drained away in long-term costs. A reinforcing loop had formed in the middle, causing a death spiral of mutually detrimental actions.

"ACCIDENTAL ADVERSARIES" TEMPLATE

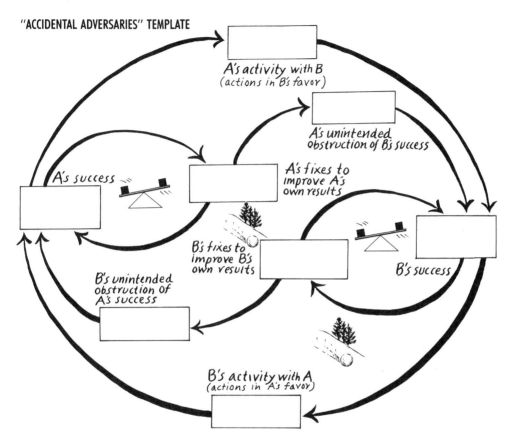

Each of the partners recognizes that they could mutually support each other's success—as shown by the large outer loop. However, as they take independent action to improve results, they respond more attentively to their local needs than their partner's. Each partner's "solution" turns out to be unintentionally obstructive to their counterpart's success. Often widely separated, the two partners do not communicate well. They tend to be unconscious of their effects on each other. One partner feels it is merely pulling an opportunity closer, but the other partner feels as if it is being flung through the air recklessly, flailing around at the end of the first partner's rope.

Later, as the unintended obstructions are felt more strongly, each remains confident that the solution is to convince the other partner that its strategy is the correct way to improve results.

In general, at this stage, each partner has almost forgotten its original purpose in collaboration. It is much more aware of the things its purported partner—that traitor!—has done to block it. This makes the partner even more unlikely to talk, and it becomes even more unlikely that either side will ever learn the effect it is having on the other.

STRATEGIES FOR AN "ACCIDENTAL ADVERSARIES" SITUATION

■ Don't push on the well-intended fix or solution which applies to your own part of the organization. Instead, seek to strengthen your understanding of your partner's fundamental needs, how you are unintentionally undermining them, and how you could support each other instead. This may include helping to remove or weaken the constraints in your partner's system that resist your own solution.

In the case of P&G and Wal-Mart, the leverage came from bringing both sides into the same room, determined to understand the structure that they had built up. Once in the room, they discovered that the other organization's strategy seemed perfectly rational and reasonable from their local perspective. There was no "treachery" afoot. There was simply a larger system whose pieces didn't work well together. Having recognized this, they could start collaborating on a new joint strategy. P&G offered, for the first time, to stop promotions at Wal-Mart, and provide an "everyday low price." Within a few years, P&G announced that they would give up promotions entirely as a marketing tool.

Interestingly, during that group conversation, both sides realized that despite their recent commitment to a strategic alliance, they still found it difficult to describe their own fondest hopes to each other. They had never thought they could say, "If you help me realize my goals, I can help you realize yours." But their discussions about promotions became a strong first step in talking about a common vision and forging a renowned alliance.

For another approach to a similar situation, see "Seven Steps for Breaking Through Organizational Gridlock," page 169.

18 The Archetype Family Tree

Michael Goodman, Art Kleiner

Most of the archetypes are related strategically to each other. This diagnostic tool helps you work through those relationships. Start at the top, thinking about the nature of the phenomenon you want to understand. Is it about growth? Then work through the reinforcing (left-hand) trunk of the family tree.

Or are you trying to fix a problem? In that case, work your way through the balancing (right-hand) trunk.

You can also use the "tree" to move to new insights about a situation. For example, after identifying a "Fix That Backfires," a revealing question to ask is: "What is the reason why we are putting so much attention on quick fixes?" The answer often has to do with the next level deeper: a "Shifting the Burden" structure. Similarly, when approaching a pernicious "Limits to Growth" situation, it's worth inquiring whether under-investment, or a "Tragedy of the Commons," is involved.°

⟨⟨ For an example of movement down the tree by "adding loops," see page 165.

In this illustration, the letter *B* represents a balancing loop, and *R* represents a reinforcing loop.

° We have discussed the most powerful archetypes here in the *Fieldbook,* but as you will see in the following diagram, there are at least a half-dozen others. You can read about them in *Systems Archetypes: Diagnosing Systemic Issues and Designing High-Leverage Interventions* by Daniel H. Kim (1993, Cambridge, Mass.: Pegasus Communications). Or see *The Fifth Discipline,* pp. 378–90; issues of *The Systems Thinker;* and course materials produced by Innovation Associates.

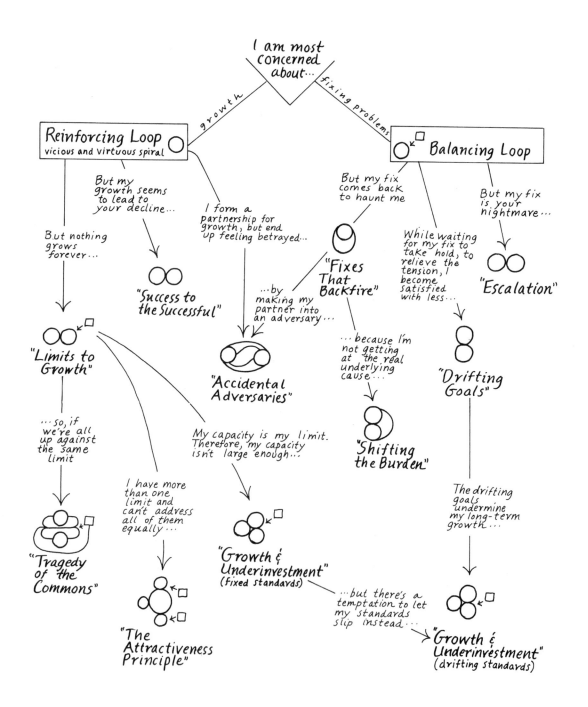

I am most concerned about...

growth

fixing problems

Reinforcing Loop
vicious and virtuous spiral

Balancing Loop

But my growth seems to lead to your decline...

I form a partnership for growth, but end up feeling betrayed...

But my fix comes back to haunt me

While waiting for my fix to take hold, to relieve the tension, I become satisfied with less...

But my fix is your nightmare...

But nothing grows forever...

...by making my partner into an adversary...

"Fixes That Backfire"

"Escalation"

"Success to the Successful"

"Limits to Growth"

"Accidental Adversaries"

...because I'm not getting at the real underlying cause...

"Drifting Goals"

...so, if we're all up against the same limit

My capacity is my limit. Therefore, my capacity isn't large enough...

"Shifting the Burden"

I have more than one limit and can't address all of them equally...

"Growth & Underinvestment"
(fixed standards)

The drifting goals undermine my long-term growth...

"Tragedy of the Commons"

...but there's a temptation to let my standards slip instead...

"The Attractiveness Principle"

"Growth & Underinvestment"
(drifting standards)

19 Systems Sleuth*

Clifford Security Trucks *Bryan J. Smith, David Wolfenden*

A STRONG SENSE OF PRIDE RUNS THROUGH THE CULTURE OF CLIFFORD Security Trucks. (Names and some nonessential details have been changed, but the story is true as presented here.) For almost 100 years Clifford has been a highly committed and dedicated armored truck carrier in communities throughout North America. It serves primarily banks, in both large centers and outlying remote regions. Their service is essential but mostly unnoticed—until money is stolen.

In the last few years, with increasing competition, Clifford's relationships with customers have come under pressure. The banking industry has successfully played security firms off against each other. Some armored car companies bid for contracts at prices well below the cost of doing business. If Clifford accepted jobs at those rates, it would lose its ability to provide desired levels of service, to train its employees adequately, and to continue reaching into remote regions. However, if Clifford's refused to bid on these contracts, it would lose visibility in its industry, and perhaps its largest (banking) clients.

Clifford's managers eventually decided they had two choices. They could participate in the price war, using the company's superior reputation and capacity to undercut and "outwait" their competitors. Or they could withdraw from the bidding for contracts in regions that were caught up in the price war and (therefore) consistently unprofitable. In withdrawing, they would not only reduce their own losses, but demonstrate to the banks that the prevailing assumptions about costs were flawed.

Which strategy would you adopt? And what systems archetypes would you use to better understand the ramifications of your decision?

The name "Systems Sleuth" comes from The Systems Thinker, *which includes one case in each issue.*

PURPOSE
To build skill with archetypes.

OVERVIEW
Read the case history and select (or discuss in a team) the archetype which seems to fit best.

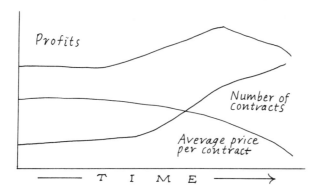

AN ANSWER (NOT NECESSARILY THE ONLY ANSWER)

Taking the bait, and reducing their costs, might "shift the burden" to low-cost pricing, involving Clifford's in an addictive bidding war. But the alternative was "hanging in there" long enough to wait for the bidding wars to run their course. How severe would the wait be? That would depend on the growth of its competitors. To understand this better, the Clifford managers analyzed it as a "Limits to Growth" dynamic:

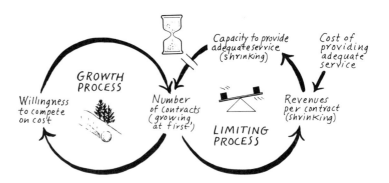

If Clifford's competitors became more willing to compete on price, their contracts would increase. But the cost of providing adequate service (particularly for the tough parts of the job, when there is the threat of theft) would remain the same. Therefore, revenues per contract and the capacity to provide adequate service would shrink. How long would it be before that affected the number of competitors' contracts? That could be estimated, based in part on Clifford's managers' knowledge of the industry.

During the next year, Clifford lost a great deal of its business to its next-largest competitor. To the surprise of clients, Clifford's sales managers did not bid on fiercely competitive contracts. This was a difficult decision; Clifford was under pressure from its union not to jeopardize jobs. About eight months after they began this policy, however, a Clifford vice president got a call from one of the largest banks in one of the problem regions, requesting a meeting to discuss giving their service back. The competitor's security had been breached at least once, and rural branches were underserved. When the bank had raised the option of leaving the contract, the competitor had threatened to sue. Clifford Security Trucks negotiated with the bank to fulfill the contract at a price that would allow for higher levels of service.

This episode has shifted Clifford's managers' perception of their role and their strategy as leaders. Aligning themselves around a vision of quality, and holding themselves firm to it, has renewed their sense of pride.

Burson-Benson Power Tool Company

Art Kleiner

Burson-Benson makes high-performance, high-quality power tools: chain saws, drill presses, and lathes, primarily targeted at affluent homesteaders and do-it-yourselfers. Since its origins in the 1920s, the company has had a widespread reputation for power and performance. There are actually clubs of Burson-Benson users, many of whom feel the equipment gives them an aura of being rough-and-tumble loggers. (Names and some nonessential details have been changed, but the story is true as presented here.)

Like many American industrial firms, Burson-Benson lost much of its market share to new Japanese competitors during the 1970s. It responded in two ways: first, through a massive licensing effort (producing shop aprons with the Burson-Benson logo, for instance), which provided enough cash to survive several difficult years; and second, through a company-wide quality improvement drive which made the most of their limited cash flow.

But Burson-Benson continued to have a terrible problem meeting the demand for its products. At any given moment, the firm has four months' or more worth of backlogs. Dealers rarely have enough products to put one in their showrooms.

The backlogs stem in part from a chronic problem with defective equipment, usually found in the last round of testing, at the end of the assembly process. Defective products are sent to the "lathe hospital"— a repair shop next door to the plant, with an excellent reputation for fixing defective products, so they can be rushed out to customers. It costs almost twice as much to produce a power tool which has gone through the "hospital," but everyone knows that without the "hospital," the backlog would be much worse.

The company has tried to improve its production process to reduce defects on the factory floor, but these improvements are expensive, and the payoffs have been slow and uncertain. Engineers who can barely make headway there have more success when they're called in to help

PURPOSE
To build skill with archetypes.

OVERVIEW
Read the case history and select (or discuss in a team) the archetype which seems to fit best.

solve urgent, complex problems on individual tools at the ever-more-indispensable "hospital."

Another problem has only recently emerged as worrisome. Thanks, in part, to tougher regulatory safety standards for machine equipment, research and development have become more expensive. A new piece of equipment used to take six months to develop; it now takes two years. Because of the mystique of the Burson-Benson image, there's unrelenting pressure to keep introducing new models, but the last four new models were all far behind schedule, and their improvements were all cosmetic—not the performance/design breakthroughs upon which Burson-Benson rests its reputation.

All of these charts cover a four-year period:

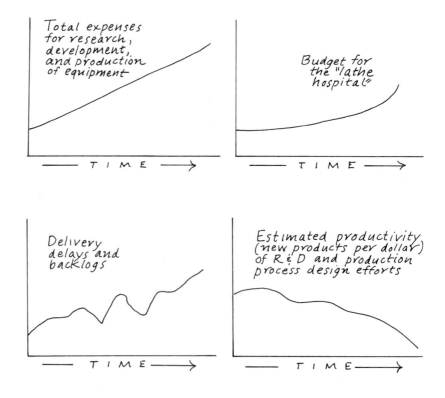

What archetype or archetypes are in play here? What strategy would you advise Burson-Benson's top managers to pursue?

AN ANSWER (NOT NECESSARILY THE ONLY ANSWER)

A "Shifting-the-Burden" structure (see page 135) underlies the company's addiction to the "lathe hospital":

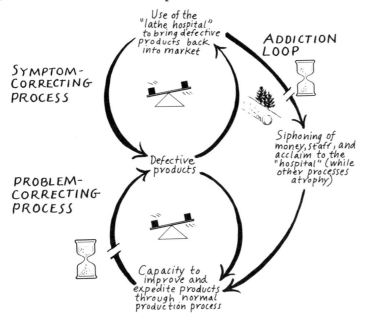

Burson-Benson's problem symptom is a high rate of defective products. In order to get the equipment out the door, the company depends increasingly on the "lathe hospital," whose success drains money, staff, and acclaim away from the slower efforts to improve the normal production process. In short, the better the "lathe hospital" becomes at doing its job, the more "addicted" the company will become. Because it's so much more expensive to produce a machine tool that goes through the hospital, profits (and R&D capabilities) will continue falling.

Fewer people should be devoted to fixing power tools, and as many resources as possible should be put into increasing first-run capability. Beyond that, there are hard choices to make, and the company can move forward only by determining its own vision and goals. If the managers can't meet all their targets for success at once, which do they want to meet *first?* For example, the company might shut down product development efforts and focus on improving the manufacturing capabilities. This would require explaining to the sales force and dealers why the Burson-Benson product line will have to be limited to the same old products for a few years. Gradually, as it solves the production problems, it will acquire resources for more new development.

Alternatively, if new products are a first priority, then process design engineers should collaborate in their design, to help make production reliability a more intrinsic component. That would ultimately ease the company's production pressures, but in the meantime, it would retain a steady backlog.

The option it doesn't have is trying to do everything at once.

The Water of Ayolé *Charlotte Roberts*

PURPOSE
To bring a team through the stages of systems thinking, through the archetype stage, in the context of fundamental but obscure solutions to problems.

OVERVIEW
The story of the Water of Ayolé contrasts two communities in Togo, West Africa, each of which handled the same problem differently. You suggest an archetype, consider another suggestion, and apply the insights to your own organization.

STEP 1: THE WATER OF AYOLÉ
View the entire videotape.

The video tells this story:

Drinking water is a great problem for villagers in rural Togo, West Africa—particularly during the long dry season. Women had to get up at 3 A.M. and walk twelve miles to the Amou River, bearing water basins which weigh as much as eighty pounds when filled. This left little time for anything else.

Even so, this water is not safe. Guinea worms lay eggs in the water, hatch in villagers' bodies, and burrow outward. People sometimes faint from the suffering.

To bring clean and accessible water to villagers in less-developed countries, governments and international aid organizations have spent $70 billion on drilling wells and installing pumping equipment. As a result, broken and abandoned pumps now dot the African landscape, skeletons of a dream deferred. Each cost over $10,000 but in some areas, 80 percent of them are no longer working.

One would expect villagers in Amoussokopé to be able to maintain their pump. The town is on a main road in Togo. It has a health center, a high school, small businesses. Even a train stops here. But the pump broke down in less than two years. "We wanted to fix it," says a woman villager in the film, "but we don't know how. We don't know anyone who can fix it for us." The villagers tried to raise $300 to fix the pump, but the money seemed to vanish. Nobody knew how much had been raised, and no one had been responsible for it.

Another village, Ayolé, has succeeded where others failed because Ayolé's pump was made a part of village life from the very beginning.

Extension agents helped villagers to organize a pump committee, and designate an overseer. A mechanic was found and trained in the village.

"Everyone used to suffer from guinea worm, before the pump arrived. People were bedridden. But since we've had the pump, that disease has disappeared. We're so free now! No more water problems. We feel so healthy!"

To get this kind of village commitment, extension agents had to go through some reorientation of their own: "In the past I just *gave* what I knew to the villagers. But now I arrive in a village, and *together* we find solutions. Previously, women didn't have clearly defined roles in running the village, because that was men's business. Now women also make decisions in these villages."

To get the money to maintain their pump, the villagers decided to work together in a communal field. This has always been a traditional way to raise money for funerals or celebrations, but now it has become part of an ongoing activity. And with the profits, they've opened a bank account in town. Villagers have organized to build latrines, a new school, and a second pump. Theirs is not a rich village, but it is a determined one.

"In the past, each person lived for himself. No one came to visit. No one had time for anyone else. We hold meetings about the pump. We're organized now."

STEP 2: ARTICULATING THE STORY

Which systems archetype applies to the story of Ayolé? Start by using this checklist to help determine the key variables of this story:

〈〈 In this exercise, we follow the procedure described in "Applying an Archetype" (page 121).

a. Rate of drilling new wells
b. Total number of working pumps
c. Efforts of women to collect water
d. Degree of potability of available water
e. Government workers' acceptance of villagers
f. Villagers' fear of government workers
g. Villagers' sense of responsibility for well
h. Quality of life
i. Quality and amount of villager training for pump repair
j. Skill of government workers to lead village meetings
k. Villagers' ability to raise money consistently

PARTICIPANTS
Ideally, a team involved in planning or in working with long-term situations—or a group of people from diverse parts of one organization.

SUPPLIES
Videotape player, flip charts, and copy of the videotape The Water of Ayolé.*

° *The Water of Ayolé,* 30 minutes, produced and directed by Sandra Nichols Productions, Oakland, CA. Published by, United Nations Development Programme, Division of Public Affairs, New York, NY. For information about the Togo assistance project, contact W.A.S.H., (703) 243-8200.

l. Villagers' capacity for envisioning individually
m. Villagers' capacity for envisioning collectively
n. Distance to "natural" water source
o. Receptiveness of extension agents to new ideas
p. Villagers' sense of community
q. Quality of parts distribution system
r. Simplicity of mechanics for pump
s. Pump durability

Add to the list any other variables that you consider important. Then pick four or five key variables and draw the pattern of behavior, over time, for them. For example, the pattern of behavior for the number of working pumps probably looks somewhat like this, as the pumps begin to fall off-line and then as the new extension program takes hold:

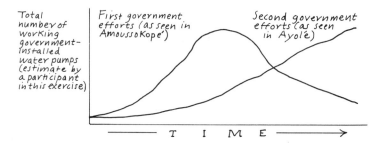

Of the variables which you selected as important, which appear to be associated? Draw links which express the causal relationships that you see. For example, the villagers' self-reliance seems to have a direct affect on the enthusiasm of the government agents.

STEP 3: SETTLING ON AN ARCHETYPE

Now we ask you to put the details aside, and step back mentally so you can answer the question, "What archetype (or archetypes) seem to best fit this story?" (Running the segment of the video again may help you spot recurring patterns of behavior.)

As a team, draw the archetype which you believe fits best. Label all the elements.

Then answer these questions:

■ What is the goal of this system?
What was the vision held by the villagers of Amoussokopé? What

was the vision held by the government? What do the people of Ayolé want to achieve? Did those visions or goals change as the story progressed? If another vision emerged, what was that, and where did it come from?

■ What is the system capable of?

What structures dominate this system? What can those structures achieve? What can't they achieve? What factors limit the villagers, the government, or the relationship between them?

■ Where is the system going?

If it continued in the same direction, either in Amoussokopé or in Ayolé, what would be the system's natural result?

■ What should be changed?

If you were the leader of these villages, or of this government, what systemic changes would you put into effect?

AN ANSWER (NOT NECESSARILY THE ONLY ANSWER): "SHIFTING THE BURDEN"

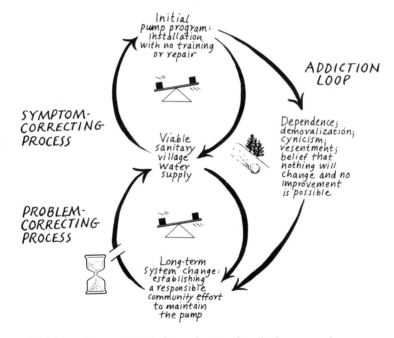

One applicable archetype is "Shifting the Burden." The upper loop represents the quick fix solution, as implemented at Amoussokopé. The bottom loop represents the fundamental solution implemented at Ayolé.

Note that in both loops, mental models played a significant role. At

Amoussokopé, the villagers thought the government agents couldn't be trusted, and the government assumed the villagers were lazy. At Ayolé, change could take place only when the agents recognized the villagers as responsible. The level of communication among the villagers also had to change, including the relationships between men and women. (Looking between the lines of the Amoussokopé story, you can see how the mistrust and competition between men and women made it impossible to save up the money to fix the pump.)

STEP 4: STRATEGIES AND RAMIFICATIONS

Consider these questions:

- In the fundamental solution at Ayolé, who is the primary actor? Whose understanding first led to a change from the old pattern? Could the understanding have come from anywhere else?
- The real solution implied the reorganization of the community. Why would that have been a difficult solution for the extension agents? Why would it have been difficult for the villagers?
- Could anything have been done to make the shift of orientation easier for

    the villagers of Amoussokopé (the first village)?
    the extension agents?
    the elders of Ayolé?

- Did the delay make it difficult to distinguish the quick solution from the fundamental solution? If so, why?

STEP 5: YOUR OWN "WATER OF AYOLÉ" STORY

Now consider a "Shifting the Burden" story from your own organization. Either individually, or as a group with someone at a flip chart, sketch a diagram of the system involved:

- "Shifting the Burden" usually implies reliance on an "addictive," or otherwise unsatisfying chronic crutch. What crutches and dependencies exist in this situation?
- To achieve the fundamental solution, who would have to be the primary actor?
- At Ayolé, the real solution implied a reorganization of the community. Would any reorganization of human relationships be required for *this* fundamental solution?

- Could anything be done to make the necessary shift of orientation easier for the people involved?
- Is there a delay which makes it difficult to see the value of your fundamental solution, or a lack of delay which makes the "quick fix" appealing?
- As you look at the system, what is it capable of? At its best, what would be the most desired outcome which your system could achieve?
- What is it *not* capable of? What future is not possible, because of the way the system is constructed?
- To achieve the most desired goal, what parts of this system would have to be changed further?

20 Enriching the Archetype

Once you have settled upon a promising archetype, it still remains to convert your understanding to strategy. Where do you intervene? How do you redesign or reengineer the system? How do you move from your diagnosis to a prescription? Moreover, if you can implement your strategy so that your understanding (and ability to understand) continues to increase, then you don't have to worry about "getting it all right" at the start.

We call this the "enriching" stage. In our work, it's often the point where people start to see things coming together.

Widening and deepening Michael Goodman, Rick Karash

CONSIDER THIS SIMPLE STORY: THE GENERAL MANAGER OF A MANUFAC-turing division faces a series of budget crises. She is told to pare her facility down, to make it run "lean and mean." So she reluctantly decides to reduce her head count. She furloughs some employees and lets others go. She also reduces preventive maintenance. And she cuts back on marketing activities. Her costs go down for a little while, but then creep up again. So she reluctantly pushes harder—reducing head count a bit more, and cutting back maintenance and marketing.

If this were your story, how would you diagram it? You might conclude that the story can be represented as a simple balancing loop, in which you respond to the problem symptom of financial problems ("budget pressure") through a quick but painful fix, reducing head count, which lowers costs and eases your budget pressure.

But to be fair to the full story, you would have to add two other corrective actions: reducing preventive maintenance, and cutting back on marketing:

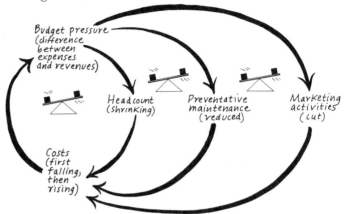

If you put them together you would have a balancing loop with three parallel activities. All of them have some effect on your costs. Adding extra loops represents your first level of enrichment, but the story is still unfinished. What are some of the unintended longer-term consequences of your actions? When you reduce head count, or change the maintenance schedule, what else is affected?

Reducing your marketing activity could impact your market share, slowing or reducing revenues and creating budget pressures. Pulling back on maintenance can lead to serious equipment failures, eventually raising costs. Head count reductions could generate morale problems and affect productivity. Eventually, costs will escalate.

In workshops, where we use this diagram as an exercise, we have seen many possible ways to diagram effects of each of those elements. In your own setting, you will find that discussions about additional loops become a productive way to jump-start inquiry about the situation. Notice that all of the secondary loops are vicious cycles, and have the opposite impact on revenues and costs than is desired.

> In this example, we have progressed down the archetype family tree from a balancing loop to "Fixes That Backfire"; see pages 125 and 149.

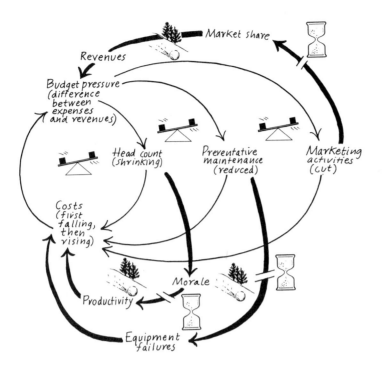

GUIDELINES FOR WIDENING AND DEEPENING

- Start by asking: "What else is affecting this element?" Then see if you can trace those elements into your picture and make them into new loops. For example: "Budget pressures are affected by revenue. Revenue is affected by market share. What affects market share . . . ?"

- Don't be shy about searching out and including interrelationships that were never discussed (or noticed) before. This adds high value to a team's learning process.

- It's helpful, as you add links, to test them also as "loops." Identify each new loop as "balancing" (moving toward stability) or "reinforcing" (pushing growth or decline) based only on its behavior: regardless of the number of factors or elements it contains, or its position in the diagram.

- The loops should be relevant and important to the story. Theoretically, you could keep adding potential causes and effects to any systems story, until the diagram begins to resemble a plate of spaghetti. But after a few interdependencies become apparent, your team will find itself facing the underlying question: "What theme is emerging? What are the implications of this structure? Have we moved to a new archetype? How do we redesign this to meet our purposes? Where do we have leverage?"

Looking for mental models

Michael Goodman, Jennifer Kemeny

AN ARCHETYPE IS NOTHING MORE THAN A MENTAL MODEL MADE VISIBLE. With the archetype before them, one person says, "This is how I think it works." Then, typically, a colleague replies, "No, that's not how it works at all." The team starts to recognize how both viewpoints are true; they each see different aspects of the same interrelationships. As they continue, the structure begins to reflect the collective thinking of the team. As more and more people comment, confidence grows that this archetype speaks to reality as people know it.

Even if you agree on what structure is involved, you will have varying perceptions of the implications. "We agree it's a 'Limits to Growth' dynamic, but you think the constraint is our succession policy, and I think it's our customer relations." You may agree that the fix has backfired, but not on what to do about the undesirable consequences. But you now have a language for describing what each person sees, clarifying the differences, and building more choices (not answers) into your thinking.

ADDING THOUGHT BUBBLES

Look at the arrows between elements in your system diagram. Many arrows represent choices people are making. Add a "thought bubble," like a bubble in a cartoon, to indicate the thinking which leads to this choice instead of others. (See page 102 for an example.)

As you consider thought bubbles, avoid making your own judgments about the rationale. Simply think about the thoughts behind the links. This has led to some profound (and sometimes painful) "ah-ha's," as people realize how disconnected their thinking is from the results they have produced. For example, a group of managers asked themselves, "What thoughts compel us to jump from budget pressure to immediately cutting head count?" Their replies showed how much they were governed by knee-jerk assumptions:

"I don't have any choice."

"I'll just do this once."

"I'll manage the consequences later."

QUESTIONS TO HELP BRING OUT MENTAL MODELS

- Assume for the moment that *all* the people involved are acting reasonably and responsibly, from their point of view. What might they have been thinking that made these actions seem reasonable and responsible to them?

■ What might the diagram look like from the factory manager's point of view? From the customer's? From the union president's?

⌇⌇ For an exercise to help ask this question, see "Multiple Perspectives," page 273.

■ What mental models do you carry that might affect how you see this diagram?
■ What mental models prevent you from breaking out of this structure?

⌇⌇ The mental models techniques—Ladder of Inference, Left-Hand Column, and Balancing Inquiry and Advocacy—are very useful in these "introspective" discussions. See page 242.

System redesign: "adding loops" and "breaking links" *Michael Goodman, Rick Karash*

YOU KNOW YOU'VE FOUND A HIGH-LEVERAGE INTERVENTION WHEN YOU can see the long-term pattern of behavior shift qualitatively in a system: when, for example, stagnation gives way to growth, or oscillations dampen dramatically. This kind of breakthrough happens most readily when you can make alterations in the structure you've mapped out. You either add new elements and create new desirable loops, or break linkages that produce undesirable impacts.

In the real world, "adding a loop" translates into designing and implementing a new process, monitoring information in a new way, or establishing new policies. Breaking a link means eliminating or weakening undesirable consequences of your actions or ceasing strategies which are counterproductive in the long run. These are not mechanistic or arbitrary acts; before you implement them, you must run mental experiments in which you test their effects in your imagination. Also, ask yourself: Is the measure viable in the real world? Do you have the power to implement it?

⌇⌇ The ramifications may be so complex or hard to predict that you want to go to a computer model (see page 173); or you may want to run prototype experiments (see page 168).

A small "Ma and Pa" lawn care company used both forms of redesign to help cope with a spiraling debt problem. Facing cash shortages, they had been forced to borrow from credit lines. Unfortunately, the fix had backfired; high interest payments on their accumulated debt pushed them into severe cash flow problems.

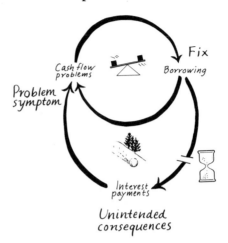

They used the "Fixes That Backfire" archetype to look for ways out. Slowing or eliminating borrowing would have been ideal, but nearly impossible. Therefore, they needed to focus attention on the sources of the problem: low income and high spending. They conceived of these new measures as two new balancing loops.

They tightened their budget, invested in better financial management software, extended their hours, and started offering additional services, such as pool maintenance. These measures worked in real life only because they committed themselves to clear goals for their spending and income, and allowed themselves realistic time delay expectations.

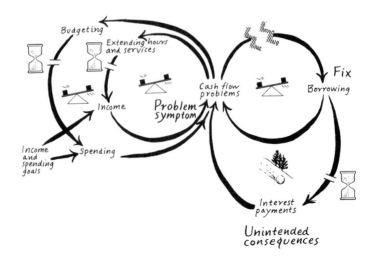

If you turn the diagram (bottom of page 166) on its side, you'll see that what started as a "Fix That Backfired" was in fact a "Shifting the Burden" system. This revealed the need to focus efforts on the fundamental problem-correcting process (the left-hand side of the diagram).

At the same time, they weakened the link between cash flow problems and borrowing, by setting (and following) a policy of borrowing less and postponing new borrowing whenever possible. They had to give up the mental model that "buying now, paying later," was workable. When you add loops or break links, it's critical to try to make such mental models explicit, because the reasons underlying peoples' actions are fundamental to the system's structure.

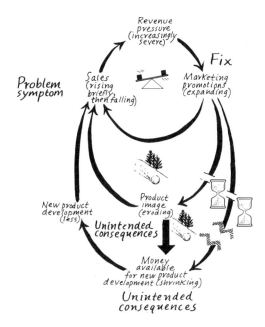

In an article in *The Systems Thinker,* Daniel H. Kim described another "breaking links and adding loops" case. A consumer manufacturing company was caught in a "Fix That Backfired" over marketing promotions and rebates. The more promotions increased, the more the company diverted resources from new product development and the more it tarnished its product image. The resulting sales drop increased the pressure for more marketing promotions. Finally, a systems thinking effort suggested breaking the link from "marketing promotions" to "money available for new product development": setting a policy that no matter how high the perceived need, promotions would not be funded out of the product development budget.[°]

° "Seven Steps for Using 'Fixes That Backfire' to Get Off a 'Problem-Solving Treadmill,' " by Daniel H. Kim, *The Systems Thinker,* September 1992, p. 5.

Another suggestion was made to add a link between "erosion of product image" and "money available for new product development." This would mean building channels so that market information passed quickly to research and development, and making sure that new product development was funded only if it was informed by the customer data coming in from marketing.

Prototyping your implementation *Jennifer Kemeny*

I GET NERVOUS WHEN, AFTER FINISHING A CAUSAL LOOP DIAGRAM, TEAM members say, "Now, we understand the system." All you have done so far, I want to tell them, is codify your group intuition. You have created hypotheses about what has happened, and where opportunities for leverage might exist.

Before committing yourself to any large-scale actions, run several small, relatively self-contained experiments. With a bit of ingenuity, you can pick out ahead of time a few early indicators of success. If you changed the system successfully, what new patterns of behavior would you expect to see? Financial indicators—the way corporations normally measure success—tend to be useless here. By the time a system dynamic has affected finances, the dynamic is already entrenched. But chances are, your archetype structure already contains clues to more appropriate indicators. Ask yourself: If the intervention works, what elements of the archetype will change first, and how might they change?

For example, I recently worked with a circuit board manufacturer with severe financial woes, despite high sales rates. Circuit board manufacturing is typically a two-step process; before they win a contract to make a new chip, manufacturers must construct a prototype for the prospective client—a loss leader, at a high per-unit cost. It turned out that only a small percentage of this manufacturer's customers chose to follow their prototype with a full production run. This statistic (the percentage of prototypes leading to full production) would be an ideal indicator, but it had never been separated out in the financial statement. It only emerged from asking a question in a systemic context: "If profits are your problem, then where do your profits come from?"

If you can perform this technique, it does not matter whether you have come up with the "right" systemic archetype. In fact, even if your systemic understanding is completely wrong, if you are willing to take action and reflect on your action, you will be able to act consistently and make genuine improvements.

THE BREAKTHROUGH STRATEGY by Robert H. Schaffer (1988, New York: Harper Business).

Robert H. Schaffer's book is about picking the right pilot projects for large system change. He has some very convincing stories and useful criteria. For example, pick indicators that show results in a few months, not two years down the road. Look for experiments which don't need more resources thrown in.—JK

21 Seven Steps for Breaking Through Organizational Gridlock*

Daniel Kim

An expanded version of this section was published in *The Systems Thinker*, February 1993, p. 5.

Gridlock results when individual actors continue to behave as if they were *independent of everyone else*—each pulling in a different direction, although the delayering has made them more interdependent.

In an automobile development program, for example, gridlock can occur when two functional teams, each responsible for a component or subsystem, want to optimize their work. In each case, the "quick fixes" to problems seem easy and effective at first, but they raise rivalry and resentment, which make it more difficult to follow the more fundamental improvements that both teams could reach only by working together.

These Seven Steps, using the Shifting-the-Burden archetype, can help teams find their way out of the gridlock loop.

PURPOSE
Despite the delayering that is taking place in many organizations, walls continue to persist between functions and divisions. Tremendous energy is wasted fighting through the obstructions. The result is organizational gridlock, which often actually increases as an organization is brought more tightly together.

STEP 1: IDENTIFY THE ORIGINAL PROBLEM SYMPTOM
Look back over a period of time and identify a class of symptoms that have been recurring. For the auto manufacturer, the problem symptoms

might include missing specifications, wrong part numbers, and incompatible parts—all of which may fall under a more general heading of "coordination problems."

STEP 2: MAP ALL "QUICK FIXES"

Next, try to map out all the fixes that have been used to tackle the identified problem. The objective is to identify a set of balancing loops that appear to be keeping the problems under control. For example, in the car product development effort, a Noise, Vibration, and Harshness (NVH) team encounters a noise problem and fixes it by adding reinforcements to the car's chassis.

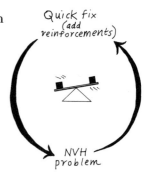

STEP 3: IDENTIFY UNDESIRABLE IMPACTS (INCLUDING IMPACTS ON OTHERS)

Solutions aren't implemented in isolation, however. Actions taken by one group almost always affect others in the organization. The persistence of gridlock suggests the presence of a reinforcing process that locks the players into a patterned response.

In our example, NVH's fix for the noise problem increases the car's weight and presents a problem for the Chassis team. Chassis, in turn, "fixes" its problem by increasing the tire pressure, which worsens the harshness and leads to another NVH problem. Another round of NVH quick fixes leads to another round of Chassis quick fixes in a vicious reinforcing spiral.

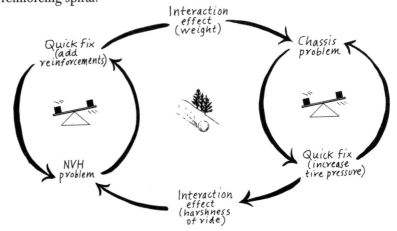

STEP 4: IDENTIFY FUNDAMENTAL SOLUTIONS

Having identified the undesirable effects of your quick fix, you need to find a solution that will more fundamentally address the problem(s). In the case of gridlock, or any other situation involving several players, this will mean looking at the situation from everyone's perspective.

A fundamental solution for NVH and Chassis might start with improving the quality and frequency of communication between the two groups so potential problems can be highlighted early and tackled together.

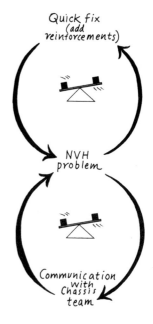

STEP 5: MAP ADDICTIVE SIDE EFFECTS OF QUICK FIXES

Remember, in a "Shifting the Burden" structure there are usually side effects of the quick fixes that steadily undermine the viability of the fundamental solution. This leads to a reinforcing spiral of dependency. In our product development example, the fixes may lead each team to focus more and more on meeting its own timing targets, which leads the team to invest even less in cross-team communication.

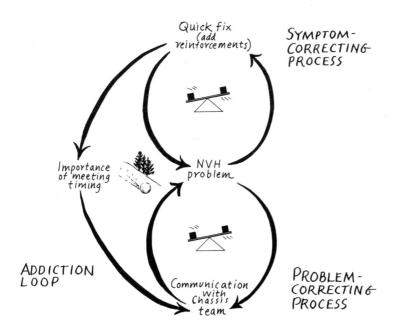

STEP 6: FIND INTERCONNECTIONS TO FUNDAMENTAL LOOPS

Side effects can lead to myopia, but they usually are not strong enough to create organizational gridlock. Finding links between the interaction effects and the fundamental solution can identify some reasons why functional walls grow thicker and higher over time. In our example, we essentially have two addictive "Shifting the Burden" structures linked together, each contributing to the other's problem. The "interaction effects" (in which each team's solution causes a problem for the other team), creates spiraling resentment, which leads to an increasing unwillingness to communicate with the other team. The "us versus them" mentality becomes entrenched as another addictive force, making the fundamental solution even less likely.

STEP 7: IDENTIFY HIGH-LEVERAGE ACTIONS

When you are in the middle of gridlock, it is difficult to see exactly where you are or how to get out. But if you are able to get a bird's-eye view, you can see the larger grid. For this reason, the process of mapping out a gridlocked situation can be a high-leverage action. It can stop the finger-pointing and blaming that often occurs in gridlock and provide a starting point for communicating across the walls.

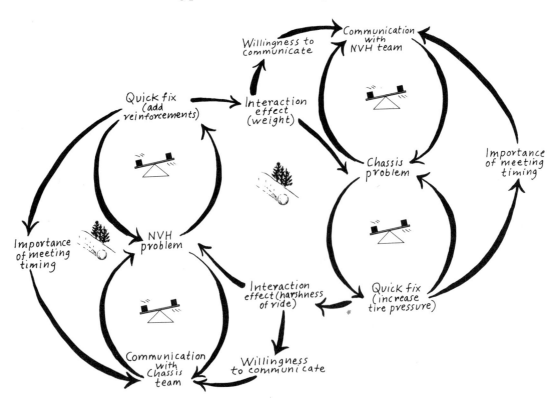

22 Moving into Computer Modeling

Michael Goodman

In the world of archetypes, all the elements of a system remain vaguely defined, and we can only speculate about what patterns of behavior the systems will produce. On a computer model of a system, we can see what happens when we take these assumptions to logical conclusions. This makes modeling an extremely valuable form of inquiry—it provides new (and less risky) ways to test hypotheses before acting on them, and gives us the basis to design "learning laboratories" that serve as transforming environments for a team or organization.

In practice, models have been used to:

- Show how systems structures directly produce patterns of behavior.
- Test whether a structure replicates the performance that was observed in the real world.
- Explore how behavior will change when different aspects of the structure are altered.
- Unveil points of leverage that might otherwise be ignored.
- Engage teams in a deeper set of systems learnings and allow them to experiment with the consequences of their thinking.

To see what models can do, consider even the simplest balancing loop with an explicit target guiding its actions. A firm has set a target for the number of employees it requires. It adjusts (increases or decreases) its staffing based on the gap between its current staff level and its target. But there are significant delays involved: the time it takes to recognize the gap, to act on it, and to hire or lay off staff:

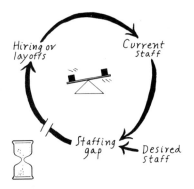

The loop provides a general description of the staffing process, but gives no indication of how it actually plays out over time. For instance, if the company has too small a staff, will there be a smooth transition to the desired level? Or will it happen suddenly? Will there be a tendency to overshoot the desired staff size?

Enter the computer. It can unambiguously trace the behavioral implications of the interrelationships you've put together, and bring the loops to life. But to do this, we must rigorously translate this general description into the software's terms. What's the exact number of staff we desire? Let's say, two thousand. The current staff? Fifteen hundred. We tell the computer we want to move staff 30 percent of the way toward our desired goal each month, and we expect it to take three months to feel the effects of hiring people or laying them off.

Moreover, each link *between* elements contains a mathematical relationship, which we must define within the program. Some elements become "stocks": a container or vessel, like the amount of current staff (often shown onscreen as a rectangle). Stocks are influenced by "flows," like the rate of hiring and layoffs (often shown as an arrow with a circular valve attached). Flows are like taps on a faucet, controlling the contents streaming into or out of the stock. There are also other types of influences, shown as solid arrows, that link elements together.°

° This model was constructed with *ithink!* from High Performance Systems.

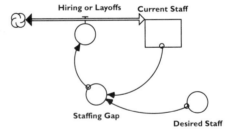

We specify relationships using mathematical formulas (here, the "staffing gap" is defined as "desired staff" minus "current staff," and a three-month delay is built into the formula for "hiring or layoffs.") When we "run" the model as a simulation, we can "play out" different scenarios and see a pattern-of-behavior diagram showing how the system performs over time. In the model we created here, the current staff levels tend to oscillate toward our goal, in the typical pattern of a balancing loop with delay—first too many people (after six months), then too few (after twelve).

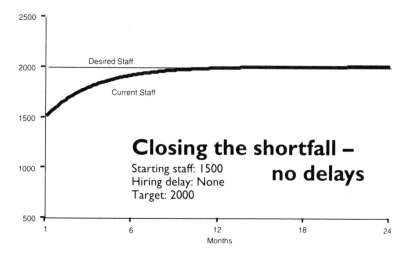

Why would staffing bounce around the desired level? Shouldn't it head straight to our goal? With the model, we can learn more by removing the delays from the structure. This dampens the oscillations—something easy to try on the computer, but not so easy to do in reality.

What if we downsize, dropping a third of our staff? Just as we overshot hiring, the same structure will overshoot the new target in the opposite direction. The delay means more people will be removed than needed, and rehiring will have to occur—a costly and demoralizing surprise, not obvious from the paper and pencil sketch of the simple balancing loop.

The concept of leverage points came out of computer modeling. As

Jay Forrester discovered in his industrial dynamics work, executives who are given command of a computer model, and asked to make it run better, usually make it run worse. They continue the most obvious actions and fail to find leverage points; or they find leverage points, but push them in the wrong direction.

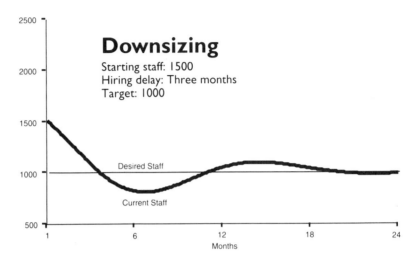

The difficulty of systems modeling comes not so much from learning to use the computer software, but from learning to represent current reality faithfully: continually testing and researching our assumptions until the computer model reflects our best understanding and behaves with a reasonable amount of credibility. Many people think that somehow using the computer will take care of those assumptions magically, but the opposite is true. When we move to the computer we have many more assumptions to make, and we must express them in quantitative, numeric terms. In a few rare cases, the formulas are straightforward and self-evident. But in most business problems, we must codify ambiguous decision rules and actions into quantitative relationships. In that sense, if an archetype is like an artist's rendition of a building, a computer model is like a full set of blueprints, complete with engineering ratios, plumbing details, and analysis of materials' tolerances.

That is why there is a more formidable learning curve here. Someone can learn to use *ithink!* in a few hours. But how long does it take to learn to design a model which produces usable results and advances a team's learning? Translating a complex organizational issue into a model that makes sense is still a high-level craft, and the modeling programs contain no built-in criteria for helping you see whether a model is credible or appropriate. As system dynamics professor John Sterman says, "These programs are very efficient ways to make bad models quickly."

Moreover, even a great model doesn't allow you to bypass the work with disciplines, despite its allure. One of the prerequisites for creating effective models is the ability of teams to take a hard look at their own assumptions and challenge their beliefs about tough issues.

For a buyer's guide to modeling and microworld software, see page 543. To see how model-building has been used in the development of microworlds and learning laboratories, see page 529. To see how system dynamics model-building is revolutionizing education, see page 487.

Beyond Training Wheels *John Sterman*

We asked Professor John Sterman of the MIT Sloan School to introduce other tools from the system dynamics tradition. John developed the "People Express Management Flight Simulator" (page 537) and many other widely used management flight simulators, and directs the System Dynamics group at MIT. He is a long-standing champion of the idea that systems understanding, in all of its forms, should be available to as many people as possible. He also takes issue with this book's emphasis on system archetypes. The archetypes have provoked a spirited debate in the system dynamics world, and we felt it important to include a significant voice from another perspective.

No one denies that spreadsheets are useful. But they also lowered the technical barriers facing people who wanted to do financial modeling. As a result, in the first few years after the introduction of spreadsheets, the average quality of financial models plummeted. Today, many financial models are not only useless, but downright harmful to decision makers who build them.

There is a danger that something similar may take place with the systems archetypes. As a first approach to understanding systems, they are valuable and revealing. (Peter Senge has referred to them, correctly in my opinion, as "training wheels.") Unfortunately, some people regard the archetypes as literal templates, where understanding your situation is just a matter of picking one, filling in the blanks, and applying the story's "moral." Where that happens, systems thinking, which should be a disciplined and creative process, becomes mere multiple choice.

Once they've picked an archetype, people often believe they can predict the behavior of the system. "If it's a 'shifting the burden' situation," they assume, "inevitably we'll become dependent on the symptomatic solution." But there are many counter-examples where addiction does not take place. The archetypes were the result of a long, inductive process in which people building formal models saw the same structures and dynamics arising repeatedly in very different systems. They formulated the archetypes to capture the general principles they saw operating. However, the formal models provided a rigorous underpinning for these generalizations. Using the archetypes alone, without the knowledge derived from working directly with formal models, can be dangerous. Predicting the behavior of even the simplest archetype would mean solving a high-order nonlinear differential equation in your head. Human beings do not have the cognitive capacity to do so. Many studies have shown that people's intuitive predictions about the dynamics of complex systems are systematically flawed.

These two problems—the "multiple-choice" tendency and the difficulty of assessing an archetype's behavior—suggest that archetypes, in the long run, are inadequate. Among system dynamics practitioners, there is disagreement about which archetypes are correct; not everyone agrees, for instance, that "Fixes That Backfire" (page 125) is a valid archetype. Other tools are available which may take a little longer to learn, but are much more powerful and flexible. They also offer greater fidelity in representing the issues of concern to managers.

CAUSAL LOOP DIAGRAMS

Causal loop diagraming uses the same "language" as the archetypes—causal links from one element to another. But the structure is more flexible; causal loop diagrams don't presume a preexisting template into which you've got to force-fit the situation. Causal loop diagrams also show the character of the relationship between each pair of concepts; for example, indicating whether an increase in one variable causes the other to increase or decrease.

The process of causal loop diagraming might typically include these steps:

- Select a problem and gather data about it.
- Identify key variables (the factors vital to understanding the problem).

- Plot the behavior of those key variables over time.
- Map the causal links between key variables, identifying the most significant relationships. Your diagrams can have as many or as few elements as you need to capture what is happening in the system, and to provide an appropriate level of detail for effective communication with your audience. You map the system as you see it.
- Identify the reinforcing and balancing feedback loops implicit in your map.
- Formulate hypotheses relating the structure in your map to the dynamics of the problem you identified.
- Test these hypotheses through data collection, modeling, and other means.

This very simple causal loop diagram describes bank panics during the Great Depression. Arrows indicate the flow of causality (fear of bank failure causes people to tend to withdraw their personal savings) "Plus" and "minus" signs indicate the polarity of the relationships. A "+" indicates the two variables move in the same direction. For example, if the fear of bank failure *increases,* the tendency to withdraw personal savings *increases.* If the fear of bank failure decreases, the tendency to withdraw savings also *decreases.* Conversely, a minus sign indicates the two variables move in the opposite direction from each other: If the perceived solvency of the bank *increases,* the fear of bank failure *decreases.* If the perceived solvency *decreases,* the fear of bank failure *increases.* The overall polarity of the feedback loops is indicated by the plus or minus signs in the center of the loops.

Here, the withdrawal of savings by people who fear bank failure reduces the solvency of the bank and increases the likelihood of failure in a self-reinforcing or positive feedback loop.[*]

STOCK-AND-FLOW DIAGRAMS

As I write this, Washington, D.C., is consumed with debate over the 1993 budget bill, and its potential impact on the deficit and the national debt. Passions run high on the subject. Yet many people, including many politicians, news writers, and other informed people, are confused about the difference between the debt and the deficit and find it difficult to understand their dynamics.

The deficit is a "flow"—a stream, in this case, of borrowed money, like the amount added to (or subtracted from) a credit card bill every

[*] *Feedback Thought in Social Science and Systems Theory,* by George P. Richardson (1991, Philadelphia: University of Pennsylvania Press), p. 83.

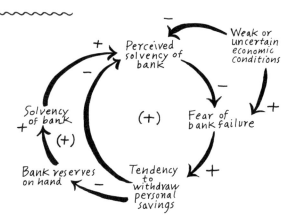

month. The national debt is the "stock" into which the deficit stream flows—a pool of accumulating credit, like the revolving balance on the credit card.

Many politicians have described the impact of the 1993 budget bill by saying that it will reduce the national debt by $500 billion over the next few years, but this is incorrect. In fact, the only way to reduce the debt is to run a surplus—that is, to have more cash coming in to government coffers than is spent. The federal government hasn't run a surplus since 1969, and the current deficit is a flow of more than $300 billion per year—more than $570,000 per minute, adding to the debt. Under the bill, though the deficit would be smaller, there would still be a deficit, and therefore the debt will continue to grow (though at a smaller rate). The only way to reduce the debt is to take in more than we spend; just as the only way to lower the water level in your bathtub is for water to drain out faster than it's pouring in.

The relationship between stocks and flows is one of the core concepts of system dynamics. However, the stock-and-flow structure of systems is not represented in archetypes and causal loop diagrams. Many studies have shown that it is difficult for people to grasp stock-and-flow concepts intuitively. However, stocks and flows are responsible for time delays; they give systems inertia and memory; they can amplify or attenuate disturbances; and they are fundamental in shaping the dynamics produced by systems.

To fully understand a delay, for example, you need to recognize the stocks and flows involved. If you mail 100 letters inviting people to a party, why are the letters not delivered instantaneously? A cynic might say, "Because you didn't use e-mail;" but actually the letters sit in various "stocks": the mailbox where you drop them, the mail carrier's bag, the truck carrying the bag, the bins at the post office where mail waits to be sorted and relayed, and all the other way stations in the postal system. Even using e-mail doesn't eliminate the stocks and flows; there is a short delay between the time I send my electronic message and the time it is received. During this time, the message resides in a stock of undelivered e-mail in a computer's memory.

Stock-and-flow diagrams can include causal loops. The notation we use was developed by Jay Forrester at MIT and published in his ground-breaking book *Industrial Dynamics* in 1961. Today, leading simulation software packages for dynamic modeling generate system maps that explicitly portray the stocks and flows along with the feedback loops in the system.

The accumulation of the deficit into the debt (a flow accumulating into a stock) would be represented like this:

National debt

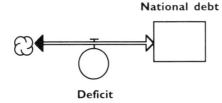

Deficit

Stock-and-flow diagrams are not as difficult to learn as you might expect. When I teach introductory system dynamics courses, I often start by displaying the diagram of the debt and deficit shown here. I then invite students to suggest the causal loops which influence the deficit flow. They call each factor out: expenditures, entitlements, interest payments, the pressure to cut spending, the tax base, tax rates, and so on, describing the effects of each. In ten minutes, we have covered the blackboard with feedback loops they've suggested. Each loop clearly captures a real process, including the physical processes and the institutional structures in it.

The students can see that they've built a macroeconomic model of federal fiscal operations, one more sophisticated than the model presented in typical economics classes. Unlike an archetype, the model's structure was not predetermined, but includes the loops that students believe are real and important.

WHY SIMULATION IS ESSENTIAL FOR SYSTEMS THINKING

Also unlike an archetype, the deficit model is too complicated to reliably simulate the economy by intuition. To understand the dynamics of the economy, you would need to simulate the system using a computer to do the calculations.

The example of the federal deficit shows how the complexity of nonlinear system maps can quickly overwhelm our ability to understand the dynamics they produce. As Herbert Simon, winner of the 1978 Nobel Prize for Economics, puts it, "The capacity of the human mind for formulating and solving complex problems is very small compared with the size of the problem whose solution is required for objectively rational behavior in the real world, or even for a reasonable approximation to such objective rationality."[*]

Simon's "principle of bounded rationality" presents us with a dilemma. The only system maps we can interpret correctly will be trivial and incomplete compared to the complexity of the systems we seek to understand. Alternatively, we can create more complex and realistic maps of our systems, but our intuition is then insufficient to provide guidance into their dynamics or help us find high-leverage policies. One resolution of the dilemma is the use of computer simulation. Computer-based models accurately calculate the consequences of the assumptions in our system maps, no matter how complex.

Simulation is an essential part of one's systems thinking training for another, more important reason. When you create a map of a system, whether via archetypes, causal loop diagrams, or stocks and flows, you have done nothing more than propose hypotheses. These hypotheses require testing. Yet in many of the systems of interest to us, we cannot run the experiments that would shed light on our theories. We can't run the business under one strategy, then go back in time and try another. Simulation is the only practical way to test the theories we propose in our system maps. And it is thus the only practical way to learn about the relationship between the structure of our systems and the dynamics they produce.

Does this mean everyone who wishes to think systemically must become a computer modeler? I believe the answer is no, as long as we understand the limits we place on ourselves as a result. For instance, some people believe that if children could be taught systems thinking from an early age, they would grow up with a deeper understanding of how systems work, enabling them to identify high-leverage policies "in their heads." It is true that studying systems thinking can enhance our intuition about the dynamics of complex systems, just as studying physics can develop our intuition about the natural world. Yet even if children began their study of physics in kindergarten, it is ludicrous to suggest

[*] *Models of Man,* by Herbert A. Simon (1957, New York: Wiley), p. 198.

that they could learn to perform the necessary calculations in their heads to predict what would happen if two galaxies collided, or even when the next rainstorm will come. Many human systems, including businesses, the economy, and the political system, are just as complex. Even if children learn how to think systemically—which I believe is vitally important—it will still be necessary to develop formal models, solved by simulation, to understand these complex systems.

Moreover, systems thinking without computer simulation can short-circuit the process by which we develop human intuition. Without modeling, we might think we are learning to think holistically when we are actually learning to jump to conclusions. A well-crafted and well-tested computer model enables us to close the feedback loop by which we learn, by showing us the implications of our assumptions.

ACCESSIBLE LITERATURE ON MAPPING TECHNIQUES John Sterman

Over the past ten years, computer technology and software have evolved so that anybody—from grade school students to CEO's of Fortune 100 firms—can develop and work with his own simulation models. People no longer need a technical or mathematical education to use simulation, though of course the more training in math and science you have, the better.

Introduction to System Dynamics Modeling with DYNAMO, by George P. Richardson and Alexander Pugh III (1981, Portland, Or.: Productivity Press). A clearly written college-level text covering causal loop diagraming, stocks and flows, modeling, and simulation, and emphasizing the process of model building. It gives very good guidance to how you should go about doing modeling well.

Study Notes in System Dynamics, by Michael Goodman (1974, Portland, Or.: Productivity Press). Clear and easy-to-use treatment of causal loop diagraming, stocks and flows, and simple simulations, in a workbook format.

Modeling for Learning, edited by John Morecroft and John Sterman (1994, Portland, Or.: Productivity Press). A collection of papers describing the uses of models and simulation for individual and organizational learning.

An Introduction to Systems Thinking by Barry Richmond and Steve Peterson (1987, 1992, Hanover, NH: High Performance Systems).

More than a computer manual, this guide to software functions as a readable introductory textbook. While it stands alone, you will get the most out of it if you use it in conjunction with the *STELLA* or *ithink!* software.

23 Systems Thinking with Process Mapping: A Natural Combination

Rick Ross

Because process mapping and systems thinking are superficially similar, there's a lot of confusion between them—which is a shame, because the two types of tools, while distinct, are complementary. Process diagrams show a flow or sequence of activities. The labels are verbs, tasks, or steps. The arrows show sequence and chronology. A change in one element does not necessarily change other elements. One famous process diagram is W. Edwards Deming's "PDSA" circle at left:

However, most process cycles are illustrated in a straight line:

$$A \xrightarrow{then} B \xrightarrow{then} C \xrightarrow{then} D$$

Causal-loop diagram (from system dynamics) represent cause-and-effect relationships. The labels on system diagrams represent variables (not actions), usually nouns or noun phrases. Changing any variable will produce change in all the variables in the loop. The arrows indicate influence or causality, not merely chronology.

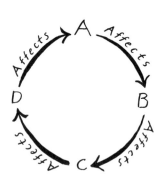

In a typical company, with its hundreds of internal and external customers, there are many process cycles operating, all interrelated, all running on different clocks, and many of them feeding back on each other. Things don't move in just one direction. A process map, while it does demonstrate interdependencies, tends to be a static picture of what's going on, unlike the systems thinking view which always looks at dynamic interrelationships.

Thus, all fast-cycle-time efforts should involve causal-loop thinking as well as process-map thinking. Studying "the billing process" by itself may help you save time, but it will not show you how the billing process affects and is affected by other critical processes in the company.

IMPROVING PERFORMANCE by Geary Rummler and Alan P. Brache
(1990, San Francisco: Jossey-Bass).

Improving Performance is an excellent introduction to understanding the process relationships of an organization. They open their book by describing an eye-opening exercise. Ask people to draw a picture of their organization—a business, a department, a business unit, or a team. Nine out of ten people draw a picture of the hierarchy—the organization chart. Then say, "What's missing from this picture?" One by one, sheepishly at first, replies will come back. "There's no customers there . . . or products . . . and it doesn't say how things get done . . ." As Rummler and Brache demonstrate, this mental model—that the organization chart represents the structure of the business—is a primary cause of the difficulties people have accomplishing anything across functions or silos. Hence their subtitle: "How to Manage the White Space on the Organization Chart."

FAST CYCLE TIME by Christopher Meyer (1993, New York: Free Press/Macmillan).

Chris Meyer's book *Fast Cycle Time* is more specifically about improving the speed of performance in an organization—not by trying to move faster, but by redesigning your work. This is a more recent, more sophisticated book, which refines many of the techniques from Rummler and Brache. As you might expect from a book for which Peter Senge wrote the foreword, there are a lot of synergies between Meyer's approach and our own. For example, Meyer describes how to identify the varied rhythms in different processes that seem unrelated, and how to design a team that can bring those rhythms into synch.—**RR**

CREATING THE CORPORATE FUTURE by Russell Ackoff
(1981, New York: John Wiley & Sons).

Russell Ackoff originated the extreme reengineering question: "Imagine that you could redesign your business at once. What systems would you put in place?" This book is an extended answer to that question. For example, Ackoff suggests creating a free-market economy within an organization, where each component must serve internal customers. (He calls this the "multidimensional organization.") There's also a lot of material on designing information systems to give managers the material they need to look at, instead of drowning them in data. We do not necessarily endorse everything Ackoff suggests; it should always be instituted with an eye toward unintended consequences. But it is the single most comprehensive, most insightful guide we know to re-creating the mechanisms of the enterprise. —CR, Suzanne Thomas

Five years of "delicious adventures" John Parker

At the start of the events described in this story, John Parker ran a manufacturing plant at Martin Marietta Astronautics. Like many pioneers in the learning disciplines, he was considered a maverick at his company. But now, thanks in part to the work described here, John is the head of manufacturing. He and his colleagues had learned how to use systems thinking as a language for creating learning teams throughout the company.

Martin Marietta Astronautics has always been known for its ability to manage crises. Whenever there was a threat, we took great pride in our ability to band together in cross-functional "tiger teams." We put aside our differences, focused on the task at hand, and produced remarkable innovation in a hurry. It took us a startlingly long time to figure out that we could behave the same way even when times were good.

In 1987 we won a contract to produce 108 instrumentation and flight safety systems for the U.S. Air Force Peacekeeper missile. This was a triumph in every respect but one—the price. When our in-house estimators analyzed this project, they found that we would overrun $19 million if we approached it with our current way of doing business. At that time, the Defense Department was revamping its policies so that contractors would share the overrun costs.

Thus, during the next five years we re-created our entire production and development system—incorporating quality improvement, faster cycle times, new relationships with suppliers, high-performance teams, and redesigning our work flow as a system. From the beginning, we recognized that all of these methods would reinforce each other in a virtuous cycle. And indeed, every time we found an improvement, two more possibilities seemed to open up. That's why I described our project in a technical paper, two years ago, as a series of "delicious adventures"—a phrase which provoked more comment than the rest of the paper did. But to make the adventures delicious, and not disastrous, we had a great deal to learn about looking freshly at our own systems, and about finding leverage within them.°

° *Peacekeeper IFSS—A TQM Success Story* by J. Parker (Martin Marietta, Denver, Co.; AIAA/ADPA/NSIA National Total Quality Management Symposium, November 1–3, 1989, Denver, Co.; American Institute of Aeronautics and Astronautics, Washington, DC 20024).

THE REAL LEVERAGE

One clear source of leverage existed with our bottoms-up supplier policy. Every component part had a cost, a schedule, and a level of reliability designed separately by us and the supplier. We'd add up all the aggregate pieces, and that would be the cost, the schedule, and the quality of the whole unit. Now we had to reduce the cost—which, according to the rules of most government contract work, means giving the piece part order to the lowest bidder. Instead, we shifted our attitudes. Our real leverage would lie not with individual components, but in the way we assembled and integrated the pieces together. We needed to get our suppliers to work together with each other and us, designing their work in synch, before the parts ever got to the assembly stage.

Having decided to do this, we needed teammates (suppliers) who shared that same vision. In our first stages, this was *the* most critical step. Even though we were effectively $19 million in the hole, we didn't look at the suppliers' costs. Instead, we asked, "Do you want to play with us?" These were sophisticated organizations in their own right, makers of transmitters, antenna systems, and other complex hardware. In every case but one (where they possessed a unique technology), if they were not kindred spirits we went out and got new partners. As an example, our own factory in Denver refused to participate with us in reexamining the system. We took back their welding and cabling work, and gave it to another Martin Marietta group.

Moving the work to new sites was such a sweeping change that there was doubt we would get the go-ahead. Fortunately, however, our Defense Department contract, with its $19 million overrun, presented a severe threat to the company. I recognize the irony of that statement, but it provided a rationale for making dramatic changes. We actually lobbied to have our program rating changed to "red"—to look worse to corporate headquarters back in Bethesda.

During the next year, we prototyped many processes with our associated contractors, who would never before have been privy to our innovations. We purposefully created opportunities for people from different disciplines to work together face-to-face, and we raised acceptance of continuous improvement, as a value to be treasured and celebrated. We discovered that people at the sites—at both Martin Marietta and our suppliers—knew why they were not productive. They asked for revamped procedures, new tooling, and on-time delivery of parts.

Of all the changes we made, we were most startled by the amount of leverage that came from speeding up our cycle times. We had set ourselves a seemingly impossible goal: to equal the fastest time performance ever seen in our industry. We made the goal—but that was only the first step. With the productivity that resulted, we could have laid off half the "touch labor" (the people who actually work on the product) and taken the profit. But in low-volume production like ours, the cost of "touch labor" is fairly small. The major money drain is support staff, such as engineers, planners, supervisors, and finance people. We realized that if we kept all our touch labor, we could cut cycle time in half again—and *that* would allow us to halve the number of support staff per component. "My God," we said, "we could save 40 percent of our labor costs, without a single layoff."

We also discovered that if you do things quickly, you don't make as many mistakes. The literature said that might happen, but I don't think we expected it until it did happen. We noticed that while doubling speed, we also reduced manufacturing defects by 75 percent. Things get lost and broken when they sit in a queue, and I believe all of us are in a better frame of mind when we're kept busy.

Martin Marietta had six supplier companies in this project, and unless all of us increased velocity and designed the speedup together, we would not realize this improvement. So we had to enroll all six of our suppliers, without paying them anything extra. (That, in itself, violated a tradition; whenever you want something different from a supplier, you have to pay for it.) The suppliers had to see that they would realize the same cost reductions which we had seen. They gradually let us put people in their plants—not to look over their shoulders as had been done so often in the past, but to give-and-take so we could each benefit from the other's experience. Before long, the six subcontractors had also doubled their production rates.

By 1989 manufacturing defects had been reduced by 75 percent. Our project had gone from a $19 million overrun to a $33 million *under*run, a fact which was read into the *Congressional Record*.

CLOSING THE LOOP ON "THE LOOPS"

Near the end of this project, I was appointed Director of Manufacturing, and given the charter to instill the entire organization with the teamwork and thought processes that gave us our notable results on the Peacekeeper Program. Many key people from the project joined me on this new team. Almost immediately, we found that we did not have the tools to communicate what we had learned to the rest of the organization. The techniques and terminologies of the five learning disciplines, which we began to learn with Rick Ross's help and Peter Senge's *The Fifth Discipline,* provided those tools.

I used to be fond of saying, "There are no lessons learned." A technician might go through a thinking process, and be convinced to use number 5 lubricant instead of number 4. The "lesson" is recorded as: "Use 5 instead of 4." Which, of course, is not a generalized "lesson" at all. But now, with the ability to capture their own thought processes by explaining the cycles of cause and effect in a systems diagram, the technician (or engineer or planner) becomes a teacher who can pass on the lessons learned. With the language of causal loops as our primary communicating tool, we have developed flexible manufacturing approaches that allow our internal customers—program managers, like I was on the Peacekeeper project—to insert their immature products into a more mature environment. I call it "mature" in part because our processes have improved, but more importantly because our factory personnel have become systems thinkers, ready for new adventures.

24 Where to Go from Here

Charlotte Roberts

■ **To shared vision:** As you become more aware of systemic structures, and feel compelled to redesign them, the question will inevitably emerge: "Design them to what purpose?" This is a good reason to do some shared vision work during the early stages of your systems work (or before). Otherwise, being steeped in awareness of the forces of the system may cause you to limit your vision to what you think is possible. See pages 337 and 340

- **To mental models and team learning:** A systems effort will almost always suggest that you reexamine the assumptions that underlie your practices. Otherwise, you will be unprepared to deal with the emotions and "bad news" that starts to pop up. Some of the saddest work of our experience is with teams who were genuinely committed to understanding the systems they worked within, but who—when an archetype or story was brought up in front of them—did not know how to talk about it effectively. See segments on balancing advocacy and inquiry (page 253), conversational recipes (page 260), skillful discussion (page 385), and reframing team relationships (page 407).

- **To scenario planning:** We find systems thinking and scenario planning (page 275) are natural complements. Both provide analytical tools which bring your team's assumptions about the future to the surface.

- **To personal mastery:** Finally, every one of us is a significant part of the systems we work within, and the most significant leverage may come from changing our own orientation and self-image. This requires work in Personal Mastery: developing our personal vision (page 201), and learning to see the world from not just a reactive point of view ("They're doing it to me!") but also a creative and interdependent perspective. For more on this, see "Intrapersonal Mastery," page 226.

Personal Mastery

~~~~~~

25 Strategies for Developing Personal Mastery

A striking number of business people tell us that of all the learning disciplines, they are most drawn to personal mastery. They are hearteningly generous; they want not only to increase their own capabilities, but improve the capabilities of the other people around them. They recognize that an organization develops along with its people. Some of them recognize the central tenet of this discipline: no one can increase someone else's personal mastery. We can only set up conditions which encourage and support people who want to increase their own.

Why offer that encouragement and support? Because it is increasingly clear that learning does not occur in any enduring fashion unless it is sparked by people's own ardent interest and curiosity. When the spark is not present, people compliantly accept training in a subject—statistical process control, executive development, or planning for reengineering. The effects of that training last for a while, but without commitment, the trainees stop using the new skills. Gradually, they systematically forget them, often beginning with the principles and theories which made the training seem so worthwhile in the first place.

On the other hand, if learning is related to a person's own vision, then that person will do whatever he or she can to keep learning alive. But instead of encouraging what Dr. W. Edwards Deming called "intrinsic motivation," many organizations are set up to block it. For example, there may be a gauntlet of forms and requisitions to run every time someone wants to pursue their own training; or there may be policies and attitudes which discourage people from speaking openly about current reality, or which subtly denigrate efforts to articulate a lofty personal vision.

The enthusiasm for personal mastery has, in fact, outpaced the development of ideas about how to instill it in organizations. We expect that to change during the next few years, as personal mastery becomes a more respectable subject for learning organization research.

Some of that research will hopefully include tracing the guiding ideas which underlie this discipline. Work historian Philip Mirvis suggests that a full survey of the field should include the work of psychologists Kurt Lewin, Carl Rogers, Jean Piaget, Abraham Maslow, and Milton Erikson; management writers Frank Barron, Jay Ogilvy, Robert Quinn, Tim Gallwey, Jane Loevinger, and William Torbert; and concepts from both Eastern and Western spiritual disciplines. But the key concepts which we have found valuable for this discipline were developed and articulated by composer/teacher Robert Fritz. He designed a three-stage process for adopting a "creative" orientation to life: articulating a personal vision, seeing current reality clearly, and choosing: making a commitment to creating the results you want.

See the reviews of Robert Fritz's books on page 197.

MASTERY

The term mastery descends from the Sanskrit root *mah,* meaning "greater." (This is also the source of "maharajah.") Through the centuries, in Latin and Old English, the meaning of "mastery" as domination over something else ("I am your master") has endured. But a variation of the word evolved in medieval French: *maître,* meaning someone who was exceptionally proficient and skilled—a master of a craft.

Mastery, as we use the word today, reflects *maître.* It means the capacity not only to produce results, but also to "master" the principles underlying the way you produce results. If someone can create great work only with constant struggle, we wouldn't call him or her masterful. In mastery, there is a sense of effortlessness and joyousness. It stems from your ability and willingness to understand and work with the forces around you. —AK

A conversation within yourself

THE CENTRAL PRACTICE OF PERSONAL MASTERY INVOLVES LEARNING TO keep both a personal vision and a clear picture of current reality before us. Doing this will generate a force within ourselves called "creative tension." Tension, by its nature, seeks resolution, and the most natural resolution of *this* tension is for our reality to move closer to what we want. It's as if we have set up a rubber band between the two poles of our vision and current reality.

People who are convinced that a vision or result is important, who can see clearly that they must change their life in order to reach that result, and who commit themselves to that result nonetheless, do indeed feel compelled. They have assimilated the vision not just consciously, but unconsciously, at a level where it changes more of their behavior. They have a sense of deliberate patience—with themselves and the world—and more attentiveness to what is going on around them. All of this produces a sustained sense of energy and enthusiasm, which (often after a delay) produces some tangible results, which can then make the energy and enthusiasm stronger.

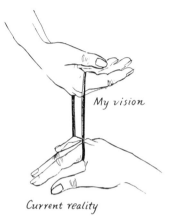

My vision

Current reality

We may not be able to command ourselves to snap instantly into this frame of mind, but the discipline of personal mastery suggests that we can, as individuals, cultivate a way of thinking that leads us gradually to it. The more we practice this way of thinking, the more we will feel competent and confident, and the more we will allow ourselves to be aware of the tension which can pull us forward if we cultivate it.

Some people think, "I will never accomplish my vision, because of the way I was raised—I *know* I can never have what I want." Or they feel, "I can only force myself toward my vision if things get bad enough," or "It's up to me to push ahead through sheer willpower, against the obstacles thrown at me." As Fritz notes, all of these fears are manifestations of "emotional tension"—basic beliefs that we are unworthy or powerless to obtain our deepest aspirations. How do we cope with emotional tension? Not by denying it exists, but by trying to see it more clearly, until we can see that emotional tension, too, is part of our current reality.

Personal mastery teaches us not to lower our vision, even if it seems as if the vision is impossible. And, paradoxically, it teaches us that the content of the vision is not important in itself. "It's not what the vision is," says Robert Fritz. "It's what the vision does." There are many stories of people who achieve extraordinary results with extraordinary visions—where the results happen to be different from their original intent.

Personal mastery also teaches not to shrink back from seeing the world as it is, even if it makes us uncomfortable. Looking closely and clearly at current reality is one of the most difficult tasks of this discipline. It requires the ability to ask yourself, not just at quiet times but during times of stress, "What is going on right now? Why is my reality so difficult?"

See, for example, the "Moments of Awareness" exercise on page 216.

Finally, personal mastery teaches us to choose. Choosing is a courageous act: picking the results and actions which you will make into your destiny.

Practicing personal mastery is like holding a conversation within ourselves. One voice within us dreams of what we want for the future. Still another casts an (often baleful) eye on the world around us. A third voice, often well hidden, is willing to say, "I have chosen what I want and accepted that I will create it." In this discipline, we try to hear all these facets clearly, knowing that the power which pulls us toward our vision emerges from the relationship between them.

The leader as coach

CULTIVATING CREATIVE TENSION PUBLICLY (BY BUILDING SHARED VISION on one hand, and helping people see the systems and mental models of current reality on the other) can move a whole organization forward, because organizations are as propelled by creative tension as individuals are. The first step in learning to create that larger-scale tension is learning to generate and manage creative tension within yourself.

Admittedly, the notion of encouraging personal mastery in the workplace is intuitively difficult for some leaders. There is a feeling, usually under the surface, that personal vision lies at odds with organizational purpose. During the time they spend at work, employees are supposed to be totally dedicated to the enterprise, and to check their own goals and desires at the door.

To the great relief of many people, this paternalistic attitude is turning out to be both unpersuasive and ineffective. What, then, can a senior manager do to encourage personal mastery in others? We recommend taking on the stance of a coach. No coach can make a difference unless the player has an intrinsic desire to achieve something. But given that intrinsic desire, a coach can draw out efforts and understanding which the individual might not access as easily on his or her own.

The first task of a coach is to model, with your own behavior, the increased personal capacity that develops when you accept and generate creative tension. During any shared vision process, someone will inevitably ask the senior leader: "Well, how do you feel *personally* about where we should go?" If, as leader, you don't have a good sense of your own vision, you won't be able to draw out other people to create their own or consider yours. Similarly, if you can't describe current reality clearly, you will have little credibility when you suggest other people look at it with you.

"The leader has a responsibility to pursue personal mastery," says our colleague Alain Gauthier, "not just for his or her own sake, but for everyone else in the organization. Unless the leader has a degree of self-knowledge, and self-understanding, there is the risk that he or she may use the organization to address his or her own neuroses. This can have a tremendous impact on the other people."

A typical personal mastery coaching task might involve helping someone see how clouding their own vision with worries about whether the vision is possible. "Is that what you really want? If you had it, would you take it?" Or it might involve helping people develop better pictures of what's really going on in current reality. "What is happening *right now* at this moment?" As people learn to coach more effectively, the techniques cascade up and down the organization, because coaching, like most of the methods of personal mastery, is best learned by example.

For more about learning to be a coach, see *"Finding a Partner,"* page 74. Also see "Drawing Forth Personal Vision," page 201, and "Leadership Fields," page 65.

THE PATH OF LEAST RESISTANCE by Robert Fritz (1989, New York: Fawcett-Columbine);

CREATING by Robert Fritz (1991, New York: Fawcett-Columbine).

Robert Fritz, who started his career as a musician and composer, got sidetracked along the way by his interest in the creating process. What attitudes made it easy or difficult? For twenty years, he has tested his conclusions in seminars of his own design. Both of these books, targeted primarily at the individual level, offer exercises and ideas for developing your own personal mastery and creativity.

The Path of Least Resistance, from which *The Fifth Discipline* and this *Fieldbook* draw heavily, covers the basic methods for generating creative tension (which Fritz calls "structural tension"), building on momentum, and avoiding the emotional surges and depressions which sidetrack you from your vision.

Creating describes how to build an effective frame of mind for producing new work. As a veteran of many creative projects, I can attest to the value of his suggestions: develop a simple plan of action, and then experiment with it. Let each stage of the work build on the previous stage. People who have been discouraged all their lives from "being creative," for whatever reason, can reverse that process starting here.

Fritz writes clearly and simply, but these are not easy books to read. Every section challenges some old way of thinking—at least in me. Quite possibly in you.—**AK**

26 What You Can Expect . . . from the Practice of Personal Mastery

Charlotte Roberts

Are you and your organization ready for it?

IMAGINE AN ORGANIZATION FULL OF PEOPLE WHO COME TO WORK ENTHU-siastically, knowing that they will grow and flourish, and intent on fulfilling the vision and goals of the larger organization. There's an ease, grace, and effortlessness about the way they get things done. Work flows seamlessly among teams and functions. People take pleasure and pride in every aspect of the enterprise—for example, in the way they can talk openly, reflect on each other's opinions, and have genuine influence on the structures around them. That's a lot of energy walking in each day, accomplishing an ever-increasing amount of work and having fun along the way.

Is this scenario energizing or frightening? If you don't want people to bring this much passion, caring, and focus to their work, then don't practice this high-voltage discipline. It will make unfamiliar demands upon everyone, and particularly upon senior leaders. Some learning organization efforts do well to begin here; others should work their way in gradually, letting people discover this set of practices in an evolutionary process.

Treating emotions respectfully

WORKING WITH PERSONAL MASTERY MEANS ENTERING THE REALM OF matters of the heart. Developing a personal vision means tapping into a deep well of hope and aspiration, including the longing to serve something greater than oneself, and the desire to have a joyful life.

Making choices and looking closely at current reality can also bring deeply buried emotions to the surface. It may depress people at first: "I didn't want to see how much I dislike my life currently, and I don't want the burden of trying to improve it." It will also probably energize people: "I always thought the world did it to *me*. Now I realize I'm pulling my own strings." None of these emotions are bad in themselves; but as they come to the surface, people should be prepared for them.

Investing in personal mastery

TO PROVIDE CONDITIONS IN WHICH INDIVIDUALS CAN DEVELOP THEIR CA-pacity to create what they care about, organizations must invest time, energy, and money far beyond what most managers today consider appropriate. Less than 13 percent of American workers have ever received extensive training in how to do their work better (as opposed to perfunctory "on-the-job training.")[*] No doubt only a small fraction of those have ever felt that the management of the firm focused on improving their personal development. Personal mastery implies a willingness to invest what is necessary to create an environment that helps employees become high-quality contributors.

For more on the mechanisms of making this investment, see page 220.

[*] This statistic comes from several sources. A figure of 13 percent was presented at the 1992 annual meeting of the Ohio Manufacturers Association. Also see "Worker Training: An Investment in Safety" by Gregg LaBar in *Occupational Hazards*, August 1991 (vol. 53, no. 8), p. 23.

Rethinking traditional models of motivation

MANAGERS OFTEN TURN TO PERSONAL MASTERY BECAUSE THEY ARE weary of traditional forms of motivation. Some have depended on the "carrots and sticks" of rewards and punishments. Other managers have spent years using fear and desperation ("the doom and gloom talk") to motivate people. They always have a bit of bad news to share, about the difficult environment around them and the wolves at the door. People indeed respond to incentives for a short time, and they may respond to difficult times even more heartily, pulling together with extra effort, as long as they feel the difficulty is real. But once they realize these incentives are intended to manipulate them, they stop immediately in their tracks.

Unfortunately, by that time the management has often fallen into a "Shifting the Burden" dynamic, losing its fundamental ability to motivate people in any genuine way and therefore relying even more on carrots, sticks, and "doom-and-gloom" speeches. Gradually, the continual introduction of new motivation efforts grinds a nearly indelible cynicism into the organization.

⟨⟨ See "Shifting the Burden," page 135.

At this stage, some managers decide to build "aspiration" and "inspiration" by promoting personal mastery. They tell themselves that they can catch more flies with honey than vinegar. (When I first heard my grandmother use this expression, I asked why she wanted a supply of flies anyhow.) But the change in the rules of the game still doesn't work. The cynicism typically worsens; members suspect that the pursuit of personal mastery is just another game.

Why doesn't it take? Because a personal mastery effort depends on setting aside the assumption that people are primarily motivated by money, recognition, and fear. Instead, you must assume that in the right atmosphere, people will contribute and make commitments because they want to learn, to do good work for its own sake, and to be recognized as people. This attitude may be difficult to change. One approach is to begin an in-depth shared vision effort simultaneously, in which you allow your employees to tell you exactly what personal mastery efforts will contribute to the evolution of the whole.

Wherever you are, start here

PERSONAL MASTERY OFFERS AN OPTION FOR PEOPLE WHO FEEL THEY want to change their organization, but can't accomplish much from their position. You can always move, as an individual, to develop your personal mastery.

Drawing Forth Personal Vision*

Charlotte Roberts, Bryan Smith, Rick Ross

° This material has been adapted in part from two separate Innovation Associates exercises: "Vision Escalation" and "Power of Choice."

Preparing to do the exercise

THIS EXERCISE BEGINS INFORMALLY. YOU SIT DOWN AND "MAKE UP" A few ideas about your aims, writing them on paper, in a notebook, or with a word processor. No one else need ever see them. There is no "proper" way to answer and no measurable way to win or lose. Playfulness, inventiveness, and spiritedness are all helpful—as if you could again take on the attitudes of the child you once were, who asked similar questions long ago.

Pick a locale where you can sit or recline in privacy, a quiet and relaxed space to write, with comfortable furniture and no glaring light or other visual distractions. Play a favorite piece of music (or work in silence if you prefer). Most importantly, give yourself a block of time for this exercise—at least an hour, on a day relatively free of hassle. Hold your phone calls and visitors for that duration.

STEP 1: CREATING A RESULT

Begin by bringing yourself to a reflective frame of mind. Take a few deep breaths, and let go of any tension as you exhale, so that you are relaxed, comfortable, and centered.

From there you may move right to the exercise; or you may prefer to ease in by recalling an image or memory meaningful to you. It could be a favorite spot in nature (real or imagined), an encounter with a valued person, the image of an animal, or an evocative memory of a significant event: any time where you felt something special was happening. Shut your eyes for a moment, and try to stay with that image. Then open your eyes and begin answering the following questions:

Imagine achieving a result in your life that you deeply desire. For example, imagine that you live where you most wish to live, or that you have the relationships you most wish to have. Ignore how "possible" or "impossible" this vision seems. Imagine yourself accepting, into your life, the full manifestation of this result. Describe in writing

PURPOSE

This exercise will help you define your personal vision: what you want to create of yourself and the world around you.

OVERVIEW

Because a personal vision requires commitment—it does, after all, influence most of the decisions you make thereafter—it is not a casual affair. The self-examination in this exercise takes place on a level that may be unfamiliar to some readers. But if you persevere through all four steps, you will see how powerful the question "What do I really want?" can be.

(or sketch) the experience you have imagined, using the present tense, as if it is happening now.

What does it look like?

What does it feel like?

What words would you use to describe it?

STEP 2: REFLECTING ON THE FIRST VISION COMPONENT

Now pause to consider your answer to the first question. Did you articulate a vision that is close to what you actually want? There may be a variety of reasons why you found it hard to do:

■ *"I can't have what I want."* Pretending you could have anything you want may not be an easy task. Many people find that it contradicts a habit held since childhood: "Don't think too much about what you want, because you might not get it." In a preemptive strike against disappointment, they denigrate any object of their deep desires. "It'll never live up to expectations anyway." Or they may feel they have to trade it off against something else: they can have a successful career *or* a satisfying family life, but not both.

In this exercise, you are trying to learn what your vision is. The question of whether it is possible is literally irrelevant. (That's part of current reality.) Suspend your doubts, worries, fears, and concerns about the limits of your future. Write, for the moment, as if real life could live up to your deepest wishes: What would happen then?

■ *"I want what someone else wants."* Some people choose their visions based on what they think other people will want for them: a parent, a teacher, a supervisor, or a spouse. For the duration of this exercise, concentrate on what *you* want. You may find yourself articulating that you want a good relationship with (for example) your spouse; you want the time to devote to that relationship, the understanding to act wisely within it, and the ability to live up to the mutual commitments you have made to each other. But you should include it only if you want it for yourself—not because you think your spouse would want it.

■ *"It doesn't matter what I want."* Some people assume that what they want is not important. They scribble out whatever comes to mind quickest, just to get "any old vision that sounds good" down on paper. Later, when they need a coherent personal vision as a foundation for further learning, their haste turns out to have been counterproductive. Do not belittle yourself; if, like many of us, you have doubts about whether you deserve rewards, imagine the rewards you would want if you *did* deserve them.

■ *"I already know what I want."* During this exercise, you may create a new sense of what you want, especially if you have not asked yourself this question for some time. A personal vision is not a done deal, already existing and waiting for you to unearth and decode it. It is something you create, and continue to re-create, throughout your life.

■ *"I am afraid of what I want."* Sometimes people say, "Well, what if I didn't want to stay at my job anymore?" Others are afraid that if they let themselves start wanting things, they'll get out of control, or be forced to change their lives.

Since this is *your* vision, it can't "run away" with you; it can only increase your awareness. Nonetheless, we suggest that you set your own limits on this exercise. If a subject frightens you too much, ignore it. However, the fact that you feel uneasy about something may be a clue to potential learning. A year from now, or two, you may want to come back to that subject—at your discretion.

■ *"I don't know what I want."* In *The Empowered Manager*, Peter Block offers an effective approach with people who say they don't have a personal vision ("of greatness," as he calls it) for themselves. In effect, he says, not to believe them:

> The response to that is to say, "Suppose you had a vision of greatness: what would it be?" A vision exists within each of us, even if we have not made it explicit or put it into words. Our reluctance to articulate our vision is a measure of our despair and a reluctance to take responsibility for our own lives, our own unit, and our own organization. A vision statement is an expression of hope, and if we have no hope, it is hard to create a vision.°

° *The Empowered Manager: Positive Political Skills at Work* by Peter Block (1991, San Francisco: Jossey-Bass), p. 113.

■ *"I know what I want, but I can't have it at work."* Some people fear their personal vision won't be compatible with their organization's attitudes. Even by thinking about it, and bringing these hopes to the surface, they may jeopardize their job and position. This attitude keeps many people from articulating their vision or letting this exercise go very far.

This is really a question of current reality. As such, the perception is worth testing. Occasionally, someone we know does test it, by asking other members of the organization what they really think of this "dangerous" proposed vision. More often than not, the answer is: "It's no big deal." When approached directly, organizations tend to be far more accepting of our goals and interests for ourselves than our fears lead us to expect.

See "Ways to Test Personal Vision Against the Company's Culture," page 222.

Nonetheless, you may be right about your vision's unacceptability. If you can't have it at work at *this* place, then your vision might include finding another place to work which will allow you to grow and flourish.

STEP 3: DESCRIBING YOUR PERSONAL VISION

Now answer these questions. Again, use the present tense, as if it is happening right now. If the categories do not quite fit your needs, feel free to adjust them. Continue until a complete picture of what you want is filled in on the pages.

Imagine achieving the results in your life that you deeply desire. What would they look like? What would they feel like? What words would you use to describe them?

Self-image: If you could be exactly the kind of person you wanted what would your qualities be?

Tangibles: What material things would you like to own?

Home: What is your ideal living environment?

Health: What is your desire for health, fitness, athletics, and anything to do with your body?

Relationships: What types of relationships would you like to have with friends, family, and others?

Work: What is your ideal professional or vocational situation? What impact would you like your efforts to have?

Personal pursuits: What would you like to create in the arena of individual learning, travel, reading, or other activities?

Community: What is your vision for the community or society you live in?

Other: What else, in any other arena of your life, would you like to create?

Life purpose: Imagine that your life has a unique purpose—fulfilled through what you do, your interrelationships, and the way you live. Describe that purpose, as another reflection of your aspirations.

STEP 4: EXPANDING AND CLARIFYING YOUR VISION

If you're like most people, the choices you put down are a mixture of selfless and self-centered elements. People sometimes ask, "Is it all right to want to be covered in diamonds, or to own a luxury sports car?" Part of the purpose of this exercise is to suspend your judgment about what is "worth" desiring, and to ask instead: Which aspect of these visions is closest to your deepest desires? To find out, you expand and clarify each dimension of your vision. In this step, go back through your list of components of your personal vision that you have written down: including elements of your self-image, tangibles, home, health, relationships, work, personal pursuits, community, life purpose, and anything else.

Ask yourself the following questions about each element before going on to the next one.

If I could have it now, would I take it?

Some elements of your vision don't make it past this question. Others pass the test conditionally: "Yes, I want it, but only if . . ." Others pass, and are clarified in the process.

People are sometimes imprecise about their desires, even to themselves. You may, for instance, have written that you would like to own a castle. But if someone actually gave you a castle, with its difficulties of upkeep and modernization, your life might change for the worse. After imagining yourself responsible for a castle, would you still take it? Or would you amend your desire: "I want a grand living space, with a sense of remoteness and security, while having all the modern conveniences."

Assume I have it now. What does that bring me?

This question catapults you into a richer image of your vision, so you can see its underlying implications more clearly. For example, maybe you wrote down that you want a sports car. Why do you want it? What would it allow you to create? "I want it," you might say, "for the sense of freedom." But why do you want the sense of freedom?

The point is not to denigrate your vision thus far—it's fine to want a sports car—but to expand it. If the sense of freedom is truly important to you, what else could produce it? And if the sense of freedom is important because something else lies under that, how could you understand that deeper motivation more clearly? You might discover you want other forms of freedom, like that which comes from having a healthy figure or physique. And why, in turn, would you want a well-toned body?

To make love for hours every night? To play tennis better? Or just because . . . you want it for its own sake? All those reasons are valid, if they're *your* reasons.

Divining all the aspects of the vision takes time. It feels a bit like peeling back the layers of an onion, except that every layer remains valuable. You may never discard your desire to have a sports car, but keep trying to expand your understanding of what is important to you. At each layer, you ask, once again: If I could have it, would I take it? If I had it, what would it bring me?

This dialogue shows how someone handled this part of the exercise:

My goal, right now, is to boost my income.
What would that bring you?
I could buy a house in North Carolina.
And what would *that* bring you?
For one thing, it would bring me closer to my sister. She lives near Charlotte.
And what would that bring you?
A sense of home and connection.
Did you put down on your list that you wanted to have more of a sense of home and connection:
[Laughs] No, I didn't. I just now realized what is really behind my other desires.
And what would a sense of home and connection bring you?
A sense of satisfaction and fulfillment.
And what would that bring you?
I guess there's nothing else—I just want that. [Pause] I still do want a closer relationship with my sister. And the house. And, for that matter, the income. But the sense of fulfillment seems to be the source of what I'm striving for.

You may find that many components of your vision lead you to the same three or four primary goals. Each person has his own set of primary goals, sometimes buried so deeply that it's not uncommon to see people brought to tears when they become aware of them. To keep asking the question, "What would it bring me?" immerses you in a gently insistent structure that forces you to take the time to see what you deeply want.

How to be a good "drawing forth personal vision" coach

THIS EXERCISE CAN BE VERY EFFECTIVE WHEN PRACTICED WITH A TRUST-worthy partner. Taking turns, lead each other through the questions, gently prompting each other to understand: "If you could have it, would you take it? What would it bring you?"

Avoid the temptation to lead other people to a vision you prefer. Don't say anything along the lines of: "No, that vision isn't right for you. Pick another one." Your task is to support people's own choices, whether you agree with them or not. Similarly, don't analyze and dissect their vision. Merely help them bring it to the surface.

Phrase your prompts simply, and in the present tense: "What does your house look like?" instead of "What will—" or "What would—" Encourage the player to describe each scene as if it were happening before his or her eyes. Susan Frank, who has managed organizations which train people in personal mastery practices, puts it this way: "As a coach, you work with people to help them identify what they *really* want, and help them distinguish that end result from mere 'problem solving,' from a subsidiary result, or from something they think they *ought* to aspire to."

You may discover, even if you are strangers, that you share common themes. It's good to recognize that explicitly, without making a big deal about it. We have found that this exercise tends to lead people to feel a sense of mutual respect and even kinship—an inevitable by-product, perhaps, of hearing someone else's deepest wishes.

Vision for the Organization*

Charlotte Roberts, Bryan Smith

* Part of this exercise was developed in work, through Innovation Associates, for VHA East, Inc., and VHA of New Jersey, Inc.

Anyone seriously contemplating a shared vision effort (see page 312) or a leadership role in organizational redesign (see page 65) should take the time for this exercise.

- What would you personally like to see your organization become, for its own sake? What kinds of customers could it have? What sorts of processes might it conduct?

    What reputation would it have?
    What contribution would it make?
    What sorts of products or services could it produce?
    What values would it embody?
    What mission would it have?
    Who would be its clients and customers?
    What would its physical environment look like?
    How would people work together?
    How would people handle good and bad times?

- If you had this sort of organization, what would it bring you? How would it allow your own personal vision to flourish?

PURPOSE

This exercise links your personal vision to the organization's potential; to help people align the organization's purpose with their own; and to prepare individual groundwork for creating a shared vision.

WHAT COLOR IS YOUR PARACHUTE? (A PRACTICAL MANUAL FOR JOB HUNTERS AND CAREER CHANGERS) **by Richard Bolles** (revised annually, Berkeley, Calif.: Ten Speed Press).

Those of us who spend our waking hours earning a living essentially have two choices. We can come up with a vision for our career. Or we can let somebody else determine what kind of work we do, turn that part of our life over to them, and spend our time at work in a state of nonexistence.

If you choose to develop a vision, Richard Bolles's much-beloved book can genuinely help. He leads you through a creative process. What kind of people do you want to work with? What kind of product or service do you want to help create? Where do you want to work? What do you want to do when you're working? He demonstrates that it's not only possible but fruitful to have vision about your work, even in a recession. (Indeed, he wrote his first edition of this book after getting laid off.) Then he jumpstarts you to current reality, to what you have to do, whom you have to know, and what resources you need. — CR

Checklist for Personal Values

Charlotte Roberts

When you consider part of your vision, and something inside you says, "That's really not me," most likely you have felt a pang from a deeply held personal value.

Values are deeply held views, of what we find worthwhile. They come from many sources: parents, religion, schools, peers, people we admire, and culture. Many go back to childhood; we take on others as adults. As with all mental models, there's a distinction between our "espoused" values—which we profess to believe in—and our "values in action," which actually guide our behavior. These latter values are coded into our brains at such a fundamental level that we can't easily see them. We rarely bring them to the surface or question them. That's why they create dissonance for us.

As literature and spiritual guides warn us repeatedly, individuals should beware of the temptation to let their values slip when times get tough. Organizations should doubly beware. If your organization values honesty, that means it should show employees the financial books—even when the books are embarrassing. If your organization believes that "employees are our most important asset," it means that your first strategy in difficult times will not be layoffs. You may eventually have to lay off people, but it will be carefully considered because it contradicts your organization's value in action.

STEP 1: "WHAT I VALUE MOST . . ."

From this list of values (both work and personal), select the ten that are most important to you—as guides for how to behave, or as components of a valued way of life. Feel free to add any values of your own to this list.

PURPOSE
This exercise is designed to help you reach a better understanding of your most significant values.

OVERVIEW
A winnowing process in which you gradually eliminate less important concerns.

_____ Achievement	_____ Friendships	_____ Physical challenge
_____ Advancement and promotion	_____ Growth	_____ Pleasure
_____ Adventure	_____ Having a family	_____ Power and authority
_____ Affection (love and caring)	_____ Helping other people	_____ Privacy
_____ Arts	_____ Helping society	_____ Public service
_____ Challenging problems	_____ Honesty	_____ Purity
_____ Change and variety	_____ Independence	_____ Quality of what I take part in
_____ Close relationships	_____ Influencing others	_____ Quality relationships
_____ Community	_____ Inner harmony	_____ Recognition (respect from others, status)
_____ Competence	_____ Integrity	
_____ Competition	_____ Intellectual status	_____ Religion
_____ Cooperation	_____ Involvement	_____ Reputation
_____ Country	_____ Job tranquility	_____ Responsibility and accountability
_____ Creativity	_____ Knowledge	_____ Security
_____ Decisiveness	_____ Leadership	_____ Self-respect
_____ Democracy	_____ Location	_____ Serenity
_____ Ecological awareness	_____ Loyalty	_____ Sophistication
_____ Economic security	_____ Market position	_____ Stability
_____ Effectiveness	_____ Meaningful work	_____ Status
_____ Efficiency	_____ Merit	_____ Supervising others
_____ Ethical practice	_____ Money	_____ Time freedom
_____ Excellence	_____ Nature	_____ Truth
_____ Excitement	_____ (being around people who are) Open and honest	_____ Wealth
_____ Expertise		_____ Wisdom
_____ Fame	_____ Order (tranquility, stability, conformity)	_____ Work under pressure
_____ Fast living		_____ Work with others
_____ Fast-paced work	_____ Personal development (living up to the fullest use of my potential)	_____ Working alone
_____ Financial gain		
_____ Freedom		

* This exercise was adapted from a design by Robert Niles, vice president of Human Resources at the Helene Curtis corporation.

STEP 2: ELIMINATION*

Now that you have identified ten, imagine that you are only permitted to have five values. Which five would you give up? Cross them off.

Now imagine that you are only permitted four. Which would you give up? Cross it off.

Now cross off another, to bring your list down to three.

And another, to bring your list down to two.

Finally, cross off one of your two values. Which is the one item on this list that you care most about?

STEP 3: ARTICULATION

Take a look at the top three values on your list.

a. What do they mean, exactly? What are you expecting from yourself—even in bad times?

b. How would your life be different if those values were prominent and practiced?

c. What would an organization be like which encouraged employees to live up to those values?

d. Does the personal vision which you drew forth (see page 204) reflect those values? If not, should your personal vision be expanded? Or are you prepared to reconsider your values?

e. Are you willing to choose a life, and an organization, in which these values are paramount?

PAIRED VERSION

This exercise can be very effective done in pairs. Each person takes a turn as "values presenter" and as coach. We generally start with the five most important values to the presenter. One by one, the coach asks the presenter to eliminate one more value, until the list goes down to one . . .

The coach then asks, "What did you feel when I directed you to give up a core value?" Then, "Have you ever felt this feeling before, at home or at work?" And finally, "How do you want to handle this situation in the future if it arises?"

Cycling Back: Current Reality and Re-vision

Bryan Smith

W e suggest completing this exercise once a year, perhaps on or near your birthday. It should be conducted with an attitude of celebration and acknowledgment of how far you have come. Don't cover over problems and failures, but don't make them larger than they deserve to be. The point is not to say, "Look how I've failed this year," or "Look

P U R P O S E
Your first vision is generally not your final one. As you work toward your vision, your understanding of what you want gradually grows more sophisticated. Inevitably, you will

reach some elements of your vision, or reach other milestones that change your perception of what you care about. This exercise helps you "cycle back" to revisit your life's goals in light of the current reality.

how successful I've been." The point is to say, simply, "Let me look at what I want, as part of my personal vision right now. And let me look at where my current reality is now."

As you reacquaint yourself with this exercise each year, it should galvanize the creative tension in your life.

1. Answer these two questions for each of these aspects of your vision:
    a. **Self-image:** What is my current self-image?
       How has my vision changed for the kind of person I want to be?
    b. **Tangibles:** What is the real state of my tangible possessions, vis-à-vis my vision?
       How has my vision changed for material possessions?
    c. **Home:** Where do I live now?
       How has my vision changed for my living environment?
    d. **Health:** What is the state of my health, fitness, and anything else to do with my body?
       How has my health vision changed?
    e. **Relationships:** What is my current state in terms of marriage, romantic relationships, and friendship?
       How has my vision for relationships changed?
    f. **Work:** What is my professional or vocational situation?
       How has my job- and career-related vision changed?
    g. **Pursuits:** What is my current reality regarding individual learning, travel, reading, and other activities?
       How has my vision changed?
    h. **Community:** What kind of community do I live in and belong
       How has my vision for community changed?
    i. **Other:** What are any other important aspects of current reality?
       How has my vision changed?
    j. **Life purpose:** What is current reality now, in terms of my life purpose and deepest aspirations?
       How have these aspects of my vision changed?

27 Loyalty to the Truth

Charlotte Roberts

Tucked in between two Appalachian mountains stands a small glass bottle manufacturing company. I visited them some years ago to help the senior management team work more effectively together. During the first meeting we tried to nail down some ground rules. The manager of quality control proposed, "We'll be honest."

Right away, I noticed the production supervisor smirking. He was a tough, gritty man, who liked to bait people. "I can only be *flexibly* honest," he said. "For instance, if I can sneak bottles past quality control to make my production bonus, I will."

At that point, the manager of quality control rose up from his chair and rushed toward the production manager. I remember thinking he looked like an enraged grizzly bear. Had four men not jumped between those two managers, a fistfight would have broken out. We took a half-hour break to cool down, and I then asked a few questions. The production supervisor was rewarded each day, he said, for the number of bottles produced—with no regard to quality. The QC manager was punished when the quality of bottles fell too low.

Watching the two men snarl at each other, restrained by other arms, I got a visceral experience of the powerful emotions that rise up when someone says, "Tell the truth," in organizations.

Seeing and telling the truth is a fundamental component of personal mastery, and of the related discipline of shared vision. (Truth, in this case, doesn't mean the "absolute truth," but simply the truth as you see it.) Because creative tension depends on a clear understanding of current reality, it drains away as soon as people lie to themselves or each other. Why, then, is it so difficult for people in organizations to tell the truth? Why is it especially difficult when the truth helps—when it *empowers* us to take corrective actions or make choices in favor of what we truly want?

The answer stems from conflicts between honesty and loyalty. Most of us live and work in structures in which the need to tell the truth clashes with other loyalties built into the system. These loyalties—to the "boss," to rewards and incentives, or to longstanding attitudes about what is important—are typically rooted deep enough that they come first. If personal mastery enters an organization, with its emphasis on commitment to the truth, there will be an arduous stage during which the two sets of loyalties clash.

THE "PINCH POINTS" OF DISHONESTY

The production supervisor, for instance, was pinched between two untenable choices. He could tell the truth, stop production to ensure the quality of the bottles, remain loyal to the plant's overall performance—and give up his bonus (and the deeper loyalty to the CEO's true motive). Or he could continue to slip bad bottles past the QC manager and remain loyal to the incentives built into the system, doing his best to pretend there was no conflict. Since different people in the same structure produce qualitatively similar results, most of us would probably respond with the same solution—"flexible honesty," as he called it.

A similar pinch point occurs in organizations which routinely "shoot the messenger" who raises significant bad news. Surfacing the truth, while loyal to the organization's long-term improvement, is impossible, because there is no support for it. Hiding the truth means denying one's own perception. Most people end up standing in the middle, trying to balance the loyalties without conflict, taking the burden of the problem on their shoulders and doing what they can to fix it covertly. This is a particularly frustrating compromise, because the three loyalties—to the truth, their position, and the peace—can't all be satisfied at once.

The only sustaining loyalty is loyalty to the truth. All loyalties which prompt us to avoid looking at current reality, including most forms of "flexible honesty," will sooner or later run aground against the organization's environment. Indeed, the policy of "flexible honesty," and the quality problems it engendered, eventually brought that bottling plant in the Appalachians close to bankruptcy.

REMOVING BARRIERS TO TELLING THE TRUTH

How then do you reconcile loyalty to the truth with the other loyalties people feel?

■ *Look for the systemic blocks that prevent individuals from speaking out.* Look at the full range of formal and informal punishments for speaking frankly: they might include, for example, a pattern of sarcastic humor and put-downs. At that bottling plant, after the chief financial officer reminded the CEO of his own support for the "flexible honesty" mind-set, the CEO made seven harsh personal remarks about the CFO—"all in fun"—within the next twenty minutes.

Punishments for telling the truth might extend to unnecessary grunt work, demotions, and termination. At the executive council meeting of another company, a sales executive snarled to a subordinate who raised bad news, "You better fasten your seat belt, son. You're going for a ride." Thereafter, the subordinate had to call in each morning and afternoon with his sales targets—an unusual and humiliating measure. Eventually, and after much penance, he was fired. Later it was proven that the point he had made long ago in that executive council meeting was correct.

- *Provide context and training for the truth.* Members of an organization must be given the information they need to understand the truths they are told from above. A CEO at a small manufacturing firm gave an important speech to all the employees on the frightening financial position of the organization, the impact on its bond rating and the need for cutting costs drastically. He wanted to spark a spirit of problem solving and cooperation. But many people in the audience were unprepared. Lost in the details, they tried to fill in the meaning from the CEO's tone of voice and the fact that he had called this special meeting. They walked away saying, "If we don't get more product out, people's heads are going to roll." Follow up such speeches with dedicated training that helps people interpret the facts.

⟩⟩ One valuable technique for this is dialogue; see the GS Technologies story on page 364.
⟩⟩ Also see our review of *The Great Game of Business,* page 542.

- *When you can't keep loyal to the* letter *of the truth, remain loyal to the* spirit. When an employee has resigned, for example, often the whole truth from the management side cannot be told. In one management conference, the CEO explained to the assembled people why a popular senior manager would not be promoted to an executive council slot. "Some of you have voiced your concern to me about why Kathleen is not getting this position," he said. "She and I have talked about it, and we feel she is not ready for this job yet. Nonetheless, I am committed to her development." He didn't explain what "not ready" meant; nonetheless, people commented with admiration on the candor and respect he had shown, and Kathleen said she felt relieved. She felt that he had made a public commitment to her development and the whispers behind her back would stop.

■ *Set up a formal amnesty policy.* "When you begin a quality program," says Bill Conway, one of the eminent consultant/authors in the Total Quality field, "it's important to offer amnesty to anyone who tells the truth. Otherwise," he says, "people will inevitably fudge or misrepresent the data they collect. People need to know that if they are punished for telling the truth, they have a nonthreatening way to appeal." In every learning organization, some formal policy should institutionalize the concept that there is no point in blaming an individual for system-related problems.

Amnesty is always a two-way street. When senior executives make a mistake, with no ill intent or wrongdoing, and then tell the truth about it, they need to know that they will be given "amnesty" by the employees, their peers, and the board.

Moments of Awareness*

Rick Ross

* This exercise is adapted from: *You're in Charge: A Guide to Becoming Your Own Therapist* by Janette Rainwater, Ph.D. (1979, 1989, Marina del Rey, Calif.: DeVorss and Company), p. 11. Janette Rainwater's book offers many variations on this "mindfulness" exercise, and describes some other basic tools for self-knowledge: journals, autobiographies, body and health awareness, dream remembering, and meditation.

We have also borrowed some phrasing from Robert Fritz's "pivotal technique in the creative orientation" (*The Path of Least Resistance*, (1984, New York: Fawcett/Columbine), p. 135.

You can practice this exercise any time. The trick is getting yourself to practice it when you most need it—at stressful moments. You can get into the habit of reminding yourself, "Remember Ma." Then you can run through the exercise.

Pause and ask yourself:

1. What is happening *right now?*
   Stretch it out by asking yourself three subsidiary questions:
   What am I doing right now?
   What am I feeling right now?
   What am I thinking right now?
   Then ask a second primary question:
2. What do I want right now?
   In other words, ask yourself what you are trying to achieve in this conversation. Often, simply the act of asking this question will provoke a change, without your making a deliberate decision to change.
   This can lead you to a third question:
3. What am I doing right now to prevent myself from getting what I want?

Make a choice at this moment. All you need to do is to say the phrase to yourself, "I choose . . ."

And finally,

4. Take a deep breath, and move on.

Now that you know what you want, move toward it. Sometimes this means moving directly to a goal you are now aware of. Other times, as Robert Fritz suggests, just change the focus of your attention. Change the subject. Shift gears. Do whatever occurs to you; just don't remain stuck trying to push at the same stuck situation.

MOMENTS OF AWARENESS IN ACTION

I use this exercise in the midst of fast-paced argumentative conversation, when I'm most likely to forget. For instance, recently someone stood up a workshop and asked me to summarize everything I'd said for two days. Rage rose within me—hadn't he been *listening?*—and I snapped back at him: "That question is full of bull." Then I "remembered my Ma" and I asked myself:

What is happening? "I'm in a confrontation."

What are you doing? "Well, I'm arguing. In fact, I'm pushing back at this guy as hard as I know how."

What are you feeling? "I'm upset. I'm pissed off."

What are you thinking? "I've concluded that either this fellow's an obnoxious individual, or he's deliberately trying to trip me up."

How am I breathing? "I'm puffing—okay? Want to make something out of it?"

What do I want, right now, for myself?

My immediate answer to this last question usually emerges as, "What I *don't* want." And I often step myself through a series of small realizations from there:

"I don't want this guy to make me look like a dummy in front of the group. Actually, when I think about it, I don't want to continue this conversation. What *do* I want? I want him to shut up. No, I want his understanding. I don't necessarily want to understand *him* better, but I'd sure like him to have a better sense of what *I'm* saying. It's not easy to articulate this material, and I'm upset because I don't know how to answer his question, and that anger spilled out."

By now, of course, I was gradually realizing that this guy had stepped

PURPOSE

Some readers of this book are, no doubt, like me—the kind of people who habitually talk first and then ask questions later. Among the questions we ask are: "Why did I say what I just said? Why didn't I stop and think?"

Moments of awareness (or "Ma," for short) is an exercise for engaging in real-time reflection; stopping in the moment and taking a quick reading of our current reality. When practiced regularly, it gives you the ability to engage people constructively and thoughtfully, as events are taking place—which is far more effective than shooting off your mouth.

on something sensitive to me, something I didn't see before. So then I asked myself:

And what am I doing to prevent myself from getting what I want?

"Well, probably, just pushing on him, as hard as I can. If I apologized, it might be easier to figure a way out."

Okay. Take a deep breath, and move on.

In the seconds it took me to run through these questions, my attitude and behavior had changed. I hadn't planned this moment—far from it—but now I chose to use it. I apologized to the man I had snapped at and described my thought processes to the group. Some participants said later that it was a powerful part of the workshop, simply because it showed them a real-time example of how reflection helps unstick these sudden bouts of anxiety, rage, and frustration.

"Moments of Awareness" is a very simple technique to master. Getting myself to actually practice it, at the moment I need it, is another ball game, but I'm getting better at that, too. Mindfulness—the skill of being present—offers incalculable rewards for people who tend to get hung up in anxiety, anger, despair, confusion, or their own self-image.

28 The Power of Choice

Bryan Smith

In "Leadership and Mastery" seminars at Innovation Associates, we include an exercise called "The Power of Choice." We ask people to formally choose the aspects of their personal vision to which they wish to commit themselves. It feels to some people as if, with their vision, they have set a number of options out on a shelf to consider. Now they are walking up to select the things they want to keep for the rest of their lives.

In teams, at the end of shared vision exercises, we do something similar. I ask for silence and say, "If you can honestly say you're whole-heartedly committed to choosing this vision, and bringing it to reality, please stand up. And if you're not, please stay seated." This is a serious, not a rhetorical question. Although most of the room, by that time, will probably stand, there are often individuals who remain in their seats.

They are then given a chance to say what would have to be added or changed before they would stand up.

You can make such choices when facing a group, facing another person, or merely facing a mirror. But that moment of commitment is vitally important. It means you are willing to devote your time and effort to making your vision come about. This is not necessarily an easy choice. Nine times out of ten, with your limited time and energy, you must choose among alternative visions of where your life *might* go. Which choice are you going to take?

Making a choice is much more powerful than saying, "I want . . ." even when the vision itself is exactly the same. After choosing, the vision itself feels more enriched, and the task of reaching it more creative. As with any life-changing choice—a marriage, the choice to bring a child into the world, or the choice of a career—there is a custodial sense invoked. You become a servant to the vision you have chosen: a partner in the process of making it come to life.

We do not present a "choosing" exercise in this book. We believe that you should make the choices in whatever manner, with whatever rituals, suit you best. It may be as simple as returning to the pages on which you have written elements of your vision, and actively choosing those which you are ready to choose. Simply say the words, formally, to yourself: "I choose . . ." and then complete the sentence with the aspect of the vision you are focusing on. For example: "I choose full self-expression." You may want to sit with a trusted colleague or friend and state your choices to them. Or you may simply consciously decide that *this* personal vision is truly worth your time and energy. Having made that choice, the vision will become part of you—wherever it may lead.

29 Innovations in Infrastructure for Encouraging Personal Mastery

Charlotte Roberts

Not long ago, an executive vice president introduced himself at an Innovation Associates course by saying, "I've lost five good people through this program. I'm here to find out what's been going on in my organization." At the end of the course (which included much personal mastery material), he said he understood; his employees felt they weren't free to pursue their own visions at his company. "I want to re-work the structures," he said, "that made these people feel blocked."

One of the most intriguing aspects of personal mastery is the changes it induces in an organization's design. When organizations embrace personal mastery they are compelled to rethink their investment in developing the capabilities of employees. This does not just involve an investment of money. To encourage personal mastery, an organization must invest intelligence, time, and attention, taking the trouble to design new elements of infrastructure.

A "transformation and discovery" department

DEVELOPING A VISION AND PERCEIVING CURRENT REALITY CAN'T BE handed off to specialists, so the temptation to make "Training and Development" responsible for the organization's "personal mastery" should be resisted. Nonetheless, there can be a significant, and much-needed *service* role for "T&D" as the purveyors of lifelong learning for people who pursue their personal visions.

For example, I want to be a better public speaker and develop a more compelling stage presence. I take acting lessons—not because I love the theater, but because I value the education it can give me. I have seen other people, after an exercise in personal vision, seek training in carpentry, crafting a budget, using Total Quality tools, and creative writing.

A "Transformation and Discovery" department could abet this by becoming much closer to its customers—not the senior managers who typically approve training programs, but individuals (and teams) who articulate what they need to know. This T&D department would customize its offerings, using many more outside courses and trainers, and computer-aided learning, evaluating their success based on whether they actually "transformed" the learners, leaving them more capable than before.

"Discovery" would not mean teaching people how to discover. The training department would actively engage in discovering *itself:* continually anticipating people's needs and interests. "What are people likely to want to learn next year? Where is the rest of the industry, or the rest of society, going? What types of training should we begin preparing now?"

New performance appraisal systems

ALMOST EVERYONE IN ORGANIZATIONS ESPOUSES THE IDEA THAT A PERformance appraisal should be an interactive dialogue—where even good performers sit down and check their progress and purpose. But very few organizations conduct appraisals that way. Personal vision and current reality provide an appropriate vehicle for redesigning performance appraisals.

Your manager, or whoever is responsible for judging your work, would ask questions that draw forth aspirations:

- What do you want to accomplish here this year? What do you want to accomplish during the next few years? (Vision)
- What assets do you have to help accomplish this? What liabilities stand in your way?
- What do you need from the company to help?
- What do I do, as your supervisor, that gets in your way?
- What is your pattern of failure? What danger signals should I look for ahead of time, so I know to come talk to you and help you?

"Now that I'm familiar with quality techniques," a junior manager might say, "I want to learn how to lead with them. I want to spend some time as an internal consultant to other divisions." The supervisor would respond: "Well, in that case, we've got to build some connections for you. You may need to learn more skills, and you have to develop some-one to take over your current duties." Given a structure that supports mentoring in this fashion, even supervisors with rudimentary people skills may find it easier to support and develop the people who work for them.

For some managers, this type of appraisal represents a leap of faith: that what people want for their own careers would also be best for the organization. For individuals, it implies a much deeper level of respon-sibility: it's the employees' own task to see what they want, and to see current reality clearly—including the organization's need for what they might have to offer.

An early-information system

WHEN PLANTS MUST BE CLOSED OR LAYOFFS TAKE PLACE, EMPLOYEES need a clear picture of what is happening in current reality, and the opportunity to develop their personal vision. This suggests planning ahead to present the news of the downsizing as early as possible, and providing opportunities for people to rethink their goals in a supportive, knowledgeable context. We have seen some companies that close plants train their departing people to generate and hold creative tension, in place of the traditional "how-to-write-a-resumé" outplacement training. For younger managers and workers, this seems far more effective, be-cause it approaches more fundamental needs. Older employees have a tougher time; for many, their personal vision has been long tied to sta-bility and community, often based around the plant itself. Even there, it's an important step to separate the end of their jobs from the question of what they really want.

Ways to test personal visions against the company's culture

LAST YEAR, AN ENGINEER AT AN AEROSPACE COMPANY IN THE SOUTHEAST came up to me after a talk on personal vision. "I'm gay," he said, "and my vision includes coming out of the closet. I share my life with another man, and I'd like him to come with me to company picnics and gather-ings. I'd like to keep advancing here, but I'm not sure anyone here will accept me as a gay person. If they can't, then I think I ought to move on. How can I find out whether or not I would be accepted?"

I asked him, "What makes you think they won't understand and value you, despite your sexual orientation?" He mentioned some incidents at work: "I've seen them tear people apart in project reviews and make their lives miserable." I asked if he could test this view of reality quietly with an ally, and he said there was no one within the firm with whom he felt safe taking the risk. "These guys are hard-nosed, competitive, and judgmental."

That company, I realized, would lose him, because he would continue to move toward his personal vision of being open at work. If he couldn't even test the possibility there, his vision would provide him the momentum to find another employer.

This sort of conundrum is typical among people who begin thinking about their vision. It need not involve anything controversial like sexual orientation. It could start with not wanting to relocate, or being told to implement a policy that feels inappropriate. When they can't test that block, because they're afraid to raise the question, they move on. Organizations that hope to avoid losing these people need an inviolably discreet ombudsman, who can show people how to test these questions more effectively: "How do you know the barriers are as strong as you think they are? What can we do to check out our assumptions about them?"

Hold regular meetings *Susan Frank*

It seems so simple at first glance . . . but personal mastery takes a lot of practice. Only 10 to 15 percent of all participants who attend training programs can consistently apply the insights and skills they learned back in the workplace. Typically, they simply run out of steam. Under stressful situations, they can't generate the energy to master and apply new skills, so they revert back to old habitual ways of doing things.

Organizations can help by providing structured opportunities for practice. For example, holding weekly meetings to talk about vision and current reality give people a structure in which to reestablish and revisit creative tension. People can use one another as a resource. They can coach each other in articulating and enriching their vision, based on what matters to them. They can learn more about current reality from recent experiences, and develop small experimental projects that reveal the strengths and limits of their own creative skills.

30 Instilling Personal Mastery at Beckman Instruments

Wilson Bullard

Wilson Bullard is product development group leader at Beckman Instruments, one of a very few managers who has personally carried the ball on a personal mastery effort, relying on his own perseverance and conviction. When people don't get immediate results, they often want to shut down an experiment. Wilson said, "Let's give it some time." He was right: it took six months or more for Beckman to show results. This may seem like a simple story, but it's one of the most powerful in the book, because it shows what it takes to be a champion of this material.

Last year, when I read *The Fifth Discipline,* the "Personal Mastery" section struck a particularly strong chord with me. As a scientist at a technology-based company, I have the good fortune of working with an organization which is open to experimentation. (Our group develops instrument systems and reagents for the medical diagnostics industry.) Some of our openness has to do with the pressure we feel to improve our overall process for new product delivery. No one has the road map to that improvement, so we're willing to look at opportunities. People at Beckman Instruments go through a lot of team training, but we generally talk about teams only in an operational sense—What is this team going to *do?*—rather than in any kind of personalized, behavioral, individual sense. We rarely talk about how our personal values relate to the purpose of the team or company.

Personally, I have always felt that the quality of human relations is fundamental to an organization's performance. When I read about the personal mastery discipline, I thought I might have found a vehicle for exploring the power of human relations at Beckman. Perhaps this discipline could help us realize some of the potential which I knew existed. It was at least worthy of experiment.

So I started looking around for an outside consultant who could work with my department. We hired Dr. James Milojkovic, a Bay Area organizational learning consultant, to lead my team in a two-day workshop.

Our objective was to learn about the disciplines, particularly building shared vision and team learning.

Our two days of contact time were very intensive. I can't say they were a lot of fun. Before long, the balance of conversation began to shift toward the personal mastery material. We began to talk, fairly stridently, about the behaviors that were personally important to us, and vital to our success as an operating team. Some of the behaviors came out of the learning disciplines; others were based on our own priorities. Trust was number one. Also near the top of the list was presence—the ability to shake off the dogs that are biting at you, and focus yourself clearly on what the team is trying to accomplish. Honesty was important, along with openness—the willingness to consider different points of view and perspectives. We included the abilities to surface mental models, to balance advocacy and inquiry, and to participate. We went so far as to create a matrix chart that allowed us, as individuals, to assess ourselves and each other. Having agreed that certain behaviors were important, we needed a way to test if we were practicing them.

This was the first time people had talked about their behavior in any structured way, with any mutual openness, and it had a profound effect. It brought up a new level of trust among us, especially as fears surfaced and were resolved. As the organizer of that session, I came out of it realizing that these new behaviors had to be tied to our deeply held personal values. This concept was not new to the world, but it was new to me. A very compelling feeling was growing within me, that I could not begin to address personal mastery organizationally until I dealt with it myself.

THE CHRISTMAS BREAK VISION EXERCISE

Thus, over the Christmas break the following month, I spent some time writing out my own personal and professional vision. What really mattered to me? How did I see my future in terms of my values? Who, what, and where did I want to be? I committed all of the answers to paper—then signed and dated it. The bottom line, for me, was a single statement: "My job will merge with my life."

Since then, I have been asking around, and I have found that very few people conduct this exercise. I did it because I felt inspired at that moment. I didn't expect anything specific to come from it. But writing out my personal vision was an unexpected breakthrough. Only after this did I know how to talk to people about aspirations—how to ask them what they felt the organization should be, for example.

I started with my own staff—people who, like me, had never spent much time thinking about their aspirations. Now I invited them to try to visualize what their future might be, and to articulate their desires for a professional future at Beckman, keeping in front of them their personal values. This is not routinely done, anywhere in our organization, and it required some new ways of thinking and behaving. For example, I struggle to be as much of a colleague as I can be with my staff, but the model still holds that it is *my* staff and they have to go along with me. I had to work the fine line between their "doing it to satisfy me," and doing it because they saw intrinsic value in it.

This phase of the personal mastery effort began four months ago, but we already have enough experience to know that the energy that fuels this transformation comes from personal values. If you can find out what really matters to individuals, and only then pull in the other disciplines and start developing a strong shared vision, you kick the whole learning effort into high gear. We've discovered that taking an experimental approach, in which we invite people to move at their own speed, produces a much greater level of enthusiasm and commitment than if I commanded them to "get together behind a vision." I now firmly believe that this is the right thing to do; and if we can pull it off, we will be very successful.

31 Intrapersonal Mastery

Charlotte Roberts

During the last several years, I (and other practitioners of the learning disciplines) have begun to wonder if something significant is missing in our descriptions of personal mastery. Is vision limited to our *personal* appetites and aspirations? Or can the discipline help us look beyond ourselves, to develop a sense of where our aspirations come from, how and why they call to us, and what they are made of?

Traditional personal mastery practice is centered around a shift in people's view of their relationship to the world. In Robert Fritz's terms, it's a shift from being "reactive" (responding to events), to "creative" (creating the future you want). I now believe that, as people practice personal mastery, they can begin to pass into a third orientation: "interdependent," in which you and the world are intimately interrelated. The shift between orientations is significant because it affects every aspect of a person's ability to participate in the work of learning organizations. It affects how individuals draw knowledge from experience; how they understand and act upon systems; and the types of visions they create.

It's important to remember that we do not live in any of these frames of mind all the time. We might have an "interdependent" attitude toward civic life, a "creative" attitude toward work, and a "reactive" relationship with our significant other. More likely, in all arenas of our lives, our orientations may constantly shift. Herein lies the need for intrapersonal mastery—if you can understand how you see yourself, you can more deliberately shift from one orientation to another. In the long run, this could have a dramatic effect—not so much on your ability to achieve results, as on the type of results you seek and achieve.

The "reactive" orientation: "the world is happening to me"

THE WORLD, FROM THE VIEWPOINT OF THIS ORIENTATION, IS FULL OF forces which exist outside you and act upon you. You play the hand you're dealt and consider yourself smart if you can figure out ahead of time what cards are coming your way. Your learning is political: you are skilled at finding unfriendly forces to blame. Was it the economy? The weather? The in-crowd? The politicians? You respond "pro-actively," often with political gamesplaying and heroic fire fighting of your own. When you study systems, your purpose is defensive: to see what the system is doing, and avoid its unpleasant consequences. Your personal visions are similarly negative: "I want to get out of this situation," or "I want to be left alone," or "I just don't want to be tricked again." This is, in fact, the orientation of a hero who is toyed with by the whims of god and fate, traveling down what mythologist Joseph Campbell called "the road of trials."*

Many organizations unintentionally encourage the reactive orientation, by keeping most employees out of any meaningful participation in decisions, planning, or learning. With no opportunity to take responsibility themselves, people learn to keep their defenses up, duck blame, and avoid initiative. They are toyed with, in their view, not by gods and fates but by "those people on the top floor"—the senior managers who lay people off, raid pension funds, and make arbitrary policies. The boss,

What do they want now? Who did this to me?

* See *The Hero with a Thousand Faces*, by Joseph Campbell (1949, Princeton, N.J.: Bollingen), p. 97.

meanwhile, feels beset by a different level of gods and fates—the demands of customers, competitors, and employees. Reactive orientations tend to reinforce each other in organizations, breeding fear, hostility, apparent laziness, and apathy. I have known people, enmeshed in these sorts of organizations, who have never seen evidence of any other way of working.

The reactive orientation, of course, is equally common outside the organization. For many people, it's borne out by their life stories (as they see them). Disease, loss, and untimely death affect our lives; we can't brush aside such tragedies just by saying, "Get a vision." And yet . . . people who can escape this orientation seem to have more strength of character for handling tragedy. Perhaps it's because the way we interpret these bad events affects our self-esteem and effectiveness; people in the reactive orientation see the world as a basically unfriendly place, separate and apart from them.

What do I want to create for myself and the people I care about?
How did I create this situation?

The "creative" orientation: "I create my future"

IN THE CREATIVE ORIENTATION, YOU MOVE THROUGH LIFE ASKING: "What do I want to create?" Instead of blaming the world, you ask how you caused your circumstances to happen, and what you need to do to change them. You learn rapidly from experience, and continually improve your ability to take effective action and produce results. You know how to effectively investigate systems, using a variety of tools to find leverage points and propose innovative solutions. Your visions are equally far-ranging and effective: you know what you want to bring into the world, and how you want to make your mark. You don't feel limited by today's reality. People think of you as a leader because you know where you are going and you can get people to go along. If you are successful, they call you "self-made." (They may also call you "self-centered.")

When a creative orientation is part of an organization's culture, people work long hours. The culture expects them to "do what it takes." The reward system acknowledges outstanding performance, and yet, it's challenging to stand out in such a field of stars. As they continue increasing their capabilities to create the results they want, the people in this organization become more confident and competent. By nearly every yardstick, including the ability to appear ethical and responsible, this is a dynamic organization, an organization of winners.

And yet . . . there's still something unsatisfying about the creative orientation. Don't get me wrong; for many people it represents a genuine triumph over the reactive orientation. But it is the opposite side of the same coin: like the reactive stance, the creative stance sets you "apart from" the rest of the world. Creatively oriented business people, for example, may see how they are strategically dependent on customers or suppliers, but they establish sharp, distinct, impenetrable boundaries between themselves and these others. It's as if they say to themselves, "I'll get out there and 'do it' to those other people." They do not permit themselves to identify with anyone but themselves.

Physicist David Bohm uses the word "fragmentation" to describe the fundamental assumption that we are separate from the world. As Bohm points out, this is a fundamentally unfulfilling way of thinking. Perhaps that explains why, despite its worthwhile qualities, the creative orientation often leads to vicious rivalry and extraordinarily self-centered behavior in organizations. It seems to breed a fast-paced, exhausting way of life, where you are always expected to do, to create, and to shape the world in your image.

The interdependent orientation

THE INTERDEPENDENT ORIENTATION PROVIDES A MODEL WHICH, WHILE not swallowing you against your will, gives you the personal, visceral sense that you are part of a greater whole. There is a kinship between your internal awareness and your external reality, because both are part of the same system. Although you recognize your integrity as a separate person, you also feel "a part of" the system which is your environment. This "a-part-of-ness" is dynamic, evolving over time.

This orientation—which has surfaced in many forms throughout human history—represents an alternative to efforts to control the world. As Joseph Campbell reminds us, "No tribal rite has yet been recorded which attempts to keep winter from descending."° The interdependent orientation recognizes that you can't command the larger system, any more than a cell can command a body.

° *The Hero with a Thousand Faces,* op. cit., p. 384.

You cannot even fully know the vast web of interrelationships which enmesh, affect, and (in a sense) create you. But you can learn, as MIT professor Fred Kofman puts it, to "touch the web." You can distinguish those interrelationships which are significant. Personal vision evolves away from getting what you want. Instead, you ask, as Fred Kofman puts it: "Who is the 'I' that wants when I say 'I want'?" You realize that, as much as you "want" your vision, you are also its instrument—the steward and servant of a larger purpose, as if the web itself were pulsing with a purpose, and you are the expression of that purpose. You feel no desire to gain at the expense of anyone or anything else—not because of your sympathy or altruism, but because you recognize that the fate of the larger world inevitably comes back to affect your own fate. This desire for "rightfulness" is surprisingly common; people working to clarify their personal vision often wrestle internally, trying to balance what they want for themselves with what they want for the larger system: the organization, nation, or planet.

Perhaps the best articulation I have heard of this worldview came from the physician/author George Sheehan, who spoke at a national conference I attended in 1979. "Unless you are an identical twin," he said, "you are a unique, never-to-be-repeated event. Your parents could make love a million times and never again reproduce the same genetic pattern. You are the only chance this planet has for your unique contribution. Will others' expectations, rules and roles be your focus? Will you be only what you think you should be? *Or will you occur?*"

I left that talk deeply puzzled. How could I possibly know if I was or wasn't "occurring"? At first, it sounded like a good opportunity to heap responsibility and guilt onto myself. Yet the question kept returning to me during reflective moments. If I were unique, as he said, what would be calling me to occur? If I am an expression of the world, then why would I need to make a commitment? And to whom would I make this commitment? In my own past, there were threads that seemed close to the commitment I had made: for instance, a drive to teach which dated back to my earliest experiences at school, when I regularly helped other children with their work. For most of my life, I had regarded this drive as simply "what I did"—now I began to think of it as a calling, something which the world around me called forth from me. The most relevant and enduring component of my personal vision was completely mine, but I had no feeling that I had generated it myself.

Intrapersonal mastery

LIVING EFFECTIVELY IN THE INTERDEPENDENT ORIENTATION REQUIRES an expansion of personal mastery. My term for this discipline is "intrapersonal" mastery. Intrapersonal mastery embraces the interdependent orientation, but in order to be masterful in the outside world, it is necessary to start the practice of mastery deeply within oneself.

Do you remember the child's game "Electricity"? Children stand in a circle holding hands. One child stands in the middle, tagged as "it," watching closely to see the flow of "electricity" (which passes when each child squeezes the next child's hand). If a child in the circle is caught by surprise and doesn't squeeze the next hand in time, then that child can be tagged by the child in the middle. The surprised child becomes "it," and moves to the center of the circle. In this game, children learn to be aware of the flow of squeezes; otherwise, they will be tagged when it comes back to them.

The practice of intrapersonal mastery is similar. We ready ourselves for the conversation, thoughts, emotions, déjà vu, resources, options, problems, opportunities, trials, and questions that flow between us and the rest of the system. We become more attuned to the passage of time, developing a stronger innate sense of how soon we should expect to see change after we act. We learn to recognize when our actions are consistent with the flow of the greater system around us. Knowing how we create each other's world, we develop a stronger sense of responsibility.

In organizations, intrapersonal mastery leads us to think of all resources as shared—from the secretarial pool to the rationed water supply to the social responsibility for generations to come. The nature of the vision for the organization changes. Don Burr, former founder and CEO of People Express, was asked by MBA students at Harvard why he started the airline. He said, "M.A.B.W."—his own acronym for "making a better world." Many executives have stepped over the invisible psychological line to intrapersonal leadership—as servant, steward, and teacher. When it is time to develop strategies, they ask: "Who will our actions impact? How will we involve them in the decisions and planning? On what basis will we conclude that our actions are right or wrong?" In developing an interdependent vision, people begin to ask themselves such questions as: How can we grow an organization where our great-grandchildren might be proud to work?

An interdependent vision can be realized only through collaborative action, so relationships at work become central. We need to find others who serve the grand vision and are willing to tenaciously collaborate to make sure the vision occurs. The organization becomes a living entity, of which each member of the collective body is a guardian, engaged in bringing about the group's purpose. Building shared understanding of the grand vision is a continuous process of endless dialogue. As customers and suppliers are brought into this process, the distinctions between them and employees begin to blur.

The frontier of personal mastery lies within. As you work with personal vision and current reality, reflect on the orientation from which you perceive them. When do you view the world reactively? When creatively? When interdependently? Which of these orientations do you choose, for which aspects of your life? Seeing the orientations more clearly will help you see the sources of both your fears and aspirations.

32 Where to Go from Here

Charlotte Roberts

- **To mental models:** One key ability for personal mastery is reflection. Your own theories and models of the world are part of your current reality. Personal mastery gives you a compelling reason to reflect on how your underlying assumptions may block you from realizing your vision. You may be able to develop and test new mental models, such as the idea that intrinsic motivation is more effective than "carrot-and-stick" motivation, which allows you to direct your own learning and development more effectively. See page 242.
- **To shared vision:** Personal mastery leads naturally to shared vision. To realize your individual vision, you will inevitably need the help of other people, which means galvanizing others to help create that vision. See page 297.
- **To systems thinking:** Once you realize that you can create your future, you will see how you have contributed to creating your present. Understanding and deepening your appreciation of current reality requires understanding the interrelationships and connections among our internal structures (values, beliefs, and attitudes) and external structures (family, work, career). A good starting point is page 94.

Mental Models

33 Strategies for Working with Mental Models

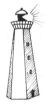

A man visits a therapist and says, "I've just gotten fired, for the seventh time in the last five years. I'm having trouble with my wife, and I've already been divorced three times. I desperately need you to help me understand: Why are there so many screwed-up people out there in the world?"

Imagine that instead of a therapist, this man came to you. And you genuinely wanted to help him. What would you say? You might find yourself speaking empathetically: "Yes, a lot of bad bosses exist, and I'm sure there are some unpleasant spouses out there." But if you wanted to do any good in the long run, sooner or later you would have to show him how his problems were not created "out there." They stemmed, at least in part, from his own assumptions and beliefs about other people. Unless you found a way to help him see this, all your other attempts to help would be short-lived and probably doomed to failure.

Mental models are the images, assumptions, and stories which we carry in our minds of ourselves, other people, institutions, and every aspect of the world. Like a pane of glass framing and subtly distorting our vision, mental models determine what we see. Human beings cannot navigate through the complex environments of our world without cognitive "mental maps"; and all of these mental maps, by definition, are flawed in some way.

A common workshop exercise involves asking people to arm wrestle with a neighbor. We tell them that "winning" means bringing their opponent's arm to the table, and we ask them to "win" as many times as they can in fifteen seconds. Most people pit themselves against their opponent, struggling to push the other person's arm down. But a few partners look at each other, and then spend the fifteen seconds flipping their arms back and forth, without any resistance, a dozen or more times. They are not held back by the mental model that only one person can "win."

Differences between mental models explain why two people can observe the same event and describe it differently; they are paying attention to different details. Mental models also shape how we act. For example, if we believe people are basically trustworthy, we may talk to new acquaintances far more freely than if we believe most people can't be trusted.

But because mental models are usually *tacit,* existing below the level of awareness, they are often untested and unexamined. They are generally invisible to us—until we look for them. The core task of this discipline is bringing mental models to the surface, to explore and talk about them with minimal defensiveness—to help us see the pane of glass, see its impact on our lives, and find ways to re-form the glass by creating new mental models that serve us better in the world.

Experts are particularly susceptible to difficulties with mental models. Among educators, there is a widespread tacit assumption that "parents don't really know much about what their children need." As a result, well-intentioned school reform efforts have alienated parent groups. The health professionals' mental model that "hospitals are foremost repositories of scientific knowledge for healing the seriously ill" has diminished opportunities for hospitals to serve as community health centers. In manufacturing companies, the deep-seated mental model that "poor quality is caused by laziness or sabotage by hourly workers" endures even among managers who espouse the principles of the quality movement. In work with systems thinking, many insights directly confront our mental models; unless we can suspend and test our attitudes, we will tend to react by saying, "That's interesting . . . but not really relevant to us," with no deeper consideration of the implications.

MENTAL MODELS

The concept of mental models goes back to antiquity, but the phrase (to our knowledge) was coined by Scottish psychologist Kenneth Craik in the 1940s. It has since been used by cognitive psychologists (notably Philip Johnson-Laird of Princeton University), by cognitive scientists (notably Marvin Minsky and Seymour Papert of MIT), and gradually by managers. In cognition, the term refers to both the semipermanent tacit "maps" of the world which people hold in their long-term memory, and the short-term perceptions which people build up as part of their everyday reasoning processes. According to some cognitive theorists, changes in short-term everyday mental models, accumulating over time, will gradually be reflected in changes in long-term deep-seated beliefs.° —AK

° Research by Faith L. Florer and Thomas Fritsch of Miami University and conversation with Professor Johnson-Laird contributed to this lexicon.

Reflection and inquiry

TWO TYPES OF SKILLS ARE CENTRAL TO THIS WORK: THEY ARE REFLECTION (slowing down our thinking processes to become more aware of how we form our mental models) and inquiry (holding conversations where we openly share views and develop knowledge about each other's assumptions). The techniques we most favor for learning these skills emerged from "action science," a field of inquiry developed by theorists and educators Chris Argyris and Donald Schön, aimed at exploring the reasoning and attitudes which underlie human action, and producing more effective learning in organizations and other social systems.

The tools of action science are deceptively simple. For example, the ladder of inference (see page 242), which shows how rapidly we can leap to knee-jerk conclusions with no intermediate thought process, as if rapidly climbing up a ladder in our minds, is a modest metaphor. Yet incorporating it into everyday conversation, so that we internalize the principles of the ladder, has proven to be a pivotal component of learning organization work.

The value of these skills is perhaps most apparent in their absence. Individuals who are undisciplined in reflective thinking have difficulty hearing what others actually say. Instead, they hear what they expect others to say. They have little tolerance for multiple interpretations of events because they often "see" only their own interpretation. In teams and groups, people who have not mastered a threshold level of inquiry skills will spend hours arguing their ideas. Eventually, in frustration and exhaustion, they end up with some kind of compromise, in which no one wins—or they defer to the most senior person in the room, who wins through authority: "This is the strategy. Thank you for your input." The strategy turns out to be far less than it could be.

And what of people who have learned to reflect, talk more openly, and make their assumptions explicit? As you might expect, they have more penetrating conversations, in which talk of strategy always considers their mental models of (for example) where the world is going, what customers want, what competitors will do, how the marketplace is evolving, and what technologies will exist. Moreover, their conversations tend to be more naturally suffused with openness and humor. This makes working with mental models a natural antidote for the typical political gamesmanship bred by conventional "command-and-control" hierarchies. People find ways to diffuse defensiveness by laughing good-naturedly at themselves. At GS Technologies, whose work with labor-management dialogue is described on page 364, the union members went out and bought one of the plant managers a stepladder. He keeps it in his office, and jokes with visitors, "They tell me I live my whole life up on the top rung."

Scenarios and learning laboratories

THE FRONTIER OF THIS DISCIPLINE LIES WITH CREATING INNOVATIONS IN infrastructure where work with mental models can take place. One of the most influential such innovations, scenario planning, has become increasingly widespread and diverse in the last few years. Scenario work, which emerged in the "nonintrospective" culture of Royal Dutch/Shell, traditionally encouraged people to look outward, using stories of the future to surface assumptions about the business and political forces of the present. Gradually, this work seems to be embracing more of an ability to increase interpersonal understanding. For example, former Shell planner Adam Kahane has adapted the scenario approach to work with political leaders in South Africa. He has found that diverse, even antagonistic participants could safely talk about even the most emotionally charged issues. By describing plausible futures, they developed a better understanding of each other's tacit beliefs. The scenario, when used this way, becomes a shared "memory of the future": as people rehearse their views of what will happen, they reveal the differences and similarities in their current views of the world. Says Kahane:

> You may wonder what keeps people, in these highly charged meetings, from walking out. Conservatives and radicals kept coming back because they felt they were learning a great deal—and enjoying themselves. The advantage of scenarios is that, unlike in a negotiation, people don't have to commit their constituents, but they can see a common language—a common way of understanding the world—emerging fairly early in the process. Once the scenario process is over, that common language should make subsequent negotiations easier to conclude successfully.°

° 66 "Scenarios for Building Community," by Adam Kahane (1994; Emeryville, Ca., Global Business Network).

Mental models work is also very central to the design of learning laboratories. When the reflection and inquiry exercises are built into them, laboratories become mental model practice fields, where people develop the skills to talk about their assumptions in "real time"—in the moment that they are dealing with an issue. To talk coherently about attitudes and beliefs, to allow others to point them out, to hear comment about them with involvement but without rancor, and to look more clearly at the sources of our own actions—these capabilities all improve with practice, and particularly with well-structured, supported team practice.

⟩⟩ See, for example, the Ford Learning Lab cameo on page 554.

34 What You Can Expect . . . in Working with Mental Models

Charlotte Roberts

This discipline offers the highest leverage for change. Though it seems to some, at first glance, to be strictly an intellectual exercise, with little relevance to the "real world," it is probably the most practical of the five disciplines. As teams which incorporate this work into their practice will attest, it directly enhances the ability to navigate through changing times.

Unfortunately, it is also the most difficult place from which to *start* building a learning organization. It takes a great deal of perseverance to master this discipline, perhaps because very few of us have learned how to build the skills of inquiry and reflection into our thoughts, emotions, and everyday behavior. When we begin practicing those skills, we bring to the surface some of our unconscious, automatic responses. We see, perhaps for the first time, what we have done to ourselves and others through automatic or incomplete thinking. Even after we get glimpses of our mental models, knowing how to act differently is not obvious.

Practice together over time

THE MOST PRODUCTIVE WAY TO LEARN THESE NEW SKILLS IS WHILE TRY-ing to get to the bottom of the mental models which have created chronic business problems. Hold regular sessions with the same team, perhaps for a period of months. Be prepared to have someone who is skilled in this discipline assist the team for the first few sessions.

Prepare for dealing with strong emotions

PEOPLE WHO ACCEPT DIFFERENT POINTS OF VIEW INTELLECTUALLY MAY have trouble with the emotions raised by this work. When the assumptions behind your models are exposed, they will often be shown to be flawed or incomplete. People will now know why you do the "stupid," "irritating," or "bureaucratic" things you do. You may be chagrined to discover (unfortunately, at the same time as everyone else), that your actions (or those of your team or organization) are based on erroneous data or incomplete assumptions. At the moment of discovery, feelings may rise to the surface: anger at the reasons you gave for your actions; embarrassment at an incorrect assumption; uncertainty about how to challenge someone else; reluctance to talk about a heretofore "undis-cussable" concern; confusion about how to proceed; or fear of retalia-tion.

Because most management teams have little experience as a team at dealing with such fierce emotions, they often let the emotions escalate;

dismay and uncertainty turn into opposition and feelings of betrayal, instead of genuine inquiry and learning. Or, worse, they change the subject and deny that these emotions exist; which paralyzes the group until the subject can be resurfaced and understood. The alternative is to set time aside for dialogue or skillful discussion about the emotions that have been raised.

Exercises that may help include "Moments of Awareness," page 216, and "Undiscussables," page 404. Also see "Dialogue," page 357, and "Skillful Discussion," page 385.

Use frustration as a source of new inquiry

TEAMS STRUGGLE IN MENTAL MODELS WORK, EVEN WHEN IT'S ORIENTED to a business problem. Sometimes they sense that their ability to communicate together is not yet up to the task. Sometimes members need time to reflect, or time to build up a sense of comfort. The team needs to develop strategies for pacing itself—for knowing when to pause, when to pick up again, and how to deal with impasses.

An atmosphere should be established in which frustrations can be brought up for inquiry. If people feel the group lacks enough knowledge to have an adequate mental model of (for example) their customers' needs, they can use questions to explore that perceived inadequacy:

What do we know as a fact about our customers?

What do we sense is true but cannot support with data?

What don't we know? What are our questions and ponderables?

What is unknowable?

What limited experiments can we design to test our current model of our customers?

Beware of excitement and unbridled action

WHEN THE TEAM BREAKS THROUGH THE LIMITATIONS THEY HAVE PUT ON themselves, and they feel that at last they "see" the truth about themselves, their work, or their customers, they will be tempted to take grand action immediately. "No, our customers don't buy on price! They only care about prompt delivery!" They have merely constructed another mental model which, without testing, will produce more blinders. They might rush out to build speedy delivery systems, when the customers really cared about breakage and better packaging. This is the time to pause and reflect upon strategy. Design small experiences to test the new model before making it a standard part of the infrastructure of the organization.

You can create new mental models

MENTAL MODELS MAY BE GENERATIVE; YOU CAN SET ABOUT TO CREATE an attitude which you do not have. The scientists who created the space program (and who still provide that program with its successes) had to envision unimagined possible futures. They conceived of changes in travel, in the ability to create environments, in research, and in energy use that have still not fully taken place.

Generating new mental models, if they are to hold, can take place only by linking imagination with action. Ask yourselves, "If we *did* hold a better model of our customers, how would we behave?" Then try the behavior, and over time see if the new view of the world feels closer to reality.

* Our ladder of inference material includes concepts and examples adapted from *Systems Thinking: A Language for Learning and Acting: The Innovation Associates Systems Thinking Course Workbook* (1992, Framingham, Mass.: Innovation Associates); suggestions from Philip McArthur and Robert Putnam; material from *Overcoming Organizational Defenses* by Chris Argyris (1990,

35 The Ladder of Inference*

Rick Ross

We live in a world of self-generating beliefs which remain largely untested. We adopt those beliefs because they are based on conclusions, which are inferred from what we observe, plus our past experience. Our ability to achieve the results we truly desire is eroded by our feelings that:

■ Our beliefs are *the* truth.
■ The truth is obvious.
■ Our beliefs are based on real data.
■ The data we select are the real data.

For example: I am standing before the executive team, making a presentation. They all seem engaged and alert, except for Larry, at the end of the table, who seems bored out of his mind. He turns his dark, morose eyes away from me and puts his hand to his mouth. He doesn't ask any questions until I'm almost done, when he breaks in: "I think we should ask for a full report." In this culture, that typically means, "Let's move on." Everyone starts to shuffle their papers and put their notes away. Larry obviously thinks that I'm incompetent—which is a shame, because these ideas are exactly what his department needs. Now that I think of it, he's never liked my ideas. Clearly, Larry is a power-hungry jerk. By the time I've returned to my seat, I've made a decision: I'm not going to include anything in my report that Larry can use. He wouldn't read it, or, worse still, he'd just use it against me. It's too bad I have an enemy who's so prominent in the company.

In those few seconds before I take my seat, I have climbed up what Chris Argyris calls a "ladder of inference,"—a common mental pathway of increasing abstraction, often leading to misguided beliefs:*

Needham, Mass.: Allyn and Bacon), pp. 88–89; *Reasoning, Learning, and Action* by Chris Argyris (1982, San Francisco: Jossey-Bass) pp. xvii–xviii, pp. 176–78; *Action Science* by Chris Argyris, Robert Putnam, and Diana McLain Smith (1985, San Francisco: Jossey-Bass), pp. 57–58. See *Fieldbook*, p. 264 for more on these books.

* *S*ee *Overcoming Organizational Defenses*, p. 87.

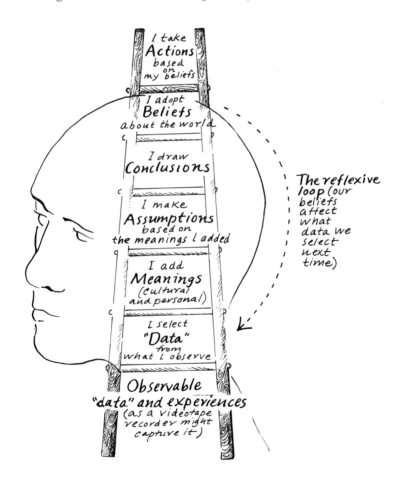

I take **Actions** based on my beliefs

I adopt **Beliefs** about the world

I draw **Conclusions**

I make **Assumptions** based on the meanings I added

I add **Meanings** (cultural and personal)

I select **"Data"** from what I observe

Observable "data" and experiences (as a videotape recorder might capture it)

The reflexive loop (our beliefs affect what data we select next time)

- I started with the observable data: Larry's comment, which is so self-evident that it would show up on a videotape recorder . . .
- . . . I selected some details about Larry's behavior: his glance away from me and apparent yawn. (I didn't notice him listening intently one moment before) . . .
- . . . I added some meanings of my own, based on the culture around me (that Larry wanted me to finish up) . . .
- . . . I moved rapidly up to assumptions about Larry's current state (he's bored) . . .
- . . . and I concluded that Larry, in general, thinks I'm incompetent. In fact, I now believe that Larry (and probably everyone whom I associate with Larry) is dangerously opposed to me . . .
- . . . thus, as I reach the top of the ladder, I'm plotting against him.

It all seems so reasonable, and it happens so quickly, that I'm not even aware I've done it. Moreover, all the rungs of the ladder take place in my head. The only parts visible to anyone else are the directly observable data at the bottom, and my own decision to take action at the top. The rest of the trip, the ladder where I spend most of my time, is unseen, unquestioned, not considered fit for discussion, and enormously abstract. (These leaps up the ladder are sometimes called "leaps of abstraction.")

I've probably leaped up that ladder of inference many times before. The more I believe that Larry is an evil guy, the more I reinforce my tendency to notice his malevolent behavior in the future. This phenomenon is known as the "reflexive loop": our beliefs influence what data we select next time. And there is a counterpart reflexive loop in Larry's mind: as he reacts to my strangely antagonistic behavior, he's probably jumping up some rungs on his own ladder. For no apparent reason, before too long, we could find ourselves becoming bitter enemies.[*]

Larry might indeed have been bored by my presentation—or he might have been eager to read the report on paper. He might think I'm incompetent, he might be shy, or he might be afraid to embarrass me. More likely than not, he has inferred that I think *he's* incompetent. We can't know, until we find a way to check our conclusions.

Unfortunately, assumptions and conclusions are particularly difficult to test. For instance, suppose I wanted to find out if Larry *really* thought I was incompetent. I would have to pull him aside and ask him, "Larry, do you think I'm an idiot?" Even if I could find a way to phrase the question, how could I believe the answer? Would *I* answer *him* honestly?

[*] The "reflexive loop" was first published in William Isaacs's 1992 working paper, *The Ladder of Inference*, published by the MIT Center for Organizational Learning.

No, I'd tell him I thought he was a terrific colleague, while privately thinking worse of him for asking me.

Now imagine me, Larry, and three others in a senior management team, with our untested assumptions and beliefs. When we meet to deal with a concrete problem, the air is filled with misunderstandings, communication breakdowns, and feeble compromises. Thus, while our individual IQs average 140, our team has a collective IQ of 85.

The ladder of inference explains why most people don't usually remember where their deepest attitudes came from. The data is long since lost to memory, after years of inferential leaps. Sometimes I find myself arguing that "The Republicans are so-and-so," and someone asks me why I believe that. My immediate, intuitive answer is, "I don't know. But I've believed it for years." In the meantime, other people are saying, "The Democrats are so-and-so," and they can't tell you why, either. Instead, they may dredge up an old platitude which once was an assumption. Before long, we come to think of our longstanding assumptions as data ("Well, I know the Republicans are such-and-such because they're so-and-so"), but we're several steps removed from the data.

Some ladders of inference :

We can't count on John. He's unreliable.

John always comes in late.

John knew exactly when the meeting was to start. He deliberately came in late.

The meeting was called for 9 AM and John came in at 9:30. He didn't say why.

Using the ladder of inference

YOU CAN'T LIVE YOUR LIFE WITHOUT ADDING MEANING OR DRAWING CONclusions. It would be an inefficient, tedious way to live. But you *can* improve your communications through reflection, and by using the ladder of inference in three ways:

- Becoming more aware of your own thinking and reasoning (reflection);
- Making your thinking and reasoning more visible to others (advocacy);
- Inquiring into others' thinking and reasoning (inquiry).

    Once Larry and I understand the concepts behind the "ladder of inference," we have a safe way to stop a conversation in its tracks and ask several questions:

- What is the observable data behind that statement?
- Does everyone agree on what the data is?
- Can you run me through your reasoning?
- How did we get from that data to these abstract assumptions?
- When you said "[your inference]," did you mean "[my interpretation of it]"?

This boss shouldn't be supervising women.

He picks on Jane because she's a woman.

The boss thinks Jane's work is unacceptable.

The boss is chewing Jane out.

"Jane, your performance is not up to standard," says the boss.

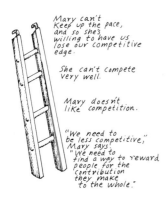

I can ask for data in an open-ended way: "Larry, what was your reaction to this presentation?" I can test my assumptions: "Larry, are you bored?" Or I can simply test the observable data: "You've been quiet, Larry." To which he might reply: "Yeah, I'm taking notes; I love this stuff."

Note that I don't say, "Larry, I think you've moved way up the ladder of inference. Here's what you need to do to get down." The point of this method is not to nail Larry (or even to diagnose Larry), but to make our thinking processes visible, to see what the differences are in our perceptions and what we have in common. (You might say, "I notice I'm moving up the ladder of inference, and maybe we all are. What's the data here?")

This type of conversation is not easy. For example, as Chris Argyris cautions people, when a fact seems especially self-evident, be careful. If your manner suggests that it must be equally self-evident to everyone else, you may cut off the chance to test it. A fact, no matter how obvious it seems, isn't really substantiated until it's verified independently—by more than one person's observation, or by a technological record (a tape recording or photograph).

Embedded into team practice, the ladder becomes a very healthy tool. There's something exhilarating about showing other people the links of your reasoning. They may or may not agree with you, but they can see how you got there. And you're often surprised yourself to see how you got there, once you trace out the links.

The Left-Hand Column*

Rick Ross, Art Kleiner

STEP 1: CHOOSING A PROBLEM
Select a difficult problem you've been involved with during the last month or two, the kind of tough, interpersonal difficulty that many of us try to ignore.

- You can't reach agreement with your close associates.
- Someone else is not pulling his or her weight.

° This exercise is based upon the two-column research method developed by Chris Argyris and Donald Schön. The research method was first presented in their book *Theory in Practice* (1974, San Francisco: Jossey-Bass).

- You believe you are being treated unfairly.
- You believe your point of view is being ignored or discounted.
- The rest of the organization is resisting—or you believe they will resist—a change you want to implement.
- You believe your team is not paying much attention to the most crucial problem.

Write a brief paragraph describing the situation. What are you trying to accomplish? Who or what is blocking you? What might happen?

STEP 2: THE RIGHT-HAND COLUMN (WHAT WAS SAID)

Now recall a frustrating conversation you had over this situation—or imagine the conversation that you *would* have if you brought up the problem.

Take several pieces of paper and draw a line down the center:

(You can also enter this in a word processor with a two-column feature. Use side-by-side columns, or "table" columns, rather than newspaper or "snaking" columns.)

In the right-hand column, write out the dialogue that actually occurred. Or write the dialogue you're pretty sure *would* occur if you were to raise this issue. The dialogue may go on for several pages. Leave the left-hand column blank until you're finished.

STEP 3: THE LEFT-HAND COLUMN (WHAT YOU WERE THINKING)

Now in the left-hand column, write out what you were thinking and feeling, but not saying.

A SAMPLE CASE

Here is an example of the format. An R&D project manager (Jim) assumes his supervisor (Todd) feels harshly about him. In the right-hand column, Jim writes down his last conversation with Todd. In the left, Jim recalls his own thoughts.

PURPOSE

To become aware of the tacit assumptions which govern our conversation and contribute to blocking our purpose in real-life situations, and to develop a way of talking about those tacit assumptions more effectively.

OVERVIEW

Analysis of a transcript of a real exchange— probably recalled, possibly tape-recorded.

TIME

One and one-half to two hours.

What I was thinking	**What we said**
We're two months late, and I didn't think he knew. I was hoping we could catch up.	TODD: *Jim, I'd like to come down there next week. We're a few weeks behind, and I think we might all benefit from a meeting at your office.*
I need to make it clear that I'm willing to take responsibility for this, but I don't want to volunteer for more work.	ME: *I've been very concerned about these deadlines. As you know, we've had some tough luck here, and we're working around the clock. But of course, we'll squeeze in a meeting at your convenience.*
He never offers this help in the planning stages, when I could really use it. It's too late now to bring that up.	TODD: *Well, it's occurred to me that we could use better coordination between us. There are probably some ways I could help.*
The changes he keeps making are the real reason we're late. He must have another one.	ME: *Well, I'm happy to talk through any changes you have in mind.*
	TODD: *I don't have anything specific in mind.*
It's a shame I can't tell him that he's the cause of the delays. If I can hold him off two more weeks, I think we'll be ready.	ME: *I'd like to have a prototype finished to show you before you come down. What if we set up something for the twenty-seventh?*

STEP 4: REFLECTION: USING YOUR LEFT-HAND COLUMN AS A RESOURCE

You can learn a great deal just from the act of writing out a case, putting it away for a week, and then looking at it again. The case becomes an artifact through which you can examine your own thinking, as if you were looking at the thinking of someone else.

As you reflect, ask yourself:

■ What has really led me to think and feel this way?
■ What was your intention? What were you trying to accomplish?
■ Did you achieve the results you intended?

- How might your comments have contributed to the difficulties?
- Why didn't you say what was in your left-hand column?
- What assumptions are you making about the other person or people?
- What were the costs of operating this way? What were the payoffs?
- What prevented you from acting differently?
- How can I use my left-hand column as a resource to improve our communications?

For example, I (Rick) have developed a way of describing my left-hand column to others in a nonaccusatory, nonjudgmental way. I'll use language like this: "Look, I feel like I'm between a rock and a hard spot. The rock is our conversation, my right-hand column. You're saying you want to move ahead with this project rapidly. On the other hand, my own thoughts, my left-hand column, say that if we move ahead with it, we're likely to lose Joe's and Bill's participation. I'm leery of raising this with you because in the past, when I've asked you to slow down for other reasons, you've gotten upset with me."

In group meetings, when you feel angry or frustrated, the left-hand column is particularly valuable. You can stop the action and say, "I realize we've got important work to do, *but* once again I don't think we're focusing on the real issue. Can we check some of our assumptions before we go any further? Let me tell you what I've got in my left-hand column . . ."

In other cases, leverage lies with the conversation itself. Begin by rewriting the previous conversation as you *might* have held it. How could your right-hand column (what you said) bring some of your important left-hand column thinking to the surface? How could you have revealed your thoughts in a way that would contribute to the situation turning out the way you wanted? What could you have said that would effectively inquire into the other person's left-hand column?

For a reality check, show the revised case to a third party (such as a partner; see page 74).

You can also show selected parts of it to the person with whom you had the original conversation. If handled with a sense of inquiry and care, that might be a way to break through your impasse: "I have been making some assumptions about our last conversation, and I wanted to check them with you." Sometimes you may find you both remember the same conversation completely differently. Even when you agree on what you have said, you may have been thoroughly unaware of each other's unvoiced concerns.

When you show your case to the other person, don't approach it as a way to finally clear the air and get your points out in the open. Nor is your purpose to "prettify" your left-hand column by redefining your thoughts in a cosmetically kinder, gentler context. As Robert Putnam notes, some of your left-hand thoughts probably *should* stay hidden. Our internal censors often have a good chunk of wisdom; sometimes these comments would wreak havoc if voiced. Your purpose is to raise the assumptions and mutual misunderstandings whose resolution will most contribute to more fruitful future conversations.

Two good points to continue from here are "Opening Lines" (see page 263) and "Recipes" (see page 260).

Risks and opportunities with "the left-hand column" *Robert Putnam*

Robert Putnam is a long-standing associate of Chris Argyris, and a partner in Action Design, a consulting firm that helps organizations incorporate and implement reflection and inquiry skills. He helped us quite a bit in articulating this chapter. When he read over this material, he said that we should emphasize that achieving the learning potential of this exercise, in particular, requires a skilled facilitator. Because we think the exercise is both conceptually and practically significant, we asked Bob to expand upon his comment. For Bob's insights on using "recipes" to promote learning, see page 260.

When left-hand column cases are discussed in pairs, the learning potential is limited by the abilities of the partners to coach each other effectively. Fundamental learning often requires talking about issues that are difficult to face without being defensive. There are three ways that a coach's ability to help may be limited:

- The coach may share the assumptions and blind spots that limit the case presenter's effectiveness;
- The coach may join in commiserating with the case presenter; "Look how screwed up those other people are." That establishes a sense of good feeling, but it distracts attention from the case presenter's tacit assumptions.
- The coach may not know how to raise the subject of the case presenter's "shortcomings" in a way that promotes inquiry. Imagine that

you are a case presenter, and your coach says, "In a spirit of learning, I think you really screwed it up. You say you want to be honest, but *this* is not honest." You might feel self-conscious, or wonder if you had revealed too much. If you felt misunderstood, you would probably stop yourself from saying so (thereby further diminishing inquiry), for fear that the coach would see you as defensive.

In groups of six to eight people, there is more chance of someone having a valuable insight into the way case presenters create their own difficulties. But most groups are even worse than pairs at raising shortcomings in ways that promote inquiry. A case presenter may receive a barrage of comments that are abstract, attributive, and bluntly advocated. The danger of a poor learning experience is especially high when only one or two members of a group have their cases discussed. They may feel unfairly singled out or ganged up on.

Discussing cases in an intact team creates opportunities for greater impact, but also poses difficulties. As one manager said to me privately, "You want me to lay out my real left-hand column before the group? But that's like my secret sauce. It's helped me survive all these years. If others know what it is, it might not work anymore!"

More serious problems can occur if members of a team give in to the temptation to "let each other have it" with resentments and hitherto-unvoiced judgments that have been building up for months or years. There is often good reason that people have not told each other what is in their left-hand columns. Getting unexpressed thoughts and feelings on the table may be an essential first step, but few teams have the capacity to turn these lemons into lemonade on their own.

At a recent meeting of a business unit, a regional sales manager stood up and said, "Our biggest problem is marketing. They don't know what they're doing. I've been saying this for years, and nothing happens!"

At this moment, Bill's left-hand column might have read: *I'm the only one who's responsible around here for raising this key organizational problem. But I'm not from headquarters, so they figure they can ignore me.*

The others, meanwhile, might have had something like this in their left-hand columns: *Here goes Bill ranting again. He's never willing to take responsibility. Demanding we hire more marketing people is not real-world; we are under pressure to cut expenses. How can we get past this ranting to get something useful done?*

Suppose that this team decided everyone should speak openly about their left-hand columns. Bill would advocate his position, adding that the others were irresponsibly ignoring him because he was from out of town. Others would advocate the opposite position, adding that Bill was an irresponsible obstructionist, and would he please shut up? People would feel angry, tense, and hopeless about resolving the matter. In the best case, some might feel a sense of catharsis at expressing their feelings. Participants would have reason to decide this "left-hand column business" was unproductive.

A skilled facilitator might inquire into each party's reasoning: "Do others confirm Bill's view that too few leads is a major problem? What leads you to doubt that hiring a marketing person is the answer? Bill, when others say we don't have the money to hire someone, do you have any information to the contrary? If not, what leads you to keep arguing for it?" The facilitator might prompt Bill to consider if he is acting from a mental model that says: *My responsibility is fulfilled when I tell people about the problem.* Similarly, the others might consider if they are acting from the mental model: *When someone points out a problem, we can hold them responsible for telling us how to fix it.*

SHOULD YOU HAVE A TRAINED FACILITATOR?

Revealing left-hand columns creates enormous opportunities for learning. To take advantage of these opportunities, it is important that at least one participant has the willingness and skill to promote inquiry, the presence of mind to recognize subtle mental models at play (including his own), *and* an eminent enough position that everyone else in the room will listen to him. In many cases, this requires an outside facilitator.

Here is a way that I imagine a team could test itself to see if it has the necessary skills, before making the decision to go ahead on its own. Bring together some core members of the team, and ask yourselves: imagine what we think is really on the other team members' left-hand columns. Now imagine if everybody actually said those things in a room together. Could we handle it? Would it lead to good things, or would it just be a recipe for people blowing up at each other, or getting entrenched in their own positions? Are we sophisticated enough in the mental models concepts to recognize our own potential for prodding each other's defensiveness?

36 Balancing Inquiry and Advocacy

Rick Ross, Charlotte Roberts

Managers in Western corporations have received a lifetime of training in being forceful, articulate "advocates" and "problem solvers." They know how to present and argue strongly for their views. But as people rise in the organization, they are forced to deal with more complex and interdependent issues where no one individual "knows the answer," and where the only viable option is for groups of informed and committed individuals to think together to arrive at new insights. At this point, they need to learn to skillfully balance advocacy with inquiry.

When balancing advocacy and inquiry, we lay out our reasoning and thinking, and then encourage others to challenge us. "Here is my view and here is how I have arrived at it. How does it sound to you? What makes sense to you and what doesn't? Do you see any ways I can improve it?"

Balancing inquiry and advocacy is sometimes hard on people's cherished opinions, which is one reason why it is so difficult to master. But the payoff comes in the more creative and insightful realizations that occur when people combine multiple perspectives.

We don't recommend inquiry alone. People almost always have a viewpoint to express, and it is important to express it—in a context which allows you to learn more about others' views while they learn more about yours. Nor do we recommend that you switch in rote fashion from an adamant assertion ("Here's what I say") to a question ("Now what do you say?") and back again. Balancing inquiry and advocacy means developing a variety of skills. It's as if all the "colors" of conversation could be spread out on an imaginary palette. As the creator of your part of the conversation, you should be able to incorporate styles from all four quadrants of the palette.°

This palette chart, of course, is only the beginning of a taxonomy of roles which people can play in conversation. There are probably a dozen more distinct combinations of varying levels of inquiry and advocacy, each with a different impact.

There are dysfunctional forms of both advocacy and inquiry. For example, in organizations, adroit people can skew the inquiry process by

° This diagram is an expansion of the "Inquiry/Advocacy matrix" developed by Diana McLain Smith.

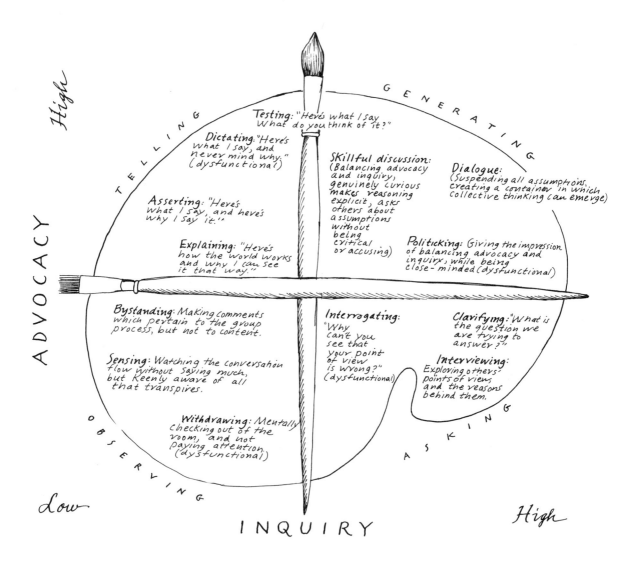

High

TELLING   GENERATING

Testing: "Here's what I say
What do you think of it?"

Dictating: "Here's
what I say, and
never mind why."
(dysfunctional)

Skillful discussion:
(Balancing advocacy
and inquiry,
genuinely curious
makes reasoning
explicit, asks
others about
assumptions
without
being
critical
or accusing)

Dialogue:
(Suspending all assumptions,
creating a container in which
collective thinking can emerge)

Asserting: "Here's
what I say, and here's
why I say it."

Explaining: "Here's
how the world works
and why I can see
it that way."

Politicking: Giving the impression
of balancing advocacy and
inquiry, while being
close-minded (dysfunctional)

ADVOCACY

Bystanding: Making comments
which pertain to the group
process, but not to content.

Interrogating:
"Why
can't you
see that
your point
of view
is wrong?"
(dysfunctional)

Clarifying: "What is
the question we
are trying to
answer?"

Sensing: Watching the conversation
flow without saying much,
but keenly aware of all
that transpires.

Interviewing:
Exploring others'
points of view,
and the reasons
behind them.

Withdrawing: Mentally
checking out of the
room, and not
paying attention.
(dysfunctional)

OBSERVING   ASKING

Low   High

INQUIRY

relentless "interrogating," without caring at all for the person being questioned. In the same vein, advocacy can feel like an inquisition if the advocate simply "dictates" his point of view, while refusing to make his reasoning process visible. People who are unwilling to expose their thinking may also "withdraw" into silence, instead of taking the opportunity to learn through observation.

One of the most destructive conversational forms is "politicking," in which there is no overt argument—just a relentless refusal to learn while giving the impression of balancing advocacy and inquiry. In workshops, we see this form sometimes when people who have read *The Fifth Dis-*

cipline play "The Beer Game." This game is a mock production-and-distribution system simulation, demonstrating how the structure of a system determines behavior. From the description of the game in *The Fifth Discipline*,* some readers conclude the best winning strategy is deliberately under-ordering beer and remaining in backlog throughout the game. When these people show up to play, they cling to their mistaken impression at all costs. Their strategy is disastrous for their team's score, and it would be disastrous in real life, because businesses which remain in backlog don't keep their customers. Nonetheless, these players refuse to consider any other course of play. When people ask them to change for the sake of their teammates, they don't argue back. They simply call attention to their "superior" status: "Look, I've read the book. Trust me. I know what I'm doing."

It is said that each of us has a natural predilection toward either advocacy or inquiry. Debate and law teach advocacy; journalism and social work (if they're practiced well) teach inquiry. Men are rewarded more for advocacy; women are more rewarded for inquiry. In the South, women are even taught that it is a sign of poor breeding to state what you want or need. (Instead of saying, "Can you get me a mint julep?" a thirsty woman would say, "It's a terribly hot day. Wouldn't it be wonderful if we all had some special refreshment?") During the 1970s, many women had a hard time with advocacy, but now that more women have joined managerial ranks in organizations, members of both genders are becoming more adept at balancing the two forms.

* *The Fifth Discipline*, p. 27ff.

Protocols for balancing advocacy and inquiry

BALANCING ADVOCACY AND INQUIRY IS ONE WAY FOR INDIVIDUALS, BY themselves, to begin changing a large organization from within. You don't need any mandate, budget, or approval to begin. You will almost always be rewarded with better relationships and a reputation for integrity.

The purpose of these conversational recipes is to help people learn the skills of balancing inquiry and advocacy. Use them whenever a conversation offers you an opportunity to learn—for example, when a team is considering a difficult point that requires information and participation from everyone on the team.*

}} Also see "Opening Lines" (page 263).

* These protocols were adapted, with many changes, from course material developed for *Leading Learning Organizations* (1993, Encinitas, Calif.: Ross Partners); from material developed by Diana McLain Smith and Philip McArthur of Action Design; and from *The Fifth Discipline*, pp. 200–1.

1. PROTOCOLS FOR IMPROVED ADVOCACY:

Make your thinking process visible (walk up the ladder of inference slowly).

What to do	**What to say**
State your assumptions, and describe the data that led to them.	*"Here's what I think, and here's how I got there."*
Explain your assumptions.	*"I assumed that . . ."*
Make your reasoning explicit.	*"I came to this conclusion because . . ."*
Explain the context of your point of view: who will be affected by what you propose, how they will be affected, and why.	
Give examples of what you propose, even if they're hypothetical or metaphorical.	*"To get a clear picture of what I'm talking about, imagine that you're the customer who will be affected . . ."*
As you speak, try to picture the other people's perspectives on what you are saying.	

Publicly test your conclusions and assumptions.

What to do	**What to say**
Encourage others to explore your model, your assumptions, and your data.	*"What do you think about what I just said?"* or *"Do you see any flaws in my reasoning?"* or *"What can you add?"*
Refrain from defensiveness when your ideas are questioned. If you're advocating something worthwhile, then it will only get stronger by being tested.	

What to do	What to say
Reveal where you are least clear in your thinking. Rather than making you vulnerable, it defuses the force of advocates who are opposed to you, and invites improvement.	*"Here's one aspect which you might help me think through . . ."*
Even when advocating: listen, stay open, and encourage others to provide different views.	*"Do you see it differently?"*

2. PROTOCOLS FOR IMPROVED INQUIRY:

Ask others to make their thinking process visible.

What to do	What to say
Gently walk others down the ladder of inference and find out what data they are operating from.	*"What leads you to conclude that?" "What data do you have for that?" "What causes you to say that?"*
Use unaggressive language, particularly with people who are not familiar with these skills. Ask in a way which does not provoke defensiveness or "lead the witness."	Instead of *"What do you mean?"* or *"What's your proof?"* say, *"Can you help me understand your thinking here?"*
Draw out their reasoning. Find out as much as you can about why they are saying what they're saying.	*"What is the significance of that?" "How does this relate to your other concerns?" "Where does your reasoning go next?"*
Explain your reasons for inquiring, and how your inquiry relates to your own concerns, hopes, and needs.	*"I'm asking you about your assumptions here because . . ."*

Compare your assumptions to theirs.

What to do	**What to say**
Test what they say by asking for broader contexts, or for examples.	*"How would your proposal affect . . . ?" "Is this similar to . . . ?" "Can you describe a typical example . . . ?"*
Check your understanding of what they have said.	*"Am I correct that you're saying . . . ?"*
Listen for the new understanding that may emerge. Don't concentrate on preparing to destroy the other person's argument or promote your own agenda.	

3. PROTOCOLS FOR FACING A POINT OF VIEW WITH WHICH YOU DISAGREE:

What to do	**What to say**
Again, inquire about what has led the person to that view.	*"How did you arrive at this view?" "Are you taking into account data that I have not considered?"*
Make sure you truly understand the view.	*"If I understand you correctly, you're saying that . . ."*
Explore, listen, and offer your own views in an open way.	*"Have you considered . . ."*
Listen for the larger meaning that may come out of honest, open sharing of alternative mental models.	
Use your left-hand column as a resource.	*"When you say such-and-such, I worry that it means . . ."*
Raise your concerns and state what is leading you to have them.	*"I have a hard time seeing that, because of this reasoning . . ."*

4. PROTOCOLS FOR WHEN YOU'RE AT AN IMPASSE:

What to do	What to say
Embrace the impasse, and tease apart the current thinking. (You may discover that focusing on "data" brings you all down the ladder of inference.)	*"What do we know for a fact?"* *"What do we sense is true, but have no data for yet?"* *"What don't we know?"* *"What is unknowable?"*
Look for information which will help people move forward.	*"What do we agree upon, and what do we disagree on?"*
Ask if there is any way you might together design an experiment or inquiry which could provide new information.	
Listen to ideas as if for the first time.	
Consider each person's mental model as a piece of a larger puzzle.	*"Are we starting from two very different sets of assumptions here? Where do they come from?"*
Ask what data or logic might change their views.	*"What, then, would have to happen before you would consider the alternative?"*
Ask for the group's help in redesigning the situation.	*"It feels like we're getting into an impasse and I'm afraid we might walk away without any better understanding. Have you got any ideas that will help us clarify our thinking?"*
Don't let conversation stop with an "agreement to disagree."	*"I don't understand the assumptions underlying our disagreement."*
Avoid building your "case" when someone else is speaking from a different point of view.	

37 Conversational Recipes

Robert Putnam

The help Robert Putnam, a partner in Action Design, gave us in this part of the book emerged from his work on this piece for us, which in turn was based upon a more in-depth article for action science practitioners: "Recipes and Reflective Learning: 'What Would Prevent You from Saying It That Way?'" by Robert Putnam, in The Reflective Turn: Case Studies in and on Educational Practice, *(1991, New York: Teachers College Press). Philip McArthur, whose "Opening Lines" (page 263) provide an example of recipes, is also a partner in Action Design.*

People who are learning reflection and inquiry skills very quickly develop a repertoire of stock phrases. I call these phrases "recipes" because most of them are used like step-by-step procedures for getting a particular response. For instance, here is a conversation where "Paul," an in-house consultant, is trying to help "Linda," a supervisor, delve into the assumptions underlying a troublesome incident where someone had been fired:

> PAUL: Are you and the other supervisors going to talk about this incident, to learn from it?
> LINDA: I'm not going to bring it up.
> PAUL: *What prevents you* from bringing it up?
> LINDA: Nothing prevents me. What do you want me to say?

Later, Paul reflected, "I seemed to get myself into trouble with that line that I couldn't get myself out of." Then he described what went through his mind at that moment: "Am I handling it right? Am I too concerned about what I'm doing? Am I getting stuck in the technique?"

The value of recipes

Paul's reflections suggest exactly the difficulties we expect in the early stages of using any new technique. It feels unnatural. When he got into difficulty, he doubted his ability to follow-through consistently. And his self-consciousness made it even less likely that he would follow through competently. At first glance, you might assume that he was in a terrible double bind; he didn't have the sophistication to use inquiry techniques with skill, so he was stuck with "recipes"—canned remarks that "parrot" (as Paul himself pointed out) what a skilled intervenor would say, and that would inevitably "get him in trouble."

But the learning of skills begins with recipes. For instance, if you decide the ladder of inference (see page 242) is useful, how do you learn to apply it? Without practice, the concept won't be second nature; but until it's second nature, you can't practice with it effectively. So you short-cut the dilemma by following a set of rules:

1. Identify the conclusions someone is making.
2. Ask for the data that lead to the conclusion.
3. Inquire into the reasoning that connects data and conclusion.
4. Infer a possible belief or assumption.
5. State your inference and test it with the person.

Working recipes into obsolescence

RECIPES LIKE THESE PRODUCE USEFUL DATA, AND THEY COME QUICKLY to the tongue. Their vividness may also aid in focusing reflection.

But there is a caveat. Rules and guidelines can play a vital role only when we deliberately use them to move beyond rule- and guideline-based behavior. Recipes must be made to work themselves out of a job.

Here are some rules and guidelines for doing so. (Of course, these are also recipes; so they, too, must be made to work themselves out of a job.)

■ *Examine your own conversations later.*

Describe and reflect upon your use of the "recipes." Paul, for instance, used "What prevents you?" as a kind of advocacy, implying that Linda was hypocritical. But through his own retrospective critique, Paul realized the prejudgment he had made: "I see now, maybe it wasn't inconsistent for her to say, 'I don't want to talk about it now.' It may have been just a timing kind of thing. But I wasn't hearing that. I was sort of forcing it into an inconsistency kind of thing." For Paul, this sort of self-judgment is an invaluable way to learn.

■ *Seek out generic strategies for improving your use of "recipes."*

When you look at your earlier conversations, try to figure out general strategies for various impasses. For instance, Paul worked with a manager named Mike, who had given a mixed message to a subordinate. Over and over, Paul asked Mike what had led him not to say more directly what he really wanted. Later, listening to tapes of the conversation, Paul realized a maxim: rather than getting people in situations like Mike's to admit they are wrong, you can be more helpful by naming how they are caught in a dilemma and focusing on how they can manage it more successfully. Paul went on to use this maxim very successfully in work with other people.

■ *Put yourself in the other person's vantage point.*

This is a difficult rule to remember to follow. Paul, for instance, with all his training and reflection, still found himself advocating his point of view in a series of highly charged meetings about downsizing. Even his "recipes" were just subtle ways of trying to manipulate a plant manager, whose name was Greg, to change his mind. But finally, when Greg responded to one of Paul's recipes by saying what he feared his boss would do, Paul (as he said later) felt something shift within him. He began to talk openly in the group about how he might think differently "if I put myself in Greg's shoes." Greg, in response, articulated a breakthrough scenario. Gradually the group worked through its impasse and developed a proposal for restructuring their division more intelligently.

■ *Ask for the perspective of the people you're working with.*

By this time, Paul had moved beyond recipes. He was able to ask the people he worked with, "Am I inviting enough inquiry in my own advocacy? I tried to, but I don't know if it was just pro forma." His interventions had become less stilted, more natural. And his attention had turned away from "Will I or won't I get them to do what I think we should?" and more to "What can we accomplish?"

Recipes, when you first start using them, are gimmicks. You'll use them within your taken-for-granted way of framing the situation. But as you gain experience with them, the frame too may shift. You may be able to jump, without planning in advance exactly how to do it, from superficial technique to a deeper sense of practice.

38 Opening Lines

Philip McArthur

When . . .	**. . . you might say . . .**
Strong views are expressed without any reasoning or illustrations . . .	*"You may be right, but I'd like to understand more. What leads you to believe . . . ?"*
The discussion goes off on an apparent tangent . . .	*"I'm unclear how that connects to what we've been saying. Can you say how you see it as relevant?"*
You doubt the relevance of your own thoughts . . .	*"This may not be relevant now. If so, let me know and I will wait."*
Two members pursue a topic at length while others observe . . .	*"I'd like to give my reaction to what you two have said so far, and then see what you and others think."*
Several views are advocated at once . . .	*"We now have three ideas on the table [say what they are]. I suggest we address them one at a time . . ."*
You perceive a negative reaction in others . . .	*"When you said [give illustration] . . . I had the impression you were feeling [fill in the emotion]. If so, I'd like to understand what upset you. Is there something I've said or done?"*
You perceive a negative reaction in yourself . . .	*"This may be more my problem than yours, but when you said [give illustration] . . . I felt . . . Am I misunderstanding what you said or intended?"*
Others appear uninfluenceable . . .	*"Is there anything that I can say or do that would convince you otherwise?"*

39 Bootstrapping Yourself into Reflection and Inquiry Skills

Jeff Dooley

If you are intrigued by the reflection and inquiry skills in this part of the book, you may want to delve deeper into "action science"—the body of theory and practice from which they emerged. Here is a guide to finding your way through the literature—with reviews by Rick Ross, by Harvard graduate student and Buckminster Fuller associate Amy Edmondson, and by Jeff Dooley, an organization development consultant based in Benicia, California.

Jeff set out three years ago to teach himself "action science" through self-study. He has written a longer history of his odyssey, aimed at professional consultants and practitioners, available by sending a stamped, self-addressed envelope to the address on page 573.

Can an individual acquire competence in reflection and inquiry skills through self-study? Is there a theory to guide us in acquiring that competence? If, like most people, we are not fully aware of the state of our own mental models, then how can we progress through a program of self-designed learning without being undermined by our inner defenses?

Three years ago, I set out to put those questions to the test. I began by reading the important books in the field, but that is only the first step: it's easy to espouse the principles of inquiry and reflection, but difficult to acquire a frame of mind which is open to this type of learning.

Thus, I found that I had to combine my study with regular practice. At first, before I had opportunities to use the skills in organizational consulting, my wife Lynn and I practiced them together. Talk around our kitchen table took on a lingering, almost agonizingly slow quality as we considered every word. We gradually learned to inquire into the sources of each other's views, to catch ourselves when we tried to exert unilateral control over the conversation, and to bring to the surface our long-cherished and secret, powerful defensive routines.

I have since expanded my practice with friends, colleagues, and in study groups. Over time, if you continue, you will begin to see the importance of art and creativity to this practice. During one session, for example, when participants critiqued each other's "left-hand column," they could not see that they were criticizing each other in a harsh, judgmental manner—precisely in violation of the advice they were giving. Instead of pointing this out, I asked if I could role-play as one of the critics, using his exact words, while he role-played the other person. He felt angry and defensive at hearing them, and only then could he see the seeds of ineffectiveness in his own behavior. Can you learn to do that kind of role-play from a book? Probably not—but these books are worthwhile starting points.

OVERCOMING ORGANIZATIONAL DEFENSES
by Chris Argyris (1990, Needham Heights, Mass.: Allyn and Bacon).

This is Chris Argyris's most accessible book for managers. It is a slim book, built around the idea that everyday "defensive" behavior—behavior which makes us feel most in control in the short run—is the worst possible way for people to act in organizations, because it masks the actual dynamics of a situation. Why, for instance, did the "budget whiz-kid" of the Reagan era, David Stockman, fail to stop the debt crisis he saw coming? Because infighting in the White House organization was never allowed to appear as infighting. Why did the NASA *Challenger* disaster take place, although engineers at the contracting companies reported safety problems ahead of time? Because nobody asked why higher-level managers weren't listening to them. The first five chapters show how organizational defenses come to be, and the last four chapters offer strategies for undoing them.—**RR**

"SKILLED INCOMPETENCE" **by Chris Argyris,** *Harvard Business Review,* September 1986, HBR Reprint #86501;

"TEACHING SMART PEOPLE HOW TO LEARN" **by** Chris Argyris, *Harvard Business Review,* May–June 1991, HBR Reprint #91301.

These two *Harvard Business Review* article reprints are full of examples of left-hand-column and ladder-of-inference exercises, and how people use them.

"Skilled Incompetence" focuses on the premise that the most skilled people in day-to-day communication can't unearth their mental models until they "unlearn" how to protect themselves from feeling threatened.

"Teaching Smart People How to Learn," based on Argyris's fifteen years of work with management consultants, suggests that most of us can cultivate the intellectual and emotional vulnerability of failure, without having to actually fail. — **RR**

ORGANIZATIONAL LEARNING: A THEORY OF ACTION PERSPECTIVE by Chris Argyris and Donald A. Schön
(1978, Reading, Mass.: Addison-Wesley).

Argyris and Schön introduce action maps: charts showing how dysfunctional mental models, held by different people in the same organization, reinforce and influence each other. For instance, in a case at a Third World technology institute (page 54), the local office "expert," and the central office "expert" couldn't agree on how to assign tasks to their staff. They did not recognize or discuss this lack of agreement; instead, they engaged in fancy footwork to avoid facing it, which only heightened the severity of their dilemmas. As more people get involved, these interpersonal dynamics escalate into "secondary inhibiting loops"—coalitions, group-think, and committees which spend their time second-guessing and outmaneuvering each other. Not only do these dynamics inhibit "Model II" behavior—they reinforce themselves because they are designed, in the first place, to camouflage uncorrectable errors. — **JD**

ACTION SCIENCE by Chris Argyris, Robert Putnam, and Diana McLain Smith
(1985, San Francisco: Jossey-Bass).

Halfway through *Action Science*, I began to appreciate what Argyris and his associates were trying to do: provide an account of the steps of an in-depth organizational learning process. *Action Science* is also a critique of traditional social science in which the experimenter remains aloof from the experiment.

Interventionists trying to change organizations may already possess skills such as "balancing advocacy with inquiry" and "left-hand column" analysis. But the interventionist must also set an example: avoiding any form of coercion or unilateral control of participants, even under the guise that it is in the participants' best interest to be coerced. There's a paradox here—how do you bring about free and informed consent, without controlling the group, when participants' automatic (defensive) behavior may block their chances for free and informed consent?

Part Three of *Action Science* is the road map of an escape route from this paradox. It is the account of a year-long intervention during which participants were shocked to see how they acted in violation of their own espoused values, then learned to understand and map their mental models and the causal chains of behavior reinforcing those models, and finally learned to invent and produce new behaviors consistent with "Model II" values. This section is a template for designing an action science intervention of your own. —JD

KNOWLEDGE FOR ACTION by Chris Argyris (1993, San Francisco: Jossey-Bass)

This book represents the best account to date of the learning process Argyris facilitates in his interventions. In giving this account of a five-year intervention with a team of consulting firm directors, Argyris introduces a key concept which comes close to identifying what he thinks he helps produce: "actionable knowledge." Actionable knowledge not only illuminates a strategy (for instance, a strategy a manager might use to abet someone else's learning), but it also must specify the skills the manager would need to carry out the knowledge, and the conditions that must be created in the organization.

The book's chapters are organized around key episodes in the learning process, and the transcripts of these episodes provide rich harvests of hints about what the action science process is like for an observer. Argyris gives us insights into his own approach by scoring the transcripts and providing detailed accounts of difficult episodes—accounts which include his own on-line interventions and what he intended. One empathizes with Argyris when he notes regret for a particular strategy he used in a difficult moment and contrasts it with the behaviors he might have produced instead. There is also a chapter on an episode, three or so years after the work had begun, during which two consultants went ballistic on one another, despite their increasing skill. —JD

ORGANIZATIONAL CULTURE AND LEADERSHIP
by Edgar H. Schein (1985, 1992, San Francisco: Jossey-Bass).

An organization's culture can be seen as its members' collective mental models—which is why you cannot change an organization without investigating its cultural assumptions. In Edgar H. Schein's model, cultural assumptions are deeply influenced by beliefs held by founders and leaders, carrying on for years after the founders themselves have ceased to run the company. Unlike Chris Argyris, Schein sees most organizations as essentially healthy, and willing, patients. They lack certain skills and may be handicapped by dysfunctional values, but these gaps can be remedied through careful clinical work.

Organizational Culture and Leadership contains two chapters describing a participative way to decipher an organization's culture. A researcher starts by eliciting data about *cultural artifacts* such as dress codes, ways of talking to the boss, and other visible evidence. The most recent hire is asked to start off the list, to offer the unjaded observations of a newcomer. The second level of data encompasses *espoused values*— that is, readily offered reasons for the visible cultural artifacts. This requires people to think slightly more deeply to generate explanations such as "We value problem solving more than formal authority," which, once stated, are readily recognized by everyone. The third and most subtle level captures *shared underlying assumptions,* which require some probing to be uncovered, through discussion of inconsistencies between artifacts and espoused values. Finally, the researcher pulls together the findings from the group and together they examine what assumptions may aid and/or hinder progress on the stated change goals.—**AE**

~~~~~~

Writing to Your Loyalties

Art Kleiner

P U R P O S E
This exercise has two purposes: to help you see your own mental models of key people in the organization more clearly, and to practice seeing a difficult issue through more than one perspective. It may also help you learn political acumen.

The purpose of most memos and reports is not to promote learning, or even to communicate, but to select a version of the truth to present for "the record"—for your boss, for the outside world, or for posterity. This puts writers within learning organizations in a difficult bind. Should they write the truth as the organization needs to hear it, or should they write what is politically expected of them? Fortunately, it also means that writing, if approached correctly, can be a very effective solo vehicle for surfacing mental models.

This is a tough exercise, especially for people who don't like to write. But those are the people whom it will help the most. (I have used it to help people with writer's block.) The exercise asks you to create a fair amount of "scaffolding"—three drafts of a report which no one will ever see, but which you need to create your final product. (That's why the word processing program is such a help.) Take consolation, however: writing your report this way, though it seems tedious, is probably much easier than doing it by the traditional method.°

° ⊤his exercise is based, in part, on exercises and insights developed by James L. Evers (see page 490).

STEP 1: LISTING THE LOYALTIES

Select a difficult situation or issue facing you right now. Then write a report or memo about it. Or use this fictional example:

Your organization has discovered that it is inadvertently responsible for a health crisis in your community. You have been assigned to research the potential damage, and write a report. The report will be read by the CEO, the chief financial officer, by your immediate superior, and by the Environmental Protection Agency. You know that a version will probably be leaked to the press, so all your neighbors will see it. Your career depends on how well you put together the report.

This exercise is much more effective if you focus on a current problem of your own. Begin by listing, on a piece of paper, all the people and things you expect to feel loyal to when you write the report. Whose reactions, if they were to read the report, would be important to you? List as many as you can. Some may be hypothetical or symbolic entities, buried deep inside you.

A list of "loyalties" for the health crisis report might include:

My boss	The CEO
My spouse and children	My co-workers
My peers in other functions	My subordinates
My neighbors	My sense of the quality of my work
My sense of the truth	Each of the people I talked to in gathering information
My mentor, whose attitudes I've ingrained in my judgment	Key staff people
The newspaper reporter who called me for information	The schoolteacher I met at a PTA meeting last year
My image of my own future self	My ideal of myself from when I was fourteen

O V E R V I E W
Writing three drafts of a different report to three audiences, and then examining the differences.

T I M E
Ten to twenty hours, spread over a week or two.

My concept of science   The P.R. department

The union representative   Etc. (fill in your own)

STEP 2: PICK TWO—PLUS THE TRUTH

Most likely, nearly all of these loyalties are important to you in some respect. But pick two which you care strongly about. (Later, you'll return for the others.) *Ideally, they should be two people, or groups of people, who will actually read your report when it is finished.*

In addition to the two loyalties you selected, you should also mentally select your loyalty to the truth, as you see it.

Write down, or circle, the names of the two loyalties you have chosen. In the step after next, you will write a separate memo for each of them. But for now, put their names aside. It would only get in your way.

STEP 3: THE REPORT FOR THE TRUTH

Write a description of the situation—a report—as if truth were the only loyalty you had. Write it, in other words, as if for a time capsule, to be opened after your death. What has happened—and what is the significance?

A full report might be too lengthy, so we recommend you write only three paragraphs:

a. A *"curtain-raiser" (opening paragraph).*

   Imagine that people, 100 years hence, have opened the time capsule and are reading your report. What do you want them to see first to pique their interest? This paragraph need not tell the whole story; in fact, it should probably be limited to some minor part of the plot. But it should express some aspect of why the story will be interesting.

b. A *"nut graf" (thematic core paragraph).*

   Journalists use the expression "nut graf" to describe the paragraph with the kernel of what happened: who, what, where, when, why, and what for. What, in a nutshell, happened here? What's its significance? Who was involved?

c. An *ending (closing paragraph).*

   What do you want the people of the future to feel when they've finished reading your report? What is your message for them? What has the truth suggested to you? If there is a moral, or action plan, articulate it here.

After you are finished with these three paragraphs, take a break. Come back after a day or two. (The break will clear your mind, and help you focus more coherently on the next step.) The piece you have just written will become your "control group," in the experiment you are about to run.

STEP 4: THE REPORTS FOR YOUR LOYALTIES

Now go back and write a separate report for each of the two "loyalties" you selected. As you write, keep an image in mind of that person reading every word you write. Remember, you probably will not show this writing to this person; however, it will become "scaffolding" for the actual report you eventually write.

Once again, stick to three paragraphs:

a. *A curtain-raiser.*
   What would this person want to know first? What would grab him or her? What could you say intriguing enough to make your reader continue reading?
b. *A "nut graf."*
   What's the essence of the situation, as you would wish to express it to this person?
c. *An ending.*
   Where do you want to leave him or her?

Don't worry about rewriting; just execute a first draft. After you've done the two or three reports, three paragraphs each, take another one- or two-day break.

STEP 5: LOYALTY ANALYSIS

You now have three separate reports. Read them again, as if you were reading them for the first time. Imagine that you have found them in the time capsule. You do not know the author, nor do you know any of the people they are addressed to. Answer these questions:

Look first at the report written to the "Truth."
1. What impression do you get of the author of this report?
2. What data (actual text from the report) leads you to this conclusion?

3. What impression, *only from the report,* do you get of the story and the facts? How important is this event?
4. What specific sentences and phrases actually contribute to this impression?

Now look at the report to person A.

5. What impression do you get, *only from the report,* of person A?
6. What text leads you to this impression? For example, what is written to A that does not appear in any other report? What is emphasized for A?
7. Look at the "curtain-raiser" paragraph. What does the author of this report believe A cares about?
8. What does the author want A to ignore or look away from? For example, what facts or details are omitted from this report?
9. What does the author want A to conclude? What actions does the author want A to take?
10. Imagine now that you showed this page of answers to A. Would A agree with the assessment and assumptions here? Would A be pleased or chagrined?
11. Can the assumptions in your answers to these questions be tested? Is there any reason to think that they might not be true?

Now answer the same questions (5–14) for your report to B.

STEP 6: THE FINAL REPORT

You still have a final report to write. But you now have three versions of a beginning, a "nut graf" or kernel paragraph, and an end.

You can choose parts of your final draft from among your versions. Choose deliberately, still concentrating only on loyalties A, B, and the truth. Then, when you are finished with the first draft, look it over with each of your other "loyalties" in mind. What will need to be added or subtracted for each? Articulate the changes needed to make it palatable to each of the people you would show it to. If the loyalties conflict too much, perhaps you should consider releasing two or three separate documents.

STEP 7: TESTING YOUR ASSUMPTIONS (OPTIONAL)

You now have, if you wish, a simple (albeit politically sensitive) way to test your assumptions. Show the material you have written so far to A and B. Show them their version, versus the version written for the "truth," versus the equivalent three paragraphs of your final version. Tell them you are trying to decide which material to emphasize in the final draft. Ask them which they prefer.

It is always a bit frightening to reveal assumptions in written form. However, most people are fairly tolerant of something they know is an early draft, particularly if it's marked as such. They will often critique an early draft far more constructively, and openly, than they would critique a draft they think is final. If you are willing to show some of your "scaffolding" to others, it can open inquiry on issues that were never raised before, because no one thought to raise them until they were written down.

Multiple Perspectives

Charlotte Roberts, James Boswell

The more perspectives on an issue that a team can consider, the more possibilities exist for effective action. The point is not just to look at one or two extremely different perspectives, but to capture as many differences of nuance as possible.

STEP 1: DESIGNING THE WHEEL
Create a disk about eighteen inches in diameter from thick paper which can be written upon. Lay the wheel in the center of the table. Write a title or draw a symbol for the problem in the center of the wheel.

Draw lines across the wheel as if cutting a pie, dividing the wheel into equal slices—one for each member of the team. Write everyone's name on a slice of the wheel.

Then write up cards with the names or titles of eight or more key stakeholders, for the problem being explored. Some stakeholders may be internal: the VP of finance, regional sales managers, technicians, supervisors, or hourly workers. Others will include key external groups: customers and suppliers, government regulators, competitors, and consumers. Set out one flip chart for each key stakeholder.

P U R P O S E
To open up or widen a team's perspectives—the points of view from which the team members regard a problem.

O V E R V I E W
Rotating between roles encourages members to see an important issue from as many vantage points as possible.

P A R T I C I P A N T S
An intact team, working on a real problem.

T I M E
Twenty minutes or more.

SUPPLIES
Flip charts, note cards, markers, Post-it notes, and thick paper for the "perspective wheel." If the wheel seems unwieldly, a similar effect can be achieved by handing cards from one person to the next, or shuffling and dealing the cards after each turn.

ENVIRONMENT
A comfortable meeting room with a central table and room for numerous flip charts.

Place the cards, evenly spaced, around the edge of the wheel, so it looks something like this:

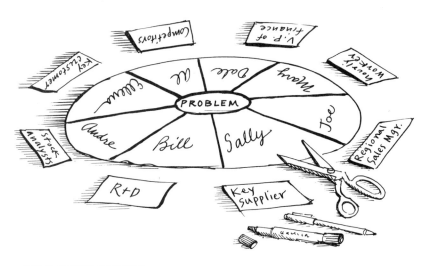

STEP 2: PLAYING THE WHEEL

When the wheel is turned one space, each person's name will stop in line with one of the key stakeholders. At each turn of the wheel, each team member must add to the understanding of the perspective to which he or she has moved.

For example, Bill's name lands adjacent to the CEO card at the edge of the wheel. Bill walks to the flip chart for that stakeholder position and completes this sentence, "From my perspective as CEO, the critical elements within this situation are . . ."

Comments may concern the problem (perhaps written in black) or ideas for leverage (perhaps written in green), but all comments should be written as if you are the person whose card you have landed on.

You are not permitted to "pass." If you feel as if you don't understand this stakeholder's perspective, ask yourself these questions, playing the role of that person:

Time: What time frame am I operating within? When did I begin to look at the problem? When will it, effectively, be a nonissue for me?

Expectation: What do I expect will happen, if all continues as expected? What do I hope (or demand) should happen? Who expects me to deal with this? What do they want me to do?

Examination: How closely am I willing to examine the problem? From how far away do I see it? What else is aggregated with this problem as I see it?

Understanding: What do I see about the problem which no one else sees? What understanding of the problem occupies my vision? What data is my understanding of the problem based upon?

STEP 3: WORKING WITH THE PERSPECTIVES

At some point, you will find yourself with full descriptions of each perspective. Now, as a team, you can talk through the situation from each of them. You may drop deeper within a vantage point: for example, you might start out with one stakeholder representing "finance." Gradually, you might realize there are three distinct "finance" vantage points, each requiring its own flip chart page.

In each case, how does the way you are thinking and seeing limit your capacity for dealing with a chronic or high-voltage issue?

40 Creating Scenarios

Art Kleiner

Contrary to what many people believe about scenario exercises, their purpose is not prediction. A scenario, as longstanding scenario innovator Napier Collyns puts it, is "an imaginative leap into the future." You don't predict what will happen: you posit several potential futures, none of which will probably come to pass, but all of which, make you more keenly aware of the forces acting on you in the present. You know a scenario exercise has been successful when you feel a premonition that shakes your worldview. Kees van der Heijden (who describes his own scenario work on page 279) calls this the "aha" experience.

A scenario planning exercise is a bit like a storytelling workshop, set up to bring forth distinctions and phenomena that the conventional wisdom ignores. Discerning the differences between Iran and Saudi Arabia, while everyone else viewed the "Arab nations" as a single bloc, helped Royal Dutch/Shell scenario planners anticipate the oil shortages of the 1970s. Seeing the demographics and economic pressures on the Soviet Union, while Western politicians saw only an "evil empire," helped Shell's scenario planners foresee *glasnost.* Looking at the slow-starting but ultimately explosive dynamics of advertising revenue in new media helped my own scenario workshop envision the current wave of mergers between telephone and cable television companies. The method can be applied to subjects ranging from the price of gold to the economic stability of East Asia; from the future of energy efficiency to the competitiveness of hospitals.

People often want to condense scenario work to a half-day or weekend session, but it's becoming clear that such efforts usually don't give people enough time to delve past their existing preconceptions. The annual workshop I lead for artists and managers at New York University's interactive telecommunications program meets twice a week for six straight weeks, supplemented by regular conversations over computer network. Even that amount of time feels cramped. Each of the steps in that six-week process is an exercise in reeducation: creating a new collective set of assumptions about the outside world, which none of us could reach on our own.

STEP 1: REFINING OUR SENSE OF PURPOSE

Scenarios provoke genuine learning only when they answer genuine concerns. Otherwise, they are merely an academic exercise. The concerns should be compelling, shared by the entire group (ideally of eight to twenty people), and best with uncertainty. "Should we move toward domestic or overseas markets?" "What sort of career should we prepare students for?" "How can we build democratic institutions in South Africa?" Articulating your focus is not a trivial task, especially because the participants should ideally be diverse people with a common interest. As with a vision exercise, it requires moving past the concerns which people *think* they have to the concerns which truly motivate them.

STEP 2: UNDERSTANDING DRIVING FORCES

Scenarios are built upon the distinction between two types of driving forces. Predetermined forces are reasonably predictable. We all know, barring unforeseen calamity, how many twenty-year-olds will exist in any country nineteen years from now. We can assume that the pace of technological growth will continue, with costs of new devices falling at a fairly predetermined rate.

But the vast majority of forces at play are *un*certain. Will investors gravitate to less-developed countries? Will consumers continue to eagerly want new media products? Will American manufacturing catch up to Japan's quality standards? You can't know the answer, but you can become far more aware of the reasons why events might move in one direction or another, and the implications of their movement.

The predetermined elements set the boundaries within which your scenarios take place; while the act of picking key uncertainties leads you to the most significant ramifications of your decision. This typically requires both intensive give and take within the group, as well as outside research. In our NYU workshop, for example, one participant demonstrated the value of outside research by investigating, on his own, how many new semiconductors it would take to develop a nationwide information highway with video available on demand. He concluded that America would have to double its chip manufacturing capacity—which dramatically changed our sense of how quickly a full-scale national digital network could emerge. For that group, whose members had tacitly assumed their immediate future was tied to such a network, this was shocking news.

STEP 3: SCENARIO PLOTS

Like working with system archetypes, developing scenarios involves considering "classic stories" in terms of your current situation. (Indeed, as a few researchers are discovering, the system archetypes on page 121 and this stage of scenario planning are devilishly complementary.)

You create several stories of your own, trying to make each evoke a future which pulls you past your own blinders. As you talk, you enrich the plots, developing sketches of what might plausibly happen.

For our scenarios at NYU about the future of global information networks, we gradually settled on the availability of capital as a key uncertainty. Moving in one direction led to a future we called "keiretsu world" (after the Japanese industrial consortia), in which information flows were dominated by large corporations, while another led to a "virtual world," in which large companies were no longer necessary, and devolved.

You don't care how likely or unlikely each story may be. You care about whether it illuminates your understanding. In fact, if a substantial drop in the demand for your product or service is undeniably plausible—even if it seems like the chances against it are 100 to 1—then you owe it to yourself to create a story around that event, to spark the necessary creativity and preparation that you might never need, but which is worth developing in any case.

° This short description has benefited from concepts developed by Shell scenario innovators Pierre Wack and Ted Newland; from conversations with more recent Shell alumnae Arie de Geus, Kees van der Heijden, and Adam Kahane; from seeing the work of David H. Mason, Jim Henry, and others at Northeast Consulting Resources, Boston; and from the insights of Napier Collyns, Peter Schwartz, Lawrence Wilkinson, and others at Global Business Network.

STEP 4: STRATEGY, REHEARSAL, AND CONVERSATION

This may be the most important step. Regrettably, it is the most often ignored. Having developed two, three, or four scenario plots, you now consider each of them. What strategies would be effective no matter which of those futures came to pass? What would it feel like to live in those worlds? Some teams go so far as to rehearse the scenarios, as if they were pieces of improvisational theater, with each participant taking the part of a different key actor. It's also important to describe the scenarios to others—to get insights from the rest of the organization that may make your pictures of the world richer.

You may find that your scenarios themselves go through several iterations. That's all for the better. When you are done, you will have a language you have created, in which collective assumptions can be voiced. "Will this strategy stand up in a 'keiretsu world'?" you may ask each other. Or, if "virtual world" comes to pass, will we be prepared?°

THE ART OF THE LONG VIEW by **Peter Schwartz** (1991, New York: Currency Doubleday).

The preeminent introduction to scenario planning. Peter Schwartz has conducted scenario work at Stanford Research Institute in the 1970s, at Royal Dutch/Shell in the 1980s, and now at Global Business Network, a future-oriented information-gathering and scenario-developing company based in Emeryville, California. A naturally gifted story-teller, Schwartz covers all the key steps of the process in detail. I helped create this book; I have also seen people use it avidly. It opens up a seemingly arcane technique, and makes it feel both accessible and compelling. —**AK**

41 Shell's Internal Consultancy

Kees van der Heijden

Giving scenarios a context in the organization

For learning to see the unexpected, scenarios alone are not enough; so in the early 1980s, planner Kees van der Heijden and others on the Shell scenario team set out to find a way to institutionalize the learning process throughout the massive network of companies which comprises Royal Dutch/Shell worldwide. Originally from Holland, Kees is now a professor of management at Strathclyde University, Glasgow.

From the beginning, the purpose of our scenario work was as suggested by Pierre Wack (the original innovator of Shell's scenario process): "to change the mental maps of managers." But it is not very easy, even with a few exercises, to establish what managers' mental maps are, let alone to change them. Asking them outright, "What are your mental models?" is obviously a waste of time.

The people who know that from experience are the designers of computer "expert systems," which try to replicate an individual's knowledge in a narrow domain. Suppose, for instance, that you agree to have your knowledge codified into this type of computer program. The designers don't ask you to list your knowledge. Instead, they conduct a comparatively small initial interview with you, go off to produce a rudimentary prototype, and sit you down in front of it. You test it by typing in a simple question. The computer comes back with a ridiculous answer, and you, as the expert, say, "Look, this is nonsense." The designers don't reply defensively. They ask: "Well, why is it nonsense?" You explain your reasoning, and they change the computer program a bit. Over the next few months, this rapid prototyping process continues. Each new iteration, in which you are confronted with the wrong information, triggers you to be a bit more explicit about your own logic, until that logic is captured reasonably well in the expert system.

For almost a decade, I have been working to develop and use a similar method at Shell—in which our consultation is a "mirror" which brings managers face to face with their own logic and assumptions. Our process is probably more difficult; unlike an expert system designer, a scenario team doesn't have the luxury of repeated iterations. If we got two or three sessions with any management team, we counted ourselves as very lucky. But our method is also very flexible, and I have seen it bring better ways of thinking to the surface—not just at Shell, but at a variety of organizations.

Our internal consultancy began in 1982. Two years before, Pierre Wack had reached the conclusion that Shell was not getting its full payout from scenarios, so he offered to take some time off, and think about how to make them more effective in the organization. After a trip around the world, he returned with the suggestion that scenarios should be part of a package aimed at strategic thinking. Arie de Geus, then the Group Planning coordinator, charged me with forming a small team to find a way to allow people to develop their own strategic thinking.

The Royal Dutch/Shell Group of companies is an unusually decentralized group of organizations. The basic organizational unit is national—Shell U.K., Shell Française, Shell U.S., and so on. Except for a few categories of large-scale allocations, the executive buck generally stops at the level of the country CEO. We could not demand that managers of these operating companies use our service, for which we charged a commercial fee. We had to sell it to them. Therefore, we designed our interventions to be limited to a handful of meetings for each person, conducted within the elapsed time of a fortnight. By the end of two weeks, we promised, they would have a clear view of their own strategic capabilities.

PHASE 1: THE TRIGGER INTERVIEWS

Scenario and strategy exercises should always begin with individual interviews. Only individually will people talk freely about their purposes and priorities. Over the years, we have developed seven "trigger" questions:

■ What two questions would you most want to ask an oracle?

This first question uncovers the primary uncertainties which people feel. Moreover, by asking them to limit their questions to two, you trigger them to say something about their priorities. I think I must have asked a thousand people this question, and only one—a senior Shell manager—refused to answer. For most people, answering this question is a game which intrigues them.

- What is a good scenario?
- What is a bad scenario?

Now you change perspective and say, "All right, this time you're the oracle. Assume the world works out well; how would the oracle answer your own questions? What if the world turned into your worst nightmare?" These questions produce most of the material you use later. Because they've already thought about uncertainties, people are ready to give you a fairly rich set of stories. However, these are just trigger questions to make people talk. You should not end up with these "most and least favorable" scenarios; the final set of scenarios, in my opinion, should be value-independent.

- If you could go back ten years (or however far you are looking ahead), what would have been a useful scenario then?

Pierre Wack introduced this question in the 1970s. We ask people to remember where they were in their own past: What would have been an illuminating scenario to produce at that point? What would it have been good to foresee? By contrast, what did we actually think was going to happen? The rule here is to go back as far as your scenarios will look forward.

- What are the most important decisions you face right now?

Some short-term issues have very long-term implications.

- What constraints do you feel from the company's culture in making these decisions?

And what decisions would fall out differently if these constraints did not exist? The very strong Shell culture, for example, has a major effect on how people see things.

- What do you want on your epitaph?

When you leave the company, how do you want people to remember you? This allows you to round off the inquiry with a sense of the values that drive people's motivations.

PHASE 2: THE FEEDBACK SESSION

As quickly as possible, we report back to the managers with an analysis of their answers—always kept anonymous, with the answers grouped thematically. This step validates our understanding of the material. The managers must have the opportunity to say, "Yes, this is correct, but over there, you didn't hear us right."

These sessions, if conducted with a team, are extraordinarily positive events. Managers discover suddenly that their colleagues have deep thoughts about a lot of areas, which they were never asked for in a functionally divided organization. The marketing manager, for instance, may have something useful to say about production, or they may all have something to say about the cross-disciplinary and cultural constraints that have held them back in the past. Often, for the first time, you open up a situation in which they feel free to talk about this. We never stop this talk from straying anywhere.

PHASE 3: THE "FOUR-BOX APPROACH"

We built our process around teaching four key strategic activities, all intended to improve communication and collaborative thinking among team members:

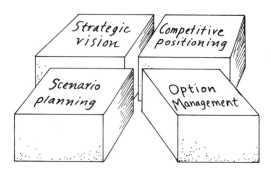

I see the *strategic vision* as the really important driving force in the background. However clever the discussions might be around the future and competitors, if they ignored this driving force—every manager's sense of purpose—then the discussions would be a waste of time. In our work, we had noticed an uncanny correlation between the success of a team and the convergence of strategic vision. We never figured out which was cause and which was effect, but our most successful companies all had management teams with cohesive strategic visions.

} } Strategic vision bears at least a family resemblance to building shared vision; see page 297.

Included in the fortnight was *scenario planning:* a relatively modest scenario exercise, sorting predetermined elements from uncertainties and trying to establish plausible plotlines for how to think about the future. To some extent, these were informed by Shell's global scenarios (which we developed in Group Planning), but in many countries, the connection was quite weak. They needed to develop their own scenarios, to focus on their own needs and concerns.

For *competitive positioning*, we adopted much of Michael Porter's approach, but recast it toward mental maps: how did the managers perceive their company vis-à-vis competitors? What should the competitive position of the company be, and what varying priorities lay under their disagreements about this question?

Finally, we wanted to help people get out from under what Pierre called the "advocative approach" to *option planning*. The more managers champion their own ideas, the less they tend to be interested in any options but the choice they prefer. If they are told to produce options for the team to consider, they will describe a few straw men alternative options, designed to be kicked down. This particularly happens in engineering environments, where managers feel very connected to the projects they propose.

Options, if you consider them carefully, are assets. They're worth money; for proof, just go to any option exchange. To develop strategies which might be effective across a series of different scenarios about the business environment, you need to generate and manage options effectively. So we tried to develop managers' tolerance for deliberately keeping their options open. For example, suppose you are planning to expand your manufacturing plant, and you can manage it at once, gaining economies of scale, or in two "bites," which are smaller and therefore more costly. If you saw the future as a one-line projection, you would choose the cheaper option. But if you started thinking about significant uncertainty in demand and plant loading, you might come to a different conclusion. Where there is uncertainty, there is value in keeping options open. There is also a cost in keeping options open, and as soon as this exceeds the value, you close the option. There is merit in learning to assess these costs carefully and manage your options accordingly.

Since managers often disagree about the value of options, the logic behind their judgment needs to come to the surface. In fact, all of these four "boxes" depend on the ability to surface and develop perceptions—of the world, and of your own strategic vision. In our internal consultancy, we took everyone through small-team exercises in each corner of the quadrant. At the end, we had a second meeting with the full team and reported back our observations: the convergence or divergence in their strategic vision, for example; their capability in analyzing their business environment; or whether they had a reasonably explicit system for managing their options. We would present this as a diagnosis and generate a list of actions to improve their capabilities.

The transition to institutional knowledge

AT SHELL, THE "INTERNAL CONSULTANCY" BECAME A REMARKABLY POPular product—even at the full Shell rate for consultation, which is fairly expensive. It became so successful that the chairman of the Committee of Managing Directors felt he had to put a stop to it. One of the cornerstones of Shell's structure is the independence of operating company management, and we could not take the risk of making their decision making depend, in any way, on our central office staff function.

Starting in 1988, instead of running an internal consultancy, the consultancy group became a local planning support group, organized and managed by long-term planning consultant Graham Galer. The local company planner is now the in-house "intervenor," interviewing and taking senior managers through the four-box approach. Group Planning provides backup, support, and training.

We have become convinced that all managers can be trained to talk effectively about their assumptions in all four "boxes" of activity. But there is still one important gap in our understanding of this process. The process by which individual managers' abilities influence the increase of institutional knowledge is still largely unknown. Mapping this link is a bit of work we still need to do.

As a clear example of what I mean, I'll describe some of my work, since leaving Shell, with a small company making machines that make microchips—an even higher-tech enterprise than the semiconductor manufacturing itself. In 1990, I conducted a "four-box" exercise there, and we spent a great deal of time in the scenario box, analyzing the main

uncertainties. One senior manager suggested that he was worried about the recession. At this time, the recession of the early 1990s was just starting, and the conventional wisdom believed it would be short, shallow, and lenient to high-technology. This manager said, "What if that assumption turns out not to be true? What if we're entering a deep, 1981-style recession? What would happen to microprocessors and then to our machines?"

Then someone else asked, "Well, how do we develop these assumptions in the first place? And how do they get worked into our cash projections?" The finance man looked at the sales man; they both looked at the marketing manager. No one knew the answer. The finance manager volunteered to find out, and he returned to another meeting a few days later.

"Well," he said, "as a small company, we cannot afford to invest a lot of money in environmental analysis, so we buy projections from Data-Quest, the top-rated high-tech market and economic research company. It makes good sense; we don't think we can ever hope to improve on their research capability."

"So," asked the original manager, "what's their assumption about the recession?"

"DataQuest," said the finance manager, "is assuming a shallow, short recession."

Now the room erupted in discussion. What if the recession wasn't to be shallow and short? The scenario exercise had shown them the value of questioning all such "inevitabilities." The CEO suggested that the finance manager ask for a new set of projections, based on the premise of a deeper, longer recession.

At the next meeting, the finance manager came back with some slides of spreadsheet numbers. "We have never done this before," he said, "but we made a few assumptions, and here's what it looks like." We gasped. If there were a deep recession, the company would be in serious trouble, because it would lose the cash influx its managers had assumed would come. They were about to commit their firm to major research investments, and it could easily fall into insolvency.

Now the CEO asked, "Are we really going to bet the company on DataQuest's prediction?" Over the next few weeks, they drastically cut back their research commitments. Today, they're not doing as well as they had hoped several years ago, but they are weathering the recession. They know that if they had committed those funds in 1990, they would now be out of business.

They were fortunate to make the jump from an individual insight to the institutional mind. It is not a leap we can take for granted. Each individual took a sensible decision from his own limited perspective. The planner making his projections, down in the finance department, was absolutely sensible to rely on DataQuest's numbers. They were the best numbers; it would be crazy to double-guess them. But nobody else in the organization knew where those projections came from, and what assumptions were driving the cash projection. If somebody said, "I wonder about the recession," nobody knew what to do with such a remark, because institutionally there were no channels to bring together the bits of information that would render the question meaningful.

Companies are absolutely chock-a-block with these sorts of compartmentalization problems. You cannot blame individuals in the system for this; it is humanly impossible to know everything. A minor lapse in communications can cause a major dislocation. People down the line may take quite sensible decisions, which can drive the company as a whole into the ground. The processes in the four-box approach need to hit at the appropriate points in the organizational system where better communication can have an impact. As in this example, the "node of productive intervention" may well be outside the management team, somewhere deep in the organization. Working through the four-box approach raises many of the right questions. But we still need to think more coherently about raising them at the place in the organization where they will make a difference.

42 Double-loop Accounting

Fred Kofman

Fred Kofman is a professor of Managerial Accounting at MIT, who also has a background as a student of the philosophy of language. The combination may sound rather bizarre, but as Fred says, "Accounting is the language of business." If we want to create a different world in business, we had better remember that old saw: "When all is said and done, the bean counters win." We'd better find some new ways to count the beans, or all our work with learning organizations will have no profound impact.

Fred's articulation of "double-loop accounting" looks at finances as a reflection of our mental models. This type of accounting may one day form a learning discipline of its own—the capacity to translate our shared understandings back into information systems, reward systems, and all the other "stuff" of an organization's infrastructure. At root is a question whose importance is as great to the heart and spirit as it is to the balance sheet: "To what should we be paying attention?"

At their first lesson in accounting, students are told that, "Accounting is the language of business." When they hear that, they think it means: "After some business has happened, the accountants come in with their language to describe it." This reflects an idea which philosophers held 500 years ago: that "language" is a means to describe the world outside oneself. But today, we realize that the speaker and the world "outside" are interrelated, and that while a speaker creates language, language is also creating the speaker. Language is a medium through which we create new understandings and new realities, as we begin to talk about them. In fact, we don't talk about what we see; we see only what we can talk about.

Being "the language of business" really means that accounting is the framework in which anything that can be perceived in business must show up. I particularly like the word "accounting" for this, because "to account" means not just to make a financial calculation, but to explain something's purpose and history. When we assume that accounting figures describe what has happened objectively, without "accounting" for the values which drove the system, we miss one of the most important levers for learning and change.

Returning the story to the numbers

WHENEVER WE OBJECTIFY A NUMBER OR A STORY, AS ACCOUNTING DOES, we face a great opportunity and a great danger. As a freestanding object, the story takes on a public identity as a vehicle for collective understanding. But when the numbers take on a life of their own, they sever their associations with us. They lose the memory of the processes which created them. The accounting system then becomes like the Frankenstein monster: a human construct which turns on its creators. The numbers appear as if they are the truth, as inescapable as destiny, muting the knowledge that the numbers are just "something we made up."

For example, a manager I worked with complained that, "I know how fuzzy my calculations were, how wide the margin of error in my measures was, how I had to combine the data to end up with a summary statement. But once my calculation is on paper, it becomes the truth and boy oh boy, you'd better not disturb it."

This might seem like a problem peculiar to a single company; but it is widespread. It is a function of the way we use accounting as a language. If we want our accounting systems to foster a learning organization, then their primary purpose should change radically. Instead of describing what already happened, accounting systems must enhance a group's ability to explore, articulate, and understand their reality. For the last several years, I have been working to develop such a system, called "double-loop accounting," combining the numbers of traditional managerial accounting with observations, questions, and models. The story which underlies the numbers, about how they were produced and what they might mean, is no longer masked within the measurements themselves.

Double-loop accounting at work: a project team

FOR EXAMPLE, IMAGINE YOU ARE MEETING A PROJECT TEAM IN A TYPICAL business, trying to decide whether to build a new component in-house or outsource it. Somebody says, "The net present value (NPV) if we build it ourselves is 20 percent, and that exceeds our hurdle rate for approving new projects, so we should go ahead." Someone else says, "No, I think the NPV should be 15 percent." A third person adds, "Have you considered the full cost of financing?" Someone else pulls out a line graph made from a spreadsheet. "When we take into account quality failure cost, we lose ten million dollars."

This language all sounds "objective," but every one of these numbers reflects a set of values. Each person at that meeting has reasons for preferring one number or another. All want to devise a number which they can sell to higher levels in the organization. As they talk about which calculation rules they will apply, they never inquire about each other's real motives. Thus, as the meeting progresses, the numbers become more and more fictitious—more divorced from anyone's values or sense of reality. The meeting is like a theatrical play, which everyone knows is a farce, but the actors keep straight faces onstage.

If the team were to practice double-loop accounting, instead of arguing about numbers created by following rules, they would hear a story. The speaker's career would not be at stake in every statement, so he or she wouldn't need to pretend to know every answer. The speaker might begin the presentation like this:

"In the time that I've had to study this problem, I've come to the conclusion that we should outsource this component, instead of building it ourselves. I want to tell you why I came to my opinion, and some basic assumptions I made along the road. There are a tremendous number of things I still don't know, so I want to check my reasoning with you . . ."

The speaker would go on to describe the view of the world reflected in the calculations. How much of the company's manufacturing capacity would be used, and for what purposes would the economy go through a cycle that would cause interest rates to vary? (And how would that affect the choice of methods for calculating ratios?) Would the market be stable? Would the learning from this new technology help the company enter other markets? If they outsourced, would the alliance with the new vendor become a strategic asset? Do suppliers exist that can provide the necessary level of quality?

Instead of attacking the number, the other people in the room would probe the story, trying to make it more complete and insightful: "So what happens if the company enters those new markets?" Each person would have something to add, and often something to ask. As they talk, the story would become a collective story. Now, instead of one "net present value" for this potential component project, there might be five or six. The story would be a model they have created together, which can spew out different numbers depending upon the assumptions they plug into it.

Preparing for a presentation

In most organizations, working groups are supposed to bring their conclusions up to the next level of management—say, the executive board. Under the old "single-loop accounting" system, before making that presentation, the manager in charge visits the board members to try to sell the proposal to them personally. Discussions and negotiation take place in offices, hallways, and carpools: "Harry told me this, but Jamie says that."

Not long ago, a vice president for manufacturing from a Fortune Ten firm described the typical negotiations to me. "Look," he said, "these guys in finance have been playing a game for the last fifty years. They come up and they tell us that they're going to set the hurdle rate at 15 percent. In other words, to get approval to invest $100,000 in a project, we should demonstrate that we'll get $115,000 back. So we prepare our capital requests to come up above 20 percent. And they come back and say, "No, it's not 15 any longer. It has to be 25." So we change our numbers up to 30. It's mutual escalation. Everybody knows everybody's bullshitting."

When the meeting day finally comes, the presenters carefully hide all the ambiguity and negotiation that went into the creation of their numbers. They pretend that the number emerged from some sort of perfect process, with no false starts, wrong turns, or cut deals. Most "false starts" and "wrong turns," of course, are turns down a path the presenter's team didn't want to take. In other words, the presenter has become a gatekeeper, choosing to hide certain options from his audience.

If all goes well, nothing happens. To quote from a manager whose company follows this pattern: "The best meeting is one where everybody sits there wondering, 'Why are we here? We've already decided we're going to do this.'" However, not all meetings go this "well." Despite the efforts of the presenter to forestall objection and cover up alternatives, everyone knows that something has been hidden. As soon as one person puts a number out, everybody shoots it down. Whatever information had survived thus far is now lost amid the advocacy.

By contrast, in double-loop accounting, there's very little effort expended in bringing people "on board" ahead of time. The presenter may visit board members, but only to ask for help: "I'm struggling with this. What do you think would make sense in this situation?" Then comes the meeting and the presenter's speech—this time with all of the assumptions and alternatives explained.

Now a member of the audience reacts: not with attack, but with inquiry. "I followed the story up to your third NPV number, but here I lost track. Can you backtrack and tell us how you came up with it?" The presenter explains; they check their interpretations against each other. "Ah, now I understand," says the executive at the table. "Let's try something else. I've learned that our supplier is offering us a deal to mass-produce another item, but only if we can outsource more parts with them. And I don't see that in your analysis."

"I didn't know that. How would that change the calculations?"

Now, the two work side by side looking at the chart, and talking freely about the implications of their changes: "Outsourcing makes me very uncomfortable because it means shutting down one of my plants. I would be lying if I said I don't feel for the people that will be out in the street if we outsource this product."

The other people in the room murmur assent, and then someone else says, "On the other hand, we ask that you understand how this whole company can go down the drain if we don't make some of these tough decisions." They may talk back and forth about all of the implications, each with its own budget counterpoints. They might have a computer spreadsheet running, where they try different numbers on the spot. Or they might say, "Let's call Joe, who worked in Japan; he may have a better sense of this." In short, instead of going to the meeting to sell, people have come to the meeting to learn.

Instilling the practice of "double-loop accounting"

SEVERAL YEARS AGO A PLANT MANAGER, A DEPARTMENT HEAD, AND I BE-gan an experiment at a Chrysler engine plant. We designed and implemented a new performance management system based on double-loop accounting principles. We started by asking the workers what would help them better understand their impact on the department's performance. Then we helped them design and produce "daily performance reports," giving them immediate feedback on performance—quality levels, scrap rates, tooling costs—in terms that they could understand. When they experimented with different procedures, they could see how those procedures contributed to the productivity of the department. Although the reports are inaccurate from a general accounting perspective, they help employees gain ownership of the numbers and redesign their work practices.

"That was the turning point of the meeting," he told me. "People began participating."

Elsewhere, I have seen environments where teams faced with financial issues are encouraged (by everyone, from the most senior managers on down) to learn together. In these environments, the team's preoccupation shifts from the final number to understanding how that number summarizes and synthesizes a much broader situation in a particular way.

How, then, can we encourage organizations to move from "single-loop" to "double-loop" learning in their financial structures? Here are a few steps that have proved effective in my experience:

- Look for the roots of the structure that determines the measurement process. This structure is simply the "way we have gotten used to doing things." It is historically dependent, and can be changed.
- Recognize that a number only makes a difference when somebody reads it and interprets it, and that the interpretations are determined by that person's mental models. Therefore, the highest leverage for improving accounting systems comes from making mental models more explicit.
- Notice that individual interpretations turn into collective decisions through communication, and adopt the principles of team learning into the accounting process.

See, for example, "Dialogue" (page 357) and "Skillful Discussion" (page 385).

- Have accounting providers and users engage in a supplier-customer relationship. In the past, financial people may have seen themselves as policemen, in charge of enforcing the rules so people did not cheat. Change their role to counselors who must help the plants improve.
- Design a continuous improvement process that will bring together accountants and operators to reflect on their mutual needs.
- Throughout this process, acknowledge difficulties, differences of opinion, and dilemmas. See the measurement process as one of mutual learning, rather than as one of mechanical application of fixed principles.

Accounting as story-telling

ACCOUNTANTS ARE THE ARCHITECTS OF AN ORGANIZATION'S NERVOUS SYStems. They design the way the organization will sense what is going on inside and outside itself. They create a context that determines the relevant questions to ask. They search for ground where the organization can position itself for maximum strength and flexibility. Their goal should be to design a structure for experiential learning.

For more about experiential learning, see "The Wheel of Learning," page 59.

Double-loop accounting springs from Chris Argyris's and Donald A. Schön's theory of "action science." (It is named after the action science concept of "double-loop learning": learning which questions deep assumptions.) However, there is an important difference between the two systems.

For more about action science, see page 264.

Action science assumes that there is a "theory-in-use" behind every action—a logical process inside the mind, reasoning, "If this, then that." Double-loop accounting assumes that there is also a *story* behind every action—a narrative process recounting. "This, then this, then this, then this." The story exists not only in our rational minds, but in our emotions and our full bodies. The theory of action science might lead us to ask: "What is the logic behind this number?" Double-loop accounting would also have us ask: "What led up to this number? What happened next?"

If the story behind the numbers is true and fully told, then people will change as they hear it—not only at the intellectual level, but down at the level of their heart, because that is where stories affect us. Truly great stories blend head and heart. They produce rational understanding, and emotional acceptance. An accounting number can be a truly great story.

43 Where to Go from Here

Charlotte Roberts

- **To team learning:** Many of the mental models techniques are similar to the practices of team learning. It is often fruitful to follow the two paths simultaneously—taking a scenario approach to planning, for instance, while participating in a dialogue (page 357) or defensive routines (page 404) project.
- **To personal mastery:** Mental models practice draws attention to personal models and assumptions about yourself and where you fit in the world. Thus, for many people, it adds urgency to the need to practice personal mastery. See page 193.
- **To systems thinking:** As you and your team uncover your dominant mental models, you will begin thinking of how to construct your organization to support the new model of business. Systems thinking will be a natural next step in the process. See page 87.

Shared
Vision

~~~~~~~~~~~~~~~~~~~~~~~~~~~~~~~~~~~~

44 Strategies for Building Shared Vision

When Czechoslovakia became a democracy almost overnight in 1989, one of the first tasks for the new leaders was planning elections. They could have designed five- or six-year terms, enough to re-create the new country's institutions. But instead, they set the terms at *two* years—barely enough time to draft a constitution.

As Václav Havel, the writer and former dissident who was elected President, explained later:

> We found ourselves in a transitional period, when everything [was] being reborn . . . The idea of democracy [had] won in every respect, but the outcome was not yet a genuine, fully fledged democracy.

Havel had plenty of ideas about what the new country should be. But he recognized the dangers of imposing a vision, no matter how worthy, on the country from above. Instead, he and Czechoslovakia's other leaders developed strategic mechanisms to involve the country as a whole in developing its future: referendums, public meetings, support for new political parties, and extensive discussion on radio.

The leaders knew they would vehemently disagree with some of the results—such as Slovakia's choice to secede. "Yet the decision," Havel argued, "is entirely up to Slovakia." In the end, the two years spent (in effect) building shared vision didn't solve many problems in itself; but it created an environment in which people believed they were part of a common entity—a community. The new Czech republic is credited with having the most vibrant national atmosphere in Eastern Europe today.°

Today many leaders seek to achieve the commitment and focus that come with genuinely shared visions. Unfortunately, too many people still think that "vision" is the top leader's job. Individual leaders' visions may succeed in carrying an organization through a crisis. But, as Havel recognized, there is a deeper challenge: creating a sense of purpose that binds people together and propels them to fulfill their deepest aspirations. Catalyzing people's aspirations doesn't happen by accident; it requires time, care, and strategy. Thus, the discipline of building shared vision is centered around a never-ending process, whereby people in an organization articulate their common stories—around vision, purpose, values, why their work matters, and how it fits in the larger world.

° This story is told in Václav Havel's recent book of political essays, *Summer Meditations*, translated by Paul Wilson (1992, 1993, New York: Random House). See p. 18, pp. 21–23, and p. 33. Also see "All They Are Saying Is Give Prague a Chance" by Stanley Meisler, *Smithsonian*, vol. 24, no. 10, June 1993, p. 66.

Shared vision: a vehicle for building shared meaning

A SUCCESSFUL STRATEGY FOR BUILDING SHARED VISION WILL BE BUILT around several key precepts:

- Every organization has a destiny: a deep purpose that expresses the organization's reason for existence. We may never fully know that purpose, just as an individual never fully discovers his or her individual purpose in life. But choosing to continually listen for that sense of emerging purpose is a critical choice that shifts an individual or a community from a reactive to a creative orientation.

- Clues to understanding an organization's deeper purpose can often be found in its founders' aspirations, and in the reasons why its industry came into being. Every telecommunications organization, for example, is tied in some way to Alexander Graham Bell's sense of the purpose for the telephone system: a vehicle for universal communication. Every medical and pharmaceutical organization is tied to the purpose of improving human health. Insurance companies exist, at root, because society has tacitly agreed to share the burden of managing risk; otherwise, life would be horribly unfair. Organizational mission or purpose statements often lack depth because they fail to connect to the industry's overarching reason for existence. When this connection is made forcefully, an individual firm's commitment can energize an entire industry toward a deeper sense of purpose.

- Not all visions are equal. Visions which tap into an organization's deeper sense of purpose, and articulate specific goals that represent making that purpose real, have unique power to engender aspiration and commitment. To be genuinely shared, such visions must emerge from many people reflecting on the organization's purpose.

- Many members of the organization, especially those who care deeply for the organization, have a collective sense of its underlying purpose. Like mental models, this shared sense of purpose is often tacit— obscured by conventional day-to-day practices, the prevailing organizational culture, and the barriers of the organization's structure. To become more aware of the organization's purpose ask the members of the organization and learn to listen for the answers.

- Thus, at the heart of building shared vision is the task of designing and evolving ongoing processes in which people at every level of the organization, in every role, can speak from the heart about what really matters to them and be heard—by senior management and each other. The quality of this process, especially the amount of openness and genuine caring, determines the quality and power of the results. That is why, in this part of the book, you will find very little material on the appropriate *content* of an organization's purpose. The content of a true shared vision cannot be dictated; it can only emerge from a coherent process of reflection and conversation.

- Finally, there is an organizational equivalent to the personal mastery concept of "creative tension"—the innate pull that emerges when we hold clear pictures of our vision juxtaposed with current reality.

For more about the link between personal mastery and shared vision, see "Vision for the Organization," page 208.

As all of these precepts suggest, the shared vision discipline is essentially focused around *building shared meaning*, potentially where none existed before. Shared meaning is a collective sense of what is important, and why. In traditional organizations, the only meaning which most members know has been handed to them from above—from a tacit hierarchy of meaning embedded in the organization's authority structure.

If people could voice their hearts as they receive the organization's "meaning from on high," they might say, "Our top management has established our organization's vision and strategy. My job has been defined within that strategy. I have been told to care about that job, but it's not my vision. I will do the best I can." People may accept this "meaning" passively, or they may feel resentful; but they will not feel enrolled.

But when members at any level have had an opportunity to actively consider what vision and purpose have real meaning for them, everything changes. Having gone through the frustration and ultimate satisfaction of creating a personal vision and a shared vision for their immediate team, they become more devoted to building shared vision and shared meaning for the entire organization. Team members will often suggest joint sessions with other teams, to share visions and develop action plans that they can implement together. As that process is repeated among many teams and multiple pairings, the whole organization is engaged and enriched, and multiple strands of shared meaning begin to bind the organization together.

Building shared vision can be an effective way to articulate an organization's "Guiding Ideas"; see page 22.

Networks and community

THE NEW INFRASTRUCTURES WE SEE EMERGING THAT ENABLE BUILDING shared vision are based on viewing an organization as a set of overlapping communities formed around shared meaning. Juanita Brown, a pioneer in applying community development principles to organizations, points out that if we began to see organizations as communities, leaders would treat members as volunteers who have chosen to give their time to the enterprise. We would realize that the ultimate "glue" that binds people is not "what they get" from the organization but what they can contribute to the community. Top management would not assume formal authority *over* the members of the organization, but would see itself as serving the community and its larger vision. We would realize that volunteers belong not just to the organization, but to multiple overlapping communities within it. Every work team, every professional subculture, and every geographic entity would be encouraged to forge its own shared sense of meaning and its own unique sense of contribution to the whole. It would be understood that meaning couldn't be handed to any of these entities. They must create it from within.

See "Organizations as Communities," page 507.

To support this creative process, people need to know that they have real freedom to say what they want about purpose, meaning, and vision, with no limits, encumbrances, or reprisals. Senior managers must put aside their fear that "We must set the limits within which people can create vision, or they will run out of control."

〉〉 See "Reinventing Relationships," page 69.

Shared visions have a way of spreading through personal contact. To link all of these multiple communities together, the organization depends on its informal networks—communication channels where people talk easily and freely, meeting at pot-luck suppers, participative events, and other informal gatherings. The organization can also support such networks with electronic mail and conferencing. However, early experience suggests that, while computer networks can help people keep in touch and compare assumptions easily, it is not adequate for building shared meaning. As members of a community, we need to meet in person when we talk about what we really care about.

〉〉 See "Bean Suppers," page 518.

Such informal networks are especially vital in bringing about the deep changes in culture and operations which management hierarchies have great difficulty achieving. Consider the case of Ault Foods, a large Canadian company based in the dairy industry, which won the 1993 *Financial Post* award for the environmentally best-managed company in Canada. Originally, the top management team, faced with increasingly strict environmental legislation, gave a manager named Pam Kempthorne the job of "keeping us out of trouble." Accepting only volunteers, she ended up with more than twenty people for a task force which began with intense work on personal values and vision.

"When they recognized their cohesiveness around those values," Ault CEO Graham Freeman tells the story, "their group caught fire. They became zealots. Our senior management committee gave them ten minutes to present their ideas. They said, 'We need two and a half hours, and not a minute less.' At the end of two meetings with them, we were completely aligned with their vision. We had shifted 180 degrees—from 'Let's comply with the law,' to, 'We're going to embrace environmental practice from top to bottom.' We ended up having a vibrant community within the organization, supporting each other; R&D people would support plant people. They were all hooking up almost outside the management system. Miraculous things kept happening in all our locations; we kept finding highly profitable ways to solve environmental problems. When I think of what other companies go through to get rid of this monkey on their back called 'environment'—well, we just didn't experience it here."

LE**XIC**ON

VISION, VALUES, PURPOSE (OR MISSION), GOALS

Although this discipline is called "building shared vision," that phrase is only a convenient label. A vision is only one component of an organization's guiding aspirations. The core of those guiding principles is the sense of shared purpose and destiny, including all of these components:

Vision: an image of our desired future

A vision is a picture of the future you seek to create, described in the present tense, as if it were happening now. A statement of "our vision" shows where we want to go, and what we will be like when we get there. The word comes from the Latin *vidēre,* "to see." This link to seeing is significant; the more richly detailed and visual the image is, the more compelling it will be.

Because of its tangible and immediate quality, a vision gives shape and direction to the organization's future. And it helps people set goals to take the organization closer.

Values: how we expect to travel to where we want to go

The word "value" comes from the French verb *valoir,* meaning "to be worth." Gradually it evolved an association with valor and worthiness. Values describe how we intend to operate, on a day-by-day basis, as we pursue our vision. As Bill O'Brien points out, Adolf Hitler's Germany was based on a very clear shared vision, but its values were monstrous.

A set of governing values might include: how we want to behave with each other; how we expect to regard our customers, community, and vendors; and the lines which we will and will not cross. Values are best expressed in terms of behavior: If we act as we should, what would an observer see us doing? How would we be thinking?

When values are articulated but ignored, an important part of the shared vision effort is shut away. By contrast, when values are made a central part of the organization's shared vision effort, and put out in full view, they become like a figurehead on a ship: a guiding symbol of the behavior that will help people move toward the vision. It becomes easier to speak honestly, or to reveal information, when people know that these are aspects of agreed-upon values.

Purpose or *Mission:* what the organization is here to do

"Mission" comes from the Latin word *mittere,* meaning "to throw, let go, or send." Also derived from Latin, the word "purpose" (originally prōpōnere) meant "to declare." Whether you call it a mission or purpose, it represents the fundamental reason for the organization's existence. What are we here to do together?

The "mission" is more popular in organizations today, but it has un- fortunate military, religious, and short-term overtones: "Our mission is to take this hill [or die in the attempt]!" I prefer the word "purpose"; it suggests more of a reflective process. You will never get to the ultimate purpose of your organization, but you will achieve many visions along the way.

Goals: milestones we expect to reach before too long

Every shared vision effort needs not just a broad vision, but specific, realizable goals. Goals represent what people commit themselves to do, often within a few months. The word may have come from the Old En- glish *gœlan,* to hinder, and goals often address barriers and obstacles which we must pass to reach our vision. — BS

Alain Gauthier develops the idea of goals in his cameo on "Strategic Priorities" (see page 344).

Is the purpose of a corporation to maximize profits?

PEOPLE SOMETIMES SAY THAT IT'S POINTLESS TO DEVELOP A SENSE OF purpose for a company. There already is a purpose, crowding out all others: "To maximize return on investment to shareholders." A loyal, dedicated officer of a company, we are told, should have no personal aspirations but providing good financial results, as immediately as possi- ble.

Obviously, making money is important. A manager who says profit is unimportant is like a coach who says, "I don't care if we win or lose." But to confuse one essential requirement for advancing in the game with an organization's purpose is a profound confusion, around which our entire industrial enterprise has been teetering. After all, every other profit-making corporation also has the purpose of making money; focus- ing on that purpose, at the expense of others, will naturally distract an organization's competitive advantage. — BS, AK

ISHMAEL **by Daniel Quinn** (1992, New York: Bantam/Turner).

When building shared vision includes ongoing reflection about our deepest problems, it lifts us out of the frame of our existing aspirations, and opens the doors to new ones. This novel does the same—not for an organization, but for the human species. Civilization has built its own hierarchy of meaning based on fragmentation, starting with the separation of man from nature and the belief that evolution ended with us. Consequently, we have become "takers" not "leavers," putting all succeeding generations at risk. In *Ishmael*, Daniel Quinn uses a fictional teacher (a gorilla in dialogue with a man) to trace the history of the story of separation, domination, and isolation "we have been telling ourselves" for thousands of years, and to suggest an alternative. Besides its potent message, the book is itself a demonstration of how a shared vision, even one that seems unlikely at first, can grow.—**PS, BS**

45 What You Can Expect . . . As You Build Shared Vision

Charlotte Roberts

New challenges for the leader

IN THE EARLY STAGES OF A VISIONING PROCESS, THE ORGANIZATION WILL seem harder to manage than it did before. In the name of achieving the shared vision, employees will demand input and influence on policies and practices.

One senior executive, talking about his newly energized team, said coming to work was like "trying to steer seven wild horses instead of beating seven dead horses to move." He was startled by the number of new skills and capabilities the shared vision effort required of him. Instead of controlling, motivating, and evaluating people, he had to learn to listen to people and channel their enthusiastic initiative without stifling it.

As the visioning process is implemented, leaders need to be present and available for talking with, listening to, and mentoring employees. Some people in the organization may not be articulate, but still feel strongly about the words. They may see the vision as an opportunity to dump all their complaints in their boss's lap; or they may think they now have a carte blanche to act independently toward the vision. Be ready for the time and patience you'll need for orchestrating collective commitment.

Momentum from previous successes

IF YOUR ORGANIZATION HAS ACCOMPLISHED A SIGNIFICANT MILESTONE— a successful new product introduction, a joint venture, a series of quality improvements, or the gaining of the #1 position in the marketplace—a shared vision effort can build on the spirit of that success. Move quickly, however, because if you allow the organization to rest too long, you will lose the momentum, and the visioning process will have to overcome the old inertia again.

Keeping the vision fluid

IT IS EQUALLY IMPORTANT TO KEEP THE VISION FLUID. DON'T HAVE THE words printed in a full-color brochure or etched in stone in the corner of the building. Visions are always evolving; they are an expression of our hearts' desire. As we work toward our vision, we learn more about ourselves and other possibilities become clearer.

Aligning the entire work force

IN THE PROCESS OF BUILDING A SHARED VISION, PEOPLE AND FUNCTIONS throughout the organization tend to naturally align. Suddenly, the scattered and isolated parts of a federation now have a sense of "magnetic north": a common orientation point, pulling everyone toward the same future.

When there is a major change such as a merger, acquisition, or downsizing, you can unify people, instead of setting them against each other, by building a shared vision of what the future will look like if the change is done well. This may mean, however, involving the entire organization in decisions about implementing the change.

46 Designing an Organization's Governing Ideas

Bill O'Brien

As president of the Hanover Insurance Company of Worcester, Massachusetts, Bill O'Brien spent twenty years refining his company's vision, values, and sense of common purpose. Since retiring in 1991, he has spent much of his time helping other organizations do the same. His example and insights greatly influence every strategy and suggestion in this part of the book.

§§ Also see Bill O'Brien on "Why Bother (A CEO's Perspective)," page 13.

For the last twenty-five years, I have personally been driven by the premise that almost every person has an enormous reservoir of potential, both for improved performance and for happiness. (By "happiness," I intend the deepest meaning of the word: the sense that your life as a whole is going well, and that you are contributing to something larger than yourself and being rewarded for it fairly.) I could see that the design of most organizations, particularly large ones, frustrated the fulfillment of this potential. I don't mean the design of the organization chart and the sequence of who reports to whom, but the arrangement of fundamental governing ideas by which the organization runs itself.

Every organization has governing ideas, whether or not they're articulated. The governing ideas of the United States Government, for example, are not the details of how a bill becomes a law. They are the principles in the Declaration of Independence, the U.S. Constitution, and the Bill of Rights. These ideas include concepts about freedom from tyranny, the rights of the individual, freedoms of press and religion, and the possibility that people, regardless of their heritage, may find opportunities to move from one level of society to another.

A COMPANY WITHOUT VALUES: HANOVER, 1970

My interest in governing ideas came out of a deep sense of frustration. I joined Hanover Insurance in 1971—not yet as the company president, but as the head of marketing. The president at that time, Jack Adam, was also relatively new; he had been placed in the post to turn around a company in serious financial trouble. Hanover was a typical authoritarian hierarchy. The governing ideas of the company, though I didn't think of them that way at the time, began with the idea that by definition, the people at the highest echelons were the smartest, and thus best qualified to make most decisions. Therefore, the more power someone had, the better they were. Success meant rising to the next higher level. Management meant figuring out how long you should offer your subordinates carrots before you started threatening them with sticks.

Every year, we would bring in the brightest, most energetic people we could find at salaries we were willing to pay. They'd discover that the name of the game was climbing up the ladder. We had many ways people could pull themselves up, including blaming people in other functions. But the most prominent method was making a good impression, so that higher-up people would say to themselves, "I like this person. I can really trust him." Eventually, however, every manager would reach a level where he would look up and think, "Uh-oh! There are not many places in the pyramid above me. But if I can't make it up there, I sure can keep from going back down." From then on, every time there was an important decision, the manager would fall back on the rules: handling things according to procedures and manuals, and channeling all his creativity and ambition into verbal gamesmanship.

I was reminded of a town I had once moved to in upstate New York, where the smell from a nearby paper mill was so strong that my wife insisted we couldn't live there. But we had no choice but to stay. Within two weeks, the smell disappeared. It was as bad as ever, but we had stopped paying attention. Organizations oriented to power, I realized, also have strong smells, and even if people are too inured to notice, that smell has implications. It affects performance, productivity, and innovation. The worst aspect of this environment is that it stunts the growth of personality and character of everyone who works there.

Jack Adam and I decided that we were going to try to overcome this problem at Hanover. We knew, even in the early 1970s, that we couldn't enforce the values we wanted by decree. We had to create them, articulate them, and see if people would sign on and improve them.

LAYING OUT A PURPOSE

We began by laying out a purpose for the company. In those days, when mainstream businessmen believed the only purpose of business was making money, it was very radical. We said that the purpose of our company was three-fold: to give the American people the maximum value for their property and liability insurance dollar, to provide each employee with the help and environment necessary to become all he or she was capable of becoming, and to earn a profit to fuel our growth, provide for a rainy day, and reward ourselves. It was a mission statement, although nobody had heard of that word yet. As soon as we had written it down, we thought we'd solved our problem.

As head of marketing, I traveled a lot. I'd come back from trips and Jack would ask if I'd talked to people about our purpose. "The first time I tell them, Jack, they think it's novel and refreshing," I said. "But by the second or third time, they think it's cornball." This is typical; most purpose statements inspire the five or ten people who sit around writing them, but do nothing for the 5,000 other people in the corporation. If it is going to enlist people's spirit, a purpose must be extended into a set of values and a vision. We needed some shared sense of what we stood for as an organization, and a way to replace the discipline of the hierarchy not with anarchy, but with self-discipline.

DEVELOPING OUR CORE VALUES

First with Jack Adam and then with other colleagues in the company and on my own, I gradually identified an ongoing series of key values—ways of behaving that we felt would help us overcome the hierarchical diseases. Three of the core values are particularly worth describing: merit, openness, and localness.

Living with a value of *merit* meant making every decision in the company on the basis of what would get the best results, not on the political clout of the advocates of any position. Anybody can intellectually grasp merit and agree on its value. The trick is internalizing it in the way the organization behaves. Senior managers had to show we really meant it, even when our own positions were at stake, and practice it through an extensive period of cynicism, which lasted for years.

Our value of *openness* came in three dimensions. The first concerned our relationship with outsiders. I had worked in four companies before Hanover, and had seen firsthand how frequently the reports to shareholders were not forthright interpretations of actual performance. A growth rate might be 3 percent, but it was described as "record-breaking," because sales were higher than the previous year. Not only did the shareholders tend to see through this, but it also made it impossible for employees to trust us—especially those who knew the real meaning of the numbers. At Hanover, starting in the 1970s, we sent the same report to front-line managers as we sent the board of directors, with no spin on the news.

The second dimension is a bit more difficult. Why do Americans watch baseball, and get bored with cricket? Because in the former, they know the rules and how to keep score. So at Hanover, in the 1980s, we began using the company magazine to explain the rules of the insurance industry. We installed a bulletin board in the lobby, and posted the most relevant financial statistics for the forty largest insurance companies.

But we also needed a sense of openness in our conversations. We were first exposed to the skills of balancing inquiry and advocacy in the late 1970s when Chris Argyris visited. Jack Adam set up a meeting with twelve of his direct reports, and within ten minutes, Chris had demonstrated how different our espoused values were from the values which governed our behavior. Ultimately, Hanover established a permanent course which we called "merit, openness, and localness," in which more than 1,500 managers were trained in skills to enhance open conversation.

⟩⟩ For more about these techniques, see pages 242–68.

Our third key value, *localness*, did not represent a geographic concept. It was based on the principle of subsidiarity: that a higher level should not make decisions for a lower level, if the lower level is capable of making the decision itself. This is a very smart principle. It suggests that the role of people at the top is to make the people who do the work self-reliant, not dependent. If you intervene from the top, the burden of proof is on you to show why the intervention is necessary.*

*For more on "localness," see *The Fifth Discipline*, p. 287 and *The Age of Unreason*, by Charles Handy (1989, 1990, Boston: Harvard Business School Press), p. 126. See *Fieldbook*, p. 65.

Creating a vision

IN 1979, I SUCCEEDED JACK ADAM AS PRESIDENT, AND BEGAN A NEW round of traveling across the country, speaking about my vision for Hanover to groups of employees. I always began by connecting our current status to our original purpose and ideals. I had seen so many corporations try to get out of trouble by importing a new executive from "company X," but like a body with an unsuccessful organ transplant, the host organization tends to reject the new entrant. So I decided to do the opposite: to go back to our roots and give credit to what had been accomplished since the company's founding in 1852. While acknowledging past ideals, I tried to portray an accurate view of realities. And finally, I tried to give them a sense of what ought to be, as I saw it.

The key to being a good visionary leader is not waking up at three in the morning struck by a white-lightning insight about where the company is going. The key is applying your vision to very mundane realities. I had thought a great deal about what I wanted Hanover to be, and what I wanted it to stand for. I wanted us to place each year in the upper quarter of our industry (as measured by combined ratio), and to grow at 1¼ to 1½ times the growth rate of the industry as a whole. These components of my vision were measurable and easy to understand. Then I told our employees I'd like to see us achieve unquestionable superiority. "I can't define it," I said, "but I know it when I see it."

I gradually came up with a definition, simple enough to use in talks and robust enough to ring true, time after time. Unquestionable superiority, for us at least, would mean marrying individual growth and economic performance. You can never separate those two factors, I had become convinced, or you will not build a very good organization. Human capital drives financial capital, and organizations without business success can't sustain individual growth. I began describing this notion as our central governing idea, and I noticed that people responded to it more ardently. Gradually, people began to offer their own descriptions of what Hanover could become.

An emphasis on individual growth, of course, meant I had to take everyone's visions seriously, including my own. So I began to tell our people that, while my personal vision got me out of the bed in the morning to go to work, it wouldn't do a damn thing for anybody else. I wasn't going to try to get people to sign on to *my* vision for Hanover, but to their own. Just as people need oxygen for physical health, we need aspirations for a healthy emotional life. I was beginning to see how transforming the day is in anyone's life when, for the first time, they go to work to build what they want to build, rather than because the boss wants them there.

When claims adjusters went out to see a car wreck, would they look closely enough to see through the fraud, padding, and deductibles of the auto body shop? Would underwriters, walking through buildings to assess them, give in to the temptation to offer insurance at too low a rate, or would they reflect long enough to reach a considered decision? If we could get 12 percent of our people to cross that line, we'd have a hell of an edge over our competitors. If we could get it up to 40 percent, we could dominate markets. But most people don't get up in the morning eager to produce high earnings per share: they are propelled by the prospect of going where they want to go.

A COMPANY WITH GOVERNING IDEAS

Our system was entirely home-grown. The only pieces that came from outside were Argyris's techniques for enriching conversation, and work with Innovation Associates on systems thinking. Everything else was born out of our own experience and needs.

Having a philosophy does not preclude bad news. If you're over-staffed, or if the economy takes an enormous dip, the philosophy will not eliminate those pressures. But it tells you, and people throughout the company, that you will deal with these pressures according to your values. There will be merit, fairness, and open information. People will get as much of an economic break as possible, and they will be treated with respect for their competence and human dignity.

Under the new system of governing ideas, we achieved far better implementation of plans, because people had a louder voice in what they were doing. People no longer deteriorated in their maturity and competence as they stayed in the company. We still made mistakes, but they were no longer buried.

In 1969, we had been one of the lowest-rated insurance companies in profitability and growth rate. When I left the company, in 1991, our sales were more than $1.6 billion, and our price per share was $40 (risen from a 1970 figure of 90 cents). None of our growth, anywhere along the line, required investment of new capital. It was all achieved by managing our internal problems, which we could accomplish only because we had a set of governing ideas.

This journey to become a mature, vision- and value-driven company took twelve years. We started in 1970 (just before I arrived), saw our first performance payoffs in the mid-1970s, and reached a point in 1982 where our economic and human performance showed us beyond a doubt we knew what we were doing. I think it's a six-year minimum job for a medium-sized corporation to reach that point. And in the end, of course, it is a lifetime's work.

47 Building Shared Vision: How to Begin

Bryan Smith

Imagine this scene: in a large hotel ballroom, 1,000 members of an organization, representing every level, sit in rows. Standing before them, the CEO has just finished a forty-five-minute presentation on the organization's vision. Now he looks out across the room: "If you want to make this vision your own and make it happen," he says, "please indicate your personal commitment by standing up."

There is a momentary buzz of excited conversation. Then, beginning at the front of the room and sweeping to the back like a thousand-person wave, everyone springs to their feet and begins applauding. The CEO joins in the cheering, laughter, and celebration, but he is no longer the center of focus. People's faces beam with pride in themselves and each other.

It has been a very effective hour—and it represents the culmination of a year of intense conversation and dialogue. Everyone in the audience has taken part in at least one shared vision session, talking about their aspirations for their lives and their work. The resulting vision is a creative synthesis of all that has emerged. It is like a diamond with many diverse facets, and each member can see through at least one facet as a personal window into the larger vision. Every member of the audience had heard his or her own aspirations reflected somewhere.

Six months later, the process continues. People throughout the organization continue to meet in small teams at work, at local gathering places after work, and even in each other's homes. Conversations focus on what they can do—individually and as teams—to move toward the vision. Their pride, energy, and commitment is even more evident than it was in the large meeting six months before.

But suppose that there had not been that year of intensive dialogue before the CEO spoke. Suppose the CEO had written out the vision over a weekend, and the "sharing" process had lasted an hour, from the moment the speech began to the collective "yes" which it evoked. An observer, watching the stage, might notice no difference in the words of the speech, the charisma of its delivery, or the enthusiasm of the crowd. However, many of the people there would feel unsure about their commitment. Yes, they would find it difficult to remain seated while others cheered, but they might not grasp the vision's implications or feel any personal responsibility for it.

It would be tempting for the CEO to conclude that the job was done. "I've come up with my vision and shared it, so now we have a 'shared vision.' Everyone in the organization has taken it for their own." But it is highly unlikely that a brief process, like a one-hour speech, can lead to a true shared vision—a vision which draws out the commitment of people throughout the organization. A vision is not really shared unless it has staying power and evolving life-force that lasts for years, propelling people through a continuous cycle of action, learning, and reflection.

After a failed shared vision attempt, I have heard senior managers say, "Once again we've just proved that these people spend all their time complaining. They're obviously not responsible. I'll just have to tell them what we're going to do from now on." Meanwhile, subordinates say, "It's obvious now that this organization has no interest in our input about the direction for the future." *Both* attitudes are actually symptoms of the fact that there was no deliberate, strategic design of the shared visioning process.

> Who carries out a shared vision strategy? It is generally handled most effectively by a partnership between the senior manager responsible for an organization, and a skilled, or committed "steward" of the vision. For more about this partnership see "Letter to the CEO" (page 328), and "Letter to the CEO's Partner" (page 333).

A strategy for building shared vision

SHARED VISION STRATEGIES SHOULD BE DEVELOPMENTAL. EVERY STAGE of the process should help build both the listening capacity of the top leaders, and the leadership capacities of the rest of the organization, so that they can move together to the next stage. To include most of the practical realities people face, I have identified five potential starting points. I believe every organization is already predisposed to one of them.

I recommend you objectively assess which stage best describes your organization now. Then develop a plan to move to the next stage using the strategies outlined in the following pages. The five stages are:

Telling: The "boss" knows what the vision should be, and the organization is going to have to follow it;

Selling: The "boss" knows what the vision should be, but needs the organization to "buy in" before proceeding;

Testing: The "boss" has an idea about what the vision should be, or several ideas, and wants to know the organization's reactions before proceeding;

Consulting: The "boss" is putting together a vision, and wants creative input from the organization before proceeding;

Co-Creating: The "boss" and "members" of the organization, through a collaborative process, build a shared vision together.

THE "BOSS" AND THE "MEMBERS"

In using the term "the boss" here, I mean any formal leader, executive, manager, or supervisor who has sufficient authority and autonomy to preside over a visioning process without being overriden by other managers. I also use the terms "CEO," "senior manager," and "formal leader" to mean "the boss."

My preferred term for other participants is "members." This term reflects the reality that all participants, even if they are not asked for their vote or opinion, end up "voting" with their behavior—which may range anywhere from active resistance through full support of the vision. To describe this role, I also use the terms "employees," "subordinates," "team members," and "participants."

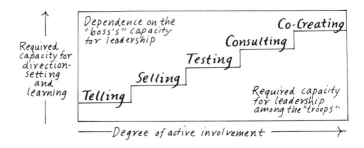

In this picture of the five stages, the further to the left, the more the organization depends on a strong leader to "tell" everyone what the shared vision should be. The further to the right, the more leadership, direction-setting, and learning capacity the organization as a whole must have. Here, the boss is less "the person with the answers," and more the convener of a robust process.

Any organization which does not adopt a somewhat formal, concerted shared vision process will probably find itself following the path of least resistance: down toward the left, falling back to the "telling" orientation. The boss will gradually become more authoritarian, and the rest of the organization more passive.

But if you climb uphill toward "co-creating," then each stage adds to your ability to reach the next stage. The boss's capacity to listen, and the organization's capacity to develop aspirations, gradually reinforce and complement each other.°

° Credit: The visual diagram and some of the points along the continuum are influenced by "How to Choose a Leadership Pattern" by Robert Tannenbaum and Warren Schmidt, *Harvard Business Review,* March/April 1958. Rick Ross also influenced the conceptual framework in this piece.

Stage 1: "Telling"

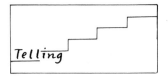

"WE'VE GOT TO DO THIS. IT'S OUR VISION. BE EXCITED ABOUT IT, OR RECONSIDER YOUR VISION FOR YOUR CAREER HERE"

People don't get to vote. When the boss says, "This is the vision of what the organization is going to look like two years from now," people know that if they disagree, or if they are caught undermining the change, they jeopardize their career. "Telling" often takes place in a crisis, when the senior managers perceive that some dramatic change is necessary.

For example, in Noel Tichy and Stratford Sherman's book *Control Your Destiny or Someone Else Will,*° Jack Welch knows he has very little time to make his organization profitable. So he proclaims his famous dictum that all of General Electric's businesses will be either #1 or #2 in their market, or sold—and tells everyone that if they don't embrace that vision, they won't survive long at GE.

° See *Fieldbook,* p. 68.

Although "telling" is a traditional and somewhat authoritarian form of instigating change, a "told" vision is still a vision, with power for galvanizing activity. I have seen effective messages from a boss that clearly and honestly describe a vision and sense of current reality in positive terms, and then say: "We can't afford anything less than a complete swing to this new strategy. Given my responsibility to the board, I'm going to be firm. After a period of time for raising concerns, people will have to leave if they can't support the new direction. We don't have unlimited time or energy for cross-currents when we're implementing such a major change."

If this is delivered in the proper mode, you can imagine people responding: "The boss is right. I don't understand it fully, but I'm willing to support it."

TIPS FOR MASTERING THE "TELLING" MODE

Inform People Directly, Clearly, and Consistently

An effective "telling" medium is efficient, revelatory, direct, and consistent throughout the organization. Letters and videos, if well produced, serve this need; so do personal speeches, especially if there are opportunities for questions and follow-up. Make sure to substantiate what you've got to say. Filling in the reasons why a change must be made is essential, if the organization is going to follow.

Tell the Truth About Current Reality

One central function of vision is to generate creative tension; to make sure people understand the difficulties of current reality, and generate the "pull" that comes from understanding your true distance from the vision. Anything less than the truth can destroy credibility. If some information is sensitive or confidential, explain why you can't disclose it.

Be careful not to build your message on a negative vision of the future that you're trying to avoid, such as: "Our vision is to avoid getting killed by the competition." There is a profound difference between "vision by desperation" and "vision by aspiration."

Be Clear About What Is Negotiable and What Is Not

There may be certain areas where subordinates have degrees of freedom to influence, and others where they literally have no influence. If so, tell them. If you are being held accountable by the board for certain results with few degrees of freedom, tell them that.

Paint the Details, but Not Too Many Details

A vision ultimately needs richness and detail to come to life. Early on, however, don't fill in too many details, because this may be the organization's only opportunity to make the vision its own. When Honda's senior managers sought to create a pattern of innovation, they set out the simple vision: "Let's Gamble." Branches of the company, in North America and elsewhere, translated that into specific ideas for action.

⟨⟨ Also see the tips for the CEO on page 330.

THE LIMITS OF "TELLING"

Research on verbal communications shows that people remember only about 25 percent of a message told to them. And everyone may remember a different 25 percent! Moreover, if the message is a "told" vision, people will comply, but few will feel any reason to commit themselves to it. Leaders who rely on "telling" often end up frustrated with what they perceive as poor communication: "I spelled out the vision, but people still don't seem to act according to it."

Unfortunately, many managers respond by repeating the same message, at a louder volume, or on a longer video. But employees can only go so far when they are passive recipients of a vision. It will be far more effective for the boss to begin moving to the right on the continuum—to "selling."

Stage 2: "Selling"

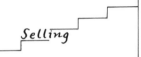

"WE HAVE THE BEST ANSWER. LET'S SEE IF WE CAN GET YOU TO BUY IN"

The leader attempts to "enroll" people in the vision, enlisting as much commitment as possible. "This is the right thing to do, and I believe in it," a CEO might say, "but we can only do it if the organization comes on board with me." The employees are like the boss's customers, and they can say "no" in many different ways, including passive resistance. Until the employees say "yes" wholeheartedly, the senior managers haven't closed the deal.

TIPS FOR MASTERING THE "SELLING" MODE

Keep Channels Open for Responses

For example, follow up speeches about the vision with break-out groups, so that senior managers can find out how much of the message is "selling."

Support Enrollment, Not Manipulation

Enrollment, as Innovation Associates founder Charlie Kiefer puts it, is "the process of becoming part of something only by choice." You do not enroll others; people can only enroll themselves. You can present them with a picture, including evidence of your own enrollment: "I'm personally committed to take the organization this way." If people see the vision is good for them, even if it takes a leap of faith, they will tend to sign on. Trusting that they will is *your* requisite leap of faith.

Build On Your Relationship with the "Customer"—Your Employees

The implicit message in a "selling" effort is: "I'm depending on you for this to work. I value my relationship with you. If you all thoroughly disagree I may not do it this way; I recognize that you have some influence over me. I will not force or manipulate you to do something you really don't want, because I know that will ultimately undermine our organization."

Focus on Benefits, Not Features

Rather than merely describing the vision, demonstrate how it will serve the needs, desires, and situation of your employees. For example, instead of saying, "This will cut our costs by 20 percent in three years," you might say, "For the first time in a decade, we'll be talking with our customers and suppliers about the *real* issues we have all wanted to address, but couldn't until now."

Move from the Royal "We" to the Personal "I"

To say, "This is the vision we endorse as a company" implies that you have taken for granted that everyone listening will be excited, motivated, and inspired by it, just because they work there. Almost by definition, this provokes resentment. Instead, speak about why it's important to you personally, and what special meaning it has for you.

THE LIMITS OF "SELLING"

The boss wants to hear a "yes." The employees want to hear that they will keep their jobs. A "compliant yes" often seems like the safest course for all. "I can go along with that," members say. "I'll give it a try." If you need more commitment, then you will probably need to move forward to "test" or "consult" about the vision.

Sometimes people don't buy the vision, despite your best efforts. Then you have a choice. You can move back to the "telling" mode, and force compliance. This may be appropriate if the survival of your organization is at stake. Or you can move forward to "test" and "consult": "What should I know before I make another proposal?"

Testing

Stage 3: "Testing"

"WHAT EXCITES YOU ABOUT THIS VISION? WHAT DOESN'T?"

The leader "lays the vision out for testing," as Bill O'Brien puts it—not just to find out whether the members support the vision, but how enthusiastically they will accept it, and what aspects of it matter to them. The results are used to refine and redesign the vision. The process of testing can galvanize response. Having been asked their opinion, people feel more compelled to discuss and consider the proposed vision. As in market research, the "test" implies that the respondents will influence the results. A shared vision which no one supports must go back, in essence, to the drawing board.

The more capacity for personal mastery that has been developed in the organization, the better results you will get. A good test depends on people's willingness to tell the truth, and on their ability to perceive current reality. If people say "count me in," then the boss will count them in—and count *on* them at the appropriate time. For that reason, a false "yes" can be much worse than an honest "no."

TIPS FOR MASTERING THE "TESTING" MODE

Provide as Much Information as Possible, to Improve the Quality of the Responses

Present the vision with all its ramifications spelled out—particularly difficulties. Otherwise, the test won't measure how people feel about the necessary changes and impacts.

Make a Clean Test

When you ask someone to choose between alternatives A, B, and C, design the test as if you really want to know the answer. Don't set it up intending them to choose A and think it's their idea. They will see through it, and you will lose your opportunity to learn what they think.

Protect People's Privacy

Design the test so people can answer anonymously, without fear of repercussion—or at least without a penalty for negative answers. You can almost guarantee, in a testing process, that you will hear unexpected bad news that had never emerged before this visioning process began.

Combine Survey Questionnaires with Face-to-Face Interviews

In many cases, questions about a shared vision are more subtle than a survey form can express. That suggests person-to-person interviews, group interviews, or large-scale conferences. The visible size of the group gives an implicit sense of "safety in numbers." Ideally, a conference should include people from every job category meeting in breakout groups. A facilitator should tally reactions without noting who said what, and amalgamate them into a report.

Test for Motivation, Utility, and Capability

Do people *want* to move toward the vision? Do they think the vision would be useful to them or to the organization? And do they think that they, and the organization, have the capability to move toward the vision? If not, what's missing?

〉〉 The discipline of Personal Mastery may be relevant here; see page 193.

THE LIMITS OF "TESTING"

Simply by virtue of being there, employees have developed a wide range of ideas and concerns about the well-being of the organization, and its ability to grow and prosper. None of this can be expressed through a test. To compensate, you can design questions about the test itself into the questionnaire: "How do you feel about this feedback process?" Or you could set up a focus group to allow people to break out of the structure, and answer their own questions. When a testing process has taken one of these steps, it is no longer testing. The organization has moved on to consulting.

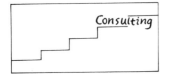

Stage 4: "Consulting"

"WHAT VISION DO MEMBERS RECOMMEND THAT WE ADOPT?"

Consulting is the preferred stage for a boss who recognizes that he or she can not possibly have *all* the answers—and who wants to make the vision stronger by inviting the organization to be the boss's consultant.

In a "consulting" process, you may say: "I want to build a vision for the organization, but before I make up my mind, I want to know what you think." You want people not just to come up with specific suggestions, but to become fully engaged in thinking through the ramifications of their ideas. For yourself, you reserve the role of judge: you still choose to accept or ignore what people say (as you would with any consultant), you determine the content of the organization's vision, and you decide how to begin moving in that direction.

Some managers are reluctant to move from "testing" to "consulting" because they fear they may be overwhelmed by options to consider. This is often a valid concern. The boss's capacity for considering options may be limited; so may the capacity of the rest of the organization. "Don't ask us to create a vision," members may want to say. "That's your job."

Even more likely, pressure to finish quickly while not offending anyone may lead the boss to accept a middle-of-the-road, all-things-to-all-people compromise vision. For all these reasons, if you are the boss, and you find yourself resisting the idea of a massive consulting effort, you may be right to move back to "testing" while you build up the organization's (and your own) capacity for surfacing the mental models which underlie the suggestions.

TIPS FOR MASTERING THE "CONSULTING" MODE

Use the "Cascade" Process to Gather Information

A typical cascade sequence, which may last several months, brings together small teams of ten to fifteen people at every level, starting with the top of the organization. I generally favor teams with natural working relationships—composed of a boss and direct reports, sometimes supplemented by "bright lights" from parallel functions or related divisions. After each meeting the team members go back to discuss the vision with their subordinate teams. Then those members carry the process one step lower. At the very end, the teams meet again to collect responses from the bottom teams, react to them at the next-higher teams, and so on back up to the top.

The cascade process works best when responsible managers run their teams, but a committed group of facilitators are available as resources— helping draw out discussion, bringing some mental models skills to bear, and making sure that responses are recorded accurately. The most difficult task in many cascade processes is ensuring that critiques survive the journey back from the bottom to the top.

Build in Protections Against Distortion of the Message

Starting each team meeting with a videotaped message from the "boss" can accomplish this. However, when the vision changes as a result of the "consulting" process, you need to update the videos. Alternatively, you can ask people to read a document, but people tend to misinterpret documents more easily.

Gather and Disseminate Results

Collect anonymous written comments from participants after every "consulting" session. This ensures that people who do not want to speak openly can nonetheless be heard. This is important not just for their sake, but because their comments may be valuable. A written report, however, should not be seen as a substitute for open meetings, where constructive disagreement and surfacing of mental models take place.

Kees van der Heijden suggests a form of this technique in his cameo on Shell's internal consultancy, page 279.

Don't Try to Tell and Consult Simultaneously

If you tell them the "right" vision, as you see it, and then ask: "What do you think about this?" you will get a ho-hum response. People will say, "Why bother replying? You've already told me what you want me to think." To keep suggestions in reasonable territory, you can lay out boundaries: "Bear in mind that any vision should deal with our attitude to customers, and should not ignore the debt from our recent restructuring."

THE LIMITS OF "CONSULTING"

The "consulting" mode (like "telling," "selling," and "testing,") is limited by a tacit, usually unquestioned assumption: that the objective of the process is to create one vision from the top for the entire organization, rather than bringing together multiple visions in an organic interdependent whole. Our experience suggests that this is a faulty premise. Especially for middle- and lower-level members, the most significant elements of a vision are almost always local, anchored to a team, work unit, or place. A shared vision is strongest when it builds from that foundation outward, connecting local visions with their counterparts throughout the organization.

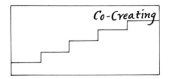

Stage 5: "Co-creating"

"LET'S CREATE THE FUTURE WE INDIVIDUALLY AND COLLECTIVELY WANT"

As Bill O'Brien says, "It's an important day in everyone's life when they begin to work for what they want to build rather than to please a boss." The organization whose leaders and members understand this is ready to benefit from a "co-creating" shared vision process.

"Co-creating" places every member in a creative orientation. Every step involves choice. Individuals begin by drawing forth aspects of their personal vision.

See "Drawing Forth Personal Vision," page 201.

Teams articulate their sense of common purpose: Are they here to serve customers, to produce better products, or to serve the organization's other members? As teams define what is of primary importance in their work, a new hierarchy of meaning emerges for the organization as a whole.

For example, the top team of an information retrieval company decided at a "visioning" meeting that their values should include "functioning with integrity." One of the participants asked, "well, does 'integrity' apply to us alone, or does it include customers?"

"Of course, we're not going to be honest with our *customers*," said someone at the table. Then they looked at each other in silence. In their industry, vendors routinely promised customers delivery dates that they knew they could not meet—and let the date slip later. The team began a three-hour dialogue, without a break; when it ended, they had changed their corporate vision. "If we're putting up integrity as a value," one senior manager said, "we need integrity in all aspects of our business."

Current reality, however, presented them with a dilemma; if they changed immediately, they would be unable to match their competitors' delivery promises, and they'd be out of business. So they developed a strategic migration plan. They visited key customers and said, "Look, this industry is based on exchanges of false promises. You know it. We know it. Nobody likes it, but we all feel stuck with it. We would like to change that, and we would like to start by being honest with *you*." Thenceforth, every delivery date they offered those customers was realistic—and honored. Within a year, their business was growing exponentially and their profits skyrocketed.

TIPS FOR MASTERING THE "CO-CREATING" MODE*

Start with Personal Vision

When a shared vision effort starts with personal vision, the organization becomes a tool for people's self-realization, rather than a machine they're subjected to. People begin to stop thinking of the organization as a thing to which they are subservient. Only then can they wholeheartedly participate in guiding its direction.

Many leaders imagine that encouraging people to identify and express their personal vision would lead to anarchy and disarray. But to expect people to veer wildly off-course is to make several assumptions: first, that members secretly harbor a desire to thwart the organization and see it fail; second, that they see no benefit for themselves in having a common purpose; third, that they can imagine no role for themselves in leading or inspiring others; and fourth, that there are no leaders link-

°We follow this progression in the intensive three-day Visionary Leadership and Planning programs we designed at Innovation Associates. First, articulation of personal vision. Second, evolving from that into a sense of organizational and shared vision. Third, gaining a mutual understanding of current realities. Fourth, beginning to take action on strategic leverage points to close the gap. For more about Innovation Associates, see p. 568.

ing teams. Experience shows that these assumptions are all unfounded. Most members are eager to link their personal visions to the team and enterprise, and most teams actually share a deep, fundamental sense of alignment—but until they can give voice to these common aspirations, teams can't build upon them.

If there *is* such a deep lack of alignment, then management should be concerned about it—whether or not there is a shared vision effort underway. In any case, the "co-creating" process promotes alignment, not anarchy. As an evolving understanding of the vision and its implications cascades through the teams, there is time for skeptics to understand the process and for everyone to begin thinking freshly about their relationship to the whole.

Treat Everyone as Equal

In the rest of the organization, the boss may wield the decision-making power, but in this exercise bosses should only get one vote. Similarly, no one team should get more votes than any other. During these exercises, discourage status differences however you can—through process design or by tapping people's innate sense that their personal visions are equal to anyone else's. Make sure that views travel down *and up* in the hierarchy with equal speed and efficacy.

Seek Alignment, Not Agreement

The temptation will be strong to paper over differences for the sake of reaching resolution and producing a coherent output. Teams should discourage this. Instead, they should use team learning practices such as skillful discussion and dialogue to look for the assumptions beneath the disagreement, and see what mental models have led to this unreconcilable view.

See "Skillful Discussion," page 385, and "Dialogue," page 357. The GS technologies story (page 364) portrayed a group of managers and steelworkers that has learned to be aligned and disagreeing.

Among Teams, Encourage Interdependence — and Diversity

In most organizations, people do not talk about their visions in a vacuum. Each team of ten to twelve people is linked to its superiors, subordinates, and peers. Every team leader, as a member of at least two teams, is a crucial leadership link between different articulations of a shared vision.

When team members begin talking about their vision, avoid telling them what other teams have said. Instead, ask each team first: "What do *we* really want?" Once the team's vision has been articulated, then members who also belong to other teams can later serve as communicating agents: "Here is what they said about this in Purchasing." Over time, as teams become curious about each other's visions, two or more teams may discover a strategic value in meeting together, comparing notes, and creating a shared vision in tandem. This should be encouraged; it can be very powerful. But even here, seek alignment instead of forcing agreement. It's dysfunctional to insist that team B's vision echo the wording of team A.

Avoid "Sampling"

A common trap for senior management seems on first glance like a reasonable resource-saving measure: "It's too darned hard and expensive to talk to everybody, so let's talk to a sample of people and analyze the themes. They'll be representative of everyone." This strategy might be effective in "consulting." But in "co-creating," it undermines whatever opportunities people feel to take on personal leadership. Instead of taking a stand within their own team, and saying, "Here's what I think the vision for our part of the organization ought to be," people simply answer the questions passively.

Have People Speak Only for Themselves

In our Visionary Leadership and Planning sessions, we do not permit participants to talk about how other people in the organization may react to their vision. It's important to remember that these other people are not in the room, and any inferences about their reaction are just that—inferences. Without that attitude, there's an inescapable temptation to say, "Well, if we use the word 'integrity,' what will Pat think?" Moreover, by alluding to any outside individual or group, the team in the room is giving away the power to determine its own vision, which is the most fundamental driving force in this process. What is left is no longer vision, but the anticipation of frustration. Later, there will be time to see how this team's vision fits with others—based on real give and take, not fears and guesses.

Expect and Nurture Reverence for Each Other

When a real diversity of opinions occurs in a group, a reverence for each other's vision will often take hold. I have seen people stop short, their breath taken away, and then say, "I have never seen things from that angle." In one session in the United States, a team member was a recent immigrant. "In my old country," he said, "freedom was only a vague concept. Your notions of freedom to participate in the firm's direction are completely inspiring to me. They even have meaning for my religious beliefs, which were persecuted overseas." Other people in the room sat back, startled; they had taken the atmosphere of freedom in the company for granted. Sparked by that member's vision, they realized they wanted to create an atmosphere which would not just preserve, but promote that sense of freedom, both internally and in the communities they lived in.

In my experience, it is rare to see people interrupting someone who is in the middle of describing his or her personal vision. No one says, "You've got your vision wrong. Let me tell you what your life's purpose and vision should be." This is one reason why a co-creating exercise is so valuable: once you appreciate each other's vision, it's easier to understand each other's perspective on current reality, and each other's ideas about courses of action.

Consider Using an "Interim Vision" to Build Momentum

It may be useful to get some interim vision on the table initially. Even if it's brief, rough, and intuitive, this will give team members an initial point of reference. If it comes from higher in the hierarchy, do not distribute it in a memo. Refrain from revealing it right away at team meetings. Wait until the team members have started to get some clarity about their own vision. Then, typically, their fear and cynicism (generally supported by past history) will be triggered. "We're starting to build some momentum and commitment here. What if we run into roadblocks from above?" Now the formal leader can take out the interim vision and say, "Here's what we came up with at the next level. I want to show you how our vision here actually aligns with the team's above us, even though the words are very different." Handled with the right personal leadership, that exchange is crucial. It represents the heart of the aligning process.

Focus on the Dialogue, Not Just the Vision Statement

Visions often translate into vision and purpose statements, which seem cryptic to outsiders, but have enormous meaning for the people who struggle to craft each word, so that everyone can sign off on them and feel the statement is meaningful. The process is more important than the product. Participants actively instill meaning and inspiration into the words and give them symbolic value; the words on their own mean nothing. That's why the test of a vision is not in the statement, but in the directional force it gives the organization.

CREATING SHARED VISION **by Marjorie Parker** (1990, Oslo: Senter for
Ledelsesutvikling A/S [Norwegian Center for Leadership Development]).

Hydro Aluminum Karmøy Fabrikker, a Norwegian company which is Europe's largest producer of aluminum, spent two years co-creating a shared vision. Marjorie Parker, the organizational consultant who helped them through the process, describes every step along the way. In this story, the pictures really *were* worth 1,000 words: virtually every employee had a chance to sketch their personal version for the organization and then link it with images others had created. The final "vision statement" was not a piece of writing at all, but an extraordinary mural of a flourishing garden, painted by a local artist, in which every plant and element had rich metaphorical meaning. For example, the management was the water supply, feeding into the soil underground and providing essential irrigation, but not visible on the surface. For planners and designers of a "co-creation" effort, *Creating Shared Vision* shows what is possible.—**BS**

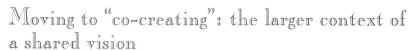

Moving to "co-creating": the larger context of a shared vision

EVERY ORGANIZATION WILL FIND ONE OF THESE STAGES MORE APPROPRIATE than others. Nonetheless, wherever you start on this continuum, building your capacity to "co-create" shared vision has many intrinsic benefits. People repeatedly say how deeply satisfying and fulfilling it is to be part of a vibrant creative process that is directly shaping their individual and collective future. In building and realizing a shared vision, I believe a deep yearning for co-creating within a community can also be satisfied.

I also believe that sooner or later all organizations will move to co-creating, because that is where the larger world culture and society are moving. As Peter Senge points out (see page 563) we are currently twenty years into a process of fundamental redistribution of power and authority in social and political institutions around the world. I see that redistribution process as essential to the very survival of those institutions and, perhaps to society itself.

Traditional models of centralizing power and authority at the top are becoming increasingly dysfunctional. Authoritarian organizations have a hierarchy of meaning, but it is set by a few decision makers. It is typically narrow: the purpose of the enterprise is to beat the competition, or to keep paying stockholders, or to reward members in carefully defined ways. Policies, decision criteria, and infrastructure designs all flow from this tacit vision and direction. As long as that tacit purpose holds sway, then opportunities to "participate" in decision making and even in organizational design will be a manipulative sham. As one control-oriented (but typical) CEO once quipped to me in a candid moment, "I'm glad to promote participative management and let people make decisions at virtually any level, as long as I control the values and criteria that they use."

Organizational members will "settle for" the lower levels of participation available in these cases, perhaps even willingly as a development step. But the competitive advantage which comes from building learning organizations is not possible without members' full participation in setting direction and priorities. Anything less is suboptimizing. If learners learn only what they want to learn, then only a deliberate effort to create collective aspiration will move people to "want to learn" what the organization needs; and vice versa.

Given the way societies are evolving along these lines, I think the question is no longer whether organizations will move to meet people's deep need to feel their aspiration fit with a larger purpose. The question is only when, and how. The choice in today's organizations is to lead in this process or fall behind.

48 Letter to the CEO

Bryan Smith

If you are a CEO, manager, or any leader responsible for a relatively autonomous organization, my first advice to you is: *find a partner.*

This is an essential first step. It is simply too much for one person—even the most tireless CEO—to lead, set direction, formulate strategy, and manage the process all at the same time. A shared vision effort is like a theater production, and you will need a strong anchor person backstage to help you be successful onstage. Your partner will have at least three key roles: keeping track of the process while you focus on the content, extending channels of communication between you and the rest of the organization, and helping you find perspective. This last role is especially crucial if you "co-create" a shared vision. In that case, you are part of an improvisational theater piece, with full audience participation throughout.

Ideally, your chosen partner should be a trusted insider, with insight into your dynamics and those of your organization. If that's not possible, then choose an outsider whom you can trust. If that individual doesn't know the internal players and norms, he or she will have to learn about them to support you effectively as a partner.

Assessing yourself

YOUR FIRST STEP, TOGETHER WITH YOUR PARTNER, WILL PROBABLY IN-volve your own self-assessment—including determining where on the continuum from "Telling" to "Co-creating" (page 314) you should begin.

WHAT IS MY PREFERRED COMMUNICATION METHOD?

If you are a salesperson by background or nature, and you take naturally to "telling and selling," then you will tend to favor that mode in creating vision. Some leaders, by contrast, feel more comfortable with the give-and-take, two-way, inquiry-oriented dynamics of consulting and co-creating. If that includes you, it will be easier to move your organization to the right-hand side of the spectrum, but you will still need support from your process partner in setting boundaries and communicating clearly about your priorities.

WHAT PRESSURES AM I UNDER, AND HOW AM I RESPONDING TO THOSE PRESSURES?

You may feel some urgency because outside pressure is bearing on you, from your boss, the board, the bank, key customers, suppliers, the government, an industry association, or competitors. If all you do is pass that pressure on, you are not leading—you aren't using your role to add value or meaning to the external pressure. Instead, your implicit message is: "Do it because I said so, based on information which I have [and you do not]." Or "These changes are based on pressures which only I can see. If you could see them, you'd be terrified into taking action, too."

Your concerns may be legitimate and real, but if you pass on fear as a motivator, then when the fear abates, even temporarily, motivation to change will go away. "Phew, we can relax," people will say. Nothing will be learned except, "When we're scared, it's good to take some action to get away from the things we fear."

On the other hand, if you offer a three-part combination—a clear picture of current reality, including the reasons for your fears; a vibrant image of your vision; and a strategy for addressing the gap as a challenge—people will generally pitch in and help. They will see that you aren't conjuring up nightmares, or obscuring and confusing reality.

HOW MUCH TIME, AND WHAT NEW SKILLS, WILL THIS REQUIRE OF ME?

How much time do you have for a shared vision effort? Even a well-organized "telling" effort will be a serious drain on you, because everyone will depend on your articulation and heroically visible efforts.

When you move along the continuum toward co-creation, other capacities are called for: listening for people's vision and aspiration; inquiring into values and mental models; sharing responsibility and accountability, and demonstrating trust. These skills are often more difficult to master, and they may feel awkward at first. But without the skills, you risk suppressing the natural co-creating abilities of the rest of the organization, squeezing them down, as if pressing down on a powerful spring.

Eventually, that spring will recoil in the form of excess resistance. Unless you are prepared to increase your capabilities and change your own management habits, it's pointless to attempt participative "co-creating." Take advantage of your strengths by moving back to the "telling" mode. Recognize, however, that you will not be able to draw upon the same level of commitment from your organization.

The single most effective index of your readiness for co-creating may be the extent to which you are *already* aware of the visions, goals, and feelings of the rest of the organization, or are curious to find out.

Tips for moving forward

HERE ARE SOME DO'S AND DON'TS TO CONSIDER. THEY PARTICULARLY apply to "Telling" and "Selling" modes, where you articulate your vision for the organization.

REFLECT PERSONALLY AND KEEP IT PERSONAL

Vision building requires the leader to clearly understand his or her own *personal* vision. Bill O'Brien, former president of Hanover Insurance, suggests that vision meetings flop unless the leaders have spent "lonely time sitting and thinking . . . and looking at what they would really like to achieve themselves." When you begin talking about your vision, share its personal meaning for you, including references to your own formative life experiences.

See "Drawing Forth Personal Vision," page 201, and Wilson Bullard's cameo, page 224.

DON'T CREATE YOUR ORGANIZATIONAL VISION IN ISOLATION

Books, articles, and speakers proclaim regularly that without a vision, your organization might face serious decline. Many senior managers today interpret that message to mean: "*I* must come up with a vision. It had better be charismatic and blow the socks off the troops, while exceeding our customers' expectations and transforming our commercial capability. And it's entirely up to me to do it."

Naturally, this is a terrifying prospect, but they see no alternative. So, perhaps with an image of themselves as the seeker going off to the mountain, they begin crafting a vision draft. Soon, they realize how difficult it is, and they may delegate the task to an ad agency or speech writers. But by doing that, they further isolate themselves from the organization. Filtered through that isolation, all the demands they hope to meet—from shareholders, customers, suppliers, employees at different levels, managers of different divisions—seem to cry out with equal force. Under these circumstances, it's just about impossible to create a statement meaningful to all those groups. To make matters worse, people within the organization are probably waiting for directions from you that will save the day.

The way out of the trap is to forge meaningful connections with one or more partners from *within* the mainstream organization. Be open and receptive. Try to learn as much as possible about the organization's needs and capabilities, and try to discern what people aspire to.

This may mean borrowing some of the "testing" or "consulting" techniques described on pages 318–22.

DON'T BRUISE PEOPLE

The head of a major company once stated publicly that he saw mediocre management throughout the company. It took a long time for him to live that down. A head-on accusation like that usually turns out to be wrong, and even if it's correct, most people will resist it. Particularly avoid characterizing people's motivation: "Nobody cares in this organization any more," or "People here are lazy." The subgroup that fits the description probably won't hear it, and everyone else will be justifiably offended.

Deliver your messages in a way that acknowledges respect for people, while letting them know change is inevitable. I saw an example of this in an all-day meeting with a management group not long ago. The CEO opened the day by saying, "Our bankers are soon going to withdraw their support. We've got to move. Here are the realities." During the entire day, he refrained from belittling people or telling them what to do. Instead, he made it clear how little time they had to institute complete reform. He asked for, and got, dramatic action.

BE ACCOUNTABLE FOR THE VISION

If you are asking people to make fundamental changes, you need to show that you, too, are ready to be counted on. Don't change direction in the middle of the effort. Give people the support and training they need to achieve what you ask of them. Embody the values you describe.

Bill O'Brien puts it this way: "I believe what distinguishes organizations that transform themselves around new values is the passion that the leadership has about the values and—most important—the practice. I would say walking the talk, by the leadership, is the most fundamental way of bringing visions and values to the organization."

For more about the general value of choosing a partner, see "Finding a Partner," page 74.

As a first step, you and your partner might review together the stages of a shared vision process, and the strategies for designing one (see pages 312–28). Read the guidelines for "telling" first, so that if you're starting there, you can avoid some common early pitfalls. If you have difficulties "walking the talk," you and your partner may want to talk through the advice for "When the Boss Blows a Fuse" (page 335).

49 Letter to the CEO's Partner

Bryan Smith

At some point in your career, you may take on the role of custodian, nurturer, or steward to building a shared vision. This role may or may not be formal; it often emerges naturally when an organization begins to think collectively about its purpose. A steward might be an assistant to the senior manager of the organization, a member of the corporate staff, a trusted line manager, or an outsider. Whatever his or her formal role, every shared vision custodian faces the same challenge: to produce a spirit of partnership among the members of the organization, across organizational levels, so that a collaborative process can take place that yields a vision shared by all.

For the accompanying "Letter to the CEO," see page 328. This letter builds on the description of the modes of shared vision—"telling," "selling," "testing," "consulting," and "co-creating"—beginning on page 312. Also see "Finding a Partner," page 74.

Your first step in this role should be to forge a strong partnership with the CEO, senior manager, or formal leader of the organization (or relatively autonomous work unit). Your focus is not so much on the content of the vision, but the process—gently, relentlessly guiding the collective initiative toward richer, broader engagement.

You may prefer to instigate a full-scale "consulting" or "co-creating" process. But if 90 percent of organizations today are actually in the "telling" mode regarding vision, then "telling" efforts will take place whether we approve of them or not. The question then becomes, "How can we work with organizations as they are, rather than as we would like them to be?" Taking part in a "telling" exercise is an opportunity to move the organization gradually but persistently toward "co-creating." Many change-from-within efforts begin as an exercise in helping the boss "tell it well."

Here are some questions for you to consider in getting started.

HOW READY ARE THE MEMBERS OF THE ORGANIZATION TO GENERATE VISION?

In their enthusiasm for moving forward, some process partners thrust "co-creating" on an organization before it's ready. Co-creating a vision demands a great deal from employees, especially when an organization needs fundamental, across-the-board change. Just as we wouldn't ask people to carry out surgery on themselves without anesthetic, you can't always ask people to fundamentally restructure a company in traumatic times, in ways that will affect their own and each other's careers. I have worked in situations where self-managing teams have had to sit down, as a result of their shared vision, and determine which two of them would be laid off. Teams don't achieve that level of functioning overnight.

Thus, your strategy requires a clear-eyed assessment of the gap between the organization's capacity to create a vision, and the demands that will be placed on it:

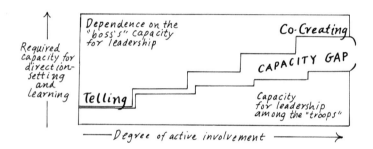

How much exposure, for example, have the employees had to personal mastery? How much opportunity and practice have members had with setting goals, perhaps at a work team level? As shown in this illustration, the greater the capacity, the smaller the gap you'll have to bridge, and the farther to the right (toward "co-creating" you and your boss can quickly move. I like to follow a model attributed to community organizer Saul Alinsky, who apparently never tried to move any community further than one degree of self-reliance at a time. Otherwise, he knew he'd trigger a reactionary response and the whole initiative would suffer a major setback.

THE RELATIONSHIP WITH THE "BOSS"

If you have a directive boss, you'll have your work cut out for you. To be effective, your own approach must be pro-participative. But your boss will often want you to "help tell them what their vision is," and compel everyone to sign up. To be effective, you have to understand why the boss resists moving beyond "telling," and not argue with that point of view—which may, in fact, have validity. Your ability to forge a relationship with the boss depends on your willingness to listen *fully* to his or her vision, mental models, attitudes, and motivation. If you can come to understand the boss's vision, *and* sense of current reality, then you will have created a sense of shared meaning between the two of you.

From there, you can work on generating and managing creative tension—helping the boss, and the organization, move forward together. If, for example, you hear that the boss feels tremendous pressure to fundamentally restructure the business, and you have a good understanding of the thinking behind the decision, then you may be in a position to better influence how that restructuring is carried out.

At first, you may be the only channel that provides the CEO with reliable information: "Here is how your message was received or misperceived. Here are the territories where we can most profitably invest follow-up energy." As you move forward, you may focus more on design: "Let me work with you to carry through your "telling" mode, but in the process, let me try to help you build in more mechanisms for getting some honest feedback from the organization."

BRINGING THE BOSS AND ORGANIZATION TOGETHER

At one organization, I said to the boss, "I think you should consider increasing everyone's participation in setting direction because the organization's sense of purpose is too dependent on you. If you leave, it's going to crash. Leaving a mess behind you is not a great legacy."

The boss replied, in effect, "All right, I'll shift a little bit toward this consult strategy, but I don't trust it."

I then said to the subordinates: "The boss wants to let go of the reins more, but if you don't fill in the gap with your own vision, leadership, and responsibility, then we're all in trouble."

When they agreed, I went back to the boss. The process felt almost like shuttle diplomacy. I think this "bridging" role is often required to break out of an impasse in the visioning process, by encouraging modest risk taking on both sides. As each side moves a bit further, that gives the other side more reason to trust the process.

When the boss blows a fuse . . .

SOMEWHERE ALONG THE LINE DURING A "CONSULTING" OR "CO-creating" process, the senior manager may abruptly turn away from the process. He may reprimand a subordinate when an uncomfortable subject is raised. Or he may insist, against evidence to the contrary, that "our quality is the best in the industry." This tightening is a sign of the "boss" reaching some limit of capacity. Some criticism or bad news coming up from below has been unexpectedly difficult to handle. This may even lead to the boss saying, "Halt!" and suspending the entire process temporarily.

Essentially, a fuse has been blown, in a circuit that never before existed. In most hierarchies, the boss is like a 5,000-kilowatt hydroelectric generating station, connected to the rest of the organization through a thin lamp cord. People are attracted to the power, but they can get jolted by the current. The chain of command acts as a transformer, diffusing the power at each stage. But in a "co-creating" organization, the current is suddenly reversed. Subordinates extend more effort and enthusiasm, and the "transformers" of the old hierarchy are rigged to amplify it. A high-voltage surge of innovation and demand can suddenly burst through. If the boss's "wiring"—his or her capacity for inquiry and open exploration—isn't prepared, the boss becomes a trip point, like a fuse, and blows out.

As the boss's partner, what should you do? First, it's important to realize that crying "Halt!" is a breach of an implicit promise—the promise to let the effort run its course. It will be seen as a big event in the life of the company. People will now feel as if the authority and respect they've been given can be taken back from them at any time.

Don't try and squeak by, or merely return to normal. Instead, the boss needs to show why he or she laid aside the momentum, in favor of some larger reality. Whatever the boss says should be as close to the real reason as possible. He or she may be able to say, for example, "I called time out because I'm not comfortable any longer. I've lost faith in the process, and I need to think things through to get it back." Or if the banks and the board of directors have redoubled their pressure, the boss needs to say *that*. Or "We based this implicit promise up on a set of assumptions about our business environment. I believe we're now outside the bounds of those assumptions and therefore I'm taking actions that I feel are crucial." If the explanation is truthful, the boss is often startled to discover that most people appreciate the company's position and are willing to help.

The key to your success here, and the CEO's, is recognizing and dealing with the capacity limits underlying the "blown fuse." The strength, openness, and trust in your relationship with the CEO is crucial here. You need to add your personal capabilities to those of the CEO, so that together you can bring the emotional tension to the surface, and better understand it. Once the causes of this emotional tension are clearer, you can return to the shared vision process.

"What Do We Want to Create?"

Charlotte Roberts

Talk through the following sets of questions. Spend time only with the questions which are meaningful to your team; different groups are attracted to different questions. The words, phrases, and ideas that emerge from this exercise become the seed thoughts for building a shared vision.

STEP 1: THE VISION OF THE FUTURE

It is five years from today's date and you have, marvelously enough, created the organization you most want to create. Now it is your job, as a team, to describe it—as if you were able to see it, realistically, around you. Consider these questions one by one, painting an ever-clearer shared vision of your future organization.

Make sure each member of the team has an opportunity to comment on each of the questions. Note the main points on a flip chart that everyone in the group can see.

1. Who are the stakeholders of this organization we have created (five years from now)?
    How do we work with them?
    How do we produce value for them?
2. What are the most influential trends in our industry?
3. What is our image in the marketplace?
    How do we compete?
4. What is our unique contribution to the world around us?
    What is the impact of our work?

PURPOSE
At a team level, defining common vision and purpose.

OVERVIEW
A series of questions which bring pertinent issues to the forefront.

PARTICIPANTS
An intact team, with or without a facilitator, working on "co-creating" a vision.

TIME
An hour or more.

SUPPLIES
Flip charts and felt pens.

ENVIRONMENT
A meeting room.

5. How do we make money?
6. What does our organization look like?
   How do the important elements of the infrastructure interact?
7. How do we handle good times?
   How do we handle hard times?
8. In what ways is our organization a great place to work?
9. What are our values?
   How do people treat each other?
   How are people recognized?
10. How do we know that the future of our organization is secure?
    What have we done to ensure its future for ourselves?
    What have we done to ensure its future for our grandchildren?
11. What is our organization's role in our community?

After each of these questions, ask: "How would we measure our progress?"

〉〉 These questions may help with either "Defining Your Learning Organization" (see page 50)
〉〉 or "Strategic Priorities" (see page 344).

STEP 2: CURRENT REALITY

Now come back to the current year, and look at the organization as it is today.

12. What are the critical forces in our systems?
13. Who are the current stakeholders today—inside and outside?
    What changes do we perceive taking place among our stakeholders?
14. What are the most influential trends in our industry today?
15. What aspects of our organization empower people?
    What aspects of our organization disempower people?
16. How is the strategic plan currently used?
17. What major losses do we fear?
18. What do we know (that we need to know)?
    What don't we know (that we need to know)?

How teams have used this exercise

THE TOP TEAM IN A MENTAL HEALTH SYSTEM STARTED WITH THE THIRD part of Question 1 ("How do we produce value for them [stakeholders]?") and developed an image of themselves as passionately adding value to patients' lives, beyond the psychiatric prognosis and treatment: "We empower and facilitate patients toward personal growth and effective functioning."

A team of computer engineers started with the second part of Question 4 ("What is the impact of our work?") and began to reconsider whether they should continue their focus on designing circuit boards. They ultimately described their vision as: "We are a winning, world-class component and system development group [and] the energy source to the group and the corporation as a whole."

After a "Vision" Presentation

Charlotte Roberts

1. What, for you, are the key words in this vision statement?
2. How did you first feel at the moment when you saw the vision on videotape, heard it described in the talk, or read it on paper?
3. How do you feel about it now?
4. How does it strike your sense of identification? (Do you feel as if you could "own" it?)
5. If no, how would it have to change for you to feel a sense of ownership for it?
6. How does it strike your sense of meaning and purpose? (Do you feel as if it is a meaningful vision?)
7. If no, how would it have to change to be meaningful for you?
8. Based on your own reactions and feelings, what implications do you see, from this vision statement, about your organization's visioning process?

P U R P O S E
Many shared vision sessions involve listening to other people's presentations of what they want the organization to be. After hearing a presentation, we often need a way as individuals to focus our reactions and to decide whether these ideas make sense for us. These questions provide that vehicle.

Backing into a Vision

Rick Ross

PURPOSE

This is a good warm-up team vision exercise, helpful for talking about common goals in concrete terms, without taking on a full-fledged "visioning" process. It helps bring to the surface people's feelings about their own levels of commitment or compliance.

OVERVIEW

A series of questions, beginning with people's own experience.

PARTICIPANTS

An intact team. Deputize one "scribe" to write answers on a flip chart.

TIME

One hour or more.

SUPPLIES

Flip chart, markers, and Post-it notes.

ENVIRONMENT

Any meeting room.

Tackle the following questions, one by one, putting the answers up on flip chart paper:

1. HAVE YOU EVER BEEN PART OF A REALLY GREAT TEAM?

Answer as individuals, speaking to the group. You can define "a really great team" any way you like. It should be a team where you felt personally committed, where you signed up body and soul, and where the team achieved extraordinary results. Think back to that experience.

2. WHAT WAS DIFFERENT ABOUT THIS TEAM?

People do "good work" all the time. Talk about what felt truly special about being on that "really great" team. In other sessions, answers have included: "I felt powerful." "I felt excited." "I believed in what we were doing." "We all had to pull together." "I made a difference." "I felt like I owned it." "I had a lot of passion for it." "There was a clear challenge."

The scribe should write all the significant comments down on the flip chart in the front of the room, and post each completed page on the wall.

If you have time, tell each other some details of the "great team" to which you belonged.

3. HOW CAN WE, AS A TEAM, CREATE THOSE KINDS OF FEELINGS HERE?

Ask each other: "What could we do [achieve, accomplish, create together] that would rekindle the same feelings we remember from those "really great teams"? Brainstorm ideas and find one that "fits" for everyone. This conversation leads into the fourth question . . .

4. WHAT WOULD WE COMMIT OURSELVES TO?

You may reach this point in one session; or it may require more. But when you reach this stage, the group as a whole commits itself to one or more initiatives, often including individual commitments for parts of the task. At this point, though no one has mentioned the word "vision," you have a shared set of priorities in hand, and a new way of thinking about them.

}} For a story of some repercussions from this exercise, see the cameo from Ed Carpenter of
}} Intel, page 392.

The Destiny Factor

Bryan Smith

I first heard the phrase "destiny factor" used by a Jungian psychotherapist. She said it helped her keep from inadvertently imposing her own opinions about what her clients should do. She began with the premise that each of her clients had his or her own unique "calling," which he or she was placed here to accomplish. To tamper with this destiny, she said, or to give advice without calling attention to it, was dangerous and manipulative. Her job was to help people intuit their purpose for themselves, and then help them move into alignment with that purpose.

The most successful shared visioning processes have the same goal for organizations: to develop a sense of destiny which the organization recognizes as its own, and help its members act accordingly. One compelling way to begin is by returning to the sense of purpose of the organization's original leaders.

This does not mean turning back the clock; it means using the visions of the past to help energize today's vision process. No one would rebuild a seventeenth-century cathedral today, but even a modern church building may incorporate Gothic architectural references.

STEP 1: LOOKING BACK TO THE ORIGINAL VISION

IBM, AT&T, Kellogg's, Digital, Xerox, Procter & Gamble, the Red Cross, most large corporations, many small firms and nonprofits, and even many government agencies have a visionary leader in their past—a person with a deep sense of purpose that the firm used as a reference point for decades. In many cases, the founders did not so much *invent* a

PURPOSE
History is empowering. It is easier to learn about creating your future if you know where you have come from. This exercise is particularly inspiring during a vision co-creating process.

OVERVIEW
You develop a deeper sense of purpose, by looking back to the organization's original purpose.

PARTICIPANTS
Any team working toward co-creating a shared vision.

TIME
Twenty minutes to several hours; possibly more than one meeting.

S U P P L I E S
*Markers and flip charts;
possibly reference mate-
rials.*

sense of purpose as *discover* their organization's destiny, and communicate that destiny to others.

To recapture that sense of destiny, and the particular way in which the founders envisioned it, begin by asking these questions:

1. What was the original vision and purpose of this organization?
2. What did it really mean?
3. What did it accomplish for us at the beginning?

You may decide to disband for a time and do some research. Or you may know the answers offhand. Often, the original organization's purpose, when finally brought to light again, can send chills up people's spines, by showing them that their work is connected to a powerful current of underlying purpose.

At a meeting of the building inspectors of a large Southwestern city, for example, the participants started to talk about what it meant to be a public servant. One man remembered his father, who had also been a building inspector, telling him: "There is no higher profession than to serve your country and community." In this meeting, we asked each person there to think back to when they made the choice to be a public servant. They sat there with watery eyes, and I remember feeling as if the ancient Greek originators of the ideal of public service had filed into the room, shadowy figures behind each chair, nodding in approval. "We are not just civil servants," the inspectors concluded. "We are the custodians of how this community will grow and develop. We guide the evolution of its physical structure. We have a powerful influence on the future of the entire city."

STEP 2: TRACING THE HISTORY OVER TIME

Now consider what changes affected that original sense of vision and purpose over time. As a team, ask yourselves:

1. What were the major milestones in the organization's life, relative to its original purpose?
2. Has that sense of purpose changed?
3. When did that change take place?
4. What caused the change?
5. Was the change creative and generative (toward a purpose), or reactive (reacting to events), or even desperate?

6. What parts of the original sense of purpose have remained?
7. What parts of it should be regained?

Often, feelings of betrayal rise to the surface here. Not long ago, I took part in a conversation with the senior team of a large corporation, which had been founded with great ideals of service and innovation. But beginning in the late 1960s, the company had been dominated by a group of marketing executives who came to the company from another industry. The organizational ethos had moved away from pride in technology and service. It had begun doing whatever it took to make a profit. "They stole the company," one manager said, "not by taking money, but by taking us away from our original purpose."

Did your organization's purpose get lost? In many organizations a peculiar set of oscillations takes place. The vision of the founder goes off track, and trouble ensues. So the next generation says, in effect, "We'll never do that again." The original founder's purpose becomes a negative vision—something to avoid. People do the opposite. Eventually, that goes awry, and people overcorrect in the other direction once again. You end up with a chart, over time, that looks something like this, showing how you veered from your purpose in either direction:

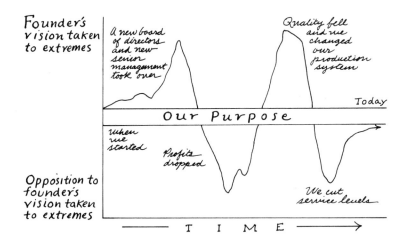

STEP 3: CONSIDERING A CHANGE OF PURPOSE
Having this memory of the original purpose helps you consider how the purpose may still apply; and how it may not. Seeing where the organization veered from its purpose, the past helps you keep from making the same mistakes again:

1. Does this earlier sense of purpose help us intuit a purpose for the organization today?
2. Does it fit with what the organization seems to be here to accomplish?
3. What current visions emerge in relation to this purpose?
4. Whom would this organization be serving under this vision?
5. How can the organization stay more closely aligned with its purpose in the future?
6. What sorts of things should we look closely at next time?
7. What practices might we put in place to carry forward a sense of "institutional memory" about our purpose?

50 Strategic Priorities

Alain Gauthier

Alain Gauthier, an independent strategic consultant formerly with McKinsey in Europe, works closely with Innovation Associates, particularly in consulting and training with health care organizations. He developed "strategic priorities" as a next step beyond co-creating a vision: a means to turn visions into specific goals.

In most cases, unless four or five strategically consequential "chunks of work" are defined and approached, the organization may never achieve much of its vision at all. For this reason, at the end of an intensive shared vision session, I always conclude with an exercise on strategic priorities. By now, this group of ten to thirty people has developed a shared understanding of the vision they want to achieve and of the major gaps (or areas of creative tension) between their vision and the current reality. They have also increased their capacity to dialogue about complex issues. I ask them to bring that capacity to bear on identifying the critical gaps they want to address first, and the milestones which will show if they are drawing close. What they choose as strategic priorities will determine a significant amount of their work during the next nine to eighteen months.

A good strategic priority is both clearly linked to the shared vision, and capable of galvanizing commitment from the people in the team (if not the whole organization). The team needs to say: "This intermediate goal deserves our best efforts." Someone—an individual or a team—must be accountable for it, enough to replace (hopefully enthusiastically) some of their other work with achieving this new priority. The "chunk of work" required can't be too narrow; it must be systemically related to the rest of the organization's vision. But it also can't be too broad; it must be distinct enough that a single person or task force can "put their arms around" what needs to be done.

These are actual examples of strategic priorities:

- "By mid-1995, 80 percent of our managers will be trained in facilitating dialogue." The team recognizes that if they don't develop this capacity, they'll lose an important opportunity for synergistic communication.
- "Within eighteen months, our community relations efforts will have led to a 30 percent increase in mutually profitable local joint ventures." This would be for a health care organization, which has resisted local cooperation for years, and only now sees its value.
- "The number of consultant-days devoted to implementation projects (instead of simply making speeches and reports to clients) will increase by 50 percent over the next two years." This came from a consulting firm which wanted to increase its effectiveness with clients.
- "Complaints from one department about another will be down 25 percent in one year." A medium-sized company beset with rival "chimneys" developed this strategic priority.

Note that all of these priorities are quantified or at least observable. You can measure or estimate whether or not you have achieved them. This grounds your vision in concrete results, for which you can establish action programs. But focusing on practical measurement is also a creative tool. Imagine, for example, a health care organization which wants to develop a better reputation for cooperatively improving the health status of its community. How would it measure its progress? The dialogue on this subject is a great spur to inventiveness and imagination, as people begin to create new measures.

Note, too, that the measurements are not prescriptive; the senior manager does not impose them on the team. The team develops them for themselves, searching for the most meaningful priorities: those crucial for the future of the organization, and where the team has real capacity to act.

Finally, the priorities are interfunctional or interdisciplinary. There is no priority which says, "By 1995, the human resource director will have her department under control," because the purpose is not to single out an individual, but to reframe a team's vision in concrete, realizable goals that can be achieved only through synergy and cooperation among peers. I always try to emphasize priorities that fit into areas where the organization has not paid enough close attention in the past, because this is where the greatest leverage tends to exist.

Once a team has agreed upon a set of strategic priorities, then they have a set of milestones. They can conduct experiments to see if they can move closer to their goals, using the milestones to measure their effectiveness. It is often useful to hold a second meeting six or nine months after the first, to monitor the team's progress and modify, if necessary, the list of strategic priorities. Additional people will have become involved, and new points of view will bring to light goals that were missed. In the end, the strategic priorities will have become a practice field in themselves: a self-contained way to experiment with significant change, giving team members a way to monitor the results.

51 Where to Go from Here

Charlotte Roberts

- **To personal mastery:** Shared vision and personal mastery are almost always simultaneous pursuits. In the context of what they want for the organization, people are inevitably drawn back to reconsider what they want for themselves, what current reality they see, and what they feel called to do. See pages 201, 208, 209, and 211 for appropriate exercises.
- **To team learning:** Team learning can be a natural next step from a shared vision effort. Collective aspiration gives team members a compelling reason to begin to learn how to learn together. Shared vision also provides a context for the more emotional challenges required

for team learning. For more about these challenges, see pages 355 and 407.

▪ **To systems thinking:** Systems thinking will be an essential tool for making any shared vision a reality. People now recognize that they need strategies for pursuing the vision, so that (for instance) two independent departments, pursuing the same ends, don't cancel out each other's actions. They see the need for finding leverage points: places to pursue their goals in a way that takes advantage of, instead of working against, the systemic structures around them. The techniques of "enriching" archetypes (page 161) are useful for this.

▪ **To mental models:** A shared vision creates an equally strong need for working with the relevant mental models, particularly the models people have of their future, and of what is possible for them. Reflection and inquiry skills (pages 242–63) will be valuable. As you begin planning to close the gap between you and your vision, you may use the tools of scenario planning (page 275), which help managers establish common mental models of the forces which can affect future actions.

Team
Learning

52 Strategies for Team Learning

In his memoir *Second Wind,* Boston Celtics basketball player Bill Russell describes one of his first conversations with his coach, Red Auerbach. "He told me that he was counting on me to get the ball off the backboard and pass it quickly to [other players]. This, plus defense, was to be my fundamental role on the team, and as long as I performed these functions well, he would never pressure me to score more points." That conversation, Russell goes on to say, "was worth a whole season of tactical coaching." It meant Russell would never have to improve his individual score at the expense of the team. Auerbach added a promise: he wouldn't bring up individual statistics when it came time to negotiate Russell's salary.

Team learning was built into the Celtics' everyday practice. They found dozens of ways to keep focused on their collective potential. Retiring players pulled aside rookies to tell them what they might expect from opponents in the league. The Celtics traded only once in thirteen years; every player knew that as long as he contributed to winning, he could stay. Auerbach made a point of telling the substitutes, the "guys at the end of the bench," how important they were precisely because they came in only when they were needed. On the court, as Russell says, "The most important measure of how good a game I'd played was how much better I'd made my teammates play."

It must have all added up to something, because the team did not merely play championship games or have a championship season. They created a championship *era* that lasted from 1957 to 1969, during which they were number one in the league for eleven out of thirteen seasons.

Many management teams simply aspire to play the equivalent of one great game. They'd be excited, they tell us, if they could improve delivery time to customers by 20 percent. We know a few teams who are trying to pull off, in effect, a great season—a string of successful results. But the real potential of this discipline is to help teams re-create themselves so that gains in capability don't just last for one season, but are sustained and self-reinforcing.

Because of the long-standing experience which many organizations have with group dynamics and team building, many teams believe that they have been practicing a version of this discipline for years. However, unlike team building, team learning is not a discipline of improving team members' skills, not even communication skills. For many years, we have used the concept of *alignment* as distinct from *agreement,* to capture the essence of team learning. Alignment means "functioning as a whole." Building alignment (you never "get there") is about enhancing a team's capacity to think and act in new synergistic ways, with full coordination and a sense of unity, because team members know each other's hearts and minds. As alignment develops, people don't have to overlook or hide their disagreements; indeed, they develop the capacity to use their disagreements to make their collective understanding richer.

The art and practice of conversation

ANYONE DOING SERIOUS WORK IN TEAM LEARNING SHOULD BE FAMILIAR with the key reflection-and-inquiry skills of the mental models discipline: balancing advocacy with inquiry, seeking to bring the tacit assumptions of the left-hand column to the surface, and becoming aware of the assumptions and beliefs that link "what we see" to "what we conclude." Team learning transforms those skills into capabilities; they become collective vehicles for building shared understanding. Team learning also draws upon the skills of building shared vision, particularly in building shared aspiration—and on systems thinking as a vehicle for surfacing how one sees the world.

See the reflection and inquiry skills, beginning on page 242; the shared vision material on page 312; and "Exploring Your Own Story" in systems thinking terms, on page 103.

Improved conversation is the primary medium with which management teams build all of these capabilities. Specifically, the most effective practice we know for team learning emerges from two conversational forms: *dialogue* and *skillful discussion.* The word "dialogue" is very often used loosely to refer to "any learningful conversation." People often tell me, "We had a dialogue about a subject," but if you were to examine the transcript, it would seldom be a dialogue and rarely even a skillful discussion. We prefer to reserve the term "dialogue" for the specific set of practices described in these pages. We have asked William Isaacs, founder and director of the MIT Dialogue Project, to introduce them here:

DIALOGUE AND SKILLFUL DISCUSSION

The word dialogue comes from two Greek roots, *dia* (meaning "through" or "with each other") and *logos* (meaning "the word"). It has been suggested that this word carries a sense of "meaning flowing through."°

Dialogue can initially be defined as *a sustained collective inquiry into everyday experience and what we take for granted.* The goal of dialogue is to open new ground by establishing a "container" or "field" for inquiry: a setting where people can become more aware of the context around their experience, and of the processes of thought and feeling that created that experience.

As we practice dialogue, we pay attention to the spaces between the words, not only the words; the timing of action, not only the result; the timbre and tone of a voice, not only what is said. We listen for the meaning of the field of inquiry, not only its discrete elements. In short, dialogue creates conditions in which people experience the primacy of the whole (see page 25).

Dialogue is an old term. There is some evidence to suggest that human beings have gathered in small groups to talk together for millennia. It does not feel like ordinary "civilized" conversation, but it does feel very natural to people once they start. That may explain why it seems to flourish in modern settings, despite a range of institutionalized barriers. The word "discussion" stems from the Latin *discutere,* which meant "to smash to pieces." Discussion is a conversational form that promotes fragmentation. However, skillful discussion° differs from unproductive discussion because the participants are not merely engaged in "advocacy wars" of one-upmanship. They develop a repertoire of techniques (encompassing collaborative reflection and inquiry skills) for seeing how the components

LEXICON

° The picture or image that this derivation suggests is of a *stream of meaning* flowing among and through us and between us. This will make possible a flow of meaning in the whole group, out of which will come some new understanding." *On Dialogue,* by David Bohm (1990, Ojai, Calif.; David Bohm Seminars), p. 1.

° The term "skillful discussion" was coined by Rick Ross.

of their situation fit together, and they develop a more penetrating understanding of the forces at play among the team members themselves.

In skillful discussion, you make a choice; in a dialogue, you discover the nature of choice. Dialogue is like jazz; skillful discussion is like chamber music. —WI

For the techniques and practices of skillful discussion, see page 385. For dialogue, see page 357.

Within and around teams

HISTORY HAS BROUGHT US TO A MOMENT WHERE TEAMS ARE RECOGNIZED as a critical component of every enterprise—the predominant unit for decision making and getting things done. Nonetheless, most aspects of existing infrastructure—such as measurement and compensation systems, as well as rewards—have not yet "captured" the significance of teams. And many people who espouse the importance of teams still believe, when push comes to the shove, that the key unit of effectiveness is individual. This will inevitably change.

The prevailing definition of "team" will change as well.

TEAMS

The word "team" can be traced back to the Indo-European word *deuk* (to pull); it has always included a meaning of "pulling together." (The modern sense of team, "a group of people acting together," emerged in the sixteenth century.)

We define "teams" as any group of people who need each other to accomplish a result. This definition is derived from a statement made by former Royal Dutch/Shell Group Planning coordinator Arie de Geus: "The only relevant learning in a company is the learning done by those people who have the power to take action."° —AK

° "Planning as Learning" by Arie de Geus, *Harvard Business Review,* March/April 1988, p. 70.

Building on this definition, we should be prepared to include many people who have been traditionally excluded from important team learning processes—internal and external suppliers, customers, and associates. These people must be brought into the learning unit at some point, even if they can't participate as regularly.

Large technologically oriented organizations, such as AT&T and

IBM, have already learned to design their infrastructures around these wider definitions of teams. A "team" might mean a worldwide network of specialists, communicating through electronic mail, telephone, and occasional face-to-face meetings. Team learning is as vital to these types of teams as it is to the face-to-face team which gathers at 11 A.M. every Tuesday. Thus, one critical element of team learning, still at the frontier of this discipline, is developing a collaborative way to design the broader infrastructure which determines how teams are identified and supported in their work.

See, for example, the mechanisms adopted by Hill's Pet Nutrition, on page 429; also see Douglas Merchant's description of new infrastructure forms at AT&T, page 520.

53 What You Can Expect . . . from Team Learning

Team Learning Is Not "Team Building" and Shouldn't Be Taken on Lightly. But You Can Focus Immediately on Your Organization's Chief Concerns and Issues

Charlotte Roberts

Don't even think of starting this work until you have thought through its implications and decided you want to proceed. This discipline goes well beyond conventional "team building" skills such as creating courteous behaviors, improving communication, becoming better able to perform everyday work tasks together, or even building strong relationships. This discipline inspires more fundamental changes, with enduring application that will ripple out through the organization.

Team learning is also the most challenging discipline—intellectually, emotionally, socially, and spiritually. The process of learning how to learn collectively is unfamiliar. It has nothing to do with the "school-learning" of memorizing details to feed back in tests. It starts with self-mastery and self-knowledge, but involves looking outward to develop knowledge of, and alignment with, others on your team. Most of us have had no training in this. This discipline will lead you there. Do you have the necessary patience, with yourself and others?

Members of the team should know that there will be times of frustration and perhaps embarrassment, as they develop their collective capabilities. Ideally, they should have the opportunity to choose the practice of team learning, with no penalty if they say "no" (although this may be unrealistic if the rest of the team says "yes").

Characteristics of a learning team

FOR A TEAM WHICH PRACTICES THIS DISCIPLINE, IT IS HELPFUL TO HAVE a reason to talk and learn—a situation that compels deliberation, a need to solve a problem, the collective desire to create something new, or a drive to foster new relationships with other parts of the organization. This first concern will become the preliminary "practice field" for the team's development. As it gains confidence and ability, the team will move on to consider other matters.

The team facilitator

THE TEAM CAN DEVELOP SKILLS FASTER IF IT HAS AN OUTSIDE FACILITA-tor who is trained in techniques for building reflection and inquiry skills, as well as dialogue facilitation. Team members often unknowingly collude to misrepresent reality to each other, and cover up the ways in which they do so. Only an outsider can see these learning disabilities clearly enough to lead the team to deal with its undiscussable behavior or issue. That is why a member of the team, no matter how skilled, is not the best facilitator. However, if there are limited funds, or if there is an expectation of long-term practice, then an internal facilitator may be worthwhile, particularly if this person can receive on-the-job training from a skilled outsider. This insider should be as distant as possible from the team and the team's political web. As the process spreads, the organization will need a cadre of people who can initiate, facilitate, and enable other teams, so plan from the start how the organization will increase its facilitator capacity.

Ground rules for learning

TEAMS NEED TO SET UP THEIR OWN GROUND RULES FOR CONVERSATION. These may include agreements to tell the truth as each person knows it, bring relevant information immediately to the team, or limit the time each person can speak. Teams may decide to clarify how decisions will be made and by whom, and to establish ways to safely check and challenge each other. Once the rules are set by consensus, it is important for the team to discuss how it will deal with violations. These rules are meant to help the team shape its conversations, not as an end in themselves; and they should never become so dominant that they override the team's purposes and learning.

When results don't turn out as expected, you and the other team members will need to master the art of forgiveness. Looking for someone to blame may mean abandoning the team's learning. Forgiveness means standing with the persons who were leading the experiment at hand, and helping the team discern what forces at play contributed to the unexpected outcomes. Forgiveness also means not holding the mistake as a trump card to be used some time in the future when politics would encourage it.

54 Dialogue

William Isaacs

Bill Isaacs is a senior lecturer at MIT's Sloan School of Management and the director of the Dialogue Project within the Center for Organizational Learning. As a doctoral student at Oxford, Bill became familiar with the physicist David Bohm's work on dialogue and the nature of thought, and participated in some of Bohm's first dialogue sessions in the early 1980s.

The Dialogue Project and the related Dia•Logos Institute are now established centers for exploring the role of conversation and collective thought in addressing pressing issues.

Bill's research, in particular, focuses on building an action theory of dialogue and its relationship to the nature of collective attention and listening.

A team of people sit in a circle on a stage, talking with intensity. In this form of intimate theater, they are both the performers and the audience. They are arguing, because they do not agree, but there's a quality of engagement about their argument. They listen intently to each other's language, rhythms, and sounds. The silences between statements seem as striking as the words. Every time someone says something, a texture changes subtly; something new has been seen. Everyone knows that everyone in the group has seen it, and that it represents more than just one person's model of the truth. As the people in the circle continue to talk, the sense of meaning they share grows larger and sharper. They begin to gain unprecedented insight into their fundamental views. No one can muster this form of thinking alone, and even in a group it takes a willful desire to build a context for thinking together. It takes a practice like dialogue.

Dialogue is not merely a set of techniques for improving organizations, enhancing communications, building consensus, or solving problems. It is based on the principle that conception and implementation are intimately linked, with a core of common meaning. During the dialogue process, people learn how to think together—not just in the sense of analyzing a shared problem or creating new pieces of shared knowledge, but in the sense of occupying a collective sensibility, in which the thoughts, emotions, and resulting actions belong not to one individual, but to all of them together.

As theorist David Bohm has pointed out, when the roots of thoughts are observed, thought itself seems to change for the better. People can begin to move into coordinated patterns of action, without the artificial, tedious process of decision making. They can start to act in an aligned way. They do not need to work out an action plan for what everyone should do, any more than a flock of birds taking flight from a tree, in perfectly natural order, requires planning. Each member of the team simply knows what he or she is "supposed" to do (or, rather, what's best to do), because they all fit into a larger whole.

At the Dialogue Project at MIT, we have begun to learn how to nurture this process in diverse settings—including an entire health care community in the Midwest riddled with competitive antagonisms, a group of South African professionals and leaders, a steel manufacturer (GS Technologies) with a history of severe labor/management problems, and a group of urban leaders in a major U.S. city. We have sought to translate 100 years of dialogue theory into practice, and to extend that theory, for the first time, so that reliable action can be built upon it. This has turned out to have exceedingly practical applications. As Margaret Mead put it, "Small groups of thoughtful, concerned citizens can change the world. Indeed, it is the only thing that ever has."

The theory of dialogue

As a reflective learning process, dialogue draws on the work of three key twentieth-century thinkers:

- The philosopher Martin Buber used the term "dialogue" in 1914 to describe a mode of exchange among human beings in which there is a true turning to one another, and a full appreciation of another not as an object in a social function, but as a genuine being.°
- Psychologist Patrick De Maré suggested in the 1980s that large group "socio-therapy" meetings could enable people to engage in understanding and altering the cultural meanings present within society—to heal the sources of mass conflict and violence or ethnic bigotry, for example.°
- Physicist David Bohm suggested that this new form of conversation should focus on bringing to the surface, and altering, the "tacit infrastructure" of thought. As Bohm conceived it, dialogue would kindle a new mode of paying attention, to perceive—as they arose in conversation—the assumptions taken for granted, the polarization of opinions, the rules for acceptable and unacceptable conversation, and the methods for managing differences. Since these are collective, individual reflection would not be enough to bring these matters to the surface. Instead, the group would have to learn to watch or experience its own tacit processes in action. Dialogue's purpose, as we now understand it, would be to create a setting where conscious *collective mindfulness* could be maintained.°

The theory of dialogue suggests that breakdowns in the effectiveness of teams and organizations are reflective of a broader crisis in the nature of how human beings perceive the world. As a natural mechanism to develop meaning, people learn to divide the world into categories and distinctions in our thoughts. We then tend to become almost hypnotized by these distinctions, forgetting that we created them. "The economy is falling apart," or "The people are corrupt," becomes our reality, with a seemingly independent power over us.

° See *The Knowledge of Man* by Martin Buber (1988, Atlantic Highlands, N.J.: Humanities Press International).

° See *Koinonia: From Hate Through Dialogue to Culture in the Large Group,* 1st ed., by Patrick De Maré (1991, London: Karnac Books).

° See *Unfolding Meaning* by David Bohm (1985, Loveland, Colo.: Foundation House).

Most significantly, we create and enter into these "hypnotic states" collectively. For example, there is a prevalent hypnotic state among doctors that difficult births are a "problem" which needs a "solution." When prenatal programs lower the instance of difficult births, physicians have insisted that actually, "nothing is happening." A senior nurse-practitioner listening to one such comment disagreed: "We see something happening where you see nothing." She argued that problem-free births are a tremendous advance, but represent a very different way of framing the same phenomenon. Essentially, the doctors had fragmented their understanding, preventing themselves from seeing the difference between "problems" and "characteristics."

As Bohm has suggested, fragmentation of thought is like a virus that has infected every field of human endeavor. Specialists in most fields cannot talk across specialties. Marketing sees production as the problem. Managers are told to "think" while workers are told to "act." Instead of reasoning together, people defend their "part," seeking to defeat others. If fragmentation is a condition of our times, then dialogue is one tentatively proven strategy for stepping back from the way of thinking which fragmentation produces.

Levels and stages of dialogue: the development of cool inquiry

DAVID BOHM HAS COMPARED DIALOGUE TO SUPERCONDUCTIVITY. ELECtrons cooled to very low temperatures act more like a coherent whole than as separate parts. They flow around obstacles without colliding with one another, creating no resistance and very high energy. At higher temperatures, however, they began to act like separate parts, scattering into a random movement and losing momentum.

Particularly around tough issues, people act more like separate, high-temperature electrons. They collide and move at cross-purposes. Dialogue seeks to produce a "cooler" shared environment, by refocusing the group's shared attention. These environments, which we have called "containers" or fields of inquiry, emerge as a group moves through a dialogue process. A container can be understood as the sum of the collective assumptions, shared intentions, and beliefs of a group. As they move through the dialogue progression, participants perceive that the "climate" or "atmosphere" of the room is changing, and gradually see that their collective understanding is changing it.

The following chart displays the evolution of dialogue:

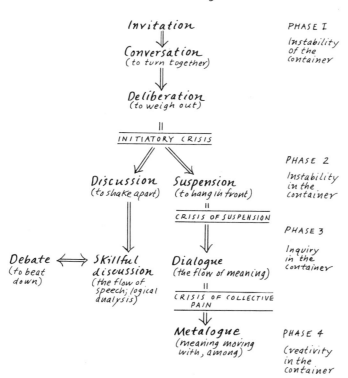

Evolution of Dialogue

Invitation — PHASE 1 — Instability of the Container

Conversation (to turn together)

Deliberation (to weigh out)

INITIATORY CRISIS

Discussion (to shake apart) — Suspension (to hang in front) — PHASE 2 — Instability in the Container

CRISIS OF SUSPENSION — PHASE 3 — Inquiry in the Container

Debate (to beat down) ⟺ Skillful discussion (the flow of speech; logical dualysis) — Dialogue (the flow of meaning)

CRISIS OF COLLECTIVE PAIN

Metalogue (meaning moving with, among) — PHASE 4 — Creativity in the Container

Passing from one phase to the next seems to entail meeting different types of individual and collective crises. Once one moves through a phase, one can return to it. In a sense, all the phases are always present, though one may seem more dominant at any moment.

Phase 1: Instability of the Container When any group of individuals comes together, the individuals bring with them a wide range of tacit, unexpressed differences in perspectives. At this moment, dialogue confronts its first crisis: the need for the members to look at the group as an entity including themselves as observers and observed, instead of merely "trying to understand each other" or reach a "decision that everyone can live with." In this initiatory crisis people confront and navigate a critical paradox: that you can intend to have dialogue, but you cannot force it to happen.

Gradually people recognize that they have a choice: they can *suspend* their views, loosening the grip of their certainty about all views, including their own. They can observe the ways they have habitually made, and acted upon, assumptions. They can question the total process of thought and feeling that produced the conflict—and everything else—in the room: "Let's see where this divergence, this chaos, this instability came from." That will move them toward dialogue.

Or the group can move to converge, avoiding the challenge of gaining insight into the barriers that are appearing, choosing instead to dissect or defend previously held positions. This convergence can take two very different forms. To the extent that people begin to defend themselves, avoiding evidence that would weaken their view, they are moving toward unproductive discussion. To the extent that they begin to surface the data that leads them to conflict, and the reasoning they use to support their positions, they are moving to skillful discussion.

Phase 2: Instability in the Container Having chosen to live with chaos, groups begin to oscillate between suspending views and "discussing" them. At this stage people may find themselves feeling frustrated, principally because the underlying fragmentation and incoherence in everyone's thought begin to appear. Normally this would be kept below the surface, but now it comes forward, despite the best efforts of the participants to keep themselves "cool" or "together." The members begin to feel as if they were in a giant washing machine. No point of view seems to hold all the truth any longer; no conclusion seems definitive. They can't tell where the group is heading; they feel disoriented, and perhaps marginalized or constrained by others.

This leads to a "crisis of suspension." Extreme views are stated and defended. All of this "heat" and instability feels distressing, but it is exactly what should be occurring. The fragmentation that has been hidden is appearing.

In our health care dialogue sessions, at this stage, people began to talk about the long-suppressed "myths" different groups felt about each other (physicians versus administrators, for example), and the anger which they felt about each other. Though expressing conflict of this sort was traditionally anathema to "caring" people, the instability in the container compelled them to explore it directly. However, instead of talking about it in terms of interpersonal issues, they could talk about their different collective images of one another. ("You think nurses are less intelligent than doctors, don't you?")

To manage the crisis of collective suspension that arises at this stage, everyone must be adequately awake to what is happening. People do not need to panic and withdraw, to fight, or to categorize one viewpoint as "right" and another viewpoint as "wrong." All they need to do is listen and inquire: "What is the meaning of this?" They do not merely listen to others, but to themselves: "Where am I listening from? What is the disturbance going on in me [not others]? What can I learn if I slow things down and inquire within myself?"

At this crisis, skilled facilitation is most critical. The facilitator does not seek to "correct" or impose order on what is happening, but to model (in his or her own behavior) some ways to suspend assumptions. The facilitator might point out the presence of polarizations, the opportunity to learn what they represent, and the limiting categories of thought that are rapidly gaining momentum in the group.

Phase 3: Inquiry in the Container If a critical mass of people stay with the process beyond this point, the conversation begins to flow in a new way. In this "cool" environment people begin to inquire together as a whole. People become sensitive to the ways in which the conversation is affecting all the participants in the group. New insights often emerge. When we facilitated a dialogue in South Africa, we found people began to reflect on apartheid in ways that surprised them. They could stand beside the tension of the topic without being identified with it.

This phase can be playful and penetrating. Yet it also leads to another crisis. People gradually begin to sense their separateness. Such awareness brings pain. It hurts to exercise new cognitive and emotional muscles, and it especially hurts to feel how you have created your own fragmentation and isolation, throughout your life.

This "crisis of collective pain" is deep and challenging. It requires considerable discipline and collective trust. As areas of lack of wholeness come to the group's attention, its members begin to change, freeing up rigidity and old habits of attention and communication.

Moving through this crisis is by no means a given nor necessary for "success" in dialogue. Groups may need a considerable period of time to develop the capacity for moving to the final level.

Phase 4: Creativity in the Container If this crisis can be navigated, the distinction between memory and thinking becomes apparent. Thinking takes on an entirely different rhythm and pace. The net of words may not be fine enough to capture the subtle and delicate understandings that begin to emerge; the people may fall silent. Yet the silence is not an empty void, but one replete with richness.

"When the soul lies down in that grass," wrote Rumi, a thirteenth-century Persian poet, "the world is too full to talk about." In dialogue's fourth phase, the world is too full to use language to analyze it. Yet words can also emerge here: speech that clothes meaning, instead of words merely pointing toward it. I call this kind of experience "metalogue" or "meaning flowing with." The group does not "have" meaning in its conversation. The group *is* its meaning. This kind of exchange allows participants to generate breakthrough levels of intelligence and creativity, and to know the aesthetic beauty of shared speech.

55 The Cauldron

Heat and Light Between Labor and Management at GS Technologies

Gary Clark, John Cottrell, Rob Cushman, B. C. Huselton, Phil Yantzi

In the early 1990s, the managers and labor representatives at GS Technologies realized they had to stop being adversaries. GS Technologies, based in Kansas City, Missouri, was at that time part of one of the largest American integrated steel manufacturers. Both sides turned to dialogue to explore intractable differences that they had maintained over a thirty- or forty-year period, to see what sort of mutual learning they could create, and to discover whether that learning might lead to performance differences in the mill.

When they started, some of the representatives from either side could barely speak without shouting or walking away. Less than one year later, the two sides have grown so accustomed to talking together that they regularly make joint presentations—not as "first management speaks, and then the union speaks," but as a common entity composed of both management and union people. It's significant that the allegiances to management and union have not disappeared. Dialogue, instead, has given birth to a metaphorical container—with their steel mill background, these people call it a "cauldron"—that is large enough to contain the allegiance to union and management within it. We could easily have included the reflections of two dozen people in this piece. For the sake of brevity, we narrowed it down to five: Rob Cushman, the president of the division (and CEO of the new entity which it has recently become); John Cottrell, the president of the United Steelworkers Local 13, which is entirely composed of workers from this plant; Gary Clark, the union local's treasurer; Phil Yantzi, the assistant chief steward (and the man whose "ballistic" moment became a catalyst for the group); and B. C. Huselton, vice president for Human Resources and Business Systems at the business.

1983–89: Rusting out

B. C. Huselton: In the 1970s, as the American steel industry started to almost self-destruct, our parent company diversified away from steel making, investing heavily in the insurance and leasing businesses. By 1983, it was clear these investments hadn't turned out as expected. By 1985, I was working with the ninth president of my career. Every president that came along had good intentions and promised to fix things, but there was an atmosphere of fear, a kind of rusting out and dying on the job.

I was part of the problem. I came to this Kansas City plant in 1987. As a human relations and labor management executive, my job was to assist with taking out 2,000 people, see what pieces could be saved, and move on to the next site. In those days, I was called the hatchet man, and it was absolutely all-consuming. I was a bear at home. I didn't want to come to work, and I was especially frustrated because I couldn't describe what was troubling me. I just knew we had to do something different.

I especially hated to be around the union. Negotiations were a joke; we never talked about anything of substance. Everybody was very angry. I'd known John Cottrell, the president of the union local, since 1973, and I knew he was a very caring, affable, outgoing guy. He must have been just as sick of it as I was.

John Cottrell: In twenty-four years, I'd seen good and bad management. But I'd never seen management willing to treat us as an equal and listen to us. At the bargaining tables we used to point across at the management side. "That one guy over there," we'd say to each other, "he's not saying anything. He's looking at you, and seeing what pushes your button. So don't let on that you're upset." So we just played games. And the plant managers never would find out what we were upset about.

1990–91: Building a foundation

Rob Cushman: When I became division president in November of 1990, we had lots of buildings that were empty and falling down. We had a terrible safety record. There were 485 grievances. There was always something breaking down, and we were always cutting back people. People weren't having a good time, and for me, having fun and productivity are directly related. Meanwhile, I felt like a pawn in a long-established union-management battle. We had one famous meeting about absenteeism in which the union grouped itself around one corner of a square table, and we managers were placed at the other point. A clash of absolute hate rose off the table. I began receiving hate mail every day.

The first changes started after a union election early in 1991, when the new officials (including John Cottrell) came to see me about some problems with workman's compensation and our plant doctor. At one point, the union vice president said, "Well, Rob, maybe I can understand how things look from your side of the table." I walked around and sat on their side. "Look," I said, "there is no other side of the table."

Somehow something clicked in that meeting, and we began to put in new policies. We changed some of our incentive systems, and hired a new doctor whom the union helped interview. We began the most massive demolition in our history, taking down 60 percent of our buildings.

John Cottrell: We built our own employee involvement program, designed by both labor and management. We'd never had that opportunity before. In the past, the company would build a program and then invite us in. And it never worked because all the rules were for them. Well somebody was smart enough to invite us in on the design; we got busy with ideas and in less than a year, we saved five million dollars just by doing a little brainstorming and communicating with each other. It was magnificent. But as we were about to see, it wasn't enough.

1991: Enter dialogue

B. C. Huselton: Both Rob and I were considered strange within the old big steel culture, outside our division. We didn't feel compelled to have all the answers, and people thought we were too "touchy-feely," as they called it. I had begun to think of those qualities as "caring" and "inspiring." But I also had a reputation of getting things done gracefully with the union, so I had survived. Now, for the first time, I felt encouraged, as Rob gave me the freedom and support to investigate ideas that might help our division further.

There was a lot at stake—especially as we pursued employee involvement. Some managers argued that the more business decision making we gave the union, the more it could hold us hostage later. To my mind, there was more potential reward than risk. I didn't know how we would survive without finding a way to create the business we wanted to craft together with the union. If we couldn't do that, then every intervention would fail, and we would eventually shut down.

Steve Buchholz, a change management thinker who had helped us a great deal, showed me a copy of *The Fifth Discipline* in 1990. The concepts connected back to questions I was asking myself: "Why do we act as if we think the union guys are a bunch of jerks? Why do we talk about real problems in the hall instead of in front of each other? Why do I feel burned out?" I went to a three-day systems thinking class that May. When they showed us the ladder of inference, I thought, that's what we're doing. We're leaping to assumptions and conclusions and doing nothing with data.

⟩⟩ See "The Ladder of Inference," page 242.

In 1991, Rob and I went to plead our case at MIT's learning center. He said to Peter Senge, "It looks like you've got a lot of well-regarded, wonderful companies here. How would you like a dog? If you really want to see if this method works, why don't you try us?" We were accepted and began to attend gatherings and I met Bill Isaacs. "What would it take," I asked him, "to get people to be capable of really talking to each other?" A few weeks later, he came to Kansas City to talk with the management group and the union group about dialogue, and give them an introductory overview.

Phil Yantzi: Unlike most of the gurus who had come in, Bill didn't begin by naming off his degrees and credentials. He sat down with us and said, "I've had a lot of education, and it's surprising how much I had to push aside when I began this work." That willingness to admit you don't have all the answers has always impressed me.

We told Bill all the horror stories about the past—how the company would sit in meetings asking, "How do we get people to buy in on this TQM?" but always pushed aside the parts of the programs that would benefit people and give us the support we needed to improve the work. For our part, all we knew how to do was beat up on each other, shout and yell, and not try to see the other side of the point. Before committing ourselves to this new system we agreed to have three training sessions of our own, off-site.

At the training sessions, Bill had some of us role-play being the managers, and we kept butting heads with them, just as we had during the last twenty-two years. No matter which side you were on, you had to go in there trying to convince the other side you were right, and not showing any weakness, even if you felt you might be wrong.

Bill told us about the container of shared meaning we'd be creating through our talks, and we started picturing that container in exercises.

John Cottrell: You can have a container in your mind. It can be anything—a cauldron, a bottle, a milk carton. It may not even be a literal container; it may be made entirely of trust. But you're all in there together, and you make up the strength of the container yourselves. You make it safe; you make it foolproof. You do that by dialoguing, bringing problems to a head, talking about them, and not worrying about blowing the container up. I get a vision in my mind of a big aluminum pot that we're all in and I can see the dents on the outside, but it's okay. It's like a pressure cooker, but it never breaks.

June 1991: The cauldron bubbles over

B. C. Huselton: We agreed to bring together about thirty-five union leaders and managers for two days. Later, I called that meeting the pin in the grenade. It was just a matter of who would let go first.

The setting was important; it was a resort, with mineral springs, where Harry Truman's presidential retreat had been located; Al Capone had holed up there. There was a lot of initial chitchat, and then about two hours into the session, things started to heat up. "Is this just another program?" asked the union guys. Right away grenades were rolled out, and people started defending themselves. "Every time we turn around you've got a new president. All you want us to do is give up wages so you can continue to run the business. We give you information and you don't use it. You tell us to do things we shouldn't be doing. You don't listen." This was all the stuff we'd heard but never wanted to respond to, and our first response was: "You guys are union, so all you know how to say is this kind of stuff."

Early the first day, we put blindfolds on. When you couldn't tell who was talking, everybody sounded the same. All of us were frustrated; none of us trusted the business. We were all insecure, and wondering about our future. We began to overlay our talk about making the business great with thoughts about what we hated. Bill, at this point, was like someone fanning the flames, saying, "I love the heat; come on, baby." At one of the breaks I went up to him and said, "Bill, I think this is going to fall apart." And he said, "Yeah, maybe it will."

⟩⟩ The blindfold exercise appears on page 384.

But then, every so often, Bill would call time out. "Let's begin to use some tools to understand our session so far before we go on." We worked the causal loop systems diagrams and the ladder of inference. At first, Bill would stop the talk and say, "Let's search for the data behind that assumption." Soon it got to the point where everybody started to catch each other and some fun started to surface in the group. Instead of accusing someone of lying, we might say, "Hey, we'd better get you an extension ladder, you're so high up there." A code of conduct started to surface among us that made us think a little bit before we spoke. Where before you might have jumped in to defend someone's comment, now you realized that that comment actually masked that they hadn't heard the previous comment.

Phil Yantzi: But after a while, the dialogue portion faded out and we stopped suspending assumptions. The conversation turned to whether the company should contract work out to "mini-mills," most of which are nonunion. We have a definite view of nonunion plants: their safety and treatment of people are substandard. They always pick a farm community where people don't know to call OSHA, so people die and get maimed. Meanwhile everyone looks up to the parent company as heroes because they're making a profit, when they're actually villains.

Jack Stutz, who had recently arrived as the manufacturing manager, said, "In our plant the other day, I stood around and talked to someone for two hours. In the mini-mills, a guy couldn't stand and talk longer than ten minutes."

"That worker didn't want to be rude to you," we replied. "He had to go play catch-up later."

But the superintendents began to talk about cutting jobs and man-hours, and finally Jack called us lazy. It was the end of the day, we were tired of sitting all day in chairs, and it raised up feelings from all those years of fighting cutbacks. I went ballistic; I started shouting. I said that I had expected Jack to bring in fresh ideas, "But this is the same old crap I've been hearing for twenty years." I told them that their hourly workers were the reason the plant was still functioning: "After twelve years of concessions, the managers squandered all that money, and didn't reinvest it here." In the heat of my anger, I used a lot of swear words. I tried to provoke Jack into jumping on me. But he stayed cool and didn't say anything.

Instead, one of the company guys said, "Well, I'm kind of offended by Phil's language. Especially if we've got a lady in the room." He meant Mary Fewel-Tulin, one of the dialogue facilitators, who was sitting between me and Jack.

"We talked to Mary," I snapped back, "and warned her this might happen, and she said she had eight brothers. If you're out in the steel mill, that's the way you talk, and that's the way I talk when I'm angry. If you don't like it, you invited me. And I can get up and leave."

Then Bill said that it was good to get this heated up. We took a break and I took him aside and apologized: "I'm trying to be a communicator here, and I blew up. I don't want to be this way."

"No," he said. "We'll discuss it more, but I want you to be yourself."

"Are you trying to get us to compromise, or what?" I asked him.

"No, I don't want you to compromise your views and opinions," he said, "but these things need to be brought out so we can look at them collectively." He said either I had to say these things to the group, or I would withdraw; and if I withdrew, nobody would ever know how I felt. And then he suggested that I spend the rest of the evening looking at myself and why I had gotten so angry.

Rob Cushman: God, it was uncomfortable when Phil got mad. It was as if the cauldron burst and all that hot metal spilled out. Later, I realized what made it so uncomfortable: up to that moment, I didn't believe any of us were telling how we really felt. We were all just playing our own parts. I didn't understand what a container was yet. I hadn't learned to dialogue.

That first night, I went to bed almost with tears in my eyes. I had had this wonderful belief in building a great facility, and now I had this terrible tension. I didn't know if anybody would want to come back. And yet the next morning we all came back and we all said, "Wait a minute. We don't want this to break. Yes, we said some harsh things, and yes, I got it off my mind." Even guys like Phil said, "I want to come back. I want to talk more." And from that moment of super heat, we became more trusting.

Phil Yantzi: The next morning, Bill said to Jack, "You brought up a problem, but you already had the solution." When you go in with your mind made up, Bill said, you end up just butting heads. Nothing gets solved because everybody's trying to push their opinion.

Jack acknowledged this, and we started talking about what my going ballistic had meant. He said it was the warrior in me, and I drew another line: "Don't call us lazy. We do too high-quality work for you to say that." We all started talking about what it's like when you're throwing material in the ladle, in 3,000-degree heat, with long underwear and safety gear on so too many sparks won't get close to your bare skin. And I thought, I'm speaking for everybody who lays their life on the line to make steel.

Now we started talking about the problem which Jack had been thinking about: the competitors had a lower level of man-hours per ton. And we started talking it through. Maybe they were lying to us. Or maybe, while we focused on man-hours per ton, they were focusing on new product lines. Or, if there was the need to cut man-hours per ton, maybe we could find a way to do it by boosting production instead of by cutting workers.

B. C. Huselton: One point that surfaced was: it's okay to be angry. We talked about how people in the steel industry were supposed to be strong. We're iron men. But really, there was a hollow spot within us; something we could still just barely talk about.

1991–92: Surfacing "union"

B. C. Huselton: For the following year, we held two meetings a month, from 8 until 11 A.M.

A concept that Phil calls "surfacing *union* as a word" came up in the second meeting. We all remembered how, with the blindfolds on, everybody sounded the same. And for many of us it was easier to talk with the blindfold on. Phil said, "We're starting to see distinctions disappear."

One of the managers said, "What distinction?"

"Well," he said, "the distinction between management and union."

From there we started talking about the business—not only what was going on but why. We started paying a lot more attention to the concepts of personal mastery: Why are we here, and what's our life purpose about? Once we had decided there was something worthy here, a lot of things started surfacing.

For example, the managers began talking about how we wanted to reduce the number of people at the mill, and we actually said, "We don't know how to do it." We ended up removing about 125 people, including a great many salaried people. The way we handled this, I think, gave us some credibility, both inside the container, and outside, back among the rest of the people, who were hearing about what was going on.

John Cottrell: We also found a way to deal with our contracting-out problem. Jack Stutz made it a dream instead of a nightmare. We do it, when we can, with our people. We had to take down an old melt shop, with enormous blue pipe on the top, that weighed tons. Normally in the past we would have contracted that out. This time, our riggers were given an opportunity, because we could say, "Jack, we can do that work." It scared me to death, having our people crawl around on top of this building, using the torches and the big cranes to hold these pipes in the air. But they did a wonderful job and came in $30,000 under budget.

Once we could see how he was thinking, it turned out that Jack Stutz was one of the most intelligent steel makers I have known. And he's a down-to-earth guy. He tells you like it is.

1992–93: What the cauldron wrought

Gary Clark: In the past, when subjects like contracting out came up, we left the room. Now, almost any topic can come up. We recognize that there is no mind scheming on their part; it's just their thoughts. We can suspend our assumptions about those thoughts, and look at them more completely.

On almost every subject, we find that management's position is not what we expected prior to dialogue sessions. And I think management recognizes that our positions are different than what they expected. They give us credit for what we believe in, instead of assuming we're trying to steal money from them. Rather than seeing the union as a hindrance, they see it as a needed force.

It all revolves around truth. We believe what they tell us. We no longer have to spend the majority of our time trying to distinguish whether what they said was true or a lie, or where they're coming from. We don't have to feel trapped by what we say, or feel like we're going to get stabbed in the back. We can suspend our thoughts without having to defend our position twenty-four hours a day. A year ago, if our union people said, "Good morning" to management, or "How was your week-end?" it was just conversation. Today, I guarantee you there's truly concern for whether each other had a good or bad weekend.

Rob Cushman: We began to spend much of our time listening and talking and walking through the plants, looking into safety problems—and acting on them immediately. Our worker's compensation costs dropped from $1.3 million to $500,000, as people began to look, think, and feel safe, and to feel good about the place where they have to come to work. We went from a backlog of 485 grievances to none. I believe dialogue has been one of the primary driving forces to allow all this to happen.

In 1992, the mother company decided that our business unit was not going to be part of their future. If we could not find some company or investors who would be interested in buying us, we would be shut down. We had a history of environmental problems, lack of investment, and labor/management hostility. We had fourteen businesses in twelve countries and forty-four locations, and a tremendous legacy burden, with approximately four retirees for every active employee. We had to go out and say, "Would you like to think about investing in the future of this?"

The people who turned out to be the principal investors in our new company were particularly interested because we could show the relationship and energy between ourselves and the union. If it hadn't been for what we did with dialogue, we would not exist as a company today.

John Cottrell: It hasn't spread throughout the plant like it has with the executive board and top management. It always takes time to drift out into the areas of the workers, because there's still mistrust in our plant. I think we'll have to learn to be facilitators ourselves; we can no longer count on Bill or any individual. We have to have the gumption and drive to go out and teach this. We're already doing a lot of teaching through our Total Quality system. Union people run that, with the support of the managers, and we hold it very sacred to our hearts.

We created a second dialogue group, and I sat in on their meeting recently. It's incredible. They're saying the same things that we were saying at the same point in our evolution. So we all have basically the same needs and problems. I chuckled. And Bill looked at me and winked.

Rob Cushman: Our largest concern is transmitting our understanding throughout middle management and front-line supervision, to the shop steward and the hourly worker. We feel bad that many times people who haven't been in the dialogue sessions don't feel the same spirit. And maybe that should be one of the key issues in this *Fieldbook:* How do you make this a looming reality throughout the whole organization?

Remember, we're working seven days a week, and three shifts a day. It's not easy to find the time and places where people can meet. We're still searching for ways to expand and include everybody. To me, generative dialogue is a foundation upon which everything else rests. Everything emanates from our ability to communicate deeply with each other.

56 Designing a Dialogue Session

William Isaacs, Bryan Smith

The setup and facilitation of dialogue is a discipline in itself, which requires respect and humility to be understood. It may take a year or more to develop these competencies, depending on where you start. Mastery is a lifetime's work.

At the same time, every practice, including dialogue, must provide immediate and practical starting points. Teams may find these precepts helpful in orienting themselves to work with a facilitator; or they may find the precepts helpful in general. As teams improve their conversation skills, they sometimes find themselves moving through the progression that leads to dialogue.

For more on this progression, see "Dialogue," page 357.

The paradoxes of dialogue design *William Isaacs*

THE PRACTICE OF DIALOGUE EMBODIES SEVERAL PARADOXES. THESE CAN require some stretching to embrace, but seem to be at the heart of dialogue work.

TECHNIQUES THAT LEAVE TECHNIQUE BEHIND

No matter how willfully you engage in the practice, you can't force dialogue to happen. You can't "will" yourself into greater awareness and sensitivity as a team. You need the techniques of dialogue to help you build a container—an environment that promotes collective inquiry—and to learn to pay careful attention to what is happening within it and within yourself.

At the same time, technique in itself cannot get you to your goal. In this sense, dialogue is like some Eastern forms of meditation whose teachers stress that it is a discipline which can be taught, and yet the ability it generates has little to do with the techniques that people teach you. (Some teachers frequently admonish their students to leave the techniques behind.)

"DON'T JUST DO SOMETHING, STAND THERE"

Many people argue that the essential strategy, when faced with difficult problems, is not to think about action, nor to talk, but to act. In dialogue, however, we don't think about what we're doing; we do something about what we're thinking. We speak in ways that catalyze insight and uncover the process of thought. This may have more power than any other step you can take, even if it looks to an outsider like not much is going on.

INTENTION BUT NO DECISION

The process of dialogue encourages people to develop a shared intention for inquiry. ("Inquiry" comes from the Latin *inquaerere,* to seek within.) Dialogue will backfire if channeled to the intent of making a decision. That would cut off the free flow of inquiry. (The word decision, from the Latin *decidere,* literally means to "murder alternatives.") It is best to approach dialogue with no result in mind, but with the intention of developing deeper inquiry, wherever it leads you.

A SAFELY DANGEROUS SETTING

People often express the desire to have a safe setting in which to explore difficult subjects and relationships. The safety of dialogue comes directly from the willingness to touch the dangerous. As one educator put it to me a while ago, "education is a process of endangering the soul in a spirit of enlightened discourse." This is the spirit of dialogue.

BEING INDIVIDUAL AND COLLECTIVE

Some of the most powerful contributions to a collective conversation can come from people who are learning to listen, not to the group, but to themselves. In that case, the voice in their heart, mind, and body is saying something because the collective dialogue is taking place around them. Are they generating this new perception? Or is the collective meaning of the group expressing itself through them? From the perspective of dialogue, both are taking place.

The facilitation of dialogue: notes for and about the dialogue "specialist" *William Isaacs*

WHILE DIALOGUE CAN'T BE FORCED, IT *CAN* BE NURTURED. YOU CAN CREate conditions under which it can occur. In fact, most of our theoretical work so far has revolved around identifying the personal and interpersonal climates which encourage or derail it. These conditions include the internal climate and point of view of the facilitator.

Dialogue does initially require a facilitator, who can help set up this field of inquiry, and who can embody its principles and intention. But this is not familiar "group" leadership. The facilitator should not be seen as the "prime mover," "leader," or "cause" of the dialogue session. Instead, it's helpful to think of dialogue as a process with no single "cause" or "prime mover." Putting the conversation together is a collaborative effort. It doesn't depend on any individual's intelligence. Over time the process should evolve toward collective facilitation, with reliance on the dialogue "expert" diminishing to nothing.

Why, then, is a facilitator necessary at all? Because the process of dialogue is unfamiliar; because it can bring up difficult emotions and misunderstandings; and because skilled facilitators know how to anticipate and help people through the "crises." This requires a wide range of skills: evoking and refining the team's collective attention, intervening in complex social systems, and actively inquiring into defensive routines. The facilitator must develop both an awareness of how his or her own defensive reactions might be triggered, and a large enough presence to embrace all sides of any intense polarization that appears.

For example, in a dialogue in Israel that David Bohm led, one participant stood up and said, "Zionism is the problem with Israel." Another person stood up, enraged, and took the opposite view. The facilitator would have to be able to embrace both views without voting externally for either, to enable the inquiry to get beyond this familiar and stuck polarization. What is the ground *between* the views? This can't be explained if the facilitators cannot help to create the right kind of space.

QUESTIONS FOR THE FACILITATOR

How am I hearing what is being said here?
Who am I as I listen here?
What am I in this scene?

Where am I listening from in myself?

Am I "them"? Am I the silence? Am I my ideas? Am I my disturbances?

Where are the factors that might stretch or fragment the container?

Who is in an emotionally tender place here?

Who's going to want applause?

Who's going to want to be constantly adjusting and improving the process?

Who's going to want to fight with the facilitator?

Who's going to want to raise objections to the process?°

° Some material in these questions derives from work by Cliff Barry about how to identify and heal fundamental identity wounds that people bring into groups.

Basic components of a dialogue session

William Isaacs

INVITATION

The invitation process begins building the container. People must be given the choice to participate. They must understand that their resistances and fears are safely answered. Dialogue can't be shoved down their throats, because that will invoke the memory of previous times when something was forced on them, whether at your organization or elsewhere. You'll get a primitive "fight," "flight," or "freeze" response. Your goal with dialogue is to evoke a higher-level response. Freeing up traditional structures of imposition and hierarchy in a group is essential to allow new energy for collective inquiry.

GENERATIVE LISTENING

To listen fully means to pay close attention to what is being said beneath the words. You listen not only to the "music," but to the very essence of the person speaking. You listen not only for what someone knows, but for who he or she is. Ears operate at the speed of sound, which is far slower than the speed of the light the eyes take in. Generative listening is the art of developing deeper silences in yourself, so you can slow your mind's hearing to your ears' natural speed, and hear beneath the words to their meaning.

OBSERVING THE OBSERVER

When we observe the thoughts that govern how we see the world, we begin to change and transform ourselves—and this is as true for a team as it is for an individual. Many of the dialogue techniques—like silence—are based around developing an environment that is quiet enough so that people can observe their thoughts, and the team's thoughts. Once that happens, things can change without conscious manipulation.

SUSPENDING ASSUMPTIONS

Dialogue encourages people to "suspend" their assumptions—to refrain from imposing their views on others and to avoid suppressing or holding back what they think. The word suspension means "to hang in front." Hanging your assumptions in front of you so that you and others can reflect on them is a delicate and powerful art. This does not mean laying your assumptions aside, even temporarily, to see what your attitudes would be if you felt differently. It means exploring your assumptions from new angles: bringing them forward, making them explicit, giving them considerable weight, and trying to understand where they came from. You literally suspend them in front of the group so that the entire team can understand them collectively.

We have found that to understand the term "suspension" we must see it as several activities, not just one. First comes *surfacing assumptions:* one must be aware of one's assumptions before one can raise them. Typically others are more aware of your assumptions than you are, and less aware of your intentions; as the team inquires into the relationship between assumptions and intentions, the suspension process is begun. Second comes *display* of assumptions: unfolding your assumptions so that you and others can see them. This act of displaying assumptions is itself a kind of suspension. The third component is *inquiry;* to suspend with the intention of inviting others to see new dimensions in what you are thinking and saying.

THE VALUE OF SUSPENDING ASSUMPTIONS

Part of the purpose of suspending assumptions is to honor the passion that underlies every participant's viewpoint, while refusing to allow that passion to become a roadblock. No one is asked to give up his views; nor do you impose one view on everyone; nor is anyone expected to remain quiet, suppressing his reactions if he disagrees with the prevailing wisdom. The assumptions hang in the midst of the room, available for all (including the person who holds them) to question and explore. In our dialogue work, we have found it useful to mention Bohm's metaphor—assumptions suspended in the air before us, as if hanging on a string a few feet before our noses.

Suspending assumptions is a difficult stance to learn to take. Your assumptions are tied closely to your deepest beliefs and values; if anyone challenges them, he is challenging the feelings closest to your heart. Normally, you protect your assumptions from inquiry, instead of saying, for example, "Go on. Can you help me see something else about my deepest beliefs that I'm not now seeing?" Implicit in the willingness to suspend assumptions is a sense of confidence; that if your deepest beliefs are worthwhile, they'll withstand inquiry from others, and if they're not, you'll be strong enough, and open enough, to reconsider them. —**BS**

Disagreement as an opportunity *Bryan Smith*

A DIALOGUE GROUP IS ALWAYS ON THE LOOKOUT FOR THOSE MOMENTS when an almost imperceptible disagreement rises to the surface. Inevitably there will be a temptation to think: "Let's just get on with it. The difference is just semantic." But chances are, if the difference is not easily resolved, it is not just semantic. The facilitator must say, in effect, "Our purpose is not to 'get on with it,' but to use potentially subtle disagreements to show us where to dig deeper."

The moment of disagreement is cause for celebration: "This little discrepancy is intriguing. It's a real opportunity. Let's not lose it. Let's slow down a little bit, play back the tape, and see what's really going on below the tip of the iceberg . . ." In fact, if there is no disagreement, that can be a sign that the group is moving too quickly.

Often, an affection develops between members of the group with the most opposing views, as if the affection itself is fueled by diversity: "Isn't that amazing," someone might say, "that you have such a different idea? Why do you feel that way? How did you come to it?"

General guidelines for dialogue sessions

William Isaacs, Bryan Smith

THERE ARE NO RULES FOR A DIALOGUE SESSION: INSTEAD, WE OFFER guidelines that may be helpful, based on experiences that people have recorded.

Allow at least two hours, or more if possible, for every session.

"Checking in" is one of the most powerful ways to kick off a dialogue session. At the beginning and end of every session, give every participant an opportunity to simply speak for a minute about what he or she is thinking, is feeling, or has noticed. Stress the value of speaking from personal experience. When everyone knows that they will have some air time, people tend to relax.

Avoid agendas and elaborate preparations; these inhibit the free flow of conversation.

While meeting over a meal may break the ice, we recommend that you avoid the temptation; restaurant service and eating can be distracting.

Agree, as a group, to hold three meetings before you decide whether to continue or disband. Anything less may not be a fair experiment; it can take time to grow into the dialogue form of conversation.

Speak to the center, not to each other. While challenging to execute, this guideline underlines the creation of a pool of common meaning, not interpersonal dynamics.

Dialogue in a business context *Bryan Smith*

Not long ago, an American chemical company held a meeting of its worldwide distribution network, intending to write a mission statement. One of the first sentences included a phrase about being an international distributor. A soft-spoken executive from Germany named Helmar said, "I want to change the word 'international' to 'global.'" The Americans protested that the two words meant the same thing.

Helmar just looked at the facilitator, also an American, who said, "Apparently they don't mean the same thing. Helmar, would you describe the difference in your mental model?"

Helmar tried but couldn't seem to find the words. At every breath he took, the Americans said, "Well, then, they are the same. Let's move on." Finally, he stepped up to a flip chart and drew a picture of a wheel, with the United States as the hub and all the other nations as spokes. "That," he said, "is 'international.' You people make the decisions. You decide how much product we get. You even push product on us that we don't want and tell us we have to sell it."

Then he drew a picture of "global": a wheel with the company's mission and values at the center. The United States appeared as one spoke among many. "The United States gets one vote," he said.

For two hours they talked about this—not seeking a decision, but trying to grasp the implications of this distinction. Did success overseas really depend on switching from "international" to "global"? The Americans realized, as they talked and listened, that they had systematically hurt their ability to reach markets in other countries, and they couldn't attract talented people in (for instance) Peru or Singapore, because there was no career path for non-Americans involving a stint at the home office. But if the only remedy was a full-fledged switch to "global," could the American executives of the parent company accept the change?

"I agree with you," the most senior manager at the meeting finally said to Helmar. "I want global. I don't know how to practice it or even how to think about it. But we'll continue to talk about it, and to move toward it, until they tell us to stop." He began by initiating new dialogue sessions at the company's worldwide affiliates, in each case agreeing to appear himself to show that he understood the significance of the word "global" in the company's mission statement. This dialogue session became a model for the conversations the company continued to hold among managers at its many locations around the world.

Exercises for Deeper Listening

William Isaacs

Each of these exercises is designed to evoke particular states of consciousness in someone who is entering a dialogue session. This is somewhat akin to physical stretching. When you stretch certain muscle groups, you allow them to move in a way that they might not be capable of during the full exercise that follows.

These exercises are also designed to isolate certain aspects of the totality of a person, and to develop the tone and quality of your attention.

Exercises in breathing and being present in your thoughts are also very helpful for building the capacity for dialogue. See, for example, "Moments of Awareness" (page 216).

Projector and Screens*

° This exercise was inspired by Cliff Barry, and developed for work with his "four-quarter" model of personal leadership development.

This is an exercise in "seeing" beneath the surface. It draws upon the capacity to see multiple and different points of view as each having a "logic" or sense to them, and the willingness to notice the ways one can become stuck in a single point of view.

PURPOSE

To practice seeing the collective mind in action; to see two polarized perspectives displayed and to learn to disidentify with ordinarily rigidly held positions.

OVERVIEW

People role-play the holder of a significant choice or problem, and two points of view about that choice or problem.

PARTICIPANTS

Any number, divided into groups of three.

TIME

Twenty minutes.

STEP 1: THE PROJECTOR SPEAKS

Divide into groups of three people, ideally composed of people who don't know each other well.

One person in each group volunteers as the "projector." The projector describes a dilemma or real-life choice, on the job or at home. The projector should feel comfortable discussing this problem, because it will be examined in detail. But it must be an important decision: something real, imminent, and not resolved. Examples might include: whether to hire someone for a critical position, or how to choose between pressing alternatives. The topic can be personal: in one rendition, the projector was a woman who was trying to decide whether or not to have a baby.

Ideally, this dilemma should have two alternatives, between which the projector feels caught, polarized. The projector should lay out why this is an issue, and the two alternative points of view.

The remaining two people are "screens." The projector chooses which of them will represent each side of the dilemma. It is as if the projector is displaying the necessary thoughts onto their screens:

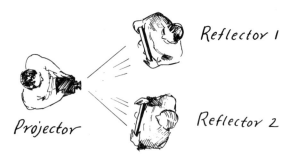

Reflector 1

Projector

Reflector 2

The screens should listen especially for the underlying feel of the position they are being asked to take. They should step fully into their role, embodying the position in every aspect of their posture, voice, and manner, if possible. The projector may suggest a pose that the screen may take physically to better display the meaning of that side of the listener's mind.

STEP 2: THE SCREENS SPEAK

When both screens are ready, the projector should deliberately take one step back, stepping temporarily out of the pattern of disagreement that the two screens now own.

For the next several minutes, the two screens debate the dilemma. If you are a screen, do not articulate what *you* think the projector should do, but represent the point of view you are "embodying," to the best of your ability. The projector, meanwhile, will be silent throughout this step, listening to the debate.

STEP 3: THE PROJECTOR RECONSIDERS

The projector reports back to the screens on what it felt like to listen to them. Typically, all three members of the team will begin to see the assumptions and thoughts of this dilemma suspended before them. Before completing, the projector should "de-roll": acknowledge *out loud* that the screens are people in their own right, not images or reflections.

STEP 4: THE LARGER GROUP DEBRIEF

After the smaller groups have finished, reconvene the large group. Bring out a few examples from the small groups' experiences. This exercise reveals how we all share each other's thoughts. We can step into another's patterns effortlessly. Equally, we can apply patterns to others without knowing it. To suspend these processes, to become conscious of how they work, opens the door for insight and dialogue.

HOW PEOPLE FEEL AFTER "PROJECTOR AND SCREENS"

The value of this exercise is most evident, perhaps, in comments made by some of the "projectors":

"It was like watching 'Firing Line,' except they were dealing with one of my problems. I had to catch myself to keep from making a decision: 'Yes, she's right,' or 'No, he's right.' "

"I was amazed at how familiar and comfortable the debate sounded. It made me more comfortable with the two voices inside my head."

"It wasn't comfortable for me. My anxiety came up. I wanted to jump in and make some decisions, or encourage the other reflector to jump in with a stronger argument."

"Neither voice had the whole picture by itself. I now see why, with some problems, you can't simply make a decision and then move forward."

"It's not the same as taking a tape recorder, arguing both sides of the question to yourself, and playing back the tape. Some resonance is clearly added by having these two other people involved."

A dialogue can itself be a "projector and screens" exercise with thirty different perspectives instead of two. One can begin to see externally the many voices that exist in oneself and in the overall community, and discover new patterns of relationships among them. This exercise can stimulate the capacity to see in this manner.

Blindfolds

PURPOSE
To give people access to an experience of deeper listening.

OVERVIEW
The dialogue group talks together while wearing blindfolds.

PARTICIPANTS
The team practicing dialogue, or any intact team.

FACILITATOR
One person is responsible for being the time-keeper and eyes for the room.

This is an *extremely* delicate exercise that requires careful set up and a clear atmosphere so that people feel safe and free to speak. The blindfolds will greatly increase many people's sense of safety. For others, it will evoke anxiety. The meaning the exercise has for people will depend on the prior context of the group.

Pass out the blindfolds. Encourage people to sit quietly, and wait until *real* stillness has emerged before beginning. People should be reminded that they are free to speak about anything they wish; the aim is to notice what happens.

For twenty minutes or more, have everyone in the room wear blindfolds over their eyes as they talk.

To the facilitator: During the exercise, remain quiet in yourself and notice your own reactions. Ask yourself: What is this telling me about myself and the group?

After the allotted time, maintain a quiet stance in yourself. Quietly say that you are about to end the exercise, and could people complete the conversation they are having. Gently ask people to remove their blindfolds, and to look around the circle to see who is there. Keep the group in the circle, and have members report on their experience.

It is possible to have more than one group practice this at once, in a large room. If you have set it up that way, have all the groups remain in their groups while they reconvene afterward; then let each group report its experience in turn.

Notes on the process: People listen in this exercise in a way that extends an "ear-field" to others. People often notice that instead of multiple conversations, they have one. There is a simultaneous blurring of boundary and focusing on the single voice that speaks.

THE VALUE OF "BLINDFOLDS"

This exercise gives people a very good taste of what deep listening can be. The group's attention level goes up five notches. The amount of internal talk, within each person, goes down, and that reduces the "noise in the system." People often don't know who is talking. It makes them realize how much they judge the credibility of a statement according to who is speaking. —RR

TIME
Twenty minutes to one hour.

SUPPLIES
We find the most effective blindfolds are airplane sleeping blindfolds or tennis headbands, which slip easily over the eyes. Get good, "stretchy" tennis headbands. There should be one for everyone in the room. Flip charts will not be needed.

ENVIRONMENT
A quiet, private room.

57 Skillful Discussion
Protocols for Reaching a Decision — Mindfully

Rick Ross

From the standpoint of building shared meaning within teams or between groups, traditional discussion is dangerously oriented toward advocacy. People "discuss" to win; they heave ideas against each other, as Bill Isaacs puts it, to see whose ideas will be the strongest. It is a dismal way to conduct teamwork, not just because it undermines learning, but because ideas and "solutions" rarely get the consideration they deserve. They are judged according to who said them, and whether or not they match conventional wisdom. Most teams need new tools and skills to both broaden and focus the scale and scope of their conversations — to make them both more divergent and more convergent — when appropriate.

The most effective vehicle I know is the form of conversation which

I call "skillful discussion." You can think of it as a midpoint on the continuum between dialogue and "raw," advocacy-filled discussion:

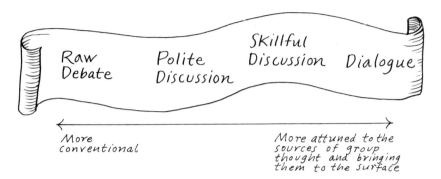

The primary difference between dialogue and skillful discussion involves intention. In skillful discussion, the team intends to come to some sort of closure—either to make a decision, reach agreement, or identify priorities. Along the way, the team may explore new issues and build some deeper meaning among the members. But their intent involves convergent thinking.

In dialogue the intention is exploration, discovery, and insight. Along that path, the group may in fact sometimes come to a meeting of the minds and reach some agreement—but that isn't their primary purpose in coming together.

Teams unquestionably benefit from dialogue—from exploring shared meaning—but they also have the everyday need to come to a pressing conclusion, decision, or plan. To accomplish this work productively, skillful discussion incorporates some of the techniques and devices of dialogue and action learning, but always focused on tasks. Meetings have agendas; people leave with priorities and work assignments in hand. Nonetheless, the team also learns to make their thought processes visible, to surface and challenge assumptions, and to look more closely at sources of disagreement. Gradually, within their team setting, they improve the quality of their collective thinking and interacting.

For the past two years, I've been training teams to conduct their business this way, and most of them have found it a far more effective means of getting to the results they want. Practicing the tools and techniques encourages openness and teamwork, builds trust within the group, and makes visible unseen assumptions which typically block progress toward the results the team members want.

Personally, I believe that everyone should conduct *all* their meetings using these tools and techniques. And I would also encourage them to engage in dialogue on a regular basis, because the two types of conversation enrich each other. But far too few teams in organizations, particularly in business, are willing to experiment with either form. Many teams will spend hours improving their billing or materials-handling processes, but will not construct the practice fields they need to improve the quality of their thinking processes, which might then leverage the quality of everything else they produce.

A facilitator is not as essential to skillful discussion as for dialogue. It helps a great deal if one or more team members are familiar with the mental models tools (see pages 242–63): the ladder of inference, the left-hand column, and the balancing of inquiry and advocacy. The most essential ingredient is an agreement which team members make: to follow five basic protocols. The protocols are clear, and not difficult to grasp; but they require practice. Any team using the protocols will observe its own behavior and effectiveness improve dramatically.

1. PAY ATTENTION TO YOUR INTENTIONS

As an individual, make sure you understand what you hope to accomplish in this discussion. Ask yourself: "What is my intention?" and "Am I willing to be influenced?" If you are not, what is the purpose of the conversation? Be clear on what *you* want, and do not mislead others as to your intentions.

2. BALANCE ADVOCACY WITH INQUIRY

In most management teams, the pendulum between advocacy and inquiry has swung far over on the advocacy side. Some teams take great pride in "challenging each other," but they don't actually challenge each other in any meaningful way. They're merely "in your face" with each other, one-upping each other with trivialities. Other teams pride themselves on how constructively they deal with confrontation. My experience, however, is that they just sit there and listen, in turn, to each other's position statements. Assumptions are not even surfaced, much less challenged. What they are really thinking will be heard only after the meeting—in the hallways or in the bathrooms. While there is essentially nothing wrong with this sort of advocacy, it is the lack of balance that causes misunderstanding, miscommunication, and poor decisions.

⟨⟨ See the protocols for balancing advocacy and inquiry, page 253.

3. BUILD SHARED MEANING

All words are symbols, and as such are abstractions. They often have different meanings to different people. If most people understood this—if they assumed that they did not understand what an individual meant by a particular word unless they inquired about it—then everyone would routinely check the meanings behind the words being spoken more often and there would be far less miscommunication. In most teams, the discussion moves at such a fast clip, and people use words so loosely, that it becomes very hard to build shared meaning. People walk away with vague ambiguous understandings, or even gross misunderstandings, of who meant what and who will do what. Decisions made in such an environment won't stick.

Thus it is important to use language with great precision, taking care to make evident the meaning—or lack of meaning—in a word. Avoid having phrases in your team lexicon where you assume everyone agrees on the definition, but nobody actually has any idea what it is. This practice is most important with the simplest phrases:

"You said 'Get it done.' But what's 'done'?"

"Well, finish the marketing plan."

"Oh. So you're not including shipping."

"I hadn't intended to. But what leads you to suggest that our definition of 'done' should include shipping?"

When talking about definitions, particularly for abstract concepts like 'inferences' and 'mental models,' it helps to start out with some sloppiness—so that everyone gets a chance to "feel around" for the right meaning of the word you are using together. "I just want to exaggerate for a minute," you might say, "so take this with a grain of salt, but I think when we say 'empowerment,' we're actually talking about . . ." As you talk around the issue, you may get closer to a precise definition which you can all agree on. If the word is important to you, then converge on the meaning with as much precision as possible.

4. USE SELF-AWARENESS AS A RESOURCE

Ask yourself, at moments when you are confused, angry, frustrated, concerned, or troubled:

1. What am I thinking? (pause)
2. What am I feeling? (pause)
3. What do I want at this moment?

You will often end up with insights about the team's assumptions or your own concerns, which you can then raise before the group, without casting blame: *"You know, this action implies an assumption about our customers . . ."* or *"When you say such-and-such, I find myself disagreeing because . . ."* or simply, *"I notice that I'm feeling uncomfortable, and I'm not sure why."*

See "Moments of Awareness," page 216.

5. EXPLORE IMPASSES

Ask yourself: What do we agree on, and what do we disagree on? Can we pinpoint the source of the disagreement or impasse? Often the sources of disagreement fall into four categories:

1. Facts—What exactly has happened? What is the "data"?
2. Methods—How should we do what we need to do?
3. Goals—What is our objective? (A "vision" exercise may help bring the disagreement over this into clarity.)
4. Values—Why do we think it must be done in a particular way? What do we believe in?

Simply agreeing on the source of disagreement often allows people to learn more about the situation, clarify assumptions that previously were below awareness, and move forward.

Three moves in particular will help:

Listen to ideas as if for the first time. Work at being open to new ideas.

Consider each person's mental model as a piece of a larger puzzle. Look at the issue from the other person's perspective.

Ask yourself (and everyone else): What do we need to do to move forward?

THE SKILLFUL DISCUSSION TENT CARD TEMPLATE

I have found it helpful to print the protocols on the back of name (tent) cards, so that team members have them handy throughout meetings. It's hokey, but it works!

A sample card might read:

1. Pay attention to my intentions
   What do I want from this conversation? Am I willing to be influenced?

2. Balance advocacy with inquiry
   "What led you to that view?" "What do you mean by that view?"

3. Build shared meaning
   "When we use the term ———, what are we really saying?"

4. Use self-awareness as a resource
   What am I thinking? What am I feeling? What do I want at this moment?

5. Explore impasses
   What do we agree on, and what do we disagree on?

PREPARING THE GROUND FOR SKILLFUL DISCUSSION

1. Create a safe haven for participants. Because people from different parts of the organization may join this team, the "turf" of the meeting must belong to no one. The symbols and trappings of power, prestige, and status should be minimized. As another power equalizer, all participants in a skillful discussion should expressly agree to "treat each other as colleagues." Curiosity, respect of, and support for each other's opinions and feelings are essential.

2. Make openness and trust the rule rather than the exception. People must feel secure that they can speak freely, without fear of being the target of criticism, ridicule, or retribution. Thus, there must be a ground rule that people will not have their remarks attributed to them outside the room, unless they agree. Everyone who attends must be given complete immunity for what they say during these discussions.

   Agreeing on a set of ground rules is only the beginning. Trust develops only if every participant continues to act in a trustworthy manner.

3. Encourage and reward the injection of new perspectives. For groups which meet often, it is useful to find external sources of new perspectives—such as outsiders invited to join in for one or several sessions. Regardless of who is present, the discussion will broach issues, ideas, and approaches typically given short shrift in day-to-day work. Right

and wrong are not of concern. The exchange of perspectives and points of view, not the selling of them, is the issue.

4. Plan the agenda, time, and context to allow for concentrated deliberation. The best way to assure a single focus is to make sure that every participant expects to talk about the same subject. Agendas should be developed and agreed upon in advance. Also, creative discussions take time. Less than two hours is unacceptable, even for the most experienced groups. Keep distractions—especially phone calls, other appointments, and interruptions—to a minimum.

HOW TO LISTEN IN SKILLFUL DISCUSSION (OR ANY TIME)

1. Stop talking: To others and to yourself. Learn to still the voice within. You can't listen if you are talking.

2. Imagine the other person's viewpoint. Picture yourself in her position, doing her work, facing her problems, using her language, and having her values. If the other person is younger or more junior, remember your early days in the company.

3. Look, act, and be interested. Don't read your mail, doodle, shuffle, or tap papers while others are talking.

4. Observe nonverbal behavior, like body language, to glean meanings beyond what is said to you.

5. Don't interrupt. Sit still past your tolerance level.

6. Listen between the lines, for implicit meanings as well as explicit ones. Consider connotations as well as denotations. Note figures of speech. Instead of accepting a person's remarks as the whole story, look for omissions—things left unsaid or unexplained, which should logically be present. Ask about these.

7. Speak only affirmatively while listening. Resist the temptation to jump in with an evaluative, critical, or disparaging comment at the moment a remark is uttered. Confine yourself to constructive replies until the context has shifted, and criticism can be offered without blame.

8. To ensure understanding, rephrase what the other person has just told you at key points in the conversation. Yes, I know this is the old "active listening" technique, but it works—and how often do you do it?

9. Stop talking. This is first and last, because all other techniques of listening depend on it. Take a vow of silence once in a while.

58 Skillful Discussion at Intel

Ed Carpenter

Ed Carpenter is the manager of a testing and assembly plant at Intel, where about 700 people work. His team has been one of the key testing fields for the practice of skillful discussion and other aspects of team learning.

While hundreds of people are responsible for the extraordinary results described at the end of this cameo, a few deserve special mention: Scooter Belew, Tom Eucker, Dave Johnson, Steve Megli, and John Muhawi. All five worked long and hard to help prepare their working sessions and make this team learning effort really take off.

I was first introduced to the techniques of skillful discussion in a roundabout manner. The plant I manage, known as A4/T11 at Intel, had embarked on a shared vision effort late in 1991. As we finished up that work in mid-1992, we began to think, "What are we going to do with this?" For example, we had placed a high premium on the value of teamwork, and said we would create a team-oriented organization at Intel. I wanted to implement that vision at our plant—a semiconductor assembly and testing plant, based in Arizona, producing primarily 486 series computer chips—but I felt we did not yet have a coherent way to translate the ideals into action.

Intel was a member of MIT's Center for Organizational Learning, from which Peter Senge referred us to Rick Ross. Rick began working closely with us in late 1992 to design a regular practice in skillful discussion. We chose skillful discussion almost by default. Some of us strongly wanted to learn the "links and loops" of systems thinking first, but the mental models material seemed to address our immediate need—staff development. We had serious teamwork problems.

In fact, those problems were the first significant topic I raised at our first full session in March 1993. I said, "You know, whenever someone giving a speech asks, 'How many people have been on a great team?' everybody always raises their hand. But in my twenty years at Intel, I've only been on two great teams, and I really believe that a majority of people haven't been on *any*." I made a joke about how the question was like a test of your manhood, so of course everyone claimed a great team or two in their past, and then I made the comment which triggered the eye-opening discussion. "For instance," I said, "I don't think *this* staff is performing as a good team, at all."

In retrospect, perhaps I should have followed up by talking about the attributes that I felt weren't being demonstrated. Members of the senior team, for instance, were optimizing their departmental functions, but they weren't acting for the good of the whole organization. They hardly talked to each other and rarely tried to figure out how to help each other. As one of my staff members later said, they didn't really care about each other's success. Until they could, I felt, our plant couldn't succeed. However, I didn't say much more at that meeting, and after a moment of shocked silence, the conversation drifted elsewhere.

About a month later, in preparation for another session, Rick talked to some members of my staff. My comment, it turned out, still rankled them. "Ed made that statement," they said, "and we still don't know what he means. He never told us what he thought good teamwork should be, and we don't feel very good about what he *did* tell us." Part of Rick's job, of course, was to relay those sentiments to me in a way which didn't make the staff people feel threatened. When he did, I realized how significant my comment had been.

In our second meeting in May, a discussion blossomed out of their contention. It felt to some of the staff as if I were leading them around in the wilderness, without much plan or guidance about what I expected. Rick pointed out to me later that leaders often get into this type of conundrum: the staff thought I should lay out a clear-cut progression to the teamwork I wanted, while I hoped they would participate with me in figuring out how to get there. Of course, none of these clashing expectations were ever talked about.

So now we began to talk about them. "I think you're putting too much of the overall responsibility for the plant on my shoulders," I said, "and I need more help than I'm getting." I praised their capability as individual managers, but I said I wanted them to be leaders—empowering people and helping them to do their jobs.

We spent the next five or six hours using the skillful discussion tools. In my opinion, my staff made more progress that day than they had in the previous year and a half. Within a few hours, they began to feel more confident with their own sense of teamwork and leadership. And some remarkable breakthroughs followed. For instance, we started talking about one of our process flow difficulties. To solve it, we would have to make a small change in one of the manufacturing groups' work. Unfortunately, this group (call them "Group A") had a reputation as one of the toughest, most resistant teams in the plant. Group A's stubbornness had always been undiscussable in the past—and even the fact that we couldn't discuss it had been undiscussable. Now, at last, we had brought it to the table.

"Look," said one of the managers who needed Group A to change, "we're even afraid to come to you, because we know you won't listen to us. You'll just come up with excuses. So why should we even bother asking?"

"But I thought I was doing everything you wanted," said a Group A leader. "In fact, you didn't tell me any differently. You just reinforced my feeling that I was doing a good job."

Ironically, it turned out that the change which everyone wanted was already in place. Group A had implemented it independently, for its own reasons, but hadn't told anyone else. Since the other managers were sure the answer would be no, they hadn't asked; they had only seethed about how difficult Group A was to work with.

The subset of managers involved with that process pursued it further over lunch. Now that they understood each other better, they hammered out a plan for making more complete improvements. Within a week or so they had most of the details worked out and much of the change underway.

That's one of several stories I could tell. The fact that they all happened at the same time isn't coincidence. A convergence of factors had clicked into place at the right time, making it possible for people to bring their complaints to the table. We know this, in part, because another group from A4/T11 went through similar sessions with less success. In fact, they inadvertently became the "control group" for our experiment, helping us see which factors make the most difference. The significant factors, in my judgment, included these:

- The involvement of the boss or leader. I personally take part in every skillful discussion session among my direct reports and senior managers. The team can see that I feel this is important.
- A consistent critical mass of committed people. All but two or three of our fifteen members have been with us since the original session. It's easy to bring new people up to speed, but it would be very hard if the rest of the team were more unstable.
- An atmosphere of trust. This type of conversation works only when people feel comfortable exposing some of the sides of themselves

which they normally protect. I had to demonstrate that no one would be nailed for something they said at a meeting, particularly by me.

- Treating each other as colleagues. We developed specific ways to suggest collegiality. For example, at most Intel meetings, people sit at square tables with the senior managers at the front. Here, we sat in a circle. No one was placed on a higher plateau.

- Raising questions with no hard and firm answers. I have developed the habit of starting the day by saying, "I've been thinking about something . . ." Once I asked what the role of leadership should be in our group. Another time, I asked whether we were really getting anything useful out of our skillful discussion work—and if we were, how could we bring it to the rest of the workplace? I always try to show that I don't know the answer and want to learn from what everyone says. It gives the meetings a different ambiance than if I walk in saying, "How do we cut throughput time to ten days?" (Throughput time is the time it takes to move the product through the entire assembly and test process.)

Interestingly, the day I asked whether we were getting anything useful out of the work was the first session we held without Rick present. We had become fairly skilled at using the techniques in open-ended discussions, but not in more task-oriented topics. So we decided to take on a subject related to our ordinary work: "We've got to operate with fewer head count next year. How are we going to do that?" This was more difficult. We found ourselves reverting to brainstorming, and we lost some of the ability we had gained to listen respectfully and treat each other as colleagues. I think the reason is simple: focused topics remind us more of work, and the old conversational habits creep in. But everyone agrees, in principle, that the new conversational habits are better as a rule.

While it's difficult to establish a one-for-one correlation, we have had breakthroughs in critical factory measures which correspond to our increasing capability at skillful discussion. Our throughput time was reduced by more than 40 percent. The quality measure of yield (the percentage of chips coming into the factor that leave as shippable units) was significantly improved by cutting losses in half!

Then there are less measurable, but equally impressive, human results. Two members of my staff, whose work affected one another's, had some historical baggage between them. They couldn't work together, and I could never figure out why. During the May session, they started talking to each before the group.

"You know," said one, "I made the inference years ago that you weren't competent. I concluded that if I needed anything from your area, I'd have to do it myself. So I never wasted time, as I saw it, trying to get you to help me."

"I had the feeling you felt that way," said the other, "but I never realized that was the reason."

I started to worry: Would this continue constructively, or would it break into more anger and hostility? But as they kept talking, they gained a kind of mutual understanding. Since then, they've met regularly to talk about what support they needed and expected. At one of the skillful discussion sessions, one of them turned to us and said, "You know, I've taken this stuff to heart. I'm really trying to go ahead and work with this guy as if I own his success."

Fishbowl

Charlotte Roberts

See the skillful discussion protocols on page 387. (For an example of the use of this exercise, see "Building an Organization That Recognizes Everyone's Uniqueness" by Michele Hunt, page 417).

Come to this exercise with a topic in mind—a difficult one. It might be a recurring chronic problem; a downsizing or product introduction failure; or an undiscussable subject which needs to be surfaced and dealt with.

PURPOSE
To get immediate feed-back on your communication style, in a skillful discussion setting.

OVERVIEW
Half the team (the inner circle) discusses an issue, while the other half (the outer circle) watches. Critiquing takes place in pairs, not in the whole group, which makes people more comfortable exchanging comments.

STEP 1: ESTABLISHING RAPPORT
Each team member chooses a partner from whom he or she will not mind getting feedback. Partners sit together in pairs and ask each other these questions:

1. What strong opinions do you hold (as an individual) about this topic?
2. What observable data (facts, not opinions) can you bring to the group's skillful discussion?
3. Are you willing to be influenced?
4. What is your vision for a satisfactory outcome of this issue?

The purpose of this review is to make sure both partners understand each other's assumptions, values, and aspirations for this topic, and for the team's evolution.

STEP 2: GROUP A IN THE CENTER (TWENTY MINUTES)

Arrange the chairs in two concentric circles, with no tables. From each pair, one partner joins Group A, and one joins Group B. These two groups will take turns talking and observing.

The first talkers (members of Group A) take seats in the inner circle and begin the conversation. They follow the basic protocols for skillful discussion, defining and pursuing the issue however they think best.

Members of Group B, in the outer circle, take the role of observer/ coaches. They sit opposite their partners, so that they can see and hear them easily. In your turn as observer/coach, use these questions as guidelines; take notes about *specific instances* (including comments) that seem to illustrate your sense of your partner's skill.

When **advocating**, how often did your partner:

1. State his or her opinions and ideas so clearly that those listening could picture them in their own minds?
2. Offer the assumptions on which his or her opinions and ideas are built?
3. Provide observable data (facts, not opinion or anecdotes) to support and illuminate a line of reasoning?
4. Invite others in the group to add to his or her ideas?
5. Refrain from defensiveness when questioned?

   When **inquiring**, how often did your partner:

6. Ask questions about others' assumptions and data without evoking defensiveness?
7. Ask questions which increased the group's understanding of someone's opinions?
8. Listen without judgment (attentively, and without interruptions) as others spoke?

STEP 3: THE FIRST CRITIQUE (FIVE MINUTES)

After about twenty minutes, stop the group and return to pairs. Now, during the next five minutes, the observer/coaches review their feedback notes with the talker. When you make your critique, use the protocols of

PARTICIPANTS
A team with enough experience with skillful discussion that they can deal with a potentially volatile subject.

TIME
Two hours or more.

SUPPLIES
Notepads and pencils or pens for each member. Handouts of questions and skillful discussion protocols.

ENVIRONMENT
A room with comfortable chairs that can be arranged in two concentric circles or in pairs.

skillful discussion yourself. For example, instead of saying, "You were really defensive out there," say, "I interpreted *this* comment as being defensive."

For tips about effective coaching, see page 207.

STEP 4: REFINEMENT AND NEW CRITIQUE (TWENTY-FIVE TO THIRTY MINUTES)

Group A returns to the inner circle and resumes their skillful discussion on the same subject for another twenty to thirty minutes. Once again, the Group B observers sit opposite their partners and take notes.

Again, when the time is up, the partners return to their pairs. The observer/coaches, once again, review their feedback notes with the talkers. This time, however, observer/coaches should focus on what has changed. The purpose of the feedback is to build competency, not catch someone doing something wrong.

STEP 5: GROUP B IN THE CENTER (TWO SESSIONS AND TWO CRITIQUES)

Repeat steps 2 through 4, with Group B as the talkers in the inner circle, and Group A as the observer/coaches. Remain in the same pairs; take advantage of the rapport you have already built up.

STEP 6: FULL GROUP SELF-OBSERVATION AND RESOLUTION

Now, as a full group, reconvene—ideally after a short break in which people can reflect on their reactions to these sessions. Then talk for several minutes about the group's competency in generating a broader understanding of its own behavior. What new behaviors worked particularly well?

You will then probably want to continue the skillful discussion, on the same subject, in one large group. After an hour, break again into pairs so that the members of each pair can give each other one last critique on their role in the team's learning.

Most teams will generally use the "Fishbowl" exercise only once in their practice; it gets stale. But after this, it will be easier to practice the skillful discussion protocols in future conversations.

PURPOSE AND OVERVIEW
We sometimes prefer this more technically involved version of "Fishbowl," because people tend to notice more details of the conversation on a videotape, and tend to regard the behavior more compassionately.

PARTICIPANTS
Two intact teams.

FACILITATOR
There should be someone to set up and keep watch over the equipment.

TIME
One full day.

SUPPLIES
Two sets of videocassette equipment. Each set should have a videocassette camera, tripod or stand, playback machine, audio microphone, and monitor.

ENVIRONMENT
Two meeting rooms, and one room in which the entire group can gather.

Video Fishbowl

Charlotte Roberts, Rick Ross

Instead of an inner and outer circle, have each team ("A" and "B") practice skillful discussion by itself, focusing on a situation vital to that team. Videotape all discussions. After an hour, each team exchanges its videotape with the other team. After watching each other's videotapes, the teams make a presentation to each other: "Here's what we saw. Here's what we would do differently. Here are our impressions of each member of your team."

After it's over, the teams may want to look at their own videotapes—or, individuals may want to borrow the tapes to look at portions of them. It's more valuable to do this *after* you have heard the other team's critiques, because you know what to look for. Looking at the videotapes gives you a chance to check the other person's perception of you against the actual data. At the moment when you were seen as advocating vociferously, was that your intention? If not, why did you come across that way to others?

59 Popular Postmortems

Rick Ross

This is a simple device for improving the way we think and act in meetings, by asking ourselves: "How well did we do?"

Draw a scale on a flip chart, showing the range of satisfaction with the meeting, from 1 to 7. Each person writes the number he or she feels is appropriate on a card and passes the cards up front. Then the results are tallied on the flip chart with hatch marks:

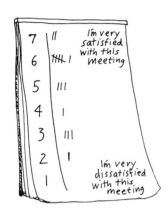

Any score less than 4 is bad news, because most people feel more harshly about meetings than they will say, even anonymously. Thus, if you are the moderator or group leader, say, "Would any of you who marked a 2 or 3 be willing to say why this was an unsatisfying meeting?"

I've conducted this exercise dozens of times. No one has ever refused to speak. (Certainly the atmosphere must admit a certain degree of openness for this to work.) Frequently, the reasons for the 2 or 3 are illuminating precisely because they're overlooked by most of the group. After one meeting, a man said, "Rick, I gave this a two because you had said we were going to deal with a personnel issue, and we skipped past it."

He was right. So we took the next five minutes and dealt with this relatively minor issue. This individual had had no other venue for raising his frustration. Left unaddressed, this could have poisoned his relationship with the rest of the team.

Months later, the same individual told me how the postmortems had affected his participation. "I'll sit in a meeting and think. 'This is terrible. I ought to award it a 2 in the postmortem. But then I'll be asked why, and I'm going to have to say that I was bored. They'll ask why I was bored, and I'll have to say that we weren't talking about anything of interest. So I'll be asked what would have been of interest.' And at that point in my internal dialogue, I find myself raising my hand and asking if I can add things to the agenda."

The rankings of the previous meeting go into the next meeting's minutes, along with comments about what should be done differently. This helps the next meeting get off to a much better start.

60 Silence

Charlotte Roberts

Imagine a team of ten managers talking for hours about a business issue vital to them. Despite recognition that they need to act with unity, they don't seem to get any closer to a solution. Tempers have frayed. They can hardly bring themselves to listen as each person explains his view, more and more vociferously. Yet there's also a feeling that, underneath the rancor, some sort of common understanding is waiting to be heard.

This is a good moment for calling a period of silence—not in frustration, but in anticipation. Collective thoughts have a force and vitality of their own. Anyone in the group can access them, as if the ideas are held in a reservoir waiting to be tapped, but only if the group is poised to hear them. Hence the value of a period of silent time to tap into the "gathered mind."

After a few minutes, someone may break the silence with a comment that clarifies the group's intent and redirects the conversation as a whole: "What we're really talking about is . . ."

Silence may allow other points of view to enter the thinking of the group: "What isn't being said is . . ." Or "When I think about this issue as a customer would . . ."

CALLING FOR SILENCE

When the conversation seems scattered and fractious, nobody is listening to one another, side conversations have broken out in corners, or the team is at an impasse, then the facilitator (or any participant) can call for silence simply by pointing out how the team has drifted out of focus. "Let's take a few minutes to reflect."

The group must agree to use this tool earnestly or the time will be wasted. All members remain in the room; even though no one speaks, there is still a collective "gathered mind" which depends on people's presence. The period usually lasts three to five minutes, but may go as long as fifteen, especially if people have a reason to take notes. The facilitator keeps track of the time and, when the time is up, gently brings the group back together.

Sometimes, after a heated discussion or impasse, there needs to be a longer break for reflection—twenty minutes or more. Members separate and go to a quiet space where their thinking will flow freely. Or, as a day closes, members may agree to spend some time before the next day in reflection, noticing their dreams and thoughts, preparing for the following day. It is important not to use time set aside for reflection to call the office, read the mail, or do anything that engages you. There is a task at hand: to refresh your mind so insights may emerge.

DURING SILENCE

Many people report that, in their first experience with a period of silence, their minds do not quiet down. Hundreds of thoughts race through their heads, wanting to be expressed. There may be an irresistible temptation to take advantage of the break to get your words in full view (no longer just in edgewise) by blurting out your thoughts. But resist that temptation; it would harshly interrupt others' efforts, and your own, to look more deeply into collective thought.

Getting skilled at silence takes practice in letting the cacophony of your own thought wash through you, without letting it push you. To do so, you can use several techniques.

Focus on your breath. Don't count breaths, or "see" them going up and down, or listen to them. Merely become aware of your breathing.

Focus on an object or location in the room. Don't stare at it; just notice it passively and, in the process, let your mind quiet itself. Relax your body as you do this.

Focus on the memory of a sound. Some people report that the vowel sounds (a, e, i, o, u) have a calming, silence-engaging effect on them. Imagine yourself letting the sound spill out of yourself as you exhale: "Aaaaaaaaaaaaaaaaaaaaaaayyyy . . ."

Once you are centered in the silence, expand your awareness to encompass the entire group. Replay the conversation in your mind. Hang the thoughts which you and others expressed out in front of your mind like flying kites. Try to pick out a pattern in the comments which illuminates where the dialogue "wanted to go," as opposed to where it was going. The group's intent is often different from the path the discussion was following, and upon reflection, you may be able to feel that intent pop out of your memory of the whole conversation.

THE ABILENE PARADOX **by Dr. Jerry B. Harvey** (1988, Toronto: Lexington Books, and San Diego: University Associates).

Jerry Harvey's *Abilene Paradox* is the most telling description we know of a group's inability to manage its agreement. Nobody wants to reach a particular destination ("Abilene"), but for fear of offending or contradicting each other, they all end up there. There are many Abilene stories of disasters which nobody wanted, from the Bay of Pigs to possibly your last staff meeting.

The Abilene Paradox is available as a book or a very funny video.° We find it most effective to show the videotape, and then invite people to describe their own. When was the last time you went to Abilene, and who joined you on the trip?—**RR, BS, CR**

° *The Abilene Paradox*, with Dr. Jerry B. Harvey, produced by C.R.M. Video (28 minutes); available from Monad Trainer's Aids, Whitestone, New York.

THE ELECTRONIC MAZE

A learning simulation for teams. This seven-by-ten-foot rectangular carpet is laid out in a pattern like a checkerboard. When you step on a square, it may beep. Teams work together to find a beepless path from one side to the other, with no opportunity to talk to each other during the play. To accomplish this effectively, you must develop effective nonverbal communication and a collective memory. When someone discovers a beeping square by stepping on it, they do not *fail;* they add to the team's collective knowledge. Learning to value the discovery phase of performance is a simple understanding, but because it's not viscerally ingrained in us, we often don't. The maze helps change that sensibility. It also tends to bring out some of the dysfunctional feelings which teams harbor in their relationships. The first time you play it, it's often every man or woman for themselves. Everyone tries to remember the pattern on their own. Gradually you discover that the team's knowledge of the maze is greater than any individual's knowledge can be.

To be used effectively, the maze requires about an hour and a half. There should always be a debrief to draw out principles and compare the experience to everyday team experience. People suddenly begin to realize: "We are so tactical that we overlook our purpose. We don't deal with mistakes well. We don't acknowledge learning. All we ever do is count the numbers." It's an effective way to bring together two functional teams that must work together, but can barely speak because of their hostility to each other. They start to realize that if they can't get across on electronic maze, how are they ever going to bring a product to market? You can also play it a second time, changing the pattern unannounced, and notice how you and others tend to cling to your memory of the old pattern.°—CR

° The electronic maze was developed by Richard Kimball and Boyd Watkins and is distributed by Action Learning, Colorado Springs, CO.

° The term "undiscussables" is derived from the explication of defensive routines in *Overcoming Organizational Defenses* by Chris Argyris (1990, Needham Heights, Mass.: Allyn and Bacon), p. 27ff. See *Fieldbook,* p. 265.

Undiscussables*

Charlotte Roberts, Rick Ross

A significant barrier to team learning is the existence of topics that team members feel are important to discuss, because they might offend someone or violate an unspoken taboo. When people are willing to talk about them, these topics often turn out to be critical factors in forming the strategic plan, solving the current problem, creating the team's vision, or developing the team's ability to learn.

For example, there is a home health-care organization in which the director of nursing withholds information that is critical to the day-to-day performance of those who directly report to her. She regularly threatens to destroy the career of anyone who crosses her. Therefore, during staff meetings, people dare not ask for information she has not offered. Nor will anyone raise the issue in an open forum.

At one point this director overburdened the system by requiring each home care staff person to make three times as many observation reports as federal safety agencies required. No one felt they could ask her to explain her reasoning, even as the burden on the system grew overwhelmingly oppressive. Because the director's defensiveness could not be discussed, and the fact that it could not be discussed could not even be discussed, people had to act as if there were no root causes of their problems—which made it impossible to think about solving them.

If you have a similar situation, this exercise can help.

Agree upon the following ground rules before beginning:

- Respect the fear that accompanies this exercise.
- Reflect and take notice of your initial response to each undiscussable as it is read aloud.
- Listen for what is said and not said.

PURPOSE
To unveil and learn from taboo topics, where even the fact that they are undiscussable is usually undiscussable.

OVERVIEW
A card game in which people can anonymously raise the questions that never get raised.

PARTICIPANTS
An intact team that has discovered itself blocked or failing, and no one can talk about why. A facilitator may be helpful.

- Challenge ideas and assumptions, not people.
- Beware of untested attributions, especially of peoples' motives.

STEP 1: GATHERING DATA

Each person on the team is given three three-by-five cards and equivalent writing tools, so everyone has the same color ink or pencil. Without discussion or collaboration, each person writes one "undiscussable" statement on a card—describing it in enough detail for any reader in the room to understand. If someone's behavior is part of the undiscussable, then refer to that person by job title and not by name, because the undiscussable is intended as a statement of a problem, not as an attack on another person.

Some examples of undiscussables from other people's sessions:

The owner/founder's children are not interested in the business and have said so to other workers. We need to talk about a succession plan without them in it.

There are not enough resources to fund the current strategic growth plan. If we proceed on the current plan, the company will probably crash and burn.

The president of the company is not open to dialogue. He must always have the last word, even when people are using humor. So no one talks to him about what is important.

All of our performance reviews are three to six months late.

We have a problem with people burning out, but when I try to get more time for myself, or more resources to do my work well, I'm treated as if there's something wrong with me.

STEP 2: DEALING THE CARDS

The blackjack option: Someone collects the cards and either shuffles and deals them, or puts them in a stack and allows people to draw them. Team members, as they draw or receive a card, place it face up on the table in front of them.

The treasure hunt option: At the end of five minutes, everyone leaves the meeting room, holding their cards. One at a time, team members reenter the meeting room and hide their three cards. Two cards should not be hidden in the same spot. Once all the card are hidden, everyone reenters the room. Each person finds three cards that are not his or her own, and sits down. This feels silly to some people, but has the advantage

T I M E
At least two intensive hours. These conversations can last five or six hours, if you uncover deep issues that are affecting the team.

S U P P L I E S
Three-by-five-inch cards; writing tools for each person in the room; a wall covered with paper; tape or glue sticks.

E N V I R O N M E N T
A comfortable meeting room.

that no one ends up reading from his or her own cards. it is also a physical reminder of the hidden structures debilitating the team.

STEP 3: UNCOVERING COMMON THEMES

Each person in turn, reads aloud the three cards from step 2, and then posts them on the wall. When all cards have been read, team members group them to reflect common themes. The team must also decide how many themes will be tackled in this meeting and how to deal with the rest. (Leftover undiscussables should be discussed soon, before they go underground again even deeper.)

Starting with an "easy" undiscussable builds the team's ability to talk about the more difficult topics. Some cards may provoke discussions that can last for hours; thus, every thirty minutes, pause to decide how much more time the team wants to spend on this topic before moving on to the next card. Time checks keep the dialogue on track, and help the group determine its progress.

These questions may help guide the dialogue

1. What is the threat behind the undiscussable?
2. What mental model has allowed this hidden structure to persist?
3. What has kept this issue from being discussed seriously?
4. What are the unintended consequences of the undiscussable, in the past, present, and future?
5. How does this undiscussable support or block our ability to learn as a team?
6. How does this undiscussable fit with our espoused vision and values?
7. What do we want to do about this undiscussable?

61 Reframing Team Relationships

How the Principles of "Structural Dynamics" Can Help Teams Come to Terms with Their Dark Side

David Kantor, Nancy Heaton Lonstein

This is a brief glimpse into a rich body of theory and method called structural dynamics (not to be confused with system dynamics). David Kantor and Nancy Heaton Lonstein are principals in Origins, Inc., a Cambridge, Massachusetts, consulting firm. David also trains therapists and consultants and conducts research at the Kantor Family Institute in Cambridge, where many of these ideas were developed over a period of twenty-five years.

For more about the work with families, see Inside the Family *by David Kantor and William Lehr (1975, San Francisco: Jossey-Bass).*

A few years ago, we began to help teams in organizations using a structural approach originally developed by David Kantor for family therapy and organizational consultation. We discovered that teams and families, while their purposes and histories may differ dramatically, have very similar patterns of behavior that lead to very similar problems. These might come to the surface as "inexplicable" personality clashes, anger, jealousy, hostility, and incompetence. These feelings are usually kept hidden, and unacknowledged, until there's a crisis where they boil over and reveal themselves, often with their most destructive power.

A serious effort to explore the learning disciplines, especially if it goes very deep, may provoke exactly that sort of crisis. We have seen some of the most sophisticated practitioners of learning disciplines become blocked—damaging friendships, splitting up organizations, and upsetting the flow of learning around them—because they were blindsided by these dark interpersonal feelings and patterns of behavior "that we shouldn't have to deal with, since we know what we're doing!"

The structural dynamics viewpoint suggests that the two most common reasons why close working groups seek help—impasses in their relationships and problematic behavior they feel they can't control—are not solely rooted in individual factors, like a person's early childhood.

Instead, these problems are manifestations of *invisible structures* in the relationships among people—including not just their histories together and separately but the assumptions they make about each other and the actions and stances they take in response to the demands that they perceive as coming from the institutions around them. There is less leverage in approaching behavior and relationship problems through individual therapy, and more leverage in studying the family or the team as a system.

A partnership collapses: the silent hand

For example, consider the Silent Hand—a composite story, based on two actual (and similar) cases.

When Thomson Wood and Tom Woodman met on the first day of engineering school, they knew their fates would twine as their names did. Both fashioned themselves as inventors. Each could boast of having a patent pending before entering college. Thomson was a genius with an angry edge, more honored than adored by fellow students and faculty. Only Tenacious Tom, the numbers wizard and ideas man who knew how to inspire people, could handle him—as he did so many others.

It was Tom's idea to name the company they formed after college, Silent Hand, after Thomson's invention: a highly sophisticated, robotic prosthetic arm. Thomson wore one himself. He had invented it after losing his arm in a motorcycle accident. The two comanagers worked famously together, bickering in synergistic cacophony that made others wonder if they'd murder one another.

"Try it this way!"

"No, stupid. That won't work!"

The two played a subtle game that amused other members of the executive team. When Thomson disagreed with anyone who was speaking, he would plant his elbow on the table, lower his forehead onto his prosthetic fist, and then hold it there, looking down at the table. As his objections grew, he would remain silent, but he would unbend his elbow. His fist would leave his forehead and cantilever out across the table at a forty-five-degree angle, a grim sentinel of disapproval. Still, Thomson would not say a word. All the while, the hapless victim-to-be would bumble on—encouraged by Tom's questions: "How did you come to that opinion? What would happen next?"

Finally, Thomson would explode at the person whose idea had displeased him. "Tell me, don't you like your job? What in flaming hell do you have in mind? Are you trying to drive us out of business?" However brutal it seemed, Thomson's fire tended to liberate the thinking of the entire executive team, particularly Tom (even though Tom was surprisingly often the object of Thomson's wrath). Everyone there had come to think of the "silent hand treatment" as a necessary price they had to pay for these surges of creativity.

For ten years, the company thrived and grew to forty million dollars in sales, with sixty employees and a team of competent managers. Then sales leveled off, at exactly the moment when the company needed to decide whether or not to invest in a new manufacturing facility. The team which had made so many decisions competently before, now suddenly seemed paralyzed, especially to its own members.

Tom had hired a chief financial officer named Wendy—a savvy, nononsense woman with a Harvard MBA whom everyone, including herself, joked about as the firm's "money man." Tom relied on her judgment with unquestioning trust and Thomson had grudgingly admitted that she could handle herself. When the company's fortunes fell, however, Thomson began to single her out with hostility, challenging her at meetings, undermining her directives elsewhere, and questioning her judgment at every opportunity. Thomson's "silent hand" lowered itself more and more often when Wendy was speaking.

Tom's behavior changed as well. At "Synergy Meetings," held every Monday at 3 P.M., he would begin to lick and audibly smack his lips. He rarely expressed any appreciation for Thomson anymore. One day, Wendy made the mistake (as she saw it) of asking Tom, her champion, if everything was all right with his health. Thereafter, Tom no longer backed her up; he began to snap at her in meetings.

Privately, Wendy confided some of her qualms about Tom to two other members of the executive team. Randall, the vice president of Human Resources, had joined the firm only one year before, hired to use his considerable skills to hold the team together during the hard times. Tom had suggested that his assignment might last only a year or two. Randall cut Wendy off before she could finish. "Tom's under a lot of stress because of this factory decision," he said. "There may be something wrong, but we'll have to wait until these more pressing matters are decided."

Previn, the company's unofficial father figure, was the vice president of marketing. Twenty years older than any other executive team member, he could read economic signs that most experts could only faintly glean.

Lately, however, Previn's radar had seemed a bit off-kilter. And when Wendy began to feel him out about Tom, he surprised her by beating her to it. "Just between us, you should look sharp," he said. "I'm not sure how much longer I'll be able to do any good here." He refused to say anything more, because it "wouldn't be helpful."

Finally, the decision about the factory could be put off no longer. The executive team gathered for what was intended to be one final go-round on the issue:

TOM: I thought I made it clear. I'll say it again. Stay on the path.

THOMSON: [*elbow on table, fist clenched, head upright*] Tom . . .

WENDY: There's a related cost item on the agenda—

TOM: You're shifting venue, Wendy. I need support, not distraction.

WENDY: Loss is not a distraction, Tom.

THOMSON: [*fist to forehead, speaking softly but ominously*] Tom . . .

TOM: [*hears but clearly ignores Thomson*] Well, we're not talking about costs now.

RANDALL: I believe in your reading of the figures and support you.

THOMSON: [*softly*] . . . as you usually do. [*With fist extended, clenched tightly, studied, and in a louder voice*] Tom . . .

PREVIN: I'm trying to figure out what's coming down here and . . . and . . . I don't know [*frustrated sigh*] Let me try some . . .

TOM: [*Raising voice to drown Previn out*] Doesn't anyone here have an idea but me? This is pissing me off.

[*Silence*]

THOMSON: [*Fist extended, loud now*] Tom! That's not an idea, it's a suicide note, damn it. You're dead-ending us again, Tom.

TOM: [*Talking over Thomson's voice*] Read these figures, Wendy.

PREVIN: [*soto voce*] It's painful; not to be listened to.

WENDY: I see, I see. I've already given my note. But shouldn't we— I mean—Previn?

TOM: Previn is an ass.

THOMSON: Previn is an ass, and I am an ass who's been lobotomized. What I think, if anybody is interested anymore, is—

TOM: This whole firm is lobotomized.

PREVIN: I agree, I agree.

TOM: If no one has anything constructive to add, I vote to end this meeting now and let's move on.

The action stances of members of the team

THERE'S NO DENYING THAT THIS COMPANY, FOR ALL ITS RECOGNITION OF the forces at play, has serious "organizational psychology" problems. Moreover, it would be pointless to blame any single person or factor. No single individual (including Wendy, the seeming "victim" of the process) can evade responsibility. This may be what Previn intuitively feels when he says it wouldn't be "helpful" to press the matter further.

But Previn is wrong. There is a great deal of leverage in looking at the psychopolitical "action stances"—the roles taken by the "players" of the drama.

For example, in most work situations, someone takes the role of *mover*—the initiator, offering a position or direction to the group. At Silent Hand, that role is traditionally played by Tom, the inspirational core of the firm, who brought everyone together and still presses for expansion.

Someone else acts as the *opposer*—the skeptic, challenging the action of the mover. Thomson is the opposer at Silent Hand, depended on to spark creative and innovative solutions.

Others may be *followers*, agreeing with either the mover or the opposer. Randall is a valuable follower, while Wendy (who had originally been a mover herself) is now increasingly forced to follow or leave.

Finally, others are *bystanders*, observers who critically witness the actions of others. Previn is a gifted bystander, capable of stepping back and offering valuable reflection.

To see these roles, we focus not on the content, but on the patterns of conversation; the recurring interrelationships. Here is the most consistently observable principle of psychopolitical diagnosis:

In healthy structures, all members are free to switch between the four stances interchangeably. But when there are problems, two or more individuals find themselves locked in a pattern of actions, stuck in stances that snare them over and over again.

Once, anyone could say anything at Silent Hand. Wendy was a strong mover whom Tom could follow at times. Previn occasionally took the mover role himself.

But now Silent Hand has become a faulty, authoritarian system. Tom is increasingly tyrannical and arbitrary; he yields the mover role to no one. The previously valuable opposer (Thomson) has become disabled (and his impotence on the team is almost as difficult to get used to as the loss of his hand had been). The bystander (Previn) has been silenced, his role as wise counselor reduced to caricature. Followers are required to walk in lockstep and not question their leaders, and some team members (such as Wendy) find themselves shoehorned into roles, intimidated whenever they try to break out.

In this type of executive team (just as in a dysfunctional family), destructive sequences are triggered over and over, reinforcing the same problematic behavior. Each time, people say to themselves, "Here we go again."

People stay with the roles that frustrate them because of the dynamics of the structure. Something about their own lives, relationships, or position makes each person "right" for the part he plays. It all seems so predetermined, yet the factors that create this may, individually, be quite inconsequential. People may even be drawn into roles which clash with their personalities. Then, horrifyingly, their personalities may change over time to match the role they have been given.

The roots of the psychopolitics at Silent Hand

ONE FACTOR WHICH CREATED THE STRUCTURE AT SILENT HAND WAS Tom and Thomson's ambivalent relationship. Tom was the only person in the company who knew the full story of the motorcycle accident where Thomson had lost his arm. Thomson was only fifteen; he was riding behind his older brother, who had been drinking, who crashed the bike, and who died.

Tom, meanwhile, had been raised by alcoholic parents. His father was a tyrant, who beat his children, and who was the only person allowed to speak at the dinner table. In response, Tom learned to be as engaging and creative as possible. Once, he tried bravely to breathe some of this enthusiasm in the dining room—and got the beating of his life. Tom looked to his much older brother for help. His brother remained silent.

In college, Tom found the brother he'd never had in Thomson—a brilliant and bold warrior who would not be silenced. Thomson, for his own reasons, felt protective of Tom. Years later, Thomson was the only one in the company who knew that Tom had a severe drinking problem. But Thomson was unwilling to mention it.

The interpersonal dynamics of the executive team also depended on Wendy's feelings about appropriate behavior, Previn's discomfort with his role as impotent "elder statesman," and the veiled threat implied in the fact that Randall would be gone "as soon as things got better."

Some might argue that all these factors should be brought to the surface: let everyone on the team know, for instance, about Tom's alcoholism and the part it plays in Tom's role. (Some would argue that everyone probably knows about it already, at least on some level.) But to articulate these deep personal problems too abruptly can be very dangerous for a team which is still, after all, stressed by some important *management* decisions as well as its members' psychodramatic factors. Instead, they need some tools for rebuilding the flexibility they once had—so that once again, members can adopt different stances appropriate to different situations and to their own styles.

Imagine that you are a member of the executive team of Silent Hand (or any similar company), and you recognize these unhealthy psychopolitical dynamics. What might you do? Your immediate goal might be to change the stuck behaviors, by helping people expand their repertoire of actions. You might encourage Wendy, Randall, and Previn to become active bystanders who intervene more freely and reflectively. You might try to show Thomson his own recurring patterns, knowing that if he sees them clearly, he may be able to teach himself to take on other roles, such as bystander, instead of feeling compelled to always oppose. In some cases, you might feel you lacked enough expertise or power. What if Thomson refuses to acknowledge the dynamics at play? What of Tom's alcoholism? Thus, you may call in an interventionist. Whatever you do, it's important to remember that this is foremost the *team's* problem. It's not Tom's, or Thomson's, or Wendy's problem, and they cannot meet it effectively unless they meet it together—uncovering the reasons for these blocks that "should not exist," so they can begin to change them.

An intervention with Silent Hand

DAVID KANTOR WAS THE CONSULTANT CALLED IN TO HELP THE COMPANIES on which the Silent Hand story is based. The first phase of the work, the change phase, typically begins with mapping the system—gathering information about the politics of relationships through a series of individual and paired interviews, and by attending several management team meetings to observe the dynamics firsthand. After a "diagnosis" is made of the structures that maintain "the problem," an off-site meeting is planned. In role-play exercises, the interventionist may try to re-create ritual impasses—structural sequences which repeat over and over—and reframe them in a more productive pattern.

Kantor first asked the team members to place their chairs in a circle and listen without speaking (taking the role of inactive bystanders). He then asked Tom and Thomson to place their chairs within the circle and to talk about the good old days. Their conversation began slowly, a bit stilted and self-conscious at first. The group's patience allowed them to begin sharing their common memories. Since no one else was speaking. Tom could not ignore Thomson, and Thomson could not be silenced. Their talk changed from recall to arguing (their original structure) and ended when Thomson mentioned that he thought the trouble began when Tom began drinking heavily. Thomson said, "You deserted me" (in effect, dying as his brother had). Tom replied, "*You* deserted *me*" (failing to rescue him, as *his* brother had). Now the unspeakable could be mentioned, without throwing all the blame on Tom. The other members of the team were spellbound throughout. Afterward, they offered reflections and support, describing their own roles in helping to expand the conflict, and their own feelings.

In this moment, the team members' awareness and understanding of their impasse was raised. Tom and Thomson reconnected with the original sense of bonding and unity that brought them together years ago. But deep challenges remain: to resist retrenchment into the same old dysfunctional patterns once they're back at work, and to cultivate better structural dynamics throughout the team. This experience has opened the door for the Silent Hand management team to contemplate becoming a true learning team—one capable of surviving hard times and resuming the company's climb to excellence.

Deeper levels of structure

MANAGERS OFTEN ASK WHETHER THE SOLUTION TO THEIR TEAM PROBLEMS lies with the person or the organization. "Joe can't get along with anyone, and he's intolerable right now. Should I fire him, or will he change if I change the organizational structure around him."

The answer is "both." Maybe you shouldn't *fire* Joe, but simply changing the system without regard for his personal history leaves out an important part of the system. Typically, something "outside" the individual, probably at the team level, triggers something "inside" the individual, who explodes or becomes paralyzed. Although the structure which causes this explosion or paralysis is invisible, most of us can feel its presence, and we can usually describe it: "We fall into a trap where Sam and Roberta lock horns, and the rest of us can't seem to find anything to say to help." Thus, the most powerful models of change operate at the systemic and individual levels simultaneously.

A skilled structural dynamics consultant would begin to diagnose the system based on four levels of the system's structure. All of these levels operate at once. All affect the quality of team performance and relationships.

- **Qualities of action:** the most accessible level of structure to detect and understand, this includes the psychopolitical stances (mover, opposer, observer, bystander) as well as other unspoken messages embedded in people's behavior. Qualities are most evident not in the words, but in body language, eye movements, facial expressions, voice tone, breathing, and gesture.

  ⟩⟩ Dialogue (see page 357) helps a team become more aware of the qualities of its actions.

- **Domains of purpose:** The goals and desires which are fundamentally driving people. Many situations get confused because one person is operating in the *affect* domain—seeking nurturance and intimacy. Another converses in the *meaning* domain, searching for validation, a sense of belonging, or the opportunity to learn more about the world. A third, perhaps unnoticed by the rest of the team, operates in the *power domain,* pursuing efficacy, competence, freedom, constraint, or dominance.

- **Paradigms of the system:** The overriding set of assumptions embedded in the organization's values about authority and boundaries. People may expect their system to be *closed* (emphasizing stability, group loyalty, security, clear boundaries, and tight controls); *open* (emphasizing flexibility, collaboration, consensus, and authentic communication); or *random* (emphasizing variety, individuality, high achievement, excitement, unpredictability, and fun). Any of these may be healthy or unhealthy.

- **Critical identity images:** The deeply guarded views which we hold of our own identity, and which predispose us to act in habitual ways. One hallmark of "lifelong learners" is their ability to transform their own images as they grow older. In the Silent Hand story, Tom and Thomson carried their identity images from their dysfunctional adolescences into their relationship as partners.

All of these levels are interrelated; reactions and counterreactions ripple between them. A boss's moves in the power domain feel like the oppressive moves of father. Our identity image influences us to take the role of "bystander," even though we have something to say as an opposer.

Examining a team's behavior: starting with action roles

THERE IS MUCH MORE TO BE WRITTEN ABOUT ALL OF THESE LEVELS: WE look forward to the day when people understand them well enough to be able to see a much fuller range of dynamics in their own team's behavior. In the meantime, we believe that anyone who takes part in a team or group can find value in paying attention to the "roles" of the team's actions. This gives people a way to bootstrap themselves into a capability for reframing some difficult team problems.

Examining roles takes place most effectively in dialogue and discussion. As people develop more open knowledge of each other's drives, preferences, and sensitivities, their ability to diagnose their problems increases. These reframing questions can help a team begin to genuinely examine its roles, without much chance of treading into areas too deep or painful:

1. Are the action stances flexible on this team?
2. Can we all expand our repertoire? For example, can our best "mover" shift when necessary to the "follower" or "bystander" role?
3. What would happen if the chief opposer on our team let go of that action stance and nobody filled the void?
4. What would happen if the bystanders were formally given the opportunity to initiate a proposal?
5. Have we put in place structures that systematically shut down certain action stances? For example, has dominating leadership foreclosed all opposer moves, or worse, all effective bystanding?
6. What ineffective sequences do we see take place over and over again? Can these rituals be interrupted? For example, would a disabled bystander who finally decided to break his silence lose his job?

62 Building an Organization that Recognizes Everyone's Uniqueness

The Herman Miller Experience

Michele Hunt

Some of the most persistent, thoughtful work on developing a learning organization approach to diversity issues has taken place at the Herman Miller Company of Zeeland, Michigan—producers of high-quality, innovatively designed office furniture. Michele Hunt spent more than thirteen years at Herman Miller, first as the equal employment officer and then as vice president for quality and people development. During the last two and one half years, she led a vision education process on customer-focused quality. This led to a noteworthy accelerated education program on quality, diversity, and change. Hunt was recently appointed head of the Federal Quality Institute; she is working with Vice President Gore's National Performance Review to transform government.

Diversity is natural and brings richness to the world. Nature is diverse, and there is a critical balance that requires an understanding of how all the pieces fit together and how each is important to the whole. This kind of understanding is just as important in organizations. At Herman Miller we approached diversity through a vision for quality, not through a sense of social responsibility or federal mandate. As an international organization—in the United States, Europe, Japan, and Mexico—we wanted our organization to be a global reference point for excellence from the customer's perspective. We had a legacy of traditional teams, where people reported to the working leader and manager, but with our new focus on quality, we realized we had to move to another generation of teamwork. Cross-global teams include not only speakers of different languages from different countries, but also people from countries with deeply rooted histories of warring with each other.

The concept of diversity took precedence at Herman Miller because we recognized we could never get to high-performance participation without valuing the uniqueness that each person brought to the organization. We knew that this was not possible without a specific effort both to understand diversity, and to help people work together more effectively. For most of the participants, the process has been an enlightening, even life-changing experience. We have discovered that the teams which work best together are those which have struggled together to appreciate each other.

Developing an organizational approach for a personal understanding

It is wrong to stereotype or categorize people because of any group they belong to. I don't want to be categorized. I can't afford it. I have spent my whole life building up who I am with all my multidimensions and complexities, and I get offended when I'm put into a category as (for example) a feminist or an African-American. It's saying that I walk, talk, and think like one whole group of people. That's the danger of some of the ways in which diversity is addressed today. The discussion threatens to *increase* categorization, not diminish it.

At the same time, my uniqueness—which includes being a woman, an African-American, and everything else that I am—is what I want to have valued. I need to be allowed to bring my uniqueness to the table. It's not just a matter of race and gender: I'm also a single parent, and I needed my organization to understand what that means. When they understood the importance of my balancing the needs of my daughter with my work, it began to set a tone that allowed the men to have the same focus. You don't have to sacrifice your family to work at Herman Miller, and in fact if you're doing that we're not getting the best out of you anyway.

All of these issues may be personal, but we learned that all of them need to be worked collectively. This requires superior dialogue and communication skills. We realized from the beginning that this was a journey, not a quick fix, and that the concepts of quality, diversity, and change could not be learned in isolation from each other.

There are many processes for learning such skills. We chose one designed in partnership with the Aspen Institute, where different groups of senior managers engage in three-day dialogues on leadership and values. More than seventy of the Herman Miller managers attended. They read excerpts from works ranging from Plato's *The Republic* to Martin Luther King, Jr.'s "Letter from Birmingham Jail"; letters from Abigail

Smith Adams and John Adams; *In a Different Voice* by Carol Gilligan; *The Life and Times of Frederick Douglass* by Frederick Douglass, Confucius's *Analects;* and to Maya Angelou's inaugural poem.

Along with that, we designed our own three- to four-day workshops, working directly with the cross-functional, cross-level teams we have developed. More than 400 people have gone through this seminar this year and there is still a waiting list at Herman Miller of 400 scheduled for next year. These are small workshops of about 24 people, so it is a significant investment for the organization to make.

The workshops are focused around providing a process for common understanding, and the creation of a common language. By keeping the discussion personal and not making blanket statements of fact, we avoid gross stereotypes and gross generalizations. Every individual's pattern of thinking and expression is unique, rooted in his or her personal experiences, and every one of us, if we want to work effectively, must learn to communicate with people who have different patterns. In a version of the "Fishbowl" exercise (page 396) we pull out a group of men, a group of men, or a group of African-Americans from the team, and put them in a circle to talk about their experiences while everyone else observes. This is a useful exercise in creating awareness and bringing issues of the inner group to the surface.

The question of gender balance

Issues of diversity are so interconnected that it can be dangerous to narrow the focus to a particular category. However, some issues, such as gender, sometimes need to be pulled out and illuminated against the backdrop of the wider picture.

In my own experience I found that there were many times I would speak in a meeting, and it was as if my mouth was moving but no one heard me. Five minutes later, when a man voiced the same idea, everyone would say "Great idea!" I used to become very frustrated. I was taught that people treat you as you treat them, so it was not in my character to jump to the conclusion that it was because of my race or gender. But I did discover that many women had similar experiences. In nearly every dialogue session on diversity women bring up this pattern of behavior.

Part of the problem involves differences in communication styles. It's important to avoid stereotyping, because all women don't talk one way and all men don't talk another. Nonetheless, we found that many women tend to explore an idea from several different angles before being decisive. This gives the impression that we are being wishy-washy or vacillating, when in fact we are brought up to ask questions before jumping to the answer. Men tend to be more immediately decisive and expect women to be the same. Once we talked about this difference, our conversational styles didn't need change, but our group style did. Now, in meetings when people get frustrated, someone will call out the question, "Do we have our filters on?"

From diversity to shared vision

At Herman Miller, we understood that we could not expect people to be proud and take care with the making and selling of a product unless we recognized them as individuals, as members of families, and as members of communities. Ultimately, every diversity effort will raise questions about people's personal visions, and how they expect they might bring their personal visions together, no matter what their background may be.

If we value differences, we have to learn to listen to voices different from our own. Any kind of prejudgment or shutting down communications is going to get in the way of a team of people attempting to create something special together.

YOU JUST DON'T UNDERSTAND: MEN AND WOMEN IN CONVERSATION **by Deborah Tannen** (1990, New York: Ballantine Books).

Deborah Tannen shows, fairly vividly, how men and women spend their lives reacting to phantom images of each other, based on mental models which begin to form in childhood. In organizations, for instance, as everywhere, men often assume that the purpose of a conversation is to determine who has more status, while women assume that the purpose is to negotiate for closeness, and maintain the appearance of equality. Both assumptions, unexamined, are equally confounding.

I have found the insights very practical on a day-to-day basis. When a man comes home with problems from work and wants to talk about it, the woman instinctively says, "Oh, poor baby, I'm so sorry. They're bad people." When she comes home from work with her problems, he instinctively says, "Well, take step one, step two, and step three." Now, when we come home from work, my significant other and I tell each other how we want to be heard. Sometimes we say, "Give me advice. What should I do?" Other times we say, "Would you just do a poor-baby for me while I tell you this?"—**CR**

63 Tools for Discovering Learning Styles

Rick Ross

The LSI and LSQ

EACH OF US HAS OUR OWN LEARNING PROFILE—OUR OWN PREFERRED strategies for learning. Your learning style governs how you approach new projects, how you increase your own capabilities, how you contribute to a team's results, and whether you find it easy or difficult to get in synch with a particular team. Getting (or developing) a good mix of learning styles can be critical to a team's long-term success.[*]

 See "Wheel of Learning" for a description of these styles, page 59.

Two diagnostic instruments exist that can help you discover your team's profile of learning styles, and improve the team capability—either by bringing in someone proficient in the styles which you lack most, or by training yourselves to pick up the slack. Both instruments have long-standing success in team practice. Both were designed for training and development departments, but I've seen them used effectively in line management teams which are learning to train and develop themselves.

Both of these instruments are set up as questionnaires with explanatory booklets. After answering the questions, people begin to appreciate their own learning style, and to value other people's different styles.

The choice between the two instruments comes down to style and format. The Learning-Style Inventory (LSI), developed by McBer and Company, is brief and straightforward. There are only twelve questions, asking you to describe your learning habits directly.

The Learning Style Diagnostic Questionnaire (LSDQ), from a psy-

[*] See *Experiential Learning* by David A. Kolb (1984, Englewood Cliffs, N.J.: Prentice-Hall), pp. 63ff.

° *Learning Style Inventory* by David Kolb (1981, Boston, Mass.: McBer and Company); *Learning Style Questionnaire* by Peter Honey and Alan Mumford (1983, 1989, Carmarthen, Wales, U.K.: Management Learning Resources, and King of Prussia, Pa.: Organization Design and Development, Inc.)

chologist/management consultant (Peter Honey) and a management trainer (Alan Mumford), is more oblique. Eighty true-or-false questions ask about your opinions and behavior. For example: " 'I like the type of work where I have time for thorough preparation and implementation.' True or False?"

Both instruments provide graphs where you can plot your profile and see its relative tendencies at a glance.°

Human Dynamics International

Roger Peters, Peter Senge

Roger Peters is CEO of Terratron Inc., an organization of Hardee's fast-food restaurants, based in Salt Lake City. For more of their story, see "Bean Suppers," page 518.

Roger Peters: The greatest breakthrough for us, in terms of harmonizing contributions from diverse people came from Sandra Seagal and David Horne's work with "human dynamics." They look at *people* as distinct whole systems. They identify three basic organizing principles—the mental, the emotional, and the physical—which combine in people to form fundamental patterns of functioning. Five combinations of these principles predominate, and can be found in people across the globe, regardless of culture, age, or gender. These combinations are mentally-centered, emotional-objective (emotional-mental), emotional-subjective (emotional-physical), physical-mental, and physical-emotional.

It was fascinating for us to discover how people who function according to each of these patterns learn, communicate, develop, solve problems, respond to stress, and contribute to teams differently, and how each complements the others. We have provided Human Dynamics training to people throughout our organization, from senior managers to entry-level kids on the work force.

The first time I came to a Human Dynamics seminar I felt as if a fog had suddenly lifted. As a young student, I thought I couldn't learn, but now I recognize that the structures provided for learning in schools didn't fit my pattern. I am what Seagal and Horne call a "physically centered" person. Physically centered people tend to be concrete and systematic in the way they learn, and therefore often slower in their responses. This doesn't mean that they're less intelligent. Sandra's experience suggests that many kids who are identified as slow learners or problem children have simply been mismatched with their natural learning processes. I think this is one reason that many people come into our organization wounded. They have never been able to function as they are meant to function. But this process can be reversed.

Our people have shown an enthusiasm for this training that has never waned. They learn, essentially, how to understand what happens when people who represent the different personality dynamics work together—what the difficulties are, and how to use the differences for creative synergy. We've found a tremendous thirst from husbands and wives for this type of learning experience—it helps them understand the relationships within their families and in the community. We've used the training to understand how to bring people together in groups, and have them work together, respecting their differences and using the contributions of each for the advantage of the whole.

Peter Senge: To develop their system, Seagal, Horne, and their colleagues have interviewed or observed 40,000 people representing more than twenty-five cultures, and produced extensive video documentation. Their videotapes show people at all ages, from infants to elders, having dinner, working, playing, and talking together. Once your attention is drawn to it, you see how the human dynamics patterns are embodied in the way that people move, eat, and speak—and particularly in the way they work (or play) together. As Seagal and Horne put it, "These [characteristics] indicate distinctions in the underlying processes of communication, the way learning unfolds, the way people problem-solve, and the dynamic contribution each person makes on teams."

The Human Dynamics seminar programs are wonderful: they open doors within oneself, and offer opportunities to talk about subtleties of relationships that would otherwise never come to light. Instead of being tested, seminar participants identify their own dynamics through self-discovery. In nearly all other personality inventory schemes, you can sense the values of the creators coming through after a while. The Human Dynamics system seems to be value-free. Once people understand it, they seem to never forget it. It's like rediscovering something we knew, but didn't know that we knew.°

° *An Introduction to Human Dynamics* by Sandra Seagal and David Horne (1986–92, La Topanga, Calif.: Human Dynamics International).

64 Bringing Diverse People to Common Purpose

Learning in the South Africa Forums

Louis van der Merwe

For several authors of this Fieldbook, *friendship with Louis van der Merwe has been a significant source of insight and inspiration. Louis is a sort of vagabond innovator of tools and techniques for improving team understanding, and a perceptive critic of same. Based in South Africa, he was formerly an executive of Eskom, that nation's primary electric power utility, where he contributed to their remarkable turnaround and restructuring in the 1980s. Currently, he works on organization alignment and community development at the Center for Innovative Leadership, in Rivonia, and he delivers Innovation Associates programs in South Africa.*

As a nation, South Africa has struggled with a host of social, economic, and political challenges in our transition from apartheid to a democratic political system. "Apartheid," which literally means apartness, has represented massive fragmentation of our country, system, people, and culture, all of which are actually unavoidably interdependent. Most South Africans agree that we need to make fundamental changes in many of our basic policies and institutions. While the limelight is currently on the political process, economic, organizational, institutional, and societal transformations will inevitably follow. But it has not been clear how to go about making these changes.

Out of this need, the South Africa Forums were born. These forums have sprung up almost overnight at national, regional, and local levels. Their purpose is to discuss, develop, implement, and eventually negotiate plans and procedures for changing institutions. Some forums meet for months in recurring two- or three-day sessions; others, for a single day. The number of participants ranges from 10 to 100 or more.

These are not blue-sky sessions or "town meetings"—there is urgent work to do, particularly when political changes have brought together former antagonists to design a new system. Forum topics include a national electrification strategy, a regional development planning strategy, and a national policy on science, technology, and environmental education. Many forums were initially sponsored by organizations such as the Development Bank of Southern Africa or Eskom. In all cases ownership has rapidly passed to the community of people who represent constituencies with a stake in a favorable result.

In the forums where I have been involved, we have discovered that the learning disciplines are crucial. We particularly rely upon the principle of creative tension—the idea that people can move deliberately by drawing on their personal vision and sense of current reality. Becoming aware of this tension, particularly in a group, seems to awaken the sense of self in many individuals. In addition, within the framework of these meetings, there is a great deal of work on making mental models visible. This is vital for the mutual understanding which makes working together palatable.

I think people seeking to bring diverse people together, in any context, can learn from our experience. In fact, groups of Japanese firms are now beginning to send managers to South Africa to experience our workplaces. They believe that our racial mix and history of turmoil have given us a kind of unique expertise. South Africa is arguably one of the most diverse places in the world, and not just in its people. It is ranked number three in the world on the international biodiversity scale. South Africans are discovering that our diversity can be a strength, not a problem.

The Eduspectrum workshops

THE EDUSPECTRUM WORKSHOPS PROVIDED A PROCESS MODEL WHICH WAS later used during our forum work. These workshops were sponsored by the South African Broadcasting Corporation working in collaboration with Network International and the Centre for Innovative Leadership (my organization), which provided the process design and facilitation support. The first meeting took place in February 1992, and the work that followed resulted in an initiative to use national television to bring education to the entire spectrum of society.

The sponsor of the Eduspectrum workshops, Madala Mphahlele, was the first black executive to be appointed as a general manager in the national broadcasting industry. He had been instrumental in producing Nelson Mandela's first televised speech, and had steered the establishment of a new national channel called CCV.

Mphahlele wanted to devote some of his time, and CCV's time, to the national education crisis. Approximately 60 percent of the population is school-aged, under seventeen, and more than 80 percent of that population is black. The relatively large number of people of color who have had impoverished educational experiences represent a massive underinvestment in learning and development. The entire public school system, including the previously inadequate institutions which taught blacks, has to be reformed into a nonracial integrated system. All this is coming at a time when new democracy requires widespread literacy and mutual understanding, and the global economy requires knowledge in engineering, math, science, and initiative management.

To chair the session required people with appropriate stature. One chair was Ian McRae, then chief executive of Eskom, and a well-respected white public figure. The other chair was Dr. Nthato Motlana, founder of a major health clinic in Soweto and Mandela's personal physician. For decades he had been an activist for the removal of the apartheid system and he is considered an elder statesman for the entire nation, as well as a highly respected leader in the black community.

Having a useful dialogue implied the need to hear from all of the groups with an interest in this issue. Therefore, as in all these forums, the entire spectrum of South African political opinion was represented, from the Africanist left wing through the bureaucratic establishment and everything in between. There were representatives from the Pan Africanist Congress (PAC), a black group in which many of the key intellectuals in the country operate. Members of Azasco—essentially a student wing of the PAC—and Azapo, a further-left organization, were also present. We had members of the African National Congress (ANC) attending, as well as representatives of several corporations. There were also people with a stake in making sure that reforms did not overturn the established educational structure. These people represented the Committee of University Principals, the Committee of Technicon (technical school) Principals, and government departments, specifically the Department of Manpower. Many of the participants came to the sessions with a mental model of the other groups as adversaries, or, worse, as beholden to special interests, or, even worse, as actually corrupt.

Most interesting and useful, however, was what all the groups had in common. All of them cared about the future of the system, despite frustrations which all the groups had endured over the years. If they had not cared, they would not have come.

Developing a sense of shared vision

OUR FIRST STEP WAS, I BELIEVE, SIMPLE AND ELEGANT. WE EMPHASIZED the commonalities among participants. We encouraged people to converse with not only their opposites, but simply with anyone they did not often talk to. Then we asked the participants, as a body, a series of questions to elicit their personal visions for the whole.

We spent several hours surfacing the views, always recorded and posted in front of the entire group. By the time we were finished, there were forty concise statements in full view, all representing aspects of a vision for education. People talked about revising the syllabus, creating a learning culture, developing community outreach, using Eduforums for public education and debate, and focusing on education for employment.

We encouraged people to identify and talk about the relationships among these components, and indicate which seemed to fit together. As they talked, we physically moved the postings on the wall to accord with people's groupings. Clusters of vision statements began to emerge. People began to see how their ideas of a desirable future might fit with ideas from people who were politically opposed. Gradually, they began to talk about the values and assumptions implicit in each cluster—for example, their sense of what they stood for as individuals. Despite their diversity, they moved astonishingly quickly into this process, and we began to identify areas of common interest and natural alignment.

We moved from there to a session on current reality. Given what we all want, what have we now got? What areas should we focus on to move toward what we want? We listed on flip charts a wide range of items which represented the current situation. Once again, we clustered people's thoughts into five or six areas of primary focus.

The clustering process emphasizes interconnectedness and a view of the system as a whole. One member says, "Teacher support." Another member volunteers: "Resocialize the youth." Yet another suggests, "Level the playing field." These points of view are placed together where everyone can see them as components of a future picture they would like to see.

"You can see," said one of the leaders at the conclusion of this part of the session, "how most South Africans have strong common beliefs, and yet the past political culture has made a national pastime out of emphasizing the differences."

Creating a productive conversation

WE NOW DESIGN ALL THE FORUMS TO MOVE RAPIDLY TO A COMMON SU-perordinate vision. By doing this in a transparent way, through a process of dialogue rather than discussion and decision, we diffuse most of the win-lose positions which people wish to occupy. By putting vision and current reality in relationship to each other, we release the energy and creativity required to move. People want to resolve the tension through practical action steps, with clear accountability for their execution. This mutual desire to act has itself been an important basis for creating alignment among the participants. °

Facilitators must continually bring forward people who have not spoken, and prompt them to add their views. They must regulate the flow of conversation, following a model of dialogue which invites people to suspend their assumptions and treat each other as colleagues. All the while, the facilitators must ask people to explain why they said what they just said—to urge them to describe what's behind their thinking. If the facilitator has credibility, then people are quite willing to talk in this way.

⟩⟩ For more about dialogue facilitation, see page 357.

By the end of the forum, people want to get things done. So we have them develop action plans, much like Alain Gauthier's "strategic priorities." We tie this up with what we call the "accountability matrix," a chart which allows the entire group to assign duties and schedule milestones democratically, so that no one feels singled out to do the dirty work. We have now created a diverse team which will continue to work together during the months ahead.

⟩⟩ For more about strategic priorities, see page 344.

We set up the recording process so that a full record of the proceedings emerge for people to take away at the end of the workshop. Even the last twenty minutes are included; we use them to develop ground rules for the team, which I record on an overhead transparency. At the last moment, we photocopy the transparency I am writing and add it to the packet. Through this, we have taken away every excuse not to act.

The sense of empowerment that is developed in these workshops comes both from exercising choice, and from being heard and seen by the other members. People develop what I see as the essence of leadership—the ability to declare a position on an issue but remain open to influence. People start taking responsibility for self within the context of

° These forums are heavily influenced by the Innovation Associates Visionary Leadership and Planning process. See p. 568.

the community, and feel fully accountable for achieving their shared purpose. I feel that something magical happens in the process—I have never seen it fail to release tremendous energy within an alignment with a purpose.

Leadership people in teams that have been through these processes usually report back many months afterward that the energy levels are still high, and the group's work is continuing. Some people, in fact, see these forums as emerging de facto structures which can form the basis of a participative democracy. There is an interesting national dialogue ahead of us about deciding whether the forums are to be permanent, and what their roles in the political and social structures of the new country might be.°

° The report, *Tomorrow's Foundations: Forums as the Second Level of Negotiated Transition in South Africa*, published by the Center for Policy Studies, South Africa, represents the first substantial research in this dialogue.

65 Designing a Company-wide Strategy for Team Learning

How the Managers and Employees of Four Very Different Plants Learned to Learn Together

Joe Douglas, Walt George, Bill Walker, Marc Swartz, Ed Oblon, Jerry Krueger

This is the story of a senior management team that set out to create a manufacturing system that is a model of quality and learning. Joe Douglas, Vice President of Operations for Hill's Pet Nutrition (a division of Colgate-Palmolive), is the leader who conceived and implemented many of the strategies described here.

Part of the process of becoming a learning organization, for Joe and his colleagues, is telling their story to the world, which they do assiduously. In this case, it took two four-hour sessions to get it told, with at least four of these managers at each of the sessions.

Walt George was the facility director at Hill's plant in Topeka, Kansas, a union plant which is in the process of being retrofitted; Bill Walker was

the facility director at Hill's plant in Bowling Green, Kentucky, a nonunion plant; Marc Swartz is the facility director at Hill's recently opened plant in Richmond, Indiana; Ed Oblon is the manager of High-Commitment Work Systems, at the Richmond plant; Jerry Krueger is the Director of High-Commitment Work Systems for Hill's operations, based in their corporate offices in Topeka.

Hill's makes nutritionally balanced food for dogs and cats, typically sold through pet retailers and veterinarians, not supermarkets.

Building shared vision (1988–90)

Joe Douglas: Our story began in the late 1980s, when we decided we wanted to create a different culture at Hill's to deliver better business results. This effort was championed by our executive vice president, Warren Schmidgall, who has played a critical supporting role throughout the process. At that time, there were three Hills plants, each located in a different part of the United States, all very different from each other. Topeka was a very traditional union plant, with tough labor-management issues; Bowling Green was a nonunion plant that needed a complete redesign; and Los Angeles was a smaller plant, with a very diverse ethnic workgroup. (Our plant in Richmond had not yet been built.) Although their managers talked, there was no formal ongoing communication structure or process among them, and we realized that we wanted to transform all of them, and our entire organization, into workplaces where employees would become thoroughly involved in the business. We also realized we would have to design the process by which we got from "here to there."

Jerry Krueger: During the early 1980s, Hill's had been grown 15 to 20 percent per year, due primarily to an increasing demand for premium pet food and an expanding international presence. In 1988, Warren looked at the trends in our industry and concluded, "Our growth is going to decelerate as more competitors enter this category." Specifically, he said, we would need to learn how to leverage manufacturing as a competitive advantage. To do so, we would need to reassess our values and our organizational structure. That was a watershed moment for our company. We knew that these were uncharted waters for us, and would present significant challenges for the future.

Marc Swartz: Hill's had decided to build a new plant in Richmond, Indiana. Warren suggested that this new plant could catalyze the change to a "a team-based technician system." ("Technician" is the Hill's name for the people who perform the operations, maintenance, and shipping tasks at the plants.) When asked what he meant by that, he said, "I don't know what it looks like, but I can tell you what it feels like. We must have all of our people participating."

Bill Walker: We had started up our plant in Bowling Green, Kentucky, in 1987, and had built it to look just like our established plant in Topeka, Kansas. The only major difference was that Topeka was unionized, and Bowling Green was not. We had expected that change to make a dramatic difference, but we saw the same kinds of performance in both plants: people did only the work they were told to do. The results, in both quality and production effectiveness, were below what we wanted. Seeing this was a catalyst for Warren, Joe, and others among us to say, "There's got to be a better way to do business. It's incumbent upon us to find it, define it, and make it work."

This statement would ultimately include a decision to invest in the training and development of people. In the past, there had been no focus on training. "Getting the product out the door" had been the main job of managers. Now we consciously gave ourselves permission to take technicians off-line and spend the money to increase their capabilities — as resources for the entire company.

Joe Douglas: We knew from the beginning that the order in which we tackled these changes would be extremely important. That's one of the reasons why *The Fifth Discipline* had a great deal of meaning for us. Many of us had been exposed to the Innovation Associates "Leadership and Mastery" program through our work with Charlotte Roberts, who had helped shape our understanding of the critical importance of systemic thinking, developing shared vision, and working with mental models.

We decided Richmond would be a learning center that would benefit all the plants. At the same time, we decided to use the same manufacturing vision and principles for the retrofit of the three other plants. Each existing plant would then develop its own charter, emphasizing its own distinctive competencies.

By the end of 1989, the senior management team of operations had developed a vision, mission, and strategy. We intended to be known as a world-class manufacturer, based on our strengths in quality, people systems, technology, continuous improvement, flexibility, and reliability. We decided to bring all the manufacturing managers from Hill's together and get them on board and enrolled as one group, not as separate sites.

Jerry Krueger: I remember sitting in Joe's office when he said, "What do you think people would say if I suggested we take all of the managers out of the plants for two or three days of meetings?" Not knowing for sure, we asked them. Company leaders said, "Good idea. What weekend would you like to do it?" Joe protested; he wouldn't penalize the managers by tying up their weekend. He wanted to meet during the week. The plant managers said they could spare about 60 percent of the management team, and what week should they set aside? "You don't understand," said Joe. "I want every manager from all four plants at the meeting. We all need to hear and understand the manufacturing strategy together."

"Then who's going to run the plant?" we asked.

"The technicians will do it themselves," he said.

Walt George: We met in April 1990. During that week, the Topeka plant actually ran better. The technicians set productivity records. They had no personnel issues or attendance problems. They got a taste of self-management. When they had a vendor supply problem, traditionally they would have had to call a manager to solve the problem. There was no one to call that week, so they dealt with it themselves.

When we came back from the meeting, we knew the plant would never be the same. Now, if someone tried to intervene in the traditional, command-and-control way, the technicians could say, "We ran this plant without you guys." We may have stumbled into that result, but in retrospect, it was a key turning point in the Topeka plant.

Marc Swartz: We were still setting up the Richmond plant when we heard about the meeting. We were scared to death of leaving the plant for several days. We looked at the start-up schedule and said, "Kiss that week good-bye."

At the off-site meeting, Joe brought the managers together to discuss and think about our manufacturing strategy. The focus was on the vision: What would it be? What tools would we be given? What would we all understand differently when we left? The old behaviors would have to change. I personally think Joe had already thought through these questions: he needed to show us techniques and applications that we could practice by ourselves when we returned to the plants. We also needed to recognize that we would have to create our own improvement plans to be successful.

When we got back, the technicians had completed everything we wanted done—mostly equipment checkout and system qualifications—and had moved on to the next steps. We had a huge celebration. The managers came in and cooked steaks and baked potatoes. It was really the beginning of a new era.

Joe Douglas: During the next three months, we shared the vision, mission, and strategy outlined at that meeting with all the technicians in every plant. Every manager and every technician talked in groups, not only about where we were going as a company, but about how their role would change and what was in it for them. The results of these meetings are still evident when you visit the plants. In the Topeka learning center, there is a hand-drawn data scroll, using pictures to show the evolution of where the plant had been, and where it was going. At Richmond, in the long corridor leading to the offices, each individual's vision is written out, signed, framed, and posted.

Learning to think and learn as one (1991)

Bill Walker: While we all had the same basic mission and were looking for similar behaviors, each of the plants had its own unique competency to develop. For example, given the management background and design opportunities at the new plant at Richmond, their competency would be developing leadership talent and new technology, particularly in a sociotechnical environment. Bowling Green's competency was reliability n high-volume, high-output production, and pioneering information systems. Topeka's was flexibility and long-standing technical experience.

Walt George: Our unique competencies allowed us to divide up the work of innovation. Each plant could focus on just a few things and learn to do them better than anybody else. We then relied on each other for knowledge. For instance, I would eventually bring my technicians from Topeka to Richmond, so they could see the new systems working. I wouldn't have to sell them; they could *see* it.

Jerry Krueger: With the Richmond plant in mind, I hired sociotechnical consultant Paul Gustavson to help us with our organizational design and change process. Paul's model for change rapidly became a common mechanism to talk collectively about plant systems and processes. Walt in Topeka, Bill in Bowling Green, Marc in Richmond, and the people in L.A. could all now speak with a common language. This would be increasingly important as we began working together as a four-plant system.

Joe Douglas: In early 1991 we began to have managers from all four plants come together monthly to review results and talk about business priorities. We began to operate not as four plants, but as one; we shared resources, learnings, and decision making. We actively encourage travel by managers and technicians from one plant to the other.

Ed Oblon: When we started building Richmond, we named it "Project Quest." A couple of months later, Warren came to us and said we had to simply be the Richmond plant—just like the Topeka plant, the Bowling Green plant, and the L.A. plant. He did not want one plant to be a "star." It doesn't take many such statements before you figure out that we're all in this together.

Bill Walker: It could have been a really explosive situation when Richmond came up. We could have felt, "The company is trying to find a way to push us out the door." But we managed the plants in such a way that all of them have grown together. When one of us finds something the others adopt it. For example, Richmond had strong information systems. Marc actually transferred two of his key staff members to our plant, to provide continuity in implementing the systems. We made some improvements on their system, which we are passing along back to them, and also to Topeka and Los Angeles.

Marc Swartz: Late in 1991, we were still struggling to come on-line at Richmond. The company needed us to produce 40 percent more than we dreamed we could manufacture. We agreed about the need to make that much product; but we knew in our hearts we couldn't do it in time. Then Bill, Walt, and Mark Bruland, the plant manager at Los Angeles, stepped in and said, "Our plants will cover you next year. We don't want you to take on that volume. We want you to learn what you're learning, so that in 1993 or 1994 you can do what we need you to do, and then teach us what you have learned." Putting a message like that in the system is worth its weight in gold.

Our collaborative learning, between plants, was not an experiment. It was not a program. It's a long-term commitment, a very, very serious commitment. And our management has made that commitment for all time. It has helped make our improvements in team learning within the plants possible, and it has begun to spin out into innovations in infrastructure—new methods of performance appraisal and reward systems designed to reward teamwork and cooperation. We struggle with all of these, and make mistakes sometimes, but nobody doubts that we're in for the long haul. We have a saying at Richmond: once you decide to dance with the bear, you can't decide to get tired.

Joe Douglas: As we have become more of a global business, competition has intensified. In order to be as successful in the decade ahead as we were in the 1980s, we simply cannot operate in traditional ways of having only management involved in the business. Each of us needs to learn to contribute more. We need the ideas of every man and woman in the organization in order to achieve world-class results.

In order to do this we need a different structure that eliminates artificial barriers such as management rights and job descriptions. The only limit a person ought to have is his own ability to learn, grow, and develop. When we are limited *only* by the restrictions we place on ourselves, then world-class results will follow.

66 Executive Team Leadership

Team Learning Among the Senior Managers of an Organization

Charlie Kiefer

Charlie Kiefer is the founder and chairman of Innovation Associates in Framingham, Massachusetts (see page 568). In his central role at IA over the last twenty years, Charlie has contributed immeasurably to the conception, design, and development of a wide variety of programs and initiatives. However, his most enduring passion has been in-depth work with senior teams in client organizations. He is widely recognized in professional and business circles for his insights into the dynamics, functioning, and aspirations of top teams, and the fundamental challenges facing those groups.

Over the past fifteen years, as organizations have grown more interested in encouraging high-quality teamwork, many organizations are making a significant shift at their most senior levels. Despite the focus by the press and Wall Street on the heroic personality of the CEO, these organizations are moving away from the "great individual" model of leadership, and moving toward being *led by a team* of executives instead. This new leadership is sometimes formalized in structures such as "Office of the President" or "Office of the Chief Executive"—the "office," in actuality, being a decision-making team of four to nine people. At General Electric, the hub of the company is Jack Welch's "Office of the CEO," consisting of Welch and his three top vice chairmen. Similar structures have been employed at Electronic Data Systems, Dayton-Hudson, and Polaroid, to name just a few.°

° See *Control Your Destiny or Someone Else Will,* by Noel Tichy and Stratford Sherman (1993, New York: Currency Doubleday), p. 150; *Fieldbook,* p. 68.

Even when an executive team is not formalized in this manner, it is less frequent that the individual sitting at the top of the pyramid is the sole leader. Rather, we see a group of people with shared responsibilities and clear accountabilities strategizing together, reaching decisions by consensus, coordinating implementation and generally performing many, if not all, the functions previously performed by a chief operating officer. Through this *executive team leadership,* these organizations are seeking ways of realizing *all* the talent and intelligence of the most senior people.

There are at least two good reasons why the executive team leadership form is on the rise. First, the problems our organizations face today are enormously complex and have political ramifications within the company. The most difficult issues that an executive team faces are often cross-disciplinary or cross-functional. They require a deep expertise in specific areas, complemented by insight into the interrelationships between functions. Few, if any, individuals have the intelligence and breadth to deal with this kind of complexity on their own, yet it must be dealt with. Consequently, major breakthroughs in *team and organizational intelligence* are required.

Second, within the past decade there has been a "sea change" in the governance of organizations. Leaders and managers, reconceiving their own job as setting forth broad visions and strategies, now grant subordinates much more power to plan and implement. In an organization led by influence, people are moved and convinced when they see a group of people at the top truly sharing a vision and strategy, and modeling it in their behavior. When they don't see that commitment and congruency, their confidence and commitment will be less.

Creating a competent, learning-oriented executive team is a new field in management—and a demanding one. It may be a discipline in its own right. Collective leadership is as different from individual leadership as collective learning is different from individual learning. Mastering team leadership means mastering a larger and more complex learning agenda, often under more difficult circumstances, than any other team in the organization.

The leadership team learning agenda

IN WORKING WITH EXECUTIVE TEAMS OVER THE PAST SEVERAL YEARS, WE have discovered that the circumstances in which their mastery must be developed are generally more difficult than those faced by any other team. They have an even more complex and far-reaching agenda because of the responsibilities inherent at the executive level, and the issues which this level must deal with competently.

Your executive team must, for example, become good at the core issues that any team must master, such as alignment around a shared vision, the ability to discuss current reality without bias, clarity of roles and accountabilities, and methods for capturing and accessing collective knowledge. The ability to dialogue openly and truthfully holds wondrous promise for the executive team. Unfortunately, divergent points of view show up too often as tensions and unspoken conflicts. Methods are either mastered for handling these tensions and conflicts constructively or the team's potential is never realized.

There are other elements, as well, to an executive team's learning agenda—the development of skills and capabilitiies that members may not have needed until now in their careers. For many managers on the team, the agenda is unfamiliar, since their previous teams required these skills to a far lesser degree, if at all. Thus, most executives have had little opportunity in the past to develop them. Nonetheless, each of the elements is significant, and each will require some deliberate work, both among the members of your executive team, and with the people who will eventually become your successors.

Shared Vision While any team must develop shared intent within self, you must master a process that appropriately involves a whole organization in what amounts to a collective creation.

Organizational Assessment Perhaps one of the most difficult tasks for an executive team is to know with high accuracy what is going on within its organization. Information-gathering mechanisms seem to evolve in ways that result in the top of the system having a limited, incomplete, and even biased understanding of reality. You must develop methods that surface and rectify these mechanisms, so that, for example, bad news is as likely to come to your attention as good. Face-to-face, two-way communication must be developed deep into the organization, and a norm must be established of responsibly surfacing and naming the truth as completely as possible.

Strategy as a Learning Activity "Strategy as a team learning activity" stands in stark contrast to "strategy developed by experts." The best strategy formulation reconceives the firm and its environment in line with the construction of new mental models, and new organization intelligence. The promise of such an effort is a more accurate, more robust view of the future, but it will require that everyone on your team (and many other key individuals) actually think about life differently. A great example of this kind of strategy is the invention of brand management by Procter & Gamble; it completely reconstructed the manner in which consumer nondurable manufacturers did business. Beyond the formulation of strategy, the bulk of learning may occur in strategy verification—probing and testing the strategy for internal inconsistencies, running pilot experiments in the marketplace, and computer-modeling strategic elements.

Organizational Strategy The executive team should set aside time regularly to ask and discuss this question: "What characteristics of our organization must change to accomplish our business strategy?" Reward and information systems, recruiting systems, performance standards, and appraisal systems may all have to be radically different.

Organization Change As an executive team, you must master managing organization change—design, structure, and implementation. This must be accomplished through methods that get the entire organization engaged and committed, both in favor of the shared vision and in a rigorous search for the truth. If you want to create an organization committed to a new way of being and a new business concept, then the processes that must be employed must foster commitment. Any coercive process, no matter how well intended, simply cannot ultimately result in commitment.

Unique learning problems of the executive team

YOUR EXECUTIVE TEAM WILL ALSO HAVE ITS OWN UNIQUE DIFFICULTIES in learning. First, for the executive team member, life is more a "zero sum game" than ever before. Earlier in the executive's career, on teams lower in the organization, he or she could get ahead without necessarily "winning" at the expense of another team member. Generally, this is not true for the executive team. One person getting ahead often means another getting left behind, a phenomenon particularly evident around the issue of succession. Lip service to collaboration notwithstanding, this is a very real dynamic on many executive teams.

Next, on the executive team there is generally no appellate court—no tie breaker or higher court of last resort. In most other teams in the organization, if an individual finds himself in conflict with the boss or the team becomes caught in dysfunctional conflict, the team leader's boss can provide a bystander or a third-party perspective. Few boards, if any, do this for the CEO. The CEO or executive team leader, who may or may not be impartial, makes the final decision.

Third, the makeup of the executive team, in and of itself, is a challenge. Typically, executive teams are populated by aggressive "movers" who are used to getting what they want and getting things done. "Group maintenance" skills may be less developed, ironically, than they are elsewhere in the organization. Such skills are typically much less rewarded on executive teams.

Finally, if you are a typical executive team, you operate in an environment that is particularly unforgiving. The organization still longs for heroic leadership. People are intolerant when executives make mistakes, or when the executives fall short of their efforts to model teamwork, however sincere and well conceived those efforts may be. While undesired vestiges of an earlier culture, these habits nevertheless are still ingrained. When mistakes are made at your level, subordinates can be particularly quick and ruthless in following the all-too-human habit of seeking to place blame.

Taken all together, these circumstances offer a daunting challenge that many teams cannot meet. Sadly, the ultimate shortcoming is often in the team's interpersonal dynamics, which are frequently disastrously bad, and many times mirror those of dysfunctional families. Failing to surmount these difficulties, the team is blocked and its potential unrealized. The resulting blocked condition is much worse for the enterprise than if the group were to abandon becoming a "learning team" and instead operate in the former rigid, hierarchical, and noncollaborative style.

Your agenda

THE FIRST STEP IS TO DESIGN YOUR OWN TEAM LEARNING AGENDA. HERE are some suggestions about how you might proceed.

- Have a heart-to-heart talk within the team about what you sincerely want, both in terms of business results and how you want to work together. Don't settle for stock answers from each other. Talk about what is really important to you.

- Next, have an open and honest discussion about the current reality you now face relative to those aspirations. Don't limit yourself to the problems; be sure to include the good things, too! Pay careful attention to what you can and *can't* discuss. Are there "undiscussables"? Can you be fully truthful? If not, can you be truthful about the fact that it is difficult to be truthful? Then, think about a plan to get from where you are to where you want to be.

- Identify those areas in which there is a significant team knowledge or capacity deficit and create methods for learning in these areas. Look at your plan. Anything that you don't know for certain how to accomplish is a candidate.

- Determine whether the team has an appetite and commitment for learning. If so, look for ways to reconstruct things that you are already doing to make them learning activities. Try to view problems, mistakes, and shortfalls as moments with learning potential. Then develop some behavioral pledges that you make together to keep yourselves on track.

It is difficult to establish new habits, particularly at the executive level. As Tod White, the chairman of Blessing/White, once said to me about executive development and change: "It's rare for a person holding four aces to ask for a new deal." You should at the very least consider assigning a team member to coach the team in regular "reviews" to keep yourself honest on your progress. It may become necessary or desirable to contract for these kind of services from a skilled outsider, particularly if you encounter some difficulties in team dynamics. Given the potential for total organization performance if the executive team realizes its full potential, this is a justifiable investment.

However, like so many important things in organizational life, executive team learning is one area where another's *prescription* is of little value. The executive team that learns together and truly learns to lead cannot be photocopied from some other organization. Nor can it be adopted from a consultant's textbook. It must be invented by the team itself.

67 Where to Go from Here

Charlotte Roberts

- **To mental models:** You will already be engaged in this discipline, as your team begins surfacing and testing mental models held about the perplexing situations you face.
- **To systems thinking:** As the team begins to explore the forces at play and consider the interrelationships within the system, it will need the skills of systems thinking. Designing experiments to test its hypotheses will demand acting systemically. Start, as a team, with "The Five Whys" (page 108), or with "Exploring Your Own Story" (page 103). "The Water of Ayolé" (page 156) is an effective, self-contained team systems exercise.
- **To shared vision:** The team will need to consider its vision of this organization before it can proceed very far. The shared vision gives context to the team's work. Start with "Backing into a Vision" (page 341), "What Do We Want to Create?" (page 337), or "The Destiny Factor" (page 341).

Arenas

of

Practice

~~~~~~~~~~~~~~~~~~~~~~~~~~~~

The reports in this part of the book cover a variety of organizational endeavors, each with its own particular concerns. Total quality efforts, corporate environmentalism, management and employee training, family businesses, media, health care, education, government, policy making, and local communities represent some of the first "arenas" where learning disciplines have made a difference. In each case, we asked people to describe their experiences in the field, and to draw forth principles that may help others distinguish between fruitful and unpromising strategies.

68 "Our Quality Program Isn't Working"

Charlotte Roberts, Suzanne B. Thomson

Based in Providence, Rhode Island, Suzanne B. Thomson has been In-novation Associates' mentor in quality leadership, and co-directs (with Charlotte Roberts) their quality consulting practice.

Can you create a quality organization without building a learning or-ganization? Certainly, you can improve processes without putting in place any of the learning disciplines. But as organizations move from process improvement into more fundamental quality approaches, they seem to develop a lust for learning. Their ways of thinking and interact-ing shift. They begin to regard the learning disciplines as a missing link—a piece that they needed, perhaps without realizing it. They see that work on vision and values, for example, might give their quality efforts a more meaningful context.

Frequently, the symptom that something is missing comes first as a complaint: "Our quality program isn't working!" By which people mean: "The results, after an initial burst of success, are not what we had hoped for." It's hard to find a credible culprit to blame for the failure, in part because of the central tenet of the quality movement itself: that 95 per-cent of the problems are the fault of the system. But tell an executive for the ninetieth time that it is all the fault of the system, and you'll get a weary, frustrated response. "You mean it's *our* fault. But we were personally involved in this program, all the way from the top. What went wrong with all our hard work? What do I have to do to get our money's worth out of all this?"

In the past several years, more than a dozen clients have asked us to help them retrieve some value from their stagnant quality efforts. We have found that there are seven characteristics common to nearly every quality effort that goes awry. They all seem inconsequential at first, but they can have dramatic effects; and their effects all reinforce each other.

1. LACK OF A CLEAR SHARED MENTAL MODEL OF QUALITY IN THE ORGANIZATION

There are at least five dominant mental models of quality, each held by some of the managers in any organization:

Status Quo: "Quality is not an issue at our organization. We hire only the best people, and our products are as good as anyone else's. We keep them up to our usual standards."

Quality Control: "Quality is the process of inspecting and catching mistakes before they get shipped and our customers have to deal with them. We hold people accountable for their actions. Modern QC techniques make it easier to track down their mistakes."

Customer Service: "Quality is listening to the customers and solving their problems as quickly as possible at no extra charge. Mistakes and 'bugs' can't be avoided, so we have an 800 number and field service personnel ready to go twenty-four hours a day. We will do anything to satisfy our customers."

Process Improvement: "Quality is using statistical process control, reengineering, and other quality tools to understand and eliminate unacceptable variation in our processes, products, and services. We believe people, particularly in teams, are a resource for learning about inefficiencies and making changes. We are constantly engaged in improving how we operate."

Total Quality: "Quality is a transformation in the way we think and work together, in what we value and reward, and in the way we measure success. All of us collaborate to design and operate a seamless value-adding system which incorporates quality control, customer service, process improvement, supplier relationships, and good relations with the communities in which we operate—all optimizing for a common purpose."

Each mental model directs managers and executives to behave in particular ways. For example, managers with the "quality control" frame of reference are more likely to look over people's shoulders to measure and assess their performance, making all important decisions themselves. Managers with a "process improvement" mental model may make employees responsible for redesigning processes. When two managers of a quality effort don't share the same mental model of quality, they tend to promote different behaviors, teach different skills, and use different measures of performance and success. If their spheres of influence overlap, their mixed messages can confuse and frustrate employees and inadvertently set up resistance and cynicism: "George and Pat say one thing, then they do another. They never know what they want." If these mixed messages come from senior management, multifunctional efforts may end up canceling each other out, ultimately resulting in the slow sabotage of the overall effort.

To forestall this problem, make a point of conducting early and thorough discussions, beginning with the questions, "What do we mean by quality in our organization? What should it be for us?" These meetings may be difficult; some team members have probably never articulated exactly what mental models they hold about quality. As team members begin to surface their models of quality and how they relate to your business, engage the skill of inquiry. "In your mental model of quality, how would we handle conflicts between sales and manufacturing when a shipment is going to be late?"

See "Skillful Discussion" on page 385. Techniques for balancing inquiry and advocacy begin on page 253.

Remember that within any organization, there are probably people holding each of these five mental models. The more interested they are in becoming a learning organization—in helping the organization build its capacity to create its future—the closer they probably are to the "Total Quality" end of the continuum. To some degree, the other mental models of quality are programmatic; they suggest that some "program" can be found or built which, when imposed, will create the necessary changes. The Total Quality model is transformative; it regards quality as an ongoing set of disciplines which gradually affect the way people think and interact, and leave the organization fundamentally different from the way it was when the quality effort started.

2. LACK OF SHARED VALUES AND VISION FOR THE ORGANIZATION

Shared values and vision, particularly if they hold throughout your organization, give quality context. If there is a shared vision for what the company's relationship to customers, employees, suppliers, and the community *could* be, then quality is naturally energized, pulled forward by the future. The vision becomes the answer to the questions: "Why all this talk about Quality? Is this the program of the month?"

Without a vision, people have to find some other rationale for the new quality focus. They fall back on short-term explanations which tend to lead to costly, wasteful efforts. For example:

- "The outside world wants us to run a quality program." A competitor has begun a quality program, or a customer demands a quality-oriented contract. If this is your motive, your quality effort will last only as long as necessary to measure up to the requirements set by the outside world. It will be reactive: its results will most likely be localized and fragmented. Moreover, it will demand enormous energy to manage and to keep alive—like climbing a mountain you never really wanted to climb in the first place. If the competitors or customers continually "raise the bar" on you, both you and your organization's employees will become resentful and resistant.
- "Our product and service problems are getting out of hand!" This manager wants to return to the past, when complaints or product returns were lower. Quality is seen as the path back to the good old days. Efforts based on this rationale tend to chase problem after problem, using crises, rather than the vision, to set priorities.
- "Everybody needs to talk the quality talk." Quality is delegated to the training department. Once people attend the classes and have their "tickets punched," the effort is considered complete. Without a shared vision, none of the infrastructure which quality demands—the links between people who work in different functions and new roles for managers, for example—is created.

3. COMPLIANCE RATHER THAN COMMITMENT AS THE DRIVING FORCE

To comply with a quality effort means to obediently support it, doing whatever is required. In a compliance-based quality effort, management has the continual burden of motivating and manipulating people to "get on the quality train." Contrast this with a commitment-based effort, in which people have made a choice to participate because they believe it is right for them and the organization. To make this choice, people must have enough time and information to consider the choice, compared to other options. They must believe that this particular effort is relevant, they must trust the outcome, and they must have an idea of the first steps.

If members of your organization are committed, the leadership for relating, measuring, learning, redesigning, and standardizing comes from each member. People continually learn and improve their own and others' performance. The management task is to manage ideas, coordinate resources, and create a quality work environment—*not* to generate motivation.

You may discover such commitment in places that seem unlikely at first. One of us (Charlotte) was once picked up at an airport by the corporate driver for a large pharmaceutical company. He was kind, helpful, and concerned about his passenger's comfort. He explained how long the ride would be, and pointed out landmarks. He turned out to be a witty, engaging individual who did his job with confidence and grace, and obviously loved his work. When asked what he thought of the company's highly touted quality effort, he said (with a bit of despair in his voice). "What do they think I was doing all along?" The training he had been forced to take was less demanding than the standards he set for himself. "I don't think they even know what quality is," he said. He had made the choice to do quality work a long time ago because nothing less would do.

Without similar commitment at the top of the organization, the quality effort will fail. Senior managers must be willing to admit they, too, are on a learning journey, which will last years. They must be committed to the mastery of quality leadership—learning about technical and non-technical aspects, leading a critical improvement project themselves, listening, mentoring, and supporting well-thought-out experiments. Above all, a leader must design the organization so everyone can make a valuable contribution.

4. "STEEL-REINFORCED CONCRETE SILOS" IN THE ORGANIZATION

One of the quality organization's goals is to become a seamless organization, where efforts from every part flow into an effective, satisfactory whole. People in each part of the process understand the full operation, from the customer's requirements through the final delivery. Sales, engineering, finance, production, service, and distribution collaborate. Admissions, nurses, physicians, billing, transportation, and medical records share common goals and procedures.

This is possible only if the self-imposed "steel-reinforced walls" between functions are torn down. Otherwise, many quality efforts stall or plateau. Typically, one function reaches the limits of its sphere of control and needs to implement changes beyond its boundaries. If other functions are not ready for partnering, the effort is stymied. The first group may be labeled as pushy or misguided; the second group, as recalcitrant or unaligned.

Breaking down silos is difficult. All too often, organizations apply Band-Aid measures—adding expediters, liaisons, or customer advocates, and expecting them to provide "links" that somehow should cohere an otherwise incoherent system. These remedies merely trivialize and bury the problem temporarily.

We suggest, instead, more fundamental redesign. Investigate and amend the rewards for silo-reinforcing behavior. Design customer interactions to take advantage of employees' expertise. Develop new systems, incentives, and mechanisms that encourage people to reconsider processes together, in teams that meet across functions. A leadership group such as a steering committee needs to provide oversight, pacing and integrating the quality effort across the organization. Demonstrate the new seamless, collaborative model of work on the senior management team.

5. A NON-SYSTEMIC APPROACH TO IMPLEMENTATION

In the early stages of a process improvement effort, individual functions make effective changes. Manufacturing increases process reliability and shortens cycle times. Sales streamlines order taking and entry. Engineering shortens development time. This "picking the low-hanging fruit" is a natural way to learn. Team members make a personal connection to quality by eliminating problems they have struggled with for years without being heard.

Yet, a year or so later, the effort often unexpectedly skids into a slew of new problems—the unintended, delayed consequences of those "low-hanging fruit" solutions. Improvements in one area of the organization create chaos somewhere else. Or an area upstream becomes frustrated with the demands their new quality-oriented internal customers impose on them. Unexpected financial or social costs appear. People in one function begin accusing those in other functions of attempting to sabotage their work.

A steering committee can provide coordination. With its broader field of vision, this team can lead the process to be more sustainable by using the tools and methods of systems thinking. Seek out the vital few targets (objectives, goals, results) which, if you focus on them during the first eighteen months, will give you systemwide, long-lasting positive effects.

The steering committee should not be the only team thinking and acting systemically. As each work team begins its improvement projects, its members, too, must ask themselves: Who will this impact? How will we involve them? If we're successful, what could be the unintended consequences? Planning ahead for the integration of quality throughout the enterprise increases the chances for quality to become a part of the culture.

6. SENIOR MANAGERS WITH INCOMPLETE TRANSFORMATIONAL LEADERSHIP SKILLS

This is a common thread in every case we've seen. The change management and leadership skills which most senior managers know are more relevant to directed, clearly defined change efforts than to the large-scale transformational change that a quality effort demands. Thus, if you are a senior leader in a company pursuing quality, be prepared to . . .

- . . . *change your personal style:* A sustained quality effort tends to thoroughly transform the way people—especially leaders—think about their work and their lives. You will begin noticing how you waste your time, others' time, and the organization's resources. You will see the same stupidity of policies and procedures which you might have seen in the past; but now you will feel compelled to fix them. Your choice to lead quality will also transform your relationships with employees, customers, suppliers, and other people who have a stake in the success of the organization. You will ask for feedback on how well they feel you are serving them, and you'll care about what they say (because you will know it affects the performance of the whole enterprise). You will become a mentor and teacher, motivated out of a love of your work, a respect for your associates, and a desire to see the enterprise long outlive you.

  Others, feeling the same changes in themselves, will look to you for guidance. For the first time in their careers, and often without anyone preparing them for the impact on their emotions and self-esteem, managers and employees will find themselves participating in decisions which impact their work. They will have visible accountability for results which can be measured. They will design their own work processes and reap the resulting efficiency and effectiveness benefits. They will come to see themselves as your partner, and expect you to see them with an equal sense of fellowship.

- ■ *. . . reorient training and team building:* Some managers think they can train and team-build their way into a quality culture. "Send 'em to a few off-sites and half-day seminars, and that'll be enough to get them started." But neither training nor team building will be successful unless it is reinforced by the regular follow-up of an ongoing, systematic change in how work is conducted. People are more likely to adopt quality if it is introduced as integral to their daily work. You don't need flashy programs or elaborate announcements. As a leader, you're better off starting simply—by listening to what people say about the work processes. Begin asking people throughout the company to make their own observations about the cost of poor quality and how the organization manages its resources. Spend your time hearing what works and what doesn't and reflecting upon the implications and possible systemic causes. The training you choose to implement should be informed by the resulting insights.

- ■ *. . . invest your sustained personal involvement.* Some senior managers think they can bow out after initial planning is concluded. Others delegate the responsibility to the next layer of technical managers or a specific department, such as Human Resources. But without competent leadership, any change effort is fated to fail, if only because people will put their greatest efforts where leadership draws focus. When you pull back, it won't be long before everyone else follows suit. "Oh, he's interested in reengineering now. Let's do that."

- ■ *. . . be patient. Results appear after a time delay.* Be prepared to wait three years, five years, or more before you can go to your board or boss and say, "Our quality effort is having a positive, systemwide effect. Our members are committed to quality and are making it happen."

Work in parallel: implement quick hits along with longer-term systemic changes. You can't shut down the operation while you learn quality, but neither can you wait for slow times to implement it. You may want to begin by holding dialogues with multifunctional, multilevel groups about what early implementation activities would be both challenging and realistic, how to proceed, and how to measure the impact of your actions. This fundamental (and recurring) step deserves a large investment of time, energy, and thought.

7. INABILITY TO LEARN COLLECTIVELY

Without collective learning there can be no continuous improvement. Investigate the organizational barriers to learning in your company. Consider these questions:

- **Perception:** Why do we ignore and sometimes deny data which do not match our models and expectations? When are we the last to know what our customers really want and what is happening in our industry?
- **Making Meaning:** How does our organization develop an understanding from the data it gathers? How well does it gain knowledge from the data it receives unexpectedly? What do we do to develop our capacity for thinking?
- **Turning Meaning into Effective Action:** How does our organization develop its *real* strategy? How do we build our theory of best practices and our knowledge of what is the right thing to do?

   Collective learning is enhanced if individuals can hold in their minds a shared model of the organization—how it converts resources and energy into products and services, and how those products are intended to serve customers' needs.

The lessons of the quality movement

THE QUALITY MOVEMENT IS UNIQUE IN ITS TRANSFORMATIONAL POTENTIAL, even today. It inherently focuses people on the whole system, on both "hard" and "soft" issues, on collective learning and action, and on their own desires for improvement. The failures have come, in a nutshell, because organizations expected too much from "the quality program," and too little from themselves. An organization cannot be a quality organization without the pursuit of collective learning. Learning organizations are coming under the same sorts of pressures. Taking heed of the lessons in the quality failures will help every organization that seeks to become a learning organization.

69 Springing Ourselves from the Measurement Trap

The Quality Effort at the Ford Motor Company

Edward M. Baker

Between 1987 and 1992, Edward Baker served as Director, Quality Strategy and Operations Support, at the Ford Motor Company. He was a participant in the MIT Learning Project and regularly assisted and lectured at Dr. W. Edwards Deming's management seminars.

During the 1980s at Ford, we had many visibly successful approaches to quality improvement. Evidence of our success included a significant reduction in customer-reported problems ("things gone wrong with the vehicle"), and an increase in customer satisfaction ("things gone right"). The employees participated more; we moved away from a culture of detecting errors after the fact, to one in which we prevented defects by improving the process. These results pleased top management and strengthened its commitment to improve quality. However, the same programs also led the company into an unexpected trap, which undermined our efforts to improve.

The trap had to do with our reliance on figures. Because Ford had achieved so much product and process improvement with refinements in measurement and statistical analysis, executives' traditional fondness for quantification was reinforced. They got the idea that the essence of Total Quality is measurement. They began asking for summaries of our shop floor quality results—a natural move, given Ford's management traditions. "How well is our quality effort doing?" is a valid question. But trying to answer that question by sending local measurements up the chain where they are aggregated into composite numbers did more harm than good. It actually distorted management's knowledge of how well we were doing, and thus added cost.

To understand why, you must understand that in the best quality strategy, measurements are used by the people who gather them. Automotive plants incorporate so many different kinds of processes—machining, metal stamping, molding plastic, manufacturing and forming glass—that we can't be prescriptive from our corporate or division office.

On a transmission there might be as many as 8,000 characteristics to measure, spread over as much as three million square feet of factory floor. A production team typically tracks only a handful of measurements, enough to help its members learn but not to overwhelm them. We don't specify which they should follow. We teach the general techniques. Then we leave it up to the local people to use their brains, expertise, and theory—and figure out what's right for their processes.

The trap shuts: management data requests

When management of the divisions asked its plants for more figures, a number of disastrous things began to happen. First, the plant crews now had to supply the additional information that management wanted for its reports. These data consisted mainly of numbers needed to compare the variability of a specific quality characteristic to the allowable variability specified by the engineers. Management, therefore, is pleased to see the index increase. Unfortunately, the index, even when used locally, provides no information about how to reduce variability and defects.

Billions of bits of data accumulated in company computers, adding to the overhead and busywork which the quality effort was meant to remove. Analysts at division quality offices combined the separate data from local processes to obtain averages for each plant and then aggregated them into divisionwide reports. Now the division managers could use quality numbers in the same manner they traditionally used financial numbers to compare plants (their own and supplier plants). If the "score" was too low one quarter, the plant manager had to explain why. The game in each plant changed from improvement to making the plant look good against its neighbors. Because the figures were used to compare plants, people became fearful that the numbers might be used to punish them. (Whether this perception was actually valid is not the point: many people believed this was the case.) Game playing was encouraged, since the index could be improved by widening the specifications as well as reducing variability and defects (widening a specification is equivalent to redefining some defectives as okay).

I know that these practices are widespread beyond Ford. When I mention them at industry conferences, people come up to me: "My God, you're the first person who's talked about all this complexity. The new approach to quality was supposed to make everything simpler and instead it's become an onerous chore." I ultimately came to believe that corporate leaders will not get the results they're hoping for from their emphasis on quality—whether they hope for lowered costs, an expanded market, or simply more profits—as long as traditional information reporting and control structures remain in place.

The solution: measurement at the top

AFTER ABOUT EIGHT YEARS INTO THE CHANGE EFFORT, I SAW SOME RESolution to this problem begin to emerge at Ford. The leverage comes from measurements—sales volume, inventory turns, tooling costs, warranty costs, employee absences, and accidents—that will enable senior management to improve the system from its *own* level. It took years of persistent effort, including seminars on systems thinking and theory of variation, for this change to show effect. But after senior managers began to recognize the dynamics and temporal relationships in their own systems, they developed a better understanding of systems in general. That effect cycled back and made things better on the shop floor too.

We started with the senior executives who understood quality on the shop floor but had not yet applied the theories to their own work. I knew division executives who could walk through a plant and recognize immediately that someone had been doing what Dr. Deming calls "tampering"—incorrectly attributing chance rises and falls in the shop floor measurements to a specific cause, adjusting the equipment when they should leave it alone, and thus making things worse. Because these managers understand statistical variation, they would not dream of asking for meaningless figures in the plant. But once they return to the corporate office, they forget all that. Suddenly they want to know why sales volume slipped or inventory costs jumped last month, and whose fault it was. When the pressure falls on *them*, they often fail to take a systemic look at the situation. Instead, they see a problem that must be solved immediately. Sometimes "heads roll."

But in the last few years, management has worked hard to change. For example, in former times the CEO and other senior executives would study figures on warranty costs—what we pay dealers to repair customers' cars—on a quarter-by-quarter basis. Once we put those figures into a temporal chart, the executives could see the pattern of variation over time, and relate it to other factors within and outside Ford. This not only helps them use the measurements to manage the system as a whole, but it also helps them begin to see the relationship between the measurables and the *un*measurables that must also be managed.

The second jaw of the trap: unmeasurables

FOR THERE IS A SECOND JAW OF THE STATISTICS TRAP: IT FOCUSES ATTENtion on measurement. The most important management issues (97 percent of all key decisions, by some estimates) do not appear in statistics at all. Management has no figures for them. Here are some examples:

- acceptability of a design by the public (early market research figures said the public wouldn't like the aerodynamic "jelly-bean" shape that Ford introduced in 1983, which turned out immensely popular);
- intrinsic motivation, cooperation, and other human attributes that make results happen;
- the capacity of a company for discovery and innovation of key new products;
- the potential for expansion of a market;
- the benefits of education and training.

In other words, the fundamental capability of an organization to shape its future cannot be put into a spreadsheet. By convincing people that they are doing enough, so-called Total Quality management is delaying the more fundamental transformation that we need in the way we think about organizations, structure them, design them, and operate them. Until that occurs, we must recognize that we have not gone much beyond packaging the old management-by-the-numbers methods in a new wrapper.

70 Corporate Environmentalism
The "Floorboards" Dilemma

Grady McGonagill, Art Kleiner

Grady McGonagill is a Boston-based organizational consultant who has studied with Chris Argyris and incorporated "action science" concepts into an eleven-year consulting practice. He has worked regularly with corporate managers who are struggling to understand environmentalism, and with groups of environmentalists and business people who are trying to understand each other.

* The definition of sustainable development—meeting the needs of the present without compromising the ability of future generations to meet their own needs— comes from the United Nations World Committee on Environmentalism and Development, otherwise known as the "Brundtland Commission." See *The Business Charter for Sustainable Development: Principles for Environmental Management* (Paris, France: International Chamber of Commerce), April 1991.

† *The E Factor: The Bottom Line Approach to Environmentally Responsible Business* by Joel Makower (1993, New York: Tilden/Times Books); *Beyond Compliance: A New Industry View of the Environment,* edited by Bruce Smart (1992, World Resources Institute); or any issue of the *Pollution Prevention Review,* published quarterly by Executive Enterprises, Inc., New York.

In 1992, in a Fortune 500 company with a well-known record of responsiveness to environmental concerns, a planning committee removed the phrase "sustainable development" from a draft of its proposed vision statement.* The phrase was "too radical," they said. But within a year, the phrase was back; it had begun to gain currency within the company, and senior managers were considering making it a part of their official vocabulary. In its growing embrace of a concept that would have seemed anathema ten years ago, the company is very much in the corporate mainstream. They've seen the rewards—in spurs to innovation, opportunities to cut waste, and improvements in morale—that a long-standing environmental practice offers them.† At the same time, the caution of the planning committee reflects an ambivalence and defensiveness that exist in many companies, threatening to compromise their environmental commitments. Their espoused theories may support an environmentalist imperative, but their underlying attitudes and beliefs are still resistant.

We've seen cases, for instance, where a team of managers invites an outside environmental consultant to help it navigate the company through a change effort. The team members recognize that this will involve a major cultural change within the firm. But when the outsider suggests opening up dialogue about an environmental vision, the idea is rebuffed: "Our people aren't ready for that yet." Why? "You don't need to know." End of discussion. There is clearly something about environmentalism that brings out defensive routines in full force, so that corporate managers risk failing to see and capitalize upon the potential benefits that environmentalism offers.

While the dynamic is probably strongest in companies that refuse to adopt any environmental practice, it is more visible to the public in companies that openly aspire to be "green." Typically, the environmental initiative begins when a senior manager makes a pronouncement that they will embrace "an environmental vision." But translating the vision into reality proves difficult because managers are caught between conflicting incentives. On one hand, there's the new "green" imperative from above, and their own genuine desire to be ecologically conscientious. On the other hand, established values reject rapid change, reward systems remain pegged to quarterly profits, accounting systems disregard "externalities" such as environmental impact, and there is still the ongoing reality of meeting the bottom line. Managers are told they have to change, and to diminish their pollution, but they are not told how. They are reminded how 3M saved millions with its pollution prevention program, but are often not given the tools or information they need to make similar savings themselves.[*]

Managers' defensiveness also reflects tensions left over from thirty years of warfare between environmentalists and corporations. Technologically trained managers, in particular, tend to see environmentalists as uninformed, presumptuous dilettantes, intruding judgmentally into areas where corporations once had a free hand. Corporate managers also make a point with which many environmentalists agree: environmental regulation and legislation tend to be crude tools, all too frequently enforced with more emphasis on the letter, rather than the spirit, of the law. Since the regulatory climate toughened in the late 1980s, managers are also vulnerable to personal liability for environmental infractions.

[*] *Multinational Corporations and the Environment: A Survey of Global Practices* by Margaret Flaherty and Ann Rapaport (1991, Medford, Mass.: Tufts University Center for Environmental Management), p. 13.

The floorboards dilemma: pressure to contain information

At the root of corporate defensiveness is a mental model that environmentalism, by its nature, entails significant risk. In some companies, the mental model contains truth: there is indeed the risk of litigation, extra expenses, and personal liability. But the *perceived* risk often feels much higher than it otherwise would, precisely because the company's environmental history is unknown.

The dynamic can be appreciated by anyone who has bought an old house. Every house has its secrets. There may be reason, for instance, to suspect that if you pry up the floors under the kitchen, you will find extensive dry-rot, costing tens of thousands of dollars to repair. Your lawyer may advise you not to open up the floors, because if you find damage, you will be legally bound to fix it or disclose it should you ever sell the house.

Imagine that you took that advice. Seven years later you are selling the house, and still don't know if the floor covers rotting wood. This makes you feel more defensive every time a potential buyer walks into the kitchen. It only takes some small, relatively innocent question about the flooring to provoke a truth-concealing reaction. ("This house was thoroughly checked against the codes when we bought it!")

Many companies have some "floorboards" that they don't want to pry up. Typically, the managers in charge don't feel responsible for causing the problem. It's not their fault, for example, that they own a toxic waste dump site created by a company they purchased, any more than it's the homeowner's fault for unwittingly buying a house with concealed dry-rot. Yet they may face the intimidating prospect of uncontrollable costs, or even personal legal liability, because they own that site. And because they feel that any information about their internal thinking is proprietary, they're reluctant to seek outside opinion. There may also be a "shoot-the-messenger" ethic in place, which discourages any attempt to bring forth the environmental skeleton from the corporate chest. Instead, they blame the bad faith or incompetence of the previous owners.

However, if managers continue to deny responsibility for the problem, they never feel fundamentally secure about environmentalism. They can't take advantage of environmental opportunities, or respond to the imperative strategically, because they are too anxious about what they may turn up. Instead, they opt for the strategy of short-term risk avoidance. They try to "contain" the problem—giving the impression that they are on top of environmental questions, while minimizing the chance of liability or change. This quick-fix strategy may include green advertising, and some isolated waste reduction efforts. But more likely than not, it will include an attempt to hide or play down information: "We don't want anyone to know, and we don't want to know ourselves, exactly what pollution problems we may actually have." In effect, they pass the same problem that snared *them* on to the next unfortunate "buyer of the property" (who may simply be the next manager in their position).

This "containment" strategy resolves the symptoms of their conflict in the short term, but it represents a strategy of denial. The more often managers opt for containment, the wider the gap will grow between their promises (based on the demands of the environmental imperative) and their actual practices. Their real and perceived vulnerability to lawsuits or regulation will grow stronger, because the fundamental environmental problems will remain unexamined.

Developing a strategy of inquiry

THE ALTERNATIVE STRATEGY BEGINS WITH AN ADMISSION OF *NOT KNOWing* the answers about liability or environmental impact, any more than the homeowner knows what lies under those floorboards. To follow a strategy of inquiry, you conduct an environmental audit—inventorying sites, emissions, and processes, bringing forth data that suggest methods for improvement. This audit takes time, and makes it more difficult to pretend to be on top of the problem. But in the long run, it is the only way to learn enough to develop creative solutions.

Many managers who take this route are startled to discover that, in the long run, it is less costly than the containment strategy and, paradoxically, less risky. There are undeniable short-term costs, but these would probably become higher cost burdens later on. There may be unpleasant surprises, but these may spark creative solutions that in fact make the entire enterprise better. Bringing forth data does not mean simply putting it in a report, but testing it against the reactions and other knowledge of people within the company.

The story of the Toxic Release Inventory Act demonstrates the positive outcomes that can result. Also known as Title III of the 1986 U.S. Superfund Amendments and Reauthorization Act (SARA), it required companies to report the quantities of 300 chemicals they emit into the air or water of each facility. Company leaders feared adverse public reaction, and some got negative publicity. But more typically, the gathering of information promoted mutual technical assistance among companies, the transfer of good practices from division to division, and increased contact with customers and suppliers.*

}} Also see the Ault foods story, on p. 301.

Companies may also find value, as McDonald's did in 1991, by forming partnerships with environmental groups. Staffers at the Environmental Defense Fund spent months conducting an informal audit, working at various levels in the fast-food company. The partnership produced an innovative, sustained revamping of the company's practices. Pacific

* *Managing Chemical Risks: Corporate Response to SARA Title III* by Michael S. Baram, (1990, Medford, Mass.: Tufts University Center for Environmental Management).

Gas and Electric and General Motors have similar relationships with environmental groups.

It is most effective to develop an environmental vision alongside an audit of current reality. What does your company or team really want from its efforts in this arena? Unless you can clarify what is important to you, you risk being stuck in a reactive mode, responding to "that damned environmental pressure" with no real interest. If there is no intrinsic resolve to fix problems, then uncovering them is quixotic.

The long-term implications of the dilemma

THE CHOICE BETWEEN CONTAINMENT AND INQUIRY IS A "SHIFTING THE Burden" situation in which the quick fix is addictive. The more you take the "risk-avoidance" strategy (the upper loop's "symptomatic solution," the harder it will be to switch to the "inquiry" strategy (the lower loop's "fundamental solution") later. The reasons for this are not just psychological, but material. If managers are trying to deny or stonewall information within the firm, it's much easier to make sure that information is never recorded. Ten years later, a team that decides to take the fundamental route will find it all the more difficult to gather the pertinent data. Records will be incomplete, measurements will never have been taken, and the habits of inquiry will never have been cultivated to make people skilled at learning from bad news. To cope with the anxiety, people will continue cutting corners on environmental safety, which makes it even more likely that there are hidden secrets waiting to be unearthed. This addiction will reinforce itself (as shown in the addiction loop), making it increasingly difficult to turn around.

For more about "Shifting the Burden" situations, see page 135.

Another loop in this diagram shows an extra opportunity: an organization that inquires gradually learns enough to influence the other organizations around it. Over time, it gains the credibility, ability, and willingness to influence the "environmental imperative"—helping other companies and governments set their direction. Taking—and living up to—the moral high road allows corporations to influence policy, far more than if they were being adversarial, as Dupont discovered during the late 1980s when it led the international chemical industry in moving away from producing chlorofluorocarbons (CFCs) because of their effect on the ozone layer.

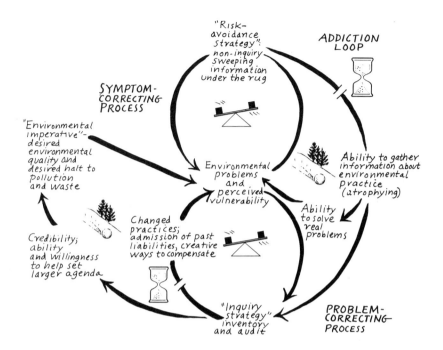

Ultimately, the purpose of corporate environmentalism is to shape the world more strategically. Companies are already involved, just by making a product or service, in shaping the world around themselves. Perhaps one day environmentalism will be seen as the front edge of corporate participation: a participation in the design of the world around the company, filling both the needs of the people within the company, and the general need for long-term ecological balance.

71 Training As Learning
A Key Element of Cultural Change

Bill Brandt

During the past twenty years, Bill has led American Woodmark through three organizational structures (he and three co-workers acquired the division of Boise Cascade in 1980, and took it public in 1986), through *significant business cycles, and through a growth in sales from $15 million to $170 million. He is currently Chairman and President. In this cameo, he describes how reshaping the training structure galvanized a renewed commitment to learning.*

In 1989, American Woodmark achieved record sales and earnings by providing a limited selection of kitchen and bath cabinets, with weekly delivery anywhere in the continental United States. We had grown through the 1980s by servicing independent distributors, large builders, and home center chains, where American Woodmark had become the industry. Although every financial measure for the company was positive, it was clear that we could no longer remain successful following our existing strategy. For example, consumers were demanding increased product variety beyond what we could yet produce. Some key competitors were providing it and working diligently to close the service gap which had given American Woodmark an advantage.

We could see that our future depended upon creating the culture of a learning organization. Our employees needed to act more autonomously and respond more quickly to changes in the marketplace. Innovation, market planning, work scheduling, and work flow design needed to take place at many levels of the organization, and we needed to make decisions more quickly. Essentially, every employee in the company, from the first line workers to me as president, needed to learn new ways to behave.

Thus we created our "1995 Vision," embracing a new culture and a six-year plan to develop separate brands for various customer categories, to produce greater product variety, to become more of a product innovator, and to develop a just-in-time manufacturing environment. Although we anticipated that changing values, behaviors, and work methods would require a significant commitment of effort and resources, we did not anticipate the many fundamental barriers to change hidden in our existing culture. The barriers were particularly strong, I believe, because we were attempting change at the moment when, from most people's perspective, we were very successful. In effect, our first steps to implement our 1995 Vision were seen by many people as the tearing part of a well-oiled machine that they had spent many years creating.

Today, we have completed four of the six years of our journey. We are on track, or ahead of schedule, with most of the strategic elements of our plan. But with the first and perhaps most important aspect of our vision—our cultural change—it has taken all this time to see the beginnings of a new culture take hold. One of the key factors which we have learned to appreciate is formal training. Our training programs have evolved in three separate phases, from a separate set of "programs" to a way of life now being integrated into every manager's and employee's workday.

Although other strategic changes (particularly in quality management and product development) may have had more immediate impact on our culture, formal training is significant in two respects. First, we use training to communicate why and how the company is changing; it puts meaningful labels on actions that have taken place informally. Second, most people still regard the cultural changes as having been produced externally *for* them. The training should enable people at all levels to learn to generate positive change for themselves—in their own area and for the whole company.

PHASE 1: PILOT TEAM TRAINING

We did not have a unified management culture at American Woodmark. Different locations and functions interpreted our common values and principles in their own unique manner. In our first phase, we set up several pilot programs to train people in specific "new skills": simplifying work flows, reducing cycle times, lowering inventory levels, and other techniques designed to produce hard measurable results. We used outside consultants to design the pilots and lead some of them; I worked closely with the consultants and monitored our progress. I expected the pilots to become showpieces, which the rest of the organization would appreciate and naturally emulate.

But for the most part, they bombed—neither producing enthusiastic response nor measurable results. To add insult to injury, they were viewed as "my" pet projects. In retrospect, I realize that the involvement of outside consultants, together with the knowledge that the company had begun to lose money, created an apprehension about the projects and where they fit in the company's priorities. The pilot teams began to feel that they were out on a limb. A team at one plant would be "empowered" to talk to a team at a supplier plant within the company, and ask them to redesign a component. The people at the supplier plant, not having been a "pilot team," would say, "We can't afford to make the change." They had no support, training, or mechanism to help them deal with the first team's request.

Because pilot teams typically didn't have the understanding or support of people higher up in the organization, there were no effective methods to resolve conflicts. Nor was there any appreciation that some conflict might support what we were trying to accomplish. If anything, conflicts were viewed as symptoms that the pilots were failing. That perception, in turn, reinforced fears among the pilot teams that their training would just be a "program of the month." The programs ran out of steam.

PHASE 2: BROAD-BASED TRAINING

We initiated a second phase of training programs during 1991 and 1992, taking the time to build a consensus among our top management team. We composed a "continuous improvement process" vision for the company, saying that all employees would learn to "make decisions in the best interest of American Woodmark." We communicated this vision in semiannual employee meetings and training sessions to about half of our 2,000 employees. We also established more than thirty new cross-functional teams, each sponsored by a senior manager. About fifty natural work groups become "Daily Improvement Process" (DIP) teams, empowered to suggest ideas and implement those within their work areas. Finally, we established an in-house training department and designed several full-time facilitators to assist in training and team development. Outside consultants were used primarily for concept development and training our own facilitators—not for implementation.

With these efforts we generated some significant performance improvements, but Phase 2 created some problems of its own. Many of the cross-functional teams proposed solutions not in step with the overall priorities of the company. DIP teams ran out of gas once their "low-hanging-fruit" was picked. People who were not yet involved in the process expressed frustration.

In mid-1992, we called a time-out to assess where we were. Upon reflection, we saw that by establishing many DIP teams before involving middle management completely in the process, we put the middle managers (who felt threatened by the involvement of outside facilitators) in the awkward position of not really understanding what their employees were trying to learn. Moreover, by going public with our vision, we had created great excitement and anticipation among many employees who were not yet on teams; they felt stuck on sidelines, waiting to enter the game. Busy creating new teams for these employees, we did not have all the resources we needed to support the initial teams as they faced hurdles. Other employees reacted with fear and anxiety. Finally, most of our people still had the impression that these new team processes were more bureaucratic "programs" to add to their normal work, instead of a way to get their normal work done.

PHASE 3: LEVEL-TO-LEVEL TRAINING

Our current phase of cultural change, begun in fall 1992, has several components:

- Every employee and manager learns the same basic management philosophy and skills. There are four core training lessons, each involving one two-hour session plus a follow-up workshop session after the team has had some practice. Lesson I covers team management practice and basic work processes. Lesson II outlines what we expect of our employees, what they can expect from us, and some basic speaking and listening skills. Lesson III is an exercise with a model company to demonstrate the principles of teamwork and continuous improvement, while Lesson IV trains employees and teams to develop client-and-provider relationships.
- Specialized training is available on an as-needed basis, consistent with and supportive of the core training.
- The management process is not only learned conceptually, but put into practice as "the way we do our work." Managers must show, for instance, that they are following teamwork principles, applying inquiry skills, and promoting continuous improvement *before requiring the same of their subordinates or direct reports.*

  I personally wrote the first version of each core lesson. I taught all four lessons to my staff, who then critiqued them. I also asked an outside consultant to critique them. I then rewrote the lessons and again reviewed them with my team. Once my team was happy with each lesson, each senior manager taught his or her team. Those members of the second level of management then critiqued the lessons, and both management levels reviewed all the critiques in an open discussion—improving the material and gaining a greater ownership of the final product.
- We conduct all core training on a similar level-to-level basis. Each supervisor trains the members of the team he or she leads; those members, in turn, train the members of the team *they* may lead.
- Each team is assigned an outside adviser, jointly accountable with the

team itself to ensure that the core training principles are practiced. Advisers, wherever feasible, are from other functions; for example, a regional sales manager might be an adviser to a plant management team. What advisers learn as outside observers hopefully helps them be more effective with their own teams.

■ At a quarterly full-day review meeting, the top two management levels meet to consider the cultural change process and foster accountability for individual, team, and overall company performance.

Today, a year after the start of this third phase, we can see more ownership and a greater feeling of responsibility on the part of senior and middle managers. We also see many small actions initiated within teams, generating significant improvements in quality, delivery, safety, cost, and other performance targets. The new process is continuing to surface inconsistencies between existing long-established practices and our stated new directions. We are addressing these issues as they arise. As we do, we are creating a significantly better alignment of goals and work effort throughout the organization.

Reflections

I BELIEVE IT IS IMPOSSIBLE AT THE OUTSET TO DETERMINE JUST THE right path for achieving desired cultural change. Although having a good initial direction is very important, it is just as important to be willing to modify the course as frequently as necessary. People throughout the organization may well view (some with relief) any significant setbacks as the failure of that new direction. Emotionally, it is critical that the leader not share this view, but rather sees setbacks as the necessary corrections needed to stay on course, just as a sailing skipper adjusts the sheets and the heading in response to changing winds and currents.

Finally, I have learned that cultural change requires both patience and perseverance. There are no quick fixes, and the greater the movement in the right direction, the greater the resistance to be faced. At this point, I am confident that our third wave of training programs will get the job done. But if it doesn't, we will create a fourth wave to take ourselves there—if not by 1995, then later.

72 Workplace Design
The Physical Environment of a Learning Organization

Janis Dutton

Janis Dutton is the managing editor of this book. Having worked edito-
rially on a variety of architectural publications, she asked one day: "Why
aren't people in the learning organization community paying more atten-
tion to the ways their buildings and environments are designed?" Here
is the beginning of an answer. We are interested in hearing from archi-
tects and their clients who have tackled the problem of creating spaces
that enhance efforts to learn within their walls.

We learn through architecture. Much of what we know of institutions
and their meanings comes from the types and styles of buildings we
encounter. That is why the design of an organization's buildings is an
important contributor to its values and relationships.

Documentation is plentiful on the effects of the physical environment
on learning, in particular. You can often feel the effect firsthand, as I did
at the last open house I attended at my sons' school. One room was
arranged as an invitation to learning. Children sat at round tables to
facilitate interaction and cooperation. A sofa and rug in the corner provided a cozy place for reading. Another room had no windows, low ceil-
ings, and beige walls. Single desks, lined up in perfect rows, clearly communicated who was in power. Though I was a visiting parent, the room
made me afraid to step out of line. I didn't want to be there, and neither
do the children. How many rooms set aside for "learning" in organizations evoke a similar feeling?

Architects, and the people who hire them, need to understand that
the practice of architecture is about the whole process involved in making buildings, as much as it is about aesthetics. Understanding this opens
up interesting possibilities. When an organization creates a new building, or retrofits an old one, there is a terrific opportunity to manifest
support for the organization's purpose and learning, in both the process
of creating the building and the form of the building itself.

The *Calgary Herald* in Calgary, Ontario, placed the day care center
for employees' children in the middle of the main floor of their building.

Since the room has glass walls, parents can see their children at play. The design takes part of the *Herald*'s vision—being an organization that takes seriously its employees' needs as family members—and incorporates it into the everyday environment.

The *Calgary Herald* story is told on page 474.

The Richmond, Indiana, plant of Hill's Pet Nutrition also incorporated some principles of a learning organization into its new building. The hallways are wide enough to allow small groups to gather without impeding traffic. In the naturally lit main hallway, a pattern of square windows is mirrored by groupings of framed, signed statements by employees telling of their own personal vision and their vision for the organization. This demonstrates that the employees are clearly important to the organization.

See page 429 for more about Hill's Pet Nutrition.

In one of my own workplaces, the city hall in my town (where I am an elected official), the building is run-down and overcrowded. No matter how empowering the management style, it is difficult to maintain morale or provide quality services. Recently, a group of architecture students at a local university worked with management and staff in an exercise on designing a new municipal building. The discussions covered such issues as: What kinds of spaces were necessary to be able to work and communicate easily as teams? What city services needed to be near each other and which could be separated? Should entrances and circulation encourage more visual and physical interaction between citizens and employees, and between departments? Who gets the corner window? Given our finances, the exercise was hypothetical, but it provided a vehicle to bring mental models of how the city should function, and shared images of its vision, to light.

ARCHITECTURE FOR PEOPLE, **edited by Byron Mikellides** (1980, New York: Holt, Rinehart and Winston);

REDEFINING DESIGNING **by C. Thomas Mitchell** (1993, New York: Van Nostrand Reinhold).

There is a great book waiting to be written on the architecture of learning organization buildings. In the meantime, I recommend two books as resources for anyone who is about to begin design or renovation of a building for a learning organization. Browse through them for ideas—to get a sense of what is possible, not only in terms of what the building looks like, but the process of making decisions about it, creating it, and starting to live in it.

The essays in *Architecture for People*, written by world-renowned authorities in a variety of fields, have one common message: we could do a better job of making buildings, homes, and cities meet the needs and aspirations of the people who inhabit them.

Written in language accessible to managers and other nonarchitects, *Redefining Designing* offers a critical assessment of architectural design philosophies and practices since industrialization. C. Thomas Mitchell argues convincingly that buildings have more often than not failed to suit their intended purposes, not so much for aesthetic reasons, but because of the design process itself. Mitchell describes international examples of user-responsive buildings, and includes comments about their success or failure over time. This is both a book about a "new" way of making architecture and a historical overview of architecture as a social and cultural process.—J.D.

73 The Tricky Dynamics of Learning in a Family-owned Business

George G. Raymond, Jr.

George G. Raymond, Jr., was CEO of the Raymond Corporation, which he inherited from his father in the 1950s. The company makes electric forklifts. As a result of George's effort to instill a culture which encouraged people to contribute, the Raymond Company began the journey to becoming a learning organization years before The Fifth Discipline *was available. People who work in warehouses talk about riding the "Raymonds." In his retirement, George and his wife Robin went to Lausanne, Switzerland, to be faculty for a year at the Institute for Management*

Development, sharing what they knew about family-owned businesses. We asked him to do the same for us—to comment on the learning organization issues which every family business top manager or family member should be aware of.

The Raymond Corporation, one of the leading companies producing forklifts, conveyor belts, and other industrial machinery, has been a family-owned business for three generations now. Looking back on our history, I attribute our current success to our efforts to become a family-owned learning organization. These efforts essentially began in December of 1949, when my father, George G. Raymond, had to step back from the business due to an illness. Out of necessity, I took control, and began experimenting with new management ideas, working closely with Dick Beckhard, an organizational change pioneer who was then at MIT.

But as the years went on, I became more and more aware of an important dimension. The "family" component of our family-owned business gave the business some added advantages, but it also introduced complexities. Since 95 percent or more of U.S. businesses are family-owned or family-controlled (according to a study Dick initiated at MIT), these complexities are relevant to many people. (A "family-controlled business" is one in which the family can control the succession to the CEO.)

Experience has taught me that a healthy family business is one in which the dynamics and relationship among family members are cultivated and attended to. *The company cannot improve unless the relationships among the members of the family are improving.* When these relationships are ignored, there's a good probability that the business will start going downhill. The most celebrated cases, such as the Binghams of St. Louis or the Campbell's Soup family, tend to follow this pattern. They fight for control, and in doing so, they ignore the needs of the company, so it begins to fall apart beneath them.

What causes these kinds of fights? Usually, I've found that someone who's not directly involved in the business—a spouse, for example—starts complaining to their closest involved family member that they're being cheated, and they'd better get a lawyer involved to protect them. Or a dispute occurs and the leaders select a "solution" that involves talking to a lawyer or an accountant to clear up the dispute and engineer an equitable arrangement. It's not unusual for the "patriarch" in a family business to look to the professionals for help in arranging inheritance. Presumably, the lawyers' accountants will get everything solved because they know what to do.

But in "Shifting the Burden" to the expert, the more fundamental issues of tricky family dynamics are ignored. The lawyers and accountants haven't got the faintest understanding of the histories of those relationships, and no family business will flourish unless the relationships among family members are also flourishing. In other words, you must pay deliberate attention to the relationships *before* trying to fix the infrastructure of wills and settlements. The relationships are an integral part of the structure of the organization. Rather than bringing in a lawyer, I would find a consultant who can work with you (as Dick Beckhard worked with us) to understand both the psychological dynamics of the family and the dynamics of the business simultaneously.

For example, sometimes an owner/entrepreneur is determined that his son or daughter should run the business after him. This determination has little to do with whether the son or daughter wants to, or whether he or she is qualified. "By God I'll see to it that they *get* qualified." Other times, the owner/entrepreneur doesn't believe in nepotism and the offspring have no opportunity, even if they *are* the best qualified. To avoid both extremes the retiring patriarch, a decade or more before retirement, should set up training in all the areas that the new top executives should know. This should probably include the diagramming of systems thinking, which I found increasingly useful for understanding the dynamics of the firm *and* the family. Make sure that the young family members have opportunities to participate. At the end of umpteen years the young family members, if they stick with it and show aptitude, will be well prepared to run the company.

CULTURAL CHANGE AND FAMILY FIRMS by W. Gibb Dyer, Jr.
(1986, San Francisco: Jossey-Bass);

KEEPING THE FAMILY BUSINESS HEALTHY by John L. Ward
(1987, San Francisco: Jossey-Bass).

Two good books about family firms. W. Gibb Dyer, Jr., author of *Cultural Change and Family Firms*, pulls out some very useful principles and techniques: how to build leadership as a catalyst for change in family firms, how to deal with conflicts and power struggles, and how to navigate the transition from public to private ownership. It's an excellent book, focused on the nexus between the managers' relationships and the family relationships.

In *Keeping the Family Business Healthy,* John L. Ward looks at the problem in terms of strategic planning, market growth, and financial issues. For example, he describes how to plan for long-term capital needs, and how to plan a succession strategy to include the personal vision of the young members of the family. —**G.G.R.**

74 Creating a Learning Newspaper

Terry Gilbert

Terry Gilbert is a reporter for the Calgary Herald *newspaper. After attending an early program on visioning at the* Herald, *she volunteered to become a facilitator in its Visionary Leadership and Planning program. Applying the tools in a variety of settings within the* Herald, *she developed a reputation for tackling tough issues head-on, including the merger of two departments and the human impact of downsizing and restructuring. In 1993 she was selected from among top Canadian journalists to study for a year as a Nieman fellow at Harvard University.*

When the *Calgary Herald* set out to become a learning organization, the majority of employees were skeptical.

Everyone else was cynical.

From all corners of the building came scorn and derision. Had Kevin Peterson, the publisher, been brainwashed? Why were we lining some consultant's pockets? Was this a sneaky way of undermining the union? And—the most pressing concern—would we have to hug?

The publisher's motivation had everything to do with other media—radio, TV, cheap printing, and electronic data. "It appeared our near and mid-term future would be dominated by a need to learn and change," says Peterson.

The principle of building a shared vision was particularly appealing to Peterson. A newspaper, he says, isn't just a business, it's part of the essential fabric of the community. It inherently has a vision: "We supply people with information so they can make a better world, make better choices, or get along better."

At first, many people were willing to learn about systemic thinking and learning organizations only because Peterson suggested it—and because those first introductory Visionary Leadership and Planning (VL&P) sessions were held in the scenic splendor of the Rocky Mountains. Those who hadn't been invited assumed the superior air of virtuous skeptics, clever enough to avoid the cult's insidious seduction.°

To understand the resistance—and the need for learning—it's necessary to understand the inherent conflicts that exist within newspapers. We have two distinct sets of customers—readers and advertisers—with clashing interests. "If Slap-em-Up Homes is building shoddy houses at cheap prices, part of our role is to tell our readers this is a bad deal," says Peterson. "However, if Slap-em-Up Homes spends a quarter-million on advertising, when we expose their business practices, they're not going to be very happy."

Maintaining credibility with readers—who contribute one dollar of every six in revenues—means being honest even if it means sometimes jeopardizing the five dollars that advertisers contribute. Internally, that integrity has always been protected by a barrier between the advertising and editorial departments. Embarking on a journey to become a learning organization meant we would have to peek over that wall. We would also have to look at the traditional conflicts between knowledge-based workers (such as those in business services, advertising, circulation, and editorial), and the manufacturing work force (encompassing compositors, plate-making, press, and distribution).

Senior managers were introduced to the learning organization concept in the fall of 1991. In spring 1992, six *Herald* employees were trained to facilitate VL&P sessions. I was one of them. At my first exposure to the notion of alignment, my stomach knotted. I imagined the reaction that would get from a roomful of my colleagues, who pride themselves on being—and are paid to be—questioning, cynical, independent thinkers.

And I wasn't sure the concept had merit in a newsroom. Even within an editorial department, not everyone is trying to accomplish the same thing. A business reporter and a labor reporter might write strikingly different stories about the same situation.

Sure enough, as we began to conduct sessions, my apprehension was well founded. There were twenty attendees in each workshop, representing a diagonal slice of the hierarchy. They became acquainted with

° The program brought in to the *Calgary Herald* was Visionary Leadership and Planning, offered by Innovation Associates of Canada (see p. 569).

the learning disciplines, then undertook some strategic planning. Many of them made it clear they were attending against their better judgment. They leaned back in their chairs, their arms folded, confident this, like other flavor-of-the-month approaches, would fade into *Herald* history. Some were clearly uncomfortable when asked to close their eyes for a couple of minutes, consider what is important, and relate it to the person sitting next to them.

But over the course of the three days, the energy level in the room invariably began to escalate. Often, what people said about their families, lives, and dreams was more personal than anything they had related in years of working in the same department. When the discussion turned to work, I was often surprised by the passion individuals felt for their careers and for the *Herald*. Even some of the most cynical people were drawn in.

The sessions were often heated, frequently frustrating, but always informative. Managers learned about the realities of work from secretaries, classified ad reps, people who ride herd on circulation canvassing crews, reporters, and technicians. Sometimes they heard for the first time about broken equipment, or about what our clients were really telling us. One reporter, emerging from an impassioned debate about how well we serve our women readers, described it as the most "frank, honest, no holds-barred discussion" she'd been part of in five years at the *Herald*. In general, we discovered one key alignment bonding us—the desire to give people as much information as possible, knowing that much of that information will be in conflict.

On some days we had five different teams meeting. By mid-1993, about 350 employees—roughly half the staff—had been through the sessions. And we began to see results. For example, the competing daily launched an aggressive attack on the $7 million in ad revenue we realize annually from home builders. Our traditional response would have been price-cutting and more advertising sales pressure. Instead, we set in place teams, including senior managers, sales and editorial reps, to meet with forty-five of our customers to learn about their advertising and editorial needs. Applying the disciplines, we ultimately revamped and restructured our approach. Designated sales teams were struck, hard-edged stories were produced, and we held a contest in which we gave away a $250,000 home. Revenue in the category climbed to $8.5 million, and one of the city's largest home builders says that every active buyer in the market reads the *Herald*'s "Homes" section. Moreover, reporters and ad sales people had found some common ground without compromising integrity.

To help extend learning beyond department walls, guests from other functions were often invited to sessions. An editorial group had people from marketing and business visit. Circulation, when it undertook a major restructuring, invited the circulation director from a sister paper. Hearing an outsider's view was, in many instances, pivotal to a group's success. When the Human Resources department, sailing along confident they were delivering the goods, heard from a printer that he didn't know why the department existed, it caused the department to rethink how it was delivering its programs.

In addition to the three-day introductory sessions, we began to hold facilitated dialogue sessions, and we undertook broad strategic planning sessions using the visioning model. More subtly, we began to change the way we tackled day-to-day issues. Instead of going into a problem-solving mode, we often started by asking: What does success look like and how are we going to get there? And we worked with a new understanding that everything we did had an impact elsewhere in the building, so we might as well enroll other departments from the beginning.

When reporters, deskers, and support staff took on the task of merging two sections of the paper—the "City" and the "Life" sections—departments as varied as marketing, business services, advertising, circulation, the composing room, and the press were involved. In the old *Herald,* senior managers would have conceived and executed the new section. Reporters and deskers, having been excluded, would have looked for flaws afterward. Other departments would have lamented that, had they only known in advance, they could have helped make it a better product.

This time, in three-day meetings, reporters, deskers, and editors debated who our readers were, how best to serve them, and crafted a vision for the new section. Then we built bridges with ad sales reps, and with the marketing and circulation departments, to design a campaign to launch the new section. Staff members devoted countless hours of their own time to make it work. A reporter and an editor who had a strong interest in developing a youth page took on the task and ran with it. A reporter with a keen interest in finding out what our readers were thinking worked with a market researcher to design an extensive in-paper survey. When we showed the prototypes to focus groups, the viewing gallery was filled every night.

In the middle of this process the *Herald,* facing economic realities, reduced staff by 15 percent. For such an event not to derail a commitment to becoming a learning organization, a CEO needs to be really upfront about the state the business is in. The payoff was that employees didn't suggest the solution to every problem was to throw more resources at it. When "City & Life" staff debated which new areas of coverage warranted designated reporters, they did so knowing that every new beat meant they had to cut back elsewhere.

Managing editor Crosbie Cotton said after the merger of the "City" and "Life" sections that he didn't get everything *he* had hoped for in the new section, but he got twenty wonderful things he had never imagined. The section also engendered an unprecedented level of enthusiasm and commitment from staff, and an understanding that diverse views needn't be threatening, but are in fact essential. Editors who didn't work directly on the merger made an immense contribution by picking up a huge amount of the day-to-day workload, and were valued for it. Moreover, by respecting those who preferred not to be involved and by being honest about the limits of VL&P—it does not offer a magic solution, just an opportunity to learn—we are gradually creating a culture in which some of the skeptics who had once voiced disdain for the process became those most anxious to participate.

I've told you about some of our terrific successes, but we also had our failures. We pulled together a diverse group to address an issue that has plagued the *Herald* for some time: marketing. The problem was, it just wasn't very clear what it was about marketing we were dealing with, and several people who had been invited were confused as to why they were there. After two hellish days we had to confess the whole thing had been, in some ways, a disaster. But when we stepped back to examine what we had learned, we discovered we knew a lot more about how to learn than we otherwise would have. And because we had learned, another group took it on and made it work.

To sum up, we don't think every newspaper should jump into this program. But any organization that has awakened to the fact it is going to have to change to thrive and prosper is going to have to learn. We know we can approach our future with confidence, not fear.

75 Health Care
How Hospitals Can Learn

Donald M. Berwick, M.D., interviewed by Art Kleiner

Four precepts for health care leadership

Donald M. Berwick is one of the leading figures in (and one of the most articulate members of) the movement to apply quality and learning organization principles to health care. An associate professor of pediatrics at Harvard Medical School, and a pediatrician at Harvard Community Health Plan, he is president and CEO of the Institute for Healthcare Improvement, a nonprofit whose mission is to encourage and support collaborative improvements in health care systems. He is also the co-author (with A. Blanton Godfrey and Jane Roessner) of Curing Health Care: New Strategies for Quality Improvement *(1990, San Francisco: Jossey-Bass). There's a message here for anyone trying to reform health care politically: the reforms will not work unless the medical community leaders build some kind of successful learning organization effort.*

Hospitals can become true learning organizations, in every sense of the word. But hospitals have some unique problems, stemming partly from the special role which professionals play, and partly from the unique relationship which hospitals have with their community. In addition, it is possible that the definitional boundaries of "hospital" must be breached or broken, if we are to invent a medical organization that learns at a level needed by society.

There are in fact many levels of medical organizations: ranging from the individual doctor-patient relationship, through traditional organizations (nursing homes, hospitals, health-maintenance organizations), all the way up to the system of health-producing activities which affect a region or society at large. In the short run, the level with the most need for learning is the local community. In local community health care, the most likely place for a first move toward building learning organizations is typically the local hospital.

Here, then, are four precepts for anyone who is starting a learning organization effort in health care:

1. START AT THE TOP

The most important lesson I've learned over the years has to do with the critical role of leadership, whether embodied in a single individual or in a group. Without the backing of formal leadership, the possibility for systematic change will be blocked.

This was a hard lesson for me to learn. But after observing the same dynamics take place again and again at hospitals, clinics, and nursing homes, I now believe that unless the board or CEO is willing to launch a full-scale dedicated effort to change the entire culture of the hospital, including the relationships among all its functions and operations, a learning organization effort is likely to move very slowly. You will deceive yourself into two or three years of high-energy activities that end in wasted time, financial losses for the hospital, and professional disappointments.

That sounds harsh, but consider what typically happens when the senior management is not personally driving the process. Everything begins with an initial wave of enthusiasm. The CEO says, "We need to make some changes, and I have asked Mary to take the lead in installing this new learning organization program."

Mary—who used to be the associate vice president of planning, the assistant director of nursing, or perhaps the director of the pharmacy—couldn't feel better. She's the coach for change. She's been promoted three levels. She sits in on the highest-level executive meetings. The CEO couldn't be more pleased because he's got someone to rely on to spearhead the project. The activities begin with a presentation full of declarations, using the latest catchwords and phrases: "We're going to develop personal mastery and shared values! We'll break down barriers! Trust will grow, and there will be vision, vision, vision!"

Newsletters are developed and quality management teams are formed. The first- and second-line supervisors, who had never been involved in thinking about the place as a system before, are suddenly put to work brainstorming, drawing diagrams, and developing their understanding. It's marvelous!

But soon there are signs that the first set of changes are superficial and shallow. The CEO gives a speech and says, "We're really invested in this learning organization stuff, but we mustn't forget about productivity." In private, he asserts that some people are using the effort to slack off or shirk their responsibilities. The board begins to ask questions: "We've noticed $200,000 was spent on this . . . Is it helping? Is anything happening?"

"Yes," say Mary and her staff. "We've shortened the waiting time in the emergency room by ten minutes, and we've saved $30,000 in pharmacy stocks. But it's difficult to give any more specifics yet. Maybe next quarter . . ."

Mary starts to feel more and more out on a limb. She gets invited to fewer meetings. People tire of the vocabulary. The chief financial officer and the chief operating officer get fed up making and hearing empty promises. Soon the organization feels teased. The "learning program" gets folded into the training budget. It becomes yet another disappointing example of the pointlessness of trying anything new.

It's not Mary's fault. The CEO was never really committed to re-creating the entire enterprise. And it's unlikely that he or she would be. Paradoxically, the same factors that make leaders so influential and vital tend to make them unwilling to get personally involved. Most hospital communities still seem to believe that the executive leadership always knows what's best for the organization, and the rest of the hospital does not. When there are problems, when capabilities are suboptimal and production is low, the belief holds that leadership can institute effective changes from the top—not through their own learning, but by exerting controls. This approach will never result in learning because it is focused on the rules of the health care system, and not the human relationships and capabilities that underlie the system.

For example, imagine that the leadership wants lower cost, greater access, and more dignity in care—while employees work the same hours for the same salary. According to the prevailing view, top leaders could change the incentive structure and capabilities would automatically improve. However, if individuals at all levels aren't equipped to work in this new fashion—if they don't have training, support, encouragement, and opportunities to raise questions—the organization is wasting its time.

2. ENABLE EVERYONE TO PARTICIPATE IN IMPROVING THE WHOLE ENTERPRISE

Even when the top leadership recognizes the problems inherent in the "teach and control" method of management, it often continues inadvertently to "suboptimize": to encourage individual units to excel at the expense of the system as a whole. For example, an operating room (OR) group could set up a local process for recording and using information—improving its own efficiency, but providing no access to the overall medical record system of the hospital, to the purchasing department, or to the physician training program.

In health care, it seems as if we're congenitally ridden with arrogance. Everyone's usually especially angry at the doctors and nurses for not being team players: "They're arrogant," people say. But nobody reflects on where this arrogance comes from. I have come to believe that it is really pride in disguise, channeled by a system of suboptimization. People want to be proud of their work, and they are willing to think about the whole hospital system as part of their work. But what happens when they are denied participation in the improvement of the system beyond their bailiwick? They draw a tight boundary—a fence, a wall—around themselves. Within that space, they work with all the dignity and beauty of craftspeople doing something wonderfully well. But to others, they say, "Please stay out! It's my thing, I built it!"

Once I conducted a staff survey of a hospital unit's quality. The waiting room environment was particularly poorly rated. Magazines weren't up to date. Walls were dirty. Patients were upset. When I presented this information to the unit's doctors, one of them took the report, rolled it up in a ball, and threw it in my face. "Waiting rooms," she said, "have nothing to do with me." She had defined her system, the environment in which she worked, as beginning not when the patient walks into the hospital, but when she walks into the examining room to meet the patient. We've denied many such doctors the access to participate in improving the system as a whole.

Once the leadership of the hospital has accepted that it wants to create a learning environment, the next step is to find ways to open up opportunities to participate. The methods for doing this may involve some sort of shared vision effort; they may require extensive systemic thinking and quality-oriented work. They almost certainly require an explicit reframing of the relationships between functions: an invitation for everyone to care and comment about every aspect of the hospital. This is not the kind of thing that an individual doctor or administrator can change unilaterally.

3. FOLLOW YOUR CURIOSITY, AND ENCOURAGE OTHERS TO FOLLOW THEIRS

In order to learn, you must start with a question in mind. As you pursue the question, learning will follow. Thus, health care organizations need what my colleague Paul Batalden calls "CEO curiosity," although it can apply to any senior leader, and should also apply to the hospital board. There must be a sense that business as usual won't work. Something must open the mind of these executives, so that they ask: "Is there anything we should be doing fundamentally differently? Is there a way of acting that would be more responsive to the sense of creative tension that we feel?"

Curiosity will not surface if it is driven only by desperation and outside pressures. Another source for asking questions is more intriguing. I call it the "intellect as driver." The health care community is blessed with many leaders who are driven simply because they're fascinated by learning. They love it for its own sake. We can draw upon this reservoir of energy when we use the learning organization as an image to guide us.

If that sense of search and exploration is missing at the highest levels—if the CEO shows no sign of interest in his or her own learning—then I become worried. Then the old model, the old crutch, still holds sway—that the CEO is there only to teach and control the organization.

The difference between "learning" and "teaching" hospitals has been explored through the exercise, "Designing a Learning Organization: First Steps." See page 57.

4. LINK THE HOSPITAL TO ITS COMMUNITY

Sooner or later, medical administrators will realize that it is better business to function as a whole, instead of as fragments. I'd like to see this concept applied not just within hospitals, but at the community level as well. Unfortunately, right now, most of the leadership in the health care world feels that it's un-American to operate health care cooperatively. For example, recently I was talking with a chief executive in a big health care system in a U.S. city. He told me that his city needed only one magnetic resonance imaging (MRI) unit. But between them, the city's hospitals had a dozen or more. If they only had one, the community would probably get better service, lower cost, and they would reduce the burden on their system for supplies and maintenance.

"This is a great business opportunity!" I said. "You should get together with the other hospital administrators, and downsize into one shared MRI unit."

"I'd like to," he said, "but they would think I was out of my mind." Having an MRI unit of your own, he said, fits the image hospitals hold of their own growth.

Nonetheless, there have been some early indications of what communitywide learning might look like, and it's very exciting. For example, in Twin Falls, Minnesota, a group of community leaders just completed a citywide project cutting emergency room visits for bicycle injuries by 40 percent. Significantly, they had to touch every part of the community to do it—through the cooperative efforts of the superintendent of schools, political and economic leaders, health care chief executives, and medical society leaders. I believe they'll make similarly impressive accomplishments in the future if they stay together.

For more about learning communities, see page 502.

Communities can't be managed by vision alone. They must work toward understanding the community as a whole. One approach would be to map the structure of an organization onto the community: to figure out its overall finances, its human resource systems, its controls, its training and education, and so on. This is the frontier for learning organizations, and I believe that learning in medical organizations will inevitably draw us further out along that frontier.

76 Education

Emily R. Myers, Frank Draper, James Evers

Design for a learning laboratory in a learning school *Emily Myers*

Perhaps the most impassioned audience for "learning organization" work consists of educators and people who care about schools. Yet realizing the promise of learning disciplines seems so elusive in education.

Emily R. Myers is an example of someone who has taken steps to realize that promise. She is leading a group of twenty-four parents, students, teachers, and administrators, from public and private schools, to collaborate in defining a "Learning Habitat" based on their experience with the Mobius Project described here. The proposal they produced for the America 2000 project was the origin of this piece.

When I took on the assignment five years ago to bring computing into the Chadds Ford, Pennsylvania, elementary school, I had very high hopes. I could imagine elementary school students designing bridges with computer-aided design, creating their own interactive videos, or using "microworlds," as the education innovator Seymour Papert had suggested, to simulate the real world and build their own learning environments.[*]

In particular, I knew we could use LOGO, the learning-oriented programming language which Papert had invented. Known for its "turtle geometry," LOGO is a compelling way for kids to discover problem-solving techniques and explore the interrelationships of math and logic. Using the computer, children draw insight out of themselves and their experience; they learn without having to be force-fed facts through memorization. The students took to the LOGO language just as Papert's writings suggested they would. In fact, the results were so good that the district hired me to offer in-service training the following year, so that regular classroom teachers could carry LOGO back to transform their own lessons.

The in-service course soon evolved into a prototype for a new type of learning laboratory, an intergenerational workshop which met every morning for one week. We had about twenty-five attendees, evenly divided among parents, teachers, and schoolchildren, working side by side on computers, learning from each other as much as they learned from me. The children pulled us all forward. They skipped lunch to keep working and would have stayed all afternoon if I could have let them. Seeing their excitement, learning, and growth convinced teachers of the value of interactive learning. As a parent, I was delighted that I could make such a valued contribution to my child's school.

Although the district gave me an award for outstanding service, the concept of computer-based interactive learning didn't begin to make a dent in the rest of the school system. As a system, schools have their own learning disabilities, and it happened that introducing technology into teacher training revealed them. Even the most receptive teachers found it hard to go back and apply LOGO within their classroom, because it didn't directly relate to the textbooks or curriculum. The teachers were talented and hardworking, and the equipment they had, while it wasn't state-of-the-art, was certainly good enough. The limiting factor was the lack of understanding about what computers in the classroom could do—and an us-versus-them management structure that virtually incapacitated teachers by setting them against the administrators. Eventually, I resigned.

[*] See *Mindstorms* by Seymour Papert (1980, New York: Basic Books) and *The Children's Machine* by Seymour Papert (1993, New York: Basic Books).

THE MOBIUS PROJECT: THE LEARNING HABITAT, PRESENT AND FUTURE

Two years ago, I began designing a learning laboratory at the Media-Providence Friends School, a Society of Friends (Quaker) private school in Media, Pennsylvania.° I was fortunate; the school had raised $40,000 in contributions for a computer lab, which we built from scratch. We now offer week-long "Computer Survival Expeditions," comprised of groups of students aged thirteen through adult. Many teachers attend because the course is approved for Pennsylvania continuing education credits.

Yes, we have state-of-the-art equipment, but a far more important factor is the transition to an open, learning environment. Traditional centralized school districts, burdened by regulations and their own large sizes, do not engender a commitment to supporting the kinds of multifaceted, in-depth relationships between people that facilitate learning.

Our prototype learning habitat, the Mobius Project, aims at producing continuous, cooperative, lifelong learning—learning, like a möbius strip without an end. We've held workshops in which grandparents and their elementary-age grandchildren compute in pairs, establishing a common bond for learning and conversation.

The first assignment asks students to design the cover of their workbook. They are thrown into it without background or instruction, and must learn through trial and error. As they get stuck they ask their neighbors, consult reference books, or ask the workshop leader. Classes are small, and participants have a tangible result in less than an hour—and the beginning of a lifelong appreciation of their own potential resourcefulness.

Later, teams of students build computer images of the components of a town: roads, houses, and offices. Then teams connect their parts to build a community. In another exercise, the entire class becomes a team to solve a survival puzzle. Each individual must communicate critical information over the computer network to succeed.

Most importantly, we try to set up our program to reinforce the view that every person is gifted, in his or her own unique way. In Quaker schools, this guiding principle is based on the religious belief that every person contains the light of God within himself. It makes a profound difference; it provides a constructive mental model against which students and faculty may flourish. And it provides an alternative to the competitive mechanisms of most schools (such as tests, where "cheaters" are punished), that punish teamwork and collaboration.

° Readers should not infer that this example, from a private school, is irrelevant to public education. For example, many people write off private schools as overexpensive, but this one has a tuition near the state average for public school expenditure per pupil.

A vision of what school might be

IMAGINE, THEN, A SCHOOL AS A NICHE WHERE PEOPLE JOIN TOGETHER TO learn, regardless of their age, occupation, or home address. Relationships between people are encouraged, because they facilitate learning. Common goals and expressed values shape the habitat. Each school-age student has an individual instruction plan, with at least one advocate who helps the student refine and shape it. The length of the learning day and the number of days per year are determined by individual achievements, and the needs of the students, their families, and the community. The length for periods of instruction varies by subject. Drill and practice activities are most effective in short bursts. Exploration and creative activities require longer periods of time. Some activities, including the use of microworlds and other computer- and noncomputer-based practice fields, might go on intermittently, possibly for weeks.

The habitat-community interface is permeable. The "classroom" extends beyond the school building, into museums, science centers, colleges and universities, health care and social service organizations, businesses, and homes. Teachers move into local businesses or organizations for summers and sabbaticals, to experience more of the world they are bringing students into. Nonschool employees return to spend weeks in the learning habitat regularly, to renew their own learning, and to teach others. Gradually, the community evolves its own sense of collective intelligence, greater than the sum of its individual parts.

I have come to believe that continuous learning is an innate vehicle for building shared visions of schools themselves (as an integrated part of the community around them). Simply to show up is to ask a question of yourself and other learners: "What can we create together?" As schools and communities evolve together, using examples and processes from prototypes like the Mobius Project, how will we know quality when we see it? How will we know our efforts are on the right track? Different communities will come up with different answers, based on what they learn. For now, we take our measure of success in the faces of the people in the room, and in the fact that they return freely for more.

Systems thinking in the classroom *Frank Draper*

When Jay Forrester, the founder of system dynamics, learned we were doing this book, he asked: "Are you including anything about the Orange

Grove Middle School?" At this school in Tucson, Arizona, with help from retired MIT faculty member Gordon Brown, a series of experiments have shown that systems thinking can revitalize the classroom by replacing the dreariness of receiving answers with the engagement of investigating systems. Many of the experiments took place in the biology classrooms of Frank Draper, who has taught middle school and high school science since 1979, and has served as the systems thinking mentor for his school district since 1990. Parents reading this may be most interested in the way boredom and discipline problems seem to dissipate, only to return when the systems learning stops. In place of boredom comes a renewed sense of responsibility, among the students, for their own education.

In 1989, with a fellow eighth-grade science teacher named Mark Swanson, I decided to convert our curriculum so we could teach life sciences systemically. I wanted students to learn how different parts of biological and ecological systems are structurally and dynamically connected to each other, and to work with the principles they were studying dynamically. They would not just stuff themselves with facts for a test, but make informed decisions about managing ecological systems, in a form as close to the real world as we could create in a classroom: StellaStack computer simulations, which Mark and I had designed.

For more on *StellaStack,* see page 547.

For example, during a unit on populations, students managed computer-simulated deer herds, compared human population growth trends in various regions of the world, and designed their own food chain by creating two simulated herbivores and one predator. They selected from a palette of skulls, legs, and behavior traits—such as the degree of parental care and the strength of herd behavior.

Before setting the animals "loose," the students had to draw graphs showing the ways they thought the populations of their three new animals would behave over thirty years. The computer showed how closely reality would mirror their expectations. They then redesigned their animals, and reran their system, until it matched their goals.

My role, as the teacher, was to help them learn to understand the feedback control relationships between predator and prey populations.

By November, Mark and I were impressed with how well the year was going. The number of classroom behavior problems seemed unusually low for eighth grade. We agreed that we were incredibly lucky to be teaching these motivated, well-behaved, and responsive students. But in February, our lesson unit on cells came up. We had not had time to convert this lesson to a systems approach, so we taught it the ordinary way: with lecture notes, a few labs, worksheets, a review, and a test.

Ten minutes into the introductory lecture, I began seeing all the typical eighth-grade behavior familiar from ten years of teaching thirteen-year-olds. Kids were writhing glumly in their chairs, whispering, calling back at me, staring out the window, and passing notes to each other. I was just about to respond the way I had responded for ten years (by shouting for order) when I realized that I had created this behavior myself. For fourteen weeks, my students had been active learners, making informed, real-world decisions. Now I was asking them to become passive vessels again.

I stopped the class, and with the help of some new causal loops on the blackboard, I explained what I thought was going on. There was a "Shifting the Burden" dynamic at play, and we had just regressed back to a way of life—traditional teaching methods—which I had never realized before was a symptomatic solution. We discussed the issue as a class, and the students agreed to meet me halfway. I agreed to work in as much systemic explanation as possible, and return to the systems approach for the rest of the year.

See "Shifting the Burden," page 135.

Since 1989 our classrooms have undergone an amazing transformation. Our jobs have shifted from dispensers of information to producers of environments that allow students to learn as much as possible. Students come early to class (even early to school), stay after the bell rings, work through lunch, and work at home voluntarily. When we work on a systems project—even when the students are working on the book research leading up to systems work—there are essentially no motivation or discipline problems in our classrooms. Not only are we covering more material than just the required curriculum, but we are covering it faster (we typically have five or six weeks left over at the end of the year), and the students are learning more useful material than ever before. "Facts" are now anchored to meaning through the dynamic relationships they have with each other.

Now, when behavior problems occur, I often find the problem exists because the students are not as engaged with the content as I thought they would be. For example, students may focus on completing the worksheet and turning it in, rather than learning the material. That means I haven't fully done my job. I need to redesign the unit to engage students more effectively—to help them see more clearly how this material is part of a system that encompasses not just the other learning in this class, but their lifelong learning about the world.

Changing the schools: first steps *James Evers*

How, then, can public schools be turned in the direction of becoming learning organizations? James Evers suggests some starting points. He draws on experience as both an award-winning public school teacher and as a co-founder of the Rockland Project School, a successful experimental private school based outside New York City. Evers also consults on learning and writing for several large corporations and self-publishes a warmly accepted writing guide for managers called The Effective Writer's Kit.

In the thirty years that I've been involved with some aspect of education, I have seen all kinds of new programs. Each was supposed to be the answer to our schools' problems, yet schools continue to be seen as ineffective. In part, the reasons have to do with America's open, diverse culture. Every religious, political, and academic orientation has a vested interest in our schools. Many even have pressure groups that demand, for example, longer school days and longer school years with no change in educational philosophy. These groups may mean well, but their demands are not based on a systemic view of current reality.

In the 1970s, I was involved with an alternative private school. Its philosophy centered on teaching the whole child through learning-centered teaching, respect for individual style differences, and an integrated curriculum. Parents, students, and teachers developed a shared vision together. Personal mastery, team learning, and mental models were a part of the program, though we didn't know those terms. (We called mental models "personal metaphors".) The school had no hierarchical administration; each teacher was considered a co-director of the school. Parents, students, and teachers were all considered board members. Students had a great say in their school, were a part of the school's administrative problem-solving processes, and learned the values of independent thinking.

That school did quite well during the twenty years that it lasted, and our approach toward collaborative decision making helped us succeed. I felt then, and still feel today, that this approach should be available in public schools. Even "good" schools—schools with many students who go on to college and successful careers—are falling further and further behind the realities of a changing world. An authority, called teacher, stands before a group of students called a class, even though the learning styles of the students are individually unique, and the teacher presents lessons in a single mode of presentation. Then the divergent learners and the school are judged by standardized tests created by people outside of that community culture.

For more about divergent learning styles, see page 421.

The assembly line model is firmly in place, while computers, televisions, encyclopedias, and modems in many homes (at least affluent homes) have eclipsed the power of the classroom to provide information.

During the years to come, students will barely need to come to the school building to get information. But they *will* need to come to get some basic skills, including the skills of collaborative learning and process judgment: learning how to put together, reflect upon, and use knowledge. New employees today are not arriving at the workplace with these crucial survival skills because schools do not provide them effectively. To provide them would mean getting the teacher out of the front of the room and into the role of guide and model, helping students find and manage the information they need or want. Nonetheless, against this backdrop, there is promise for public schools. Change can come through the practice of the five learning disciplines.

- *Use systems thinking as an incremental starting point.* You might be tempted to start with shared vision, but the prevalence of pressure groups can make any discussion of common vision difficult. Consider, for instance, the complications when communities attempt to revise the social studies curriculum. Each group wants to have the curriculum reflect its perspective of history and no one else's.

  The discipline to start with, I feel, is systems thinking. It is not just a politically neutral vehicle, but a powerful way to involve students in generative learning. Already, grass roots activities are spreading in schools, through the enthusiastic efforts of individual teachers and administrators. In Ridgewood, New Jersey, for example, Information Management Systems director Richard Langheim and elementary school principal Tim Lucas have begun incorporating system dynamics models in classrooms, all the way down to kindergarten. A teacher might take a children's literature story and lead the class in building a systems map of the strategies the protagonist used. Then the teacher would discuss how the story might turn

* The Ridgewood systems thinking courses were developed by Richard Langheim, Executive Director Information Management Systems, Ridgewood Public Schools, Ridgewood, New Jersey. A recently published book on systems thinking and modeling in schools is *Classroom Dynamics* by Ellen B. Mandinach and Hugh F. Cline (1994, Hillsdale, N.J.: Lawrence Erlbaum Associates).

out if the protagonist followed some other leverage options. "Because we found it easier to ask for forgiveness than to ask for permission," says Tim Lucas, "we just began doing it in small but incremental ways."*

Starting with this small grass-roots effort, students and teachers will gain the capability to expose the points of leverage needed to reform the schools themselves, from the inside out.

■ *Weaken the stranglehold of fragmentation on curriculum and subject content.* Calls for curricular integration are not new, but they always seem to fail. On many school levels, chair people of curricula areas are like lords of fiefdoms; they are not about to give up their positions of authority to move toward an integrated, systemic curriculum. Practitioners of educational innovations tend too often to promote one "breakthrough" at the expense of another, instead of implementing them to complement and reinforce each other. For example, "writing as process" teaches children to approach a writing assignment as a series of steps, as well as an end product. Meanwhile, the "whole language" movement argues that reading should be taught in terms of whole pieces of literature, not through the fragmented method of phonics. The most extreme practitioners of both camps get locked in philosophical battles, ignoring the fact that some students learn from each approach and many would be best served by integrating both approaches.

■ *Promote dialogue between parents, bureaucrats, administrators, teachers, students, and government leaders.* Again, start small and work incrementally. Schools which fail to open dialogue will find themselves giving in more and more to pressure groups. The work of suspending assumptions and treating each other as colleagues will not be easy, but schools cannot improve unless the "pressure" to reform them is generated by the community as a whole, not just by particular groups.

Some people argue that because public schools are a monopoly, run by the government without competition, the "pressure-group" style of governance is unshakable. But schools are not a monopoly. If they continue to fail, then the culture will turn for its learning to another, less influenceable source—perhaps one which we know today as "MTV" or "Nintendo."

77 Can Large Government Learn?

The challenge of strategic change at the Australian Taxation Office *Bill Godfrey*

When Rick Ross met him, Bill Godfrey was a Second Commissioner to the Australian Tax Office (ATO). This is the Australian counterpart to the U.S. Internal Revenue Service. They have 18,000 employees, and a highly bureaucratic tradition. The ATO Commissioner, Trevor Boucher (who is presently the Australian ambassador to the Organization for Economic Cooperation and Development), wanted to start busting the bureaucracy and bring the ATO into the twenty-first century. Bill's need to implement the learning organizations concepts in practice led to the development of a prototype seminar on learning organization leadership, which more than seventy ATO managers and fifty executives from other organizations attended during the first year. As a result of this and subsequent experience, Bill is in a unique position to judge the effectiveness of learning organization work in large governments. Bill continues to be a leading proponent of these concepts in Australia, in both the public and private sectors.

Since 1984, we have been trying to increase the capacity of the Australian Tax Office to learn. The ATO, the Australian equivalent to the U.S. Internal Revenue Service, employs 18,000 people. It is charged with collecting income and sales tax, enforcing tax laws, and administering Australia's child support laws. Our experience, I believe, shows that it is possible—even for a large government agency—to change from a typical inward-looking bureaucracy to a responsive, flexible service organization. It is too early to call our journey a complete success, and we may never "get there," in the sense of reaching our goals completely, but the indications are that our direction is right.

Arguably, no organization needs to adapt to changing times as much as large national governments, but governments are difficult soil for learning organizations to grow in. Unless all these conditions apply or can be arranged, the chances of success are very low indeed.

- First, there must be leadership at the top of the organization—ideally a highly visible, active, and persistent chief executive. In most countries, this "chief civil servant" would be the permanent head of an agency. (Sir Humphrey Appleby held such a post in the British television show "Yes, Minister," although he did not preside over a learning organization.) The American system, in which there is a change in permanent head every time there is a change in government, may be structurally hostile to learning.

- The leader must be prepared to stand up publicly for a direction and set of values which are compatible with learning. (I hesitate to use the word "vision" because that implies a clarity which may not initially be present.)

- There must be support from the organization's political head, such as the Minister or Secretary (the Jim Hacker character in "Yes, Minister").

- There generally must be a crisis: some situation or event which prompts the organization to plan in a longer time frame than usual.

- There must be a sensibly ample amount of time allowed for the changes to take hold.

- Finally, I suspect there must be some willingness, by the government managers and workers, to think of themselves as delivering "service" to identifiable "customers" (even if the "service" is extracting taxes from their hard-earned income!). For a variety of reasons, this customer-oriented attitude is rarer than it should be: government offices cover an astonishingly wide range of activities, and it can be difficult to delineate precisely who the customer is of a State or Commerce Department function.

Even if these conditions are met, there is still the bureaucracy to contend with. Of course, bureaucracies everywhere fiercely resist flexibility. But consider how many pressures exist that particularly entrench bureaucracy in national governments such as Australia's:

- Most pay structures effectively prevent anyone from entering public service above a base-level post. There is little chance for outside, experienced private sector managers to join our ranks in any responsible position.

- It can be quite difficult to reward good performance or deter poor performance, in part because there are very few promotions available, and severe restrictions on pay scales.

- The formal structures common to government service reinforce loyalty to narrow chimneys and functions, not to the whole agency—let alone the whole government or nation. The Australian Public Service Act even *defines* a public servant as "the holder of a position."

■ When I first entered government service, after a managerial career in the private sector, I was staggered at how difficult it is for civil servants and politicians to give praise. It is difficult even to praise highly visible success—let alone honest experiments which did not work. Yet praise and encouragement are crucial intrinsic rewards, especially when more formal raises are limited.

■ Government officials work in an atmosphere of investigation: by auditors, parliamentary committees, commissions, lobbyists, political parties, factions within the government, and news media. All of these entities inquire publicly into the most minute details of day-to-day administration, and use evidence of error as part of their political maneuvering for advantage. This encourages (among government employees) a defensive mind set, a preference for avoiding the controversial, an emphasis on correct process even at the expense of good outcomes, and a strong underpinning for central "command and control" in an attempt to prevent local error. And, of course, no matter how much an individual manager within a government agency may hate this form of control, the more we view it as inevitable and unavoidable, the more we reinforce it.

■ The heart of the problem is the way public servants are regarded. In Western culture, there are two primary philosophical views. In the "Anglo-Saxon" view, based on English "public/civil service" tradition, the purpose of public administration is creating quality outcomes— delivering a service. In the "European" view, derived from the Napoleonic Code, the dominant goal is the quality of process—how well the organization conforms to regulations, rules, and the policy dictates of *fonctionnaires.*° Designers and critics of government aspire to choose both. They want perfect service *and* perfect adherence to the rules. But in a fast-changing world, this is not an option. Empower front-line staff to deliver, and orient them to customer service, and ordinary common sense will recognize that some of the rules will cease to be relevant.

° I've gained some of my perspective on these issues from hearing a talk given by Otto Brodtrick of the Canadian Auditor-General's office.

Thus, a very important debate is just beginning in many governments. Can large governments redefine their accountability and control mechanisms in the interests of becoming more effective? Will mechanisms for building unity—such as shared vision and articulating mental models—help, or does the political fixation on error undermine those too completely? This debate has particular urgency, because the viability of nations and communities depends on the ability of governments to learn. If we don't learn, people will seek to bypass the political process. Perhaps describing what we've learned along the way at the Australian Tax Office, and what we still want to achieve, will add some hopefulness to the debate.

Building a system for trusting taxpayers

WE DID NOT SET OUT TO BECOME A "LEARNING ORGANIZATION." INDEED, we were not aware of the similar journeys in the United States and elsewhere which led to the term being coined. Our aim was to improve tax administration. The change process really began with the appointment of a new commissioner in 1984. The vision of what we were trying to become, and to achieve, evolved over several years.

Besides having a committed strong leader in the new Commissioner, and receiving strong encouragement and support from a powerful and reformist minister, we also had an opportunity in the 1983 Public Service Reforms. These laws were designed to "free up" control by central agencies and encourage greater use of private enterprise–style management practices, including the decentralization and devolution of authority.

Moreover, we had the impetus of a crisis. The Australian assessment system (in which the ATO laboriously checked all tax returns) was sinking under its own weight. We had to move to "self-assessment" (in which taxpayers calculate what they owe). This meant that, for the first time in our history, we would have to adopt a philosophy of "voluntary compliance." We would have to assume that, given the right help and information, taxpayers would get their taxes right.

All types of taxpayers exist—including those who should not be trusted. So we had to choose at ATO to be optimists—to deliberately see the full half of the glass of beer, not the empty half. Moreover, instead of operating without trust, we had to find ways to build trust, and reasons for people to work with us.

We first introduced the idea of formal market segmentation in 1988. At the time, there had been little attempt to analyze who our customers were, and what they wanted from us, anywhere in the public service. For example, we now realized that in addition to collecting revenue, it was part of our job to *minimize the cost to the community in time and effort.* Many taxpayers would need effective help and service, while audit processes would educate and support taxpayers, as well as performing their traditional enforcement task. Eventually, for business customers, we would combine separate functions into multidisciplinary teams: "one-stop shops" of tax advice.

It took about two years before these imperatives began to replace the "We're right, and they're wrong" mind-set within ATO. Even then, progress was very uneven. We began to formally recognize that success in achieving our goals depended on our skill at building partnership with customer groups. This, in turn, gave us a valuable platform for building self-managing teams, an endeavor which is still in its very early stages.

Training teams to work together

LIKE MOST BUREAUCRACIES, ATO INHERITED A HIERARCHICAL, FUNC-tionally based style of management. Work groups typically consisted of groups working in parallel on a single specialized process—often in competition with their peers in other parts of the service. There was little scope for initiative and no tradition of participation. Management-union relationships were strongly adversarial.

The first triggers for change were a massive new computer project, and a public service–wide move to simplify our appallingly complicated pay and classification structures. The computer project was technologically complex and audacious, but its effect on staff and the way they worked was, if anything, even greater. While the government needed assurances that there would be a return on its one billion dollar investment, the union insisted on full work force participation in whatever changes were decided. Against the background of these complex negotiations, the pay structure review provided the opportunity to pilot new ways of working and new forms of relationship. Before long, 8,000 or more jobs were redesigned. Processing a tax return had previously involved thirteen different areas of the office, but was now conducted by multiskilled teams. For many staff, this was their first experience with having their opinions asked and working in a team or project style.

We are continually revamping the promotion process to reward more flexible career paths—a slow process in a climate of economic constraint. But there is more leverage, we have found, in the realm of intrinsic rewards—perhaps precisely because they had been treated so cynically in the past. To use this leverage, our top leaders had to show that they were committed to the changes we were putting in place. The Commissioner, for example, devoted a huge amount of time and effort explaining in public forums what ATO was trying to do, why it was doing it, and where we were succeeding. This was done partly to gain public support, but equally to demonstrate support to ATO staff.

As we began to change our infrastructure, we quickly saw weaknesses in our traditional approaches to training. At the lowest levels, this meant reliance on the "sit by Nellie" approach—which perpetuated practices that had been passed on through generations of clerks. In higher echelons, we relied heavily on universities, professional bodies, and specialists. Rarely was the training linked to work being done in the field, nor was learning time well integrated with the cycle of peaks and troughs in work pressure. As a result, neither managers nor staff felt much commitment to training and development, which was viewed as either "time off" or an annoying interruption.

We recognized that we needed to re-create training and development as one part of a whole system of policies (job design, rewards and promotion, work force planning, career planning) which might help us change attitudes and behavior. The most successful approaches, we have found, begin with whole teams. In one program, we brought the top management team together for a program of building technical, interpersonal, and self-awareness skills, particularly reflection and mental models skills. The rest of the organization's reaction to this program was largely bemusement, partly because the participants found it so difficult to explain what they actually *did* during the sessions. But the program sent a clear message that learning organization skills are significant for everyone. In later programs, we made sure to invite participants from other organizations—public and private—which helped increase our awareness of others' practices and mental models.°

° These follow-up programs were based upon a Leading Learning Organizations program conducted in Australia by Rick and Joyce Ross. Rick Ross has also made a one-hour video which we used widely within ATO to "spread the message."

Even after eight years, our vision of our goal is continually being reframed. Some new practices are well established. Others, such as systems thinking, have barely begun and have certainly not yet taken strong root. But the organization is well past the point where reversion will occur. Too many people have changed their view of the ATO world and of their own role in it. The Commissioner's faith in people is being amply justified by the number of people who are working together to create visions which they share for their programs.

The challenge to "Pooh bears"

I<small>T IS BECOMING A BIT FASHIONABLE IN PRIVATE ENTERPRISE CIRCLES TO</small> say: "We need transformational change. Governments are incapable of it. Therefore, it's up to business to do the job." That shows a dangerous error in logic for society as a whole. Business must take a lead role—that is a necessary condition, but it is not sufficient for success. An untransformed government process has immense power to block much of the learning which business, acting alone, might engender. But transforming government process probably means changing not just the systems of particular agencies, but political culture as a whole.

Any major effort to transform a public sector body makes it painfully clear how hostile the accepted forms of political debate and public accountability can be to organizational learning. When Pooh Bear was asked, "condensed milk or honey?" he said, "Both." So do politicians. Good current service and blind obedience to the rules are incompatible. Yet most designers and critics of government are unwilling to give up one or the other. The ultimate result will always be poor service and no learning.

78 A Letter to an Aspiring Policymaker

Donald N. Michael

This article is for people who have aimed themselves at a career in policy—people driven by a desire for a viable ecology, Third World development, building more livable cities, the content and delivery of large-scale health care, education both for work and for citizenship, profitable economies, or simply a successful strategy. But can policy-making institutions, whether public or private, become learning organizations? More than twenty years ago, Donald N. Michael's 1973 book On Learning to Plan—And Planning to Learn *(1985, San Francisco: Jossey-Bass) as-*

serted what was then a radical idea: policymakers should deliberately give up the presumption that they knew what they were doing. As Don continued to talk and write about the learning implications of governance, his ideas have influenced a generation of planners—including most of the people who reintroduced "learning organizations" to the business world in the early 1980s.

What does it mean to be responsible as a policymaker in an increasingly interdependent, interconnected, and constantly *changing* world? *You won't know—and nobody knows—what is necessary* in advance for formulating policies that fulfill your intentions. This is because people are unavoidably ignorant in three ways:

1. We do not comprehend our complex circumstances; we have no viable theory of social change under turbulent conditions. (We can't even correctly predict birthrate changes or the economy beyond two quarters or so! And the complexities of large scale, nonlinear, human systems may always elude us.)

2. Even if we knew all the data we would still disagree about their meaning. There are always multiple stories to be told about why the human condition is as it is and no way to settle on the one true story.

3. What we choose to pay attention to, and to seek or avoid, mostly depends on our unconscious needs and motives—some genetically inbuilt, some culturally provided, but all essentially hidden from ourselves as we conduct our daily affairs, even as we claim rational reasons for what we do or don't do.

Is this letter, then, a counsel of despair? No! There is a way to meet our enthusiasms and ethical obligations—*by learning our way into the future.* Most people, especially those in the institutions and organizations with whom you will be policy-making, don't know or want to know that they can't know the answers. But you know better! Having eaten of the tree of knowledge, you can no longer remain in the Eden of ignorance about our ignorance.

PLANNING AS LEARNING

To meet your ethical responsibilities, you must conduct your activities as *learning*—exploring, discovering, experimenting—activities. Learning depends absolutely on being able to *acknowledge specific uncertainties*—unsettled questions for which we will never know the answers. Consider, for example, the variety of uncertainties—about which policymakers could admit uncertainty, but generally do not—in health care, nuclear waste disposal, economic strategy, childhood education, and adolescent socialization.

The acknowledgment of specific uncertainties becomes the basis for building a learning system via *error embracing*. Competent policymakers know that errors will happen as policies are implemented. Based on specific uncertainties, they design organizational capabilities in advance to embrace possible errors as soon as they occur, and use the resulting understandings to continually adjust the policy.

In themselves, acknowledging specific uncertainties and embracing error will engender honesty and integrity. And they are the operational preconditions for resilience—the capacity to adjust and change. But they, in turn, depend on other norms and skills:

- *Boundary Spanning:* Understanding the inevitable differences in turf control, time frames, conceptual perspectives, and human relationships, and using them constructively. (For example: design the policy so that recipients monitor the results as part of the error-detecting processes.)
- *Coping with Role Ambiguity:* Understanding that, in a learning mode, your role is not well defined, and you must learn to protect yourself from possible serious emotional upset.
- *Developing Interpersonal Communication Skills:* For example, learning to listen carefully without interrupting, and making sure you understand what the other person means without rushing on to make your own case.

〉〉 See Balancing Advocacy with Inquiry, page 253.

THE EDUCATIONAL IMPERATIVE

No one can make policy by him- or herself. Not only do you need political clout to carry the day, but your emotional stamina depends on having a support group. Thus, to enlarge your community of allies, you must become an educator, teaching others about the imperative to conduct policy making as a learning activity.

Consider, for example, the possibilities of training community members to participate in planning the implementation of an education policy that affects them, so that they learn to monitor its impact, and they can participate in the revisions of the policy.

Uncertainty and error make for feelings of vulnerability; you must accept the serious risk of living with what you don't know. But this has always been the condition of creative humans. Welcome to the world of policymakers as learners!

79 The Local Community as a Learning Organization*

Charlotte Roberts

* We are grateful to Jackson Bundy and Preston McLaurin of the Greenwood Chamber of Commerce for their help with this story.

How far can the boundaries of an effective learning organization extend? To 100 people within the same building? To 1,000 in the same function or metropolitan area? Many of us are coming to believe that the most effective boundary of the "learning organization" is larger than the organization itself—it extends to the geographic community in which the organization (or its facility) resides.

Increasingly, community leaders are realizing that their communities or regions need to build shared vision and plan for the future—as a whole. Citizens are recognizing that if they do not participate in defining the future character of their community, it may slip to the lowest common denominator. The process of building community vision often starts with the political, business, or public education leadership, but it picks up steam when a critical mass of people from all sectors begin to ask together: What does the community need to do to thrive in the future years? How will we be able to flourish, not just survive? How do we get every member excited and learning about our collective future?

One such community, whose experience has educated me about the potential of a "learning community," is Greenwood, South Carolina. Greenwood is located in the western part of the state, about an hour's drive south of Spartanburg. A group of community leaders—including Chamber of Commerce executive vice president Jackson Bundy, CEO Matt Self (of Greenwood Mills, a textile manufacturer based in the area), school superintendent Jim McAbee, and many others—have led Greenwood's journey. It began with a collaborative effort among local business people to pursue the study and practice of quality, as taught by Dr. W. Edwards Deming. They quickly began to recognize the pivotal role of the rest of the community. To *really* build a work force capable of carrying on the principles of quality, the public schools, hospitals, religious organizations, local government, and others would have to be involved.

Greenwood, like all of America, faced deep, persistent quality of life issues: teenage pregnancy, poor health conditions, youth violence, poverty and hunger, illiteracy in and out of the workplace, dissatisfaction and rebellion against traditional education, unemployment, and so on. Many dedicated individuals and groups had tackled these issues in isolation; but the efforts were only successful in part, because no one group had leverage over all aspects of any problem.

Building a learning community

CHOOSING TO CREATE A LEARNING ORGANIZATION THROUGHOUT A GEOgraphic community leads to an ongoing journey, with more than its share of pitfalls and hurdles. First, the community must develop committed leadership. Who really cares enough about the vision to take a public stand in favor of it, even in the face of cynicism and chronic problems? At first, a small group of believers tends to emerge—people who can reinforce and coach each other. The leadership of this cadre becomes sustained not through their personalities or influence, but through their concepts; they refine and shape the goals of their learning community, so that their vision becomes more than just a "do-good" idea. Through their concerted effort, including the use of well-crafted presentations and open, inquiry-filled meetings, the word spreads to others in the area, and more people begin to see the value.

Involvement of others creates another hurdle. In some communities, different constituencies have never collaborated. If the business sector proposes a noble and lofty vision, the educators and lower economic levels may be suspicious. If the churches start the effort, businesses and government may shy away. And if the original leaders come from politics or government, others see it as a gimmick for reelection. It may be especially difficult to cross the gap between ethnic and racial groups, in both major cities and smaller communities.

As others become involved, the original leadership group typically experiences a crisis of diversity, in which they must either yield influence to other people with different styles, or see the effort's impact dwindle. The skills of team learning and dialogue are vital at this stage, so that people can learn to learn and lead together, encompassing their varied perspectives.

As they explore their common problems, the Greenwood groups have found high leverage in the discipline of mental models. "It's about telling the truth and encouraging others to do the same," said Superintendent of Schools McAbee.

The "learning community" effort will inevitably expand into new parts of the community's systems. Greenwood's leaders even involved the state department of education to build a wider network of support. Learning begins to affect more aspects of individual lives, including self-esteem, aspirations, perception of authority, and relationships. In Greenwood, they have gone all the way to the maternity ward of their hospital with the "Born to Read" program, which demonstrates the importance of reading and talking with young children, and in the process, shows parents that they can be capable and competent. To make this sort of accomplishment, a basic assumption must be encouraged: every person deserves the opportunity to be seen and heard as a valuable person who can contribute to the community.

We believe learning communities are possible and the efforts to build them are vitally important. We look forward to hearing more from people who have begun implementing a vision of a community where each person is whole and productive in his own right. Stay tuned!

DISCOVERING COMMON GROUND by Marvin Weisbord and thirty-five international co-authors (1992, San Francisco: Berrett-Koehler).

"Future search" conferences can be applied in many different situations, but they are particularly appropriate for community issues, where dozens of people all seem to be blaming each other, and nothing seems to get accomplished. You bring together as many different stakeholders as possible. They focus on a theme. Suddenly, the whole community is in the room solving the problem together, instead of having an expert come in with a solution. Order emerges out of chaos.

This book, compiled by Marvin Weisbord, is a collection of case studies that shows search conferences used in a wide variety of circumstances—including several organized by the originators of the technique: Fred and Merrelyn Emery, and the late Eric Trist. Full of correspondence, "notes from the field," and artifacts, the book is like rummaging through a conference organizer's file drawer—which may appeal to professional practitioners more than managers. But if search conferences interest you, then the book is vital: it goes into practice and pitfalls in detail. — RR

Frontiers

~~~~~~~~~~~~~~~~~~~~~~~~~~~~~~~~~~~~~

"Frontiers" are broad areas of learning organization practice that don't quite fit into any of the five disciplines and that may even evolve into significant learning organization disciplines in their own right. In this Fieldbook, we focus on two significant frontiers: "organizations as communities," a body of theory and practice grounded in democracy and the community development tradition; and "learning laboratories," or the art of creating and using environments (abetted by, but not limited to, the use of computer-based models) that expand managers' capabilities.

80 Organizations as Communities

Bryan Smith

When I was growing up, my parents owned and ran a summer resort north of Toronto, Canada. People often returned for the same two weeks each year, for thirty years or more. It was fascinating to watch the community reemerge each summer. I had a sense that my family was the glue that created and maintained that environment. Everyone who stayed there regularly became a friend of our family. I think organizations are similarly defined by the commitment which people build to each other and to something they value in common. That is the purpose of the work described here.

On the most practical level, redefining organizations as communities means using the approaches of community development in organizations, particularly business organizations. It also means seeing organizations as centers of meaning and larger purpose to which people can commit themselves as free citizens in a democratic society. And it involves developing new answers to such nuts-and-bolts questions as how and why people get hired and fired, who makes what decisions, and how to assure people's contribution to success is fairly rewarded. Finally, "organizations as communities" reflects a growing body of thought about an organization's conscience—the role which corporations, for example, must play in our nation and in the world if they are to attract and retain the people with the most to offer.

81 Merging the Best of Two Worlds

The Core Processes of Organizations as Communities

Juanita Brown, David Isaacs

Juanita Brown is an organizational strategist with twenty years' experience integrating business strategy with community development practices. David Isaacs is a leadership coach with experience promoting organizational learning in both nonprofit and for-profit organizations. Innovators in this emerging field, Juanita and David have developed the material included here in collaboration with their colleague Sherrin Bennett of Interactive Learning Systems. Juanita and David are based in Mill Valley, California.

When you think of the word "corporation," what images, thoughts, or associations come to your mind?

Now, think of the word "community." What images does that word suggest?

The responses people make to these questions are surprisingly consistent. "Corporation" brings up images of authority, bureaucracy, competition, power, and profit. It also evokes images of machines, where order prevails and the chain of command is reinforced by "superiors" directing "subordinates."

By comparison, people describe a flood of varied images of "community." Some talk of barn raisings, or volunteers helping out in community campaigns. Others think of town meetings, democracy, and personal responsibility. Still others talk about the feeling of living in a town or a neighborhood where there is cooperation and a high quality of life. People think of commitment, team spirit, and fun—of education where they feel involved with their children's lives, and of helping to maintain a clean environment. Whatever the specifics may be, the images always evoke a richer, more involved sense of ourselves in relationship to a larger whole.

COMMUNITY

The word "community" has old roots, going back to the Indo-European base *mei,* meaning "change" or "exchange." Apparently this joined with another root, *kom,* meaning "with," to produce an Indo-European word *kommein:* shared by all.

We think the idea of "change or exchange, shared by all," is pretty close to the sense of community in organizations today. Community building is a core strategy for sharing among all its members the burdens and the benefits of change and exchange. —JB

For millennia, communities have been the most powerful mechanisms for creating human cooperation and reliable interdependence. By contrast, corporations and large-scale organizations have been a powerful force only for the past hundred years or so. By fulfilling their economic mission, industrial enterprises improved living standards for many millions of people. But they also separated us from our traditional ties to the land, to our families, and to communities of place—without filling the vacuum left by diminished sense of common purpose and social values. We see the results in the workplace in drug abuse, personal stress, family crises, and health problems—all of which cause as many problems for the organization as they do for society and for the affected individuals.

People have always found their sources of meaning where they spend the majority of their time. Most of us today spend that time in the workplace. But even the term "workplace" hearkens back to an era before industrialization, when people used to live and work in one locale. That place was where people learned, through practice, the skills of local democratic participation and the meaning of the common good. Today, if we want to avoid further breakdown of the web of meaning anywhere in society, then organizations can best serve that purpose by becoming practice fields for the skills that will lead to democratic behavior. This is not primarily a humanitarian question or a moral issue; it represents a corporation's *real* opportunity to contribute to the renewal of a democratic society. It is also a practical requirement for maintaining the health, vitality, and productivity of the people who will interact directly with the organization throughout its life. It's no coincidence that the call today for "empowerment" and "self-management," as keys to competitiveness, is linked to the need to develop the fundamental skills of informed participation.

We don't think organizations should ever replace local communities. In fact, most people will probably continue to belong to several communities at once, including the community of work. Nor should the old "company town" be revived. Company towns and all other forms of benevolent paternalism discourage the active personal responsibility and self-management required to sustain the vitality of true workplace communities. Finally, the reconception of organizations as communities does not mean throwing out the entrepreneurial spirit of the business world. Instead, it provides the chance to merge the best of community traditions with the best of the free-enterprise system. There is a growing body of evidence that, in the years to come, a combined organization-community form can produce better performance than any of the traditional forms of organization. But it needs to be designed not only to support the personal *experience* of community, but also to assure the long-term *sustainability* of community. This means that any designer of organizations as communities will immediately get into questions of infrastructure, and how the people in these new workplace communities will govern themselves.

The action techniques for this work emerged from the community development movement and from voluntary organizations. Miles Horton and the Highlander Institute were pioneers. Paulo Freire's work in Brazilian education, the tradition of Scandinavian study circles, and the community activism of Saul Alinsky's Industrial Areas Foundation are key influences. More recently M. Scott Peck and the Foundation for Community Encouragement have added to the range of approaches. Marvin Weisbord's work in developing Future Search techniques (see page 504) are an extension of community development tradition. And whether people agree with their methods or not, there's no doubt that Gandhi, Martin Luther King, Jr., and Cesar Chavez were all gifted leaders in designing creative approaches for engaging large numbers of people to work together toward a shared vision of a better future.

In business circles in the past, the idea of gathering and encouraging high emotional involvement by hundreds or thousands of people made corporate leaders nervous. But times are changing. Today, to capitalize on shifting markets and customer needs, fast responses by large numbers of people are critical. Community development helps break down the "corporate arthritis" and "hardening of the categories" which slow down effective action out on the front lines.

It is also worth noting that the concept of community organization is rooted solidly in our democratic traditions. The United States and Canada have a history of voluntary associations in which people regularly helped each other and collaborated as responsible citizens. The Quakers and New Englanders in their town meetings, and the establishment of the frontier communities of the West, were all based on people living up to their commitments to themselves and each other. All of these communities governed themselves through local, informed, democratic participation. The tradition continues today in Neighborhood Crime Watch groups, town councils, Little Leagues, the Cancer Society, the Heart Association, the United Way, and a myriad of other community efforts. These remain as a living legacy of our capacity as a people to support and serve the common good, as well as our individual interests.

You could argue that the American dream can only thrive if our business organizations also tap into that same vitality, and that same community tradition of service, informed participation, and contribution to the common good. Luckily, we are beginning to see businesses experiment with community building practices. For example:

■ Motorola has made a huge investment in capability and learning, not only with its own employees, but with the local school districts that provide the continuity of future talent for the company. Retirees, the "elders" in the community, are serving as adjunct faculty at learning sites, thus bridging between the past and the future of the Motorola community.

■ At Steelcase, managers have created physical "neighborhoods" where product and business teams work together in proximity. They have designed a type of community "commons" adjacent to these office neighborhoods to encourage the kind of informal conversation and collaboration that we associate with small towns.

■ Herman Miller has focused on the nature of the organization's "covenant" with employees—both the rights and responsibilities of membership in the corporate community, as well as the idea of leadership as community service.

Over the last several years, together with key people at a number of organizations, we have identified several core processes which are fundamental to creating and sustaining organizations as communities. We call these the "C" words. They involve processes, similar to business processes, for enhancing *Capability, Commitment, Contribution, Continuity, Collaboration,* and *Conscience.*

CORE PROCESS #1: CAPABILITY

Vital communities are capable: they have the skills, knowledge, and personal qualities to renew themselves and reinvent their future. They do this by encouraging learning and improvement among their citizens as a *collective* undertaking.

"Embracing this governing idea in organizations," says Bryan Smith, "requires managers to have a higher level of faith in the capability of people to develop over the long run." Company leaders must ask: Are we the unique kind of community that can inspire our members' best thinking? That people want to be a part of? Where members can really learn, grow, and increase their overall capacity even during times of crisis and change?

In an organization based primarily on democratic principles, learning can come only from members *wanting* to learn things they care about. For example, people learn to run great meetings when they see that great meetings need to take place. This style of "just-in-time" learning (where coaching, training, and the actual work are integrated into a common process) is enhanced by community support. In healthy work communities there are also "replays," where members gather in the twilight of a common undertaking—anything from a meeting to a new product introduction—and reflect together, as if surveying the field of play, on how it might be improved next time.

The lifeblood of the organization as community is the capacity for dialogue—not just within a team, but throughout the enterprise. If intellectual capital is the key asset in the knowledge era, then the capacity for great conversations about things that matter is essential for breakthrough thinking and collaborative innovation.

See "Dialogue," page 357.

CORE PROCESS #2: COMMITMENT

Commitment builds when people are an active part of the experience of creating something they value together. Using common language, symbols, and metaphors which evoke positive emotion also help bring people together. That's why using the language of "community" can be valuable. It calls forth an intuitive image of mutual commitment and contribution—as opposed to training people how they "should behave" in a "high-commitment work system."

To build community in an organization under the stress of unrelenting change, serious attention must be paid to mutual commitment: What commitment is the organization asking of its employees, and what commitments will the organization make and keep in return? The answer will vary from situation to situation.

Many employees are willing to commit themselves to a truly engaging purpose, larger than just personal self-interest. They are willing to give of themselves to help create the collective enterprise. But we live in a free-enterprise system. Therefore, the employees also seek concrete evidence that the collective enterprise is committed to them. They prefer to see tangible results from the investment of their efforts. For example, it's hard to build strong commitment when thousands of members of the community see themselves being cast out by losing their jobs. If people are given the hard economic truths, they will be willing to share the pain during hard times. But as key stakeholders, they reasonably want to share in the tangible rewards from helping to save the day.

Recently, faced with a budget crunch, a division of Intel instituted a graduated pay cut. The highest-paid employees, including executives, reduced their pay by 10 percent while the lowest-paid employees lost nothing and there were no layoffs. Volkswagen Europe, in similar circumstances, moved to a shortened, four-day, twenty-nine-hour workweek to save 30,000 jobs among its 100,000 work force. In other companies employees have volunteered for early retirement or temporary leave without pay. These are all examples of community development principles at work. A critical factor is for executives to be honest with everyone about the realities of life in the business, so that people can actively join together at all levels to determine fair ways to solve common problems.

CORE PROCESS #3: CONTRIBUTION

Every day, people in stultified offices moan to themselves: "We're overwhelmed with paperwork. If we could only have computers." But in a community-oriented organization, those people might collectively embark on a drive to get computers. They might conduct their own analyses, and discover how their computer needs linked to the company's overall technology strategy. They would end up making far better use of the tools than if someone had imposed them. By contrast, many computer introductions have failed, with huge resistance, because simple principles of community development have not been applied.

Essentially, people want to give, especially if it's to something they think is needed and worthwhile. That's why it's important to develop ways for people to see clearly how their daily work makes a real contribution to the organization's success. Business process improvement incorporates this concept. However, unless it is seen as one key to building community, people feel like *they've* been reengineered, rather than the work process.

Healthy communities provide opportunities for the full diversity of members' talents and contributions to the community's sustenance, not just in narrowly defined roles. Each person's gifts are unique; each enables the community to continue developing and serving the common good.

For example, at a large, very technologically advanced plant, we involved all the employees in strategic planning. One of the maintenance workers became a lead member of a plant-wide singing group which began to write and perform songs about the strategic planning and visioning effort. His music helped engage everyone in a common image of the future—and was a lot of fun. No one would ever have known his talents if we hadn't had a "volunteer sign-up" process where people could offer whatever they thought would help out the overall effort.

In a community model of contribution, a company's hiring and interviewing systems track the multiple talents people have that they never shared on the job before because no one ever asked. Reward systems recognize people for volunteerism—for tasks they undertake, on their own initiative, outside of their ordinary scope.

CORE PROCESS #4: CONTINUITY

Communities can't survive without some measure of continuity. If we want to gain the benefits of healthy communities in the workplace, we need to become more creative about how to build some sources of continuity. Otherwise, the knowledge of mature citizens literally gets lost in the constant "churn" of career moves.

For example, in many companies, there is a tacit mental model that managers who stay in their jobs longer than two years are considered "dead wood" or "unmotivated." A community-oriented workplace would foster a different view of career paths, allowing people to develop continuity and longer term accountability for results, without sacrificing their careers. Already, in many workplaces, employees can be compensated at higher levels without having to change job locations, by gaining a broader range of skills or taking on more tasks. In the future, if people *do* change jobs or work sites, part of their compensation could be based on how well they serve as bridges of continuity to whoever replaces them. Some people might have rotating assignments, while continuing to serve as mentors and resources to their "home units" for a time.

See "Free Agency, Employment Stability, and Community Boundaries," page 520.

An institutional memory is one of the most critical factors for community continuity. In preindustrial times, the community's memory was transmitted by word of mouth. Elders kept and shared knowledge of "best practices": "How we planted, harvested, and distributed the fruits of our labor." Today, the organizational counterpart to that knowledge ("How we developed and marketed a new product") can be captured and shared through computer networks and data banks. Technology supports a common knowledge base that the community can draw on for years.

Other aspects of institutional memory must be carried person-to-person. For example, organizations have difficulty maintaining continuity unless they create ways to help new members understand the rights, responsibilities, and practices of the learning community. To provide continuity in self-managing teams, it is also valuable for organizations to encourage rotating team leadership, even at very senior levels, through innovations in personnel practices, performance standards, and pay systems. If one person moves on, others retain the history, vision, and values. A team doesn't have to start all over because a new leader comes in who wants to "make his own mark."

CORE PROCESS #5: COLLABORATION

Developing reliable interdependence is the essence of effective collaboration in a community. Community development is interested in building collaboration across very large populations by creating a web of multiple constituencies and stakeholders—engaging, involving, and mobilizing members until there is a critical mass of perhaps hundreds or thousands of people who can move together on a common path. They may move autonomously in many different locations, but they move with a clear shared vision and overall strategy in common. Organization development and team building, by contrast, have often focused on building collaboration in smaller groups.

Collaboration does not live in the abstract. It depends, for example, on the web of information which, in thriving communities, flows freely in all directions. When members know what's going on in the community and why, they can act together autonomously to achieve common goals without being supervised or monitored. Town criers served the public information function in medieval communities; local newspapers and radio play that role in towns and cities today. In organizations, the function is often served by computer networks and electronic mail, as well as by organization-wide learning processes. For example, in new interactive forms of strategic planning, people gather regularly to share information about progress and clarify direction, in an ongoing *organization-wide* collaborative learning process.

Collaboration is also strengthened through weaving the web of personal relationships. Even in the most technologically advanced organizations, people need face-to-face meetings and communication. Community builders recognize that, as human beings, we need the opportunity to respond *personally* to each other, and, as importantly, to feel known and "seen" as valued community contributors. Ultimately, a focus on personal relationships allows people to develop a web of mutual trust in which the members of the workplace community know they can count on one another and on their leaders for honesty and support. All of these factors—stakeholders, information, relationships, and trust— can be delicately woven together in a way that nurtures and sustains the process of collaboration for results.

CORE PROCESS #6: CONSCIENCE

All healthy communities incorporate processes which could be described as "conscience" mechanisms. The organization finds ways to embody or invoke guiding principles, ethics, and values such as service, trust, and mutual respect. These, in turn, translate into daily actions and concrete decisions. But most organizational conscience mechanisms are tacit. Even when there is a value or mission statement, the question, "To what are we going to be responsible?" is rarely raised explicitly. Community building brings that question to the surface.

We often associate conscience with guilt—we speak of having a "guilty conscience." But it's more useful to think of people and organizations having a "positive conscience," stemming from the choice they have made to be responsible individual and organizational citizens. This is the basis of maintaining a democratic society.

We are beginning to accumulate evidence that having a conscience also pays off in the bottom line. A recent study showed that over an eleven-year period net profits grew 756 percent in companies which had an ethic of multiple stakeholder satisfaction and involvement, compared to a 1 percent increase in a comparable set of companies that kept to traditional management practices.°

Organizational conscience may ultimately take its shape as a Bill of Rights and Responsibilities for organizational citizens. Workplace constitutions, credos of conscience, and "green" policies have also been formed. The "famous" Johnson & Johnson Tylenol case is an example where a credo helped provide guidelines for practical decision making. When tainted Tylenol was discovered, J&J's leaders could quickly make the decision to immediately, publicly, remove all Tylenol from the nation's shelves, because they were following the organization's credo—which said that J&J's first responsibility was to provide quality products to doctors, nurses, and patients. This dramatic action helped ensure a reinstatement of both public trust and employee pride in the integrity of the company, and led to higher long-term sales.

Exploring the question of conscience is a first step toward repositioning the organization within *its* larger community. When corporations start to see themselves as active members of a larger interconnected web of concern for a positive future for all key stakeholders, then the community approach will begin to yield benefits in increasingly larger systems.

° The study was cited in "The Caring Company," a review of *Corporate Culture and Performance* by John Kotter and James Haskett, in *The Economist,* June 6, 1992, p. 75.

82 Bean Suppers
Building Capability for Learning at Hardee's Salt Lake City Franchise

Roger Peters

Roger Peters is a builder and architect who is now in the restaurant business—CEO of Terratron, a Hardee's franchise organization in Salt Lake City with about 3,500 employees.

According to Juanita Brown, the "bean suppers" which Roger describes are part of a long-standing tradition in community development work—"house meetings," where people gather together to create and reinforce a base of mutual support. "When everyone brings food to a potluck dinner," she says, "even if they feel too shy to speak, they have a way of actively connecting and contributing to something they believe in. Just as you would never refuse someone the chance to eat because they aren't 'important' enough, house meetings with food reinforce the idea that everyone is 'important' enough to contribute."

Though our company operates restaurants, I don't consider the business of food to be our most important activity. We are in the people business. Our organization is a gymnasium where people can exercise their learning. A lot of our people are wounded when they first come to us: they don't have any belief in their own original gifts or capabilities. Until their self-esteem can develop, learning doesn't take place. It certainly won't take place if we simply ordain it, or if we lecture people about "how to learn." We need to do fundamental work to bring people in the community to a level where they can truly participate. That fundamental work starts with being open in our conversations.

We call our gatherings "bean suppers." The term goes back to Rochester, Minnesota, where young doctors joining the Mayo Clinic were invited to Sunday night bean suppers. According to Mayo Clinic legends, the bean suppers on the third floor of the clinic's "Plumber House" had no agenda, but the conversations sometimes went on until the wee hours. Real breakthroughs for the future of the clinic took place at those bean suppers. In the early 1980s, as a builder, I was involved when this old house was demolished. While it stood abandoned, I went to the third floor and tried to capture in my imagination what had happened there.

But I soon forgot about it. I went into the business of Hardee's restaurants. I sometimes met with members of my management team in my house, but we always had an agenda. Then at a conference two years ago, while talking with Juanita Brown about dialogue and community, I remembered the Mayo Clinic experience. So I returned home and held our own first bean suppers—evening dinners, with food, with no agenda, with people from the organization who wanted to be there.

Those bean suppers were tremendously successful. People were contributing, proposing new projects, and talking freely about how they might learn more and how the organization could help them. At the office, they began to make contributions to the organization that were more powerful than anyone could anticipate. We began to think about where that motivation came from. People were thirsty for something meaningful to happen between them. Those bean suppers began to build our community.

We've had many bean suppers now. We have some of them in my house, some in others' houses. I had a special round table built, which fifteen or more people can gather around, with a view looking out over the city. The fact that people bring food and ideas ends up bringing the group together. On any night, there may be a bean supper for our organization occurring some place in Salt Lake City. There is a need for repeated contact to counteract the unwitting damage done in relationships every day.

Anyone is welcome to the bean suppers; no one has ever been told he or she has to come. That would be the epitome of the death of the whole feeling. We say there is no agenda, but people bring their own agendas. If they want to talk about something, we talk about it. People sometimes come to talk about something specific and return next time because they feel involved.

At first, we were so pleased that we began trying to add structure to the meetings. That destroyed what we were accomplishing and we went back to the original form. It took a while to realize that there was value simply in coming together. Sometimes the greatest value was apparent when others joined us—spouses who didn't work at Hardee's, but who became part of our expanded community. By including spouses in the relationship the company has with its people, we have improved the happiness of our families substantially, with real benefit to ourselves.

We've had a tremendous surge of success in the company since we strengthened this new community-oriented approach. The success is not just measured in numbers, but in the initiative which people take. For example, the teams from seven restaurants got together, approached the corporate leaders, and asked for "the opportunity to be responsible for the success of what we do." They asked to pick their own community leader from within their group. (By that time, "community leaders" had become our name for the leaders of the teams.) Only a year before, there wouldn't have been a chance of their asking for that degree of self-management. Now there was a strength which we have solidly appreciated.

83 Free Agency, Employment Stability, and Community Boundaries

Douglas Merchant

Three innovations in infrastructure for serving the community at AT&T or elsewhere

Douglas Merchant works for AT&T in the Corporate Human Resource Strategy and Planning organization. His career has been, as he puts it, "a twenty-three-year random walk throughout AT&T, beginning at Bell Labs." The breadth of his concept of community reflects some of the economic and policy planning he has done, as well as his experience managing a field sales branch. Merchant's colleague RuthAnn Prange, who joins him in describing the "Resource Link" mechanism on page 524, is in strategic human resource planning at AT&T. "I have come to feel that I can't be a high-quality 'community of one,'" she says, "unless I pay attention to the community aspects of the organization which I am part of."

Before the 1982 divestiture agreement which broke up the Bell System, AT&T had a purpose which had been stable for more than fifty years—providing the United States with universal telephone service. Many of us inside the Bell System took that fundamental purpose very seriously; it engaged and aligned the work of a million people.

Today, AT&T is roughly one-third its predivestiture size. The ideal of helping to bring people together from around the world taps a similarly deep well of emotional energy inside the company. Nonetheless, our global ideal alone is not enough to align 325,000 employees around the world, no matter how individually committed and capable they are. If you're going to create a truly global corporate community, you need to build infrastructure mechanisms at every level.

We saw this in the late 1980s, when AT&T decentralized to a business unit structure, moving decision making closer to our customers. To gain a clearer understanding of our costs, we set up an internal contracting process. Traditional staff functions such as information systems, human resources, and building services were now required to *sell* their services to AT&T's various business units.

We soon discovered we had created new problems. A sort of centrifugal force had been set into motion. The new relationships and communication channels (and a new approach to measuring costs of internal transactions) tended to draw people closer to their diverse customers, whether internal or external, and away from their old loyalties to the management team or staff colleagues which formerly provided the glue of the enterprise. People within the company began to feel pulled apart. At various levels, AT&T leaders started exploring for a concept of exactly what should hold AT&T together in the future.

We knew cohesion would become even more difficult to sustain as the corporation increased its global scope. Today, if an AT&T business unit based in New Jersey moves some jobs from Oklahoma to Indiana, people do not perceive it, internally or externally, in terms of national or cultural identity. The AT&T manager in Oklahoma may not be pleased with the decision, but he or she will not view it as AT&T trying to curry favor with the Hoosiers at the expense of the Sooners. Yet imagine a few years from now, when the company may make a similar move—but this time a Japanese business unit decides to reduce staff in the Ukraine and move the work to India. How will people within and beyond AT&T's boundaries perceive this decision? When the Ukranian managers involved in the decision go home at night, what will they tell their friends and family? Will such decisions magnify the centrifugal force in the organization?

The challenge for global corporations will be to develop a sense of collective identity, spanning the planet, so that local decision makers in Tokyo, Kiev, New Delhi—and Basking Ridge, New Jersey, as well—are willing to defer their provincial self-interest to the interest of the global community. It should be possible to set up mechanisms that benefit the community at large. Three mechanisms stand out for me as important: "free agency," "employment stability," and the maintenance of community boundaries.

FREE AGENCY

It is unreasonable to expect "empowered" community members to feel responsible for serving AT&T's customers, if they have limited ability to find and choose meaningful work within AT&T for themselves. A "free agency" policy might address this. The policy would simply mandate that employees could always seek and accept positions anywhere in the global enterprise, without fear of local reprisal. People would commit their work lives not to one business unit, but to the overall enterprise—which, after all, can more effectively return that commitment because of its larger size and greater resources.

With this kind of policy in place, individual business units have more freedom to engender diverse local cultures and leadership styles. If they create an attractive environment, they will attract more high-quality people. The corporate leadership role shifts from one of command and control to market regulator and consultant: "Sure, you can try that policy," a senior manager might tell a local unit leader. "But it could drive your best people away to other business units." The central management of AT&T does not determine the attractiveness or diversity of its units; unit cultures shape, and are shaped by, where the employees choose to work. There is, in effect, a continuous plebiscite in which employees vote for or against local leaders without having to vote for or against AT&T as a whole.

Even without a specific policy, many organizations have an informal "free agency" effect. When I was a field sales branch manager, I learned that if I gave a 110 percent effort to the development and movement of the people in my group, they would give 125 percent back to our customers. Even though I sometimes lost people when they moved on to better opportunities, my business gained. I had a slate of high performers standing in line to join, knowing they could advance their careers.

EMPLOYMENT STABILITY

Investment in the corporate community requires both obligations and entitlements, including some form of employment stability. Many people reject the idea of entitlements, particularly where people claim they are entitled to lifetime employment, no matter what they contribute. But entitlements are simply the rights earned as a result of membership. Without a mechanism to establish and protect membership entitlements, there can be no community. That is why local downsizing imposes a community-wide cost: If members of the AT&T community live in fear of losing their jobs, then membership in AT&T is worthless, and the entire community finds it harder to attract and retain qualified people.

In discussions about this, some managers argue, "Maybe our responsibility is not to provide lifetime employment, but employability. We can help people develop marketable skills, so that if they have to leave, they will still feel their time with us has been of high value."

However, if your company can acquire a skill from the outside labor market (by hiring or by purchasing training), then your competitors can acquire it just as easily. To have competitive advantage, a company must develop skills which are specific to itself, beyond the reach of other companies. Employees will invest their time and effort in learning "how we do things at AT&T" only if they expect to get a long-term return on their investment. If they're told, "Tomorrow morning, you may be gone," they will invest in skills that can be sold on the outside. They will pursue their MBAs and their résumés, but they will not commit themselves to the corporate community. Unfortunately, the recent trend of downsizing, "right-sizing" and reengineering is teaching employees that company-specific learning is not a wise investment.

COMMUNITY BOUNDARIES

At AT&T, we have found that the quality of community depends on conscious attention to community boundaries: the process by which membership is extended to newcomers or withdrawn, and the process by which community-wide standards for members are developed and maintained. For example, we have periodically implemented organization-wide hiring controls. These have two purposes. First, they make membership in the community more valuable to incumbent employees by making sure that new jobs support the employment stability of people already inside AT&T. As some parts of the business grow, new job opportunities compensate for lost jobs in the parts of the business that are shrinking.

Second, the hiring controls make it more likely that someone hired at the local level is potentially a valued member of the overall corporate community. By elevating the boundaries to community membership, corporate hiring controls may impose a local cost to individual business units. But they also benefit the larger organizational community by making sure more explicit attention is paid to the criteria for new members, and whether prospective members meet that criteria. Having hiring controls also makes it easier for the organization to deliver employment stability.[*]

*Some of these issues are dealt with in more depth in *Governing the Commons* by Elinor Ostrom (1990, Cambridge, England: Cambridge University Press), p. 91 (in which one of her design principles is "clearly defined boundaries").

Resource Link: A vehicle for providing continuity at AT&T *Douglas Merchant, Ruthann Prange*

IN 1991, WE RECOGNIZED THAT AT&T NEEDED TO REDEPLOY PEOPLE more effectively. Without necessarily discussing it in terms of a community infrastructure, we were looking for some fundamental mechanism that would increase the stability and value of community membership. Thus, we established Resource Link, an internal agency similar to an employment agency, that leases full-time employees back and forth across the organization. When people leave a position because a local business unit has downsized, or because their skills are no longer necessary there, they can now join the internal Resource Link agency. As part of Resource Link, they join other business units on a temporary basis. Some people move from Resource Link to a permanent position elsewhere; other people remain with Resource Link indefinitely, as they would with a temporary employment agency. This also creates a web of interpersonal relationships that span unit boundaries—a sort of corporate neural network—increasing the cohesion and continuity of the AT&T community and giving people a broader perspective of AT&T's resources, needs, and opportunities.

Every organization has an internal labor market with various degrees of market imperfections. Resource Link improves market efficiency by reducing barriers to employee movement within the boundaries of the AT&T community. Ideally, it should be easier for employees to move to another part of AT&T than to move out of AT&T's boundaries. This principle is somewhat like the "free agency" policy: the more information and choice employees have in their employment, the more commitment they will have toward their jobs.

Resource Link is also a mechanism for increasing the community's ongoing capacity to learn. The movement of people through the system is actually a way that the company stores information about itself—about which business units are successful, and which are failing, in the market. In part because of Resource Link, employees now have more options within the corporate community; they can more easily "jump ship" to other units. When people "jump ship" en masse, then it's a signal to both the unit and corporate leadership. Is the business unit being led well? Is it losing market opportunity? Does the community have unrealistic expectations for the unit? The community can then decide whether to lower near-term financial objectives and bail out the unit, or provide additional life rafts for the unit members. And if the community must abandon ship and let a unit sink, Resource Link allows AT&T to do so without drowning the employees.

Initially Resource Link was seen by some as a place to "park" people who weren't immediately needed elsewhere, but now it's coming to be regarded as a valuable community asset. Its employees are full members of the AT&T community; they're not seen as temporaries. We're exploring the possibility of contracting that talent outside of AT&T. Then people would bring experience of the "outside world" back into our community.

We continually benchmark Resource Link against outside agencies and it compares very well on all key performance measures including resource utilization and customer satisfaction. Intriguingly enough, Resource Link itself is becoming known as a desirable place to work—a career enhancer rather than a parking lot.

84 Operating Principles for Building Community

Juanita Brown, Bryan Smith, David Isaacs

Here are some of the techniques we know for bringing people together, and enabling them to mobilize their collective efforts.

We don't see these techniques as primarily useful for formal "change agents" or outside consultants. They're more for anyone who feels, "I wish I worked in a place that was more like a community."

- Focus on the real work. Successful community development work starts with the challenges people face in real life. There are gangs afoot, so we begin a neighborhood crime watch. There is garbage in the streets, so we get together for a cleanup campaign.

  Similarly, in a business, avoid a narrow focus on "building community" in the abstract. Focus on the immediate things people care about. "We're drowning in piles of paper; our workload is overwhelming; the communication system is wacky; we need better training to do a good job with the company." Later, the group can broaden its interest.

- Keep it simple. What one specific thing could you and others do that will have multiple business and personal payoffs? Generally, the simplest, most effective initial approaches are those which touch concrete business issues, but also touch people's hearts and spirits—like informal gatherings and celebrations.

- Act. Action learning—"learning by doing"—is a key strategy in community development. Take a step and see where it takes you, in the context of where you want to go. One thing leads to the next and the learning, excitement, and self-confidence build.

  ⧙⧘ See "The Wheel of Learning," page 59.

- See the glass as half full, not as half empty. Community developers say: "Build from good, expect better, make great." Even in organizations with lots of problems, focus on the best, most life-giving forces which are already present. Involve the people associated with them. Look for the wellness and wholeness which exist even in the sickest organization, and start there. For example, in a large organization, some people may already be doing a great job with customer service or improved paperwork flow. What can you learn from that, and how can you propagate that spirit further?

- Seek what unifies. As you talk with people, try to find not only what pulls you apart, but what brings you together. Sniff out the people who care, and bring them together, using dialogue, problem-solving approaches, potluck suppers, or house meetings. Start a small group talking about what the issues are, what its members have tried, and what worked well or less well. Your only power might be providing them with lunch. The important thing is to start great conversations about things that matter.

  ⧙⧘ See "Bean Suppers," page 518.

- Do it when people are ready. Timing is everything in community development. It's often better to wait until you sense that people are ready to move forward. For example, some managers wonder why they hear so much complaining and groaning and so little positive suggestion. They are tempted to say to their subordinates, "Don't you have any vision?" But when there is a sense of injury, comments like that will simply squelch the needed collective healing process. It's more effective to be subtle. Do what you can to help alleviate the immediate pain, while encouraging people to focus on their best hopes. When the pain is acknowledged, ideas about larger vision will start to emerge on their own.

- Design spaces where community can happen. How would organizations be designed physically to support community? Maybe you would create the equivalent of a central plaza or common square where people would come to have coffee and conversation. The watercooler would not be a forbidden place. In one factory, the teams developed the "Blue Room"—a living room right in the middle of the plant floor, which had been a storeroom before. When people needed to think together they would go there.

⟩⟩ See Workplace Design, page 469.

- Find and cultivate the "zoysia plugs." Zoysia is a grass, originally indigenous to Asia, which people sometimes use to start lawns. You water and fertilize plugs of grass scattered far apart. Eventually they find each other and meld into a carpet covering the whole lawn. In organizations, "zoysia plugs" are people who share your passion. They are also the informal leaders who know how to "make things happen." Find them, wherever they might be, and support them however you can. Eventually, when you reach a level of critical mass, you may feel the atmosphere of the entire enterprise shift.

- Learn how to host good gatherings. Any community builder should know certain fundamental skills of hosting great conversations and designing gatherings. These may be different from the traditional skills of good organizational meeting management. Look for meeting sites that feel relaxing. Avoid formal conference rooms, because of the stultified associations people have with them. Sit at round tables, or better yet, choose a living room atmosphere, with informal comfortable seating. Try to have food available as often as possible, and stop periodically for "fun" breaks.

  When you can, have a scribe capture people's ideas on flip charts so they can "see" what they're talking about. Record decisions and points of focus in clear view of everyone. Encourage the group to take responsibility for deciding what should be done next right there on the spot. Find out what people can contribute. Get volunteer "sign-ups." Finally, take time for sharing "learnings" and "yearnings": What have we learned? What do we want to do to improve our next get-together?

■ Acknowledge people's contributions. One of the most fundamental tools in community building is acknowledgment. Everyone who contributes should be thanked and honored for what they have done. One organization we know concluded its visioning effort with a mock Academy Awards ceremony, in which every one of the organization's two hundred people was nominated for at least one award. Some awards were hilarious: for example, a "foot in the mouth award"—to acknowledge the biggest gaffes that people could remember. Others were quite serious: a "beyond-the-call-of-duty" award. Each person (including the "foot in mouth" award recipient) left knowing that others appreciated what they had contributed.

■ Involve the whole person. Use music, art, symbols, and drama to tap deeper sources of knowing and intuition. In one mass visioning and strategy effort, a large hot-air balloon floated outside the plant to symbolize the importance of a larger perspective. We started a series of volunteer "balloon meetings" with groups of employees, customers, suppliers, and other corporate stakeholders. For the first time in the organization's history, members brought food to their meetings. Muralists sketched what people envisioned the plant might become. Employees drew possible logos for the plant. Eventually, the strategy teams, made up of both managers and line workers, made creative presentations together about the plant's future direction. These presentations included skits, murals, and music. The managers contributed an understanding of the business focus, so that all the visioning and strategy work was tied directly into the improvement of the business. That plant became the highest-producing plant of its type in the world. Eight years later, results continue to be sustained.

■ Celebrate. What's the point of building community if you can't have fun? Community development work has to engage people's hearts, minds, spirits, and bodies. A key vehicle for this is celebration. In one company, we began the community building effort with a kickoff extravaganza for all employees and their families in the local high school. The international singing group *Up with People* was invited to come in and perform. The members of the group are mostly high school students from all over the world. They lived in the homes of managers and hourly employees for several days before the event. The kids from the singing group talked to everyone about what it was like to work with people from different cultures. This happened to be a locale with severe racial issues, and the celebration gave people an opportunity to see how that tension might change.

Celebrate and recognize success, even if it's small. Celebrations don't have to cost lots of money. The only real requirement is imagination.

85 Microworlds and Learning Laboratories

Peter Senge

A recent *Business Week* article talked glowingly about "reshaping education" through computers and multimedia technology. Schoolchildren might become "active rather than passive learners," loving the excitement of making discoveries, gaining more control over what they learned, and "never being called stupid" for making mistakes. Nowhere in the article was there any mention that these same principles and technologies might have relevance for adults, or for learning in the workplace.*

Unfortunately, the prevailing mental model of computers in business today does not differ fundamentally from what it was thirty years ago. Computers are number-crunching machines, or vehicles for gathering and storing data—not *learning tools* that might reshape our understanding and alter the ways we make sense out of the information we receive. Using computers for learning may be fine for children, but not for adults.

At the base of this mental model appears to be an assumption that what managers lack most for effective decision making is adequate information. Yet, research results directly contradict this assumption. Even knowledgeable and experienced decision makers often filter their information through nonsystemic mental models, construing symptoms as causes and reacting in ways that make problems worse rather than better.* While increased access to information may be a step in the direc-

* "'The Learning Revolution" by Larry Armstrong, *Business Week,* Feb. 28, 1994, p. 80.

* See *The Fifth Discipline,* pp. 27–54, and "Misperception of Feedback in Dynamic Decision Making," by John Sterman, *Organizational Behavior and Human Decision Processes,* Summer 1989, vol. 43 no. 3, p. 301.

tion of enhanced learning, more information is not always better. It can overwhelm and paralyze decision making; it can direct attention to highly visible but highly misleading facts; and it can place greater control in the hands of information system designers, who might not necessarily have the best understanding of business issues.

How, then, might computers enable learning in organizations? Microworlds and learning laboratories comprise an important frontier in which people are developing answers. I believe this frontier will eventually be crucial for realizing the vision of learning organizations. But progress is not guaranteed. Using computer simulations to promote learning is a complex and challenging endeavor, with many possibilities for short-lived gains and superficial advances.

The technological aspects—creating and refining more useful tools—are the easy part. More challenging, and more significant, are the conceptual aspects. Many management simulations available today have sophisticated user interfaces, but few have sophisticated theories laying behind the interfaces. The result is more entertaining than enlightening. At MIT, the new "management flight simulators" typically take two to four years to develop and test. Often they are based on prior system-dynamics theories developed over many years.

The most challenging aspect of this frontier is organizational. Major payoffs for organizations will only occur when tools like microworlds become integrated into the fabric of how organizations operate. Yet today, the theory and technology of these tools is well ahead of our ability to get them into widespread effective use. This will require new learning processes—such as the management learning laboratory, a "practice field" where teams will regularly go to reflect on how they are thinking and interacting, to surface and improve their mental models, and to enhance their capacity for high-leverage coordinated action.

We're just beginning to learn how to successfully design and implement learning laboratories. We are realizing, for example, that this job is too important to be delegated to technical staff specialists. One of the first successful learning laboratory implementations, the Claims Management Learning Laboratory at Hanover Insurance, was developed by a team led by the claims vice president and two direct reports.° Thus, one of the most daunting cultural challenges posed by learning laboratories is the redefinition of managerial work—to include accountability for producing results *and* for producing knowledge about how the results were produced.

° *The Fifth Discipline*, p. 325.

The material in this section of the book will give some feeling for the current state of the art and, hopefully, shed light on key elements for future progress.

MICROWORLDS, MANAGEMENT FLIGHT SIMULATORS, AND LEARNING LABORATORIES

Educator/artificial intelligence researcher Seymour Papert coined the term "microworld" in the late 1970s, to define a computer-based learning environment for children, in which they could program the environment, see how it responded, and draw out their own understanding of the principles of mathematical relationships. Gradually, the word "microworld" has come to mean any simulation (often, but not always, created with computers) in which people can "live" in the simulation, running experiments, testing different strategies, and building a better understanding of the aspects of the real world which the microworld depicts.

For more about Papert's microworld, see "Design for a Learning Laboratory in a Learning School," page 484.

Perhaps several dozen microworlds now exist for use in management. They are also called "management flight simulators," after the People Express [Airlines] Management Flight Simulator, one of the earliest managerial microworlds. "Management flight simulators" are not limited to the airline industry. They are in use in such diverse businesses as insurance, automobiles, photocopiers, health care, utilities, consumer goods, and real estate.

The term "learning laboratory" has come into use in the last couple of years. It refers to an innovation in infrastructure: a "practice field" where teams can surface, test, and improve their mental models. Learning laboratories represent a natural context within which tools like management flight simulators seem to have the greatest impact—as tools for learning, rather than tools for predicting. Without that context, experts may develop "management flight simulators" with little clear idea of how they will be used, and managers may play them as if they were playing a computer game—with little learning. Conversely, without a management flight simulator, the learning laboratory lacks one of its most effective elements. Other tools, such as the mental models tools described on pages 242–63, are equally critical components.—**AK**

86 Where the Organization Develops a Theory About Itself

Daniel Kim

Flight simulators—the type used to simulate aircraft—actually have two uses. The first is for training pilots and helping them gain experience in maneuvering the aircraft, gaining a feeling for its responsiveness, and understanding some of the counterintuitive actions that are needed to fly a plane. The second use is for the improvement of aerodynamic design—developing principles and methods for making the aircraft interact more effectively with the air in flight.

Similarly, management flight simulators have two uses. First, they help managers understand better the interconnected nature of their organizations, and the consequences of their own actions. But the frontier of this work involves the second use, where managers build a theory about the organization through an ongoing process of refining their understanding and translating that into the simulator model.

Consider how most management flight simulators come into existence. A team of managers typically sets out to understand some dynamic of its industry. The team members have no interest, per se, in creating a microworld. But as they approach their question systemically, they begin to develop a theory that explains how they contributed to creating their own problems. Once they can put that theory into words, they don't know what to do with it. They can't just summarize the main points and present them to other people in the organization. People won't swallow a theory whole, because the action that the theory recommends usually runs counter to everything else they're doing.

So the original team decides to replicate its own learning experience for other people to go through. The team builds a microworld—a working model, on computer, of the system the members saw. They test it, first among their own team, and gradually with more and more people. This doesn't happen in isolation; through the archetypes, the mental models tools, and other concepts, the team members talk through the theory with other people in the organization, and evolve a shared understanding which makes their work on the microworlds more effective.

This is how the Hanover Claims Learning Lab evolved, and similar approaches underlie most successful efforts to date. Gradually, the organization develops a theory about itself. It tests that theory, again and again, in relatively concrete form in the continually improving microworld.

From generic microworlds to your own theory

PARADOXICALLY, THE MICROWORLD NEED NOT BE TAILORED SPECIFIcally to the organization to be effective at first. As Seymour Papert pointed out, even something as generic as a child's doll can be a "transitional object"—an object you "fall in love with," precisely because it keeps showing you more about yourself. It doesn't hold an "answer," with an understanding about your business that will solve all your problems. Instead, it returns to you, with interest, the understanding that *you* invest in it.

Thus, as long as generic microworld sufficiently captures the main features of the real situation, people can still find an understanding of their own experiences within it. Managers at Federal Express, for example, have recognized some of their call center dynamics by using the service/quality microworld originally developed for Hanover Insurance. The same questions come up: "Why do we get focused on the production numbers at the expense of other factors? What is the relationship between our productivity and the backlog of customers waiting? Why doesn't the erosion of our quality show up in any aspect of the system to which we pay attention?"

But there are limits, in the long run, to the value of an off-the-shelf microworld module. I think there is an innate tendency for people to abdicate their responsibility as a decision maker—to accept the "answer" given by the computer. Learning laboratories try to compensate for this tendency by bringing a team together to talk about the conclusions and assumptions they draw from the model. The model itself is simply an explicit set of assumptions, and its principal value is in helping make implicit assumptions explicit.

Reframing the organization's design

THAT'S WHY I IMAGINE THE FUTURE OF MANAGEMENT FLIGHT SIMULAtors will probably include a great deal more theory building—revision of the model and its underlying logic. Many microworlds today do not permit the users to see or change the theory embodied in the management flight simulator. There is no way to say, "Whatever strategy we try in this model, we're screwed up. What if we could change the assumptions underlying the microworld itself?"

In many microworlds, for example, there is a "hard-wired" (unchangeable) hurdle rate: the rate of return on investment needed to make a project viable. The hurdle rate is based on prevailing assumptions held by the organization. As long as those assumptions hold, no matter what kinds of parameters and scenarios are entered, the team may not get anywhere close to its goals.

But if the players of the game could rewrite it to change the hurdle rate—perhaps by suggesting some plausible new mechanism that could be added into the model—then they would have a creative tool with which to extend and test the current theory of the organization. According to conventional wisdom, it might be impossible to change the hurdle rate; that's probably why it was hard-wired into the game in the first place. The designers of the microworld may never have conceived that someone would want to change it. But conventional wisdom itself is based on past assumptions and structures, and it's reasonable to think that using the microworld would crystallize an understanding of how to make more fundamental changes.

87 Using Microworlds to Promote Inquiry

Michael Goodman

In the right context, microworld simulations are powerful learning experiences for teams. But research shows that people can easily draw the wrong conclusions from them. This problem stems from the microworld's seemingly greatest strengths: the ease with which people can design and run experiments, and the apparent ability of the computer to translate "soft" assumptions into "hard" statistics.

How then can we design a setting to maximize the inquiry and learning from a microworld? Design precepts are now emerging as we accumulate experience:

- Construct the context within which people engage the computer just as thoughtfully as the simulation. While a typical learning lab lasts from two to three days, less than half that time should be spent on the computer. Participants need to be able to interpret what's happening on the screen in terms of the real world. If they are thinking in new ways about tough concerns, they need to explore what the microworld's implications mean to them personally, and to the organization. A natural progression is to ask them to formulate new "real-world" experiments that might confirm or challenge the theory emerging from the microworld.
- Design the rest of the learning laboratory around archetypes and systems concepts that relate to the microworld's underlying model. A well-designed learning lab leaves its participants with the skill to communicate the stories of the microworld without depending on a computer. The systems archetypes are ideal for this. We generally build the understanding of archetypes *before* they are witnessed on-screen, and we ask them to construct their own paper-and-pencil models of the business issue they came to explore. This gives participants a framework for observing why events unfold as they do, and makes it far easier for participants to relate to the microworld and the understandings that emerge from it.
- Design the lab so the group pays attention to all four levels of systems thinking: events, patterns of behavior, structure, and mental models. Because a single keystroke can generate hundreds of data points, people tend to be transfixed at the event and pattern levels, fending off crisis after crisis in the model and sinking into the same kind of short-term reactive behavior that has plagued them in the real world. As in the real world, discipline is needed to keep their attention on structural relationships and their own habits of thinking. We generally ask teams to mentally simulate what they expect to happen, and why, *before* executing a new strategy. After the simulation, we ask them to compare their prediction with the results, and explain why there was a difference (assuming there is one) and how they were surprised. This "before and after" exercise is critical to the learning process and keeps the team in an inquiry-oriented mode.

For more about the four levels, see "The Acme Story," page 97.

■ You don't need a custom-built microworld to conduct a learning lab. We hold many introductory learning labs in which people play with generic management flight simulators, such as "People Express" (see page 537). After several hours, the participants say, "It's just like our organization. We're growing like gangbusters, and we haven't paid attention to our service capacity. We're starting to see some indicators that we may get into the same types of problems." While the microworld isn't focused on their particular situation, it has enough in common to focus a team on the dynamics which they should be thinking about.

88 A Buyer's Guide to Off-the-Shelf Microworlds

W. Brian Kreutzer

W. Brian Kreutzer is a one-person Consumer Reports *for the field of systems thinking. An interface designer, systems modeler, and educator based at Gould-Kreutzer Associates, in Cambridge, Massachusetts, he has written similar "buyers' and builders' guides" for the* Whole Earth Review *(see page 570),* The Systems Thinker *(see page 91), and for a pivotal book,* Managing a Nation, *edited by Gerald O. Barney, 1990, Boulder, Colo.: Westview Press. He has taught courses in system dynamics to master's degree candidates at colleges and business schools, as well as to managers. Here he presents a consumer's guide to the most effective examples of "ready-to-use" management flight simulators and microworlds.*

Sally stared blankly off into space. What had started out so well had turned into a nightmare. She had taken over an airline company that had three planes and gross revenues of thirty-two million dollars a year, and in just four years she had grown the company to a half-billion-dollar firm with a fleet of 100 aircraft. She had sweated over decisions in the areas of human resources, aircraft acquisition, marketing, pricing, and service scope, and in each case, her airline had triumphed. But then, she had reached a turning point. Her market had collapsed. Her service quality had eroded. Losses had piled up so fast that the ability of her company to absorb them was in doubt. It would all turn around though, it had to. All she needed was one more quarter . . . But instead of the next quarter's financial reports she received notification that her creditors were forcing her into bankruptcy. Time had run out. Her creditors began to liquidate her company.

"What did I do wrong?" she thought. All her decisions had seemed to make sense at the time. She reached over and pressed the save button. She would have to analyze her decisions to see what went wrong later. Right now, she had another strategy she wanted to try out. She hit the restart button to begin the simulation. She was back to having three planes and gross revenues of thirty-two million dollars . . .

Sally was exploring a management flight simulator based on the story of People Express Airlines. Created by John Sterman at the Massachusetts Institute of Technology, it was designed to illustrate a generic problem which is common in many rapidly growing organizations: the difficulty of maintaining a balance between rapid growth and the necessary investment to keep quality standards high.

Ready-made management flight simulators are sophisticated management-oriented microworlds which have been adapted to a wide audience. There are two reasons to explore them. First, your situation may have enough in common with the flight simulator that you can come away with a valuable experience. Second, if you're going to design your own management flight simulator, then you should expose yourself to several existing examples, and build on their work instead of starting from scratch. These management flight simulators are fairly easy to learn, inexpensive, and well worth the time it takes to explore them:

Management flight simulators from the MIT Sloan School*

THE PEOPLE EXPRESS MFS†

People Express, an innovative, low-cost, and "people-oriented" airline formed in the early 1980s, experienced explosive growth and then a dramatic fall. What happened? Was it poor management or the side effects

* People Express Management Flight Simulator by John Sterman (Macintosh and MS Windows™ versions); B&B Enterprises Management Flight Simulator by John Sterman, Mark Paich, Ken Simons, and Eric Beinhocker (Macintosh and MS Windows versions); Commercial Real Estate Management Flight Simulator by Bent E. Bakken and John Sterman (Macintosh only); International Oil Tanker Management Flight Simulator by Bent E. Bakken and John Sterman (Macintosh only). All are available from: John Sterman, Sloan School of Management, Massachusetts Institute of Technology, Cambridge, Mass. or MicroWorlds, Inc., Cambridge, Mass.

† Peter Senge describes the logic underlying this flight simulator in the chapter on People Express, "The Art of Seeing the Forest *and* the Trees," pp. 127–35 of *The Fifth Discipline*.

and delayed interactions of the company's innovations? Or was it something else? With this simulator, you become the president of People Express, vary your policies, and make your own judgment.

As president you make decisions about aircraft acquisition, hiring, marketing, fares, and scope of service. You base your decision on information the MFS provides you every "quarter," about human resources, finances, capacity, the market, and other key factors. Whether you "fly" People Express into the clouds or crash it into the ground, you learn about (as the users' guide puts it) "the difficulties of coordinating operations and strategy in a growth market; and the dynamic interconnections among a firm, its market, and its competitors."

Like all of the simulators produced by John Sterman's group at the Sloan School of Management, this MFS requires little or no training and no prior computer or modeling experience. The documentation is excellent, and people who have never used any type of computer before are running their own company in twenty minutes.

B&B ENTERPRISES MFS

Managing a product through its life cycle is tricky: When do you raise or lower prices? When should you push or ease up on marketing? When should you expand capacity? And how should your competitor's decisions affect yours? The B&B Enterprises Management Flight Simulator allows you to consider these questions, and others, in the context of a consumer durable product company. Placed in the role of president you determine your product's price, marketing strategy, and target capacity. Since real CEOs don't have complete access to information about their products, competitors, and markets, neither do you. You have the information that a real CEO would have: financial information on your company and on that of your competitor, market research on your company versus the competitor, and production information which shows information like costs, capacity, and the order backlog. To test your strategy in a variety of outside environments, you can select from five market scenarios and four sets of competitor strategies—or a "mystery world," in which you don't know in advance what sort of market and competitors have been chosen for you.

COMMERCIAL REAL ESTATE MFS

This allows you to try your hand at managing a real estate portfolio in the volatile office building market, a system rife with delays and unintended consequences. You start with thirty buildings. You can buy or sell buildings or build new ones; you make money through sales and rentals, making decisions based on construction activity, your company's finances, leasing activity, and the market. You can set scenarios that determine such factors as the amount of time it takes to construct a building, the lifetime of a building, the growth curve of demand, and how much cash you start out with.

INTERNATIONAL OIL TANKER MFS

The oil tanker market is perhaps even more volatile than the commercial real estate market. The International Oil Tanker Management Flight Simulator gives you an opportunity to experience this volatility firsthand, by putting you into the role of a tanker developer and operator. Your goal is to navigate through twenty to thirty years of volatile market activity without sinking into bankruptcy.°

Management flight simulators from Gould-Kreutzer Associates*

THE COPEX MFS

The simulator opens with a briefing on the problems facing COPEX, a high-end copier manufacturer. "We originally produced this game for an organization which had a dilemma," says Jennifer Kemeny, one of the developers of the game. "The company was considering a fix of downsizing their service personnel. Some managers thought this would backfire on the quality of service and sales. The financial people thought the impact on profits would be much stronger. We used the model to help them investigate which effects would be more dominant under various circumstances and strategies."

⟩⟩ This MFS is based upon "Fixes That Backfire," page 125.

THE ELECTRONIC BEER GAME

An electronic version of the popular and evocative "Beer Game" (*The Fifth Discipline*, page 27). It can be played in both "gaming" mode (in

° The company I work for participated in the creation of these programs. They run only on Macintosh computers. *The Competitive Dynamics Simulator and Scenario Impact Simulator* by David Kreutzer, Janet Gould-Kreutzer, and Brian Kreutzer; available from Gould-Kreutzer Associates, Cambridge, MA; *The COPEX Management Flight Simulator* by Brian Kreutzer and Jennifer Kemeny; and *The Electronic Beer Game* by Brian and David Kreutzer and Michael Goodman; demonstrations available only through special arrangement with Gould-Kreutzer or Innovation Associates (see p. 568); *ShareBuilder*, created by and for the ShareBuilder Consortium of companies, available through the ShareBuilder consortium, c/o Gould-Kreutzer.

which you play on a simulated version of the board game, and enter your beer-purchasing decisions each week) or a "simulation" mode (in which you select a policy at the beginning and the simulation plays out the results. It is well adapted for answering questions after students and managers have played the board version.

THE COMPETITIVE DYNAMICS SIMULATOR

You have just been promoted to the presidency of a consumer durable company—one of two dominant players in a mature market. By making careful decisions about marketing, R&D, SS&A, and capacity expansion, you attempt to become the leader in both market share and accumulated net income. This is a very tailorable generic simulation of the systemic implications of competitive strategy.

SHAREBUILDER

This executive strategy system, with a spreadsheet program incorporated into it, allows managers to test their business plan. Your goal is to grow your market share and your profitability against several distinct competitors. You control the characteristics of the strategies that these competitors pursue. Output is viewed in a number of formats including line charts, bar charts, and animated bubble charts.

Vensim's demo disk*

THIS DISK CONTAINS FIVE DIFFERENT MANAGEMENT FLIGHT SIMULATORS created in the Vensim modeling language. Not only can you use these models as management flight simulators, but with Vensim's extensive documentation features you can easily explore the underlying structure of the models that were used to create them. The three most exciting are:

*Vensim's Demo Disk is available from Ventana Systems, Harvard, Massachusetts. These programs require an MS-DOS computer.

MAINTENANCE AND SERVICE STRATEGIES EXPLORER

You move from a reactive to proactive maintenance schedule, controlling values for parts availability and labor use. Unlike most generic microworld programs, this one allows you to change the underlying assumptions of the model. You can also use Vensim's "optimization" feature to find what values to assign to variables to maximize the aspects of performance which you consider critical.

WORLD3-91 EXPLORER

The "Limits to Growth" archetype was based on a series of insights about global population, pollution, and resource dynamics. This explorer was set up to allow you to explore those dynamics. It lets you run all thirteen scenarios described in the book *Beyond the Limits* (see page 135) and others.

URBAN GAME

You are in charge of a city that is falling apart. Your population is so discouraged by lack of employment and adequate housing that it is leaving in droves. Your job is to save the city by using job training, housing, and business development programs.

Management flight simulators for teams

FISH BANKS, LTD.*

This team-based board game allows you to experience firsthand the issues, problems, and potentially tragic consequences associated with the management of a renewable resource, such as fish, forests, and groundwater. Each team, representing a fishing fleet, must decide how many ships to buy and where to send them. One member of each team moves the boats on the game board so everyone can see where the fleets are fishing. Because the players are too busy discussing their potential decisions and outcomes with their team members, or negotiating with other teams, only the facilitator uses the computer, which simulates the results and then displays each team's catch.

° *Fish Banks* was developed by Dennis L. Meadows, Thomas Fiddaman, and Diana Shannon and is available from Dennis Meadows, the University of New Hampshire, Portsmouth, N.H.

FRIDAY NIGHT AT THE ER*

Your team is responsible for making decisions about resource use and service availability in a hospital's emergency, surgical, and critical care departments. The game covers a twenty-four-hour period from Friday

° *Friday Night at the ER* by Betty Gardner (1993, Morgan Hill, Calif.: Gardner and Associates).

noon to Saturday noon—the busiest time for a hospital's emergency room. Your job is to keep service quality high as well as control the financial impact of that increased demand. While *Friday Night at the ER* is based on health care, it offers valuable lessons on systems thinking and Total Quality for professionals in any service industry.

THE GREAT GAME OF BUSINESS **by Jack Stack** (1992, New York: Currency Doubleday).

At the Springfield Manufacturing Company (SRC), the whole company is a learning laboratory. Jack Stack, president, CEO, and instigator/designer of his "great game of business," tells the story of how that came to pass.

The "game" is built around the financial scorecard of the entire business—the same set of numbers which senior managers generally assume is their sole responsibility. At SRC, everyone educates themselves, and each other, about these numbers and their implications. Stack argues that an extensive, carefully designed employee stock ownership plan is vital for making people feel that they are part of the game. You can play the game without giving people equity, Stack says. "But you will never complete their education."

With SRC's help, encouragement, and investment, some players of the Great Game of Business go on to start their own businesses—freestanding subsidiaries that generate earnings back for SRC.—**AK**

89 Creating Your Own Management Flight Simulator

A Step-by-Step Builder's Handbook (with Software Reviews)

W. Brian Kreutzer

STEP 1: ASSEMBLE THE TEAM

Systems models and management flight simulators are not built in isolation. Your team should consist of several people, including:

- at least one experienced modeler
- at least one experienced computer interface designer; the interface designer should be in on discussions from the beginning
- at least one (and probably several) key managers from your organization

STEP 2: DEVELOP A SENSE OF YOUR PURPOSE

All other considerations are subordinate to this. MFS's can fulfill several purposes:

- **An Aid to Model Building:** With an MFS, you can make a system dynamics model accessible enough that other people can use it, test it, and critique it intelligently. This helps you see the model from several different perspectives, including the all-important perspective of a less technical person.
- **Learning:** Most management flight simulators are created for use in learning laboratories. Typically, you would design not just the model, but a briefing where the case is introduced and the simulator is put into context, and a debriefing where the experience is put into the framework of system dynamics. Often explanations of relevant causal loop diagrams and archetypes are included in the labs, to give the user a glimpse at the underlying structure of the model.

■ **Practicing Decision-Making Skills:** MFS's give managers the chance to experiment with the results of choices, as well as learn about the structure and dynamics of the systems in which they find themselves—before they actually need to make their real decisions. Playing CEO, you can bankrupt a company hundreds of times and hopefully learn how to avoid doing it in real life.

■ **Scenario Planning:** In scenario planning, policies are tested against several plausible futures. A system dynamics model can capture the scenarios that are of interest to your company and permit you to test your policies against them.

For more information on scenario planning see page 275.

STEP 3: CONSIDER THE SOPHISTICATION OF YOUR TEAM AND YOUR AUDIENCE

I like to divide management flight simulators into two categories, based on the audience's needs. This will help determine the type of software to use:

Basic Management Flight Simulators have a minimal computer interface. You won't be able to animate the results, or present it in sophisticated graphic forms, such as three-dimensional bar charts or an "animated bubble" chart. But this type of interface takes the shortest amount of time to design and build. It works extremely well for developing the first prototype of your microworld, or for creating a microworld which simply, cleanly, shows the results of the model and nothing more.

Sophisticated Management Flight Simulators let you build help and explanatory screens, automatic messages that "kick in" when a variable reaches a certain point, hypertext features that respond to user's choices, animated graphics (as good as most computer games), and a variety of other sophisticated software features. You have more control over what users can and cannot do; your microworld can guide them in particular directions at particular times. If your audience consists of many unsophisticated users, it will probably be necessary to use software tools from this category.

Most of the available modeling software is extremely powerful—it can produce extensive models which play out ramifications of your decisions over long periods of simulated time, with great numbers of simulated causes and effects. Unfortunately, that power is not free. Its complexity requires either the help of a professional model builder or a technologically and mathematically sophisticated manager—or both.

Sooner or later, most management teams end up hiring someone with expertise to help them. That creates its own dangers. Much of the real learning about your system occurs in the model building itself: converting the system to equations, and exploring the relationships between variables in the greatest details. If you leave the task entirely to specialists (whether in-house experts or outside consultants), you will lose the benefit of that insight. That is why at least one or two managers should always go through some system dynamics training and work on the modeling team. When the consultants and specialists are finished, the manager-modelers can still refine and learn from the structure of the model.

STEP 4: CONSIDER YOUR PRELIMINARY DESIGN

This is a brainstorming job, ideally with the entire development team present. Before you even choose your software, begin to develop a sense of what you want the management flight simulator to look like. What will people see on the screen? What reports will they be given? What decisions will they be asked to make? What plots will they be introduced to? What sorts of events and problems should be sent their way? How slick and elaborate do you want the interface to be? This is a good time to run and critique some generic models (see page 536) as a basis for your own creativity and judgment.

A word of caution: fancy flight simulator interfaces can often hide mediocre understanding. It is important to have a very strong, validated model as the engine—either a literal mathematical model, or a well-thought-out and *tested* understanding of the causal loops and enriched archetypes of the system. If you have a small budget most of it should go into the model, rather than the luxury of bells and whistles in the interface.

STEP 5: CHOOSE THE SOFTWARE YOU WILL USE FOR MODELING AND INTERFACING

Once you have thought about your purpose (as in Step 2), you are in a much better position to choose the software most useful to your purposes.

Check recent issues of *The Systems Thinker,* reviewed on page 91, for more up-to-date reviews.

You will probably need at least two separate programs. Start by selecting a flight simulator (MFS) development language. These are the programs with which you design the outer "shell" of the flight simulator: the buttons and commands which users see.

Then choose a modeling software package—the program with which you create the underlying model. Make sure you choose a modeling language with which the MFS development language is easily compatible. This chart shows the appropriate combinations of the software packages I am about to describe:

COMPATIBILITY CHART OF MFS SOFTWARE:

	Modeling software (used to build the underlying model of your system)	Basic MFS language (for building relatively simple microworlds)	Sophisticated MFS language (for highly interactive, graphically sophisticated microworlds)
Macintosh software combinations	Microworld Creator	Microworld Creator	
	ithink! (core version)	Microworld Creator	
	ithink! (authoring version)	ithink! (authoring version)	
	ithink! (core version)		S°°4 and HyperCard
	ithink! (core version)	S°°4	
MS-DOS and Microsoft Windows software combinations	ithink and STELLA II	ithink! and STELLA II (authoring version)	
	PowerSim	PowerSim	
	VenSim	Vensim	
	Professional DYNAMO Plus	DYNAMO for Windows	Mosaikk and SimTek
	SimTek		Mosaikk and SimTek

- *Microworld Creator* (**Modeling and Basic Flight Simulator; Macintosh**) Most of the MIT flight simulators, including the People Express flight simulator, were created with it. The interface itself is separated into four boxes. The first lists your input variables, the second lists your custom-designed reports (a report here consists of texts, graphics, and values), the third lists your plots and tables, and the fourth is the display area for your reports, plots, and tables.

- *S°°4* (**Sophisticated Flight Simulator and Executive Strategy System; Macintosh**) A more sophisticated, complex version of *Microworld Creator.* It has the same basic interface, divided into four boxes. But it includes many more features, including the ability to use arrays and a lens feature that makes it easy to trace through the cause-and-effect relationships in your model and track down unusual behavior.°

° *Microworld Creator* and *S**4* developed by Microworlds, Inc., Cambridge, Massachusetts.

- *ithink!* **Core Version (Modeling; Macintosh and Microsoft Windows)** Because of its powerful features and ease of use, *ithink!* is one of the most popular system dynamics modeling tools. It allows you to draw stock-and-flow diagrams on the computer screen, completely mapping the structure of the system before you enter equations. You can add more detail and then group elements into submodels, zooming in for more detail in complex models. The manual is such a good introduction to systems modeling that we recommend it even if you use another program.

  A cousin of *ithink!* called *STELLA II* is designed for academic use. People familiar with HyperCard, the Macintosh educational/programming tool, can use older versions of *STELLA*, the latest HyperCard, and a discontinued but still-useful interconnecting program called *StellaStack.*

〉〉 Educator Frank Draper used *STELLA* and *Stellastack* to teach systems thinking in public schools; see page 487.

- *ithink!* **Authorizing Version (Modeling and Sophisticated MFS; Macintosh and Microsoft Windows)** This version gives you the ability to customize and control the user's MFS experience. Some of its more exciting features include the ability to have messages displayed when certain conditions are met; exploration of the systems structure through mapping tools; a "browse" mode which allows users to interact with your MFS without being able to change the structure of the model; and navigation capabilities which allow the user to control the pace and direction of their interaction.°

° All forms of *ithink!* and *STELLA II* developed by High Performance Systems, Hanover, New Hampshire.

- ***PowerSim* (Modeling and Basic MFS; Microsoft Windows)** *PowerSim* is a flow-diagram-based modeling language that gives you the ability to open multiple models simultaneously, and connect separate models to each other. You can also build a basic MFS using slide buttons (like the ones on your stereo's graphic equalizers) to handle your input and reports, plots, and tables for your output. You can also add causal loop diagrams as a form of on-line documentation.

- ***Mosaikk — SimTek* (Sophisticated MFS; MS-DOS)** Mosaikk is a very sophisticated authoring tool for the PC that can run video CD players. It connects directly to *SimTek*, a *DYNAMO*-like modeling language with a great deal of versatility.°

- ***Vensim*—The Ventana™ Simulation Environment (Modeling, Basic, and Sophisticated MFS; Microsoft Windows)** *Vensim* is an extremely powerful model development language for the PC and Unix world. You begin a modeling session by using the sketch tool to enter the causal loop diagrams which will become the basis of your model. *Vensim* automatically documents your model as you go along, creating trees that allow you to trace cause-and-effect relationships throughout your entire model. It offers sophisticated statistical and graphics features and allows you to create menus, input screens, and text screens to help guide people through the flight simulator.°

- ***Professional DYNAMO Plus* (Modeling; MS-DOS)** *Professional DYNAMO Plus* allows you to build extremely large models (with up to 8,000 equations) with a variety of sophisticated programming features. However, you start by typing in equations, based on diagrams you have drawn on paper. *PD Plus* may have a daunting learning curve, but it repays that challenge with greater programming power. Since much of the literature in the system dynamics field uses the *DYNAMO* language, you will have no trouble finding models to study and adapt.

- ***DYNAMO* for Windows (Basic Flight Simulator; Microsoft Windows)** *DYNAMO* for Windows allows you to easily attach *Professional DYNAMO Plus* models to basic flight simulator interfaces. You can include text to introduce and document your model, and create custom-designed reports which allow your user to see the output in a manner similar to balance sheets or other real-life formats.°

° PowerSim, Mosaikk, and *SimTek* developed by ModellData AS, Fevik and Bergen, Norway.

° *Vensim* developed by Ventana Systems, Harvard, Massachusetts.

° *Professional DYNAMO Plus* and *DYNAMO* for Windows developed by Pugh-Roberts Associates, Cambridge, Massachusetts.

STEP 6: BUILD THE MODEL

Now create a causal loop map of the system as you see it. Share it with your colleagues to improve it; resist the temptation to have the modelers dictate what the "system should be."

Eventually you need to convert the data you have gathered, and your map of the system, into a mathematical set of equations, using one of the modeling software packages. Your model will go through a great deal of debugging and testing before you converge on a final draft. Bear in mind that you must validate the model, as you did your map, with other managers in various parts of the organization.

STEP 7: BUILD THE INTERFACE

At this stage, the interface designer creates a prototype interface based on the model and all previous discussions. The modeling team reviews the interface and uses it to further test their model. Gradually, the interface designer refines the final draft.

STEP 8: DESIGN AND IMPLEMENT THE LEARNING LABORATORY

It is particularly important for managers, especially if they were not part of the modeling process, to know that a model is just that—a model. It is not the real world but a simplification of that world, and should be used to make general conclusions about the behavior and nature of the system, rather than to predict specific events.

For all of these reasons, designing and implementing the learning laboratory workshop setting is a crucial part of the process of building a flight simulator. The entire team should be involved in the setup of the room, the design of the debrief, and the selection of other learning. The entire team should also help test the microworld in a learning laboratory setting, observing the first people who "play" the flight simulator, and changing either the program itself, or the debrief and introduction, to bring it closer to the team's purpose.

90 The Du Pont Manufacturing Game

A Global Maintenance Network Develops Its Own "Hero's Journey"

Winston Ledet

Here is a step-by-step story about the development of a board game which has led to dramatic improvements in Du Pont's handling of maintenance problems. The game itself doesn't make an appearance until the final round of this story, at which point it crystallizes the details of everything that came before. That's happened in real life, too. Trained as a chemical engineer, with a background in research, Winston Ledet had worked in human relations before becoming a manager of chemical plant maintenance for Du Pont. Ledet's work, described here, was based in Kingwood, Texas, near Houston, but it affected all of Du Pont's "CMLT network"—the international network of maintenance specialists.

Most people think "maintenance" means "building maintenance"—keeping floors clean and air conditioners running. But chemical plant maintenance is a much more sophisticated job. Our large plants are massive assemblies of pumps, valves, pipes, huge tanks, rotating and packaging equipment. They operate at unusual and extreme temperatures and high pressures, and they endure constant chemical corrosion. We restore them periodically because of normal wear and tear; we inspect them for leaks and other problems that might have safety or environmental consequences.

Beginning in the early 1980s, Du Pont's maintenance costs had steadily increased, enough to become a serious problem. So in 1986, looking for solutions, we embarked on a benchmarking program. Over a period of several years, we discovered the cost savings of "planned maintenance"—keeping our equipment in good shape, instead of paying to fix it. This means doing inspections to catch problems before they cause a full-scale breakdown, and then planning the repairs in advance. It's like inspecting your car's fan belt every year instead of waiting for it to snap. This changed our focus from the old "problem" (as many saw it) of keeping a large, costly repair staff on hand, to the new goal of having equipment that ran well.

"If they could see the situation as we did . . ."

BEGINNING IN LATE 1989, I PRODUCED A SERIES OF *STELLA* MODELS, using the system dynamics approach to show how better-planned maintenance could cut costs.

⸰⸰ For a description of *STELLA* software, see page 547.

We kept correcting the models based on people's experiences in the plants. For instance, we had originally modeled planning and scheduling as one activity. But as someone on the shop floor told us, planning has to do with how well you lay out the material and equipment. Scheduling is a question of time coordination: how to make sure that maintenance can take place when the equipment and facilities are available. It turns out that handling these tasks together frustrated people. The two tasks had to be separate, but integrated. This simple shift in thinking about our operations allowed us to dramatically improve productivity and install a number of common-sense innovations. For instance, one plant has a highly erosive chemical stream that eats up parts of the pump through which it flows. Instead of waiting for the pump to fail, now they keep a spare pump in place on wheels (planning). When they see (through a scheduled check) that the erosion is too bad, they shut the pump down, replace it with the new pump, and then repair the old pump in the shop.

We gradually got around to a simple idea: if we reduced the number of defects in our equipment, then all the other variables got better. Maintenance would now mean discovering the defects as soon as possible, and removing them before we had a failure. We tested this extensively in the model, in analyses of the benchmark studies, and in our own prototypical experiments. We became certain it was the optimal approach to maintenance.

But it was counterintuitive; it meant going in the face of long-established procedures and ways of setting up the work. Even when we showed maintenance managers and employees the results from the computer models, we had a great deal of trouble getting our point across. The maintenance community is not wild about computer models; there's no easy way to make any intuitive sense about the numbers coming out of a computer. So we began to look for a way to express this understanding in terms which people could appreciate.

We wrote some articles for the internal Du Pont audience, but we still didn't make our case effectively. The "solutions" for eliminating defects were too complex and diverse to translate into a set of rules and guidelines in a published piece of writing. We still didn't know how to reply effectively when someone said to us: "I understand that defects offer great opportunities for us. But what do you suggest I do about it?" If only they could see the situation as we saw it, then they would know what to do.

Thus, in early 1991, we created the Manufacturing Game—a board game which Du Pont maintenance people play in teams. We modeled our game after the Beer Game developed at MIT, and like the Beer Game, the underlying structure is based on the cycles of the computer model. But the model itself does not explicitly appear. The board in our game is three feet by five feet, divided into a maintenance area, an operating area, and a business services area, with one person playing each role. We use black poker chips for equipment, green for maintenance resources, and blue as spare parts. The team has to work together to keep the equipment—like the pumps in a chemical plant—in working order.°

We built a financial element into the balancing loop at the heart of the game; you measure success by the amount of money the group makes. Each turn, you can make different types of moves: you can conduct breakdown maintenance or proactive maintenance, or you can improve the reliability of the equipment. These mimic the decisions you would make in an actual plant. Most importantly, simply playing the game helps people make a transition from a reactive mode, where the maintenance problems seem to happen to them, to a proactive mode, in which they recognize they're responsible for their own problems.

° Tony Cardella, Winston P. Ledet, and Mark Downing developed the Manufacturing Game, based on the Operating Value computer model developed by the Du Pont CMLT Measurements Team. Vince Flynn provided some of the inspiration, and technical help, for the game. Mark Paich, a system dynamics consultant with High Performance Systems, contributed to the design of the model and the game. The game is available through Winston Ledet (see page 574).

Watching heroes at their journey

WE WERE SURPRISED AT THE LEVEL OF UNDERSTANDING THAT PEOPLE got from the game, compared to anything else we tried to do. The complexity of the game is pretty demanding at first. People see their own embarrassment kick in when they make some mistake and let the other two guys down. Then they see how the embarrassment causes them to become overly cautious next time; for instance, if they run out of spare parts once, they'll overstock during the next round, because running out was so damn embarrassing.

"In the models, it always makes so much sense to do the right stuff. I always wondered why people don't just do it," said Mark Paich, the systems consultant who helped us. "But then I played the game, and I saw that the emotional element interferes."

People play the game as part of a learning laboratory. There is always a debrief, and an opportunity to talk through their experiences and potential strategies. They create an action list and many have gone back, taught their colleagues the new methods, and cut their pump failures by, typically, 50 percent in three months. Over time, we have refined the game, incorporating (for instance) icons on the board. We are now working on a series of expanded "phases" covering different aspects of the maintenance system, from process control through organizational structure. We have even demonstrated our games at the MIT System Dynamics Group, where some of the students said that in our jeans and tennis shoes, we were more credible and down-to-earth than some slick Harvard MBA's in suits and ties.

In watching people play the game (and we've analyzed a lot of videotapes), we like to use Carol Pearson's metaphor of a hero's journey. Each new strategic round is a Road of Trials. Players start out as Innocents, and then become Orphans (refusing the call to change the way they think), then Warriors ("Okay, I'll get the best of this thing"), then Caretakers (teaming up to handle the whole production system rather than just their job). At the end, they're Creators—they can make sense of their experience, and create a plan. Now, like all heroes, they must return to their own home. Can they really apply the lessons they've learned back there?

91 Creating a Learning Lab—and Making It Work

Fredrick Simon, Nick Zeniuk, Julie Petrucci, Richard Haas, Ford Motor Company, 1995 Lincoln Continental (FN74) Team

The American auto industry has come a long way since the late 1970s. This cameo shows how far there still is to go, and what the terrain ahead looks like from the point of view of a particularly farsighted automobile development team.

The Ford Lincoln Continental (or FN74, to use its internal name) will be introduced on December 26, 1994.

We could have easily included worthwhile comments from dozens of members of the team. The contributors here are Fredrick Simon, program manager (overseer of the entire FN74 project); Nick Zeniuk, business planning manager and a primary mover in the learning lab effort; Richard Haas, team leader for the interior and electrical system; and Julie Petrucci, engineering supervisor in vehicle development. Daniel Kim, who has worked closely with this team, also helped us produce this cameo.

Fred Simon: We began our learning lab effort in 1991, when the new 1995 Continental team (or, to use our code name, the "FN74 team") was only six months old. I was looking for a way to counterbalance the force of Ford's functional chimneys. Even though I am the program manager for this new car, and totally responsible for everything that happens on it, only a few members of the team actually work for me. Most of the 300 people working full time on this car work for other functional organizations: finance, assembly division, body engineering, climate control, plastics, et cetera. I have no leverage over their rewards, promotions, performance reviews, or other traditional incentives.

Imagine that you are an automobile designer in the climate control division. You return to your chief engineer and say, "I've just accepted the task of surpassing the performance of the best cars on the market in cooling, but with larger windows. I think we can do it with smaller ducts, and for a lower cost." Your chief engineer might recognize that this might produce a better overall car. But he will give you a less than acceptable performance rating, because if your innovation *doesn't* work, then you've put your division's performance statistics in jeopardy.

As that engineer, you wouldn't go back to your boss with that objective unless you felt genuine commitment to the other people on your car team. If you're not committed, you haven't got a chance of convincing anyone back home. Therefore, if I wanted to improve the quality of this car, my greatest leverage was in helping my team members develop better personal relationships and see each other more as people.

Nick Zeniuk: I had just come from the launch of the 1990 Lincoln Town Car, which had been awarded Car of the Year, and we were very proud of it. But with that car, we had depended a great deal on heroic effort at the last minute—we called it "managing by panic"—because somehow we weren't able to put the right processes in place early enough. I wanted to avoid that this time. In fact, because of budget reductions that we could see were coming, we would not be able to rely on doubling the team at the last minute to get us out of the hole. Instead, management expected us to make significant process improvements, but it didn't know how. Nobody knew how, ourselves included.

In the summer of 1991, I began to think systems thinking might be a useful tool for the changes we wanted to make. At various times during the next few months, Fred and I met with Peter Senge, Fred Kofman, Bill Isaacs, Dan Kim, and Chris Argyris. They wanted to make sure we were serious; that we were willing to do most of the work ourselves; and that we would have support from top management so that we could proceed to the end.

Fred Simon: I had a problem with this attitude about top management involvement. There's a mind-set that before you can put a new way of working into practice, you have to convert the chairman. But if we started by trying to convert the chairman, we would be entering into a holy crusade, with nothing to base it on except trust and, "Read this book" or "Go to this course." That wouldn't sell. So we resolved to see what would happen if we tried to put a learning organization practice together for our own FN74 team.

Our first move was a three-day off-site meeting at the Renaissance Center. We brought Peter Senge, Dan Kim, and others in to speak about process improvement and systems thinking. I was the skeptic in the group; frankly, I was less interested in the content than in getting people together so they'd get friendly.

The core team

Nick Zeniuk: In retrospect, Fred was right to be skeptical. I thought I had it all figured out. We would set up a cross-functional core team of five or six senior managers, which would create a "monster" system map and see all the leverage points. Then we would simply follow the insights from this map.

But almost from day one of the core team meetings, we ran into a wall. Each participant, as a senior manager of one or more functions, had his or her own view of what processes to change, and where the problems lay. It was always somebody else's fault. We spent much of our time arguing about old war stories. I began to realize that our biggest challenge was getting ourselves in order as a management team.

Fred Simon: The core team met monthly for most of that year, mostly with Dan Kim's guidance. Ostensibly, we were concentrating on the early technological and organizational problems we faced in designing the car, but we were actually learning how to talk to each other. We used mental models tools like the ladder of inference, and archetypes and process maps to chart the relationships among our problems.

From what I've seen at other companies, most people go directly to setting up learning labs, without spending time working on how people understand each other first. We couldn't have made any progress if we hadn't generated some basic trust among ourselves through tools like the ladder of inference and left-hand column.

For more about these tools, see pages 242 and 246.

Eventually, we came to see that a few core emotional issues had generated all the rest of our problems. There was a fear of being wrong that led to people not sharing information. People did not trust others to help them; they expected everyone else to one-up whatever they did. And there was the bosses' need to control every detail. Throughout my twenty-nine years at Ford, I had heard talk about the value of having open, honest communication; now, for the first time, I was beginning to experience it. Of course, while the senior team met, the rest of the FN74 people were working on the car. But even they were beginning to be impacted by the changing relationships in the core team.

Rick Haas: We didn't know what was going on at the time. But we noticed a change: "Gee, Fred's acting a little differently," we would say to each other, walking out of a meeting. "We didn't get beat up that time."

Julie Petrucci: Everybody wants to go into the boss's office and bring great news. But now there seemed to be more of a willingness to listen to bad news. "It's better that we know now," they would say, "than when it's too late for us to do anything about it." The change was very subtle; I didn't really see it until I looked back on it.

Creating the learning lab

Nick Zeniuk: By September, we believed that we were ready as a core management team. Now how would we deploy learning to the rest of the people working on the car? We decided to bring in 20 members at a time. We chose people who worked on the same teams, so they could reinforce each other's new behavior in their daily work.

We wanted to create a collaborative practice field where team members could work on real problems that they were all involved with. We worked with Dan Kim to design the first two-day session, for a team of key people working on the interior of the car: the instrument panel, electrical system, climate control system, seat, and door.

Fred would not be invited; his high rank might inhibit some of the discussion. But to show this was important, I would participate, as a key executive on the project. During the first day, we would review the Argyris tools, creative tension, and the archetypes. During the second day, we would delve deeper into archetypes and take people through a computer-based management flight simulator. We would use a simulator developed by Dan and Donald Seville, another MIT researcher, based loosely on our product-development process. Working in pairs in front of the computer, team members would make decisions about (for instance) adding or removing engineers, changing deadlines, or resetting goals. By watching how the behavior of the system changed, they would see underlying system relationships.

In retrospect, the flight simulator was interesting, and it gave us a threshold from which to talk about systems issues. But the noncomputer-based parts of the learning lab had the most impact. They gave us ways of talking more directly and effectively about our issues.

The "tragedy of the power supply" story on page 142, and the "organization gridlock" exercise on page 169 emerged from this learning lab.

Rick Haas: It was important that Nick was the type of person to whom we could say what we were really thinking. Most senior managers, if you disagree with their opinion, tend to lunge back at you. Nick had trained himself to sit quietly and listen, without trying to defend himself right off the bat.

Julie Petrucci: The learning lab wasn't structured like the training environments we were used to. Nick didn't begin with an overview: "Here are the ten things we're going to tell you." Instead, he said, "We're going to learn together as we go along." This felt foreign, particularly in an engineering environment. It was uncomfortable that the boss was learning with us; that he didn't have the answers; that we were going to figure it out together. And yet it was exciting, because we could see that we were all going to be in on this together.

After the learning lab was over, we went back into the team and began practicing the ladder of inference. We were clumsy at first; not exactly sure what we had learned. But when Rick and I used the tools in meetings together, we saw positive results. A supplier would tell us that in the past he hadn't owned up to the fact that he was two weeks late because he did not want to tell us it was our own purchasing department's fault. Now that we had shown the suppliers that they could talk freely, without repercussions, we would find things out.

Fred Simon: After the learning lab, every time we had a success, the story would spread and make others more willing to raise questions themselves. On one of my business trips, I was in the hotel shower at 7:30 A.M. when the phone rang. It was an engineer, about six levels below me. He said, "Listen, Fred, the car bodies are building too wide, and I don't know why. I want to stop the prototype build and take a week to figure out what the problem is. And then fix it and resume the build."

To appreciate this, you should know several things. First of all, no engineer at his level would ordinarily call someone at my level—let alone call me off-site at seven-thirty in the morning. Moreover, build schedules are sacred at Ford. We never stop a build for any reason. Finally, for an engineer to say, "I have a problem, and I don't know what the answer is," would typically be seen as a confession of failure. But this combination all took place, and it was the right thing to do. On any other team, he might never have called. We would have built the cars with the body too wide. This would have made the instrument panels seem too low. We would have fixed the instrument panels. But before the next round of builds we would have noticed that the body was too wide and narrowed it; which would mean that, in the next round, the instrument panels would be too high. It would have led to a never-ending cycle of correcting the fixes we had made the time before.

Nick Zeniuk: Even the archetypes, which seem at first like they're so tied to processes and systems, lead to this kind of understanding. In one learning lab follow-up, two team leaders were trying to use an archetype to pin down something they disliked about the engineering change management system. It took some time and encouragement before they could bring themselves to spell it out. "Nick," they finally said, "you are making our lives miserable. We can't get anything approved without coming to you for permission. Why do we need such a cumbersome system?" And as we talked, I realized why I insisted on that. "It's because I don't trust you," I said.

In any other context, I would have found that almost impossible to say. If I had said it, it would have been a deadly insult. It would have cut the cord of communication. But in this context, it opened up the discussion. They accepted that this was my opinion. And we began to talk meaningfully about the specific issues which had led us to such mistrust and resentment.

Spreading the learning further

Nick Zeniuk: In the last year or so, we've brought five or six more teams into the learning labs. We waited a long time before we conducted the second one. We wanted to convince ourselves that this process would work. We also needed our top management support in order to continue funding the project. They were reluctant initially, until we presented some of the results and benefits of the project to them.

We keep improving the format. We've reduced the amount of academic theory, and put more emphasis on our day-to-day work. Every group has its own dynamic and works at its own pace, which means the learners have to direct the agenda. We provide the tools; they decide what problems to work on.

In the last learning lab, we added an hour and a half of dialogue. I honestly had no idea how it would work. I was elated. We have some people who never stop posturing and instructing others; and in this setting, they complied with the rules about listening, reflecting, and not making speeches. As a result, we've begun to hold dialogue sessions once a week. We're trying to use that to reinforce the camaraderie of the labs themselves.

Fred Simon: By now, we've had seventy-five people go through the labs. When they begin to act differently, and act positively about going through it, then people begin to come to us and complain: "Why haven't I been able to go through it yet?" That makes it easier to spread.

Nick and I are now talking to other program managers within Ford about the value of the program. By now, we can point to unequivocally dramatic measurements of quality improvement and time savings. Some results are directly tied to good coordination between different functions. There's a risk that people might attribute the success to Nick and myself, and not to the process we've used.

The other way of spreading it through the system will take place automatically when this car is completed and the program's over. The people will scatter throughout Ford. If enough of them wind up in the same place, they can reinforce each other and begin to change the people around them. If they're alone, they may feel out of place. We're hoping to keep them together in groups large enough to have an impact.

Nick Zeniuk: As the project continues to unfold, we realize that the most challenging issues may lie beyond the boundary of the team and the learning laboratory itself. The more successful the team becomes, the more it comes in conflict with the larger organization system's expectations and norms. The challenge ahead is to figure out how the team can engage the bigger system to cooperate with the learning and progress being made.

Endnotes

92 Coda

From the Foreword to the Chinese Edition of
The Fifth Discipline

Peter Senge

Around the same time that this book appears, in mid 1994, a Chinese translation of its predecessor, The Fifth Discipline, *will be published. We feel the Chinese translation is particularly significant because of the impact this emerging economy is likely to have on the rest of the world. Like emerging economies in Asia, Africa, South America, and elsewhere, the Chinese society will face the unique challenge of entering the twenty-first century without destroying the knowledge and wisdom that has taken more than fifty centuries to develop. As they pursue economic growth, will they follow the same path through industrialization that Western nations did? Or will they develop a new form of capitalism with an innate sensitivity to the subtleties of process and interdependence, integrating industrial and traditional thinking?*

Peter's friend and colleague, Professor Showing Young, asked him to write a foreword to the Chinese edition. "Just meditate," he suggested, "and imagine that there are thousands and thousands of Chinese sitting in front of you, and that they want to hear some very plain and personal words from your mind, your heart, and your soul."

Once upon a time, human beings did not distinguish themselves from their world. Our awareness was one of unbroken wholeness. We and nature were one. Then, we learned to distinguish ourselves, to see ourselves as separate. We discovered a differentiated awareness, an independent will, personal needs and aspirations. We evolved a sense of self that distinguished ourselves from one another, and from the rest of God's creations. This was a great gift, and a curse, of our evolution.

Without the separation of "self" and "environment," intelligence as we now know it would not have evolved. The scientific method of analysis of a "physical universe" separate from ourselves would not have been possible. And the technological progress from which we all now benefit immeasurably would never have occurred.

Yet, separation quickly became fragmentation and isolation. With the agricultural revolution, and then the industrial revolution, there came increasing specialization. We eventually came to see ourselves not only as standing apart from nature, but as having a right to rule over nature. Today, with diminishing exceptions, our worldwide culture tells us that the natural world actually exists for our benefit, and that it is a mere collection of natural "resources" (a word meaning, literally, "standing in reserve") awaiting our use.

Now, we stand at a sort of crossroads. Our culture tells us that humankind has found the correct path. It is our destiny to rule. Yet there are signs all around that maybe the path is coming to an end.

We have learned how to influence our environment, to the extent that our very survival as a species is now at risk. We have evolved our ego, to the extent that we now think that our personal happiness is somehow separate from the happiness of those around us. We have separated ourselves from nature, to the extent that we have lost our sense of awe at the mystery of life, and our sense of belonging to something larger than ourselves.

In the West, our primary social institutions are in a state of breakdown because of fragmentation. We have fragmented physical health from mental and spiritual health, to the extent that people now stay alive longer at a lower state of health than ever before, at ever greater cost to society. We have fragmented education into the banal transmission of disconnected facts and dry academic exercises, to the extent that school is increasingly detached from personal growth and genuine learning, and is increasingly ineffective. We have fragmented government into a cacophony of "special interest groups" who fight to maintain the status quo, to the extent that we are paralyzed by "gridlock." Virtually everything about our modern system of management is based on fragmentation, and the inevitable competition that results. Marketing departments are at war with manufacturing. Frontline managers have a hostility for corporate management that borders on hatred. People within the organization often compete more with one another than with external "competitors."

As best as I can understand, the traditional Chinese culture evolved along a slightly different path. Chinese culture has not quite lost its appreciation of the interconnectedness of life, of life's continuing unfolding, of the mystery. We in the West see a world composed of things, while you see a world of processes. We act individually, while you are still tied to family and community. We believe in simple cause and effect and continually search for the all-encompassing "answer," while you tend to reason from concrete particulars, and seek more to understand the web of interdependencies within which effective action must be taken. We think in days and months, while you think in decades and generations. For us, time is an adversary, while I believe for you, it is more of an ally.

Thus, we watch with special interest as the Chinese society enters the modern economy. Make no mistake: the forces of industrialization are powerful forces of fragmentation. The seeds of an isolating, specializing culture planted in the agricultural revolution will grow at an even faster pace in the climate of smokestacks, factories, and traditional industrial management practices.

So we have natural questions as we watch your unfolding. Will you follow the deeply grooved path of industrial societies toward increasing material affluence and increasing arrogance, seeing human growth as the center of the "natural order of things"? Will you develop your "economies" at the expense of your communities? Will you become another "taker" society, as author Daniel Quinn called societies that take from the natural world in an unsustainable manner?* Or will you find a different path into the future?

° See the review of Daniel Quinn's *Ishmael, Fieldbook*, p. 304.

The answers will lie, at least in part, in the predominant system of management that develops in China. The system of management in a society determines the character of its institutions of business, government, and education. The character of these institutions in turn shapes the type of society that emerges. In the modern era, the spiritual life of the community is inseparable from the spiritual life (or lack thereof) of its large institutions. Our harmony or disharmony with nature is inseparable from the harmony or disharmony of those same institutions with nature.

So it is with deep humility and great sense of honor that I dedicate the Chinese edition of *The Fifth Discipline* to those Chinese leaders and managers who will have the heart to seek a new path. I believe the principles and tools described here provide an initial outline of such a path. It is a path based on reflecting on our deepest aspirations, honoring personal visions and conversation, being more intelligent together than we can ever be separately. It is a path based on the primacy of the whole, rather than the primacy of the parts. It is a path fundamentally different from the path along which industrial development in the West has progressed.

Ironically, it is now a path that many corporations, schools, and other institutions in the West are attempting to discover. There is a ferment in management worldwide. It is being driven not just by global competitiveness, but by the growing awareness that keys to success in the twenty-first century may be quite different from the keys to success in the nineteenth and twentieth centuries. We are leaving the era where cheap natural resources were the key to a nation's economic status, and its system of management was designed to exploit those resources. The rise of Japan, Korea, Singapore, and Taiwan as world economic powers has signaled a new era when tapping the creativity and imagination of people is now the central management challenge.

Finally, the management ferment is also driven by an even deeper realization: there must be an antidote to fragmentation. The politics, games playing, and internal competition that characterize modern organizations sap people's energy and commitment, and can never be a foundation for a great enterprise *or a sustainable society*.

In writing *The Fifth Discipline* I was acutely aware of the enormous debt I owed to the intellectual pioneers on whose work the book builds. When people ask, "How long did it take to write *The Fifth Discipline*?" I often respond that, "It only took me a couple of years, but that was only because of one hundred years of work by some of the leading thinkers of this era." These extraordinary people include Jay Forrester of MIT (my mentor for many years), inventor of "core memory" and leader of the team that built the first general-purpose digital computer, whose work on "system dynamics" has contributed a general approach to understanding human systems; Chris Argyris, one of the world's leading authorities on the counterproductiveness of management teams; David Bohm, one of the leading theoretical physicists of this era, whose work on dialogue grew out of his lifelong inquiry into how thought and reality influenced one another; Robert Fritz, an immensely talented musician and composer with deep insights into the creative process; and Charles Kiefer and other experts on organization change, who have begun to show how change might arise out of people's dreams rather than their fears.

I can imagine no greater way to repay this debt than to bring their work to China. As you learn, so will we all.

93 Acknowledgments

M any people contributed time and effort to improve or enhance *The Fifth Discipline Fieldbook*.

Foremost is Janis Dutton, who served as the managing editor for this manuscript. She gathered, coordinated, and refined much of the *Fieldbook*'s contents, working diligently and creatively to help a project with many contributors emerge as a coherent whole.

Michael Goodman, director of the Systems Thinking program at Innovation Associates, took on a role as emcee of the Systems Thinking chapter. Its quality is a direct result of his critical eye, imaginative insight, and unrelenting drive to make the section as cogent as possible.

Robert Putnam, partner in Action Design, gave us significant guidance and generous criticism on the Mental Models chapter.

William Isaacs, director of the MIT Dialogue Project, helped develop and conceptualize the Team Learning section, adding perspective and overseeing the framing of the conversational forms described there.

Joyce Ross, principal in Ross Partners, provided invaluable in-depth critique for nearly every section of the book, and significant help in developing the Leadership section and many exercises.

The idea for the *Fieldbook* emerged originally in conversations with Harriet Rubin, Currency Doubleday editor-in-chief. In a hundred different ways, she made it possible for the book to exist. The quality of the book also owes a great deal to the suggestions, critiques, and perseverance of Currency Doubleday editor Janet Coleman, who oversaw its critical stages during the editorial and production process. We also wish to thank Lynn Fenwick and Rob Earp. Donna Sanford's work defining the book's public presence has added to our understanding.

Thanks to copy editors Chris Pavone and Estelle Lawrence, designers

Terry Karydes and Chris Welch, associate managing editor Susan Newe, publicist Gabrielle Brooks, and production manager Randy Lang for their talent, patience, and resourcefulness.

Joe Spieler, literary agent, shepherded this project through its contractual process, contributed to its finding an audience worldwide, and helped us think about how to build a foundation for future *Fieldbooks*.

Martie Holmer created the rich array of hand-illustrated drawings, charts, and diagrams in the *Fieldbook,* adding ideas and improvements, and working under difficult deadlines. Calligrapher Herb Florer produced the Chinese characters for "learning" (page 49).

The *Fieldbook* benefited from a number of readers who critiqued all or part of the initial manuscript and provided invaluable perspective: Philip Mirvis, Dan Simpson, Jim Evers, Edward Urow-Hamell, Peggy Hanley, Jim Boswell, Emily Myers, Avé Carta, Adam Kahane, Faith Florer, Louis van der Merwe, Graham Freeman, Peter Spellisey, Tom Keenan, Bill Dever, Karen Allen-Keenan, Larry Morden, Terry Hildebrand, David Wolfenden, and Harris J. Sokoloff.

Colleen Peacock handled with aplomb the difficult job of being the *Fieldbook* project's business manager. Tom Fritsch and Jim Evers edited and refined some of the cameos. Chris Haymaker, Betty Quantz, and Betsie Jones took on important editorial coordination jobs. Judi Webb's tape transcriptions were a key part of this book's nervous system; we also benefited from transcriptions by Julia Sager and Nancy King. Sheryl Erickson helped us begin to foster a community of readers and practitioners.

Arie de Geus, Philip Mirvis, Ed Dulworth, Adam Kahane, Judith McCrackin of SEMATECH, Ed Josephson and Philip Macedonia of Textron Defense Systems, Robert Hargreaves, Sue Miller Hurst, Richard Kimball, Jackson Bundy, Preston McLaurin, Tom Sugalski, and Nancy Margulies made insightful contributions to drafts of various segments of the *Fieldbook.* We were also grateful to have read the "Study Notes on *The Fifth Discipline,*" an abridgement developed by Robert Levi of Corona, California.

This book benefited from the support and encouragement of the following organizations:

■ *Innovation Associates,* Framingham, Massachusetts. Innovation Associates is a learning organization offering consulting and training services to enable clients to collectively create the results they most care about. Many of the techniques and tools developed in this book, including the original concept for the system archetypes and several of our personal mastery and shared vision techniques, were developed here. We are grateful to Charlie Kiefer, Steve Tritman, Jennifer Kemeny, Joel Yanovitz, Rick Karash, Steve Ober, Robert Hanig, Suzanne Thomson, Bill Moon, Bill Latshaw, Henry Frechette, Shirley Stahl, Sharon Lash, Wendy MacPhedran, Ilene Fischer, Erwin Mesch, Pat Hartlen, Susan Frank, Neil Baird, John Donovan, and Bruce Elkin.

■ *Innovation Associates of Canada,* Thornhill, Ontario. The Visionary Leadership and Planning Program, developed here, has been a key laboratory for the evolution of many of the ideas in this book. I.A. Canada also provided invaluable administrative and support help. We want to thank Claire Dela Cruz and Frances Spatafora.

■ *The Center for Organizational Learning,* Massachusetts Institute of Technology, Cambridge, Massachusetts. The Center is a consortium of corporations and researchers, working to advance the foundations of theory, methods, and understanding that can make learning organizations a way of life. Much of this book reflects experience and research developed in association with the Center, or with the Dialogue Project which is associated with it. We particularly benefited from the insights and work of Edgar Schein, Fred Kofman, Chris Argyris, Sue Miller Hurst, George Roth, and Jeffrey Clanon, and from the support and help of Vickie Tweiten, Laura Tawater, Doreen Sullivan, Michelle Martin, Robin Doughty, Jane Punchard, and Angela Lipinski.

■ *Ross Partners,* Encinitas, California. This consulting and training partnership, in collaboration with Innovation Associates, developed the Leading Learning Organizations course from which much of the *Fieldbook* material derived. It also provided necessary administrative underpinnings, without which this project could not have gotten off the ground.

■ *Pegasus Communications,* Cambridge, Massachusetts. Publishers of *The Systems Thinker* newsletter (p. XX) and conveners of the annual Systems Thinking in Action conference, this organization worked collaboratively with us to ensure that both of us would gain from the experience and material of the other. We are particularly grateful to Daniel Kim, Colleen Lannon-Kim, and Kellie Wardman.

■ *The Learning Circle,* Sudbury, Massachusetts. This partnership-oriented organization develops and fosters a variety of interesting projects and joint ventures, dedicated to fostering learning organization concepts and practice throughout the world in business, health-care, government, education, and community development. We benefited from the interest, encouragement, and suggestions of Sheryl Erickson and Rita Cleary.

- *Dia•Logos,* Cambridge, Massachusetts. This nonprofit institute is a leader in developing the theory and practice of dialogue around the world, with the purpose of promoting generative learning and collaborative social action. We wish to thank William Isaacs, Jody Isaacs, John Parrott, Risa Kaparo, and others.

- *Action Design Associates,* Newton, Massachusetts. This consulting firm helps organizations design and implement changes that require fundamental shifts in people's assumptions and behaviors. Much of our Reflection and Inquiry Skills section builds upon materials developed here. Diana Smith, Robert Putnam, Phil McArthur, and Sam Borelli helped us.

- *Global Business Network,* Emeryville, California. We developed most of our material on scenarios with the courtesy and help of this organization, which invited us to attend their annual scenario development workshop. We wish to thank Napier Collyns, Lawrence Wilkinson, Peter Schwartz, Pierre Wack, Kees van der Heijden, Adam Kahane, Roberta Gelt, Stewart Brand, Danica Remy, and Nancy Murphy.

- *The Whole Earth Catalog* and *Review,* Sausalito, California. Published by the Point Foundation, these publications inspired some of the format and approach of *The Fifth Discipline Fieldbook.* If you enjoyed the informal tone and eclectic approach of the *Fieldbook,* we highly recommend looking at the *Whole Earth Review.* John Sumser, Howard Rheingold, and others offered encouragement and help.

Others whom we wish to thank for their help and encouragement include Bill O'Brien, Alain Gauthier, David Kantor, Louis van der Merwe, Peter Wendel, Carole and David Schwinn, Shoji Shiba, Myron Tribus, Juanita Brown, Richard Beckhard, Bill Conway, Barbara Lawton, Kevin Cushing, Thomas Dutton, David Elder, Michael J. Hanley, Sandra Seagal and David Horne, Jim Roberts, Jim Collard, Sandra Nichols, Susanna Opper, Pat Walls of Federal Express, Lorrie Zimmerman of AT&T, Lee Goodman, Grady McGonagill and Lanng Tamura, Ralph Waldo, Nathan Gray and Yumi Sera of EarthTrain, Stephanie Spear, Dana Meadows, George Richardson, Joe Seamans, David Mason, Robert Weber, Jim Henry, Clare Crawford-Mason, the WELL writers' conference, David Langford, and Eric Siegel and Jeff Wagoner of Ford.

Our "lexicon" etymologies derive from three primary sources: *Dictionary of Word Origins* by John Ayto (1990, New York: Arcade); *Origins: A Short Etymological Dictionary of Modern English* by Eric Partridge (1958, New York: Greenwich House), and the writings and speeches of David Bohm.

Creating a book of this size and scope inevitably involves the support and attention of the people with whom we are closest in our lives. Therefore, we particularly wish to acknowledge, with love and appreciation, Jim Boswell, Faith Florer, Joyce Ross, Diane Senge, Nathan Senge, Ian Senge, Linda Zarytski, Michael Smith, and Anthony Smith.

94 How to Stay in Touch with The Fifth Discipline Fieldbook Project and other resources

In keeping with the purpose of this *Fieldbook,* to provide access to tools for people engaged in building learning organizations, we encourage you to send us one of the mail-in forms on page 573, so that you can stay connected. Consider it your *"Fieldbook* Owner Registration Form," linking you to new tools and resources as they develop. You can also fax it to us at 905-764-7983, or call 1-800-636-3796.

Here is one resource that is available now: Pegasus Communications is offering *Fifth Discipline Fieldbook* readers a free three-month subscription to *The Systems Thinker* (page 91), a monthly newsletter that explores how to put systems thinking and the other disciplines of the learning organization into practice. To receive it, check the appropriate box on the mail-in form.

■ **Help in obtaining resources:** If you would like help obtaining resources that are reviewed or identified in the *Fieldbook* (including videotapes, computer software, simulations, and additional copies of this book and *The Fifth Discipline*), or information on consulting resources, training, and speakers, please write to us, or use these telephone numbers: 1-800-636-3796 (voice), 905-764-7983 (fax).

- **Contributions to future *Fieldbooks:*** We plan to continue gathering and disseminating information about strategies and tools for creating learning organizations. We expect to produce future *Fieldbook*s incorporating this material every two or three years. If you would like to contribute a description of your experience and learnings to be considered for the next *Fieldbook*, please send it to us by mail, typed double-spaced, with your address and phone number included.

- **New developments and materials:** We also expect to produce, sponsor, or offer access to other materials, possibly including bulletins, newsletters, electronic media, computer network links, collections of tools and practical tips, and other resources. To keep informed of these Fieldbook Project developments as they unfold, please check that box on the mail-in form.

- **Credit:** We have done our best to track down and credit the sources of all the material in this *Fieldbook.* However, we recognize we may have inadvertently omitted some important sources or credits. If you feel someone is not properly acknowledged, please let us know by mail and we will do our best to correct future printings.

- **Comments:** If you have found this book valuable and would like to tell us why, or if you have responses or suggestions of any sort, we are interested in hearing from you. Please write to us, or use the blank space on the front or back of the mail-in form.

The Fifth Discipline Fieldbook Project
PO Box 943
Oxford, OH 45056-0943
USA

The Fifth Discipline Fieldbook Project
PO Box 270
Richmond Hill, Ontario
L4C 4Y2 Canada

Fifth Discipline Fieldbook Owner Registration Form

> **Use this "*Fieldbook* Owner Registration Form" as a way to stay connected with new developments, tools, and resources as they emerge.**

Mail to:
The Fifth Discipline
Fieldbook Project
P.O. Box 943
Oxford, OH 45056-0943
USA

or
The Fifth Discipline
Fieldbook Project
P.O. Box 270
Richmond Hill, Ontario L4C 4Y2
Canada

or fax the form to:
905-764-7983
or call:
1-800-636-3796.

☐ Please send me a complimentary three-month subscription to *The Systems Thinker*.

☐ I'd like to be informed of new developments and resources for building learning organizations. I'm particularly interested in: _____

☐ I would like to offer comments on *The Fieldbook* (use back of form).

Name _____
Title _____
Organization _____ *# of employees* _____
Address _____
City _____
State/Prov. _____ *Zip/Postal Code* _____ *Country* _____
Phone # _____ *Fax #* _____

☐ Please send me a complimentary three-month subscription to *The Systems Thinker*.

☐ I'd like to be informed of new developments and resources for building learning organizations. I'm particularly interested in: _____

☐ I would like to offer comments on *The Fieldbook* (use back of form).

Name _____
Title _____
Organization _____ *# of employees* _____
Address _____
City _____
State/Prov. _____ *Zip/Postal Code* _____ *Country* _____
Phone # _____ *Fax #* _____

95 Contributors to The Fifth Discipline Fieldbook

ART KLEINER: PO Box 943, Oxford, OH 45056-0943

CHARLOTTE ROBERTS: 4613 Welbourne Drive, Sherrill's Ford, NC 28673

RICK ROSS: Ross Partners, 412 West F Street, Encinitas CA 92024

PETER SENGE: MIT Center for Organizational Learning, 1 Amherst Street, Building E-40, Room 271, Cambridge, MA 02139

BRYAN SMITH: Innovation Associates of Canada, 7070 Bayview Avenue, Thornhill, Ontario L3T 2R4, Canada

•

EDWARD M. BAKER: PO Box 279, Farmington, MI 48332

DONALD BERWICK, M.D.: Institute for Healthcare Improvement, 1 Exeter Plaza, Boston, MA 02116

JIM BOSWELL: 4613 Welbourne Drive, Sherrill's Ford, NC 28673

BILL BRANDT: American Woodmark, Box 1980, Winchester, VA 22601

JUANITA BROWN AND DAVID ISAACS: Whole Systems Associates, 166 Homestead Boulevard, Mill Valley, CA 94941

WILSON BULLARD: Beckman Instruments, 200 South Kraemer Boulevard, Brea, CA 92621

ED CARPENTER: Intel Corporation, A4/T11, 5000 West Chandler Boulevard, Chandler, AZ 85226

JEFF DOOLEY: Department of Anthropology, San Jose State University, San Jose, CA 95192

JOE DOUGLAS, WALT GEORGE, BILL WALKER, MARC SWARTZ, ED OBLON, and JERRY KRUEGER: Hill's Pet Nutrition, Inc., PO Box 148, Topeka, KS 66601-0148

JANIS DUTTON: PO Box 943, Oxford, OH 45056-0943

FRANK DRAPER: Catalina Foothills High School, 4300 East Sunrise Drive, Tucson, AZ 85718

JAMES L. EVERS: 10 Rockland Avenue, Nanuet, NY 10954

SUSAN FRANK: % The Fifth Discipline Fieldbook Project

ALAIN GAUTHIER: Core Leadership Development, 1 Fernhoff Court, Oakland, CA 94619

TERRY GILBERT: *Calgary Herald*, PO Box 2400, Station M, Calgary, Alberta T2P 0W8, Canada

BILL GODFREY: 8 Reibey Place, Curtin ACT 2605, Australia

MICHAEL GOODMAN, RICK KARASH, JENNIFER KEMENY, CHARLIE KIEFER, SUZANNE THOMSON: Innovation Associates, Inc., Three Speen Street, Suite 140, Framingham, MA 01701

MICHELE HUNT: Federal Quality Institute, 1900 E Street NW, Washington, DC, 20415

B. C. HUSELTON, ROB CUSHMAN, JOHN COTTRELL, GARY CLARK, PHIL YANTZI: GS Technologies, 7000 Roberts Street, Kansas City, MO 64125

WILLIAM ISAACS: Dia • Logos Institute, PO Box 42-1149, Cambridge, MA 02142

DAVID KANTOR AND NANCY LONSTEIN: Origins, Inc., 7 Shepard Street, Cambridge, MA 02138

DANIEL KIM: Pegasus Communications, PO Box 120, Cambridge, MA 02142

FRED KOFMAN: Sloan School of Management, 50 Memorial Drive, Cambridge, MA 02142

W. BRIAN KREUTZER: Gould-Kreutzer Associates, River Court, 10 Rogers Street, Suite 120, Cambridge, MA 02142

WINSTON LEDET: The Manufacturing Game, 3230 Rambling Creek Drive, Kingwood, TX 77345

GRADY MCGONAGILL: 41 Westbourne Terrace, Brookline, MA 02146

DONELLA MEADOWS: Dartmouth College, Environmental Studies Dept., Hanover, NH 03755

DOUGLAS MERCHANT: AT&T Human Resources, 295 North Maple Avenue, Basking Ridge, NJ 07920

EMILY MYERS: Mobius Project, PO Box 113, 82 Bullock Road, Chadds Ford, PA 19317

WILLIAM O'BRIEN: 22 Red Gate Lane, Southborough, MA 01772

JOHN PARKER: Martin Marietta Astronautics, PO Box 179, Denver, CO 80201

ROGER PETERS: Terratron, 7050 South 2000 East, Salt Lake City, UT 84121

RUTHANN PRANGE: 16 Harrison Brook Drive, Basking Ridge, NJ 07920

ROBERT PUTNAM: Action Design, 66 Amherst Road, Newton, MA 02168

GEORGE RAYMOND: 7920 Grand Bay Drive, Naples, FL 33963

FREDRICK SIMON, NICK ZENIUK, JULIE PETRUCCI, RICHARD HAAS: Ford Motor Company, Car Product Development, Danou Technical Center, 16630 Southfield Road, Suite 4000, Allen Park, MI 48101

PROFESSOR JOHN D. STERMAN, Director: System Dynamics Group, Sloan School of Management, 50 Memorial Drive, Cambridge, MA 02142

KEES VAN DER HEIJDEN: University of Strathclyde, Graduate Business School, 199 Cathedral Street, Glasgow G4 0QU, United Kingdom

LOUIS VAN DER MERWE: Centre for Innovative Leadership (Pty) Ltd., PO Box 1779, Rivonia 2128 South Africa

DAVID WOLFENDEN: Innovation Associates of Canada, 7070 Bayview Avenue, Thornhill, Ontario L3T 2R4, Canada

Index